# The Nixon Defense

Also by John Dean

---

*Blind Ambition:*
The White House Years

*Lost Honor*

*The Rehnquist Choice:*
The Untold Story of the Nixon Appointment
That Redefined the Supreme Court

*Worse Than Watergate:*
The Secret Presidency of George W. Bush

*Warren G. Harding*

*Conservatives Without Conscience*

*Broken Government:*
How Republican Rule Destroyed the Legislative,
Executive and Judicial Branches

*Pure Goldwater*

# THE NIXON DEFENSE

What He Knew and When He Knew It

---

# JOHN W. DEAN

VIKING

VIKING
Published by the Penguin Group
Penguin Group (USA) LLC
375 Hudson Street
New York, New York 10014

USA | Canada | UK | Ireland | Australia | New Zealand | India | South Africa | China
penguin.com
A Penguin Random House Company

First published by Viking Penguin, a member of Penguin Group (USA) LLC, 2014

Library of Congress Cataloging-in-Publication Data

Dean, John W. (John Wesley), 1938-
The Nixon defense : what he knew and when he knew it / John W. Dean.
pages cm
Includes bibliographical references and index.
ISBN 978-0-670-02536-7 (alk. paper)
1. Watergate Affair, 1972-1974.   2. Nixon, Richard M. (Richard Milhous), 1913-1994.
3. Dean, John W. (John Wesley), 1938-   I. Title.
E860.D385 2014
973.924092—dc23
2014020821

Printed in the United States of America
1   3   5   7   9   10   8   6   4   2

Set in Minion Pro and Steelfish
Designed by Amy Hill

*This book is dedicated to the staff of the
National Archives and Records Administration,
who made it possible to locate and listen to
former President Richard Nixon's self-recorded
conversations relating to Watergate.*

It occurs to me that at this point the central question . . . is simply put: What did the president know and when did he know it?

*Question asked by Senator Howard H. Baker, Jr., during the testimony of John W. Dean before the Senate Watergate Committee, June 28, 1973*

# Contents

# Preface

The report of the arrests in the early morning hours of June 17, 1972, of five men who had broken into the Watergate complex offices of the Democratic National Committee (DNC), wearing business suits and surgical gloves, their pockets stuffed with hundred-dollar bills, was something like a scene from a circa 1940s low-budget black-and-white gangsters B movie. This caught-in-the-act stupidity seemed too dumb to be ours, since the undertaking was so conspicuously illegal and inexplicably risky, not to mention obviously bungled. But this political surveillance debacle *did* turn out to be ours, the work of a ham-fisted team of amateurs assembled by G. Gordon Liddy, a former Nixon White House staff member who was then serving as general counsel of the finance operation of the Committee to Re-elect the President (CRP). This was, in fact, the opening scene of the worst political scandal of the twentieth century and the beginning of the end of the Nixon presidency. It was the start of Watergate, a story that has been told and retold, but never as I am going to tell it in the pages that follow.

The central character in Watergate was, of course, the president of the United States, Richard Nixon. From beginning to end Nixon sought to defend himself and his presidency from the political and legal consequences that followed the arrests at the DNC on June 17, 1972. This is the story of Nixon's defense, the story I found when trying to understand how someone as politically savvy and intelligent as Richard Nixon, a man who surrounded himself with those he thought the best and brightest, allowed this "third-rate," bungled burglary to destroy his presidency. The story of the Nixon defense is Richard Nixon's Watergate story.

Most of Nixon's Watergate-related activities were secretly self-recorded. These surreptitious recordings eventually revealed that his public Watergate

defenses were colossal deceptions, patent lies that eventually forced his resignation. Nixon's secret recordings provided much of the overwhelming
evidence that sent his former top advisers to prison, not to mention forced
his own early retirement. So some of this story has been around for several
decades. Investigators and prosecutors, however, were not interested in the
context and circumstances of Nixon's ill-conceived defensive efforts; rather,
they focused only on select portions of conversations that could provide
evidence establishing wrongdoing beyond a reasonable doubt, so as to end
any malfeasance and punish malefactors. Historians, in recounting the Watergate story, have relied largely and almost exclusively on the information
gathered by the Watergate investigators and prosecutors. Remarkably, historians and other students of the Nixon presidency have chosen to ignore
the full collection of secretly recorded White House conversations relating
to Watergate, which slowly but surely have become almost fully available
over the past four decades.

Before now, no one has attempted to catalog and transcribe all of Nixon's
Watergate conversations, and to examine and reconstruct this history based
on this primary source material, the likes of which has never before existed.
The account in the pages that follow is based on this unique collection, and
it is presented not as transcripts but rather as narrative and dialogue drawn
from and based on them. The story that follows is a first-person account of
what I found in this unique historical record. In telling this story I have only
edited the transcripts to make them readable and understandable, correcting
the obvious anomalies that inevitably occur in spontaneous conversations
and often compressing material to report its essence.[1] Almost all the conversations from which this account is drawn are available online at the Nixon
Presidential Library's Web site: http://nixon.archives.gov/virtuallibrary/
tapeexcerpts/index.php; the exceptions are those from June 1972, which are
available at the Miller Center, which is devoted to presidential scholarship
at the University of Virginia: http://web2.millercenter.org/rmn/audiovisual/
whrecordings/ (see chron1).

The Nixon defense—both legal and political, because they were
inseparable—was assembled behind closed doors in a process that began
in the days following the arrests at the Watergate headquarters of the
Democratic Party. The first public statement of a defense was made by
Nixon on June 22, 1972—that nobody in his White House was involved in
this bizarre incident—and Nixon's final firewall explanation of his defense

was issued eleven months later, on May 22, 1973; the latter followed the firing of his top aides, including your author, who had become the centerpiece of his defense. Because I was deeply involved in and later the focus of the Nixon defense, I always hoped someone else would tell this story. I also understood such an undertaking meant the not easily accomplished task of transcribing all of Richard Nixon's Watergate conversations. Of course, we knew the broad outlines of his activities that led to his resignation, and he did provide some additional details in his memoir. But he, too, relied primarily on conversations that had been transcribed by investigators and prosecutors, leaving most of the historical facts buried in his secretly recorded conversations. Having now transcribed all those conversations, and grasping the content of the newly transcribed material, I understand why he wanted no more information than was already easily available made public, for while this additional information explains many of the activities he was responsible for, those rationales do not redound to Richard Nixon's glory.

The National Archives and Records Administration (NARA), which Congress charged with the preservation of this historical Nixon material, has prepared, and continues to update and refine as it has released more of the Nixon recordings, a detailed "subject log" highlighting all the content of all the recorded conversations. This can be used to identify topics and the persons addressed, along with times and dates. No one has ever bothered to identify all the Watergate conversations that can be located with these subject logs. Today that can be done digitally. When I did it in 2009, I had to do it manually, which took several months, although given the volume of material, even today it would take almost as long. Depending on how you count them—as it is not always clear when one conversation ends and another begins—there are approximately one thousand Watergate-related conversations. Some of them run only minutes while others run many hours.

After "my" assembling a list, I first determined which of the conversations had previously been transcribed. Virtually all existing transcripts had been prepared from the analog recordings first made available by NARA. However, it is now possible to digitize these recordings, and when that technology became available, NARA began releasing digital editions. When I started this project in 2009, I was way ahead of the NARA release schedule for the Watergate-related material, so I decided to digitize that material before NARA had done so. Because the sound on these is improved, making it easier to understand and transcribe the conversations, my project became somewhat less challenging. But today, the best copies of the recordings are found at NARA, for they prepared copies from the best editions of the analog tapes and have used the latest technology.

For example, the Watergate Special Prosecution Force (WSPF) transcribed all or parts of eighty Watergate-related conversations. When I checked the quality of the transcripts using the digital recordings, I found it was sometimes possible to hear material that those who prepared the WSPF transcripts had been unable to. Also, I found that those used in the cover-up trial, *U.S. v. Mitchell et al.*, were of better quality than those not used in the trial. Clearly the Watergate defendants had taken the time to listen to them carefully, and to make corrections, so those used at trial are more reliable than the drafts prepared by FBI secretaries; often the secretary was not sure who was speaking, so some were identified incorrectly, along with other such conspicuous errors.

Former University of Wisconsin historian Stanley Kutler, working with Alan Morrison's Public Citizen Litigation Group, successfully sued NARA to make public Nixon's so-called abuses of government power recordings long before the former president wanted them released, and these covered Watergate as well as earlier abuses of power. Professor Kutler published partial transcripts of 320 Watergate-related conversations from the first release by NARA in 1996, along with portions of hundreds of other unrelated ones, in *Abuse of Power: The New Nixon Tapes* (New York: Free Press, 1997). These, however, were all based on analog recordings. When I began using modern digital listening equipment for the audio of randomly selected conversations transcribed by Professor Kutler's team, I discovered I could hear things they had missed. I further found that information I thought important had not, for one reason or another, been included in the transcripts he published. Professor Kutler selected portions of conversations he felt relevant and interesting, and understandably he did not include Nixon's almost obsessive-compulsive repetition of information related to Watergate; he had to trim many conversations, because there was simply too much material for one book, and he excluded most conversations previously transcribed by others. While I also had to trim material for this book, I focused on abuses that fall within the term "Watergate" (as it was later defined by Congress to mean both the break-in and the cover-up), and I did so only after having examined the entire available conversation.

In addition, in private conversations with his staff Nixon had a highly repetitive nature—and only those who may someday go through all these conversations will ever fully appreciate that my describing it as "obsessive-compulsive" is an understatement—that created something of an editorial problem. I did not want the repetition to become tedious for the reader, yet while drastically digesting and compressing these conversations as I have, it is also my hope to give the reader a feel for Nixon's behavior, and clearly he was obsessive about Watergate.* And as Nixon obsessed over Watergate, particularly starting in April 1973, as well as later, he was constantly reinventing what happened, and this is vital to understanding the story. Accordingly, I have tried to trim as tightly as possible without removing this very Nixonian character trait in his dealings with Watergate.

Available transcripts also include those transcribed by the Nixon White House and turned over to the House Judiciary Committee's impeachment inquiry: forty-seven conversations (a collection running thirteen hundred pages) on April 30, 1974, that were published in a document known as the *Submission of Recorded Presidential Conversations to the Committee on the Judiciary of the House of Representatives* (SRPC). Because of the poor quality of the transcripts prepared by the White House, not to mention selective edits and omissions, many of these were retranscribed by the committee. When working on his memoir, Richard Nixon had one of his longtime secretaries, Mrs. Marjorie Acker, prepare transcripts of all his Watergate-related conversations with aides, chief of staff Bob Haldeman, assistant to the president for domestic affairs John Ehrlichman and special counsel to the president Charles Colson for the first month following his return to the White House after the arrests at the Watergate; that is, from June 20 through July 20, 1972. He included as well transcripts of his conversations with Haldeman in May 1973, but only when they were reconstructing what they remembered about the events of June 23, 1972—the date of the so-called smoking-gun discussion, when Nixon authorized Haldeman to meet with the CIA "to limit the FBI's investigation of Watergate."[2] Neither Nixon nor his estate has ever made his completed transcripts publicly available, although the material he drew from them is presented in the narrative of his memoir, which I have checked and noted as this book unfolds. By my count, Marjorie

---

*I have asked other Nixon historians familiar with his behavior and recorded conversations in other areas, such as the war in Vietnam and the planning for his China initiative, if he was similarly obsessive when discussing other matters, and I was told that to some degree he was but, from what I can gather, not as obsessive as he became with Watergate.

Acker transcribed, at most, about forty Watergate-related conversations, based on Nixon's description of her work.

In summary, I found (roughly) 447 Watergate conversations had been transcribed. Most were only partials, but a few were of complete conversations, plus the material used in Nixon's memoir. (More specifically, I found 80 Watergate conversations transcribed by WSPF; 47 by the White House, including those retranscribed by the House Judiciary Committee; and 320 by Stanley Kutler.) Based on my list of all Watergate conversations, this meant that 634 conversations had never been transcribed by anyone, nor likely even listened to by anyone outside the NARA staff involved in processing them for public release (i.e., removing information that is classified for national security or designated personal/private, such as most of the conversations between the president and his wife or daughters).

Because all these transcripts were prepared from analog recordings, and most are only partials, I realized I needed to start from scratch and prepare ones of all the conversations to really be sure I understood what had occurred. There are good reasons no one had done this. Not only was it not easy to obtain digital copies of it all, but even with them, it is challenging work.

Most of the audio from telephone conversations is of relatively good quality compared with that obtained in other locations. Telephones in the Oval Office, the Executive Office Building (EOB) and the Lincoln Sitting Room in the residence and the telephones in the president's study in Aspen Lodge at Camp David created near-broadcast-quality recorded telephone calls. In the Oval Office, if the speakers were seated not too far from the president's desk, where the microphones were embedded, conversations are discernible with patience. Recordings made in the president's study at Camp David are similar to those from the Oval Office. But those from the EOB office are consistently challenging, when not totally impossible, because of where people typically sat: They were usually out of the range of the microphones. Similarly with the Cabinet Room: It is possible usually to pick up only the gist of the president's remarks, while others almost never can be understood.

Because of the poor sound quality, transcribing Nixon's recordings is extremely arduous and time consuming, sometimes not even possible. It can take many hours to transcribe less than a minute of conversation from the poor-quality recordings in the president's EOB office; sometimes these efforts are especially essential, as particularly important discussions were often held there. Most people who have transcribed these tapes discover that listening over and over and over enabled them to better understand what is being said, as does listening on different audio equipment, with different digital software, and at different speeds—and I occasionally employed all these techniques to the same conversation to tease out important information.

I found the most efficient, if not most reliable, process was to have someone else prepare a first draft, because it takes far longer to prepare the initial one than to correct someone else's. Accordingly, in 2010 I hired graduate students and created an evolving team to prepare them. Cherity Bacon, a former legal secretary working on her graduate degree in archival science, worked relentlessly and became the de facto team leader. It required almost four years to transcribe all the Watergate-related conversations, and the project continued when I started writing. And while writing this story, when the material was important I would listen to the conversation myself, for I am often able to hear words and phrases others do not because of my familiarity with the players and the subject matter.

There was far more Watergate material than I expected, for in addition to the Nixon tapes, I pulled over 150,000 pages of related documents from NARA. But had I known what I was getting into with the tapes, I might never have taken on the assignment of transcribing them all. Yet there was no other way to do the project and be sure I knew everything that could be known, so once I committed to it, there was no turning back. Actually, I am not sure which has been more challenging—transcribing about a thousand Watergate conversations or digesting and condensing the four million transcribed words into this story. Suffice it to say, neither could be done quickly.

The conversations fall into four general categories, which give form to this story. While not every conversation is quoted, they were all reviewed to write the following: Part I, Covering Up, is based on 35 conversations that occurred between June 20 and July 1, 1972; Part II, Containing, on 158 conversations held from July 2, 1972, through December 1972; Part III, Unraveling, on 110 conversations from January 1973 to March 23, 1973; and Part IV, The Nixon Defense, on 669 conversations from March 23, 1973, to July 16, 1973, when the recording system was dismantled. To give a full picture, other information relevant to the break-in is reported in the Prologue. The Epilogue summarizes events after the recording system was disconnected, on July 16, 1973, when Watergate became Nixon's fight to prevent the disclosure of his tapes, among other battles. In telling this story, which has much new information with which I certainly was never familiar, as a general rule I have not tried to highlight it as such; rather, I have allowed the story to unfold as it happened, only occasionally noting extraordinary new material.

These recordings also largely answer the questions regarding what was known by the White House about the reasons for the break-in and bugging at the Democratic National Committee headquarters, as well as what was erased during the infamous 18½-minute gap during the June 20, 1972, conversation and why. Because these questions have had enduring public interest, they are addressed in Appendices A and B. (Appendix C is a listing of Nixon's Watergate-related recorded conversations, as well as other data. See www.penguin.com/thenixondefense.)

Finally, in assembling this story I have not, except in a few instances, recounted my own involvement in these events, as I already have, first in testimony (in 1973 and 1974) and later in my autobiographical account, *Blind Ambition: The White House Years*, which was published in 1976. However, when listening to these secretly recorded conversations, or in reading the transcripts, I have recalled countless facts and actions I had forgotten, for the recordings provide information that was not previously available to me. Accordingly, I have, from time to time, flushed out some autobiographical details, usually in endnotes or footnotes, but occasionally in the narrative as well. Other than a meeting on September 15, 1972, I had no Watergate conversations with the president until eight months after the scandal commenced. It was not until late February 1973 that the president started calling on me to discuss it. Alex Butterfield, who knew the workings of the Nixon White House intimately, accurately described where I fit in the pecking order early on to the House Judiciary Committee during its impeachment inquiry, which may add some perspective to the material that follows.

> Now, Mr. Dean . . . was the counsel to the president, but I must say the president never did know this. The President may have heard his name, the President may possibly have seen him in one or two meetings prior to the summer or fall of 1972, but I would rather doubt it. Dean was young, he was very bright. I speak of him as though he were no longer with us, but he is. He is young, he is bright, affable, highly intelligent, gets along well with everyone, and was very effective. But he just could not, through no fault of his own, penetrate the system. He could not get close

to the President. I don't think he tried. . . . And the President never stopped looking to John Ehrlichman as his counsel on legal matters, or on matters which bordered on or which involved legal matters or had some legal aspect. He called on John Ehrlichman. . . . John Dean . . . was put into a somewhat untenable situation at times, because he did have two masters; he was responding to both Haldeman and Ehrlichman.[3]

While this is my account of what I found in Nixon's recorded conversations, I have tried to stay out of the way and let that information speak for itself. These recordings certainly answer Senator Howard Baker's question about what the president knew and when he knew it. Behind the closed doors of the president's office we also learn most of the details of what happened, when it happened and how it happened, not to mention how I became the centerpiece of the Nixon defense. Fortunately for everyone, his defense failed.

# List of Principal Characters

*(Positions at time of the story)*

| | |
|---|---|
| Robert Abplanalp (1922–2003) | Founder of Precision Valve and friend of the president |
| Jack Anderson (1922–2005) | Journalist; syndicated columnist |
| Sen. Howard Baker (R-TN) (1925– ) | Vice Chairman, Senate Watergate Committee |
| Richard Ben-Veniste (1943– ) | Assistant Watergate Special Prosecutor |
| Patrick J. Buchanan (1938– ) | Special Assistant to the President; speechwriter |
| Stephen Bull (1941– ) | Special Assistant to the President; personal aide |
| Alexander P. Butterfield (1926– ) | Deputy Assistant to the President; Haldeman aide |
| J. Fred Buzhardt (1924–1978) | Special White House Counsel for Watergate |
| Joseph Califano (1931– ) | Washington attorney; partner Williams & Connelly |
| Dwight Chapin (1940– ) | Deputy Assistant to the President; Haldeman aide |
| Ken W. Clawson (1936–1999) | Special Assistant to the President; Colson aide |

Charles W. "Chuck"         Special Counsel to the President
Colson (1931–2012)

Archibald Cox              Watergate Special Prosecutor
(1912–2004)

Kenneth Dahlberg           Fund-raiser, Committee to Re-elect the President
(1917–2011)

Samuel Dash                Chief Counsel, Senate Watergate Committee
(1925–2004)

John W. Dean               Counsel to the President
(1938–   )

John D. Ehrlichman         Assistant to the President for Domestic Affairs
(1925–1999)

Sen. Sam Ervin (D-NC)      Chairman, Senate Watergate Committee
(1896–1985)

W. Mark Felt               Assistant Director, Federal Bureau of Investigation
(1913–2008)

Fred F. Fielding           Associate Counsel to the President
(1939–   )

Leonard Garment            Special Assistant to the President; Counsel to the
(1924–2013)                President

L. Patrick Gray            Acting Director of the Federal Bureau of
(1916–2005)                Investigation

Alexander M. Haig, Jr.     Aide to Kissinger; White House Chief of Staff
(1924–2010)

H. R. (Bob) Haldeman       White House Chief of Staff
(1926–1993)

Richard Helms              Director, Central Intelligence Agency
(1913–2002)

Lawrence Higby             Haldeman aide
(1947–   )

E. Howard Hunt             Consultant, White House; former aide to Colson
(1918–2007)

Leon Jaworski              Watergate Special Prosecutor
(1905–1982)

| | |
|---|---|
| Herbert Kalmbach (1921– ) | Nixon's personal attorney; campaign fund-raiser |
| Sen. Edward Kennedy (D-MA) (1921–2009) | Chairman, Administrative Practice and Procedure Subcommittee |
| Henry A. Kissinger (1932– ) | Assistant to the President for National Security |
| Egil "Bud" Krogh (1939– ) | Deputy Assistant to the President; Ehrlichman aide; Undersecretary of Transportation |
| Fred LaRue (1928–2004) | Mitchell aide, Committee to Re-elect the President |
| G. Gordon Liddy (1930– ) | General Counsel, Finance Committee of the Committee to Re-elect the President; former aide to Krogh and Young |
| Clark MacGregor (1922–2003) | Assistant to the President for Congressional Relations; Director, Committee to Re-elect the President |
| Jeb Magruder (1934–2014) | Deputy Director, Committee to Re-Elect the President |
| Robert Mardian (1924–2006) | Deputy Director, Committee to Re-elect the President; Mitchell campaign aide |
| James W. McCord (1924– ) | Chief of Security, Committee to Re-elect the President |
| John N. Mitchell (1913–1988) | Attorney General; Director, Committee to Re-elect the President |
| Richard A. Moore (1914–1995) | Special Counsel to the President |
| Pat Nixon (1912–1993) | First Lady, wife of the president |
| Richard M. Nixon (1913–1994) | President of the United States |
| Manuel Ogarrio | Mexican attorney; clients include a contributor to the Committee to Re-elect the President |
| Henry Petersen (1921–1991) | Assistant Attorney General, Criminal Division |

Raymond K. Price, Jr.　　Assistant to the President; speechwriter
(1930– )

Charles G. "Bebe" Rebozo　Friend of the president
(1912–1998)

Elliot L. Richardson　　Attorney General; Secretary of Health, Education
(1920–1999)　　　　　and Welfare

Rep. Peter W. Rodino, Jr.　Chairman, House Judiciary Committee
(D-NJ)
(1920–2005)

Chapman "Chappie" Rose　Private Nixon adviser
(1907–1990)

Sen. Hugh Scott (R-PA)　Senator Minority Leader
(1900–1994)

Donald Segretti　　　California attorney; friend of Chapin and Strachan
(1941– )

John Sirica　　　　Chief Judge, U.S. District Court for the District of
(1904–1992)　　　　Columbia

Hugh Sloan　　　　Treasurer, Committee to Re-elect the President;
(1940– )　　　　　former Haldeman aide

Maurice Stans　　　Chairman, Finance Committee of the Committee to
(1908–1998)　　　　Re-elect the President; former Secretary of Commerce

Gordon Strachan　　Haldeman aide; General Counsel, United States
(1943– )　　　　　Information Agency

Fred Thompson　　　Chief Minority Counsel, Senate Watergate
(1942– )　　　　　Committee

Vernon "Dick" Walters　Deputy Director, Central Intelligence Agency
(1917–2002)

Sen. Lowell Weicker　Member, Senate Watergate Committee
(R-CT) (1931– )

Rose Mary Woods　　Personal Secretary to the President
(1917–2005)

David Young　　　　Special Assistant to the National Security Council;
(1936– )　　　　　Kissinger aide; Ehrlichman aide

Ronald L. Ziegler　　Press Secretary to the President
(1939–2003)

# The Nixon Defense

# Prologue

Although President Richard Nixon was enjoying the best days of his presidency, he was looking forward to a few days of rest from his busy schedule as he departed from the South Grounds of the White House for the Bahamas on an early Friday afternoon, June 16, 1972.[1] The president had reason to feel good about his accomplishments, both foreign and domestic, not to mention his prospects for reelection, since it had become increasingly clear that his opponent would likely be South Dakota senator George McGovern; he had all but locked down the Democratic Party's presidential nomination. McGovern was Nixon's challenger of choice, given the senator's hard-left positions on many issues, and the president did not want the Vietnam war any more than McGovern did, but Nixon wanted to resolve it with honor rather than merely quit, which the president felt would have long-term negative consequences for the nation.[2]

When Air Force One landed at Grand Bahama Island the president was met by his close friend Charles G. "Bebe" Rebozo, owner and president of the Key Biscayne Bank and Trust Company, and together they climbed into the president's awaiting helicopter for a brief flight over to the smaller Grand Cay Island. There they would stay with their mutual friend Robert "Bob" Abplanalp, founder of Precision Valve Corporation (inventor of the aerosol valve), who owned the 125-acre island and had refurbished a separate house just for the president's use. It would be a relaxing stag weekend of walking, swimming, boating (Abplanalp's fifty-five-foot yacht was docked there), good food and a few movies, courtesy of the motion picture industry. Other than the usual retinue of Secret Service agents and a White House physician, who always accompanied the traveling president, the only other aides on the trip were White House chief of staff H. R. "Bob" Haldeman, accompanied by his wife and daughter, and the president's press secretary, Ron Ziegler. The White House staff would take up residence for the extended weekend over on the mainland, at the Key Biscayne Hotel near the president's Florida vacation home where both Rebozo and Abplanalp also had homes.

The White House Communications Agency (a special unit of the Army Signal Corps) had set up a secure telephone line from the president's study in the Abplanalp house to the living room of his chief of staff's villa at the Key Biscayne Hotel, but there had been no communication until the president called upon his return to his Key Biscayne home on Sunday morning, June 18, 1972, and even then they did not discuss the breaking news of the weekend. Haldeman called the story "the big flap" in his contemporaneous diary, a record that would not be published until some two decades later.[3] His diary entry for that Sunday evening noted that he had spoken briefly with the president that morning, but not about the news reported to him "last night [Saturday, June 17, 1972], then followed up with further information today, that a group of five people have been caught breaking into the Democratic headquarters (at the Watergate). Actually to plant bugs and photograph materials."[4] Haldeman learned the details about what had transpired at the upscale Watergate hotel, office and apartment complex from John Ehrlichman, his longtime friend (Ehrlichman had been a classmate of Haldeman's at UCLA, and both were veterans of two Nixon campaigns) and professional peer on the White House staff, where he served as assistant to the president for domestic affairs. Haldeman also spoke with Jeb Magruder, a former member of his staff at the White House, whom he had sent over to serve as the deputy director of the Committee to Re-elect the President (also known as "CRP," "reelection committee" or, because the offices were located across the street from the White House at 1701 Pennsylvania Avenue, NW, "1701").

Ehrlichman, who had remained in Washington, had himself learned on Saturday evening, June 17, 1972, of the arrests of the five men shortly after midnight that day by the District of Columbia Metropolitan Police at the offices of the Democratic National Committee (DNC) in the Watergate complex, first from Lilburn E. "Pat" Boggs, an assistant director of the U.S. Secret Service. Boggs reported that the men had electronic surveillance and photographic equipment in their possession. He also said that the FBI had found White House consultant E. Howard Hunt's name with a White House telephone number in an address book, as well as a check drawn on Hunt's bank account, on one of the burglars.[5] Ehrlichman asked Boggs if anybody from the White House was involved, and Boggs responded that, as far as he knew, the only connection to the White House was the material relating to Hunt.[6]

Boggs also informed him that one of the men arrested was James Mc-Cord, the chief of security at the reelection committee and the Republican National Committee. Boggs had earlier shared this information with Ehrlichman's former White House aide John "Jack" Caulfield, a retired New York Police Department detective, who had undertaken countless clandestine investigations for Ehrlichman, including several wiretappings, while working at the Nixon White House.[7] (Caulfield had wanted to be in charge of the 1972 campaign's political intelligence operation, but he was passed over for the job.[8]) It was Caulfield who suggested that Boggs call Ehrlichman to report this "fucking disaster."[9] Caulfield himself later called Ehrlichman to assure him, as he did others, that the Watergate matter was not his operation, although he had, in fact, recruited McCord for his position as head of security not only for the CRP but also for the Republican National Committee. He was also planning on going into business with McCord after the election.[10] Notwithstanding later statements to the contrary by McCord, Caulfield claimed he had no knowledge of McCord's involvement in the bungled break-in.

While Ehrlichman was doubtless relieved that Caulfield was not implicated, and that to Caulfield's knowledge no one in the White House had any relationship with McCord, Howard Hunt was another story. Hunt's involvement raised serious potential problems for the White House and Ehrlichman. Both Ehrlichman and Haldeman had been directly involved in Hunt's coming to the White House, at the urging of Charles W. "Chuck" Colson, the latter's friend and fellow Brown alumni. Colson, a special counsel to the president (a title that enabled lawyers to keep their law licenses active when not practicing at the White House), was actually the president's special political handyman; he worked at building good relationships with friends while trying to destroy the president's perceived political enemies. It was Ehrlichman who had assigned Hunt to the Special Investigations Unit, which was created in July 1971 to investigate sensitive information leaks in general and that of the so-called Pentagon Papers (a top secret study of the origins of the Vietnam War prepared for the Johnson administration) in particular. Leaks had long plagued the Nixon presidency, and the disclosure of the Pentagon Papers in June 1971 had pushed the president to take action. When the FBI failed to investigate the matter aggressively, the president created his own clandestine unit within the White House, which later became known as "the plumbers."[11] Ehrlichman had once called the deputy director of the CIA to request that the agency "assist" Hunt (who wanted false identification and disguises as part of his work for Colson and the plumbers), notwithstanding the fact that such domestic activity was a violation of the CIA's charter.

But Ehrlichman had a far more troubling potential problem involving Hunt: Ehrlichman had approved—for reasons of "national security," he later claimed—a botched and illegal operation undertaken by Hunt with another White House plumber, G. Gordon Liddy, to obtain information from a psychiatrist (who had turned down the FBI's inquiries) who had treated the man who had leaked the Pentagon Papers, Daniel Ellsberg. This supposedly covert operation, which took place on September 3, 1971, had been a debacle, a conspicuously overt and unusually sloppy break-in at the offices of Dr. Lewis Fielding in Beverly Hills, California, that had produced nothing while putting the White House at considerable risk. After this fiasco Ehrlichman closed down the plumbers' covert operations and quietly found propitious ways to move both Hunt and Liddy out of the White House.[12]

After his conversations with Pat Boggs and Jack Caulfield, Ehrlichman called Chuck Colson, because he considered Hunt to be Colson's man. Or, more specifically, as he later explained, Hunt was a fellow who would do dirty deeds for Colson, and since Colson did dirty deeds for the president, Ehrlichman could not rule out the possibility of Nixon's involvement.[13] But Colson protested innocence regarding Hunt and the Watergate break-in, claiming that Hunt had departed the White House in April, although he could not explain why Hunt still had a White House telephone number and an office in the Executive Office Building (EOB), which was part of the White House complex.

Later on that Saturday evening of June 17, Ehrlichman telephoned Haldeman in Florida to share the facts he had gathered. But Haldeman was out, so he gave Ron Ziegler a bare-bones report so the president's press secretary would be prepared to handle any news media inquiries.*[14]

Alex Butterfield, a deputy assistant to the president and Haldeman aide

---

*Notwithstanding that he was highly knowledgeable and intimately involved in virtually all decisions about how to portray the White House's relationship to the Watergate scandal as it unfolded over some twenty-six months, Ziegler was never the focus of any investigation or prosecution, and he gave only a few general interviews when it was all over. Ziegler never wrote the book he once contemplated and never provided the Nixon library with an oral history; his White House files are little more than the

who handled administrative and management matters, such as liaising with the Secret Service, also learned of the arrests on Saturday, June 17, 1972. He was first notified by Secret Service Agent Al Wong, who was in charge of the service's Technical Security Division, which comprised the electronics experts who made certain no one was bugging the White House or wiretapping its telephone system, and who installed and maintained Nixon's secret recording system. As it happened, it was Al Wong who had recommended James McCord to Jack Caulfield as someone who could provide security for the CRP and the Republican National Committee, because McCord had held a job similar to Wong's at the CIA headquarters in Langley, Virginia, before his recent retirement. Wong, understandably, was troubled that McCord had been arrested in the DNC and was now in jail.

As the day progressed, Butterfield learned more. Late Saturday afternoon the U.S. Attorney's Office for the District of Columbia obtained a subpoena to search the Watergate Hotel rooms occupied by the burglary team, and it was there they found the address book with Hunt's name and White House telephone number, as well as a sealed envelope addressed to the Lakewood Country Club, Rockville, Maryland, with a $6.36 check drawn by Hunt (to pay far less costly his out-of-state dues; because he lived in-state he had given one of the burglars the check to mail from Miami). The FBI's Washington Field Office (WFO) quickly found Hunt's name in their indices, signaling that they had recently completed a background check on him for a staff position at the White House. This prompted the FBI WFO supervisor to contact Butterfield at 7:11 P.M., according to the FBI's records, to advise him of Hunt's possible connection to one of the men arrested at the DNC. Butterfield, who was home by this hour, knew that Hunt had been a consultant but thought he no longer worked at the White House.[15]

On Sunday morning, June 18, 1972, *The Washington Post* front-page headline reported 5 HELD IN PLOT TO BUG DEMOCRATS' OFFICE HERE. The *Post* story had the names of the men arrested and said that they had all been wearing rubber surgical gloves and were carrying lock-picking equipment, a walkie-talkie, forty rolls of unexposed film, two 35 millimeter cameras and twenty-three hundred dollars in cash, most in sequentially numbered one-hundred-dollar bills. The story further reported that four of

---

product of the White House Press Office. Ziegler died of a heart attack on February 10, 2003, at age sixty-three.

the men arrested had rented rooms 214 and 314 at the Watergate Hotel around noon on Friday using fictitious names. They had all dined on lobster at the Watergate Restaurant on Friday night, and after the U.S. Attorney's Office obtained search warrants, the FBI "found another $4,200 in $100 bills of the same serial number sequence as the money taken from the suspects, [and] more burglary tools and electronic bugging equipment stashed in six suitcases."[16] At the end of the account, inside the *Post* on page 23, another headline read INTRUDERS FOILED BY SECURITY GUARD. This second story reported that Frank Wills, a security guard, noticed two doors had been taped so the latches would not lock. He removed the tape. When he rechecked ten minutes later, new tape had been placed on the doors, so he went to the lobby and telephoned the police, who arrived fifteen minutes later.[17]

Ehrlichman read the *Post*'s accounts, and after church, he called Haldeman.[18] According to Haldeman's diary, "Ehrlichman was very concerned about the whole thing." At Ehrlichman's suggestion, Haldeman spoke with Magruder, who was in California for a CRP event with its director, former attorney general John Mitchell, and other CRP officials, including First Lady Pat Nixon. Haldeman learned from Magruder that an Associated Press (AP) reporter had told the CRP's press man that McCord had been identified as their chief of security, so a public statement was being prepared by Mitchell. Magruder said it "was not a good one," although it would distance the CRP from McCord and condemn such illegal behavior as having "no place" in a campaign. Jeb said the "real problem" was the fact that the break-in and bugging operation was the work of the CRP's finance committee general counsel, G. Gordon Liddy (a former White House plumber), and they were worried that it was "traceable to Liddy." Liddy claimed it was not, but "Magruder is not too confident," Haldeman noted. Magruder said their plan was for former assistant attorney general Robert Mardian, a Mitchell campaign assistant with them in California, to return to Washington to keep an eye on Liddy.[19] Haldeman, not a Mardian fan, instructed Magruder to get back to Washington immediately to deal with the problem.[20]

Haldeman and Ehrlichman discussed and approved the statement released by Mitchell on behalf of the CRP, which (falsely) denied any knowledge of or involvement with the illegal entry at the DNC. Ehrlichman later recalled that "we discussed the public statement that was going to be made on it."[21] Haldeman added in his diary that Ehrlichman thought "the statement is OK and we should get it out."[22] Haldeman said he also talked with Colson and told him "to keep quiet." He noted that Howard Hunt had been implicated, identifying Hunt as "the guy Colson was using on some of his Pentagon Papers and other research type stuff." He further wrote, "Colson agreed to stay out of it and I think maybe he really will. I don't think he is actually involved, so that helps." Finally, he added that the president was "not aware of all this, unless he read something in the paper, but he didn't mention it to me."[23]

President Nixon returned to his Key Biscayne compound from Grand Cay by helicopter on Sunday morning, June 18, 1972, touching down at 11:51 A.M. Rebozo returned with him, and they went to their nearby residences. In his memoir, Nixon recalled that when he arrived at his home he could smell coffee brewing in the kitchen, so he went to get a cup. There he noticed the *Miami Herald* front page, with a small story in the middle on the left side: MIAMIANS HELD IN D.C. TRY TO BUG DEMO HEADQUARTERS. He scanned the opening paragraphs, which said that four of the five men arrested in the Democratic National Committee headquarters at the Watergate were from Miami. After reading that they had all been wearing surgical gloves, he "dismissed it as some sort of prank."[24]

Absent from his memoir, however, is what appears to have been his delayed reaction to the Watergate story, which occurred a few hours later, when he learned more from Rebozo and then spoke with Colson. After an hour and a half of telephone calls on other business and lunch, Nixon strolled over to Rebozo's house at 2:45 P.M. But they visited for only fifteen minutes before returning to the president's house to call Colson. Rebozo, who was very active with the Miami Cuban community, knew most, if not all, of the men arrested at the Watergate, for their names had been listed in the *Herald* story: Bernard L. Barker, a real-estate broker; Eugenio Martinez, one of Barker's salesmen; Virgilio Gonzales, a locksmith; and Frank Sturgis, a soldier of fortune—all well-known anti-Castro activists who were respected in the Cuban community. After talking with Rebozo, Nixon understood that this was no prank.

Colson was later unable to recall either of his two conversations with Nixon on June 18, 1972, but he did testify that one of his assistants recalled what was said, because Colson had told him about it after he talked to Nixon. Nixon, he said, "was so furious that he had thrown an ashtray across the room at Key Biscayne and thought it was the dumbest thing he had ever heard of and was just outraged over the fact that anybody even remotely connected with the campaign organization would have anything to do . . . with something like Watergate."[25] Colson was mistaken when he also testi-fied he believed Nixon had learned of McCord's role from the newspaper on June 18, 1972, for that information was not publicly reported until Monday, June 19, 1972. It is more likely that Colson, who learned from Ehrlichman, told the president about McCord and Nixon exploded. Although when Nixon later thought about his reaction, he walked it back to a nonreaction, so that he appeared unconcerned, as his later behavior showed. But in the larger picture, Nixon's first reaction is not particularly important. No doubt he was trying to establish for doubters that he had no direct connection with the Watergate break-in, which I am confident was true.

Because of a passing hurricane late Sunday afternoon, the president de-cided to not return to Washington until Monday, June 19, 1972, but when the weather turned beautiful Monday morning, he decided to spend the day in Key Biscayne, for more boating and swimming, and to return to the White House that evening. Given the limited information the president had received, there was no reason he would have been particularly concerned about the events at the Watergate. So Nixon spent that Monday morning on the telephone with his personal secretary, Rose Mary Woods, and his daugh-ters, Tricia and Julie; he called Haldeman to advise him of his decision to spend the day in Key Biscayne; he talked with Kissinger's assistant Al Haig, and then with Reverend Billy Graham—which was the longest of his calls—discussing efforts to keep Governor George Wallace from undertaking a third-party run for the presidency, which posed a threat to Nixon's reelec-tion, as it could split the conservative vote. Reverend Graham was close to Wallace's wife and thought he could help out.[26] At 11:50 A.M. the president met with Haldeman for an hour and fifteen minutes to discuss campaign logistics and the need to place someone in the CRP to handle the adminis-trative details for Mitchell, but there is no evidence that Watergate was dis-cussed.

Back in Washington, Ehrlichman was further assessing the problem. He called me, requesting I speak with Chuck Colson to see what I could learn, and he asked me to talk with Attorney General Dick Kleindienst to see if he knew where all the Watergate investigation leaks in *The Washington Post* had come from. I told Ehrlichman that Magruder had called me to tell me that the break-in was Liddy's work and that Magruder had requested I meet with

Liddy, since they could barely communicate (Magruder claimed Liddy had threatened to kill him). Ehrlichman instructed me to do so and report back to him.

In a walk down Seventeenth Street NW (which is on the west side of the White House grounds), a shaken, slightly disheveled-looking Liddy apologized for his team's arrest at the Watergate, explaining that they had gone back into the DNC to fix bugs that were not working properly, because Magruder had pushed him for more and better information. He also apologized for using McCord, since he had promised that none of his activities would ever be traceable. He said that with Howard Hunt's assistance he had recruited the team in Miami, and he was concerned that they were now in jail, although he assured me they would not talk. Liddy said I needed to know that two of the men in jail had been used in an earlier effort—a "national security operation" at Daniel Ellsberg's psychiatrist's office in California. I asked him if anyone from the White House was involved; he said that no one at the White House had knowledge of his activities, with the possible exception of Haldeman's aide and liaison to the CRP, Gordon Strachan. As our walk ended, Liddy offered to have himself shot on any street corner if the White House wished to take him out. I told him I did not think that would be necessary.[27]

At noon I met with Ehrlichman to report all I had learned. Concerned with my own exposure, I also told Ehrlichman that I had been asked to attend two meetings in Mitchell's office, while he was still attorney general, at which Liddy had presented absurd plans for campaign intelligence gathering that involved kidnapping, prostitutes, chase planes and electronic surveillance. I said Mitchell had turned him down at the first meeting. I arrived late to the second, and when I heard talk of illegal activities, I had thrown cold water on it all by saying I did not believe such matters should be discussed in the office of the attorney general.[28] I told Ehrlichman I had reported this information to Haldeman, who had instructed me to have nothing further to do with these activities. I assured Ehrlichman that I believed Liddy's scheme had been turned off but clearly that had not happened. It was at this time I mentioned in passing that maybe we should hire an experienced criminal law attorney for the staff, for I had no such experience and was unaware of anyone on the staff who did, but he completely dismissed the idea with a wave of his hand.

At 1:45 P.M. Ehrlichman met with Attorney General Dick Kleindienst, who was in a mild state of panic. On Sunday, June 18, 1972, after he played in a golf tournament at Burning Tree Country Club in Maryland, Liddy had interrupted his lunch. He caught Kleindienst's eye, signaling that he needed to speak with him, and then told him he had a personal message from John Mitchell, and they needed privacy. They went to the men's locker room, where Liddy asked if he'd heard about the arrests the night before at the Democratic National Committee at the Watergate. Kleindienst said that Henry Petersen, the head of the Criminal Division at the Department of Justice, had called him about it that morning. Liddy then told Kleindienst that the break-in was an operation of the Nixon reelection committee and that the men arrested were people working under his direction. He said they would keep their mouths shut, but one of the men, James McCord, was an employee at the CRP. "Jesus Christ!" Kleindienst responded, and Liddy proceeded to explain that he wanted to get McCord out of jail right away, before he was identified. Kleindienst said that that would be impossible, that he had no such authority, and that it would be terrible for the president for him to even try. Kleindienst concluded the conversation by telling Liddy to tell Mitchell that if he wanted to call him, he knew where to reach him, and ended the visit. Neither Ehrlichman nor Kleindienst has ever testified about this June 19, 1972, meeting. I do not know if Kleindienst also told Ehrlichman what he told me about his meeting with Liddy and his reaction to what Liddy had told him: As long as he was attorney general he would never prosecute John Mitchell.

After the president completed his meeting with Haldeman on June 19, he headed out for a relaxing afternoon in the sun, starting with a cruise on the *Coco Lobo III*, Rebozo's houseboat. Nixon found it pleasurable to simply motor around Biscayne Bay reading or simply thinking.[29] This excursion was followed by a swim at their favorite beach, to which a crew of strong Secret Service swimmers drove them and then watched over them as lifeguards. After dinner with Rebozo, the president took a short helicopter ride from his compound to Homestead Air Force Base, and got on Air Force One for the trip back to Washington. During the last half hour of the flight the president met with Haldeman, which, Nixon later noted in his diary (contradicting Colson's testimony), was when he first received "the disturbing news from Bob Haldeman that the break-in of the Democratic National Committee involved someone who is on the payroll of the committee to reelect the president."[30]

More important, during this June 19, 1972, meeting on Air Force One the president agreed with the feelings of Ehrlichman and Haldeman, and the advice of John Mitchell, that the White House, if possible, must stay away from Watergate. Nixon wrote in his diary: "Mitchell had told Bob on the phone enigmatically not to get involved in it, and I told Bob that I simply hoped that none of our people were involved for two reasons—one, because it was stupid in the way it was handled; and two, because I could see no reason whatever for trying to bug the national committee." Nixon added, "I also urged Bob to keep Colson and Ehrlichman from getting obsessed with the thing so they were unable to spend their time on other jobs. Looking back, the fact that Colson got so deeply involved in the ITT was a mistake because it kept him from doing other things that in retrospect were more important to do. The best thing probably to have done with ITT was just to let it run its course without having the whole staff in constant uproar about it. I hope we can handle this one in that way."[31]

The International Telephone and Telegraph Company (ITT) scandal had erupted in March 1972 and gone on for months. It was triggered by a story on leap-year day, February 29, 1972, by syndicated columnist Jack Anderson claiming that ITT, a multinational conglomerate, had settled a major antitrust lawsuit filed by Nixon's Department of Justice in exchange for a four-hundred-thousand-dollar, quid pro quo pledge to the city of San Diego, where the 1972 GOP convention was scheduled although later moved to Miami. More specifically, Anderson claimed that ITT's Washington lobbyist, the "crusty, capable Dita Beard, [had] acknowledged the secret deal after we obtained a highly incriminating memo, written by her, from ITT's files." Anderson's column detailed how Dita Beard and Attorney General John Mitchell had negotiated the terms of the settlement during a lengthy conversation at a dinner party following the Kentucky Derby, given by Kentucky governor Louie Nunn, in May 1971.[32]

Democrats had jumped on the charge, led by DNC chairman Larry O'Brien and Senator Edward Kennedy (D-MA), who made the ITT settlement central to the Senate's approval of the pending confirmation of Richard Kleindienst to be attorney general. Although Kleindienst's nomination had cleared the Senate Judiciary Committee, he insisted the hearings be reopened so he could clear his name. It proved a disaster, for he lied when he said the White House had no input into the decision to settle the ITT case, as did John Mitchell on the same matter. Nixon had personally called Kleindienst on April 19, 1971, to tell him to settle the case because the Antitrust Division of the Justice Department was taking a position contrary to his philosophy on antitrust law, not to mention contrary to the positions candidate Nixon had taken during his 1968 presidential campaign. He certainly had no knowledge of ITT's pledge to San Diego (it was actually only one hundred thousand dollars), for it was made after the president's call, as was Dita Beard's purported deal with Mitchell.[33] Dita Beard told many different stories about why, or if, she had written her infamous memo.[34] In fact, it appears that she did, but she was trying to take credit for something she had not actually accomplished, and when her faux boasting became public, she disowned it, but lost her job anyway, and then lied about it all.

At the time, no one took more effective political advantage of the Anderson charges than Larry O'Brien, which particularly angered Nixon because they effectively removed the luster from the aftermath of his historic trip to China, replacing it with a sleazy government corruption sandal. Even more frustrating, the charges were unfounded.[35] Notwithstanding considerable efforts by Nixon's staff, we were unable to knock down the ITT scandal. Behind closed doors, however, Nixon renewed calls for the head of his long-time foe, hoping to expose O'Brien's hypocrisy when he learned in early 1972 that O'Brien was on the payroll of billionaire Howard Hughes.[36] The president protested to Haldeman, in words to the effect that O'Brien's not going to get away with it, certain that they were going to get proof (O'Brien's tax returns) of this relationship with Hughes.[37] Nixon had been after O'Brien since at least March 1970, when O'Brien became chairman of the DNC and the president began worrying about O'Brien's political skills; he created something he called "Operation O'Brien" to discredit him. But nothing had been done.[38] The ITT attacks on the Nixon administration renewed his interest in discrediting O'Brien, for, as Haldeman later described it, Nixon was convinced O'Brien was somehow breaking the law with a "fantastically large ($180,000-a-year) Howard Hughes retainer for a part-time job."[39] Nixon had Ehrlichman personally reviewing O'Brien's tax returns and pushing the Internal Revenue Service (IRS) to audit him.[40]

When in prison because of Watergate, Haldeman opined that Nixon had provoked the DNC break-in because of his orders to nail O'Brien, "to get the goods on O'Brien's connection with Hughes," and because he was "infuriated with O'Brien's success in using the ITT case against them." Haldeman speculated that Nixon had told Colson, who in turn instructed Hunt, to get information on O'Brien. Although I did not find a recorded conversation corroborating Haldeman's conclusion, this is not to say that the widespread efforts in the White House "to nail" O'Brien was not a significant factor leading up to the Watergate break-in, for I believe Nixon's demands for information were clearly the catalyst that resulted in seeking information at the DNC offices in the Watergate. There are clear clues in the recorded conversations as to why they broke in and bugged the DNC, for those who mistakenly believe this remains a significant mystery.*

An overreaction to the ITT scandal would result in an underreaction to the unfolding Watergate scandal. By the time the president returned to the White House from his extended weekend in the Bahamas and Florida, Haldeman and Ehrlichman were fully aware of the problems. Ehrlichman was certainly aware of Hunt and Liddy's activities when they were working for the Special Investigations Unit, of which he was the titular head. Haldeman had been aware of the development of a campaign-intelligence operation from the start.[41] He knew the Watergate break-in was the work of the Liddy campaign political-intelligence operation, which had a budget of three hundred thousand dollars that he had accepted, after being informed by Gordon Strachan in a written memorandum in early April 1972 that Mitchell had approved it. Indeed, Haldeman had instructed Strachan to tell Liddy in early April 1972 to transfer his intelligence capabilities from Senator Edmund Muskie, who had been the Democratic front-runner, to George McGovern when McGovern appeared to become the leading candidate. (Had Liddy's team not been arrested at the Watergate they had planned to proceed that night to McGovern's headquarters on Capitol Hill.[42] Should they have been arrested in McGovern's offices, their orders would have been traceable as follows: Nixon → Haldeman → Strachan → Liddy → Hunt, McCord and the Miami burglary team. Although when Nixon called for moving the "plant" from Muskie to McGovern, it is not clear that he was referring to the planting of an electronic listening device; that was precisely the kind of order Liddy would have twisted, so the responsibility would have come back to Nixon.[43]

Frankly, the actual story, as revealed in Nixon's recorded conversations, of the way the events unfolded in the first two weeks following the break-in, and then in the months that followed, surprised me. While I knew the gist of the story from information that has long been available, what actually happened behind closed doors was often not as I had thought. But I am getting ahead of myself. This story speaks for itself.

*See Appendix A.

# PART I
# COVERING UP

*June 20 to July 1, 1972*

*June 20, 1972 (Tuesday)*

# Before and After the 18½-Minute Gap

On June 20 President Nixon's day began as did most throughout his presidency. He had breakfast in the residence, on this morning at 8:40 A.M., where he scanned *The Washington Post* and the *New York Times*, both of which had front-page headlines on the Watergate incident: The *Times*'s was EX-G.O.P. AIDE LINKED TO POLITICAL RAID, by Tad Szulc, and the *Post* had WHITE HOUSE CONSULTANT TIED TO BUGGING FIGURE, by Bob Woodward and E. J. Bachinski. Both reported Hunt's connection to the break-in, the *Times* connecting him through his ties with the Miami Cubans and the *Post* reporting that Hunt's name and White House phone number had been found in the address books of two of the arrested men. Both stories reported that Hunt had been a consultant to Chuck Colson and that White House spokesman Ron Ziegler had said from Florida that he would not comment on "a third-rate burglary attempt." But Ken Clawson, a former *Washington Post* reporter who now worked for Colson, told the *Post* that Hunt had left the White House and Colson had no knowledge of his Watergate-related activities. The *Post* account also noted that Larry O'Brien said the Democrats were considering a lawsuit.

When the president arrived in the Oval Office at 9:00 A.M., he signed a few documents and then scanned his news summary, a document prepared every weekday by White House aides containing highlights of the coverage of the Nixon administration by network television news, wire services and newsmagazines, with occasional special issues on media coverage of issues of interest to the president, who was not a television viewer. The document summarized a vast amount of information from the preceding twenty-four-hour news cycle (or for forty-eight hours over weekends) and served as both an information and a management tool. When the president finished reading it, the staff secretary reviewed his marginal notes and directives and prepared an "administratively confidential" memorandum to inform various staffers of the president's requests or directives. Because the summary could become voluminous, Haldeman often reviewed it beforehand, underlining with a blue felt-tipped pen the material that he thought might be of particular interest to Nixon.

Watergate was a lead item in that day's summary (with Haldeman's underlining reproduced here): "3-4 minutes on all nets on what [NBC's John] Chancellor called '1 of the most fascinating and exotic stories ever out of DC.' The GOP, said Chancellor, is 'scandalized and fit to be tied.' Mc-G[overn] and [the Republican National Committee chairman, Senator Robert] Dole on all nets; O'Brien on 2 shows w/HHH [former vice president and again senator Hubert Humphrey (D-MN)] and [Senator Edmund] Muskie [D-ME] getting in their licks as well on CBS. Dems will file a court suit Tues."

On page 16, under the heading POLITICS and the subheading "DNC Break-In," the following item caught the president's attention: "On CBS Hubert Humphrey said RN and cabinet 'owed country an apology and explanation for this incredible act' although he had no evidence GOP behind the incident. Humphrey acknowledged such things can happen in US politics, he discounted a Democratic investigation because it would be politically motivated and said the Department of Justice would have to be trusted."

After reading this, the president wrote questions for White House aide Pat Buchanan: "Haven't there been some other break-ins in political and government offices? Where were the cries of anguish when the [*New York*] *Times* and [Jack] Anderson got [Pulitzer] prizes for publicizing stolen top-secret government documents [referring to the Pentagon Papers]?"

As Nixon was reading the summary, Bob Haldeman and John Mitchell were joining John Ehrlichman in his office, on the second floor of the West Wing, directly over the Oval Office. I was asked to join this meeting, which was in progress when I arrived. I was told that Attorney General Richard Kleindienst was in the West Wing lobby and would soon be joining us.[1] Kleindienst would later adamantly claim that he had never attended this meeting, and Mitchell, Haldeman and Ehrlichman would later claim that they could not recall what had transpired during the forty-five minutes before I arrived, although they did not dispute my recollections, or that Kleindienst had attended as well. As I later summarized:

I expected some weighty decisions to be made in this company. Wrong. All parties were guarded. The White House faction did not trust the Justice Department faction, and, moreover, no one wanted to acknowledge how serious the problem might be. . . . Ehrlichman raised the only matters of substance, and even they were marginal. He told Mitchell that the White House would steer all Watergate press inquiries to the Re-election Committee. Mitchell nodded, not happy, not objecting. Then Ehrlichman asked Kleindienst about the Watergate leaks. Kleindienst replied that they were coming from the Metropolitan Police. He said the problem would soon be solved, since the FBI was assuming jurisdiction over the investigation.[2]

Haldeman, however, did record in his diary that evening: "I had a long meeting with Ehrlichman and Mitchell. We added Kleindienst for a little while and John Dean for quite a while. The conclusion was that we've got to hope the FBI doesn't go beyond what's necessary in developing evidence and that we can keep a lid on that, as well as keeping all the characters involved from getting carried away with any unnecessary testimony."[3]

Ehrlichman went from our meeting to the president's EOB office, where they talked from 10:25 until 11:20 A.M. Honoring the president's request, Ehrlichman did not mention Watergate, but just as they were parting, the president made the point to Ehrlichman that he had noted on his news summary that the press was all excited about the Watergate break-in but that they passed out Pulitzer Prizes to the *Times* and Anderson for stealing documents.[4] He would repeat that complaint in later conversations throughout the day.

After Ehrlichman departed the EOB office, the president ordered a bowl of soup for lunch and complained to a Secret Service agent about the dictating equipment he had used in the Bahamas and on Air Force One over the weekend. From 11:26 A.M. until 12:45 P.M. the president met with Haldeman.[5] While Watergate was not the focus of their discussion, the subject did arise in passing early on and again at the end. But this June 20, 1972, conversation lives in infamy because when the recording of it was later subpoenaed by the Watergate special prosecutor, it contained an 18½-minute gap consisting of a buzzing sound that experts determined had been caused by five to nine deliberate erasures of the tape. This gap created a media frenzy when it was revealed, and it was the basis for a mystery that has lasted to this day.*

---

*It is clear today what was erased and why, but as to who did it, while the list of candidates can be narrowed, the actual culprit cannot be established beyond a reasonable doubt. The gap story is 99.9 percent news media hype and 0.1 percent significant to understanding Watergate. See Appendix B.

The conversation began with talk of the good weather they had left behind in Florida, followed by a discussion of the president's schedule. Because Nixon expected poor weather in July, when they were to be in California, he told Haldeman he would return to the Bahamas in August. After going over routine matters, Haldeman mentioned that the Republican governor of South Dakota was having some political trouble, and the president began to dictate the outline of a letter. South Dakota was, of course, the home base of his likely reelection opponent, Senator George McGovern. It was while discussing this letter to the governor, some seven minutes into the conversation, that the 18½-minute buzzing begins.

The fact that they next spoke about Watergate can be determined by notes Haldeman made during the meeting; read as a record of the meeting they do not reveal anything of particular importance.[6] Haldeman's note-taking procedures have been misunderstood; he did not make a record of or even cite the highlights of what was said at any given session but instead recorded only matters that called for further attention and follow-up. It was in his diary he made an effort to record the actual gist of meetings and events, or of matters he thought of importance on any given day. Haldeman made his diary entries at the end of each day with uncanny discipline and regularity, and given the often highly incriminating information they contain, it does not appear he filtered information if he remembered it. Accordingly, Haldeman's diary entry is often more revealing but adds little to his notes for June 20, 1972.

Per Haldeman's notes (which I have translated from his abbreviated shorthand[7]), the following Watergate matters were raised during that morning's meeting: The president instructed Haldeman to be sure his EOB office was thoroughly checked for bugs at all times. He wanted to know what the White House "counter-attack" to Watergate would be. He wanted to launch a public relations offensive that would undermine Watergate by charging his opponents with their own questionable activities. Nixon had always been annoyed by the well-known fact that Jack Anderson had gotten away with bugging (and at the time of Watergate there was a rumor that McGovern's staff had tried to bug Nixon's reelection committee). The president wanted to point out that libertarians had created a callous public attitude toward bugging and wiretapping, and "the public didn't give a shit about it." Finally, he repeated to Haldeman the complaint that his detractors were making a big deal out of stealing information from the DNC while justifying the theft of the Pentagon Papers and Anderson's publishing of national security secrets. He told Haldeman that they "should be on the attack" regarding Watergate, if for no other reason than diversion. The 18½-minute gap also covered material unrelated to Watergate, according to Haldeman's notes, for the president asked him to find out the schedule of the Senate Foreign Relations Committee hearings on the Strategic Arms Limitation Talks (SALT) agreement, and they discussed details of an upcoming trip to California.

After listening to countless hours of Nixon's conversation, I can confirm what he wrote in his memoir about the gap in the June 20 conversation: "It has always been my habit to discuss problems a number of times, often in almost the same terms and usually with the same people. This is the way I tried to elicit every possible piece of information and advice and examine every possible angle of a situation before making this decision."[8]

I would add that Nixon also had the habit of ending a discussion by going over key points he had made during it, and that appears to have been the case for this June 20 conversation. At its conclusion he returns to the subject of Watergate, as Haldeman's notes recorded, but in a slightly different form: "If I can come back on this thing more intently, I can be very, very serious on the hypocrisy. There's no question there's a double standard here." Haldeman agreed and made an inaudible counterpoint, which Nixon dismissed. "I don't give a shit about that. Also regarding political money, and contributions, too. They're all doing it. That's the standard thing. Why the Christ do we have to hire people to sweep our rooms?"

"Because we know they're—"

Nixon finished Haldeman's sentence, "Yeah, they're bugging. And why—"

"Sue 'em," Haldeman quietly interjected, as the president was making his point.

"We have been bugged in the past, haven't we?"

With this question the recording ends abruptly, and it is followed by 2 minutes and 53 seconds of a specific tone added throughout the recordings by NARA to indicate that personal material was withdrawn. The NARA Tape Subject Log for this conversation (No. 342-16), prepared by people who listened to this redacted portion, indicates that Nixon's rhetorical question referred to his "previous campaigns"—namely, the 1968 presidential campaign. Nixon raised this particular topic throughout Watergate, believing that if he could make an issue of what had been done to him, it would place the DNC break-in in context.

Haldeman's diary entry about this June 20 conversation is consistent with

Nixon's account of it in his memoir (which undoubtedly his postpresidency staff checked) concerning the information missing in the 18½-minute gap: "The P was concerned about what our counterattack is, our PR offensive to top this. He felt we have to hit the opposition with their activities. Also put out the point that the libertarians have created public callousness. Do they justify this kind of thing less than stealing the Pentagon papers, or Anderson's files, and so on. He feels we should be on the attack for diversion, and not just take it lying down."

Nixon further explained in his memoir: "I am confident that our discussion about the break-in covered much the same points at 11:26 in the morning as it did just five hours later at 4:35 in the afternoon: that if any of our people, at any level, had embroiled us in such an embarrassing situation; and that the investigations and depositions, if they went too far in pursuing all angles available, would hand the Democrats a major campaign issue."[9] Haldeman's diary confirmed that Nixon raised the subject again several times during the day, "and it is obviously bothering him. He had Colson over to talk about it, and then later called me a couple times on various specifics. He called me at home tonight, saying he wanted to change the plans for his press conference and have it on Thursday instead of tomorrow, so it won't look like he's reacting to the Democratic break-in thing."[10]

At 2:16 P.M. Nixon called Colson, whose office was right beside his in the EOB, and asked him to come over. They met from 2:20 P.M. to 3:30 P.M.[11] Watergate was discussed for approximately twelve minutes at the outset, and then fleetingly at the end. The president tried to boost Colson's spirits—he was already being implicated in Watergate by news accounts—while sharing his thoughts about how the White House should deal with the problem.

"Now, I hope everybody is not going to get into a tizzy about the Democratic Committee," Nixon said, sounding as if he is stretched out in his favorite easy chair, beside his desk.

"It's a little frustrating. Disheartening, I guess, is the right word," Colson replied, with something of a pained tone, adding, "Pick up that God damn *Washington Post*. See you're guilty by association." Colson was annoyed about the story linking him to the Watergate break-in because Hunt had worked for him, although he had been off the White House payroll for three months.

The president listened to Colson complain about how his family wondered if he had been involved but dismissed such speculation, because Nixon said he would not have someone that careless on his White House staff; "A lot of people think you ought to wiretap. Or knew why the hell we're doing it. They probably figure they're doing it to us." Then Nixon added, "Which they are." When Colson concurred, the president asked, "That's why they hired this guy [McCord] in the first place, to sweep the rooms, didn't they?"

"Yes, sir. Frankly, sir, I haven't gotten into all the details that we want to on this. But I assume he was hired to protect their offices," Colson added regarding CRP offices.

"Well, they'd better. Better have someone." With political espionage on his mind, the president told Colson that Haldeman was working with Nixon's political mentor, Murray Chotiner, who had a political operative known only as "Chapman's Friend." This individual, posing as a journalist, was in fact a spy at the McGovern campaign reporting to Chotiner, and his information was shared only with Haldeman and Mitchell. The president explained, "Chotiner has some guy with McGovern, aides he had on the road, the plane, the bus. I just said to Bob: Get it out, make a good story. Get it out." Nixon wanted to leak some of the gathered material to go after McGovern. Then, after speculating on whether they had spies in their own ranks, Nixon returned to Watergate. "On this thing here," he declared, but then, apparently reconsidering, said in a near whisper, "I've got to, well, it's a dangerous job."

"Well, Bob is pulling it all together. Thus far, I think we've done the right things to date," Colson reassured him.

The president raised a central issue with respect to what would become a quickly developing cover-up: "I think the real question is whether we want it to remain with the people charged, whether they'll hold up. I understand, basically, they're all pretty hard-line guys." Colson agreed that was correct. "Or if we are going to have this funny guy take credit for that," Nixon wondered, probably thinking of Liddy, whom he later characterized as "a nut," or perhaps McCord. He often confused the two men in the early days, and it is not clear if he knew of Liddy's role until the following morning.

Colson, however, thought Nixon was referring to Hunt, and became defensive. "'Course, I can't believe he's involved. I think he's too smart to do it this way, he's just too damned shrewd. Too much sophisticated techniques. You don't have to get into [*unclear*] with heavy equipment like that, put it in the ceiling. Hell of a lot easier way."

"It doesn't sound like a skillful job," the president noted. "If we didn't know better, we'd have thought it was deliberately botched."

"Yeah, I thought of that this weekend," Colson said. "And then I figured, maybe it's the Cubans that did it. Organizing it on their own, because, you know, they had good reason." Mention of the Cubans immediately caught the president's attention, not as an explanation of what had actually happened but as a way to cover it up. He told Colson about having seen a Cuban newspaper, on Bebe Rebozo's desk in Key Biscayne, with an article headlined TED KENNEDY, PUBLIC ENEMY NUMBER ONE, which Colson made a note to obtain. He then explained to the president that the Cubans in Miami hated McGovern, because they saw him as a Kennedy stand-in. They were concerned that the United States might recognize Castro, and if so, all Cuban nationals would be considered fugitives and returned to their homeland, with no possibility of political asylum in the United States. This information surprised and interested Nixon, and Colson concluded by saying that they would therefore be willing "to resort to something pretty serious." Since Nixon was now well aware that this had not been a Cuban operation, but rather one initiated by his own CRP, he cut Colson off, bringing the conversation back to the real world and a discussion of the hostile press coverage, complaining again about the Pentagon Papers and Jack Anderson.

Before turning to other matters, he wanted Colson to understand that, concerning responsibility for the Watergate break-in, "We are just going to leave this where it is, with the Cubans."

"I think that's the only thing you can do," Colson agreed. In an effort to exonerate Hunt, he added, "The fact that they had Hunt's name was the most logical thing in the world, because he ran and trained the chief of brigade that went to the Bay of Pigs. He's the fellow that came up and cried at John Kennedy's office to send a second wave. Conservative syndicated columnist Bill Buckley is his children's godfather. He's a very hard-right, hard-running guy."

Nixon played the matter down, saying he hoped Hunt would not have a problem, and explained, "I'm not going to worry about it. I've—shit, the hell with it. We'll let it fly, we're not going to react to it."

Colson mentioned Larry O'Brien filing a lawsuit but had no further information on it. After a discussion of leaks, Chuck wanted Nixon to know he understood that they were not going to deal with Watergate the way they had ITT: "Back then, we were riding so damned high, and I guess we couldn't do much about it, but they dragged us into it." Then, referring to Watergate, he added, "But the press, the media and the Democrats are so God damn desperate for any issue that they can lay their hands on that it's something which normally wouldn't amount to that much. They're just going to blow the hell out of it, because they haven't got any other place they can lay a glove on us. And that was the case with ITT, which came after China, the economy was picking up, wage-price controls were working, they had nothing, so they went into ITT viciously." When Nixon agreed, Colson added, "I think they'll try to," but noted, "You can't make a case out of this the way you could out of ITT. The weakness in ITT was that it fed the public suspicion that the Republicans are dedicated to big business."

"Oh shit, that's right," Nixon said. "I couldn't agree more. You've got to keep all your people away from it."

The conversation went on for almost another hour, addressing matters such as Colson's suggestion of using the Securities and Exchange Commission to make life difficult for The Washington Post Company, because he believed that Katharine Graham, the publisher and head of the company, was a "vicious" woman who was primarily interested in her social status in Washington, DC, and who wanted someone in the White House who would "kiss her ass." Watergate came up again toward the end of the conversation, and the president labeled it "the dumbest thing," but he said he understood that "there are going to be all sorts of things in the campaign." Most important, he did not want anyone to think the Watergate situation meant the "world's coming to an end." Rather, it was merely "a development," not a scandal that was going to lose them the election. While he was concerned about the Democrats possibly filing a lawsuit, he did not think any judge would force his campaign manager, John Mitchell, to give "a deposition in the middle of the campaign." Chuck agreed and departed.

Haldeman returned to the president's EOB office at 4:35 P.M. and remained for almost an hour.[12] Although Nixon writes that "Haldeman ran through some of the other information he had picked up during the day,"[13] Haldeman told him nothing that he could not have recounted earlier during the 18½-minute gap. Nixon asked, "Have you gotten any further on that Mitchell operation?"

"No," Haldeman answered softly, and they began to talk over each other, about Mitchell, speculating about his knowledge of the bugging operation at the DNC. Clearly audible is the fact that neither of them thought that Mitchell had advance knowledge. "I think he was surprised," the president said. "I think that's right," Haldeman said, cautiously adding a qualification: "I don't think he knew they were going to break in." Haldeman's tone suggested that Mitchell knew generally about such intelligence-gathering activities, as in fact he did, but not specifically about the DNC matter. Notwithstanding the bungled nature of the operation, Haldeman assured the president, "these guys apparently are a pretty competent bunch of people, and they've been doing other things very well, apparently." Haldeman proceeded to provide Nixon with a strikingly detailed account of the break-in: "My goodness, the stuff, all they had in there. They had a three-channel transmitter. Two of the channels went out. They went in to get those untangled, and get the pictures of stuff."*

The president, still thinking about Mitchell, said coldly, "It's his problem."

Haldeman had more information about the Democrats' lawsuit: "They directly sued the committee for re-election and the Republican National Committee for a million dollars. One hundred thousand dollars damages and nine hundred thousand dollars punitive. Quite a sum. They want to take depositions on all this crap. Dean said that's the kind of thing, once they file and a judge orders, sets the thing, and starts the suit going and all, you could stall it for a couple of months, probably down to the election, with technical delays and pleadings."

Nixon remained concerned about Colson being attacked by *The Washington Post* and thought the situation called for "a little more sympathy." Haldeman agreed, noting, "I know he's sensitive, hypersensitive." But Haldeman wanted it understood that Colson did, in fact, have ties to Hunt, so the story was not baseless. With the point noted, the president said, "It's fortunately a bizarre story. Don't you agree?" Haldeman did, and added, "Its bizarreness almost helped to discredit it."

"On McCord, how was he employed?" Nixon now asked.

"He was on a regular monthly retainer fee," Haldeman replied.

"Does he have other clients?"

"He had a regular monthly fee at the [Republican] National Committee also," Haldeman said.

Nixon wanted to know about McCord's relationship to the Cubans: who was working for whom; what McCord might say, if he said anything; and how Howard Hunt fit in the picture. Haldeman speculated, "McCord, I guess, will say that he was working with the Cubans, who wanted to put this

---

*This information had to come from Ehrlichman, Mitchell or Magruder, because it had not been reported in the newspapers. Before hearing this tape, I was unaware of this information.

in for their own political reasons." As for Hunt, Haldeman had some new intelligence. "Hunt's disappeared, or is in the process of disappearing. He can undisappear if we want him to do so. He's planned for this day all along and has a whole process set up to disappear to a Latin American country. At least, the original thought was that that was good, that he might want to disappear, mainly because he can, on the basis that the Cubans see he was in the Bay of Pigs thing. One of the Cubans, Barker, the guy with the American name, was his deputy in the Bay of Pigs operation, and so they're kind of trying to tie it to the Cuban nationalists business."

"We are?" Nixon asked, surprised, and Haldeman explained that this was originally the press's doing. "Now, of course, they're uncovering these ties to Colson, to the White House. The closest they come was that Hunt was a consultant to Colson."

"Do we know what Hunt did, somewhat the nature of his consulting fee?" Nixon asked. The usually well-informed chief of staff did not know of, or perhaps decided not to report, Ehrlichman's relationship with Hunt, and replied, "I don't know about this."

"You don't know what he did, then?" the president asked, with a tone of displeasure in his voice. In fact, there was probably no information Richard Nixon needed more at that time. But with Haldeman pleading ignorance, both men speculated a bit on Hunt, and then the president reported, "Colson's protested his innocence in this. As I've told you, I've come to the conclusion that Colson's not that dumb."

Haldeman agreed, "In fact, we all knew that there were some—"

"—intelligence things," the president finished the sentence.

"Some activities, and we were getting reports, or some input here and there. But I don't think Chuck knew specifically that this project was under way or that these people were involved."

"But Mitchell, if he did—ah, well, I'm second-guessing," the president said, checking his thoughts about the obvious.

"Mitchell seems to take all the blame himself," Haldeman added.

"Did he? Good."

"He was saying this morning that it was damn stupid for him to not learn about the details and know exactly what was going on."

After a brief tangent, the president inquired again about White House security protection against eavesdropping, just as he had during the 18½-minute gap. Haldeman advised him that the Secret Service swept his office and telephones twice a week. As for their own secret recording system, the president told Haldeman that the Oval Office conversations were the most important. "They say it's extremely good. I haven't listened to the tapes," Haldeman said, to which Nixon explained, "They're just kept for our future purposes." Haldeman reassured him, "Nobody monitors those tapes, obviously. They are kept stacked up and locked up in a supersecure area, and there are only three people that know they exist."* "There's nothing we can do to help Mitchell out," the president said plaintively, returning to their previous topic, and said he thought that Mitchell was "in for a fall" because of the arrests.

"I feel like this is a nightmare," Haldeman said. "When you think about it, you think it can't be true. Something like this just doesn't happen." He worried that Mitchell might "perjure himself" and "end up part of it," although that was not inevitable. "As is, fortunately, John [Ehrlichman]† thinks, circumstantially, Mitchell hasn't done the specifics." Haldeman believed that the best evidence of that was that "if he had, it probably wouldn't have happened."

As the president attempted to piece together everyone who might have been involved, Haldeman responded, "It's everybody with any knowledge all the way through. It may be it's better to plead guilty, saying we were spying on the Democrats. Just let the Cubans say, we are with McCord because we're with the Republicans. We figured he was a safe guy for us to use."

"Well, they've got to plead guilty and get this stuff behind them, as fast as they can," the president said, with a tone of frustration. The conversation turned back to Howard Hunt and some of his activities for the White House, such as interviewing Lucien Conein, a former CIA compatriot of his who had been deeply involved in the CIA's activities in Vietnam and was believed to have knowledge of the assassination of Vietnamese president Ngo Dinh Diem.

"How was Hunt directly involved at the Watergate?" the president asked.

"He was in the Howard Johnson Motel with a direct-line-of-sight room,

---

*Haldeman was referring to the White House staff only, namely himself and aides Larry Higby and Alex Butterfield. The Secret Service, which installed and monitored the recording system, similarly kept knowledge restricted to only those who were needed to keep it functioning properly.

†There are many Johns who come up during the recorded conversations: John Ehrlichman, John Mitchell, John Connally, John Dean, etc. Typically both the president and Haldeman refer only to Ehrlichman as John, while for others they use the last name. For clarity, when confusion is possible I have either replaced the "John" with the appropriate last name or added it in brackets.

observing across the street. And that was the room in which they had the receiving equipment for the bugs."*

"Well, does Hunt work for McCord, or what?"

"No. Oh, we don't know. Something I haven't gotten into is how, apparently, McCord had Hunt working with him, or Hunt had McCord working with him, and with these Cubans. They're all tied together. Hunt, when he ran the Bay of Pigs thing, was working with this guy Barker, one of the Cubans who was arrested."

"How does the press know about this?"

"They don't. Oh, they know Hunt's involved, because they found his name in the address book of two of the Cubans, Barker's book and one of the other guy's books. He's identified as 'White House.' And also because one of the Cubans had a check from Hunt, a check for six dollars and ninety [sic]† cents, or something like that, which Hunt had given to this Cuban to take back to Miami with him and mail. It was to pay his country club bill. And one of his identities is a Cuban base, or I mean, a Miami base, and he uses. Probably so he can pay nonresident dues at the country club, or something. But anyway, they had that check, so that was another tie."

Maybe this was not too bad, the president thought aloud: "Well, in a sense, people won't be surprised by the fact that Hunt's involved with the Cubans, or McCord's involved with the Cubans, and so forth, here are the Cuban people [who don't like McGovern]."

As the conversation wound down, Nixon returned to the subject of Colson, who he did not think should be concerned; they would get someone to defend him in the media. Both felt Colson could take care of himself. "If Colson knew about it, he was not involved with it, I'm sure," Haldeman said, and Nixon agreed. The only note that Haldeman would make of this discussion is from an inaudible or withdrawn portion of the tape, in which the president ordered: "Colson stay away from [the] press." It was a telling instruction, and he added: "[D]on't give P[resident] details."[14]

"My God, the Democratic National Committee isn't worth bugging, in

---

*Haldeman, who was still sorting out the facts, had this particular one wrong. He would later learn it was Alfred Baldwin, who worked for James McCord, who used this line-of-sight room. After the arrests on June 17, Hunt went there to give Baldwin instructions to pack up the listening equipment and get out of town. Hunt and Liddy had been in the Watergate Hotel rooms that had been occupied by the Miami-based burglars.

†Often there are misstatements in the conversations, and I have not given them a sic; rather, when it is an important fact, or a clear effort to mislead, I have noted it either in the narrative or a in footnote.

my opinion. That's my public line," Nixon declared. Haldeman, however, reminded him, "Except for this financial thing. They thought they had something going on that." Wearily, Nixon conceded this point: "Yeah, I suppose, I suppose."*

Haldeman assured the president that his point was well taken, adding, "I've asked that question: If we were going to all that trouble, why in the world would we pick the Democratic National Committee to do it to? It's the least fruitful source." On this note the conversation ended, and at 5:25 P.M. Haldeman and the president left the EOB office together, with the president heading for the barber.

At 6:08 P.M. the president called John Mitchell. The conversation lasted only four minutes, and the recording system was not used. When the president returned to his EOB office after dinner, he phoned Haldeman, at 7:52 P.M. Inexplicably, all of the conversations he had made on the EOB office telephone on June 20 were inaudible, but the room recording equipment did pick up the president's report to Haldeman, and Haldeman made notes of this rather significant conversation.[15]

"I gave Mitchell a call," Nixon told him, after asking if he had interrupted Haldeman's dinner. "Cheered him up a little bit. I told him not to worry, that we might be able to control this Watergate thing. He's obviously quite chagrined." Years later Nixon would write that "Mitchell sounded so embarrassed by the whole thing that I was convinced more than ever that it had come as a complete surprise to them. He also sounded completely tired and worn out."[16]

As Haldeman took notes, the president continued, "I had one thought on the Cuban thing, on the Cuban angle, if that's the way it starts to bounce. I'd give a call to Bebe. The Cuban community down there is very much against McGovern. They could raise money for the purpose of paying these fines, and all, and so forth." Whatever Haldeman said about such a fund led Nixon to add, "I'm thinking, though, of having it publicized. Not something in private. In other words, making an issue of the fact that, given the politics of these people, there's real concern in the Cuban community about the importance of this election, which is why they're doing it. You know, there's an anti-McGovern attitude in Miami."

Explaining the logical connection between the Cuban community and

*See Appendix A.

the men arrested at the DNC's Watergate office, the president explained, "They are all tied in, apparently, with the Bay of Pigs." Nixon reminded Haldeman that Miami's anti-Castro community was, as the news accounts of the arrested Cubans had reported, "all anticommunists."

Haldeman recorded the president's thoughts and added a note to himself to "talk to E[hrlichman]." Years later Haldeman explained that Nixon had instructed him, "Tell Ehrlichman this whole group of Cubans is tied to the Bay of Pigs." Haldeman said he had asked for clarification but that Nixon only said, "Ehrlichman will know what I mean" and dropped the subject. Haldeman later wrote that he followed the president's instructions and told Ehrlichman the following morning after the staff meeting. Ehrlichman took this to mean that the president was referring to a disagreement he was having with CIA director Richard Helms over getting the CIA's complete records on the Bay of Pigs invasion, a matter in which Ehrlichman wanted no further part.[17]

It was now clear to Haldeman that Nixon wanted the White House to think about how to help Mitchell. He also realized that Nixon was thinking in very human ways about the Cuban Americans who had been arrested and that they would need money to survive the ordeal ahead. Haldeman felt there was a touch of political genius as well, typical of Nixon, in the way he saw the opportunity to counterattack when he was in trouble and to effectively "kill two birds with one stone. Get money to the boys to help them, and maybe pick up some points against McGovern on the Cuban angle."[18]

After a brief conversation with Colson and another with Haldeman, the president worked until 11:22 P.M., including updating his personal diary, in which he wrote that he felt reassured by Haldeman and Colson that no one at the White House had been involved in the break-in. Watergate, he concluded, was "an annoying problem, but it was still just a minor one among many."[19]

*June 21, 1972 (Wednesday)*

# Creating the Cover-up Scenario

I n the *New York Times* of June 21 the Watergate story had moved below the fold on the front page. Tad Szulc's report offered nothing new: Ex-G.O.P. Aide Rebuffs F.B.I. Queries on Break-In.[1] *The Washington Post* coverage, meanwhile, was escalating, with another front-page headline and story by Bob Woodward: O'Brien Sues GOP Campaign: Lays Blame for Bugging on White House. On page A-7 the *Post* featured the Cast of Characters Involved in Democratic Office Bugging Case, which listed Charles Colson (and characterized him as "a specialist in delicate assignments for the President") after Howard Hunt and the men arrested at the DNC, plus a lawyer, Douglas Caddy, who had shown up to try to bail the burglars out despite the fact that those arrested had made no telephone calls to anyone.[2] (Hunt had retained Caddy and given him this assignment.[3]) Another *Post* story reported Espionage Possibility Probed in 2d Break-in at Watergate, and described an earlier break-in attempt at the complex, noting that the men arrested on June 17 had been registered at the Watergate Hotel on another night when a break-in had been tried at two other offices in the Watergate Hotel. On May 28, 1972, "the police records show someone attempted to unscrew the locks on the offices of the Democratic National Committee [but had been] unable to gain entry, investigators said."[4] A *Post* editorial titled Mission Incredible opined: "*Mission Impossible* it wasn't; experts in these matters all agree the job was bungled at almost every stage of the way. *Mission Incredible* it certainly is, both in terms of the execution and, more important, in terms of the motives that could conceivably have prompted so crude an escapade by such a motley crew." The piece questioned whether the Nixon administration could "bring itself to use every means at its command to prosecute perpetrators of the Watergate raid."

That day's presidential news summary contained disquieting information. NBC News had reported that those arrested at the Watergate "may have been involved in [an] earlier DNC break-in (May 28)" and "DNC lawyer Edward Bennett Williams plans to take depositions from [Nixon's reelection committee] and White House staffers next week." CBS and ABC quoted Larry O'Brien boldly claiming, "[T]here's a clear line of direction to the Committee for Re-election and a developing clear line to the White House."[5]

According to the desk diary log kept for Haldeman by his secretary, Mitchell and Ehrlichman returned with him after the 8:15 morning staff session to his office, where they spoke from 8:45 A.M. to 9:25 A.M., when the president buzzed for Haldeman. Although none of the three men could later recall much about it, their meeting that morning was a pivotal one, for it was here that they concocted the first scenario for a Watergate cover story. Haldeman, however, described it in his June 21 diary entry: "The bugging deal at the Democratic headquarters is still the main issue of the day. Mitchell and Ehrlichman and I talked about the whole thing again this morning and Ehrlichman came up with the possible scenario of moving the guilt level up to Liddy. Having him confess and going from there.* The problem is apparently we can't pull that off because Liddy doesn't have the authority to come up with the amount of money that was involved and that's now under the campaign spending act requirements. So it would have to go up to Magruder in order to reach a responsible point. And that they, I'm sure, won't want to do."[6] Haldeman shared some of this information in his subsequent briefing with the president.

Mitchell, in fact, had totally reversed his opinion regarding the White House and Watergate. He originally urged Haldeman to have nothing to do with the matter. His new position was prompted by what he had learned the preceding evening from his top lieutenants, Bob Mardian and Fred LaRue, who earlier that day had met with Gordon Liddy in LaRue's Watergate apartment.[7] Liddy had confessed to his participation in the Watergate operation, which they already knew about, but also told them of his involvement with Hunt in the White House–sponsored California break-in at Dr. Fielding's office during the Ellsberg investigation, and he revealed that two of the men

---

*Ehrlichman would be indicted and convicted for perjury for his grand jury testimony on May 3, 1973, when he denied any knowledge of Liddy's name coming up during any meetings he attended during the week following the arrests at the Watergate. The prosecutors, however, did not have this remarkable information recorded by Haldeman. Count Eleven, Indictment, *U.S. v. Mitchell et al.* (March 1, 1974).

involved in that operation were now in the DC jail in connection with Watergate. This disclosure stunned Mardian, who, as assistant attorney general in charge of the Internal Security Division of the Justice Department, had been deeply involved in the Ellsberg investigation and prosecution. Mardian undoubtedly understood that this could result in a mistrial for Ellsberg, who was then being tried in federal court in Los Angeles.

To assure them that he would never get caught over Watergate, Liddy told Mardian and LaRue that, unbeknownst to all, he had worked with Hunt in getting Dita Beard out of Washington during the Kleindienst hearings (Hunt had, in turn, interviewed her to see what she knew wearing a disguise), suggesting he was as elusive as Hunt. Liddy also revealed that he had shredded all the new, serialized one-hundred-dollar bills in his possession, as well as all other evidence relating to the Watergate break-ins, including wrappers from the hotel's soap that he had brought home for his wife. Liddy also claimed he and his men had commitments for bail money, maintenance and legal fees, and told Mardian and LaRue that Hunt felt this was CRP's responsibility.*

Mitchell was alarmed by this report, and when later testifying before the Senate Watergate committee would refer to Hunt and Liddy's activities as the "White House horrors."[8] Based on my meeting and conversation with Mitchell on the evening of June 19, I had thought he might well step forward and admit to his role in the break-in. But in the days and weeks that followed, after I learned what LaRue and Mardian had told him, I noticed Mitchell's changed attitude.[9]

Mitchell urged Ehrlichman to call L. Patrick "Pat" Gray, the acting director of the FBI, to get him to rein in the FBI's investigation. He also enlisted Ehrlichman for assistance in devising an appropriate cover-up scenario.

When Haldeman stepped into the Oval Office at 9:30 A.M. he and the president conducted routine business until Nixon finally asked, "What's the dope on the Watergate incident? Anything break on that since we talked last night?"[10]

"No," Haldeman said flatly. He explained that Watergate was off the table at the senior staff meeting, which was as he wanted it. Haldeman did, however, tell the president he had additional thoughts on the matter as a result

---

*Liddy falsely claimed I had made the commitment, but I told Mardian and LaRue that it was untrue, not to mention that I certainly had no such authority. Today I realize this was a standard Liddy manipulative tactic.

of his later discussion with Mitchell. "Mitchell's concern is the FBI, the question of how far they're going in the process. And he's pretty concerned that that be turned off, and John's [Ehrlichman] working on it."

"My God, if you are talking to Gray, it's got to be done by Ehrlichman," the president insisted.

"Well, we were told yesterday in the discussion on this with Mitchell and Kleindienst that we should not go direct to the FBI. Mitchell said today that we've got to, and he asked Ehrlichman to talk to Gray. John's doing it right now," Haldeman explained.* He continued, "The question that Ehrlichman and I raised, both of us have been trying to think one step away from it and look at a strategy. See whether there's something that we can do other than just sitting here and watching it drop on us bit by bit, as it goes along. And it's pretty tough to think of anything. Ehrlichman laid out a scenario which would involve this guy Liddy, at the committee, confessing and taking the blame, moving the thing up to that level, with him saying, 'Yeah, I did it, I did it; I hired these guys, sent them over there, because I thought it would be a good move and build me up in the operation; I'm a little guy, that nobody pays any attention to.'"

"Liddy? Who's he? He the guy with the detective agency?" Nixon asked, confusing him with McCord.

"No. Liddy is the general counsel for the Re-Election Finance Committee. And he is the guy who did this."

"Oooh," the president groaned softly. This new fact prompted him to ask again if John Mitchell knew about the Watergate break-in before the arrests.

"Mitchell? I'm not really sure," Haldeman replied, even more guarded than earlier. "He obviously knew something. I'm not sure how much. He clearly didn't know any details."

---

*According to the telephone logs of acting FBI director Patrick Gray, Ehrlichman called him at 9:35 A.M., as Haldeman was meeting with the president. Gray later said that Ehrlichman simply told him (which I had not in fact been informed of): "John Dean is going to be handling an inquiry into this thing for the White House. He's expecting your call." Gray further claims he told Ehrlichman, "As far as the FBI is concerned, we're treating this as a major special with all our normal procedures in effect. It's going to be an aggressive and thorough investigation, and I expect we will be interviewing people at the White House. We'll need to set up procedural safeguards against leaks." L. Patrick Gray III with Ed Gray, *In Nixon's Web: A Year in the Crosshairs of Watergate* (New York: Times Books, 2008), 63. Gray's reconstruction is highly doubtful: There was no White House inquiry conducted by me, and if Gray was bracing the White House for an aggressive "major special" investigation, Ehrlichman would likely have shared this fact with someone—which he did not—for he would very much be subject to it. At the time, Gray hoped to be nominated director, and such a statement to Ehrlichman would have assured that he would not get it. Ed Gray, who authored this book, relied on the reconstructed conversation in his father's testimony. This was surely a conversation both Gray and Ehrlichman later wanted to forget had taken place.

"Couldn't have," Nixon said, dismissing the possibility. If Mitchell was involved, the whole affair was closer to the president, so he asked: "Isn't there some way you can get a little better protection of the White House?" Before Haldeman could respond, the president repeated his ongoing concern about Colson, who he felt was "taking a bad rap," and, of course, "if he's taking the rap, basically the White House is taking the rap, regarding the White House consultant business." The president noted rhetorically, "Hell, yes, Hunt worked for Kennedy, he worked for Johnson and he worked for the White House. That's the whole story about him."

Haldeman advised Nixon that they had been dealing with this situation as best they could, which satisfied the president, who again raised the subject of Colson. "You're convinced, though, this is a situation where Colson is not involved, aren't you?"

"Yup, I'm completely convinced of that as anything. As far as I can determine, it is," Haldeman assured him. Relieved to hear this, the president said, "I'm not concerned at all, I am just concerned, or I just want to be sure we know what the facts are."

At this point Haldeman cleared his throat, unconsciously telegraphing that he felt he had a duty to convey important information. While it is not clear how much Haldeman actually knew at this stage about Liddy, Hunt, and the Cubans' prior activities on behalf of the Nixon White House, he had certainly been told by Ehrlichman that they were a potential time bomb, and accordingly decided he must at minimum warn the president: "The problem is that there are all kinds of other involvements, and if they started a fishing thing on this, they're going to start picking up threads. That's what appeals to me about trying to get one jump ahead of them."

The president interrupted to probe for more information, but Haldeman was not inclined to share more bad news, though Haldeman remained in control of the conversation and tried to diminish the problem by quickly adding, "Hopefully, cut the whole thing off and sink all of it. See, Ehrlichman paints a rather attractive picture on that, in that that gives you the opportunity to cut off the civil suit. The civil suit is potentially the most damaging thing to us, in terms of those depositions." Haldeman apparently believed the FBI could be controlled.

"You mean you'd have Liddy confess and say he did it un-, or authorized?"

"Unauthorized," Haldeman clarified. "And then, on the civil suit, we'd plead whatever it is, and you get a summary judgment or something. I forget what the legal thing is. But Ehrlichman saw that as the way to cut it off, too, and then let it go to trial on the question of damages, and that would eliminate the need for the depositions."

The president went silent, digesting "other involvements" and the "unauthorized" Liddy, since he knew that Mitchell typically ran tight operations. When he finally spoke after a long pause he asked, "What do you think that they have to show as far as White House involvement is concerned? I am not too concerned about the committee."

"Well, we're getting a bad shot to a degree, because it's one hundred percent by innuendo. The only tie they've got to the White House is that this guy's name was in their address books, Howard Hunt, and that Hunt used to be a consultant—"

"And he worked for the CIA," the president added. "He worked in the Bay of Pigs. I mean, he's done a lot of things." The president wanted to make Hunt's activity an "isolated instance."

Again Haldeman sought vaguely to warn him, without volunteering any hard information. "You've got to be careful of pushing that very hard, because he was working on a lot of stuff."

"For Colson, you mean? Well, the declassification, then?" Nixon was using a code word—declassification—referring to a project that Hunt worked on to declassify national security documents embarrassing to the Democrats.

"No. It was that among other things."

"Well, did he work on that ITT thing, too?" Nixon asked.

"Yes, see, and if they track that down—"

"He didn't accomplish anything," the president added, still apparently unclear about Hunt's "other involvements" and "a lot of stuff."

"He's the guy that went out and talked to Dita Beard, in Denver," Haldeman offered, as an example of one of Howard Hunt's less offensive but controversial activities.

"I see, I see. Hunt is the Dita Beard contact," the president said, acknowledging this problem might resurrect the ITT scandal.

"Among other things. They've used him for a lot of stuff, apparently," Haldeman added darkly. After a pause, though, Haldeman made it clear he was not telling Nixon everything. "It's like all these other things, it's all fringe bits and pieces that you don't want to know, that's why I've challenged this question of Hunt disappearing, and they say there is no question it's better for Hunt to disappear than for Hunt to be available. And there's no question that Hunt would be called in this."

As Nixon responded with a neutral "hmmm," Haldeman continued, "But the effectiveness of the Ehrlichman scenario or something like it is that you establish the admission of guilt at a low level and get rid of it, rather than letting it imply guilt up to the highest levels, which is, of course, what they're trying very hard to do. By 'they,' I mean the press and the Democrats."

"Well, sure, that's the same thing," Nixon added.

"I think our people deluded themselves, and I have to a degree, in thinking this was a Washington story that would not be of much interest to the networks," Haldeman said, explaining that, because there was not much news, the media was "investigating those Cubans, and they're bound to find and follow some of these strings." They discussed the Cubans' activities, as they had been reported by the media, on behalf of the Nixon campaign before Watergate, which would help establish the break-in as a Cuban story. But they ultimately agreed that with Ehrlichman's scenario—having Liddy confess—the Cuban angle was not needed. But losing the Cuban version also presented a problem. "That's one argument against the Liddy scenario, because you can claim that Howard Hunt and all the other guys have ties to the Cubans," Haldeman noted, adding that Liddy's confession would not include everyone involved.

"An elaborate deal, wasn't it?" Nixon finally noted. "Mum, hmm," Haldeman agreed. The president added, "Apparently they said or they implied that they had some plans to bug McGovern headquarters, too?"

"Oh, I don't know. They found a plan of—" Haldeman wanted to correct the news media's speculation, which was correct, however. "That's a pretty shitty bit of journalism, incidentally, which they haven't pointed out and we shouldn't, but the reelection committee can. They had a plan that showed the layout of the ballroom area at the Doral Hotel, which is going to be McGovern's headquarters. What the press didn't point out is, the Doral Hotel is also going to be the Nixon headquarters. And we had a lot of plans of the Doral Hotel all over here, because it happens to be where we're going on our room arrangements."

"But who's over there at the committee that can do a little slam-banging on that sort of thing?" the president inquired. "I think that you ought to chip away at things of that sort that are so obvious."

"We should and we will. I've made a note of that one," Haldeman responded, yet nobody was ever enlisted for that role. But this prompted further conversation about the press coverage of Watergate, and Haldeman continued to sort out the players; also, the president soon returned to the press coverage of Colson.

"I was not of the opinion that it would just be a Washington story," Nixon said, but he had had second thoughts. "I think the country doesn't give much of a shit about it. You see, everybody around here is all mortified by it. It's a horrible thing to rebut. And the answer, of course, is that most people around the country probably think this is routine, that everybody's trying to bug everybody else, it's politics. Now, the purists probably won't agree with that, but I don't think they're going to see a great uproar in the country about the Republicans' committee trying to bug the Democratic headquarters. At least, that's my view."

"Well, that line of reasoning seems to me argues for following the Liddy scenario, saying, 'Sure, some little lawyer who was trying to make a name for himself did a stupid thing,' " Haldeman suggested.

"Is Liddy willing?" Nixon asked.

"He says he is.* Apparently he is a little bit nuts. I have never met him, so it's not fair to draw any judgment. But apparently he's sort of a Tom Huston–type guy." Haldeman's reference to Tom Charles Huston, a right-wing zealot who had worked at the White House, was no doubt meant to characterize Liddy as a similar radical, a beat-the-bastards-any-way-and-every-way-possible character. "Well, he sort of likes the dramatic. He said: 'If you want to put me before a firing squad and shoot me, that's fine.' Kind of like to be like Nathan Hale."

"The beauty of the Liddy scenario is that as far as anybody under him is concerned, he's where it came from. Even if we can't count on those guys," Haldeman continued, referring to the Cubans and McCord, "if Liddy admits guilt, then those guys can think any way they want, and it won't matter. Because it'll all tie back to Liddy, and he says: 'Yeah, I got the money and I

---

*This information could only have come from Mitchell, and it appears, at best, to have been pure speculation. When Liddy had spoken with Mardian and LaRue on the afternoon of June 20, 1972, his position was that his involvement would never be discovered, and he resisted Mardian's suggestion that he give himself up. See testimony of Robert Mardian, 6 Senate Select Committee on Presidential Campaign Activities (SSC), 2359. Rather than confessing, Liddy was busy creating new problems—a conspiracy to obstruct justice by demanding money to take care of all those involved in the mess he had created.

paid them the money and I told them to bug the place and I was going to be a hero.' And then, we ask for compassion: This is a poor misguided kid who read too many spy stories, a little bit nutty, and obviously we'll have to get rid of him, we made a mistake in having him in there, and that's too bad."

"Breaking and entering and so forth, without accomplishing it, is not a hell of a lot of crime," the president observed. "If somebody was going to ask me whether I agree with Ziegler's cut, calling it a third-rate burglary, I'd say, no, I disagree; it was a third-rate *attempted* burglary. That's what it was. And it failed." The president suggested checking the law, and based on his earlier conversations with Ehrlichman and Mitchell, Haldeman told him, "Well, they don't think they can be hurt much on that. If they take a guilty plea, the lawyers all feel that they would get a fine and a suspended sentence, as long as they're all first offenders." And Haldeman added, "Which they apparently all are."

"Yeah, yeah, yeah. So who's going to talk to Mitchell today about this?"

"We have," Haldeman reported.

"He's thinking about the Liddy thing," Nixon said, and then continued. "My inclination is, you have to do it, due to the fact that, if that's the truth, the truth, you always figure, may come out, and you're a hell of a lot better doing that than to build another tissue around the God damn thing. Let me say this: If it involved Mitchell, then I would think that you couldn't do it, just because it would destroy him."

"Well, that's what bothers Ehrlichman. He's not sure it doesn't," Haldeman noted.

"Does it involve Mitchell?" Nixon asked.

"I put it almost directly to Mitchell this morning, and he didn't answer, so I don't know whether it does or not," Haldeman answered.

"Probably did," the president surmised, quickly adding, "but don't tell me about it. But you go ahead and do what you want. But if Liddy'll take the rap on this, that's fine." Nixon would later tell others, and state in his memoir, that he never confronted Mitchell with the direct question of whether he had been involved in or had known about the planning of the Watergate break-in. As he explained, "[Mitchell] was one of my closest friends, and he had issued a public denial. I would never challenge what he had said; I felt that if there were something he thought I should know, he would've told me." (Nixon once told Haldeman, suppose he did call Mitchell and confront him, and Mitchell said, "Yes, I did it." What would Nixon say and do next?[11])

Now that he had more information, Nixon told Haldeman, "I wouldn't try to shove it in Miami direction," meaning the Cuban fund-raising approach, "but I think that if you're going to have Hunt on the lam, that's going to be quite a story, he's disappeared and so forth."

"Except they've got no direct tie from Hunt, at least up until now," Haldeman pointed out.

"The fact that he's missing bears out the fact that he's associated with the arrested Cubans, for the man on the street," the president observed.

"That's why it's important to get to the FBI," Haldeman explained. "There's, as of now, nothing that puts Hunt into the case except his name in their notebooks, along with a lot of other things," Haldeman claimed, oblivious to his conflicting conclusion.

"Why did the FBI put out all of that stuff?" Nixon asked. "It seems to me a rather bad thing to do. I mean, when you're investigating a case, you don't put out the fact that you found this bit of evidence, you found names and notebooks and the rest."

"The Bureau didn't. The DC police did," Haldeman corrected him.

"Oh, I see. Okay, that would add up. They're sort of stupid. Some press man gets to them, you know."

Haldeman told the president that he thought the Democrats had control of the investigation, since Joseph "Califano's got two men right in the U.S. Attorney's Office." Califano was a prominent Democratic attorney and former Lyndon Johnson White House aide. This information had come from John Mitchell, who only a few months earlier had been the attorney general of the United States, so he knew a great deal about all the U.S. Attorney's Offices throughout the country. Throughout Watergate Mitchell expressed concern that the rank-and-file staff of both the District of Columbia's U.S. Attorney's Office and the FBI were filled with Democrats antagonistic to the Nixon administration. More specifically, Mitchell believed that two top assistant U.S. attorneys in the DC office, Earl Silbert and Seymour Glanzer, were hostile Democrats.[12]

"Well, we'd do the same thing, wouldn't we?" Nixon asked.

"Sure. Oh, hell, they're doing exactly what we'd do, and the lawsuit," Haldeman said. He added admiringly, "It's a damn good move. They've got Edward Bennett Williams into depositions. [He] is going to press to start immediately. And they've made no bones about it. They've said the reason they're doing it is to get the depositions."

The conversation stopped briefly, and the sound of paper shuffling on the president's desk can be heard. When the conversation resumed, Nixon, speaking softly, evenly and with no enthusiasm, said, "Well, what you need is, what you can do about it today is, for Ehrlichman to talk to Gray," tacitly approving the move to curtail the FBI. He then added, "Got to find out what the law is on the depositions, and so forth." More animatedly, he reminded Haldeman: "They're going to have Colson, for example, on depositions. And they'd probably try to unravel his whole relationship with Hunt."

Haldeman suggested, "Which he could say is irrelevant, or his counsel could say is irrelevant, but that doesn't matter in a deposition. That's the problem. At least, that's what Ehrlichman and Mitchell were explaining to me. The problem with a deposition process is that you don't have the protection like you do in court. You can refuse to answer, but then they can go to the court and get an order for you to answer."

The president pondered that in silence before responding. "Well, you don't have much of a choice there, looks like, if the Liddy guy will do this."

"Mitchell's rightly, I think, a little afraid, 'cause of Liddy's instability. Because, obviously, they'll see that as a way for us to get out of it, and they're not going to let Liddy off any easier than they have to."

Nixon groaned, to which Haldeman responded, "For sure, that," and then reminded the president, "John [Ehrlichman] just developed this scenario as we were talking this morning. And he and Mitchell and I all thought we ought not to move too fast on it. On first blush it looked like it had some possibilities, but we ought to work on what's wrong with it."

After another long silence, Nixon said his intuition told him he should not yet hold a press conference, reminding Haldeman that McGovern's winning another primary would be the big story. The president thought he should learn more about Watergate, and what tactics should be used for dealing with it, before getting out before the press and commenting on it. Haldeman thought that he should not comment on it at all, to which Nixon agreed, but added, "Well, I know, but just no-commenting is hard to do, too." On this note, the conversation turned to the president's schedule, and then the decision was made to invite Colson into the conversation, to lift his spirits.

Colson arrived at the Oval Office at 10:13 A.M., and for the next twenty-five minutes, Nixon and Haldeman attempted to boost Colson's morale and get a sense of his thinking, and then sent him back to battle. "So anyway, don't let the bastards get you down, Chuck," the president said, as Colson departed, with Haldeman leaving soon thereafter.

Bob Haldeman returned to the Oval Office at 1:24 P.M. for a conversation that would last an hour and forty-five minutes. Because Watergate had been covered in detail earlier, it came up only tangentially,[13] but a discussion on the topic of anonymous campaign contributions foreshadowed the handling of Watergate two days later, during a so-called smoking-gun conversation on June 23 that would eventually prove fatal to the Nixon presidency.

In February 1972 the Congress had passed and the president had signed a new campaign finance law that called for the increased disclosure of campaign contributors. Congress provided a sixty-day grace period before the law went into effect, on April 7, 1972. Both Republican and Democratic presidential hopefuls used this grace period to raise unlimited amounts of new money from contributors who still wanted to remain anonymous, as did Nixon's own reelection finance committee. George McGovern, however, seeing a political opportunity in what his primary opponents and the president were doing, publicly declared that he would reveal all of his contributors, even before the effective date, and challenged all other candidates to do likewise. Although McGovern actually had few truly large contributors, the news media made his proposal an issue. A few other candidates from both parties agreed to disclose their contributors, but the Nixon campaign, which had raised some $10 million, declined to do so. While this was perfectly legal, the president was being criticized by the news media, which suggested that his donors were special interests who were receiving benefits from his administration.[14]

On March 13 the president had requested that Haldeman consult with Mitchell about whether there would be "a substantial problem" if they disclosed names of contributors. Mitchell said it would, as they had raised funds from many Democrats on the promise that their contributions to Nixon would not be disclosed. Since they were following the letter of the law, Mitchell told Haldeman, they should "straight-arm" the news media by announcing that "the president's not involved," and that this was the work of his reelection committee. He believed that after the grace period expired the issue would go away,[15] but instead the pressure had continued to grow, with virtually all the focus on the Nixon campaign.

As the president prepared for the June 22 press conference, his staff correctly anticipated that he would be questioned on this topic. The finance chairman of the reelection committee, former secretary of commerce Maurice Stans, was, like Mitchell, adamant that they honor their pledges to contributors, and felt that any donations should be returned rather than their donors revealed, but this was not an option anyone at the campaign wanted to consider.

It was during the June 21 conversation that Haldeman explained this problem to Nixon, and that much of the money that had been raised for his reelection was in the form of cash. As they were considering how to deal with this situation, the conversation drifted back to Watergate, first with an odd prediction by Nixon: "You will undoubtedly find that there's going to be another bugging incident, probably against us, before this is over. I'm sure." After further discussion of the new campaign law, Nixon had a suggestion: "Thing to do, I'm sure it's already occurred to you, but on the PR side, every time there's a leak from the White House or campaign headquarters, [we should] charge that we're being bugged. Don't you agree?" When Haldeman concurred, the president pushed the concept even further, explaining that Haldeman should have someone "plant a device," but cautioned, "Do it if there's anybody you can trust. Although I think you can trust, apparently, these Cubans. I think they probably are, to Hunt's credit, pretty reliable characters." The president took note of "the way they do operate, you know. They swear on this and that, their own blood, and so forth."

Then Nixon went silent for a moment, before his thoughts turned again to the PR aspects of Watergate. Referring to the overreaction of his staff to the ITT scandal, he warned Haldeman, all the while tapping a finger rhythmically on his desk, not to make the same error regarding Watergate.

At 2:15 Ron Ziegler joined them, which was the press secretary's first visit with the president since the arrests at the DNC. After discussing the mechanics and frequency of Nixon's press conferences, the president asked Ziegler, "What do you want me to say about the bugging incident, and so forth?"

Ziegler urged the president to say nothing, for, contrary to the impression in the news summary, television networks were not treating the incident as a major story. "My view is, if they ask you, and they will," Ziegler noted, "would be simply to say, 'I have nothing to say about that. The appropriate legal agencies, through the due processes of law, as Attorney General Mitchell has already pointed out, and we pointed out at the White House, obviously this has no place in the political system. Now what is the next question?' " He said the president should not take a hard tone but simply give it the "brush-off." Nixon made notes as they rehearsed responses, and the conversation moved to other topics.

At 3:11 P.M. the president departed the Oval Office with Haldeman and

Ziegler to walk over to his EOB office, and then at 4:00 met with Chuck Colson, with Watergate only a passing topic.[16] The president remained concerned about Hunt and what he might have done while working at the White House, and he asked Colson about Hunt's work on ITT. Colson said he had sent Hunt out to Denver to interview Dita Beard, but it was not a matter he was worried about.

"He didn't break any rules?" the president asked.

"He did do some stuff for me," Colson responded, vaguely.

"But not for us?" the president asked, hopefully.

"Oh, all of it was for us," Colson said, and repeated that he was not worried about Hunt's other activities. He did offer the president an idea, however: "I think that we could develop a theory as to the CIA, if we wanted to. I've not thought that out. We know that Hunt has all these ties with these people."

"He worked with them," the president agreed, momentarily warming to the suggestion.

"Oh, he was their boss, and they were all CIA. And you take the cash, you go down to Latin America—"

Nixon, however, was headed in another direction. "I'll tell you, I think that this has one plus to it, the Cubans thing works for us," he said, more interested in his own cover story than any CIA proposal. When Nixon ran by Colson the idea of Liddy's taking the rap and cutting their losses, Colson responded that he was for anything that got them out of it. But he added that he was deliberately staying out of the whole matter so that he could one day make an honest affidavit that he knew nothing about it.[17]

---

# First Watergate-Related Press Conference

T he front-page headline of Thursday's *New York Times* read 4 BEING HUNTED IN INQUIRY IN RAID ON DEMOCRATS. The story reported that, in addition to the five men who had been arrested, the investigators were looking for four more who had registered at the Watergate Hotel. (In fact, these were aliases of the Miami men who had been arrested.) It cited "Republican sources" as saying that Mitchell had ordered an investigation to determine the relationship of the CRP to the arrested parties, but that information was a ruse, for Mitchell never undertook such an investigation.[1]

By now it was clear, however, that *The Washington Post* was going to make a much larger issue out of Watergate. The city editor of the *Post* at the time of the arrests was Barry Sussman (who was soon to be appointed its special Watergate editor, and who would lead the paper to win a Pulitzer grand prize for its public service coverage). He was absolutely tantalized by the story as it unfolded, so he assigned two eager young reporters to it: Bob Woodward and Carl Bernstein. Sussman later explained that there was a collective mind-set at the *Post*, from executive editor Ben Bradlee on down, that Nixon & Company were somehow complicit in Watergate.[2]

Contrary to popular belief, the White House was not particularly well plugged into the FBI's investigation, and much of what the public (including Nixon himself) learned about it was from coverage in the *Post*, which in addition to Woodward and Bernstein had a dozen more reporters busy digging. Typical of the comprehensive coverage in the paper was Woodward's front-page story on the morning of June 22, DEMOCRATS, GOP TIGHTEN SECURITY AFTER WATERGATE "BUGGING" CASE, in which he reported that Larry O'Brien said that diagrams of his personal offices and living quarters in Miami had been found in the belongings of the five arrested men.[3] The *Post* also had three additional Watergate features, including one about the disappearance of Howard Hunt.[4]

After eating breakfast and scanning the morning newspapers, the president went directly to his EOB office, arriving at 9:20 A.M., where he planned to spend the day going through Pat Buchanan's briefing books, in preparation for his press conference at 3:00 P.M., his first in months. At 9:40 he summoned Haldeman, and after a brief discussion about how politically effective the president's family had become, he turned to Watergate.[5]

He told Haldeman he would respond to any questions about the matter as he had been advised by Mitchell and Ziegler but was certain he would be asked if there was any White House involvement. Here he needed some further guidance and thought, for the responses drafted by Buchanan sounded too much as if they had been drafted by a lawyer. As he paraphrased them aloud— "Nothing has happened to reduce my confidence in members of the White House staff"—he complained, "Well, that [is] too much of an obvious [reply], in my opinion. I think I should state there's no White House involvement." But he wanted to be sure that that was not too broad a statement, since it had not been suggested by whoever had prepared the briefing material.[6]

"I don't know what, it may be that their concern is that there is some White House involvement?" the president asked.

"No," Haldeman answered quickly. "The only question is whether that technically puts you in a—"

"—a position of commenting on it?" the president interrupted.

"Well, no, in a sense that, on a direct basis of White House involvement, I think you're absolutely clean," Haldeman replied hesitantly. Only days earlier, on June 20, he had reminded the president that a number of members of the staff—including the president and himself—were aware of the reelection committee's intelligence operation: "We all knew that there were some," he had said, a sentence the president had completed with "intelligence things." Haldeman now rephrased the statement more prudently: "Some activities, and we were getting reports, or some input here and there." When Haldeman responded to Nixon's question on June 20, his choice of the words "on a direct basis" regarding the White House was a careful qualification of the potential involvement of the staff, including that of Colson and myself, but particularly his own.

"Hunt's the only line to the White House," Haldeman continued, but he raised the concern that both Gordon Liddy and Jeb Magruder had once been members of the White House staff.

"But they aren't White House now," Nixon pointed out.

The president now took a call from Ziegler,* and after he hung up summarized for Haldeman the Watergate strategy they had agreed on.

"Well, I think I'll just say Mr. Ziegler's covered that, because he said he was asked about Hunt, and he said he left the White House three months ago. He said he was asked about Colson the first day, he checked with Colson, he was not involved. I'll say Mr. Ziegler has covered that. It keeps me from getting into it, and then they bring up another story, the president says White House was not involved."

Haldeman did have some good news to report: "We're in pretty good shape. Today's news is all good. In the first place, we got Judge Richey for the civil case. The civil case is kind of worrisome. The Democrats outsmarted themselves. They made a fatal legal error. They filed the suit on behalf of all Democrats, thereby disqualifying any Democratic judge from hearing it. And according to [former attorney general and current secretary of state] Bill Rogers, [Richey's] programmable, and knows exactly what's going on. Richey's played it just beautifully." Haldeman described how the Democrats had planned to "move immediately on depositions," but Richey would "entertain all sorts of delaying motions."

"He also knows he has a possibility of moving up in the world," the president added, and then turned to the fact that security at the Republican National Committee and the CRP had been beefed up, and warned that they needed to be careful, because papers had been stolen from the White House.[†] Discussing security and leaks brought the president back to reporters who published stolen classified government documents. That morning's *Post* editorial gloated over the fact that nothing had gone amiss, no national security calamity had occurred, when the classified Pentagon Papers had been published. Nixon instructed Haldeman to have a story written by at least one columnist critical of Pulitzers being awarded for such reporting. "We'll get

---

*The National Archives and Records Administration (NARA) tape for this telephone conversation, No. 25-116, is inaudible, so only the EOB room recording of the conversation is available.

†A navy yeoman, Charles Radford, had taken documents from the National Security Council and Henry Kissinger's office and given them to officials at the Pentagon, who wanted to know what was occurring inside Nixon's NSA. Some of this information had later appeared in Jack Anderson's syndicated column and became the focus of a major investigation by David Young for the Special Investigations Unit, aka the plumbers. Haldeman, though, was not certain anything had actually been taken, as opposed to copies having been made.

that," Haldeman assured him. "We've got another thing going that's taken hold a little bit, which is, we've started moving on the Hill, letting things come out from there, which is that this whole Watergate thing is a Jack Anderson thing." Haldeman reported about how members of Congress and their staffs had "started a rumor yesterday morning, and it's starting to come back already. That Jack Anderson has put all this together. He was bugging the Democratic offices and, you know, because these Cubans are tied to him," Haldeman explained (which, in fact, was correct with regard to Frank Sturgis). "These are agents he's used." Haldeman said the White House had planted the rumor that they had been working for Anderson at the DNC. "So, the great thing about it is, it is so totally fucked up, and so, so badly done, that nobody believes we could have done it. It's just beyond comprehension."

"Well, it sounds like a comic opera, really," the president added. Haldeman agreed, saying, "It really does, it would make a funny God damn movie." The president responded, "I mean, you know, here's these Cubans with their accents," and Nixon began laughing as Haldeman continued the description: "Wearing these rubber gloves, standing there in their expensive, well-made business suits, wearing rubber gloves, and putting their hands up and shouting 'Don't shoot' when the police come in. It really is like a comic opera." Then, on a serious note, Haldeman added, "Also, they have no case on Hunt."

"Why?" Nixon asked.

"They have not been able to make him. They can't put him into the scene at all," Haldeman explained. "We know where he was, though."

"But they don't. The FBI doesn't?" the president asked.

"That's right," Haldeman assured him, and added, "They've pursued him and been unable to tie him in at all to the case."

"What about the disappearance?" which had been reported in the *Post*. "So, he'll come back?"

"Well, they've got no warrant for him, so they don't care whether he disappeared," Haldeman replied. "The legal people, the FBI, who are running the investigation, have no way to fix Hunt in the case. They have issued no warrant for him. They don't care whether he disappears or not. The only thing there is, his name's in the guy's address book. But so is the hotel clerk's name."

"Is Rebozo's name in anyone's address book?" Nixon asked.

"No, I don't think so. He told me he doesn't know any of these guys,"

Haldeman said. The president thought Bebe did know Suarez, whose name had come up in Jack Anderson's commentary on the Watergate break-in and arrests. "But, hell, Suarez is one of the biggest contractors in Florida," the president noted.

Haldeman had further encouraging news: "Another good break is, they can't trace the currency."

"They traced it to a Miami bank," the president pointed out, again reporting what he had read in the *Post*.

"They traced it to a Miami bank, which was easily done. But the bank cannot trace the thing beyond that. They're not required to, and they don't maintain any record of where, or who takes it, when it's hundred-dollar bills. When it's bigger denominations, they have to keep a record, but with hundred-dollar bills, they don't. Even if there were [a way to trace the source of the funds], it wouldn't be a very great problem, unless it can go two more steps, because the funds came from a money order from a South American country. They might be able to get to the South American country and find out where the money order came from, and that isn't good. Up to that point we're all right, and they can't even go to the next place."

Referring to the CRP, Haldeman added, "They're going to continue to crank up the Cuban operation."

"How high up?" Nixon interrupted.

"Well, the FBI's investigation is beginning to look into other Cubans, and that kind of thing. These guys are allied in some other enterprises that we don't care about." Haldeman felt this was still a pretty encouraging story, as long as they didn't dig too deep—though he did not explain what they might dig up, which he apparently felt the president need not consider. "See, the thing we forget is that we know too much, and therefore read too much into what we see that other people can't read into it. I mean, what seems obvious to us because of what we know is not obvious to other people."

After a brief discussion of how little attention the networks were paying to the Cuban connection, Haldeman continued, "One thing they are thinking about doing at the CRP, which we could do, and it would be easy to cover it with no problem, just for safety's sake, is to get Liddy out of the country. They'll just have him go over to Europe and be checking on some of our financial contributions, the fund-raising drive in Europe."

"You mean, the idea being, they're not after him?" Nixon asked.

"Not yet. But they figure, maybe if he's moved around, it would be good.

They've sent him to L.A. He's had some business there. And he can as a routine matter go to Europe, and it's just as well if something does surface not to have him around, or have to move him after it does. And then they can wait and see; if we want him back, it's easy to bring him back.

"How the hell can you question him, unless somebody talks?" Nixon asked.

"If somebody talks, which is still a potential," Haldeman said. "Now, they're leaving McCord in jail to keep an eye on the other guys and maintain contact with them."

This situation surprised the president. "The guys there, they don't want to get them out on bail?"

"Apparently they'd rather leave them in right now."

"They probably don't mind," the president surmised.

"For a lot of reasons, they're better off in jail," Haldeman agreed.

The June 22, 1972, press conference was handled as an impromptu event in the Oval Office, where the White House press corps gathered around the president's desk for an informal question-and-answer session, with no radio or television coverage. A White House stenographer prepared an official transcript of the event, which was also recorded. Ziegler had set the ground rules for the event, which was limited to domestic issues. At 3:04 the president entered, nodding his greetings. Frank Cormier, the senior wire service correspondent, began the session with a loaded Watergate question, just as had been anticipated.

"Mr. O'Brien has said that the people who bugged his headquarters had a direct link to the White House. Have you had any sort of investigation made to determine whether this is true?" Cormier asked.

"Mr. Ziegler, and also Mr. Mitchell, speaking for the campaign committee, have responded to questions on this in great detail," the president began, then stepped closer to his desk and the gathered reporters. "They have stated my position and have also stated the facts accurately. This kind of activity, as Mr. Ziegler has indicated, has no place whatever in our electoral process, or in our governmental process. And, as Mr. Ziegler has stated, the White House has had no involvement whatever in this particular incident. As far as the matter now is concerned, it is under investigation, as it should be, by the proper legal authorities, by the District of Columbia police, and by the FBI. I will not comment on those matters, particularly since possible criminal charges are involved."

Two thirds of the way through the press conference the president called on Bonnie Angelo, of *Time* magazine, who began, "Mr. Mitchell has declined to make public the source of about ten million dollars of contributions to your reelection fund. I know that this is in the letter of the law, but I wonder, in the spirit of the law, of more openness, what you think about that and might you make them public?"

"Mr. Ziegler has, I think, responded to that, and Mr. Mitchell and Mr. Stans. I think it is Mr. Stans who has declined to do that. I support the position that Mr. Stans has taken," the president said. He was, in fact, making his decision on the issue as he spoke. "When we talk about the spirit of the law and the letter of the law, my evaluation is that it is the responsibility of all individuals, a high moral responsibility, to obey the law and to obey it totally. Now, if the Congress wanted this law to apply to contributions before the date in April that it said the law should take effect, it could have made it apply. The Congress did not apply it before that date, and under the circumstances, Mr. Stans has said we will comply with the law as the Congress has written it, and I support his decision."[7]

When Haldeman dictated his diary entry that evening he recorded what he considered positive developments in the Watergate matter. In fact, the investigation had taken a turn for the worst. I tried to call Haldeman that evening to report what I had learned, but he was attending a dinner at the Kennedy Center, as a member of the board of trustees.

# Firing the "Smoking Gun"

The June 23 *New York Times* ran a front-page Watergate story focused on the Cuban angle, suggesting that an organization of Cuban veterans who had served in the U.S. Army after the Bay of Pigs had been involved. It included Nixon's comment at his press conference that "the White House had 'no involvement whatsoever [*sic*]' in the incident at the Democratic headquarters."[1] *The Washington Post* moved Watergate to the Metro section and featured photos of all the men arrested at the DNC on their way to a bail hearing. An article by Woodward and Jim Mann included President Nixon's press conference statement, actually tracking what the president had said: "The White House has had no involvement whatever in this particular incident."[2] The *Post* also had a story on the Cuban exile community's view of the Watergate incident: They did not understand it.[3]

Although it was highly unusual for me to call Haldeman on his interoffice phone line, that morning I did so at the request of John Mitchell, with whom I had spoken the preceding evening. Just before that conversation with Mitchell I had met with acting FBI director Pat Gray and learned that he felt the FBI investigation was "out of control," and there was nothing he could do about it. Gray was candid in admitting that he really did not know how to keep the FBI's investigation within bounds, but he trusted the man handling the investigation, Assistant Director Mark Felt, to do so. As time and events have revealed, Felt (better know as Bob Woodward's "Deep Throat") had his own agenda: Using leaks, he would either embarrass Pat Gray out of the top job, hoping that the president would instead select an old hand like Felt for it because he could control the place, or make Gray appear conspicuously incompetent to the Senate, which would not confirm him, and then Felt would be available to pick up the pieces.[4] While Felt and the old Hoover crowd certainly did not want to see Nixon defeated by someone like George McGovern, who might relieve all of them of their jobs, they also did not want an outsider like Gray, a former assistant attorney general of the civil division, not even a law-enforcement type, running their FBI.

As a former attorney general, Mitchell was not surprised that Gray could not control the FBI. I had already told Mitchell that Assistant Attorney General Henry Petersen, the head of the Justice Department's Criminal Division and the Watergate investigation, said he would not get into unrelated issues, such as campaign contributions.[5] But also, based on what Gray had said during our meeting, it was clear that neither Petersen nor U.S. Attorney Harold Titus was providing any guidance to the FBI, which had already begun aggressively tracing the money found on the burglars and digging into campaign contributions. Gray explained that FBI agents had visited arrested DNC burglar Bernard Barker's bank, a development that had been leaked to *The Washington Post* the day before. Because of that leak, Haldeman, Ehrlichman and I were told by Mitchell that Liddy had been given checks from two "anonymous" donors—Ken Dahlberg, a CRP fund-raiser, and a Mexican attorney by the name of Manuel Ogarrio—which had arrived in Washington after the April 7, 1972, cutoff date, but which had actually been in the possession of CRP fund-raisers before the cutoff. Finance committee general counsel G. Gordon Liddy had advised that he would solve the problem, which we had now learned he had done by giving the checks to his recruited Watergate burglar Bernard Barker, who had cashed them at his bank, the Republic National Bank of Miami. Although the money had been returned to CRP in early May and commingled with other cash in the committee's safe, by pure happenstance some of that money had later been given to Liddy for his intelligence-gathering operation. Mitchell, aware of this problem, was deeply concerned that innocent campaign contributors who had been promised anonymity were now going to not only be revealed but become involved in Watergate.

During my conversation with Mitchell, I also told him Gray had said that many in the FBI thought they had run into a CIA operation at the Watergate, because of all the agency connections. This prompted Mitchell, who thought Watergate could embarrass the CIA, to request that I suggest to Haldeman that he call in Vernon "Dick" Walters, the new deputy director of the CIA, to invoke the "delimitation agreement." Mitchell explained that this was a long-standing understanding between the FBI and the CIA to not investigate each other's activities.

Until 1997, when told by the BBC during its preparation of a documentary series on Watergate, I was unaware (as were investigators and prosecutors) that Haldeman had made notes of our June 23 conversation, during which I relayed what Gray had told me and Mitchell's recommendation. Those notes were as follows:

> Invest[igation] out of control—Gray doesn't know what to do
>
> They've found Dahlberg
>
> Also $ out of Mex[ican] Bank
>
> W/[ill] know who the depositors were today
>
> informant came into Miami [FBI office]
>
> photog[rapher] devel[oped] film for [arrested Watergate burglar] Barker—pix DNC
>
> Peterson [sic]—Titus—no guidance
>
> Is at brink right now—
>
> Either w/[ill] open all up—or be closed
>
> FBI conv[inced] its CIA—Cols test[imony to FBI] cleared him
>
> Gray looking for way out—called Helms
>
> call Walters in—
>
> say don't know where going—need some help
>
> have him talk to Gray

When Haldeman arrived in the Oval Office at 10:04 on the morning of June 23, 1972, he was carrying the notes of our conversation. As he seated himself, the president was still reading documents Alex Butterfield had brought in for his signature; his first comment to Haldeman was that he wanted to get up to Camp David as soon as possible.[6] Haldeman said that Secretary of State Rogers wanted a quick meeting, and Henry Kissinger was returning from his secret trip to China. Nixon said he would meet them together and invite Henry to join him at Camp David for dinner and a full debriefing. When Butterfield departed, Haldeman turned to Watergate and the latest developments.*

*When revealed by order of the U.S. Supreme Court in late July 1974, this became known as the "smoking gun" conversation, because it was viewed as hard evidence, demonstrating beyond question, that Nixon's final defense about the Watergate break-in in his April 30, 1973, speech, followed by his May

"Now, on the investigation, you know, the Democratic break-in thing," Haldeman began, "we're back to the problem area, because the FBI is not under control, because Gray doesn't exactly know how to control them, and their investigation is now leading into some productive areas." More specifically, he explained, the FBI had "been able to trace the money" found on the burglars to the bank that issued the new hundred-dollar bills, although not to the individuals to whom the bills had been given. "And, and it goes in some directions we don't want it to go."

Haldeman shared other information Gray had given me, including that a photographer who had developed film for Watergate burglar Bernard Barker had gone to the FBI in Miami with photographs of documents on Democratic National Committee letterhead. He then turned to the reason he was raising this matter, although neither Mitchell nor I had suggested it be taken to the president: "Mitchell came up with yesterday, and John Dean analyzed very carefully last night and concludes, concurs now with Mitchell's recommendation that the only way to solve this . . ." Here he paused and prefaced the recommendation with a bit of selling, telling the president, "We're set up beautifully to do it, in that the only network that paid any attention to the Watergate story last night was NBC," and summarized NBC's coverage as "a massive story on the Cuban thing, and all that."

Haldeman then continued with his recommendation regarding the out-of-control FBI: "That the way to handle this now is for us to have [CIA deputy director Vernon] Walters call Pat Gray and just say, stay the hell out of this business here, we don't want you to go any further on it." Haldeman did not explain what business he was talking about. In fact, I had told Haldeman I was concerned that the out-of-control FBI was going where Henry Petersen had assured me the investigation would not go, and that was into campaign contributions, as I later testified, as did Haldeman.[7] Although Haldeman's

---

22, 1973, statement, was bogus, which doomed the Nixon presidency. Ironically, this conversation has been mistakenly understood as an effort by Nixon and Haldeman to shut down the FBI's entire Watergate investigation. This appears to be the case only when viewed out of context. In August 1974, when the converstion was revealed, and Nixon and his lawyers had to focus on this conversation, he had long forgotten what was actually involved; they assumed it had the same meaning as everyone else did. In reality, it was only an effort by Haldeman to stop the FBI from investigating an anonymous campaign contribution from Mexico that the Justice Department prosecutors had already agreed was outside the scope of the Watergate investigation. In approving this action, however, Nixon slightly expanded the request, saying that the FBI should also stay out of Howard Hunt's CIA-related activities. In fact, this conversation did not put the lie to Nixon's April 30 and May 22, 1973, statements, and had Nixon known that he might have survived its disclosure to fight another day. This is not to say, however, that Nixon's April 30 and May 22, 1973, statements were not a lie, as countless other conversations later revealed. In short, the smoking gun was only firing blanks.

comment to the president did not make that clear, I have little doubt that Nixon and Haldeman understood that what they were talking about was perfectly legal anonymous campaign money. Haldeman assured the president that having Walters do this would not be "an unusual development." The president agreed, and Haldeman added, "And that would take care of it"—the "it" being a campaign contribution.[8]

"What about Pat Gray, you mean he doesn't want to?" Nixon asked.

"Pat does want to. He doesn't know how to, and he doesn't have any basis for doing it. Given this, he will then have the basis. He'll call Mark Felt in, and Felt wants to cooperate because he's ambitious, and say, we've got the signal from across the river to put the hold on this. And that will fit rather well, because the FBI agents who are working the case, at this point, feel that it is the CIA."

"But they've traced the money to whom?"

"Well, they've traced to a name, but they haven't gotten to the guy yet."

Fearing the worst, the president asked: "Who is it, is it somebody here?"

"Ken Dahlberg," Haldeman said.

"Who the hell is Ken Dahlberg?"

Haldeman explained that Dahlberg had provided twenty-five thousand dollars in Minnesota, and his check ended up with Bernard Barker. But there was more money involved, Haldeman said: Funds from contributors in Texas went to a bank in Mexico, and the FBI would be tracing these names today. Haldeman had been told how Liddy, as general counsel for the CRP finance committee, had passed the checks on to Barker to cash in his Miami bank, which he then returned.

The president's first reaction was that the FBI would have nothing if these contributors did not cooperate, for he understood from his background and experience that no one had to talk to an FBI agent.[9] Sharing his thoughts, he told Haldeman, "Well, I mean, there's no way, I'm just thinking, if they don't cooperate, what do they say? They were approached by the Cubans. That's what Dahlberg has to say, the Texans, too. Is that the idea?"

"Well, if they will. But then we're relying on more and more people all the time. That's the problem. And the FBI will stop if we could take this other step." In short, rather than enlist liars, Haldeman wanted to simply curtail the FBI's investigation.

"Alright, fine. Right," the president said, approving the action.

"And they seem to feel the thing to do is get them to stop." Haldeman's "they" was an apparent reference to Mitchell and me. Haldeman was usually an honest broker in passing along thoughts from the staff to the president, which suggests that, since he was now calling for a much more aggressive approach than either Mitchell or I had ever proposed, it is possible that Haldeman had discussed this further with Mitchell when they met in Haldeman's office after we had spoken.[10] Mitchell might have suggested that Ehrlichman and Haldeman call Helms in.

"Right, fine," the president repeated, and Haldeman explained the mechanics of it.

"They say the only way to do that is a White House instruction. And it's got to be to Helms and, ah, what's his name? Walters."

"Walters," the president echoed.

"And the proposal would be that Ehrlichman and I call them in—"

"All right, fine," the president said. Having approved the plan, the president now wanted to know how Haldeman was going to deal with Helms and Walters. Given the fact that "we protected Helms from one hell of a lot of things," Nixon believed he would be receptive.[11]

"That's what Ehrlichman says," Haldeman added, regarding Nixon's earlier assistance to the CIA.

Nixon thought the way to approach Helms was by mentioning Howard Hunt, who he figured might be a sore spot for the CIA. "Of course, with Hunt, you will uncover a lot of problems," the president said, when suggesting wording for the approach. "See, you open that scab, there's a hell of a lot of things, and that we just feel that it would be very detrimental to have this thing go any further. This involves these Cubans, Hunt, and a lot of hanky-panky that we have nothing to do with ourselves." Having dealt with the FBI question, the president again returned to that of Mitchell's involvement in the unfolding mess. "One thing I want to know, did Mitchell know about this thing to any much of a degree?"

"I think so," Haldeman said ambiguously, apparently referring to Watergate, since Haldeman knew Mitchell had no knowledge of the handling of the campaign money. It is at this point that the conversation becomes somewhat difficult when they are clearly talking about different subjects and seamlessly shift between them, but I believe I have sorted it out correctly.

"Ssshiiit," the president reacted in a hushed, hissing tone.

"I don't think he knew the details," Haldeman continued, "but I think he knew," still apparently talking about Mitchell and the break-in.

But then Nixon made it clear he was talking about campaign contributions when he added, "He didn't know how it was going to be handled, though, with Dahlberg and the Texans and so forth, did he? Well, who was the asshole that did this thing? Is it Liddy? Is that the fellow? He must be a little nuts."

"He is," Haldeman confirmed.

"I mean, he just isn't well screwed on, is he? Isn't that the problem?" Nixon asked.

"No, but he was under pressure, apparently, to get more information, and as he got more pressure, he pushed the people harder to move harder on," Haldeman answered, clearly referring to Watergate.

"Pressure from Mitchell?" Nixon asked, now understanding that Haldeman had changed the topic.

"Apparently."

"Mitchell has said that everybody was concerned about ITT, or something, so do something." The president was trying to understand what had motivated Mitchell, and it appears he was referring to their June 20 conversation, for no one else had spoken to Mitchell about why the break-in had been undertaken.

The president was unhappy to learn these things, and had received enough bad news. "All right, fine, I understand it all. We won't second-guess Mitchell and the rest. Thank God it wasn't Colson," he said, referring again to Watergate.

On Colson, Haldeman had some good news, which I had given him in our earlier conversation. The FBI had interviewed Colson the day before and established that he was not involved. Rather, as Haldeman told the president, "The FBI guys working the case had concluded that there were one or two possibilities, they think it was either a White House operation and they [the White House] had some obscure reasons for it, or it was the Cubans and the CIA. And after their interrogation of Colson yesterday, they concluded it was not the White House but are now convinced it is a CIA thing, so the CIA turnoff would—"

"Well, not sure of their analysis, I must say that. I'm not going to get that involved," the president noted.

"No, sir. We don't want you to," Haldeman told him.

"You call them in."

"Good," Haldeman said.

"Good deal. Play it tough. That's the way they play it, and that's the way we are going to play it," which the president later said was a reference to the Democrats, not the CIA.

"Okay, we'll do it," Haldeman reassured him, and they moved on to other topics.

As the conversation was coming to a close, the president was still thinking about the plan to call in the CIA. "When you get these people in say, look, the problem is that this will open the whole Bay of Pigs thing, and the president just feels that, I mean, without going into the details, don't lie to them to the extent to say there is no involvement, but just say this is sort of a comedy of errors, bizarre, without getting into it." He suggested Haldeman tell them that "the president believes that it is going to open the whole Bay of Pigs thing up again. And because these people [referring to the Democrats] are playing for keeps, that they should call the FBI in and say that we wish for the country, don't go any further into this case, period! And that destroys the case." Haldeman agreed, and the president added, "That's the way to put it, do it straight now." While Nixon appears to have intended to escalate the use of the CIA beyond merely cutting off the FBI's pursuit of campaign funds, when Haldeman called in Helms and Walters, he only addressed the Mexican money, so again it is unclear whether they were on the same wavelength.[12]

Years later, Haldeman admitted he had gone far beyond anything Mitchell and I had recommended. As he explained, "Dean had suggested that I call Walters at the CIA. I knew Walters well. Normally, I would have simply called him over to my office at the White House and asked him if he would help us out. Whether he would have turned me down or not doesn't matter. The fact is, there never would have been the 'smoking gun' conversation in the Oval Office that resulted in Nixon's resignation if I had just called Walters myself, as I usually would have." While Haldeman acknowledged that he had done "something I shouldn't have done," and that it was "a crucial—even historical—error," he never did explain why he involved Ehrlichman and Helms, or why he remained silent about his notes of our conversation.

Reporters and historians (as well as Richard Nixon) have also failed to understand the brief exchange, when this matter arose again, in the Oval Office between 1:04 P.M. and 1:13 P.M. on June 23.[13] This second conversation has been viewed as further evidence of the president thrusting himself into the Helms and Walters meeting by summoning Haldeman back to the Oval

Office just before it took place. Nixon (not to mention his researchers for his memoir) got the facts wrong: The president did not, as he wrote in his memoir, call "for Haldeman to come in again" after a meeting with his economic advisers and two ceremonial meetings to further instruct him on what to say to Helms and Walters.[14] Rather, it was Haldeman who initiated the follow-up discussion. He already needed to go to the president's office in Ehrlichman's place to edit a statement on higher education legislation to be released later that afternoon. Haldeman was covering this so Ehrlichman could be in his office when Helms and Walters arrived.[15]

"Okay. Take the God damn thing," the president said, as he finished the last of the editing of the statement he was going to personally deliver on camera. Then he asked Haldeman where he was meeting with Helms and Walters. When Haldeman told him it would be in Ehrlichman's office, the president can be heard tapping his finger on his desk, a typical contemplative gesture, before sharing his thoughts about it. "I'd say, the primary reason, you've got to cut it the hell off. I just don't think, ah, it would be very bad to have this fellow Hunt, you know, he knows too damn much. And he was involved [in the Watergate break-in], we happen to know that. And if it gets out, the whole, this is all involved in the Cuban thing, it's a fiasco, and it's going to make the FBI"—he had misspoken and corrected himself—"the CIA look bad, it's going to make Hunt look bad, and it's likely to blow the whole Bay of Pigs thing, which we think would be very unfortunate for the CIA, and for the country at this time, and for American foreign policy. And he's just got to tell them, lay off."

"Yeah, that's the basis I'm going to do it on. Just leave it at that," Haldeman said.

"I don't want them to get any idea that we're doing it because of our concern about the political, and they know the, I wouldn't tell them it is not political," Nixon said. Haldeman agreed, and Nixon continued, "I'd just say, look, it's because of the Hunt involvement, just say, yeah, Hunt got involved, is involved in this sort of thing." The president wanted to use Hunt as the excuse because he thought the CIA cover—a seed Colson had planted a few days earlier—was a "good move." But it is less than clear precisely what he actually had in mind for the CIA to do. Suffice it to say that when this conversation is viewed in the context of what preceded it and what followed, its intent is not as clear as most believed at the time it became public.

Following the discussion with Helms and Walters, Haldeman met with the president in his EOB office, at 2:20 P.M., to give him a report.[16] "Well, it's no problem," he announced. "Had the two of them in, and—"

"You scare Helms to death, did you?" the president interrupted.

"Well, it's kind of interesting. Walters just sat there. Made the point, I didn't mention Hunt at the opening of it, I just said that this thing would lead in the directions that were going to create some very major potential problems, that they were exploring leads that lead back into areas that would be harmful to the CIA, harmful to the government. But Walters didn't say much." Haldeman reported that Helms said the CIA had nothing to do with Watergate: "Gray had called [him], told them what he knew, and said, 'I think we've run right into the middle of a CIA covert operation here.' Helms said, 'Nothing that we've got going at all,' and that was the end of that conversation."

Haldeman then turned to what he and Ehrlichman had told Helms. "We said, well, the problem is that it tracks back to the Bay of Pigs. It tracks back to some other stuff, if their leads run out to people who had no involvement in this except by contacts or connections, but it gets to areas that are going to be raised. The whole problem [is] this fellow Hunt, so at that point Helms kind of got the picture, very clearly. He said, 'We'll be very happy to be helpful to, you know, we'll handle everything you want. I would like to know the reason for being helpful.'" But Haldeman said that he was not sharing that information. "And it may have appeared, when he wasn't going to get such information explicitly but was gonna get it through generality, he said fine. And Walters was ready to do it, Walters said that." Haldeman chuckled. "And Walters is going to make a call to Gray, I think. That's the way we put it, that's the way it was left."

"How would that work, though?" the president asked, very clearly referring to the campaign contribution money. He wanted to know what would happen if the judge pulled in people from the Miami bank and asked them about Barker's account. Haldeman conceded this could be a problem. "The point that John [Ehrlichman] made is, the Bureau is going all-out on this because they don't know what they're uncovering. Because they think they need to pursue it. And they don't need to, because they've already got their case as far as the charges against these men, or something, so they don't need anything further on that. And, as they pursue it, they're uncovering stuff that's none of their business," he paraphrased, clearly referring to the campaign contributions, though Ehrlichman, it seems, was also thinking of Hunt's other activities, ones that predated Watergate.

"One thing Helms did raise," Haldeman said, "is, he said he asked Gray why he felt they're going into a CIA thing, and Gray said because of the characters involved and the amount of money involved. He said there's a lot of dough."

Just before six o'clock that evening the president was joined by First Lady Pat Nixon, his daughter and son-in-law Julie and David Eisenhower, Henry Kissinger and White House secretary Terry Decker for the thirty-minute helicopter flight from the South Grounds of the White House to Camp David, Maryland, for the weekend. Haldeman would travel by car to Camp David on Saturday, June 24, 1972. The president planned to use the weekend to start preparing for his nationally televised press conference, to be held in the East Room of the White House, on June 29, 1972, which was the last major commitment on his schedule before his departure for California, where the pace of work was cut back at the Western White House in San Clemente, California.

*June 24 to July 1, 1972*

# Martha's Breakdown, John's Resignation and Another Scenario

On June 24 Nixon had breakfast in Aspen Lodge, the presidential residence at Camp David. What caught his attention in the papers that morning was a story in *The Washington Post* by Helen Thomas, a United Press International (UPI) reporter, about another storm brewing. Martha Mitchell had called Thomas from California to announce that she had given her husband, John, an "ultimatum to get out of politics" or she would leave him. Thomas reported that Martha's call had ended abruptly when someone apparently tried to take the phone away from her as she protested, "You just get away!" With those words the connection was broken. When Thomas called back she was told that "Mrs. Mitchell is indisposed and cannot talk." Thomas then called John Mitchell at his Watergate apartment, reported the situation and found him amused. He said Martha never liked his being in politics and confided, "We have a compact. We have agreed we're going to get the hell out of this gambit. We aren't going to be in Washington after November 7 [the date of the election]. We're going to leave lock, stock and barrel. We have an understanding. We're going to get out of this rat race. We have no interest." Mitchell informed Thomas that his wife was in California with her sister and a secretary, who had probably sought to stop her from calling. Mitchell added, "She's great. That little sweetheart. I love her so much. She gets a little upset about politics, but she loves me and I love her and that's what counts."[1]

Nixon and his top aides had witnessed such behavior from Martha before, during the previous campaign and periodically during Mitchell's tenure as attorney general. Martha had gone (either voluntarily or involuntarily committed by John) to Craig House, a psychiatric hospital in Beacon, New York, to deal with a drinking problem before coming to Washington, and while living in the capital she had spent time in the VIP wing of Walter Reed Army Medical Center.[2] But Nixon understood that with this latest revelation the responsibilities of the president's reelection campaign were now more than John Mitchell could handle. It was a situation that had to be addressed quickly.

Haldeman joined the president at 2:29 P.M. in Aspen Lodge, where they talked briefly before continuing out by the swimming pool.[3] (The Aspen Lodge recording system had been installed only a month earlier, and it included the president's study as well as the two telephones in it.) After a brief discussion of Martha Mitchell, Haldeman reported that he had nothing new on Watergate. "We forwarded the message to Vernon Walters, and it was properly received," Haldeman said. "And no problem with the director." Somewhat wishfully, Nixon said he felt that some of those involved in the Watergate operation should plead guilty. Haldeman agreed, but wondered, "Who?"

"Fair question," the president responded. They discussed the civil lawsuit and how the Democrats hoped to move quickly on depositions and to "slap a subpoena on Mitchell," as Haldeman described it. The president figured they would go after Colson to try to learn about the White House's political activities. Haldeman was not concerned but rather found it amusing that "nobody believes the truth." When a surprised Nixon asked, "You don't think so?" Haldeman explained, "Oh, I don't think at this point, they don't. Even our own people don't think the Cubans did it. You know, the press and the Democrats are trying to push it onto us." Haldeman's bemusement belied the situation, for as he wrote in his diary later that day: "The problems on Watergate continue to multiply as John Dean runs into more and more FBI leads that he has to figure out ways to cope with."

## June 25, 1973, Sunday, Camp David

The president slept late and had breakfast at 10:30 A.M. He went to Birch Lodge to work at 11:26 A.M. and requested that Haldeman join him. They talked for an hour and a half, but there was no recording equipment at that location. According to Haldeman's diary, they discussed the campaign, which, in turn, led to Martha Mitchell, but Haldeman had little more than what had been reported the day before.[4]

The president was clearly burned by an op-ed by columnist Joseph Kraft,

THE WATERGATE CAPER, in that Sunday's *Washington Post*, for he raised it with several of his aides during the day. In his column, Kraft—unaware at the time that the Nixon White House had tried to bug his home and office to uncover his sources within the administration, and that when the first attempt failed the FBI succeeded on a second try, while Kraft was in Paris on assignment, though it ultimately never discovered who was leaking—launched a direct attack on Nixon and Mitchell. While no one believed Nixon and Mitchell were so foolish as to have been directly involved in the Watergate caper, he wrote, "you don't hear anybody say that President Nixon and John Mitchell couldn't have been involved because they are too honorable and high-minded, too sensitive to the requirements of decency, fair play and law." Rather, Kraft argued, "The central fact is that the president and his campaign manager have set a tone that positively encourages dirty work by low-level operators. The president's record goes back a long way. Every election he has fought since 1946 has featured smear charges, knees in the groin and thumbs in the eye." Kraft said Nixon had a "special tolerance [for] using unethical means for partisan purposes" and for "[b]ending the law for political advantage." Whoever had done this deed of "doing the dirty on the Democrats," Kraft concluded, did so to earn "good marks in high favor" from Nixon and Mitchell.[5]

Kraft further charged that Mitchell had, in his very brief public career as attorney general, compiled "deep associations in matters involving chicanery and the cutting of corners," citing high-profile prosecutions undertaken with an "astonishing insufficiency of evidence"; the use of unconstitutional authority (unanimously condemned by the Supreme Court) to bug domestic subversives without judicial approval; and the appointment, as head of the Justice Department's Criminal Division, of Will Wilson, a man who was then forced to resign because of "a gamy Texas scandal involving fraud and bribery."[6]

## June 26, 1972, Monday, the White House

Martha Mitchell's threat to leave her husband was now a front-page story in *The Washington Post*. Helen Thomas reported that she'd received another "tearful telephone call" from Martha, who had relocated to the Westchester Country Club in Rye, New York. Martha claimed she was "a political prisoner" who couldn't stand the life she'd been living. "It's horrible to me. I have been through so much. I don't like it. Martha isn't going to stand for it," she announced. "I love my husband very much. But I'm not going to stand for all those dirty things that go on," she hinted darkly. She told Thomas that a security man for the reelection committee had pulled her telephone out of the wall when they last spoke from California, and they had left her "black and blue." She said she had been left behind in California "with absolutely no information. They don't want me to talk."[7]

Haldeman noted in his diary that Martha's situation was the president's principal concern "throughout the day."[8] John Mitchell, Haldeman told the president when they met in the Oval Office between 9:50 A.M. and 10:45 A.M., had attended the senior staff meeting that morning but told Haldeman he was heading up to New York to get Martha to try to work out their problems.[9] "Is it the same story?" the president asked.

When Haldeman recounted the substance of that morning's coverage, Nixon remarked, "Helen Thomas ought not to be brought into this thing, God damn it, as a matter of decency. The woman's sick."

They spoke sympathetically about the situation and how it hit Mitchell harder every time it occurred. "Maybe he should send her abroad," Nixon thought, adding softly, "You know, Mexico." Haldeman noted, "Locking her up is a problem, but I think he can make the point that, and get a little sympathy for it, that she's had a nervous breakdown, or something, that she's ill." Nixon pointed out, "Any sophisticated person reading that story will realize she's sick." Haldeman agreed.

When the discussion turned to Kraft's column, Nixon observed that it showed the "left-wingers" were having trouble "laying gloves" on him for the Watergate bugging, ITT and such scandals, which he felt were not "hurting the president." He was annoyed at the lack of media response to his comments distancing the White House from Watergate: "Well, for Christ sakes, I said I completely shared the stated views of Mitchell and Ziegler that this kind of activity has no place in our political process. What in the name of Christ do they want? I think Ziegler ought to crack somebody on that one, I mean, what the hell, what do they want me to do, jump up and down and say this is a horrifying thing? No, I'll tell you, there's a plus side of all this. I'm sure you can see what it is. I think they're reaching. Do you agree, or not?"

Haldeman agreed, and after making a note, they discussed the absurdity of Larry O'Brien's calling for the appointment of a special prosecutor, since the matter was being investigated and would be prosecuted. The president again wondered, "Is there any way that Ehrlichman's crowd can get these people to plead guilty and get the hell out of the case? Or how is it working there? I don't know what kind of jackassery is going on in the handling of it, you know, because I don't have much confidence in these lawyers. Who's watching that end of it? Is that Dean?"

"Dean and Mitchell," Haldeman answered. "Mitchell, alright," the president said, satisfied. Haldeman added, "Very closely watching it. Also Mardian." He awkwardly added, "Unfortunately, I have to agree with you, though it may not be that simple. It would seem to me if they plead them guilty and get them out. But they don't have an indictment yet. They keep investigating and uncovering new things. Hopefully we've got that turned off," referring to his conversation with Helms and Walters.

This conversation ended with the president's further thoughts on Martha and John Mitchell, given the unfolding problems with the Watergate investigation. "You realize, you're looking here at Mitchell's case, we may be looking at something we may not be able to handle," the president said. "That's what I'm concerned about, you know. John is a strong man, and I don't know how in hell he got—" He did not finish the thought, but added, "This woman, if she goes completely off her rocker, I don't need that business. She was different before. She wasn't a national celebrity, but now she's a national celebrity. I mean, what the hell John's got to do is put her in rehabilitation—" On that unfinished point the conversation ended and Haldeman departed.

When Haldeman stopped by the Oval Office shortly after noon to discuss other matters, the subject of Mitchell's resignation as campaign manager arose.[10] The president had earlier asked Haldeman to speak to Richard "Dick" Moore, a retired television broadcasting executive who had worked with Mitchell on his public image as attorney general, developed a friendship with him and then joined the White House staff. The president wanted Moore to probe Mitchell's thinking and see whether he, too, was thinking about resignation.

"I talked to Moore," Haldeman began. "He said John hasn't said anything to Moore, and Moore felt he shouldn't push into it because John knows he can call on him if he wants. But he's going to do a little checking, see what LaRue might know. Apparently Mitchell's used LaRue some to keep Martha under control." Fred LaRue and Martha had developed a special bond, both being committed Southerners in the Nixon administration. "Martha's very strange," Nixon added, softly. When this subject was broached again later in the day, it concerned Ziegler, who had been advised of the situation but wanted Haldeman's judgment on whether he should discuss it publicly, since he would have a press conference in a few days. "The question I have is whether I really ought to speak about it," the president asked.

"I wouldn't worry," Haldeman said, to which Nixon replied, "Well, I naturally worry, not so much because of the effect on me but the effect on him. And on her, too. I don't want to see them hurt."

When Haldeman met with Nixon in his EOB office shortly after noon, the conversation quickly turned to Watergate: "[S]omeone raised the point this morning that, although the potential is nowhere near now, but we could get to it, there were real potential problems with Watergate."[11]

The someone was myself, for at 9:20 A.M. I had been summoned to Haldeman's office, where I found Haldeman and Ehrlichman. To my surprise I was asked if I thought both Mitchell and Jeb Magruder should be removed from their posts at the campaign. I felt it presumptuous for me to pass judgment on Mitchell, but I explained why I thought both Mitchell and Magruder might be indicted for their roles in the conspiracy to break into and bug the DNC.[12] While Haldeman did not mention my opinion to the president, when Nixon indicated that he understood the scope of the problem, Haldeman continued, "You could use this as a basis for Mitchell pulling out. That means we're going to have to fix nearly everything all over [at the reelection committee] and at the same time start trying to put a new structure together." Referring to Watergate, he added, "It isn't going to turn the other off. So if Mitchell pulls out, he's still the former attorney general, your former campaign manager, and they're not going to let up on him just because he's not the manager now. And then the only way you can do that is to hang him on it, say, well, he did it, and that's why we have to get rid of him."

"I can't do that. I won't do that to him," Nixon immediately protested. "I'd rather, shit, lose the election. I really would." Haldeman countered, "You can't do that. He won't let you do that." Nixon agreed with a somewhat philosophical "no," and continued, "He [John Mitchell] was supposed to do everything he could to find out what was going on, you know what I mean. I must say, we know that."

"Apparently, with our limited resources in that area, he used the same people for a wide range of things," Haldeman explained. "So you've got them all, you've got crossties, interweaving and all that. And if these guys were only on this thing, you could cut them loose and sink them without a trace." It appears, based on later conversations, that Haldeman was not fully aware of the illegal activity sponsored by Ehrlichman's special investigative unit, but he had sufficient information to warn the president there were problems. But either because he did not know or because he felt Nixon should not know, Haldeman remained less than explicit when pressed.

"You mean they've been on ITT?" the president asked.

"And other stuff," Haldeman answered.

"Black holes?" Nixon asked.

"Apparently a lot of stuff. There's stuff I don't know anything about," Haldeman said. "But I've been told that the lines run in various directions."

"Any other candidates?" the president asked.

"Yeah. Apparently, this is part of the apparatus that's been used for some of these surveillance projects and checking on various things. The trouble is, they're tied into, in some remote way, the people that have been doing some of the anti activity and other campaign things during the primaries. Apparently there's various lines of interlinkage in the whole damn business."

"What can we do, not to borrow trouble?" Nixon asked.

"I don't know," Haldeman answered. "Nothing, there are no specifics." Both men were very unhappy about having to deal with the president's campaign with Watergate as an issue, since all else had gone so well.

## June 28, 1972, Wednesday, the White House

The president did not arrive in the Oval Office until 10:35 A.M., telling Haldeman that he'd had insomnia and not fallen asleep until around 6:00 A.M. He spent much of the morning with Ziegler discussing logistics for his televised press conference, which was to be in the East Room at 9:00 the next evening. Both Nixon and Haldeman had concluded that Mitchell would have to leave as head of the reelection campaign. Haldeman's diary shows that he had already begun to think about Mitchell's replacement, and after discussions with others, the consensus was that former Minnesota Republican congressman Clark MacGregor, who then headed the congressional relations staff of the White House, should be given the position.[13] According to Haldeman's office log, he had already met with MacGregor, and they had undoubtedly discussed this possibility.[14]

Haldeman joined the president in his EOB office at 11:16 A.M. and informed Nixon that Mitchell and Martha were traveling back to Washington.[15] The fact that they were returning surprised the president, who was also "surprised at McGovern's bad taste" in apparently making a disparaging crack about Martha. When Colson arrived early in the course of this conversation, the discussion turned to the press's handling of the Mitchell situation. Haldeman did not think it was hurting the Nixon campaign, which had been Mitchell's concern, because there had been "so many political divorces, or marital problems," over the previous three months. Nixon noted that other people had these kinds of problems, to varying degrees, so most would simply think, "Oh, shit, it could be me."

When Colson departed, the president wondered if he'd be asked at the press conference about "crap on the bugging and Martha." Haldeman observed, "Some shit's going to lob in the bugging thing." The president then asked, "What's your honest opinion on the Mitchell thing, do you think he should resign?" When Haldeman said he did, Nixon instructed, "Okay. You and Mitchell talk about it."

Haldeman then explained, "Mitchell's come to the same conclusion." Haldeman said he had been told [by either LaRue or Moore] that Mitchell realized that he could no longer be fully effective, and he did not want to be in a position that in any way jeopardized the full effectiveness of the campaign. "Incidentally," Haldeman added, "the more I've thought about it, I think that maybe it's all a very good move."

The president then suggested rotating the secretaries at Camp David; not only did they enjoy going up to the retreat, but it was a nice way to reward the top secretaries, along with trips to California. Haldeman liked this idea, too. The president observed admiringly that Terry Decker, who had traveled to Camp David the previous weekend, was "the most beautiful girl in the White House. She could be in the movies." Haldeman added that she had a great figure as well, not to mention "spectacular legs." The president felt that they had many skilled secretaries, and none more reliable than Rose Mary Woods, but noted, "Nobody can do better than Shelley." He was referring to Shelley Scarney, the West Wing receptionist, who later became Mrs. Patrick Buchanan. Nixon instructed Haldeman to have people like Shelley, who were "good looking" and with "good personalities out front." And as for "the ones who are not quite so pretty, like Rose and Marge Acker and the rest," they should be kept working out of sight.

Returning to the subject at hand, Haldeman reported that Mitchell seemed to think he could control the Martha situation, which explained their return to Washington, but what could not be passed over was the

Watergate investigation: "I think there's also lurking down, way behind, there is the question of his involvement in the Watergate caper and the fact that—" Haldeman began, but Nixon interrupted to ask, "And that he does know about it?" Haldeman continued, without addressing the president's question, "We've got a lid on it, but it may not stay on, and his getting out might just be a good move on that, because supposedly it goes to him."

"But I don't, I think, as I understand it, and I don't want to know, because I've got to answer at a press conference," the president again advised. "But as I understand it, John did not know specifically about this crazy thing."

"As I understand it, that's right," Haldeman agreed.

"As far as you know. I mean, if people down the line, the Cubans and others working for us, working for some asshole, and they do something stupid, we can't be responsible for that." Nixon had another matter he wanted to raise. "I was glad to see that Kevin Phillips or somebody [brought out] the fact that we were tapped. You know, Lyndon Johnson tapped us, because he told us later."

"He tapped Mrs. what's her name," Haldeman confirmed, not recalling Anna Chennault's name, but noting a discovery during the 1968 campaign that Nixon believed placed the Watergate bugging in a proper and better context.

"With John Mitchell returning this afternoon," Haldeman continued, "we'll want to talk about this, but my view would be to encourage him to resign, on the basis of, it's a beautiful opportunity. He'll gain great sympathy. The Martha fans will think, isn't that a wonderful thing, that the man has given up, you know, it's kind of like the Duke of Windsor giving up the throne for the woman he loves, this sort of stuff. This has a little of that flavor to it. The poor woman hasn't been well and all, and he's going to be by her side, and all of that."

"And we would leak out the fact that she's not well, very strongly," Nixon said, and emphasized, "We'd have to." He soon added, "Incidentally, he can still do some inside jobs." Nixon could see the potential of Mitchell's operating even more effectively by not having to run the entire campaign. "Then you use him for the kinds of things he is indispensable for," Haldeman agreed. "The Rockefeller, Reagan, Buckley, the Middlebury people, putting the deal together in Missouri, and that kind of stuff."

Haldeman soon mentioned another positive in getting Mitchell out of the campaign: his record as attorney general. "Well, John's carrying a lot.

He's tarred with Carswell;* he's tarred with the failed Berrigan trial;† he's tarred with the failed Angela Davis;‡ he's tarred with the Ellsberg case, that's going to fail;§ he's tarred with the Watergate caper, in a sense, indirectly, and we know it's more than that; and he's tarred with the ITT case and the Kleindienst business; he's tarred with the Martha Mitchell problem, which is an issue, and there's just a lot of stuff there—"

"But we don't lose him, that's the point," Nixon noted, and they discussed keeping Mitchell on in an unofficial capacity. After a conversation with Ehrlichman about the press conference, the president, joined by the First Lady, flew to Camp David, where he would continue preparing for the event.

### June 29, 1972, Thursday, the White House

The president returned from Camp David at 2:32 P.M., and went shortly thereafter to his EOB office, where Haldeman joined him. While waiting for Henry Kissinger, the president asked, "What is the latest with the deal on Mitchell, and the discussion?"[16]

"He came in, said he wanted to see me," Haldeman reported. "And he gave me a very detailed synopsis of his whole situation. It's a very serious situation. And he said the net result is, there's no question in his mind, the only thing he can do is step out as campaign manager, because Martha's very serious, and not solvable." As soon as Kissinger departed, after a ten-minute discussion about Vietnam, the president returned to the subject of Mitchell, anxious to hear the rest of Haldeman's report.

"It's both mental disorder and alcohol, an enormous consumption of alcohol. She's not an alcoholic. But she gets very, very drunk. The alcohol comes with the mental disorder. It isn't the cause of it. At least, I think that's what John thinks. He says she drinks an enormous amount, and she becomes

---

*The president's U.S. Supreme Court nominee, Harrold Carswell, was rejected by the U.S. Senate.

†In January 1971, Mitchell's Justice Department indicted Philip Berrigan and others (known as the "Harrisburg Seven") for purportedly trying to kidnap Henry Kissinger and blow up federal buildings. The jury did not believe the charges and acquitted all.

‡In August 1971, black intellectual and radical Angela Davis was indicted by Mitchell's Justice Department for murder, kidnapping and conspiracy, charges relating to an escape of prisoners from a federal courtroom, only to be later found not guilty on all counts by an all-white jury.

§On December 29, 1971, Daniel Ellsberg and Anthony Russo were indicted by Mitchell's Justice Department on fifteen counts of theft of government documents and espionage in connection with leaking the Pentagon Papers. The case was pending in federal court in California, and the fact that Haldeman and the president believed the case would fail is a striking admission.

violently irrational, as we know. And she's past the point of no return. He's afraid she's suicidal, and he also has enormous respect for her ability to do what she decides to do and turn out [*unclear*]. She is devoted to you—"

"Incidentally, is she aware of Watergate?" Nixon asked.

"No," Haldeman reported, referring to any advance knowledge of her husband's role, and the fact that it involved people from the CRP. "That's part of what caused his problem, is that she found out. John didn't tell her that weekend about the fact that it was out in the papers, and after he left, she found it on television and read about it in the papers, and she blew her stack about that. That was what caused the tantrum, and she started drinking Kahlúa, putting her hand through a window in the hotel, cut her hand all up. They did call a doctor, and they did throw her down in the bed and stick a needle in her ass, because they had to, she was demolishing the hotel. Then they had a couple take her to New York, these friends of his, and he went up and spent the Saturday, he said there's no way I can do this. And I said, what about putting her where you had her before? I played this all, I saw where he was going, so I went the other way."

"Absolutely. So it doesn't appear we're driving him out," Nixon said approvingly. Haldeman assured him, "He doesn't think that at all. He can't, 'cause I argued the other side." Nixon was pleased that Martha supported him, and Haldeman continued, "[Mitchell said] the one way we can solve this for now is for the president to call Martha, and say, 'I know of all the problems and sacrifices, but John is the one indispensable man here, and I've got to have him.' But [Mitchell] said, 'I don't want him to do that, it won't solve the problem long term, and there's no way of knowing when the next thing will come up, and it's bound to within a matter of days.'"

"Really?" Nixon was surprised.

"Yeah. And he said there's no point in trying. [Mitchell] said, she's told me she's going to jump off the balcony at the Watergate. Well, you know, I can't be sure she won't."

Haldeman added that Mitchell was very upset, very calm about it all and obviously tired and wrung out. "Martha told him, John you don't need this. You're out front, and they're blaming you for all these things that happened, and I can't take that. They blame you for breaking into the Watergate, and all this stuff, and she said, we just don't need it. And you could be just as much help to the president consulting, and help him on the sidelines."

"That's pretty good," Nixon responded.

They went on to discuss how they needed Mitchell for the big plays during the campaign, particularly New Jersey, where the Department of Justice had indicted a number of state officials. As for Mitchell's departure and Watergate, the president made several points: "We have two things this accomplishes, which is, first, it gets rid of, frankly, a liability, it's with John, it's hard to carry John on this. We know it's not his fault. I frankly believe that if it had not been for Martha, he probably wouldn't have let this Watergate thing get out of hand."

"That's quite possible," Haldeman agreed.

"And actually, I really don't think he knew about this, I really don't." Nixon then mentioned the conversation, which was not recorded, that he'd had with Mitchell on the evening of June 20, 1972. "John said to me, one of the lower guys told [him], we're preparing to get information. He said, well, don't tell me anything about it, you know, that's the way you do. Thinking probably they were going to do it the way you always do, by planting a person on the other side, which everybody does. But these assholes were going around bugging people, or whatever it was, I don't know." The president paused, thinking about it. "My view on that is that that pretty well kills Watergate. I mean, I mean, as far as I'm concerned, it doesn't cover Watergate."

"Which is another good thing, and John raised that, he said, if this thing escalates, I think it would be very good if I'm out of the place now, and you could say, well, there's an all-new team over there," Haldeman reported, then added, "They fired Liddy."

"The guy who did it?" Nixon asked. "How? On what grounds? He going to blow the fact he did it?"

"Nope," Haldeman reassured. "He won't. Part of the plan to fire him, he agreed to be fired."

"We agree to take care of him some way?" Nixon asked. Haldeman's response is inaudible, and Nixon pressed for more information. "On what ground did they fire him? They're going to say that he had some, in the event, it comes out that he did have contact with—"

"Yeah. They're not making any fuss about it. Nobody will ask why they fired him unless he becomes identified. The FBI [does] have a line to him. They have questioned him, and he didn't cooperate. He answered certain questions, and then they got into other areas, and he said, 'If you're going to get into that kind of area, then I request to have an attorney here.' The FBI said, 'Well, if you have an attorney, he'll tell you not to answer the question.' Liddy said, 'Well then, I've got to take that advice,' and the FBI dropped it."

"What were the questions?" Nixon asked.

"Name what other people [were] involved," Haldeman answered. "The thing that bothers me about [the FBI's investigation] is that it's a time bomb. They can investigate until they get something else, and then lob it out whenever they feel like it."

"Yeah. Well, what do we do, then?" Nixon asked.

"I don't know. I don't think there's a damn thing we can do, except follow it." In a very soft voice the president again inquired about Mitchell's role, and Haldeman had no additional information to share. But he did speculate that if Mitchell confessed, it might end the investigation, but it would require that Mitchell make an unequivocal statement to the effect, "I was running the thing at the time, and I should have known what was happening, I'm sorry I didn't."

"But he didn't know it," Nixon said, and Haldeman continued with his assessment of what Mitchell would have to say, something to the effect that he "was diverted by some personal problems," which was also why he resigned from the campaign. Nixon next asked, "How do you think the resignation goes in terms of timing?"

"The resignation is going to be a positive story," Haldeman advised. As for timing, "It's going to hang totally on Martha." The conversation turned to the mechanics of Mitchell's departure from the reelection campaign. The president wanted to send both Clark MacGregor and Fred Malek from the White House to run the day-to-day operations, but because MacGregor had a heavy load with his White House congressional relations office, there would be a slight delay, so he could finish up those assignments.

"A great load will be lifted" for Mitchell, the president thought aloud. "Then he'll come in as an adviser, something like Connally," referring to John Connally, the former secretary of the treasury. Except, the president noted, "Connally's likely to be better than Mitchell."

At 8:55 P.M., Nixon and Ron Ziegler went to the East Room for the live radio and television press conference. From 9:01 P.M. until 9:44 P.M. the president took questions from the press but was not asked a single question about Watergate or the Mitchells. Afterward the president spent two hours in the Lincoln Sitting Room of the residence in his post–press conference ritual—taking calls from his cabinet, staff, family and friends offering their congratulations. In his diary Haldeman reported that Nixon had been effective, because while he was well prepared, "he wasn't so completely programmed. More relaxed, some good quips, no nervousness."[17]

*June 30, 1972, Friday, the White House*

The president invited John Mitchell and Bob Haldeman to lunch in his EOB office, where they discussed the Martha situation from 12:55 P.M. to 2:10 P.M.* Mitchell and Haldeman had crab soufflé, while the president had his usual pineapple and cottage cheese.[18] Nixon later described this lunch as "a painful session" and observed that "Mitchell looked worn out, and his hand shook so much that he had to put his soup spoon down after the first taste."[19] There had always been an awkward distance in Nixon and Mitchell's relationship, even though, as former law partners, they had spent almost six years working closely together. Nixon, I was once told by Haldeman, believed that he owed his election as president to Mitchell's work in 1967 and 1968. Mitchell himself once said to me that the only reason he took the post of attorney general was because Nixon had insisted, and Nixon made him one of his closest advisers during the first term. During the few meetings in which I witnessed them together, I noticed a stiffness in their working relationship that is present in their recorded conversations as well.[20]

The president welcomed Mitchell with comments about Iran's gray caviar, which he was not serving but that had been served to him on his last trip to Iran, when visiting the shah. He continued with some familiar topics, including the Supreme Court (with a negative comment about Justice Potter Stewart, one of Nixon's least favorites justices), and then proceeded to the reason for their meeting, telling Mitchell with empathy that he understood that Martha's problems had created an impossible situation for him.

"Let me say this," Nixon continued. "I've always had a theory about politics. I covered the situation somewhat in *Six Crises*. I dedicated that book, on the flyleaf, you may recall, to Pat—'she also ran'—and it's always seemed to me, and it's true for Martha as well, that for a woman, being the wife of a politician is infinitely more difficult than probably being one."

"I think you're right on," Mitchell said.

"And Martha's been a great asset to us," the president continued. "I mean, she's a star, she has star quality, she always will, but I can see what happens here, the reason she's damaged after three years as wife of the attorney

---

*The audio quality here is worse than usual, because they were seated for lunch at a small conference table a good distance from the microphones in the president's desk. Although approximately thirty-five minutes of this seventy-five-minute meeting has been withdrawn by NARA, because of personal material, the gist of the conversation can be determined.

general, that's over, all of a sudden you're out of that, in a new area, you're in the line of fire, and kicked around, and you're not home, and this, that and the other thing, she's wondering what the hell is this all about? And as time goes on, it doesn't get better, and so forth and so on. Until finally she reached the breaking point. My own view is that . . ." Nixon cleared his throat. "Probably, I say this with the greatest reluctance, but understanding of your desire and the situation, probably [your decision is] correct. I think the real problem is how to handle the timing. What's going to happen in the campaign, the pressures are never going to get less, they're going to get a hell of a lot worse, and I would never want to put her through all that. So take her back home. I just wanted to give you a little background. I totally understand. I, the affection, you know, I feel about her—"

Mitchell had a barely audible question about timing, and Nixon responded, "You're the best judge of that." He added, "But the only thing I would say, of course, [is that] you can't put amateurs in running the campaign, for example, California, or New Jersey, also some of the Southern strategy."

"Well, Mr. President, Martha's around the point where she understands it's crucial that you get reelected president," Mitchell assured Nixon. Haldeman, who genuinely liked John Mitchell, felt he should resign sooner rather than later. He noted, "Well, there's another practical point: If you wait, you run the risk of more stuff, valid or invalid, surfacing on the Watergate caper type of thing." The president picked up on that point. "That's the other thing. If there is something that does come out, we hope nothing will, it may not, but there's always the risk." Haldeman added, "As of now there's no problem there," but at any moment in the future there could be one. "Nope, I'd cut the loss fast," Nixon agreed. "That's my view, generally speaking. And I think the story is positive rather than negative," he assured Mitchell.

As the lunch was ending, the president shared, "in confidence," the fact that he had spoken with Billy Graham, "a great admirer of Martha's," who offered to help if it was sought. Nixon said he'd told Graham it was a personal problem, but he thought Graham's sympathetic reaction was typical. Mitchell agreed, and the session ended with the president saying, "Well, anyway, we'll try to work it out."

After a nap, Nixon went to the Oval Office, where he had a brief meeting with Clark MacGregor on legislative matters.[21] Not until later that day did Nixon formally ask MacGregor to take the assignment to head his campaign, although Haldeman had already made sure he would do so.

After MacGregor departed the Oval Office at 3:18 P.M., Ziegler said he needed to talk with the president before he met with newly confirmed attorney general Dick Kleindienst. Kleindienst was scheduled to go to the press room to explain the administration's request to add the death penalty to federal cases involving kidnapping, hijacking and the killing of police officers.[22] Ziegler, however, had been bombarded with Watergate questions at his 12:50 P.M. press briefing, because of a report that the FBI had found a "bugging device, maps and a loaded pistol" in Howard Hunt's White House office.[23] He was now worried that Kleindienst, who as attorney general was in charge of the FBI and the criminal investigation of Watergate, would face a Watergate feeding frenzy from the press.

As Ziegler departed, Kleindienst arrived with Haldeman. This meeting, which lasted almost an hour, was remarkable not for what was said but rather for what was not said. Without explaining the reason, the president advised Kleindienst that his press briefing on death penalty cases would be rescheduled for the following week. Twelve days earlier, the day after the arrest of his bugging and burglary team at the Watergate, G. Gordon Liddy had met with Kleindienst, revealed that his men were in jail and asked Kleindienst to get them out. Kleindienst, who had no such power, had sent Liddy packing. Yet Kleindienst's visit turned out to be little more than a shoot-the-breeze conversation, one in which Watergate was never mentioned.[24]

As Kleindienst departed, Haldeman and the president turned to the subjects they had been avoiding until others had departed: Watergate and Mitchell's resignation. Haldeman told Nixon that Mitchell had accompanied him back to his office after lunch.[25]

Nixon had not known Hunt had an office in the White House complex and was curious about what had been found in it. Haldeman explained that there had been no map of the DNC, contrary to the press reports, but there was a handgun. The president was surprised that the FBI was still pursuing Hunt. "But I understood, though, that on that Bureau thing, that they were to keep off of this guy, you know what I mean?" the president asked, thinking about his approval of Haldeman's meeting with the CIA regarding the Mexican money that he had expanded to include Hunt.

"That's what they were told. They aren't," Haldeman reported. "We're having problems here with the Bureau. That's what we were talking about with Dean and Mitchell before our meeting with you."

"I see. You mean, despite Walters going over there?" the president asked, recalling their conversation.

"Gray doesn't know how to turn them off, and neither does Felt, I guess," Haldeman replied. "They're concerned about how to do it, get the record clear on the completeness of the investigation, and all this sort of stuff. Kleindienst hasn't turned Justice off either, which is another problem. The U.S. attorney and his criminal head [Assistant Attorney General Henry Petersen] are both pushing the Bureau, and forward, now. We'll work it out. We've got to somehow get Kleindienst to tell them."

"Well, I'd have Walters go see them, too," Nixon suggested, to further exploit the CIA ties to the situation. "The gun and the wiretapping doesn't bother me a bit with this fellow [referring to Hunt]. He's in the Cuban thing, the whole Cuban business. He's out of the country now, I assume?"

"He never went out, but it doesn't matter. They say his main stock in trade is, he's a master of disguise," Haldeman said, chuckling. "He's someplace under some disguise, although he's supposed to go abroad."

The president stopped to think about the situation, then continued, "Was Colson aware he had stuff in his safe and all that sort of thing?" "Colson wasn't there when they opened the safe," Haldeman explained, "I don't think he knows what was in it. In fact, I'm sure he doesn't. They haven't told him what was in it."

Haldeman said that Ziegler had basically given no comment on the report, which had appeared in *The Washington Daily News*, although he did try to suggest that it had not been totally accurate, explaining, "The story says they found a Spanish-made gun. The reason that's not true is, they did not find a Spanish-made gun."

"They didn't find a map?" Nixon inquired.

"John Dean's the one who knows about this, and he says there wasn't any map. He says there was a road map, but it had nothing to do with the Democratic National Committee, and there was no map of the committee headquarters."

Nixon noted, "Sort of adds up that he has wiretapping stuff, of course."

"Dean hasn't discounted the possibility that we're dealing with a double agent in this thing somewhere," Haldeman reported. (Because neither Ehrlichman nor anyone else was sharing details of Hunt, Liddy and the plumbers' earlier activities with me, I was truly confused for several weeks about how all the relevant details fit together.)

"Meaning this fellow Hunt?" Nixon asked.

"Probably not this guy. Probably one of the other guys, or several of them," Haldeman advised.

"A double agent who is putting out this information, giving leads, or what?" Nixon asked.

"Well, who purposely moved this thing. It's complex, it's so ridiculous, it's still kind of hard to figure the whole thing out," which accurately described the situation for Haldeman. We were all trying to understand the situation, but Haldeman was making it difficult for the president because he was withholding information about his role in allowing Liddy's operation to proceed at the CRP, for Haldeman was way ahead of the president in figuring it all out but not sharing his knowledge.

"Well, I wonder, then," Nixon said, "in view of this break today, if that means whether Mitchell's going tomorrow is a good idea after all."

"Yes. This thing doesn't tie back to that," Haldeman assured him. "Why not?" Nixon asked, and Haldeman explained, "Because Hunt's work leads to the White House, not to Mitchell and the reelection committee. They haven't tied Hunt to the reelection committee. They're tying him to Colson."

"Well, they haven't really tied Hunt to the group [that was arrested] yet, have they?" the president clarified.

"No, except that his name was in their [address] book."

"Yeah. Or Colson, does he know about all this, so he's told the story? What does he say?" the president asked.

"I haven't talked to him, since the story just came this afternoon. But knowing Chuck, I'm sure he's very disturbed."

"Hmm. Well, there's not much we can do about it, is there," Nixon said. "No," Haldeman agreed, but as they were speaking, Haldeman had another thought. "Well, if it's Mitchell," he said firmly, "I want him to call Kleindienst and Gray in and say, look, this happened. I used to sit on the National Security Council. You know, this happens to lead to some lines that don't relate to the Watergate/Democratic National Committee caper. Your people are investigating stuff that must not be investigated. That's the signal you've gotten from the CIA. For Christ's sake, smarten up, smarten up and turn this off. Go ahead and toss your cards to the grand jury on the open-and-shut-case stuff and let it go at that." When Nixon did not respond, Haldeman continued, "McCord is developing a case, talking to the attorneys over there. He is trying to get F. Lee Bailey to handle his case. So we may be getting into an F. Lee Bailey versus Edward Bennett Williams—" Haldeman said, savoring the idea.*

---

*This NARA recording literally runs out here, resulting in a gap of unknown length. When the conversation resumes, Haldeman and Nixon are still addressing the same general topic

Nixon observed, "I don't know anything about that," pointing out, "I thought it was all over in the reelection committee." Haldeman replied, "Hunt is the only tie," referring to the White House, and he assured Nixon that Colson had told the FBI he had nothing to do with it. "What did he tell them?" Nixon asked.

"He told them the straight truth. He told them he had nothing to do with Hunt as far as this thing was concerned, that he'd worked with Hunt on totally unrelated—see, Hunt was working for—"

"We know, in a sense, the fact that his gun and wiretapping equipment is still there and so forth, it would seem to me it would be an indication that he's not afraid of anything. You get my point?" Nixon observed.

Haldeman, who was unhappy that Hunt had these things, explained that Hunt had returned to his EOB office after the arrests at the Watergate. "I can't understand why he didn't empty his safe. A lot of this just totally passes me by. I just can't put it together and have it add up," Haldeman declared. "It's just a lot of very strange things in it."

"Well, the committee contact was through Liddy. What was his job?" Nixon asked. Haldeman explained, "He was the counsel for the finance committee, this job for Stans. That was just a cover." As Haldeman reported this information, Nixon can be heard tapping his fingers on his desk, contemplatively taking it all in. Haldeman added, "And he's the guy—" and Nixon finished, "—that did this with apparently Mitchell's knowledge?" Nixon then pressed, with a questioning and doubtful "Well?" Haldeman's failure to respond caused Nixon to answer his own question, "We don't know."

"Not this, not specifically this, but—" Haldeman was carefully phrasing his response when Nixon interrupted, "—but he was getting information?" Still cautious, Haldeman answered, "Developing intelligence and so forth."

"He was off on his own, though?" Nixon asked. Haldeman evaded the question and responded vaguely, "And some counteractivity, and that stuff." "Which, as we know," Nixon replied confidently, "is standard practice."

After a long pause, Haldeman volunteered a bit more information. "See, Liddy used to work at the White House, too." Nixon, surprised, had totally forgotten that in October 1971 he had read and praised a Liddy memorandum arguing for why FBI director Hoover, for whom Liddy had once written speeches, should be removed from his position.[26] "He worked for Bud Krogh," Haldeman explained. "So did Hunt."

"Where was Krogh? What capacity?" Nixon asked.

"Narcotics," Haldeman said. Controlling drugs and narcotics had been a major push by Nixon and his White House, but this was less than a full description of Hunt and Liddy's work.

"Well, there's nothing particularly wrong with that," Nixon noted.

"No, there isn't," Haldeman confirmed. "And he worked, at the same time, on the Pentagon Papers." Haldeman then quickly changed the subject back to Mitchell's resignation and his proposed brief announcement, which would be accompanied by a longer letter to the president drafted by Moore. Haldeman had a copy of that letter, and after quickly scanning it, said, "Hey, this is pretty good" and read it aloud:

Dear Mr. President,

Your words of friendship and understanding when we met today meant more to me than I can possibly convey in this letter. I have long believed, and often said, nothing is more important to the future of our country than your reelection as president. I had looked forward to devoting all my time and energy to that result. I have found, however, I can no longer do so on a full-time basis and still meet the one obligation which must come first: the happiness and welfare of my wife and daughter. They have patiently put up with my long absence for some four years. The moment has come when I must devote more time to them. Relatively few men have the privilege of serving the president of the United States. In my service, it has been special indeed, because of the strength of your leadership. As I said today, I shall continue to work for your reelection as well as to be grateful for your unfailing friendship and confidence.

"It's an excellent letter, it couldn't be better. It's very subtle," Nixon observed, and Haldeman agreed, "Very personal, and all that." Haldeman said the letter would be released with a straight announcement: "John Mitchell announced today he's resigned as campaign director for the Committee to Re-elect the President in order to devote more time to his wife and family. He will continue to serve the committee in an advisory capacity." The president was so taken with Moore's draft for Mitchell that he decided to have Moore work up a draft response for him as well, which he outlined for Haldeman.

At 4:30 P.M. Nixon asked Clark MacGregor to join him in the Oval Office and explained to him why Mitchell was leaving, citing ITT (though clearly meaning Watergate) and Martha's health.[27] Then, speaking more candidly, Nixon added, "But due to that, John has been unable to watch the committee, it is not as well organized as we would like, but he must never know that we think that."

Haldeman joined the conversation at 4:48 P.M., and after a discussion of how to operate the congressional relations staff after MacGregor's departure, the conversation turned to Watergate. Nixon and Haldeman proceeded to assert the innocence of all the key figures, and while much of this conversation has been redacted, it is clear that MacGregor, a savvy lawyer, did not ask any questions but simply told the president, "I don't need to know anything about the past, but I need to, I guess, know something about the future. I have said to people absolutely flat-out, I've talked to congressmen and senators, that the Committee to Re-elect the President and the White House had absolutely nothing to do with the recently disclosed incident."

"That's what you've got to, that's the line you should take," Nixon confirmed.

"That's what Mitchell is doing," Haldeman added.

"I know the White House had nothing to do with it," the president reassured MacGregor. He said, "As far as the committee is concerned, I know Mitchell had nothing to do with it. As far as the Cubans are concerned, they certainly are Republicans, that's the problem."

"There are some lines of interconnection," Haldeman noted vaguely. "That's our problem."

"They certainly were doing it to hurt McGovern and support Nixon. That's the problem, and that's what Mitchell basically is concerned about," the president said. "But you can be sure that, as far as Mitchell is concerned, he, of course, had nothing to do with it. I mean, basically, the reason you can be sure, Clark, even if you figure that he was lying, which he would not do to us, is he's not a stupid man."

"Oh, no," MacGregor agreed.

"[On] the White House thing, Hunt is a former CIA agent. He's a super-sleuth, et cetera, et cetera, et cetera," the president explained with his favorite nonexplanation. "There's some story today that they found some gun in his safe over here, or something like that, but I don't know anything about it. But he hasn't been in the White House since when?"

"March, I guess," Haldeman added.

"March twenty-ninth, I think was the last day he was paid," MacGregor added, which had been printed in the news accounts.

Haldeman jumped back in. "See, when he was here he worked on a totally different thing. He was in the Bay of Pigs. He was working on the declassification thing, where we had an all-out unit going. He knew about that stuff." In fact, Hunt never worked on the declassification project. Haldeman then said that Hunt had also worked on the narcotics effort, which was a stretch at best, and in a final bit of disinformation, stated, "Now, he's also been involved, as this thing starts to develop, in other things we didn't know anything about. And this is what you get when you start dealing with these underground characters, as you know as a lawyer."

The president repeated his points, occasionally backing off a bit, as he had with Mitchell, as the conversation proceeded. "All that I know is, the White House had nothing to do with it," Nixon insisted. "I know Colson had nothing to do with it. I know Hunt was gone. So, as far as Mitchell is concerned, Mitchell is in a spot, I would have to admit, where we really don't know. You have to worry a bit about it. Mitchell is in a spot where he hasn't been watching the committee too closely, and you can't be sure that these Cubans who were hanging around didn't have some contacts in that committee. I don't know who. If we did, we'd fire them."

"Well, they did," Haldeman said, trumping the president. He added, "The Bureau has a line into one guy at the committee named Liddy."

"Liddy," Nixon echoed.

"Who was working over at the Finance Committee, not at the—"

"For Stans," Nixon interrupted.

"He worked for Stans as a counsel," Haldeman continued. "He is a guy that was in the White House office working with Krogh's office on the drug stuff. He knew these people. And they have some lines that tie him into some of this. In their [FBI] interrogation of him, they weren't satisfied with his answers, or he said he wanted to get a lawyer, and they said, well, the lawyer would tell you to shut up, and he said, well, I'll do what the lawyer says. And they said, well then, there's no point in talking to you. When the committee found out what had happened in his interrogation, they fired him. The word that they have fired him is not out yet, and we hope it doesn't get out. But Liddy has been released from the committee, from his post."

"If he was involved, and I'm not sure that he was," Nixon said, notwithstanding the fact that Haldeman had told him Liddy was responsible. (After

MacGregor left Haldeman would elaborate on the latest approach: having the cover-up rise to, but stop at, Liddy.)

"That's right," Haldeman said, backing up the president.

"This whole thing is a strange bag," the president explained.

"Well, that runs to some, flies around directly into the CIA, what they're concerned about," Haldeman said. This vague reference to even more complex activities were an effort to tell MacGregor what he might need to know but not in a way that he could possibly understand what Haldeman was actually talking about.

Nixon pushed the discussion forward, "But anyway, the Liddy thing, if he's involved, Clark, it was an unauthorized involvement. That's the point that you need to know. It was without the authority or without the knowledge of John Mitchell. That's the way I'd put it. And as a matter of fact, this has nothing to do with John's leaving, because he has to leave for other, personal reasons, but in a sense it's a good thing, because at least you're in and you know very well that you had nothing to do with anything. And if anything happens, I would assume John—"

"Yeah, but I don't think, I don't know. We purposely don't know a lot of what kind of thing was involved—" Haldeman noted, explaining their willful ignorance. And Nixon added almost simultaneously, "I don't want to find out."

"Both on the governmental side or the committee," Haldeman said, acknowledging that it was more than a CRP problem, that it was related to their government service at the White House as well.

"To me, it's such a crude God damn thing. You almost think it's a bunch of double agents," Nixon said.

"It may very well be," Haldeman added, with a tone of irony.

"Double agents, that's what I'm afraid of. It just looks to me like, almost like a fix," Nixon said, clearly warming to this potential scenario. "Doesn't it to you? How the hell, I said, why in the name of Christ did they want to bug the national committee? What in the name of God, if you're going to bug, bug the McGovern committee," the president said, apparently unaware that Liddy, Hunt and their team had planned to proceed from the DNC to the McGovern headquarters.

Both Nixon and Haldeman continued to proclaim their outrage until MacGregor finally interrupted them, saying, "My fear is that the remarkable record that you've made is going to be besmirched by these extraneous things that you have no knowledge of."

"Sure," the president commented appreciatively.

Haldeman added, "The worst thing we can do, though, is let them do exactly what they want to, which is to get us so involved in that that we don't keep shooting our guns."

Having established his innocence, and Haldeman having made his point, Nixon assumed a more philosophical and presidential posture, observing, "Well, you're going to have this sort of thing more, I guess. People do stupid things. That long agonizing ITT business—we survived. It was very stupid."

"We did some stupid things. Our people did some stupid things," Haldeman agreed. "There are a thousand stupid things like that that don't get uncovered, that we do and that they do. It's when they get uncovered that they look so stupid."

"There will be more. They're going to have a few problems, too," the president pointed out.

Given the confessional tone the conversation had taken, MacGregor now offered, "I've been asking myself, Mr. President, if there's anything in my background, political or otherwise—"

"Forget it," the president said.

"—that would redound on you—"

"Forget it."

"And I don't think that there is," MacGregor concluded.

"Let me say this. Everybody's got something in his background, everybody," Nixon observed.

Haldeman pointed out that if there was anything in MacGregor's past, it likely would have come out when he ran against former vice president Hubert Humphrey for the U.S. Senate in 1970, assuring him that they would not find anything now, because the McGovern people were "a lot more confused than Hubert's people."

"It's a bizarre business, period," Nixon said again. "I don't know that you should comment on this Hunt fellow. Did you ever meet Hunt? I've never seen him."

"No, sir," MacGregor responded.

After a speculative exchange about Hunt, and his having a gun, the president said, "The main thing, frankly, that I was concerned about was Colson, because Colson did work with him on the Pentagon Papers, whatever the hell it was they were working on." But the president said he was no longer worried, because Colson had been questioned by the FBI, and while a staffer might lie to him, it was not likely he would do so to the FBI.

Haldeman added, "I honestly don't think there is any guy in the White House" who was involved in Watergate. Rather, Haldeman explained, "I think there obviously were some contacts at the committee. There was a contact with McCord. I don't know what the hell they were, and there's nothing at any level of authority, and I don't know whether there was any contact with us in that way." Haldeman was effectively notifying MacGregor that while low-level people might have some involvement, no one of authority—meaning Mitchell, Stans, Ehrlichman, himself and the president—did.

"Well, the real problem we deal with, though, from a governmental viewpoint," Haldeman explained, "that has nothing to do with politics at all, is that the lines from these people lead to places we don't want led to."

"The CIA understands," the president said.

Again, using equivocal terms rather than identifying the FBI investigation to which he was actually referring, Haldeman said, "And the investigatory people are on those lines and don't know that they cut in, they don't know where one thing crosses the other."

The president elaborated, "Trouble is, frankly, that Helms's shop does not want to be involved in these things, we just won't say anything further about it, it could very well involve some anti-Castro activities. The Cubans are frightened to death of McGovern, frightened to death, you know, because he made this statement that he'd get along with Allende—"

After MacGregor's departure, Nixon and Haldeman assessed their visit with him.

"How did he react to the remarks?" the president wondered.

"Damn prudent," Haldeman repied.

"He has every right to know what he's getting into," the president observed, "and he asked the right questions. In my mind, he should take this job without asking about Watergate."

"I told him about the Liddy thing," Haldeman explained, "because he's going to find it out right away anyway, and it was better to let him know there was a guy." But Haldeman also had new information to tell Nixon dealing with Liddy's involvement in Watergate. "What we're talking about is, we're going to write a scenario—in fact, we're going to have Liddy write it—which brings all of the loose ends that might lead anywhere at all to him. He's going to say that, yeah, he was doing this, he wasn't authorized." Haldeman, of course, had not only been told by Gordon Strachan, his aide

and liaison to the reelection committee, that Liddy's intelligence operation budget had been approved, but he had also given Strachan instructions in early April 1972 to have Liddy change his focus from Muskie to
McGovern.[28] It was still not clear from these conversations whether Haldeman knew if Mitchell had authorized an illegal break-in and bugging at the
DNC, but he clearly suspected it. Haldeman was certainly aware, however,
that Jeb Magruder would not have authorized such an action without Mitchell's blessing, and that Magruder was directly involved in the Watergate operation.

"Well, what else?" Nixon pressed for more of the scenario.

Haldeman obliged by spinning out the story he had discussed with
Mitchell. "He thought it was an honorable thing to do. He thought it was
important. Obviously, it was wrong. He didn't think he should ask for authorization, because he knew it was something that he didn't want to put
anybody else in a position of authorizing. How did he get the money? See,
we've got that one problem, the check from Dahlberg. What happened is,
and that works out nicely, because the check came in after the spending limit
thing [on April 7]. So it was given to him with the instruction to return it to
Dahlberg. Instead he subverted it to this other purpose, deposited it in the
bank. That explains where the money came from. That explains everything.
And they're [Mitchell and his aides] working on writing out a scenario.* I
think that's the answer to this, and admit that, by God, there was some
campaign involvement."

"But without Mitchell's knowledge," the president qualified, and Haldeman repeated, "But without Mitchell's knowledge."

"Or authorization," Nixon further confirmed. Haldeman echoed, "Or
authorization."

"He's fired."

"And he's fired," Haldeman assured the president.

"What does he get out of it? What's his penalty?" the president asked.

"Oh, not too much. They don't think it will be any big problem," Haldeman
said. Then he added, "Whatever it is, we'll take care of him."

Nixon could not imagine this having taken place without Mitchell's authority, but then, he told Haldeman, he was still not sure. Haldeman speculated, "I can't imagine that he knew specifically that this is what they were

---

*When we were meeting earlier, in Haldeman's office, Mitchell had asked me to write out a bogus Liddy
scenario, but I resisted, explaining that I did not have the time or knowledge. Haldeman saw what
Mitchell was doing and backed me up.

doing. I think he said, for God's sake, get out and get this God damn information, don't pussyfoot around."

The president wanted to know about the money: "How'd he [Liddy] get the check?"

"He was processing the checks. It was an illegal check," Haldeman concluded, incorrectly placing a worst-case potential on it by blending fact with the fiction of the scenario; when all the facts were gathered, it turned out to be a legal contribution. Haldeman guessed, "You know, he was going to run it down to Mexico and put it into cash or something."

"Then what did we do, return the money to the guy? What, what happened?" the president asked, confused about what was the true story and the bogus scenario.

In fact, the check was never given to Liddy to return to the donor; instead, Liddy offered to get it cashed, and ultimately he returned the cash to the reelection committee.[29] But Haldeman explained how the scenario would handle it: "That's what they're going to say he was supposed to do. But he didn't. He on his own initiative decided this was a good source of funds for this covert operation he was running. So he took the check, processed it through this Mexican bank, and ran it up here, which is what he did do."

The president asked, "When would he do this?"

"Quickly, and hopefully, I think the thing to do is do it during the Democratic convention. The way to do it, they know [the FBI has] some lines into him, and Dean says, they've identified him as a suspect in the case, and they're on this. Before he was just a source of information that didn't pan out, so if you let them follow their routine investigation, he doesn't offer up anything, they just catch him, but he works out his whole plan beforehand, so what they catch him at—" This plotting seemed to bring it to an end. Yet Haldeman noted there were problems: "But there may be some flaw in this, and that's what they are going to kind of work out. It has the great advantage of being—"

"He thought it up?" the president asked. Haldeman did not know. "'Cause he's going to have to lie about that, you see," the president noted.

"Well, maybe we can turn it off on that basis. They know there are other lines involved. We can get them not to ask about that, maybe," Haldeman opined.

Nixon was thinking about Hunt's role and talked over Haldeman, stating, "But then, on the basis of the CIA, but the Hunt outfit was involved for other reasons?"

Haldeman suggested, "Maybe he [Liddy] ties Hunt in. Maybe that's the better way. They've got to work that out." Nixon suggested another approach: "He found this group of people that were very amenable—" Haldeman picked up Nixon's train of thought and offered his own, which was closer to the truth: "—[Liddy] met them over here when he was working on this other project, and he used them on the side, for this project." The president and Haldeman exchanged ideas about how to bring the Cubans into the scenario, until Haldeman changed the direction of the conversation with a question: "You know who Dahlberg is?"

"No," Nixon said.

"He's [Dwayne] Andreas's bagman." Andreas, a wealthy industrialist and Democratic backer of Hubert Humphrey in Minnesota politics, had contributed a portion of the money that Liddy had converted to cash for the CRP. The president was mildly surprised, but Haldeman saw other potentials for the scenario he was developing that could include the Democrats as well. "So it, all of a sudden, starts running over to the other side, too. It's kind of intriguing," Haldeman mused.

"Well," the president began, and after pausing for a bit, announced, "I agree. I think the best thing to do is to cut your losses in such things, get the damn thing down. It's just one of those things, and they were involved."

"Otherwise they're going to keep pursuing these things that lead into the wrong directions," Haldeman said, and began again to explain the entangling connections of the White House to the men arrested at the Watergate. More people than Colson were involved, he said, because there were other projects. "Hunt's tied to Krogh, Liddy's tied to Krogh. They're all tied to Ehrlichman," Haldeman reported.

"You mean they worked here?" the president asked.

"Sure."

"Well, what the hell's wrong with that?" Nixon asked dismissively.

"They're tied in to Dave Young," Haldeman added, before responding, "Nothing any more than there is with Colson." But he did not point out that they all—Hunt, Liddy, Krogh, Young, Colson and Ehrlichman—had been involved in the break-in at Ellsberg's psychiatrist's office some nine months earlier.

Again, Nixon pressed, "Yeah, that's what I mean. No, but not in any hanky-panky. The only thing that you mean is the Pentagon Papers? What the hell is the matter with that?" This question was posed with a tone of alarm and concern in the president's voice.

Haldeman answered vaguely, "The investigation, the process."

"What?"

"Just the process that they used," he answered, again using ambiguous words to describe the illegal break-in.

Not surprisingly, the president could see the problem, and he declared, "Well, that's perfectly all right."

At this extremely sensitive moment in this conversation, when Haldeman might have explained the true dimensions of the issues now confronting the White House, Ron Ziegler walked in and interrupted. When he left, it returned to Watergate, and Nixon asked, "When will this Liddy scenario [be done], is Dean working on it?"

"Dean's working on it with Mitchell," Haldeman said, but then corrected himself. "'I suggest,' Mitchell said, 'Dean write it.' I suggested that, let Liddy write it, Liddy knows more of the facts than anybody, let him sit down and spend as long as it takes to and spin out the whole web, see where it comes." Both men sat silent for a moment, until Haldeman finished, "If he's willing to take the heat, which he apparently is."

"The guy's apparently a true believer," Nixon said with admiration.

"Yeah. He says he is. He says it doesn't make any difference what they do, he will not [talk]."

"And we'll take care of him, too," Nixon said. He then added, "Well, it's good to have some people like that."

"He may have to go to jail for a while or something, but he'll survive that," Haldeman volunteered.

"What the hell, there's worse than that. His breaking into the Democratic committee, Christ, that's no blot on a man's record," the president said.

Haldeman now raised another potential problem in the scenario they were concocting: "Well, the embezzlement of those funds, too, and violation of the Campaign Spending Act."

"Yeah, that's probably a fine," the president said.

"Wrapping it all up in this way, it doesn't make much difference. After, if he gets hung on it, then we'll wait a discreet interval, pardon him," Haldeman said.

"After the election."

"Sure." After a moment of silent reflection, Nixon shared his thinking. "Let me tell you something interesting. Don't be that worried about things of that kind. How much effect did Bobby Baker's thing, where he was directly involved, where he was convicted, where everybody knew that [President Lyndon] Johnson was in the bag and all that sort of thing? How much did it affect [Johnson]?"

"Probably a lot."

"Bullshit," Nixon snapped. "Johnson, how could he be hurt when he won sixty-one to thirty-nine?"

"Oh, it didn't hurt in the election. It hurt his image," Haldeman added.

"A little," Nixon conceded. But Watergate was different. "This does not personally involve the president. We're in a different area. This involves the campaign committee, which we don't like it worth a damn. But Clark and a lot of others are terribly sensitive about this, that and the other thing. But we don't like this."

"Well, Clark's got a good right to be. If there's something there, he'd better know what he's got to cope with," Haldeman said.

"Well, I'm sorry, but I guess that's the way it has to work. You can't cover this thing up, Bob. The best thing is to cut it. That's why I was hoping to get the damn guys charged." This was the first time Nixon mentioned that they "can't cover this thing up," which he would periodically repeat in the weeks and months ahead. Based on this conversation, it appears as if any responsibility would stop at an unauthorized Liddy, although the president knew this was not true. For Richard Nixon, though, this did not constitute a cover-up; a cover-up, it seems, would result in no one's being held responsible, including those apprehended and arrested in the DNC.

"In fact, the Bureau's got the job of digging it out. The problem is, they're a proud organization, they're going to have to do their jobs, correct?" the president, being a realist, pointed out.* Haldeman agreed, but he was not pleased with this fact. Nixon continued, "It's just such a ridiculous God damn thing, it really is."

Haldeman turned the conversation to scheduling matters, a veto message, a meeting with Henry Kissinger before Henry traveled to California, and a call to Governor Ronald Reagan about Kissinger's forthcoming trip (which the president called "a pure boondoggle"). Then, as this session was ending, Nixon returned to Mitchell. "We're doing the right thing on John, don't you agree?" Nixon asked. Haldeman noted, "[Mitchell] can't carry the

---

*A statement like this further confirms that Nixon did not believe he was closing down the FBI's investigation of Watergate on June 23, 1972, in authorizing Haldeman to have the CIA intervene with the FBI's investigation of the Mexican check and Hunt's activities.

kind of personal load he does and still run a campaign. It's one of the reasons you got a mess in the campaign, because he couldn't do it, and he knew it. And locking her up, or any of those other things—"

"Wouldn't work," Nixon said.

"Well, even if it would work, it doesn't really solve the [Watergate] problem."

When Haldeman departed at 6:15 p.m., the president talked with Rose Mary Woods and told her "in the greatest confidence" that Mitchell was resigning because of Martha. As Nixon was leaving the Oval Office to head up to the residence, he told Rose that Mitchell was "a good guy" for the way he was dealing with Martha. Rose agreed. "Poor man." she said.


## July 1, 1972, Saturday, the White House

Before heading to California for eighteen days at his San Clemente home, which became the Western White House offices during such visits, the president held a ceremony in the Oval Office to commemorate the signing of the Twenty-sixth Amendment, giving eighteen-year-olds the right to vote, which had been adopted a year earlier, on July 1, 1971.

Two weeks had passed since the arrests at the DNC, and there was little new reporting in the news accounts. *The Washington Post* was rehashing earlier Watergate stories with new details about the arrests at the DNC's Watergate complex, but the *New York Times* had stopped all coverage. (In fact, the *Times* would largely ignore the Watergate story until January 1973, when they hired investigative journalist Seymour Hersh.[30])

Between Nixon and Colson, Watergate came up only in passing comments, when Nixon quizzed Colson further about Hunt, but Colson provided nothing new. Nonetheless, the president and Colson soon contrived a counterploy scheme to blame the Democrats for a staged break-in at the Republican National Committee (RNC), one that was never executed.[31]

While preparing to travel to California Nixon dictated his reflections on the Watergate situation to his diary: "The major problem on the Watergate is simply to clean the thing up by having whoever was responsible admit what happened. Certainly I am satisfied that nobody in the White House had any knowledge or approved any such activity, and that Mitchell was not aware of it as well."[32] At that point he thought he had done nothing wrong. However, when writing his memoirs some six years later, the former president better understood his actions in the days following the arrests, noting that he had taken "the first steps down the road that eventually led to the end of [his] presidency."

In his memoir he acknowledged that he did nothing to discourage the various false stories being developed to explain the break-in, and that he had "approved efforts to encourage the CIA to intervene and limit the FBI investigation."[33] He said his decisions were prompted by what he perceived "as an annoying and strictly political problem," so he "was looking for a way to deal with Watergate that would minimize the damage to me, my friends, and my campaign, while giving the least advantage to my political opposition." In short, Nixon viewed Watergate in terms of "politics pure and simple," and he played it "tough" because that's how the Democrats and their sympathetic news media partners played it.[34] But Nixon, trained in the law, surely recognized that a good motive did not justify criminal activities.

In fact, Nixon's attitudes and motives were shared by others at the highest levels of his administration: Haldeman, Ehrlichman, Mitchell and myself. No one was considering the criminal implications of our actions, only the political consequences of inaction. No one doubted that breaking into and bugging the Democratic National Committee was against the law, yet no one, particularly Ehrlichman and myself, as lawyers, paused to examine the laws that come into force in a situation like that in which we now found ourselves. Offenses such as conspiracy and obstruction of justice are not bright-line crimes that are immediately and easily discernible to those not experienced in criminal law; they are ones in which the wrongful conduct can be less than conspicuous. A striking number of lawyers found themselves on the wrong side of the law during Watergate, and almost all of them did so out of ignorance of criminal law. But ignorance of the law has never been an acceptable justification, and good motives do not excuse criminal conduct, with the classic law school example being Jean Valjean of *Les Misérables*, who stole a loaf of bread for his sister's starving children. He was still a thief.

Everyone knows the difference between telling the truth and lying, and that lying, when done under oath, constitutes perjury. In the case of Watergate, the effort to keep the cover-up contained without lying to investigators became increasingly challenging as time passed. When the president left for California on July 1, the scenario that would place responsibility for the Watergate activities no higher than G. Gordon Liddy was the theory, and the hope. But in practice, it only raised new complications.

# PART II
# CONTAINING

*July 1972 Through December 1972*

On July 2, 1972, *The Washington Post* somewhat breathlessly reported that "a force of 150 FBI agents has begun a nationwide search for Howard E. [*sic*] Hunt, the former White House consultant" linked to the DNC bugging.[1] The White House knew that Hunt could "undisappear," as Haldeman told Nixon on June 20, and today it is clear that there was, in fact, no nationwide FBI search for Hunt; actually, as the *Post* reported a few days later, Hunt's lawyer, William O. Bittman, a former assistant attorney general at the Department of Justice who had successfully prosecuted Jimmy Hoffa, had called the Watergate prosecutors in the U.S. Attorney's Office and informed them that his client was available whenever they wanted to speak with him.

Apart from the *Post*, most Americans viewed the arrests at the Watergate as little more than politics as usual, as Nixon himself had earlier surmised. In its first post-Watergate poll, Gallup reported on Nixon's standing versus both Democratic contenders: Against McGovern the president received 53 percent of the vote to McGovern's 37 percent, with 10 percent undecided, and against Vice President Hubert Humphrey the president led 55 percent to 33 percent, with 12 percent undecided. When Governor George Wallace was added to the mix, Gallup still had Nixon victorious, although his percentage dropped, as did those of other candidates.[2]

Although there wasn't any secret recording equipment installed at the Western White House at San Clemente, the president's diary, later testimony and others' memoirs reveal that Watergate remained very much on his mind during his eighteen-day visit to his California home. Several key events took place and related decisions were made during this working vacation.

*July 6 to July 18, 1972*

# The Call from Gray
# and a Walk on the Beach

On July 5 acting FBI director Pat Gray telephoned CIA deputy director Vernon Walters to ask for a formal written memorandum instructing the FBI to hold up interviewing the leads regarding the Mexican money that had passed through Bernard Barker's bank account. (Walters had informally made such a request earlier.) Although CIA director Richard Helms had not changed his own mind on the matter, Walters was unaware of Helms's thinking, and that he wanted to keep the FBI out of the CIA's relationship with Hunt, so he informed Gray that the CIA had no interest in anything relating to the FBI's Watergate investigation.[1] The conversation with Walters prompted Gray to call Clark MacGregor later that day to warn the president that his staff was interfering with the FBI's investigation.[2]

## July 6, 1972, the Western White House

Nixon reported in his diary that Pat Gray had called, "greatly concerned about the Watergate case and that Walters had come in to see him indicating that the CIA had no interest in the matter and that pursuing the investigation would not be an embarrassment to the CIA. He said that he and Walters both felt that some people either at the White House or the [reelection] committee were trying to cover up things which would be a mortal blow to me—rather than assisting in the investigation." The president further noted that when "Ehrlichman came in he was astounded to find out that I had this conversation. He then told me that the problem was that the unraveling of the case would not be particularly embarrassing as far as this instant matter was concerned, but that it would involve perfectly legitimate activities that would be hard to explain from other investigations, including "the Ellsberg case, the Bay of Pigs, and other matters where we had an imperative need to get the facts."[3] Like Haldeman, Ehrlichman merely alluded to Liddy and Hunt's earlier White House activities without explaining to Nixon that they had bungled another surreptitious burglary in September 1971.

Nixon's July 6 diary note reveals that during his conversation with Haldeman on June 23, when Helms and Walters had been sent to the FBI, the president was acting on information from Haldeman that had led him to believe that Gray wanted help from Walters in controlling the investigation. Then, he added in his diary (while the subject was still fresh in his mind), on June 30 Haldeman had again explained that the FBI wanted to limit the investigation but was under pressure from the U.S. Attorney's Office. Based on these prior conversation with Haldeman, Nixon was understandably confused by Gray's July 6 call informing him, rather bluntly, that it appeared the White House was trying to frustrate the FBI's inquiry, which is exactly what the president was saying he did *not* want to do, as it might involve the White House in Watergate. Nixon closed this July 6 entry:

> Certainly the best thing to do is to have the investigation pursued to its normal conclusion. In any event, we have to live with this one and hope to bring it to a conclusion without too much rubbing off on the presidency before the election. It is one of those cases where subordinates in a campaign, with the very best of motives, go off on some kick which inevitably embarrasses the top man. In this instance, however, how we handle it may make the difference as to how we come out. In any event, as I emphasized to Ehrlichman and Haldeman, we must do nothing to indicate to Pat Gray or to the CIA that the White House is trying to suppress the investigation. On the other hand, we must cooperate with the investigation all the way along the line.[4]

Haldeman was a bit more to the point in describing the situation in a note he made after a long meeting in San Clemente with MacGregor about the campaign: "The P[resident] and I then met for a couple of hours with E[hrlichman] afterward. Got into the Watergate caper problem. Walters apparently has finked out and spilled the beans to Pat Gray, which complicates the issue substantially."[5] Clearly Haldeman's effort to manipulate the situation to trim the Watergate investigation had failed. He had distorted the recommendation from Mitchell that I had passed along on June 23, not to mention created a ticking time bomb for the president, directly involving him in the cover-up six days after the arrests at the DNC.

Nixon's July 6 meeting in San Clemente with Ehrlichman was their first conversation of any substance about the Watergate incident. Haldeman was taking a few days off with his family and some friends during this California trip, so Ehrlichman was spending substantial time with the president, during which he shared more bad news about Watergate.[6] Ehrlichman told him about Jeb Magruder's possible involvement, and that Magruder was going to be questioned by the FBI. (Nixon, in turn, noted in his diary that "Magruder had been Liddy's immediate superior and had been responsible for authorizing money for him.") Ehrlichman explained that Magruder might have to take the Fifth Amendment, because even if the prosecutors had no evidence of "his involvement in the planning and execution of the bugging, his relationship to Liddy was such they might be able to draw him in as a part of a conspiracy."[7]

## July 7, 1972, the Western White House

Gray's call and his learning of Magruder's role remained very much on the president's mind the following day, according to Ehrlichman's contemporaneous notes. More specifically Nixon was considering his direction to Haldeman to have the CIA cut off the FBI's Watergate investigation into Mexico and Hunt. He told Ehrlichman of his concern that "the release of the Pentagon Papers has led to a demand for declassification of a lot of secret documents and may lead to grave consequences for the CIA and its former officials. They have to worry about the Bay of Pigs and Diem's assassination and other things," and he reported that Haldeman had a study by former White House aide Tom Huston on this matter. Nixon told Ehrlichman, "Howard Hunt was privy to most of the CIA's problems, you know. It all will blow! We tried, but we can't have this followed up. Gray and Walters must tell people that there is no effort to cover up either by the White House or the committee to reelect. The cover-up is the worst thing. Cover-up is how I nailed Truman. It can hurt deeply."[8]

## July 8, 1972, the Western White House

On Saturday, the president and Ehrlichman spent four hours together walking and talking along California beaches, and swimming. Both men later wrote in detail about their conversation, and their accounts largely correspond. The president again referred to Gray's call and insisted that there could be no appearance of a cover-up, "Not a whiff of it." He wanted Ehrlichman to get it out to the press that the president's feeling was, Let the chips fall where they may. Then, spinning out what Ziegler might announce, Ehrlichman quotes Nixon as saying, "No one in the White House is involved. Our own investigation is completed, and that's the finding." Ehrlichman said he wondered "what investigation he was talking about, because I wasn't aware of any that could be called 'ours.'" Both of their accounts indicate that clemency for those involved in Watergate was discussed, and they agreed that no one should approach the president on the subject. Nixon, though, did not close the door to the potential of it after the election.[9]

Ehrlichman claims that they also spoke about Hunt and Liddy's involvement in the break-in at Dr. Fielding's office. He later claimed that Nixon also brought up the subject, albeit in vague terms, during their July 6 conversation, but there was nothing vague about their conversation on the beach on the eighth. They discussed what Howard Hunt had done and what he knew and "that included his California burglary, his attempts to prove that John Kennedy had caused the failure at the Bay of Pigs and his similar project involving the assassination of Diem."[10] Ehrlichman's account in his memoir, however, conflicts with the records of both his own prior statements and that made by Nixon, not to mention the fact that, when I later gave this information about the Ellsberg break-in to Nixon during a conversation on March 17, 1973, he claimed it was the first he was aware of it.[11]

### July 9–18, 1972, the Western White House

While Nixon was in California, George McGovern was nominated by the Democratic National Convention in Miami as the party's presidential nominee, and McGovern, in turn, selected Missouri senator Thomas Eagleton as his running mate. The chaos of the convention pleased the president and his senior staff, for it only confirmed their assessment of the disorganization in their opponent's campaign. But things were not going all that smoothly for the well-oiled Nixon organization either, as they learned upon returning to Washington on July 18.

During the president's stay in California the FBI had interviewed many of the key figures on the reelection committee: G. Gordon Liddy (pre-departure June 28), who was later dismissed in a staged firing for his refusal to cooperate with the FBI; John Mitchell (July 5); Maurice Stans (July 5 and 14); and several lower-level staffers. Based on leads from these conversations, the FBI scheduled an interview with Jeb Magruder on July 20, which was a disaster waiting to happen, as Magruder had been involved in the development and implementation of Liddy's illegal plans, and he was generally not one to take responsibility for his mistakes.

To bring Haldeman and Ehrlichman up to date on this pending situation, they requested I meet them on Air Force One when they landed at Andrews Air Force Base. We met in the president's cabin on the empty plane on the evening of July 18, 1972. I reported what I knew of the FBI and grand jury investigations (which was much less than investigators and the public later assumed), as well as on Herb Kalmbach's efforts. He was an attorney who did personal work for the president on his real estate holdings and a major CRP fund-raiser who was also raising money for and distributing it to the six men Liddy had involved in the Watergate fiasco. Haldeman and Ehrlichman had authorized me to speak with him after John Mitchell had requested I do so, and I informed them that he had paid for attorneys and living expenses for the so-called Watergate gang, as those involved in the break-in were occasionally called in the early days.

Most of the concern was with Magruder's forthcoming FBI interview. Earlier that afternoon I had learned that Magruder had found a witness to corroborate his false testimony that the money he had authorized be paid to Liddy—some $199,000*—was intended for legitimate campaign security purposes. I expressed serious concern about Magruder's concocted story (which, four decades later, I have come to realize was the scenario Ehrlichman had developed with Mitchell and Haldeman on the morning of June 21), not to mention the fact that Magruder had enlisted his assistant, Bart Porter, to support his false story. I also reported to Haldeman and Ehrlichman that Hugh Sloan, who served as treasurer of the finance committee, had resisted Magruder's efforts to enlist him in lying, and they were now at odds, with Magruder claiming Sloan had stolen money and Sloan charging that Magruder was trying to get him to commit perjury.

Haldeman noted this meeting in his diary and the Magruder problem:

*This would equal more than $1 million in today's dollars.

As of now, Dean feels that they are going to move on Magruder and that the only thing we can do is to have him take the rap that they'll hit him with. And he feels that I've got to talk to him and convince him that this is what he should do. I'm not at all sure that is the way to handle it, that I can do it. But Ehrlichman called me at home later and confirmed that he thought we should do that, although he'd adjourned the Dean meeting after it became clear that he couldn't read exactly what my reaction was on it. This is a real powder keg, I guess, and John's sitting on top of it. John Dean is trying to keep the lid on, but is not at all sanguine as to his ability to continue to do so.[12]

In the days that followed both Ehrlichman and Haldeman would explain this situation to the president, as he increasingly requested updates on the status of the Watergate investigation. Until preparing this book—and discovering the conversations that follow—I was not aware that Nixon was deeply involved in the decision regarding Magruder's perjured testimony, a deceit essential to the initial phase of the cover-up.[13]

# Concern over Magruder's Testimony

*July 19, 1972, the White House*

John Ehrlichman arrived in the Oval Office at 12:44 P.M. In these early days of Watergate both Haldeman and Ehrlichman almost always waited for the president to ask before volunteering any information on this subject. Not long into a discussion about airline hijackings and making them a capital offense, Nixon asked for an update.[1] "Well, I don't know," Ehrlichman began. "I talked to Dean this morning, and Bob talked to Mitchell. I don't know what transpired there, but he sent Dean over to talk to Mitchell, and there's something cooking this morning, and I haven't been in on it. Dean came out to the airplane and briefed us after you all left, and my conclusion is that this whole scenario that they had dreamed up that was going to preserve Magruder is not going to work."

"Yeah," the president snapped, clearly not happy with the news. Ehrlichman added, "And Magruder is probably going to have to take the slide." Nixon asked, "How's he going to slide?" Ehrlichman replied rather matter-of-factly, "Well, he's just going to take whatever the lumps come. He'll have to take responsibility for the thing, and they said they're not going to be able to contrive a story that indicates that he didn't know what was going on. But I think that's what Dean's working on this morning." The president asked about Magruder, "Did he know?" Ehrlichman immediately confided, "Oh, yeah! Oh, Lord yes! He's in it with both feet."

"If he can't contrive a story, then, you know, I'd like to see this thing work out, but I've been through these. If he can't tell the story, . . ." the president began, but then he had another thought. "But the worst thing a guy can do, there are two things, each is bad: One is to lie, and the other one is to cover up." Ehrlichman agreed, and Nixon continued, "If you cover up, you're going to get caught. And if you lie, you're going to be guilty of perjury. Now, basically, that was the whole story of the Hiss case." Ehrlichman agreed, and Nixon added, "It was the story of the five percenters and the rest.* It's a hell of a God damn thing. I hate to see it, but let me say, we'll take care of Magruder immediately afterwards." The president reassured Ehrlichman that "[i]n his case it would be easy as pie, it'd be a case of [*unclear*], you could treat him like these Vietnam Veterans Against the War, and, I mean, you could just give amnesty to all of 'em."

"That'd do it. We'll have to lay that foundation, but as I say, I think Bob and Dean will have a better feel for this a little later, after they talk to Mitchell, see where we are," Ehrlichman said, and changed the subject to a morning lead story in *The Washington Post* about the lawyer who showed up to bail out the Watergate burglars without being called, Douglas Caddy. Caddy had refused to answer questions, because he claimed the information was privileged communications, but Judge John Sirica had cited him for contempt; Caddy's appeal had been denied by the local court of appeals.[2] Ehrlichman explained how this could draw in not only Hunt and Liddy but Colson as well, because Caddy was handling the divorce of Colson's secretary. Both concluded that that was too remote to be a problem and returned to the Magruder situation.

"[C]an't [Magruder] plead the Fifth?" the president inquired. "No, I don't think so," Ehrlichman said. "Never?" a surprised Nixon asked. "I don't think so," Ehrlichman replied, without offering an explanation. "But they'll convict him?" the president added with disbelief. "Oh, they'll convict him by somebody else's testimony," Ehrlichman said confidently. But this made no sense to Nixon, who asked, "Then what in the hell is he, what good does he do? Try pleading the Fifth?"

"No, no. I think he has to go in and say, Well, I did this, and it was a bad thing to do, and I got carried away and I feel terrible about it," Ehrlichman suggested.[3] Nixon, taken with that proposal, asked, "Well, can't he state it just a little different? He could say he did it, but say, I was just slightly into it?" Ehrlichman, acknowledging this was possible, replied, "Yeah, but it isn't going to change his situation." Nixon then clarified, "No, no, he'd still be [guilty], what I meant, I didn't expect it to be this way, the way they handled it, and so forth and so on. I

---

*During the Truman presidency the Senate investigated charges that presidential aide Harry H. Vaughan and others were charging a 5 percent commission for their influence in securing government contracts.

said, just get all the information you can, and I think I've just got to take the responsibility for it." "Yep, yep, he could say that," Ehrlichman agreed.

"No, it's got to be kept at the Liddy level, if possible," Nixon affirmed, and when Ehrlichman again said he did not have detailed information about Magruder's testimony, the president had another question: "What is the situation, though, with Petersen and Kleindienst and the rest? What are they doing?"

"Petersen is pretty good, but Kleindienst is one step removed from it. Petersen's been very good with Dean in trying to help to evaluate the thing as it goes along and in keeping Dean informed of the direction that things are going," Ehrlichman reported. "What the U.S. attorney is up to and so forth?" Nixon asked. "Yep, and he's managed to keep ahold of the U.S. attorney better. It's a better situation than it was," Ehrlichman explained, and again tried to change the subject, but Nixon was still focused on Watergate. "Well, the real problem here isn't so tough. The important thing is to get the God damn thing done," the president declared. "And now."

Ehrlichman assured the president, "We're urging that. I was all over Dean on that last night: We've got to get it done soon as possible, so that people have a chance to forget. He agrees with that, and he says they're not dragging their feet on this by any means. And, well, he's enlisted on that."

"Just so we keep it all in one hat here, is Dean with you, or Dean with Bob, or both?" Nixon asked. Ehrlichman reported, "Both. The two of us have been talking to him, more or less together, right along, and we've been drawing on Bob's political judgment on this. It's been pretty good." "It sure is," Nixon agreed, and Ehrlichman added, "And Dean called us on the airplane and said he had to talk to us, so we stayed on the airplane after it landed. He came out and we sat and talked for about an hour and went through all the kinds of stuff he didn't like to talk about on the phone. He had a long meeting with Petersen yesterday and—"

"So, it really gets down to Magruder?" the president asked, recognizing that this would either close down the inquiry or open it anew. Ehrlichman advised, "Yeah, that's about right." "But what does Magruder say?" Nixon asked, eager for specifics. "Well, he says that he wanted to get a lot of information, that he felt he had to have that information for a lot of different reasons, they had kind of a dirty tricks department, that—"

"Disrupting the convention?" Nixon said, raising a legitimate concern. "If he brings it up, we have these stories about Vietnam Veterans Against the War, mention that," the president suggested. Ehrlichman continued with the scenario,

"And, but he imposed on Liddy the responsibility for getting it—" The president interrupted to add his thoughts on how to embroider the story: "Also, we had our own security-protecting interests, against ourselves. Don't you agree?"

But Ehrlichman wanted the president to understand that the situation was not that simple. "The problem is that once he starts to talk, I don't know what the limitations of the scope of the examination might be, and that sort of thing—" Nixon knew where he wanted it to stop, and said, "I suppose that the main thing is just whether he is the one where it stops. Whether he goes to Mitchell or Haldeman, is that it?"

"That's it. And this is one of the questions that we raised with Dean last night. Dean said he didn't have any confidence really that Magruder was sufficiently tough and stable to be able to hold the line if he were pressed by adroit interrogators." (In fact, I argued that Magruder should not, or could not, pull off his bogus account.) "Do you think Mitchell knew?" Nixon asked again. "Yeah, I assume so," Ehrlichman replied. "I don't know that he did. Yeah, I think so. See, did, did—" Nixon interrupted, "I can't believe that!" quickly coming to Mitchell's defense. "Well," said Ehrlichman, "the fruits of this thing were around. There were memos of overheard conversations, for instance, and I just have a hunch that, and I don't know this, so this may be unfair, but I just have a feeling that Mitchell, in his situation, saw those transcripts and had to have—"

"Did Bob see them?" the president asked. "No, no. And I can't find anybody in the White House, including Timmons, that ever did, or that ever knew about this operation," Ehrlichman said. Alfred Baldwin had mentioned White House congressional relations staffer Bill Timmons as someone he thought might have delivered his reports to the reelection committee. In fact, Timmons had nothing to do with intelligence and denied ever seeing such material. "I do not think that Bob would have anything to do with it, because he's too smart," the president surmised.

"Bob and John Dean had a meeting with Mitchell and Magruder and some people about a different operation that was proposed, which they disapproved. And they have the right to feel, as a result of that meeting, that nothing like this was going on." Ehrlichman was giving the president a placid account of my two meetings in Mitchell's office, while he was still attorney general, with Magruder and Liddy regarding campaign intelligence, and that I had told Haldeman I thought I had killed Liddy's absurd plans. He continued, "But after that was disapproved, then they went ahead with this other operation without there ever being another meeting involving White House people." "But," Ehrlichman added, "the question of whether Magruder will hold and take the gaff and assume the responsibility and say Mitchell didn't know anything about this is the tough question."

"Why wouldn't he?" Nixon quizzed. "Well," Ehrlichman said, "you know that when you've got a fairly callow guy on the stand, and you work on him properly, you can get him to say things that he doesn't intend to say. I think it's a risk." "It's a risk, I agree," Nixon replied, "but I would think that Magruder on that would be just, it's just that there's so much riding on this thing. We cannot put John Mitchell in this thing."

"I appreciate that, and you can condition it for a thing of that kind, but I would be willing to bet you a new hat that a guy like Edward Bennett Williams could break Magruder down." Ehrlichman offered an example of how he would cross-examine Magruder: He would establish that Magruder had obtained approval for even the smallest of items at the reelection committee, and that therefore he had undoubtedly obtained approval for Liddy's Watergate operation.

"Well, looking at the criminal case now, the Magruder side of it, what is the best tactic there?" the president asked. After some back and forth, Ehrlichman gathered his thoughts and said, "The best tactic, if we had our way on [it], would be [to] let Liddy and Hunt go. Hold it there. If Magruder is going to be involved through third-party testimony and so on, then the next best tactic would be the one that's been proposed, which is to rationalize the story, which does, or it doesn't, lead to his conviction. That's the thing they're checking out this morning. Dean's very pessimistic, and Henry Petersen's very pessimistic about that washing. Now [Petersen, through Dean] says there's an internal problem. He says there are disloyal guys in the U.S. Attorney's Office and the Bureau who are just standing watching this thing, and who are going to second-guess any story that you come up with. So, he said, whatever we come up with has got to be watertight."

"That's why it was never a cover-up, a cover-up thing—" Nixon did not finish his thought but went silent for several seconds, and he can be heard slowly and gently pounding his clenched fist on his desk. Then he proceeded, hesitantly, still collecting thoughts, "I know, what, what we, I wonder, I wonder, I don't think that, that I would, I would, don't, I don't think it would bother me so much in the cover-up, John, and, if they had confessions and convictions of some of them. That's really what I think is the important thing." This notion that it could not be considered a true cover-up if someone at a lower level could be held accountable became central to Nixon's thinking and would recur in other conversations, if left unstated. To Nixon, a cover-up would involve letting the men arrested in the DNC's Watergate office walk free. "Well, they'll have not only the five burglars, but they would have the two mystery men, Liddy and Hunt," Ehrlichman added encouragingly.

"Both of them will confess?" Nixon asked and answered. "They'll have to be convicted. I just don't see any escape for that. And that'll give the public a lot of blood and give the Democrats a lot to chew on. Liddy and Hunt doesn't bother me too much." Ehrlichman agreed, and they discussed how the two had already surfaced in press accounts as likely being involved in Watergate, although they agreed that their having worked at the White House was a negative.

Ehrlichman steered the conversation back to the matter of Magruder's perjury: "If we can, I'm still hopeful, though, that Dean and Mitchell will conclude that the Magruder scenario will work, and it'll wash, that there are no extrinsic loose-end facts that will impeach him. So that the disloyal guys in the U.S. Attorney's don't have anything to get their teeth into. If all you've got is the testimony of Baldwin or somebody like that, who's an outsider, it might do it, and maybe it would pull it off. But there's no sense in starting it and then having it disproved, that would be doubly damaging. And we—"

"Oh, yeah, then you've got a cover-up and Mitchell," the president said, which was the worst case. "Which, I'd say, is what happened in our little investigation so far," Nixon added, mentioning again the faux investigation that Ehrlichman had earlier noted but nonetheless modifying it to cover new circumstances. "Yep, yep," Ehrlichman agreed. Then he added, "Well, and Dean's been admonished not to contrive a story that's liable not to succeed." When Ehrlichman reported this blatant subornation instruction the room went silent, until finally Ehrlichman added, "Ah, they're trying to take all the risk out of it. If there's risk that remains, he might as well just go whole hog." Again silence, until the president spoke in a hushed tone, "That's right." Silence followed, and Nixon then added, "Well, I must say that I, I can't see how—" The president paused, then finished, "Magruder should stand firm on Mitchell."

"Well, he may want to, but he may not be tough enough," the president quickly added.

When the president met with Chuck Colson and Bob Haldeman in his EOB office that afternoon, Watergate ran throughout the conversation, although with Colson the president was guarded.[4] While this audio recording is very difficult to hear, it is clear that the president was seeking Colson's reactions to the prospect of Magruder's being the stopgap of the cover-up as well as sharing the latest with Haldeman.

The president mentioned his conversation with Ehrlichman about Magruder and the need to "cut our losses." Nixon said he was not sure Magruder "will stand up as far as Mitchell," which was a serious problem, because "we just can't get Mitchell in this." When Nixon probed Colson about Hunt's potential testimony, Colson speculated that "Hunt will not think that anything he did was wrong." When Haldeman pressed the topic, Colson was more specific: "Well, if he's properly coached, and he's got a good lawyer, he's one guy that I would figure would take the rap, take the heat, and I'm not speaking for him."

The president explained that Magruder's testimony would make or break his criminal liability, as well as Mitchell's. This was a problem, he said, because Ehrlichman had no confidence in Magruder, referring to his ability to lie, without saying that. Everyone understood, though, and Colson responded, "Hell, I wouldn't put much confidence in him, but I think he's scared," and "he's scared enough that he would do it." Colson said he felt Watergate was a tragedy, because its political notoriety meant the people involved would likely go to jail. If it was an industrial espionage case, they'd only be fined and given suspended sentences. Those involved were going through a horrible experience, not to mention that their actions would forever be on their records. This prompted the president to mention pardons, and that after it was all over those involved might be pardoned in a general amnesty that included antiwar protesters with criminal records. Or as Nixon put it, "We'll just basically pardon the whole kit and caboodle after the election."

After Colson departed Nixon asked Haldeman for an update. Haldeman still did not have all he needed to know but reported that the Magruder plan was proceeding: "They've started on that path now, where we're in this thing with Magruder." His meaning was clear: Magruder was going to lie. Haldeman explained that Mitchell and Magruder had "this guy, Porter" at an FBI interview and that he had done "very well." Porter, Haldeman said, worked at the reelection committee, and his testimony "cuts it off before it gets to Mitchell."

"Is that something Magruder thought up?" Nixon asked. "Well," Haldeman said, "I'm not sure that Magruder thought it up or if it's these other guys who thought about it and recruited him. But Magruder got it in the end." Haldeman explained that Magruder's testimony was "going to come into the campaign," that that was almost guaranteed to happen, for there was "no way to contain" it. While no one wanted to see it get to Magruder, "it's a matter of trying to turn it off before it gets Mitchell, which everybody agrees is very unfortunate. Cut it off at the Magruder level, and not because I want to get Magruder."

"Can Magruder do that?" Nixon asked, and Haldeman said, "Well, that's the problem. He says he will. Some question as to whether he can. On the other hand, Dean and Ehrlichman think it's problematic." He explained that Magruder had the authority to approve funding for Liddy, and the investigators and prosecutors had this information. Haldeman could not give the president any reassurances about Magruder, adding, "It's probably better to take whatever losses we have to take."

"Yeah," Nixon agreed. "It's just a God damn shame about Magruder. God damn, he's such a good man."

That evening Haldeman noted in his diary that the "Watergate thing flared up again today with the problem on Bart Porter's testimony which will start the implicating of Magruder. He decided to go ahead with that. Mitchell and John Dean have spent a lot of time working out the details and apparently have something developed that will work out all right."[5]

### July 20, 1972, the White House

Haldeman sat in on the president's meeting with Armand Hammer, the chairman of Occidental Petroleum, who had recently signed an assistance agreement with the U.S.S.R. The real reason Nixon was meeting with Hammer was to get him to provide his executive vice president, Marvin Watson, an experienced Democrat operative, to run the Democrats for Nixon operation at the request of John Connally, who would head the organization, to which Hammer agreed.[6] As soon as Hammer departed the president asked Haldeman, "Any further developments on Watergate?"[7] Haldeman did not have any new information, which prompted the president to ask, "Who is really watching from the White House? You, Ehrlichman, who?" Haldeman responded, "John Dean is watching it on an almost full-time basis and reporting it to Ehrlichman and me on a continuing basis." "Alright, good," Nixon said, and Haldeman added, "And no one else. There's no one else in the White House who has any knowledge of what's going on there at all." When the president suggested including Colson, Haldeman disagreed. "There isn't anyone else in this, and I think it's much better that way. In the first place, there's no need for anybody to know, and there's nothing they can do about it."

"That's right, we can't." As regarded Colson, the president observed, "It's so bad for his stress. Just a few of us that know to worry about it." With a painful-sounding small chuckle, he added, "Don't let anybody else worry about it." Haldeman said that that was appropriate, again repeating that no one could do anything about the situation. Nixon modified that observation, "Except we can, of course, stretch it to [a] certain extent. The really key question at the moment, and sometime we've got to answer it, it's in regard to Magruder. Not waiting for the ax to fall, and the risk of waiting it out is that he might have to be thrown out." Haldeman said, "Let me ask Mitchell about it. Because that's one thing Mitchell wants to talk about." Nixon continued, "Right. I just don't want that to happen. I think they're going to get Magruder. My own feeling is that his good and our good will both be served by, if he's going to get it, in other words, by his statement, whatever the hell it is." Thinking that Magruder might have to leave the campaign caused the president to ask about Hugh Sloan, who he learned was at odds with Magruder over Sloan's testimony.

Haldeman explained how the prosecutors were handling his situation. "What they've done with Sloan, and which apparently is a very good break, is they've granted him informal immunity. Sloan is clean on his own involvement [regarding Watergate], but he knows things that have nothing to do with the Watergate caper, but there apparently are some substantial irregularities under the Campaign Spending Act which Sloan's aware of."

"Christ, they should have stayed the hell out of that one," the president added with alarm. Haldeman explained, "And some cash movements and things like that. And so they've granted Sloan temporary immunity, and he's going to cover what he knows about the Watergate stuff, which is nothing. And that gets him out of things. Now, what they had planned to do is, he was going to take the Fifth, but this avoids his having to take the Fifth, which is much better, because he has no guilt under the Watergate thing, he has some under the other." Haldeman coughed, and then, catching his thought about taking the Fifth, he added, "That's the one thing I wanted to raise with Dean this morning, is whether there isn't a way to give Magruder immunity, and maybe get him out from under, too. I don't see why they couldn't." With no real understanding of how prosecutors use immunity, Haldeman suggested, "Give Magruder immunity in order to get information on the Watergate caper people, and Liddy maybe, or something like that." The president, who understood prosecutorial immunity only slightly better, was confused. "If he goes in and says, 'I will say this and that and the other.'"

"Well, apparently that's the thing our people have been worried about is, if they give immunity to the wrong people and get too much of the story out, but if Magruder's given immunity, he could then go in and inculpate himself, plus the others, but his immunity protects him from prosecution, and he seals the case on the others."

The president sat silently, and then, barely audibly, replied, "I think the way that we've trusted people to stand up that, the way this [*unclear*] Magruder scenario, I don't care." He then addressed Magruder's testimony and suggested returning to his original scenario: "But if it's at all possible, it should be put in a way that the group of people who were hard-nosed and extreme on the Cuban communists, they came to express their concern about McGovern and wanted to do this sort of thing, and these people said, 'Alright, we'll finance it.' I don't know whether that'll work, or whether it was the other way around." Haldeman noted, "On the public side, that's sure what we want." Nixon agreed, "That's what I mean. It fits in with the public image, the public story." They sat wordlessly for several seconds, and when the president continued, he could not figure out how Magruder might get immunity but told Haldeman to check it out. He then asked, "Who else besides Sloan and Magruder are our people, who's this fellow, Wardman, Bart, what's his name?"

"Bart, Bart Porter." "Bart Porter," the president repeated, sounding exasperated at the involvement of another person. "Did he work for Magruder?" When Haldeman reported that he did, the president fell silent again. Then Nixon said, clear displeasure in his voice and with a tone of protest about the ever-expanding investigation, "The question is, how many people that they've involved in—" Haldeman said, "They're not going any further." Speaking to the president's frustration, he added, "Magruder's the last one they're going to call, apparently."

"Yeah," Nixon added, with something of an angry growl. "Well, it seems it would stop someplace. I mean, Jesus Christ, you can't go through the whole God damn committee. They're not going to call Mitchell, apparently?" Haldeman thought not. "No. At least not as of yesterday, that was the word." As they walked toward the office door after discussing other pending business, Nixon, sounding both concerned and confessional, mentioned that he'd had some sort of troubling premonition: "I had this strangest dream last night. I have a feeling Watergate's going to be a nasty issue for a few days. But I can't believe that, you know, or maybe I'm whistling in the dark, but I can't believe that they can tie it to me." He let that question hang for a moment, and then answered his own question: "Huh? I don't know. What's your feeling?"

"It'll be messy. But I think John [Ehrlichman's] probably right. We're going to take any heat, some tie to us, we can't avoid getting the [reelection] committee tied in somehow, so it's going to be untidy. I hope you can get over that." "Yeah," the president said, hoping so, too.

That afternoon, between 3:16 P.M. and 5:30 P.M., Haldeman and the president met again in his EOB office.[8] After discussing in astounding detail the food to be served on a cruise on the presidential yacht, *Sequoia*, that evening, Haldeman had some good news to share: "It appears that there's a very good chance that Magruder will not be indicted. On the grounds that there's a fine-line question as to whether he made a knowledgeable decision and therefore was a part of this thing or not." "Well, conspiracy is a hard case to prove," Nixon observed (incorrectly). Haldeman continued, "Well, the point is, his line will be that he did not know about this specific action, which apparently, is true."

That was true only in the sense that Magruder had no knowledge of the time of the operation, the team members, the place of entry and other specific details, although he was very aware that they had broken into the DNC earlier and bugged the place, and that one of the bugs was not working. Haldeman continued, "And that he had this guy, Liddy, and sure he authorized certain sums of money to be paid to Liddy for various Republicans and for campaigning activities, but he was not personally aware of this. Then he can say that it was stupidity on my part, bad management, but no criminal guilt. And I was the sweet young guy in a campaign, and I didn't realize all the things you ought to check out."

"Yeah," Nixon said uncertainly, unsure of what to make of this explanation. Haldeman continued, "And John [Ehrlichman] seems to feel that it's at least fifty-fifty, but he still feels that it can go that way, and maybe even better, we'll know a lot more, he's being interrogated today by the FBI. That's the end of their interrogation. It was the FBI, not the grand jury, that Bart Porter was interrogated [by] yesterday. He has not been before the jury. Pat Gray told John Dean today, he just wanted to chat, that the Bureau is going to require at least another month to complete their investigation." Haldeman added that Gray felt that the grand jury would need three to four months to do their work after the Bureau completed its own. "And Mitchell and Dean are reading [the conversation with Gray] as a message from the Bureau and Justice that this thing was not going to be brought before the election. Mitchell argues very strongly that with Magruder there'd be a real good chance of not getting any high-level campaign command involved in the case, and therefore we shouldn't let Magruder go now, because [his] going out now would really put the focus on it." Haldeman added that Mitchell felt they would have ample warning if they needed to act on Magruder.

Haldeman felt prompted to provide additional information as the president began speculating about what Gray and Petersen might do. "Well, another thing I didn't know that Mitchell told me is that John Dean [thinks] that Petersen [is on our team totally]. John Dean ran into Petersen and laid out the whole scenario of what actually happened, who was involved and where it all fit. Now, on the basis of that, Petersen was working with that knowledge and directing the investigation along those channels that will not produce the kinds of answers we don't want produced. Petersen also feels that the fact that there were some lines in this case that ran into the White House is very beneficial to you, because that has slowed them down in pursuing things, because they all are of the view that they don't want to indict the White House. They only want to indict the criminal [acts], they want to tighten up that case on the criminal acts and, and limit it back to the degree that they can. Now that's the reason, for instance, that they were partially—" At this point the conversation is interrupted by a recording malfunction, making it impossible to understand over a minute of the discussion about the grand jury, Magruder and the reelection committee. It then becomes audible as follows:

"Is anybody listening to the lawyers over there?" the president asked, about the reelection committee. Haldeman said they were, and that the two lawyers, Paul O'Brien and Ken Parkinson, were "just superb." He then explained to the president the conflict that had developed between Mitchell and Ehrlichman: "It's fallen into a pattern we've got," which he described as "the Ehrlichman and Mitchell controversy," where Mitchell is of the "totally-stonewall-it-the-hell-with-everybody" approach versus "Ehrlichman's complete-panic-cut-everything-off-and-sink-it-immediately," which was soon called the "hang-it-all-out route"—or some variation of it. Haldeman added, "They're both wrong." "Yeah," the president agreed. "Fortunately, we haven't followed either of their leads," Haldeman concluded.

## July 22, 1972, Camp David

During a conversation at Camp David, Haldeman gave the president an update on Magruder: "There were no problems. We don't have the interrogation report, but the lawyer who sat in said he did extremely well."[9] "And is he going before the grand jury now?" the president asked. Haldeman reported, "Not as of yet."

"Well, what the hell is the grand jury going to do, then? Are they going to keep, keep, keep, keep investigating? Is that the whole point of this thing?" Nixon pressed. Haldeman said, "It seems they will." On reflection, the president felt that this was not all bad: "As far as I'm concerned, that's the best of both worlds. Let it go." Haldeman suggested, "Let it go until after the election." But then Nixon simply dismissed them all, "Oh, they can, those pricks." Haldeman continued, "Again, Ehrlichman urges to get them indicted now, get them out, but I'm not really sure that's the best, if you accept as inevitable that you're going to get indictments, and then you have to get them before the election. But better yet is to have nothing happen." And Haldeman reported that there was still a reasonable chance that nothing would happen: "They're just going to let it go."

The president wanted to know who was talking with whom. "Dean is instructed to, talking to whom? Talking to you?" Haldeman answered, "He's talking to us." Nixon again wanted to be clear, "You and Ehrlichman?" Haldeman affirmed that that was the arrangement, and added the other people with whom I was talking: "On our side, Mitchell and two lawyers and Petersen at Justice and Gray at the Bureau."

"You know, at the Bureau, we ought to put a Bureau man in there somewhere. We've got to. I don't know [whom]," Nixon said. But Haldeman had a suggestion: "Well, this guy Feldman is pushing hard. Is that his name?" "Felt," the president corrected. Haldeman said Felt was "pushing to try and be our boy," noting, "he's obviously looking to be more, I guess." "He is our boy," the president observed and added, "yeah, you know, I want one that's *our* boy. I'm not going to screw around on that score." Referring to his selection of a new FBI director, the president said, "But, you see, if you take him out of the Bureau, it's very hard for anybody to piss on him," meaning that if his new director was drawn from the FBI, he would be safe.

"We ought to throw some tests at Felt," Haldeman suggested. "We could put some real sticky wickets to him and see how he bounces." Then the conversation turned to a sticky wicket for the Secret Service. The president wanted to know if they had a line into McGovern's Secret Service protection detail. Haldeman said that they did not. "We should, we can obviously try," Nixon pressed. "Well, sure, ought to try, but I don't know how to do it," Haldeman admitted. Nixon surmised that his opponents had tried to get the

Secret Service to provide information about him, but Haldeman was not so sure and thought it very risky should they get caught. Nixon backed off and said that he did not want Haldeman to try, but instead he hoped that someone in the Secret Service might "sometimes volunteer information." Haldeman thought some might like to do that, and the conversation drifted into vague talk and prospects about the potential of causing political problems for McGovern and DNC chairman Larry O'Brien.

## July 28, 1972, the White House

With the president's busy schedule and a slowdown in the investigation and reporting on it, I found no recorded conversations focusing on Watergate from July 23 through July 27. On the twenty-eighth, Haldeman mentioned relatively good news during that morning's meeting, assuring the president that the investigation was progressing nicely, with nothing amiss.[10] "It's on a reasonably good track, considering," Haldeman said. "The grand jury is going through the 1701* people, but Petersen's view to Dean is that, I think we're going to be able to finish this grand jury thing up pretty quick, and they'll bring indictments on the seven. And we can probably bring them the later part of August or wait around until mid-September. And Dean said he got the distinctive feeling that Petersen was asking for guidance as to which we wanted. But he was also telling me they were going to bring indictments on seven, and that's very good news, because that means they're indicting the Watergate five, plus Hunt and Liddy and, and then that's all. John [Ehrlichman] says, if they—"

"Are they going to put out a statement about the others?" the president asked.

"Apparently not. They'll just have to indict those, and our view, I think, is to wait, because there's a very good chance of it not going to trial until after the election." The president, who was pleasantly surprised, added an "Oh, yeah?" before Haldeman continued, "It will be called on a special calendar, and the special calendar is fairly clear, so it could come up pretty soon. But even if it gets to court, there's a set of pretrial motions they've got to go through, and all of that stuff. So, John [Ehrlichman] feels that we ought to go for a delay and hope nothing happens before the election, because we're better off with that than we are with anything. My original feeling was, get

*This is a reference to the reelection committee, whose office was at 1701 Pennsylvania Avenue.

it out now, get it done in August, and get it over with. But that might hit it right in the middle of the Republican convention—"

"No, no, no, no," the president interrupted, and Haldeman continued, "—where there's a lot of TV attention, which would be a problem, too." The president wanted to be sure he understood who was going to be indicted, so he asked, "If they indict seven, can we trust the ones they're thinking about are Hunt and the other fellow," he said, forgetting Liddy's name. Haldeman assured him, "That's almost an ideal scenario. If they would indict seven and then not get around to the trial until after the election, we're in pretty good shape. Now, on the [Democrats'] civil suit, the judge took some time off. He's out of chambers. So he's coming back, and what they're going to do there is, we have a motion, which they think the judge will probably uphold, to withhold any further steps on the civil suit pending the outcome of the criminal suit, that any action on the civil suit would damage or interfere with the rights of the defendants in the criminal suit, or something like that. They've got some legal matter, fiddling around with those, which they think they'll get, and if we do that, then we're home free."

The president had an observation on the timing of the indictment: "The trial will never be finished before the election. Well, if the people plead not guilty. If they plead guilty, it would be [before the election]." Haldeman reported, "We know some of them are going to go not guilty. Hunt is going to go not guilty."

"Hell yes. Fight it to the end," the president said. "And you know, the problem that you could have on this is that some lower-echelon shit-ass at the Justice Department or the FBI will try to leak out stuff about this and that and force, in some way or other, force it to another direction. You know that can happen. Fortunately, we have not tried to cover up Mitchell. We've allowed them to cooperate with the investigation."

"The record has to show us in pretty good shape," Haldeman said.

Clearly, based on his conversations with Haldeman, the president understood that Magruder's perjured testimony had saved John Mitchell, not to mention prevented the further unraveling of the Watergate cover-up. But he was thinking politically, not legally. He understood that Magruder had largely cooked this story up by himself. There is no evidence suggesting that it ever occurred to him that his knowledge and approval of Magruder's actions effectively placed him at the top of a conspiracy to suborn perjury. But even Haldeman's encouraging news did not mean he could relax, for

Magruder had yet to appear before the grand jury. Rather, for Nixon, it was time to start thinking seriously about getting even and dealing more effectively with his enemies now that his reelection was almost a certainty.

### August 1, 1972, the White House

During 10:33 A.M. to 11:50 A.M. Oval Office conversations with Haldeman, following a brief discussion about obtaining information from Larry O'Brien's taxes, the two men turned to the subject of news leaks about the Watergate investigation.[11] Nixon said he had noticed the wire service story about the money.* "How will that affect us?" the president asked. Haldeman said, "I don't know. Nobody knows. We'll find out today." They speculated that the information had come from the Justice Department. Haldeman said they had plugged one leak at Justice, "But apparently there's another. They said that this is inevitable."

"Well, that's not true," Nixon protested.

"We've got people in there that are against us," Haldeman said, referring to anti-Nixon attorneys, but he pointed out that they had pro-Nixon appointees as well. "They're trying to keep it all bottled up, and they've done it," he reminded the president. "Considering the explosive nature of what's there, they've done a pretty good job." After making that point, Haldeman turned to the latest information about the investigation, which he had obtained from John Ehrlichman after he'd met with Attorney General Kleindienst the day before.[†]

Haldeman explained, "Now, the scenario on that, they all seem pretty well agreed on, is that the only danger is Magruder, who does have to go before the grand jury. But Dean has gone over and over it with him, and Jeb is going to stay with his story, and stay with it solid. They think there's no problem if he does, and that he will not be indicted. They will come down

---

*The wires were carrying the story from Carl Bernstein and Bob Woodward, "Bug Suspect Got Campaign Funds" (*The Washington Post*, August 1, 1972, A-1), about the twenty-five-thousand-dollar check from Kenneth Dahlberg (an official with CRP) found in the bank account of Bernard Barker.

†On Monday, July 31, 1972, Ehrlichman requested I join him for lunch with Kleindienst. We met in the attorney general's office suite and private dining room at the Justice Department from 11:30 A.M. until approximately 1:30 P.M. Ehrlichman had called for the meeting. It was at this time that Kleindienst brought Ehrlichman up to date on the likely outcome of the Watergate investigation. But Haldeman's report to the president shows far more knowledge than Ehrlichman received from Kleindienst at that meeting; rather, it appears they had also spoken with Mitchell, who had information about Hunt's plans. Also, tellingly, Ehrlichman's calendar for the evening of July 31, 1972, shows that he attended a "Youth Reception" in the White House mess to which Jeb Magruder had been invited. Keeping Jeb happy was on everyone's mind.

with seven indictments, the five plus Hunt and Liddy. That'll be about September fifteenth that they'll bring the indictments." Haldeman explained why, with pretrial motions, the case would not be tried before the election. He noted, "We'll have to ride out the very bad story. We'll have to ride through the indictment story. But Liddy's already tarnished, and Hunt's already tarnished, so it's no great new revelation. It'll just be a confirmation of previous stuff, and it'll be bad. It'll hurt us, but not like the trial would. And Dean is not worried about that, and he also thinks that we're in good shape on holding the civil case until after the criminal."

"On the grounds it would be prejudicial," the president added. Haldeman then turned to Judge Richey's handling of the civil lawsuit. "Judge Richey is playing everything exactly right," he reported. "The only concern I've got there is that Judge Richey is the dumbest judge in the entire business, apparently. Fortunately, he's on our side, and his dumbness may help us, because he's not encumbered by any"—Haldeman chuckled—"any intellectual need to do certain things. And Judge Robb, who is a little more perceptive—"

"Roger Robb," the president injected, with a tone of surprise.*

Haldeman continued "—has taken it upon himself to, ah—"

"Advising Richey," Nixon injected anticipating Haldeman's report.

"—sort of take a fatherly interest in guiding Richey's hand. And Robb clearly sees all the implications."

"Roger would," Nixon confirmed, pleased with this information.

"So they think we're in as good of shape as we could hope to be. Here it is, we're sitting on a powder keg, and then the kind of thing, like the thing that came out this morning"—referring to the Woodward and Bernstein story—"there's all sorts of possibilities of someone—Oh, they subpoenaed Stans before the grand jury, but we got that quashed, fortunately." Haldeman overstated the case, for what actually happened was that arrangements had been made for Stans to give his grand jury testimony at the Department of Justice, given the leaks coming out of the courthouse. Stans had been outraged at being hauled before the grand jury, and while he was not involved in Watergate, Haldeman explained why Mitchell had Ehrlichman intervene:

---

*Judge Roger Robb was a good friend of Attorney General Kleindienst who, before going on the bench, had successfully handled a defamation lawsuit by Senator Barry Goldwater against *fact* magazine owner and editor Ralph Ginzburg following his 1964 bid for the presidency. On April 23, 1969, President Nixon nominated Robb to the U.S. Court of Appeals for the District of Columbia, and he was quickly confirmed by the U.S. Senate. Robb provided Kleindienst a direct private link into the closed chambers of the DC federal courts.

"And they're worried about Stans. And they don't think he's stable enough to handle the questioning very well. He gets indignant, and they just think he's not such a good witness. They don't want him under questioning. Magruder, they're pretty straight on. Magruder's scared. He asked Dean, 'Might they indict me just to get an indictment for political reasons, or whatever?' Dean said, 'No, the court won't do that, and the jury won't do that.' And Jeb said, 'Well, I just want you to know, if, if they do, that I'm staying with my story all the way. I'll go down with 'em, and there's no question about that.' And Dean said, 'The one thing I'm worried about with you, I know you'll do that. The thing I'm worried about with you is that, after you do that, if you don't get indicted, that you'll start running around blabbing about how, you know, you pulled yourself out of that. And let me explain to you that there's a five-year statute of limitations on this case. And that you're subject to being hauled in at any time in the next five years, and you keep your God damn mouth shut. Don't talk to your wife, or your mother, your kids, or anybody else.'" Nixon approved. "Damn right," he said softly. Haldeman continued with his version of my conversation with Magruder: "'If you get out of this one, just remember, you've got this cloud hanging over you for five years. And you're not out 'til that's over, so don't have a celebration when the indictments come through and you're not on 'em.'"

"He feels they will not indict him?" Nixon asked.

"That's right. They have not made a case against Magruder. A lot of lines lead to him, but they don't tie—" The president interrupted to ask about the Sloan and Magruder conflict, and Haldeman reported that Magruder's concocted account would impeach Sloan on a few details, but Sloan had done fine. "But inevitably some of what he had to say leads to Magruder. But Magruder's just going to say, and honestly believes, that Sloan pocketed some of the money. There's some discrepancy in how much money went where, and Magruder's going to say he thinks Sloan pocketed it."

"You don't think he did?"

"No. But Magruder does, fortunately. And we're just going to leave it at that. Let him go ahead and think it, because there's no possible way he could harm Sloan. Sloan will never know what Magruder says. And he can't, because Sloan's not culpable at all under this case. Now, they laid some groundwork in a grand jury record for another case, but apparently they can't use it. And they gave Sloan immunity on the other case, on anything beyond this case."

The president found this interesting, and Haldeman continued, "It's too early to say, but it would appear that, given a very difficult situation, and no cooperation from Justice, either the FBI or Kleindienst, that our guys and these two lawyers the committee's hired have done a superb job of keeping this thing—" But the president did not want to be overly optimistic, and he cut off Haldeman to remind him that the worst might still happen. "Let's just be, let's be fatalistic about the God damn thing."

"If it blows, it blows," Haldeman said. "If it blows, it blows, and so on," Nixon repeated. "And we'll ride it out," Haldeman noted. "I'm not that worried about it, to be completely candid with you," the president remarked. This surprised Haldeman somewhat, given the effort being made to prevent the worst, and he was prompted to add, "Well, it's worth a lot of work to try and keep it from blowing."

The president explained his thinking: "After all, if Mitchell's gone, and we find out that nobody at a higher level was involved, the White House not being involved, and all that stuff, and the Cuban crap in there—are the Cubans going to plead not guilty, too?" Haldeman explained that everybody was being taken care of, so they need not worry about those involved in Watergate. He began vaguely, answering Nixon's question about whether the Cubans would plead: "I don't know, but everybody's satisfied. They're all out of jail, and they've all been taken care of. And they're all—" Haldeman rephrased, "They've done a lot of discreet checking to be sure there's no discontent in the ranks, and there isn't any."

"They're all out on bail," the president noted. "Hunt's happy," Haldeman added. "At considerable cost, I guess?" the president inquired. "Yes," Haldeman said flatly. "It's worth it," the president said, giving his blessing to the expenditures. "It's very expensive. It's a costly exercise—" Haldeman said, to make the point that they were spending hundreds of thousands of dollars. "That's what the money's for," the president injected. Haldeman continued, "—but that's better spent than, than, ah—"

"Well, they have taken all the risk and they have to be paid. That's all there is to that," Nixon declared, making it clear that he approved of the payments to those involved. "They have to pay, although, I must say that I'm second-guessing whoever made the decision," the president added, regarding breaking into the DNC. "That's pretty damn stupid," Haldeman agreed. "About as stupid a thing as I've ever heard of. I mean, that is as bad as you can get it," the president said. "But whoever it is has suffered for his sins, plenty," Haldeman observed.

"I know. Oh no, don't do that. Never blame. But the poor son of a bitch, what the hell, you've got such a stupid God damn idea. He must have got it from Hunt. It sounds like him, doesn't it? Hunt, Liddy, I mean. I can't think of anybody in our, in that organization. Magruder wouldn't think up such a damn thing. I mean, he isn't—" Nixon said. Haldeman added, "I can't conceive that he did. I think it's Liddy. Liddy, apparently, is a guy that just, you know—"

"Hates 'em," Nixon speculated. "Well, he lives on this kind of stuff. I mean, he loves the—" Haldeman was starting to explain Liddy's zealotry when the president asked, "Now, he resigned?" seeking to reaffirm his recollection. "A long time, no, he was fired," Haldeman explained, and they reviewed the fact that Liddy had been dismissed when he had not cooperated with the FBI, a fact that had been published in the media. Nixon asked if Hunt's noncooperation was publicly known, but Haldeman was not certain.

"Well, he's not here," Nixon noted, and then fell silent. Given his next comments it is clear that he was thinking about the information Haldeman had provided: Those involved in the Watergate break-in were now being paid, and he was concerned.* "You know, they might just be so silly to be paying a bribe on Hunt, if they are putting him on, to make this case, the case about Watergate and so forth. Well, let me say, he's not worth that. I think, it's not that much, I hope, I mean, I know of, I never discount the kind of crap the press will put to us on a thing like this. But, Bob, it does not, we've, we've stayed completely away from it. I've stayed completely away from it, and we will, ah, MacGregor, of course, will take, as he should, a holier than thou attitude, 'I don't know anything about it.' Right?"

"Yeah, and we've kept Colson clear of it," Haldeman said, and added, "And we've held up this civil thing. It's on a discovery deal, but [a] motion will be made on the civil suit just to suspend all activity on that, pending the outcome of the criminal." The president was still thinking about pardons for those involved, and he asked Haldeman if they had gathered charges against his opponents, as they had done with a veteran's group down in Florida that had been charged for antiwar activities. Haldeman said that they were looking for more,

---

*I spent several hours listening to the poor-quality audio of the next few sentences because of their obvious importance. My transcription is based upon hearing it played with several software programs on several computers using several speaker systems, as well as on listening to the material played at several speeds, and then using the most audible to reconstruct what was said. Given the tone in Nixon's voice, he is clearly warning his chief of staff that they could be making a serious mistake in bribing Hunt, a warning that would be totally ignored.

and maybe they would catch some "bad guys" at the forthcoming Republican convention, whom they could hang on to for a while, and then let them go.

After a brief silence, the president asked: "You say no cooperation from the Justice Department? I understand the FBI."

"Well, it's been very hard. It's, it's hard. Petersen has been reasonably good, in fact, pretty, I guess, darn good," Haldeman reported. "The problem has been Kleindienst just totally washed his hands. And now he's come back in. Ehrlichman hauled him in yesterday and said, 'You know, this has gotten ridiculous. Now that you've got everything you need. Now, for God's sake, turn it off. Bring your indictments.' And Kleindienst seemed to see the light. At least he'll be on it." The president wanted to know the timing, if indictments could be handed down sooner by the grand jury, and if there was a way to speed up the process. Haldeman said that it was possible, but he did not think it was desirable to have them until after the Republican convention in August, because of the press coverage. "Well, I'm just nervous about it. Maybe there could be some problems," the president said. "Not Jeb, I'm not nervous about Magruder." Then he explained what was on his mind. "Do you think Sloan pocketed the money?"

Haldeman did not, and the president moved on to address the intelligence-gathering operation at the reelection committee, softly scolding that it "was a very bad place to have it, Bob." Haldeman explained, "Well, sure. Except this was something John was after, apparently."

"Mitchell?" Nixon asked. Haldeman gave an affirmative "hum, hmm," then explained that Mitchell's interest had been "on the finance thing." But Nixon did not understand and asked, "He had the idea of getting their contributors?" Haldeman reported, "Well, he had some log on who it was, or where it was coming from, or something. He thought he had something. There probably is something on there, money sources or business or something." Again Haldeman vaguely explained his understanding of the reason they had entered the DNC's offices.*

"Yeah," the president curtly commented, and again fell into silent thought before continuing. "You got to give Dean a lot of credit, the lawyers know everything." This observation led to a digression about a Justice Department investigation of an associate of former secretary of the treasury John Connally, in which the president felt Kleindienst had been less than helpful, as

*See Appendix A.

mentioned earlier by Haldeman. "I don't think, Bob, that you can blame anything on Gray, in the sense that he is in a very difficult position." "He doesn't have any control. He doesn't know how to do these things," Haldeman said. "Very difficult position. He cannot, he just can't do it," the president acknowledged. "I don't believe that we ought to have Gray in the job after this is over. I don't think it's the right thing. I think it's too close to us. I think if you could get Felt, he's a good man, and they're watching him, I guess. Like this [George] Bush fellow I have, he'll grow in the job.* You know, it just isn't right to have the Bureau select him," he said, referring to Felt.

"You put him in, he'd be your guy," Haldeman said. Following another brief discussion of Larry O'Brien's tax returns, where Nixon hoped to find nefarious profiting (which did not exist), Haldeman said, "This Watergate thing was stupid, but again, nobody made anything out of it. It's stupidity, but not personal venality or anything. Nobody's done anything for his own gain." This comment caused the president to raise again Magruder's charge about Hugh Sloan's taking money. Haldeman did not know Sloan's current status with the reelection committee, but he was able to report that Sloan's wife was still working at the White House. Haldeman assured the president that Sloan was not going to be indicted, although he did "know things."

### August 2, 1972, the White House

During a morning meeting, which ran some two hours, the president returned to his concerns about Magruder's testimony.[12] Nixon understood that if Magruder went down, Mitchell would follow, and maybe even Haldeman and Ehrlichman as well, not to mention his reelection bid. So once he understood the significance of Magruder's role, given his attention to detail, he could not leave this detail unattended. It is a behavior pattern that plays out time and again, as Nixon moves from issues to issue. Thus, his question that morning: "Is the game plan still the same over there this morning? When will Magruder testify?" "I don't know, soon," Haldeman reported. "I'd like to get him in and out," the president instructed, hopefully.

Haldeman had some encouraging news on another front: "Kleindienst

---

*Nixon, who had enjoyed a friendship with Prescott Bush, was trying to assist the career of Prescott's son George H. W. Bush. When George Bush ran for Congress in Texas and lost, Nixon appointed him U.S. ambassador to the United Nations, on March 1, 1971, where he remained until January 18, 1973, when Nixon asked him to become chairman of the Republican National Committee; he remained there until September 16, 1974, announcing his departure shortly before Nixon's resignation as president.

has now ordered Gray to end the investigation. He said that they've got all they need to wrap up their case."

"The problem is, do you think that's correct?" Nixon asked. "Yes," Haldeman answered with no hesitation. "I mean, if it really is," Nixon began, then started again, "if it isn't over, you can't," and then finally he hit on his point, "because otherwise it's now just a fishing expedition. They've got enough without it. The Magruder thing is the only thing that concerns me," the president said. "But, you know, I would think his case would be pretty good, Bob. I think he could just say, 'Look, I was in charge of the damn thing. I approved money, and Liddy wanted this money, and I gave it to him, but I haven't the slightest idea what the hell he was doing with it.' Correct? Or was that a stand?"

"I think that's his stand," Haldeman answered, reminding the president that Magruder had, in fact, been totally involved. Nixon continued, "But on the other hand, if somebody else testified that he received the copies of information and so forth—" The president was worrying whether there was a fundamental flaw in Magruder's concocted testimony. Haldeman attempted to assuage Nixon's concern, but ineffectively: "I don't think so. Someone that's testified, well, I don't know." Nixon raised it again, and Haldeman awkwardly assured the president that Magruder was not a target of the grand jury, explaining, "They're using Magruder as a witness to convict the other people, not as a witness to involve him—"

"Let me know when there's something that's a little bit more fundamental," Nixon said before turning to a related topic. "As you know, I have been the most intolerant with Stans as anybody, with this penny pinching. But budget control in a campaign, Bob, is terribly important. And it's because we didn't have budget control, the campaign stuck out too fat and too damn big. And it's because we didn't have much control, this kind of thing happened, in my opinion," he said, referring to Watergate. "I mean, if you can piss away two hundred thousand dollars, you know, on some cops-and-robbers thing, Jesus Christ, that's a hell of a lot of money.* Who the hell is in charge of budget control over there? I wouldn't leave this in the hands of Magruder, for example. I don't think he's that buttoned-down." Haldeman assured the president that MacGregor had been spending a lot of time on budget matters and now had it under his control.

"You know, we get so many assholes—" The president stopped, then

---

*A multiple of 5.5 can be used to get a rough estimate of 1972–73 dollars versus today's value.

corrected himself. "Christ, we've got less than others. But campaigns attract them, attracting them like flies, Bob. You know, they piss away the money." The president recalled how, despite all his other faults, Murray Chotiner, his first campaign manager when he ran for the House and Senate, was excellent on the budget. "He didn't waste one hell of a lot of money." Nixon added, "Chotiner saw to the stuff," meaning he played rough-and-tumble, "but he didn't go into personnel about it. He really didn't. God damn it, it went into things. It went into advertising. He worked the piss out of everybody, but I just have a feeling that maybe budget control was a weakness in this [current] operation. I may be wrong."

### August 3, 1972, the White House

During a morning meeting in the Oval Office with both Haldeman and Ehrlichman, the president sought an update on Ehrlichman's efforts at obtaining Larry O'Brien's tax returns.[13] Nixon was in a bad mood, still annoyed over a nasty *Washington Post* headline from the day before that, in his mind, harkened back to his infamous slush fund when he was vice president.*

Nixon continued, "But anyway, here we go. What in the name of God are we doing on this score? What are we doing about their financial contributors? Now they, those lists are made, they're there. Are we looking over McGovern's financial contributors? Are we looking over the financial contributors of the Democratic National Committee? Are we running their income tax returns? Is the Justice Department checking to see whether or not there are any antitrust suits? Do we have anything going on any of these things?"

"Not as far as I know," Ehrlichman answered, which only upped Nixon's rant a few notches: "We'd better forget the God damn campaign right this minute, not tomorrow, but now. That's what concerns me. We have all this power and we aren't using it. Now, what the Christ is the matter? In other words, what I'm really saying is this: I think we've got to get it out. Now, I'm just thinking about, for example, if there's information on Larry O'Brien. If there is, I wouldn't wait. I'd worry the sons of bitches now, because after they select somebody else, it's irrelevant, even though he's still in the campaign. It's much more relevant now, but then they drop him, because, see what I mean?"

After Nixon repeated these questions, Ehrlichman admitted, "Ah, the short

---

*Bob Woodward and Carl Bernstein, "Audit Set on Nixon Fund: Possible Link to Bugging Incident Cited," *The Washington Post*, August 2, 1972, A-1.

answer to your question is, nothing." "Boy, they're doing it to us," Nixon reminded them, and noted, "And it's never happened that way before. Johnson screwed everybody, Kennedy." He paused, then went back in time: "When we were out in '52 the Truman people were kicking the hell out of me. In '62 they kicked the hell out of me. In 1960 the bureaucracy mixed up my visit with Khrushchev, the Eisenhower bureaucracy," he said with added disdain, and continued, "That's part of the problem, the bureaucracy, and part of the problem's our own God damned fault. There must be something that we can do."

After further complaining from Nixon on this score, the extended discussion came to an end. Haldeman said he felt everybody had become especially gutless "with very good justification, because of this jackass operation at the Watergate. They are more sensitive than they would have been before, and they would have been very sensitive before." He then added, "But we do have a knack for doing this stuff ineptly."

"That's for sure," the president agreed. Both Haldeman and Ehrlichman assured the president that after the election they would move with a "vengeance" against the president's enemies, with Ehrlichman suggesting people like U.S. Supreme Court Justice William O. Douglas. "Do we have stuff on him?" the president wondered. "Well, we're trying to get stuff. He hangs around with snakes," Ehrlichman responded. And Haldeman added, "They've just got a hell of a lot more snakes than we do. And their snakes are a hell of a lot tougher than ours."

"They're vicious, brutal," the president complained.

Having mentioned the Supreme Court, Ehrlichman added that he had scheduled a private visit with Nixon's chief justice, Warren Burger. "I'm going to talk to Burger this week, and I would be inclined to indicate to him that it is to your advantage not to have the Ellsberg case tried until after the election. Unless you have any serious objection, I'm going to give him that signal."* Nixon approved, and Ehrlichman explained, "Ah, he [Chief Justice

---

*Daniel Ellsberg and Anthony Russo had been indicted by Nixon's Department of Justice for theft of government property and espionage in connection with the leak of the Pentagon Papers. Ellsberg and Russo were on trial in Los Angeles federal court and wanted the government to produce any information obtained using a wiretap relating to their case, but the government was opposing the motion, falsely denying that such wiretaps existed. Ellsberg and Russo had appealed to Supreme Court justice William Douglas, the one with jurisdiction over the Ninth Circuit, where their case was being tried; on July 29, 1972, Douglas had stayed the opening of the trial. Initially the government had opposed the delay. But then it seems that Ehrlichman wanted the trial delayed until after the election, because he believed the government might lose the case, in no small part due to the fact that recordings of wiretaps relating to Ellsberg that should have been turned over by the government to Ellsberg and Russo were in his White House safe. So Ehrlichman was taking the extraordinary action of an *ex parte* meeting with the chief justice.

Burger] has it literally within his control." The president added, "And just say, I'd put it, in my opinion, I'd say that it really would raise hell with President Johnson and a lot of other things that would be very embarrassing to our foreign policy, and it's just not a good thing right now, with the delicate negotiations on Vietnam. Put it in the basis that we had some other reason."

"Alright," Ehrlichman said. Then he added: "They've got a chance to really rub Mr. Justice Douglas's nose in it by reversing him and making the case go to trial. So they'll have to pass that lovely opportunity."

"Temptation to screw Douglas?" the president asked. Ehrlichman said it could be, but Haldeman quickly added, "That's a pyrrhic victory. Who the hell cares whether you screw Douglas, nobody, it won't bother Douglas." Ehrlichman told the president that Douglas's stay to delay the trial was "the most dishonest opinion I have ever read," although it actually created a favorable situation for them. Nonetheless, Ehrlichman added, "it may result in Ellsberg going free, and you've got double jeopardy, because they've already sworn in the jury. But I think that's a small price to pay and kind of a nice out." Haldeman reported that the Justice Department thought they would lose the case, but the president felt otherwise. There was more tough talk about Nixon's enemies, even putting one—Carl Shipley, an anti-Nixon Republican who was active in District of Columbia politics—in jail.

Later that afternoon Ehrlichman met with the president in his EOB office, and the conversation again turned to bending the IRS to the president's will, and how they could place their people in the IRS after the election. As a parenthetical, Nixon explained that he would never have become president if he had not investigated Alger Hiss. Ehrlichman wanted to know if they should start thinking about cabinet officers for the second term, but the president wanted his staff to stay focused on the election.[14] He felt Haldeman and others had become too "jumpy about the Watergate thing." He acknowledged going after others was "hard," but even so concluded, "I just think that they got to [do it], because basically they're the ones fucking us."

When Ehrlichman raised the problem of Howard Hughes, whose loan years earlier to Nixon's brother Don of over two hundred thousand dollars had become an issue in the 1960 presidential election, Nixon erupted: "If anybody brings up that God damn Hughes loan again, I'll break this [IRS stuff] over O'Brien's head," referring to O'Brien's quarter-million-dollar retainer with Hughes. Ehrlichman advised Nixon that he was meeting with Secretary of the Treasury George Shultz the next morning to request that the IRS dig out more information about the O'Brien-Hughes relationship. Ehrlichman assured the president his efforts would give O'Brien a few sleepless nights, which the president approved.

"George has got a fantasy," Nixon said of his treasury secretary. "What is George trying to do, say that you can't play politics with the IRS?"

"I don't know. I don't know. I don't know," Ehrlichman said, and then explained, "The way it came out, it didn't come up in this setting at all," referring to his request for information on O'Brien. "It came up [when] he called me, because this young fellow Roger Barth is over there."* Ehrlichman said they had been trying to put Barth in one of the few political positions within the IRS. "And we've been wanting him to be deputy general counsel of IRS, because he'd be in a position to do a lot more. George calls up and says, Jesus, I am really having trouble with this. My bureaucracy is really wild about this. This guy, who's known to be a loyalist, and a hard-ass, and so on, so I've had a lot of flak. And I said, George, that's the only guy we've got in the whole IRS."

An angry Nixon, wondering how many of those bureaucrats held secure jobs in the civil service versus political appointees, asked, "Aren't there several?" Ehrlichman estimated, "Oh, sure, at the top, six or eight guys." "Out with them!" Nixon demanded. "Every one of those bastards is out now! I think the whole bunch goes out just because of this. Don't you agree?" At moments like this Ehrlichman would typically lift his chin and, with a smirk, agree, "Sure, it would be a great move. It would be a marvelous move." The president, on reflection, decided that this was an action to be taken after the election. He would not only fire them but investigate them after they were gone. Ehrlichman would keep Roger Barth in place to get the names of who should be removed. With that subject resolved, they turned to domestic policy issues.

*August 4, 1972, the White House*

The president remained obsessively concerned about Magruder's grand jury testimony, as he made clear during a conversation with Haldeman in the Oval Office.[15] They also addressed the ongoing story in *The Washington Post*

---

*Roger Barth would later become G. Gordon Liddy's personal tax attorney and helped him win a partial reduction of the taxes Liddy was charged with failing to pay on money he received from the Committee to Re-elect the President. See *Liddy v. Commissioner of Internal Revenue* (1986) at http://openjurist.org/808/f2d/312/liddy-v-commissioner-of-internal-revenue.

about the twenty-five-thousand-dollar campaign contribution check from Kenneth Dahlberg that had ended up in a Watergate burglar's bank account; it had come up again in a General Accounting Office (GAO) audit of the contribution.

After this discussion the president asked if the plan was still for the Watergate indictments to be handed down "about the middle of September." Haldeman said that that was the case, so there would be no trial before the election. Meanwhile, the effort would be to try to control "these brush fires," like "this stupid GAO thing." But the GAO audit did not worry the president, and he was pleased that the Watergate break-in investigation did not appear to be attracting public attention. "I'm just not confident that it's that interesting," so he felt that it was not worth "brooding about it, it's called a caper, it's called all that crap. It doesn't appear to be a serious attempt or a sinister this, that and the other thing," the president observed.

Nor was Haldeman concerned. "I think if it comes to its worst, if the whole thing gets out, I don't think it's all that bad." For Nixon, however, a line had to be drawn. "Well, I just don't want Magruder to be involved," the president said. Haldeman emphasized, "I hope we can keep Magruder out, and we sure as hell got to keep Mitchell out. We can survive Magruder's involvement. We would have a real problem with Mitchell's involvement." Nixon agreed, for that was the only reason he was interested in Magruder. And on that front, Haldeman was encouraging: "And I think we're, apparently, we're home free on that."

"But Magruder hasn't testified yet. You don't know when?" the president asked. Haldeman did not know, but Nixon instructed, "Get him out of the way." Haldeman was not worried about Magruder. "But he'll do alright on testimony. I was just thinking, if you have another campaign group, it might not be a bad idea to let Magruder sit in." Such visits with the president were known as stroking sessions, and in this instance, Haldeman had a good reason for making the suggestion. His personal aide, Larry Higby, had spoken with Magruder earlier that morning and found himself apologizing for his not being invited along with his former White House peers for an evening outing on the presidential yacht, *Sequoia*. Both Haldeman and the president agreed it would be wise to give Magruder a little special attention. Haldeman suggested making it safe by including him in a large group: "Well, if you had thirty people in here, he'd be one of them. Not to get his name out, but just to put him in a sense, so he doesn't feel ostracized," although

Haldeman added that Magruder "knows that he is" ostracized.* "Well, he isn't as far as I'm concerned," the president countered. He instructed Haldeman to think about it. That afternoon, when working in his EOB office, Nixon himself called Magruder, which, as his records show, was highly unusual, for the president never telephoned him.†

When Ehrlichman joined Haldeman and the president, at 1:05 P.M., they resumed their discussion about Larry O'Brien's taxes, for Ehrlichman had an update based on his visit with Treasury Secretary George Shultz, who had assured Ehrlichman he would ensure that an audit of O'Brien was done. "Will O'Brien know anything on any of this?" the president asked. "Oh, believe me, he'll know," Ehrlichman assured him. "He'll know," he said again, and then explained the process. The audit was being undertaken in a western regional office, because that was the location of the Hughes and O'Brien files, so they would need to "bring agents around out there to conduct the investigation." The president was pleased.

After discussing Haldeman's report on Magruder, the president began quizzing Ehrlichman about his testimony. "Do you know when Magruder gets up to the grand jury?" Ehrlichman responded, "No, I don't." "How will he testify?" Nixon asked. Ehrlichman reported, "That he instructed Sloan to make money available to Liddy. He did it on the basis that Liddy was engaged in making sure that there were no demonstrations at the convention and, ah, for doing certain—"

"Security?" the president injected.

"Yeah, security and headquarters and all that sort of thing," Ehrlichman elaborated. "That from time to time he was vaguely aware that Sloan was making disbursements to Liddy, and he assumed Liddy was doing what he was told, but that he was never given an accounting as such from Sloan."

"And didn't, frankly, follow it up," Nixon injected.

"Didn't follow it up—"

"Busy with other things," Nixon added.

---

*Magruder later wrote that Higby told him they were keeping him away from the president, which he said made him angry, noting that at the time he thought, "*Those bastards, they want me to perjure myself for them, but they won't invite me on their lousy cruise.*" (Original italicized.) Jeb Stuart Magruder, *An American Life: One Man's Road to Watergate* (New York: Atheneum, 1974), 247.

†The conversation ran only a little over one minute, and fifty seconds of the conversation has been withdrawn as personal material. This was a stroking call, in which he discussed personal matters and wanted to let Magruder know he was thinking about him, just days before his grand jury appearance. The substance is irrelevant, for Nixon would not have said anything to Magruder about his testimony. Rather, it was the gesture that counted.

"Busy with other things and made a number of assumptions, but after this happened, he discovered that Liddy had grossly exceeded the scope of his employment. And so—"

"Asked for his resignation?"

"Then he was fired," Ehrlichman stated more categorically.

As the president sat silent, thinking, this bogus account hung in the Oval Office like a bad odor, with all waiting for the air to clear, yet Nixon seemed to find reassurance in going through such a drill. He then asked, "How does Sloan handle this?" "Sloan has been promised immunity, and he has not testified yet before the grand jury," Ehrlichman replied. "He's only talked to the U.S. attorney and the Bureau and, ah—" Notwithstanding the fact that Haldeman had explained all this, Nixon asked, "Why was he given immunity?" Ehrlichman repeated the question, and the president rephrased it, "Why did they have to?"

"Because he said he'd take the Fifth Amendment otherwise. And they felt he was key," Ehrlichman said. "That's good," the president concluded.

"He's not going to testify before the grand jury, is he?" Haldeman asked.

"Yep," Ehrlichman answered. When Haldeman sought clarity, Ehrlichman added, "Well, he was there very briefly. As soon as they learned that he was going to take the Fifth, they pulled him out. They brought him in for a conference with his attorney. He said he was going to take the Fifth because of technical violations of the Campaign Spending Act, or the Campaign Financing Act. So they granted him immunity, and then they've been interrogating him in the office. They're not taking it back."

Soon the president asked, "Is he, is he going to say that he was aware of all this, et cetera?" Ehrlichman said, "No. He's going to say that he was told by Magruder to—" Nixon interrupted, "So he's put the whole thing on Liddy," making clear he understood. "Gave Liddy the money and he did it," Ehrlichman explained. "He was just a conduit," the president added. Ehrlichman continued, "And what he did in keeping unreported cash and handing it out and so on is a violation. There isn't any question about that. Maury Stans's face is very long, because some of this, obviously, it comes back to him, because Sloan couldn't possibly have done all the things that it's clear he did without Maury having some knowledge of it."

"Is Maury involved?" the president inquired.

"Well, he undoubtedly had some knowledge of the fact there was a lot of cash," Ehrlichman said, stating the obvious. Haldeman added, "I would be very surprised if Maury had any knowledge of what was being done with the cash." Ehrlichman noted, "Oh, I agree with that totally, when it comes to that," referring to Liddy's illegal actions. "I'm talking about these technical violations of the Campaign Spending Act." Both Nixon and Haldeman concurred, and Haldeman added, "Maury had full knowledge of that, I'm sure." Haldeman explained his understanding of what Stans actually was aware of: "Now, he knew that there was cash there, and he knew that they were using it for intelligence and dirty tricks business. He knew that Liddy was the guy that was doing that, and he knew that was X amount of money. Maury doesn't let money go out without knowing about it."

"Well, Maury, because of Sloan, they've not called Maury?" Nixon asked. Ehrlichman reported, sounding pleased with his actions, "No, they're not. We've made sure they aren't. Ah, they did, and we stopped it. I woodshedded Kleindienst." "On what basis?" the president asked. "That it's very embarrassing to you," Ehrlichman explained. "That this guy's not just some bohunk off the street, he's a former cabinet officer. And he'd be subject to all kinds of notoriety. He hasn't any way of protecting himself against the inferences. And that it just, it would raise hell with the campaign."

"True," the president said. "And he just couldn't hack it," Ehrlichman added. Nixon said, "Well, certainly, I hope that he'll have the same view with regard to Mitchell." Ehrlichman agreed, and reported, "And in fairness to Kleindienst, this took place while he was out of town, by one of his guys, who exercised some bad judgment and called him up and subpoenaed Maury. So we're on top of that, and Maury is not going to be required to give a statement [to the grand jury, only to the Justice Department]."

"What's Maury going to say?" the president asked. Ehrlichman was not concerned: "He'll handle himself very well, I'm sure. At the same time, he is quite long in the mouth about the whole chilling effect this has on his ability to raise money." The president said he understood, and Ehrlichman added, "I just saw him. He was down in the mess. He's very happy because he doesn't have to go see the grand jury."

Ehrlichman then gave the president his view of the larger picture: "The best guess now is that nobody's going to get indicted except the burglars and Liddy and Hunt."

"And then Hunt fights like hell," the president added. Ehrlichman said, "Well, they all plead not guilty, and there are no trials until after the election." Haldeman was surprised, asking, "But are the burglars all going to plead not guilty?" Ehrlichman assured them, "The burglars are all going to plead not guilty," which at the time was correct information. "What basis?"

the president asked, since they had all been arrested inside the DNC with bugging equipment and cameras. "I can't imagine. I cannot imagine, but that's what they're going to do," Ehrlichman said, with a chuckle. "Make 'em prove it," Haldeman observed.

## August 7, 1972, the White House

On Monday, during a late morning to early afternoon meeting in the Oval, Ehrlichman shared his view that American blacks should "all be stuck in boxcars [and] sent around to one in each town, distributed around" to work as domestics, as the way to enter society, rather than congregating in cities.[16] Following his astonishing diatribe, he rhetorically asked the president, "You noticed that the Ellsberg case went over?"* Nixon asked, "That's what we wanted?" "Yep," Ehrlichman assured him, and the president asked, "Is this going to come up before the election?"

"It won't come up before the election. Everybody's planning out the victory for Ellsberg, and I just don't give a damn. That's fine. If they'd like to have this victory for Ellsberg, that's fine. The point is that the payoff is for us." When the president was not sure why this was good, Ehrlichman explained: "I talked to the chief justice, and he was kind of intrigued with the political aspects of it. He said, the natural inclination of the Court was not to be back for the summer anyway. You know, they don't want to break up their vacation." Ehrlichman added, "We can tolerate a little jubilation on Ellsberg's side for a while, I think—"

"Sure," the president said. Ehrlichman added, "Just ride along, and then after the election, I'd like a crack at Sheehan. Indict the hell out of him." Neil Sheehan was the reporter from the *New York Times* to whom Ellsberg had leaked the Pentagon Papers. "How about Jack Anderson?" the president asked, since he had no objection to prosecuting journalists and particularly despised Anderson. "Jack Anderson on the other case," Ehrlichman agreed, referring to their discovery that a Navy yeoman assigned by the Pentagon as a courier for the National Security Council had been spying for the Joint Chiefs of Staff and, they believed, had also been leaking to Anderson.

---

*Over the weekend it had been a front-page story: Sanford J. Ungar, "Ellsberg Trial Is Delayed Indefinitely," *The Washington Post*, August 6, 1972, A-1. The story said that it was "a major setback to the Justice Department" when Chief Justice Burger announced that the high court would not call a special session to determine if Justice Douglas had been justified in staying the Los Angeles trial.

"I don't feel [we can resist]," the president said, and reported that he had spoken with Henry Kissinger about the Sheehan situation. As for Anderson, the president added, "[With that guy, I'm never] giving in. I don't certainly intend to allow that son of a bitch to get away with that. I see no reason why we don't get at him. Let the Joint Chiefs take the heat."*

Ehrlichman reported the Larry O'Brien tax audit was proceeding, and the president shared with Ehrlichman the news that former Lyndon Johnson Senate crony Bobby Baker had called Rose Woods, saying that he wanted to talk with her or Bebe, that he had the goods on the Democrats and wanted to share what he knew. The president said, "I instructed Bebe to call him back. Bobby Baker got on the phone with Bebe, and he said, 'Look,' he said, 'This McGovern, I hate the son of a bitch.' He said, 'He's a pure disaster for the country.' And he said, 'I'll do anything to help.' He said, 'Now, I've got some information that involves Muskie. And I've got some also that involves O'Brien.'"

"This is good," Ehrlichman said.

The president explained that Bebe, using good judgment, told Baker he was going back to Florida but would be happy to meet with him: "So I told Bebe to follow through at the earliest, with the idea of getting information on both Muskie and O'Brien." Nixon said he wanted information on any senator except George Smathers. (Why Smathers was not of interest was not explained.) Nixon said that Bobby Baker was so close to Lyndon Johnson that "he never went to the can without talking to him." The president believed that Baker was Johnson's bagman, noting Baker "was about ten times the bagman than that poor fellow we had, Dave Johnson." Ehrlichman laughed, and Nixon added that while Dave was able, he was just not in Baker's league. The president said that if Baker had good information on Muskie, they should use it to "tear him to pieces."

## August 12, 1972, Camp David

Both the White House staff and the president were increasingly focusing on the fast-approaching Republican National Convention, which would formally convene in Miami from August 21 to August 23. They planned on (and

---

*A Watergate-weakened president in his second term did not pursue this case against Sheehan, the yeoman or Anderson. Rather, Nixon explained in his memoirs, he had not prosecuted the yeoman in his first term because he felt "it would be too dangerous to prosecute" a person who had access to top secret information, "which, if disclosed, could have jeopardized our negotiations with China and North Vietnam." Richard Nixon, *RN: The Memoirs of Richard Nixon* (New York: Grosset & Dunlap, 1978), 532.

succeeded in) taking the national political gathering to a new level of orchestrated media events. The convention would be a made-for-television extravaganza, planned to the smallest detail. Accordingly, the president wanted to focus on writing his acceptance speech, which would be delivered in prime time on August 23, and was spending as much time as possible at Camp David to draft it.

On Saturday, August 12, during a lengthy Camp David meeting with Ehrlichman and Haldeman at Laurel Lodge, where no recording equipment was installed, there was a review of Watergate—a topic that kept interrupting Nixon's work, as he explained in his memoirs.[17] Haldeman reported on this meeting in his diary, noting that the president reminded them both that they should "understand that the O'Brien follow-up and the attack on high-level Democrats [was] much more important than the [GOP Convention's] platform," and that Nixon wanted "the Watergate thing" further discussed, because he liked Ehrlichman's plan. "The thought there was that we would have MacGregor come out and give the full background story right at the time of the P[resident]'s meeting with [Japanese prime minister] Tanaka, so as to be overridden, and hope that settles our side of it prior to the issuing of indictments in mid-September."[18]

## August 14, 1972, the White House

Haldeman, Mitchell and Clark MacGregor got into "the Watergate thing" with the president in the Oval Office during a morning conversation.[19] MacGregor explained that Stans was preparing a report about the twenty-five-thousand-dollar Dahlberg-Andreas check that ended up in Barker's bank account. The president asked which lawyers were assisting the reelection committee, and Mitchell said they had hired Roger Robb's onetime law partner, Ken Parkinson, and his firm, along with Paul O'Brien and his firm, and noted that Paul O'Brien was doing more of the investigating. Mitchell added, "I think they've done outstanding in a very difficult situation." But neither Mitchell nor MacGregor told the president that they had conducted an investigation, as he soon claimed; rather, he would tell them they had done so.

This information, however, prompted an extended Nixon monologue suggesting, which was tantamount to directing, Mitchell and MacGregor on how they should handle Watergate: "The important thing to consider is, the real decision you have to face up to is, whether or not to wait until the grand jury indicts or whether you prepare the stage for it. The weakness that I see in the present situation, of course, it's a bad situation, we know, very embarrassing, and so forth and so on. The weakness I see at the present time is that we have people on the outside who will say, 'Well, they're going to need special investigators' and 'Oh, let's have a special prosecutor,' and all that sort of thing." Nixon interrupted his analysis to ponder whether anyone had called for a special prosecutor during the Bobby Baker scandal. MacGregor thought there had been but did not have hard information.*

The president said, "The main point that I want to make is this: I think that the case that has got to be made that the reelection committee [acted] with the total cooperation on this [matter], full cooperation by us. [And it] has conducted its own investigation, and this is the guy [Paul O'Brien] has done the investigation of this matter." Then, referring to the news media and the public, he added, "I think that's very important that they know [this fact]." The president said that if the committee merely takes the position that it is a matter for the courts, and "we don't give a shit," that it will have negative consequences. "Everybody knows that the people from the reelection committee are involved at lower levels," he continued, "so it seems to me that it's imperative that we would want to see this thing worked out, [having an] investigation and so forth. Then, having in mind the fact that when the grand jury indicts, and we get indictments on the people that obviously have gotten caught with their hands in the cookie jar, and does not indict others, like Magruder, Sloan, and so forth," the president felt there would be an immediate reaction: "'Well, what are the facts regarding others? What are they covering up?'"

Rather than allowing that to happen, the president was urging Mitchell and MacGregor to take the initiative. First, he would have MacGregor leak the fact that the committee had conducted its own investigation, and it was undertaken by a top law firm. Second, MacGregor would make a statement during the president's meeting with the Japanese during his forthcoming trip to Hawaii. The statement would explain "the limitation of the reelection committee's involvement" without getting into specific details. "So, do you see, your choices, it seems to me, are very, very limited. The choice is either to go down in that sort of fall, and then have a hell of a bitch, and then have an investigation demanded of everything and everybody else. Or, having in mind that this has nothing to do with law, forget the law, I mean, except for

*In Bobby Baker's memoir there is no mention of a special prosecutor. See Bobby Baker with Larry L. King, *Wheeling and Dealing: Confessions of a Capitol Hill Operator* (New York: W. W. Norton & Company, 1978). William O. Bittman, who represented Howard Hunt during Watergate, prosecuted Baker for the Justice Department.

the poor guys that are going to go to jail and be fined. But this [statement] has to do with public relations." The statement would be issued before the grand jury indictments, and "then when the grand jury indictment comes it would be sort of an afterthought."

"How do you feel about that, John?" he asked Mitchell, who liked the proposal. As far as the president was concerned, Mitchell had now approved the fact that they had conducted an investigation that had never actually occurred. The CRP attorneys did try to find out what had taken place, until they were halted—when they were at the point of discovering the truth. Only with time did they figure out what had transpired and, like me, learn much of it by accident.

Nixon then turned to his ongoing concern, Magruder and the grand jury: "Is Magruder going before them tomorrow?" Haldeman and Mitchell answered yes simultaneously, with Haldeman adding, "It's anticipated he'll be in tomorrow and Wednesday." Nixon noted, "Well, his questioning will indicate to me, to a certain extent, what is going to come out." Speaking as a former attorney general, Mitchell was not concerned: "Well, at least the grand jury proceedings will be controlled in the Justice Department." He also added, "They're not going to go off on their own over in the U.S. Attorney's Office. And that's where we've got to know what they're going to recommend to the grand jury. And once we know that, then you can stage the timing of the indictments and the timing of your statement." When the president raised the possibility of a runaway grand jury, Mitchell dismissed it.

Nixon still wanted the CRP to have a public relations plan and to release a statement about its own investigation. Mitchell reported that it had already made such statements, but they had been "washed over." But Mitchell had never requested a real investigation. To the contrary, when Jeb Magruder did start to tell Ken Parkinson the truth in mid-July, Mitchell had pulled him up short and told Parkinson that Magruder's information was not correct.[20] The president explained that he had been reading the *New York Times*, which he described as reporting, "The White House and the rest, that they're completely oblivious" to Watergate.* More discussion of public relations planning or statements followed, but no firm decisions were made.

---

*The president was referring to a commentary by Robert B. Semple, "Nixon and the Press: Why the Heat Is Off," *New York Times*, August 13, 1972, E-3. At one point Semple wrote: "The persistent silence in the White House and in the re-election committee on various inquiries into the bugging episode at the Democratic headquarters in the Watergate office virtually guarantees that tough questions will continue."

*August 16, 1972, Camp David*

The president telephoned Haldeman shortly before four o'clock to inquire about Magruder, who was still at the U.S. courthouse before the grand jury. There is no recorded telephone call of Haldeman giving Nixon a report on Magruder's appearance, although I telephoned Haldeman late that afternoon to tell him that I had called Henry Petersen at the Justice Department, who said that Magruder had gotten through "by the skin of his teeth."[21]

Clearly Haldeman passed along this information to Nixon, who stopped asking about Magruder in subsequent conversations. Undoubtedly the gist of what Haldeman told him was very close to what he wrote in his diary:

> Had a report from John Dean on the Watergate business, says that things went okay with Magruder, at an informal thing last night and then with the grand jury today. He was about two and a half hours, came off okay with no surprise questions or any new evidence. They focused on me, apparently, in trying to get Jeb to tie me into the case somehow today, although last night they focused on Colson. John thinks that things are under reasonably good control there.[22]

# Investigations, Indictment and the President Meets with His White House Counsel

B y mid-August most everyone on the president's staff, when not addressing government business, was absorbed in the effort of producing a flawless convention, of orchestrating the speakers at the podium and "spontaneous" events on the convention floor to make them engaging for television viewers. All of the prime-time events would be scripted; aides at the podium and on the floor would be electronically connected to others in a trailer outside the convention hall, and together they would make sure the script was followed.

On August 17, Clark MacGregor gave a wide-ranging interview to a number of reporters, most of whom were primarily interested in Watergate. At one point MacGregor said Liddy, as general counsel of the finance committee, had given the twenty-five-thousand-dollar Dahlberg-Andreas campaign contribution to Bernard Barker, but MacGregor did not know why. He also stated that he had not authorized the lawyers to seek postponement of the Democrats' civil lawsuit; the break-in had "embarrassed the Nixon campaign," but when more facts were known it would not be as troubling as it seemed; and they would make a detailed response to the GAO report. He added that, while all he knew was hearsay, he felt that the grand jury proceedings and the depositions in the Democrats' lawsuit would give "people now or formerly in a position of authority an opportunity to speak out."[1]

When Mitchell learned of MacGregor's remarks he phoned Haldeman, who noted in his diary, "Mitchell called, very concerned because MacGregor was putting out some stuff on the Watergate thing in self-defense. John's very concerned because what he's putting out is not the line, and it undercuts our legal posture, and so on. He wanted me to call MacGregor, tell him he's got to use the line of 'no comment' because individual rights are involved. We'll have a statement at the appropriate time and then scare him into the fact that he may blow the lawsuit and some of the individuals concerned if he doesn't stay with the line." Mitchell also worried that Mac-Gregor would be making television appearances and talking about Watergate during the convention.[2]

Also by mid-August the White House congressional liaison staff had learned that one or more committees of the Democratic-controlled Congress, both House and Senate, were considering Watergate-related investigations. On August 19 Chairman Wright Patman of the House Banking Committee announced that he had directed his staff to undertake an investigation into the $114,000 that had passed through the Committee to Re-elect the President and into the bank account of Bernard Barker via U.S. and Mexican banks.[3] In the U.S. Senate, Teddy Kennedy was preparing his Administrative Practice and Procedure subcommittee staff to undertake a Watergate-related investigation.

The president remained at Camp David, working on his acceptance speech, until August 21, when he traveled by helicopter to Gettysburg, Pennsylvania, to visit with former first lady Mamie Eisenhower. He then returned to the White House, where he got his hair cut and did some final work on his speech. On the afternoon of August 22 he arrived at Miami International Airport and greeted crowds (bused to the site), an event that was broadcast live, and that evening addressed a rally of Young Voters for the President. He spent the following day working in his den at his home in Key Biscayne, meeting with aides, going over the logistics of the convention and talking to GOP dignitaries. At 9:44 P.M. he flew by helicopter to the convention center, went to the holding room, had his makeup applied, and following an introduction by Vice President Spiro Agnew, stepped to the podium at 10:27 P.M. to deliver his acceptance speech to the cheering delegates. The next morning the First Family departed for San Clemente in California, where Nixon remained, working at the Western White House, until September 6.

The GOP convention coverage largely overshadowed several big Watergate stories that were covered by *Time* magazine and *The Washington Post*. On August 21 *Time* reported that the reelection committee had successfully bugged the DNC and operated a listening post across the street at the Howard Johnson Motor Hotel prior to the date the burglars were caught. The partially accurate story claimed that, after the arrests at the DNC, the

"Security Intelligence Squad of the Committee for the Reelection of the President, [which] grew out of a team of so-called 'plumbers,' originally re-cruited by the administration to investigate leaks to the media," had cleared out their DNC records and tapes from the motel rooms.[4] *Time* linked this squad to Howard Hunt and G. Gordon Liddy but incorrectly included Mitchell aide Robert Mardian, who was apoplectic at being so identified. It was the first story on the plumbers, but because of the convention, no one at the White House focused on it, nor on the *Post* story. The latter revealed that the GAO had cited violations of the campaign law in the CRP's fund-raising and expenditures.[5] Judge Richey, as reported in a *Post* article that was criti-cal of his actions, ordered that all pretrial testimony in the Democrats' law-suit be kept under seal.[6] In addition, there was clearly well-informed media speculation that, while indictments in the Watergate case would be forth-coming, the criminal trial would be delayed until after the election.[7] Two days later the media-sensitive Richey announced that he would start the bugging case civil trial before the election to "insure the right of the public to know and the right of the press."[8]

### August 26–30, 1972, the Western White House

Notwithstanding the absence of recording equipment at San Clemente, doc-uments and records reveal that Watergate remained very much on the pres-ident's mind during this California trip. For example, on Saturday, August 26, in anticipation of a forthcoming press conference, Nixon instructed Haldeman to have Pat Buchanan determine what Watergate questions might be asked. One that was certain to be posed was the matter of appointing a special prosecutor for Watergate, an issue that Larry O'Brien had been press-ing almost daily. On August 28 Attorney General Kleindienst categorically rejected the proposal, telling reporters it was impossible, because Watergate was "not a matter of looking into the conduct of government officials, but alleged criminal conduct on the part of private individuals." Kleindienst promised "the most extensive, thorough and comprehensive investigation since the assassination of President Kennedy."[9]

As the president gathered his thoughts for the press conference he made notes (transcribed following) about how he would address Watergate; they indicate that he had decided to announce not only a reelection committee investigation, but one of his own:

8-29-72

P.C.—S.C. [Press Conference–San Clemente]

kind of activity political

Watergate: This ^ has no place in our ^ process

1.  This is being thoroughly investigated by F.B.I., Dept of Justice,
    G.A.O. and Banking & Currency Committee

2.  For W.H.—John Dean—Counsel to Pres
    conducted investigation
    & no one in W.H. or in any govt agency was involved

3.  For Committee Mitchell initiated very
    extensive—independent investigation

4.  Those who are implicated, or who refuse
    to cooperate will be discharged

5.  Their [sic] making this their major issue

Indicates lack of confidence in Defense, foreign policy

other great issues—

Haldeman and Ehrlichman requested I come to San Clemente to update them, so I flew to California on August 28 and met with them on the morning of August 29, shortly before the president's press conference. They mentioned nothing to me about my ostensibly having undertaken any sort of White House investigation, for they knew I had done nothing even resembling one. I returned to my hotel in Newport Beach to watch the press conference on television, and by the second question the subject turned to Watergate: "Mr. President, wouldn't it be a good idea for a special prosecutor, even from your standpoint, to be appointed to investigate the contribution situation and also the Watergate case?"[10]

"With regard to who is investigating," Nixon responded, "it now, I think it would be well to notice that the FBI is conducting a full field investigation. The Department of Justice, of course, is in charge of the prosecution and presenting the matter to the grand jury. The Senate [actually, the House] Banking and Currency Committee is conducting an investigation. The Government Accounting Office, an independent agency, is conducting an investigation of those aspects which involve the campaign spending law. Now, with all of these investigations that are being conducted, I don't believe that adding another special prosecutor would serve any useful purpose."

Nixon continued: "The other point that I should make is that these investigations, the investigation by the GAO, the investigation by the FBI, by the Department of Justice, have, *at my direction*, had the total cooperation of the, not only the White House, but also of all agencies of the government." This, of course, was untrue; he went on: "In addition to that, within our own staff, *under my direction*, counsel to the president, Mr. Dean, *has conducted a complete investigation of all leads which might involve any present members of the White House staff or anybody in the government*. I can say categorically that his investigation indicates that no one in the White House staff, no one in this administration, presently employed, was involved in this very bizarre incident." (Emphasis added.)

At the time I thoughtlessly considered the president's statement about me a public vote of confidence, and I was delighted, although when reporters started asking the press office for a copy of my investigation, I had to tell Ron Ziegler that, in fact, I had not conducted one.[11] At the time it did not occur to me that the president was starting to refine and build his defense, and that he was using me as a shield he would be only too willing to sacrifice later.[12] In claiming the existence of these bogus investigations, Nixon had done himself what he had wanted Mitchell and MacGregor to do.

The president then said, addressing the points he had made in his notes: "At the same time, the committee itself is conducting its own investigation, independent of the rest, because the committee desires to clear the air and to be sure that as far as any people who have responsibility for this campaign are concerned, that there is nothing that hangs over them. Before Mr. Mitchell left as campaign chairman he had employed a very good law firm with investigatory experience to look into the matter." This was a half truth to which he then tied his new campaign director: "Mr. Mac-Gregor has continued that investigation, and is continuing it now. I will say in that respect that anyone on the campaign committee, Mr. MacGregor has assured me, who does not cooperate with the investigation, or anyone against whom charges are leveled where there is a prima facie case that those charges might indicate involvement, will be discharged immediately. That, of course, will be true also of anybody in the government." In fact, MacGregor had made no such assurance, nor had he continued any investigations.

The president then concluded: "I think under these circumstances we are doing everything we can to take this incident and to investigate it and not to cover it up. What really hurts in matters of this sort is not the fact that they occur, because overzealous people in campaigns do things that are wrong. What really hurts is if you try to cover it up. I would say that here we are, with control of the agencies of the government, and presumably with control of the investigatory agencies of the government, with the exception of the GAO which is independent. We have cooperated completely. We have indicated that we want all the facts brought out, and that as far as any people who are guilty are concerned, they should be prosecuted. This kind of activity, as I have often indicated, has no place whatever in our political process. We want the air cleared. We want it cleared as soon as possible."

Even as the president was proclaiming assurances about Watergate, the lawyers who had filed the civil lawsuit for the Democrats were beginning to realize that they had hooked something far larger than they had imagined, and they were now pursuing their action more seriously and aggressively. Their suit had begun as a fishing expedition, one based purely on suspicion that higher-ups might be involved in Watergate and on the hope that they might get lucky—that with depositions they might uncover information politically damaging to the Nixon campaign. The reason for their newfound confidence was revealed only decades later in the memoir of Joseph Califano, Jr., the lead attorney for the suit.

On August 28, a Califano associate interviewed Alfred Baldwin, the former FBI agent McCord had hired to monitor the listening equipment at the DNC's Watergate offices from the Howard Johnson across the street. Baldwin had been the lookout on the night of the June 17 arrests, after which Hunt had ordered him to get out of town. From his home in Connecticut, Baldwin hired a lawyer, John Cassidento, a former assistant United States attorney whom Califano later described as a "committed Democrat." Cassidento had tipped off Califano that Baldwin "was angry" with the people at the reelection committee because he had not been paid, and he was now talking to investigators. Califano wanted to go public with Baldwin's information, but Edward Bennett Williams, his partner, advised against it.[13] Rather, they began leaking it immediately (probably to *Time*), and soon Larry O'Brien was openly charging that the Nixon committee had been bugging his phones even prior to June 17, 1972, clearly based on Baldwin's information.

Baldwin's story made it to *The Washington Post* on September 1, 1972, when Woodward and Bernstein reported that Liddy and Hunt had been at the Watergate and, having been warned by walkie-talkie (i.e., Baldwin) that the police had arrived, narrowly escaped being arrested. The *Post* story also reported that photographs of DNC letterhead documents had been developed for Bernard Barker at a Miami photography shop, according to information given to Florida's state attorney, Richard Gerstein, who was conducting his own Watergate-related investigation. The *Post* story further noted that the FBI had not yet interviewed the man who developed thirty-eight photos taken inside the DNC for Barker.[14] It was Gerstein who had given Woodward and Bernstein leads on the twenty-five-thousand-dollar Dahlberg-Andreas check, but none of this was new information to the Nixon White House, or to the FBI.

On September 2 Democrats tried to depose John Mitchell, but his lawyers instructed him not to give anything other than his name and address, because those arrested in the DNC had filed a motion objecting to the prejudicial pretrial publicity that the Democrats' lawsuit was generating. Williams, now aware that he had a real case, demanded a Saturday session with Judge Richey, who issued an order for Mitchell to be deposed on Monday, September 5. Califano never forgot the scene. Williams sat directly across from Mitchell in his office conference room, and on the table between them he had placed three large notebooks labeled Mitchell I, Mitchell II and Mitchell III. Williams periodically thumbed through the notebooks as he questioned a nervous Mitchell about the DNC break-in and bugging, alluding to information they had from Baldwin. (When he first described this deposition to me years later, Califano roared with laughter, as those notebooks were filled with blank sheets of paper.) After the deposition, Williams confided to Califano that he believed they had "one helluva lawsuit," explaining, "I may not know much about politics, but I know when someone is lying and when he's scared. John Mitchell had to squeeze his thighs together to avoid wetting his pants."[15]

The next morning, September 6, *The Washington Post* had a front-page story about the deposition and featured a photo of Mitchell surrounded by reporters and photographers as he emerged from the two-hour grilling. Mitchell told reporters: "Neither the President nor anyone at the White House or anyone in authority at the committee working for his reelection [had] any responsibility for the break-in and alleged bugging attempt." The story further reported that the attorney for the five men arrested at the DNC, who had been named as defendants in the Democrats' lawsuit, had served notice to depose ten Democratic Party officials, including Larry O'Brien.[16]

### September 7–8, 1972, the White House

The president, meanwhile, was eager to arrange for the Secret Service to infiltrate Teddy Kennedy's world by providing protection that would at the same time supply the White House with inside information about the senator. During a morning meeting in the Oval Office with Haldeman and Ehrlichman, Nixon ordered his aides to "plant one or plant two" guys on Kennedy.[17] (The undertaking ultimately failed, because Kennedy refused the offer.) Ehrlichman then gave the president a piece of bad news: He had had his man at the IRS, Roger Barth, personally review Larry O'Brien's returns, and his taxes were in proper order. "It's a dry hole," Ehrlichman explained. Bobby Baker's information was proving largely useless.

With the FBI's investigation and the grand jury's work largely completed, Watergate came up less frequently in the president's conversations, although he did continue to ask Haldeman and Ehrlichman if a date had been set when the indictments would be handed down by the grand jury.[18] Mid-September remained the best estimate. The president also asked Ehrlichman if he had been deposed by the Democrats, which he said he had not; he explained that he had seen Hunt and Liddy on only one occasion at the White House, and he "would not know their work product" if he was asked.[19] When meeting with his top campaign fund-raiser and former secretary of commerce, Maurice Stans, the president asked about the well-being of Hugh Sloan, who Stans reported was struggling. "Well, we'll take good care of him," the president instructed Stans, if his testimony did not cause any problems.[20]

### September 11, 1972, the White House

Woodward and Bernstein broke a front-page *Post* story based on Baldwin's information under the headline BUGGING "PARTICIPANT" GIVES DETAILS: "Democratic investigators" had learned that "the telephone conversations of Democratic Party leaders were monitored, transcribed and then sent in memorandum form to high-ranking officials of President Nixon's reelection committee and to a presidential assistant." The FBI, however, had been unable to locate any of these documents.[21] Nixon asked Haldeman about the story during a brief morning meeting, but Haldeman was wrong when said he did not think the unnamed participant had been Martha Mitchell's body-guard, and he was unable to answer the president's question about whether the grand jury had copies of the memoranda in question.[22] If, as the article claimed, such information had been delivered to a presidential assistant, had anyone on his staff been called before the grand jury? Nixon asked. Halde-man assured him they had not.

The *Post* story reminded the president that they still had not developed an appropriate PR response to Watergate other than his August 29 press conference statements, and he began peppering Haldeman with questions about their plans, to which Haldeman had few answers. Nixon, eager to take the offensive, told Haldeman, "I'm just trying to think of getting a line on developments. I thought Dean would be doing it, you know? I mean, is there somebody on our side working on this? Maybe you've got to give it to Col-son? He'd work hard. Or is he the right one?"

The president was satisfied when Haldeman said that Ehrlichman was working on it, but he cautioned that they were not planning on going "too far on the offensive" because of the developing congressional investigation. When the president asked for more information on the *Post* story, Haldeman called me for an update, and then reported to Nixon that the unidentified participant in the *Post* story was Alfred Baldwin: "He was assigned to Mar-tha at one point. But he knows nothing, and everything he has, everything he does know has been told to the grand jury and will come out in the in-dictment. And whatever he's given the Democrats, he can't go beyond that. He doesn't know any more. And we think he may have made up some of that." This last comment referred to the claim by Baldwin that he thought he had delivered memoranda of the overheard conversations on one occa-sion to a presidential aide, and the only name he recognized was Bill Timmons. But that had never happened.

"Why is he talking to them?" the president asked. When Haldeman an-swered that he didn't know, Nixon wondered how Baldwin fit in the picture, since a guy who was now talking to the Democrats was "a hell of a guy" to have been involved in the operation. Nixon wanted to know if they were all "kooky," and Haldeman could not deny that analysis. "They were all kooky," Haldeman conceded. "The Cubans, in their own way, are kooky Cubans," he noted.

When they met later that afternoon in the EOB office, Haldeman reported that everything was still on track for the indictments to be issued on Friday, September 15.[23] Only those arrested in the DNC, plus Hunt and Liddy, would be named. As planned, they would "ride" the indictments with a MacGregor statement.

The president recalled that during the Hiss affair nothing seemed to hurt Hiss and his supporters until he was actually indicted. "Now, in our case," the president told Haldeman, "we've got to be very, very careful to lay the foundation for the trial." Nixon remained concerned that they would be charged with a cover-up, but Haldeman countered that the public would be getting more than anticipated with Hunt and Liddy being included in the indictment. Haldeman was thankful the indictments did not reach "upper levels of the committee or in the White House," and both men were satisfied that all who would be named had already been publicly tarnished by Watergate.

Haldeman reported that they had leaked O'Brien's tax information to the *Las Vegas Review Journal*.[24] Herb Kalmbach was doing a further follow-up with Bobby Baker, and the president hoped Baker would produce negative information on either O'Brien or Teddy Kennedy, preferably O'Brien. Both Nixon and Haldeman were disappointed that there was little press interest in Teddy Kennedy's ongoing affair with socialite Amanda Burden, a story Colson had been spreading to anyone who would listen. Haldeman reported that whenever Teddy campaigned for McGovern someone in the audience always carried a sign asking: Where's Amanda, Teddy?

*September 12–13, 1972, the White House*

Consistent with his effort to take the offensive on Watergate, the president had Attorney General Kleindienst brief his cabinet and Republican congressional leaders at a breakfast in the State Dining Room on September 12. (I was not invited, and when Ziegler's assistant, Gerald Warren, called to ask me why, I told him that I was certain it was so I would not be asked about the investigation I had never conducted.) During the closed session Kleindienst told the GOP leaders that the Watergate indictments would be handed down on Friday, September 15, and that no one at a high level of the reelection committee or at the White House would be named. Kleindienst said he anticipated claims from the Democrats and the news media of a "whitewash," so he had hard data to refute that charge (which he later used, following the indictments). He reported that the FBI's Watergate investigation had exceeded that of the Kennedy assassination inquiry, for it had involved 333 FBI agents in 51 field offices who had followed 1,879 leads and undertaken 1,551 interviews that required 14,098 man-hours.[25]

Following the breakfast the president met with Haldeman and Colson in the Oval Office and, with Watergate still on his mind, asked Haldeman, "Any more new thoughts regarding the lawsuit?"[26] Haldeman asked whether he had gotten the memo I had prepared, and when Nixon answered, "Yeah, yeah," Haldeman nonetheless walked him through a few key points: Mitchell, who had learned of O'Brien's tax audit, had suggested areas the committee lawyers might explore when deposing O'Brien. Henry Rothblatt, who represented the Cuban Americans, had learned that the DNC surveillance had revealed that both married men and women at the committee were having office affairs; he wanted to leak this information to embarrass them over the lawsuit. After Haldeman reviewed these points, the president was doubtful much would come from this litigation.[27] Still concerned that the indictments would lead to accusations of a cover-up, they discussed an idea of Colson's to create a special commission headed by former chief justice Earl Warren to examine the FBI's and Justice Department's Watergate investigations and establish that there had been no concealment. When Colson later joined the conversation, they continued exploring this problem, but no solution emerged.

The subject of the commission came up again the following morning at Camp David.[28] "I talked to Kleindienst about it, and he just burst out laughing," Haldeman explained. "And I said, 'What's so funny?' And he said, 'That's been my idea for three weeks, but John Mitchell pisses on me every time I start to raise it. And he won't even listen to it.' And he said, 'I didn't have a commission in mind. What I had in mind was one man, and the one man I had in mind was—'" "Earl Warren?" the president injected. Haldeman said that Kleindienst was suggesting former associate justice Tom Clark. Kleindienst felt that, rather than getting a commission, which would require staff and funding, they just appoint Clark, as an individual. When the president said he would feel better about these ideas if Mitchell supported them, Haldeman reported that he had already spoken to Mitchell, who was not opposed. Neither the president nor Haldeman was sure of Ehrlichman's opinion of these proposals. "When it comes to making the judgment as to what you do or don't do, Ehrlichman's advice is often coy," the president observed.

*September 15, 1972, the White House*

The president's morning news summary reported that on the preceding evening the television networks had given Nixon a 63 percent to 29 percent lead
over McGovern. All had reported that Maurice Stans had filed a five-million-
dollar libel lawsuit against Larry O'Brien. Both the networks and *The Washington Post* reported that the Democrats had found another electronic bug
in the telephone of Spence Oliver, the executive director of the Association
of State Democratic Chairmen and whose office McCord had bugged, at the
DNC, and showed photographs of it. (Earl Silbert, the original Watergate
lead prosecutor, correctly believed that the FBI had simply failed to discover
the bug during its initial investigation. The FBI rejected this idea, however,
and opened a new investigation of Oliver and the DNC, a gesture the committee found nothing short of harassment, believing the Nixon White House
was behind it. Years later James McCord acknowledged that it was his bug,
which the FBI had missed; he revealed yet another bug to prosecutors in
April 1973.[29])

As anticipated, on September 15 the Department of Justice released the
grand jury's indictment, naming the five men arrested in the DNC and two
former Nixon White House aides. The five were James W. McCord, former
security coordinator for the reelection committee; Bernard L. Barker, president of a Miami real-estate business; Frank Sturgis, an anti-Castro activist;
Eugenio Martinez, a real-estate broker in the Barker firm; and Virgilio R.
Gonzales, a Miami locksmith. The former White House aides were G. Gordon Liddy and E. Howard Hunt. The indictment charged the seven defendants with conspiracy, interception of oral and wire communications,
second-degree burglary and unlawful possession of intercepting devices.[30]
While the public was generally indifferent to this development, Larry
O'Brien stated, "We can only assume that the investigation will continue,
since the indictments handed down today reflect only the most narrow con-
struction of the crime that was committed." O'Brien added, "We will continue to press for a far more thorough explanation of the funding of the
crime that led to those indictments" and for the appointment of a special
prosecutor. Although no one at the reelection committee celebrated the limited scope of the indictments, Magruder was extremely relieved.

Haldeman briefed the president during their morning meeting before
the indictments were publicly announced and provided him with what

information was known about the alleged new electronic eavesdropping bug found at the DNC. The White House had been assured by Pat Gray that they had not missed it the first time and that the FBI was opening a new investigation.[31] September 15 was a slow schedule day for the president, who spent much of the afternoon in the Oval Office discussing his reelection campaign; then he had an unusual conversation with me in the late afternoon. Notwithstanding the fact that I had been at the White House for over two years, I really did not know the president, nor did he know me, apart from ceremonial encounters. In hindsight it is clear that we both were misjudging each other.

During a conversation earlier that afternoon Haldeman had reported that Clark MacGregor was proceeding as planned: He would announce that, since the indictments had now been handed down, it was time to "quit all this playing games" with Watergate and "hanging innocent people by innuendo."[32] After Haldeman gave the president the information I had received from the FBI about the new bug, he replied, "And Dean [has] been a real strong man in this, hasn't he?" Haldeman confirmed this, adding, "It's been interesting to watch. He's, you know, very low-key and cool about things." Nixon repeated, "He doesn't get all excited." Haldeman explained, "Well, he's good at keeping other people calmed down, which has been important in this one. Probably the most key thing of all, because keeping the Hugh Sloans, and the Maurice Stanses, and the Mardians—who has been his big cross." Nixon was horrified to learn that Mardian was still involved with Watergate, believing that he had been put out in the field to work. Haldeman explained that Mardian had "tiptoed back in."

After the president talked on the telephone with Peter Dailey, who headed his campaign advertising group in New York City, and Ron Ziegler, who wanted guidance on how to address the Watergate indictments—the White House would not comment but would leave the matter to the Department of Justice—the president complained to Haldeman how impossible it was as president to simply drop in on his staff to say hello or be "buddy-buddy." He then asked, "Is Dean here today?" Haldeman indicated that I was in my office. "Okay, why don't you have him come down."

"John's on his way over," Haldeman reported, after summoning me.[33] The president can be heard writing as Haldeman continued. "Yeah, he is one of the quiet guys that gets a lot done. That was a good move, too, bringing Dean in," he said, referring to Watergate. "He'll never gain any ground for us. He's just not that kind of guy. But he's the kind that enables other people to gain ground while he's making sure that you don't fall through the holes. Between times he's moving ruthlessly on the investigation of McGovern people, Kennedy stuff, and all that, too. I just don't know how much progress he's making, because I—" Haldeman then turned the conversation in a direction he knew the president liked to hear, continuing, "—Chuck [Colson] has worked on the list, and Dean's working the thing through IRS and some other things. He's turned out to be tougher than I thought he would."[34]

When I entered the Oval Office at 5:27 P.M., the president expressed his appreciation for my work on the Watergate situation. Although I had expected it would last five or ten minutes, the meeting lasted nearly fifty. I could sense at the time that my presence was something of a catalyst for Nixon, who was playing president just for me, as he began to discuss his thinking about his second term. What I thought at the time might be a bad-day mood was actually his norm, involving a lot of tough talk about what he was going to do to his enemies and how he was going to go about it. As the conversation proceeded, I could not resist giving him what I knew he wanted. While I could not play the sycophant, as Colson did, nor could I be a brittle and nasty son of a bitch, like Tom Huston, both of whom I knew Nixon admired, I could play the admiring staffer in my own way, which I did with a couple of appreciative remarks, such as "That's an exciting prospect," and later, "That's an exciting concept," when he talked about making government responsive to the White House.

When Nixon first released the transcript of our September 15 conversation, he claimed it showed that he was not participating in a cover-up.* It is true that I raised the cover-up rather elliptically, and he responded metaphorically, but we each understood exactly what was being said. There was no doubt in my mind about Nixon's awareness of the cover-up after our exchange, relatively early in the conversation, when I told him, "Three months ago I would have had trouble predicting where we'd be today. I think that I can say that fifty-four days from now that not a thing will come crashing down to our surprise." The president had not been listening, or had missed my "three months ago" reference to June 17, the date of the arrests at the DNC, and the fact that it was fifty-four days to Election Day. "Say what?"

---

*The ninety recorded conversations that I have drawn from that preceded this meeting clearly reveal this was not true; rather, it was merely another discussion in the ongoing cover-up that the president was not only aware of but, through Haldeman and Ehrlichman, directing.

he asked, in response to which I was a bit more direct, clarifying: "Nothing is going to come crashing down to our surprise, either—" rather conspicuously, I believed, referring to Watergate.

"Well, the whole thing is a can of worms. As you know, a lot of this stuff went on. And, and the people who worked in the thing are awfully embarrassing. The way you've handled it, it seems to me, has been very skillful, because you put your fingers in the dikes every time that leaks have sprung here and sprung there," he said. I understood his metaphor perfectly.

Toward the end of the conversation I alerted the president that he might hear from George Shultz regarding the request I had passed on to Johnnie Walters, the head of the IRS. He suggested that he would fire Shultz if he did not follow up. When the conversation was over I figured the president probably viewed our exchange for what it was—a young aide trying to please the boss. But I was wrong: It had a very different impact on him, and it probably explains why, five months later, he called on me to deal directly with Watergate when the problems refused to go away.

### September 16, 1972, the White House

The next morning, when meeting with Haldeman in the Oval Office, the president was still thinking about our conversation.[35] There was a discussion about the CIA's leak of information to CBS News and Nixon's impulsive reaction to fire everyone on the CIA distribution list who received the documents containing that information. The president injected me into that conversation. "I'd also like you to know that I am damn impressed with John Dean. I was far more impressed with him than John Ehrlichman. As far as him being a playboy, he realizes that he's good, despite being a playboy. But Dean is more steely than John [Ehrlichman]," the president declared. "More steely than John, no question with Dean, and Bob, I can't tell you how strongly I feel you've got to be steely and mean. This handout [referring to the leak], I'm sure if I'd have given it to Dean, or that stuff on O'Brien, of course he's not as busy as Ehrlichman. But something would have gotten out there," meaning some sort White House reaction. Nixon is clearly using me as a bit of a foil to Ehrlichman, so Haldeman protested, "Well, it's going to with John," noting that Ehrlichman had "narrowed it down to—"

Nixon continued, "My point is, I find that if John is too busy, also John is damned honorable, he is an honorable man—" Haldeman again protested—it was not good to be honorable in Nixon's eyes—and said, "But not like that," suggesting that Ehrlichman was not honorable when it was a matter of going after Nixon's enemies. "And Dean is not honorable," Nixon declared. "He's a crook, he is a snake. But he is good, he's good." Haldeman responded, "The key difference, the critical difference between John Ehrlichman and John Dean in the context that you're talking about is that Ehrlichman is not a hater." Haldeman repeated, "Ehrlichman is tough, but he is not a hater." Nixon then said of Ehrlichman, "He's an executer, and a very good man, he's decent."

"But he is tough. John Ehrlichman is all ambitious as hell," Haldeman said. Nixon continued on Ehrlichman, "Also, he can call someone in and cut them off at the hip pockets, rather, you're fired—" Nixon had a particular example in mind: "Like the [Walter] Hickel thing, he was delighted."* The president qualified that admiration with: "He's not the kind of man who will destroy another man." Which prompted Haldeman to ask, "And Dean?" Nixon, with a speculative tone, said, "Yeah, I think Dean is." Haldeman, liking this reading of me, added, "And he's become more so. Dean has become harder in the job, because he is a guy, in spite of his playboy image, [who] is very deceptive. He is a playboy, he's got a beautiful girl who lives with him, who's not his wife. And he changes them every once in a while."

"That's alright," the president said. And Haldeman added, "And he loves rock music and discotheques. Hard stuff, hard. But—" He was cut off by the president's observation: "You can see that he's a good-looking guy. Christ, in Hollywood he'd be knocking 'em down. But that's alright, that's, I mean—" Haldeman said, "It might even be harmless," and then, speaking over the president, reminded him, "Henry likes good-looking girls, too. But he's damn useful in other ways." The president, with a pained tone, agreed about Kissinger, and Haldeman continued, "But Dean, he's a good judge of people."

"Really?" Nixon said. Haldeman explained, "He isn't taken in by people. He tends to give the benefit, but he isn't. Some people give people the un-benefit, I do—" Nixon interrupted to agree, "Yeah, I do too." Haldeman elaborated, "Assume a guy's no good until he proves he's good." "That's right," Nixon concurred. But Haldeman said, "Dean tends to assume he's good, but he watches him. And when he proves he's no good, he turns on

---

*"Wally" Hickel, a former governor of Alaska, was fired on November 25, 1970, from his post in the Nixon cabinet as secretary of the interior after he wrote a public letter critical of the president's Vietnam policies. Ehrlichman did the deed for the president.

him." The president said he had liked what he had seen during our conversations, and explained to Haldeman, "What I mean is, I'm watching Dean, just as I'm watching [Frank] Carlucci,* and he's enough of a hater, and he's smart enough, you know, what you really need is somebody [not concerned] with screwing the other side."

"That's right," Haldeman agreed. Nixon continued, "Dean is obviously the kind of guy that likes to screw anything, that's really what he is. And that's what we need." Haldeman burst out laughing at Nixon's sexual double entendre, as the president repeated, "And that's what we need. That's what we need."

"That's right," Haldeman agreed.

"And I was impressed with this conversation. I can tell a lot about him. I know this kind. What he's like. He's very erudite. He's beautifully educated and articulate. The same kind of a guy that Bob Stripling[†] used to be," the president said, adding that, although Stripling had a modest education, he was "shit, bright, a super guy" and, most important, he "hated with a passion. He got 'em, he'd go after people and he'd slaughter 'em. And he'd play every trick in the game. And that's what Dean will do."

After the president indicated that Colson, Carlucci and I would be important for his second term, the conversation moved in other directions. Following a meeting with Henry Kissinger and some politicking via telephone with the president of the Utility Workers Union of America, the president was still thinking about our conversation, and he gave credit to Ehrlichman for having brought me into the White House. Haldeman corrected him, explaining that it was he who had brought me onto the staff. "This is one I'll take credit for. We all knew Dean was a good man, but Ehrlichman didn't want him to work for the White House."

---

*When Donald Rumsfeld joined the Nixon administration in 1969, he arranged for his former Princeton roommate, Frank Carlucci, to be transferred from the State Department to help him run—or ruin, depending on one's point of view—the Office of Economic Opportunity (OEO), the agency created by President Johnson to fight poverty. Carlucci replaced Rumsfeld as director of OEO (1971–72) and later became undersecretary of health, education and welfare. Following Watergate, President Ford made Carlucci ambassador to Portugal (1974–77). Next he was deputy director of the CIA (1978–81), then deputy defense secretary (1981–83), then Reagan's national security adviser (1986–87) and then his secretary of defense (1987–89). Most recently I've noticed that Carlucci has parlayed his government experience and contacts into an estimated $60 billion net worth. See www.dailyfinance.com/2013/05/31/frank-carlucci-plastic-into-oil-scam/.

†Chief investigator, House Un-American Activities Committee.

# Segretti Merges with Watergate

## *September 17–30, 1972, the White House*

O ther than in *Washington Post* and occasional *New York Times* stories, Watergate largely dropped from the news after the grand jury's indictments of the Watergate seven. Chuck Colson informed the president on September 17 that McGovern's comments on the indictments had not made a front page anywhere, and, better yet, the latest Harris Poll showed only 11 percent of the public thought the president was somehow involved in Watergate.[1] Nonetheless, Jeane Dixon, a newspaper-syndicated seer and psychic who had famously predicted JFK would "be assassinated or die in office" (while incorrectly predicting any number of other events), regularly shared her private prognostications with Rose Woods, who passed them on to an interested president. On September 19, Ms. Dixon sent word to the president, "the sooner you get rid of [Watergate], the better."[2]

On September 21 Colson reported that "McGovern has shut up on the Watergate; he hasn't talked about that this week."[3] On September 24, Haldeman provided the latest internal polling numbers, which revealed that Watergate was a nonissue in the campaign: 68 percent said it would have no effect on how they voted, 83 percent of likely voters thought Nixon would win reelection, and 70 percent of voters were aware of Watergate.[4] On September 26 Haldeman informed the president that Teddy Kennedy was backing off on holding hearings with his Senate subcommittee because "he's worried about Chappaquiddick, among other things."[5] Haldeman said that the only thing not under control was Texas congressman Wright Patman's Banking and Currency Committee, but he assured the president that that problem was being addressed.* "We've got everything else in good shape," Haldeman advised. "The civil suit's taken care of. The criminal suit's taken care of. The issue [of Watergate] is basically going to go pretty much down the tubes, and they know it," referring to *The Washington Post*.

The *Post*, however, did not see it that way. The paper had been featuring a front-page Watergate-related story almost every day since the June 17 arrests at the DNC, and as the presidential race was winding down it would publish as many as five Watergate-related stories each day. While it had not uncovered anything that surprised those of us in the White House following the investigation, nor was it affecting the campaign, the *Post* was often informing the president of activities about which he had little or no knowledge before reading about them in the newspaper. What troubled Nixon most was the fact that the *Post* appeared to have access to significant leaks, like one that was the basis for a September 29 article headlined MITCHELL CONTROLLED SECRET GOP FUND, which asserted that Mitchell, when serving as attorney general, "personally controlled a secret Republican fund that was used to gather information about the Democrats, according to sources involved in the Watergate investigation." When Mitchell was reached by telephone in New York, he denied the story and attacked "Katie Graham," publisher of the *Post*, with remarks that those of us who knew Mitchell understood were made when he had been drinking. While they had been edited, he clearly had told Woodward that Katie was going to "get her big fat tit in a wringer" if the newspaper continued with such stories.[6]

The president asked Haldeman at the outset of their morning meeting on September 29 about the story: "Do they have some sort of informant or something in there, or [what]?"[7] Haldeman thought (incorrectly) that the information might have come from Bernard Barker, while the president assumed (correctly) that it had come from the FBI. He was not troubled so much by the content of this story as by the fact that it had been leaked from the investigation, and that the *Post* continued to cover Watergate relentlessly. The following morning Nixon learned that his secretary of state, Bill Rogers, had accepted an invitation to participate in the dedication of the new building that would house *The Washington Post*, and he was livid. The president

---

*As I explained in considerable detail in Chapter 8 of *Lost Honor* (New York: Stratford Press/Harper & Row, 1982), the combined involvement of House minority leader Gerry Ford (who later dissembled during his vice presidential confirmation proceedings about his activities) and the White House congressional relations staff successfully closed down the Patman hearings in early October 1972.

directed Haldeman to instruct his cabinet to not attend the ceremony,[8] and that afternoon he again complained about the *Post* to Colson, telling him that anyone on the White House staff who did anything for the *Post* or *New York Times* would be fired. He ridiculed the *Post* for not even knowing Haldeman's name, having sent his invitation for the dedication to "William Haldeman."[9]

## October 3, 1972, the White House

As the president was preparing for a preelection press conference, Haldeman assured him that he had "no Watergate problems."[10] At the time there was little new Watergate information, and the *Post* seemed confined to rehashing old stories. Still, Nixon remained irate at the *Post*, and that afternoon asked Ehrlichman if he was aware of his order to the cabinet and staff to not attend the dedication event.[11] Ehrlichman himself had received an invitation, and the president barked, "Just don't respond. Don't even respond. Don't even say 'I have another engagement.'" With the presidential pique at the *Post* still cresting, Henry Kissinger, who enjoyed bolstering Nixon's darkest thoughts, told him that afternoon that he had been too generous with his media critics. "If you've shown one weakness," Kissinger said, "it's that you've been too gentle. It's certainly not that you've been threatening." To make the point, Kissinger reported that he had broken off "any social contact" with *Post*-owned *Newsweek* columnist Stewart Alsop, who had recently written several nasty columns on Watergate.[12]

Not surprisingly, at the October 5 morning press conference in the Oval Office the first question directed to Nixon asked how he planned to defend his administration against the *Post*'s corruption charges, which the president addressed by ignoring the premise of the question and giving a nonresponsive answer.[13] Watergate was not mentioned by name until the seventh question, which was so ineptly stated that it invited the dodge it received. Nixon again all but ignored it and instead made a couple of points he wanted to stress: "One thing that has always puzzled me about it is why anybody would have tried to get anything out of the Watergate. But be that as it may, that decision having been made at lower levels, with which I had no knowledge, and, as I pointed out—"

"But, surely you know now, sir," the reporter insisted.

"Just a minute," the president said sternly, putting the interruption back behind the decorum line. "I certainly feel that under the circumstances that we have got to look at what has happened and to put the matter into perspective. Now when we talk about a clean breast, let's look at what has happened. The FBI assigned 133 agents to this investigation. It followed about eighteen hundred leads. It conducted fifteen hundred interviews." He reminded the reporters that he personally understood such inquiries because he had once conducted the Hiss investigation, which was "basically a Sunday school exercise compared to the amount of effort that was put into this." But he assured his audience that he had no problem with the resources that had been devoted to the Watergate investigation. "I wanted every lead carried out to the end, because I wanted to be sure that no member of the White House staff, and no man or woman in a position of major responsibility in the committee for the reelection, had anything to do with this kind of reprehensible activity." He added that, because the grand jury had issued indictments, it was "time to have the judicial process go forward and for the evidence to be presented." He reminded the reporters that he had once been lambasted by the news media for commenting on the Manson murder case when it was pending, so he would not comment on the Watergate case.

Haldeman thought the session was one of the best press conferences the president had held in the Oval Office.[14] However, the fact that Nixon kept repeating that no one at the White House had been involved—on this occasion, not invoking any authority for his knowledge, since there was none—was beginning to trouble him, a problem he would seek to address in the coming weeks to protect himself.

*October 10, 1972, the White House*

*The Washington Post* broke one of its biggest Woodward and Bernstein Watergate-related stories on October 10 with a larger than usual front-page headline: FBI FINDS NIXON AIDES SABOTAGED DEMOCRATS. The report stated that "FBI agents have established that the Watergate bugging incident stemmed from a massive campaign of political spying and sabotage conducted on behalf of President Nixon's re-election and directed by officials of the White House and the Committee for the Re-election of the President."[15] It was a game-changing story, because it reframed Watergate as more than a mere bungled burglary at the DNC. According to Bernstein and Woodward's Watergate memoir, *All the President's Men*, they received a telephone tip on

September 28 that led them to the person purportedly running this massive spying and sabotage operation, Donald Segretti, a University of Southern California friend of Haldeman aides Dwight Chapin and Gordon Strachan, both of whom would soon be implicated in hiring him.[16] The *Post*'s information about Segretti had come from attorneys he met while in the army's Judge Advocate General's Corps and attempted to recruit for his operation.

Donald Segretti originally had become entangled in the Watergate investigation some three months earlier, in late June, because his telephone number was in Howard Hunt's telephone toll records, which had been subpoenaed by the FBI. Segretti's connection came as a surprise at the White House, and it took several days to figure out its origins. In a nutshell, the relationship developed before Liddy's illegal intelligence plans had been approved. Liddy had learned that there might be an agent provocateur in the field soliciting recruits for his political pranking from Nixon-Agnew offices throughout the country. He sent a memo to all the offices requesting assistance in identifying the person, and when Magruder learned that the always over-the-top Liddy was threatening to kill this individual, he investigated the matter and resolved it. He called Liddy into his office and explained that this rumored person (who was in fact Segretti) had been hired by Haldeman in 1971, at the suggestion of Chapin and Strachan, to perform pranks and dirty tricks against the Democrats during their primaries that appeared due to Democratic infighting. The goal was to make it more difficult for the Democrats to come together after they selected a nominee. Magruder had learned that Segretti had been paid by Herb Kalmbach from campaign funds left from the 1968 presidential race.[17]

Magruder went to Mitchell and Strachan talked to Haldeman in early 1972 and obtained their agreement that Liddy should take charge of this operation. Liddy was given contact information for a Don Simmons, which was a false name Segretti was using. Liddy (who used the name George Leonard) was joined by Hunt (who used the name Ed Warren) at a meeting with Segretti in Miami in which Liddy told Segretti he was to take instructions from Hunt. Liddy also warned Segretti to be careful with Hunt, and to follow his orders, because he was dangerous: "He sometimes kills without orders. The least he might do would be breaking both your knees."[18] Thereafter Hunt would call Segretti from time to time to check on his activities, and it was these calls (some from the White House) that left the record the FBI discovered after the arrests at the DNC. Not only had Segretti been frightened by Liddy and Hunt, but when they tried to involve him in what he thought might be illegal activities at the Democratic convention in Miami (with the Cuban Americans who were later arrested at the DNC), he wanted nothing to do it.

When the FBI contacted Segretti in June 1972, he called Chapin and Strachan, who requested I meet with him. As best I could tell in a brief meeting, he had no knowledge of or involvement in Watergate whatsoever, and had done nothing illegal, although his activities clearly would be politically embarrassing. I reported the situation to Haldeman and Ehrlichman, including the fact that I had advised Segretti to answer all the FBI's questions honestly. I also recounted telling him that, given the serious potential for leaks, he did not need to volunteer potentially embarrassing information, such as the payments from Herb Kalmbach. Segretti's activities became an issue again in August 1972, during the GOP convention in Miami, when he called Chapin because he had been summoned to testify before the Watergate grand jury. At that time I discussed the situation with Henry Petersen, who said the only information sought from Segretti was his connection to Hunt and Liddy and anything about the Watergate break-in. Petersen said it had been a long-standing policy of the Justice Department not to investigate campaign law violations during a campaign, and he knew of nothing that Segretti had done that called for investigation. Again I advised Segretti to answer all questions honestly before the grand jury. Segretti did, and while the prosecutors did not ask him who hired and paid him, one of the grand jurors did. This, in turn, led to further FBI inquiries of Chapin, Strachan and Kalmbach.[19] In short, by late August 1972 the FBI had the entire story, which it soon began leaking to the *Post* and *Time* magazine, courtesy of Mark Felt.[20] Bernstein and Woodward wrote in *All the President's Men* that the information Bernstein developed from the attorneys Segretti had tried to recruit led Woodward to call for a meeting with his infamous source, Deep Throat, aka Mark Felt. As the seniormost person in charge of the FBI's Watergate investigation he was privy to all the Segretti information. They met on October 8, 1972.[21]

The Segretti story dominated the Watergate-related news from October 10 through the November 7 election, and it became a postelection concern of the president's notwithstanding the decidedly tangential relationship of Segretti's activities to the break-in. The *Post*, however, effectively made Segretti very much a part of the Watergate story, and soon, for both the public and Richard Nixon, any reference to Watergate included events beyond the actual activities related to the arrests at the DNC.

Anticipating probing questions at his daily press briefing on the morning of October 10, given the *Post*'s lengthy Segretti story, Ron Ziegler sought the president's guidance on how he should respond.[22] "Oh, shit, I don't know," Nixon said. "That big story in the *Post* is something. Huge story, but it seems to be a different angle," he noted. Haldeman, who was part of this meeting, agreed with Ziegler that he should just say nothing. "I can do that for an hour and a half," Ziegler assured the president, who predicted "a lot more of this desperate kind" of journalism before Election Day.

After Ziegler left the Oval Office, the president asked Haldeman if this latest story could have had an FBI source or whether it came from Chuck Colson, since it had information about the inner workings of his office. Haldeman thought the FBI was more likely, and although he had only been able to quickly scan the lengthy account, he had noticed that much of the detail was from the lawyers whom this "guy named Spaghetti, or something" had tried to recruit. The *Post* had also charged that Ken Clawson, a former *Post* reporter who now worked for Colson, had boasted to *Post* reporter Marilyn Berger that he had written the so-called Canuck letter that had been published by the *Manchester (NH) Guardian* during the Democratic primaries; it alleged that Senator Edmund Muskie condoned a racial slur on Americans of French Canadian descent by calling them "Canucks." The letter had caused Muskie to cry, which in turn marked the beginning of his failed effort to win the Democratic presidential nomination. Because Haldeman could not answer a number of the president's questions, Colson was summoned to the Oval Office.

"Let me ask this question," the president asked Colson when he arrived. "With regard to that story in the *Post* this morning, the only thing that concerned me was whether or not there's a leak in your office. I just wondered if all that crap—" At which point Haldeman clarified: "Maybe Clawson had something to do with it." "Well, Clawson's explanation of that, Mr. President," Colson reported, "is that he jokingly said to Marilyn Berger, 'That was such an effective letter, I wish I could take credit for having written it.' And she misquoted him and said he'd said he had written it.* I don't believe there's a leak in the office, because there was nothing—"

"I don't mean the Canuck letter," the president clarified. "I am speaking

---

*It took a few days to get this story sorted out. Clawson finally admitted that he had, in fact, falsely made the claim to Berger. The married Mr. Clawson was visiting the unmarried Ms. Berger at her apartment, and boasting to impress her as part of his effort to seduce her, a ploy that backfired on him and accounted for the circumstances that caused him to publicly deny he had told Berger otherwise. Notwithstanding Deep Throat/Mark Felt's claim that this letter was written by someone in the Nixon

of the fact that he said [what] we were doing, you know, various things, writing letters, and all that sort of thing." Colson protested. "No, I never heard of this guy, Segretti. I don't know who the hell he is." By now Haldeman was beginning to recall the details of the situation and confirmed, "Yeah, he isn't one of your people, is he?"

"Oh, hell no, I've never heard of the guy!" Colson stated emphatically. "Well, when the FBI took my statement, they asked me if I'd ever seen the guy. I said, 'No, I've never heard of him. I don't know who he is.' I don't know where that story could—" And he again remonstrated, "It could never come out of my office, you understand."

Nixon was still angry. "I don't give one God damn about it, except to be sure your own people are always"—a thought he did not finish, but instead he began sputtering—"I mean, of course, of course, if we were out of our minds, unless we have adequate, such a way that thing's handled with regard to, to, to handling hecklers and counterhecklers. But for Christ sakes, don't have some asshole in your office go brag about it!" Colson began to explain, "The thing is, Mr. President—" but the president cut him off to continue: "That's what I worry about. They're all the same. Advance men, you know, there's, everybody wants to prove he's a big shot."

Haldeman agreed, and Nixon added, "Everybody wants to prove to you we did great, ah, and we're, ah, we're organized in all the states, and we're going to mail out eighteen million pieces of literature." "The thing about my office," Colson replied, "nothing in that article this morning has anything to do with my office. The things that I have done that could be explosive in the newspaper will never come out, because nobody knows about them. I don't trust anybody in my office." This explanation satisfied both Nixon and Haldeman, with Haldeman and Colson soon agreeing that this had to have been connected to "Liddy's operation" and the same funding that had underwritten him.

*October 12–15, 1972, the White House*

*The Washington Post*, joined by *Time* magazine, the *New York Times* and other publications, as well as by network television news programs on a

---

White House, there is absolutely no evidence whatsoever to support this, including information in the FBI's extensive investigation. The true source of the letter has never been identified.

periodic basis, had found a new angle on Watergate. On October 12 a *Post* editorial declared the break-in itself incidental, albeit significant as one element of a larger pattern of electoral misconduct it called "as deeply inimitable to the rights and the interest of a free people as anything we can think of."[23] It said that, given Deep Throat/Mark Felt's characterization of Segretti's activities as part of a "massive campaign of political espionage and sabotage" and the assertion that "Ken Clawson of the White House staff was the author of a letter bearing a fictitious signature and falsely accusing Sen. Muskie of a slur on an ethic group, [that the] burglary at the Democratic national headquarters last June was nothing compared with what we now are told was being done to prevent the people from making a free choice about who is to govern us during the next four years."

That evening Colson offered the president, who was seething at this turn of events, his counsel: "I think we should stonewall it and try to play it cool."[24] Nixon was not sure whether he should "stir it up or not yet. The God damn story is a phony." But confident he would win the presidency, he decided he could bide his time, and after the election take down the *Post* and the *New York Times* "brick by brick."

On October 13 the *Post* headline reported MUSKIE DETAILS "SABOTAGE" INCIDENTS. The senator had given Woodward and Bernstein details of earlier incidents directed at his campaign seeking the Democratic nomination a week before they had first reported Segretti's sabotage efforts. Much of this harassment of Muskie was also Segretti's work: sending liquor, floral arrangements, pastries and pizza collect to a Muskie fund-raiser in Washington and inviting African diplomats (who were picked up in limos billed to the Muskie campaign) along with two magicians; distributing a flyer in Florida on Muskie stationery accusing his Democratic opponents Hubert Humphrey and Henry Jackson of illicit sexual activity; and sending Democratic contributors in California a letter on Muskie stationery saying he did not want wealthy donors. Other such actions may have been Chuck Colson's work, as Haldeman revealed during the following conversation with Nixon on Friday, October 13.[25]

Haldeman told the president he felt that Ziegler should continue to "not answer" questions about the matter while he tried to figure out how much more such information might surface, and its source, which he assumed was the grand jury and the FBI. However, as damaging as these revelations might be, he explained, "in a way [this reporting] is pretty good." Though he did not spell it out, there was even worse information that could surface: "It's a better string to be running out than some other strings that could come out of that [that] apparently were turned off." As usual, when he mentioned such dark matters, he remained vague, which Nixon appeared to understand. "Because it would be running out to people playing these kinds of games, so I don't think it's going to make much difference. [But] if they ran it into one of Colson's operations, you know, then it could be harmful. [And] I'm [pretty sure] this Muskie stuff is a Colson operation."

Although everyone was aware that the president privately gave Colson unsavory assignments, Nixon protested innocence: "Bob, I never knew about it." To which Haldeman replied, "Well, I didn't, either." The president explained that this was why he wanted "a white paper on it," a report that would lay out the facts but would not cause anyone problems.

At the end of that day Haldeman and Ziegler had great fun keeping me on the telephone to make me late for my wedding, since I had requested two weeks off to get married, believing, as I had told the president on September 15, that nothing was going to come crashing down before the election. Although Woodward and Bernstein had informed Ziegler that they had a story about Dwight Chapin, the president's appointment secretary—that he was a contact for Segretti, and that he and Howard Hunt had allegedly met with Segretti in Miami—I knew it was false, and no one was truly concerned about it. As I explained to Haldeman, the Segretti situation was a public relations matter that others were far more able to handle than me.

On October 15 the *Post* broke it as another banner headline front-page story, KEY NIXON AIDE NAMED AS "SABOTAGE" CONTACT, reporting that Dwight Chapin was "the person in charge of Mr. Nixon's schedule and appointments, including overall coordination of trips. Chapin is one of a handful of White House staff members with easy access to the President." The *Post*'s description of Chapin's role was in fact one of Haldeman's key activities, for Chapin seldom met with the president but learned of his schedule only after Haldeman and the president had decided upon it. But given that Woodward and Bernstein had uncovered Chapin's involvement with his former USC classmate Segretti, they needed to make him, a middle-level staffer, much closer to Nixon than he actually was. While they initially had gotten the Hunt connection wrong, they corrected it before publication. Chapin had given them a statement, through Ziegler: It said that the story was based on hearsay, denied that he knew Hunt and acknowledged his knowing Segretti only from their USC days and denied meeting with him in Florida. He refused to comment further.[26] The rest of the story was based on information Segretti had given a friend of his, a California attorney named Lawrence Young to whom Segretti had confided when seeking legal advice, believing the information protected by attorney-client privilege. Young, however, thought otherwise and gave the *Post* a sworn affidavit revealing what Segretti had told him, namely that "Dwight Chapin was a person I reported to in Washington" and outlining Segretti's activities since he had been discovered by the FBI.

The president was at Camp David when this *Post* story broke, and he observed to Haldeman when they met early that day, "I think that's really a shocking God damn story on Chapin this morning."[27] While the president noted that it was all hearsay, it was nevertheless not good for the White House. "Did, is Segretti, what, is he rabid? What, did he get mad about something?" the president asked, wondering why Segretti had revealed all this information to Lawrence Young, who the story acknowledged called himself "a liberal Democrat."

Haldeman explained how it had all unfolded, about the mistaken trust Segretti had placed in Young, and noted that while the facts of the piece were largely correct, it was not the entire story. The *Post* had not reported that Herb Kalmbach had been paying Segretti both a salary and the expenses for his operation. "But what does Kalmbach say? Is he tied in there as attorney for the president? How does he handle it?" Nixon asked. Haldeman was certain that Kalmbach had already explained his role to the FBI, which meant that this information might leak at any time. "I think you better get, pretty quickly, the story ready on Kalmbach, as to what funds he was using," the president instructed. Nixon wanted Kalmbach portrayed not as a private attorney who did work for the president but rather as a fund-raiser for the reelection committee, given that this was already public. (Within hours, however, Kalmbach would be identified and thrust into the sabotage story by *Time* magazine as "the president's personal attorney"—which would be his moniker throughout Watergate.) Haldeman believed the *Post* had gone after Chapin because McGovern was giving a big speech on corruption in the Nixon White House and this provided new and timely material. He said the timing could not be worse for Chapin, who had just been informed he had been selected by the Chamber of Commerce as one of the ten outstanding young men in America—a selection likely to be withdrawn because of this story. Haldeman added that Chapin had offered to resign, but the president rejected it out of hand.

"John Dean just got married Friday night," Haldeman reported, as the conversation was coming to a close. The president wanted to know whom I had married, and Haldeman said the girl I had been living with. Then, still laughing about it, Haldeman said, "He was getting married at seven-thirty, and at seven-ten we were still talking to him on the phone about this, and I said, 'Jeez, John, don't you think you better go get ready for your wedding?'" Haldeman did not mention his order to me that morning to cut short my honeymoon and return to Washington, and that as he was talking with the president, I was heading back to Washington. That afternoon I went to the White House to prepare Ziegler to take on the *Post* on Monday, a meeting that also included Ehrlichman, Chapin, Pat Buchanan and Richard "Dick" Moore.[28]

### October 16, 1972, the White House

On Monday, back at the White House, when the president asked what Ziegler's approach would be at the press conference, Haldeman said that he would "go out with a very strong personal reaction today, of indignity and disgust, really."[29] Nixon had read the latest charges made by the *Post* and observed that what "they're trying to do is tie it to me, personally." The paper wanted "to indicate that I was not telling the truth when I said that nobody in the White House was involved in it, correct?" Haldeman acknowledged that they were trying "to link the Spaghetti thing with the Watergate."

"Are they linked?" Nixon pressed. "No," Haldeman answered. "Under no circumstances?" Nixon pressed. "Nobody, nobody knew about it, huh?" Haldeman responded emphatically, "Nobody's God damn lying," and to be clear, he added, "on the Watergate, no." Then he said, "And they are not linked, except in the sense that Howard Hunt—" Nixon now injected, clear that he understood, "—worked on both." Haldeman repeated, "Worked on both, and I guess, because he apparently was in contact with Segretti," reporting something he had discovered in the *Post* story, for he had earlier thought it was Liddy who had been the contact. "I just want to know whether Chapin or any of your guys were involved in Watergate," the president asked. Haldeman was unequivocal: "No, sir."

Nixon favored Ziegler and MacGregor both launching frontal attacks on

*The Washington Post*, a tactic that could be carried out at the press conference. Ziegler called the Chapin story "malicious" but refused to take questions. Similarly, MacGregor read a statement saying that the *Post* was "using
innuendo, third-person hearsay, unsubstantiated charges, [and] huge scare
headlines [to try] to give the appearance of a direct connection between the
White House and the Watergate," which it knew was false. The orchestrated
attack on the paper led executive editor Benjamin Bradlee to issue a statement: "Time will judge between Clark MacGregor's press releases and *The
Washington Post*'s reporting of the various activities of the Committee for
the Re-election of the President. For now it is enough to say that not a single
fact contained in the investigative reporting of this newspaper about these
activities has been successfully challenged."[30]

### October 17–20, 1972, the White House

John Connally dropped by the White House to hold a brief press conference
on October 17, which Haldeman attended. Afterward Connally reported to
the president on his Democrats for Nixon organization, more specifically
about their ongoing fund-raising efforts, and they had their first conversation about Watergate—largely a rehash of the Watergate and Segretti stories,
which the president and Haldeman protested were the efforts of *The Washington Post* and not real problems.[31]

The following morning the *Post* reported that Chief U.S. District Court
Judge John J. Sirica, brushing aside the objections of defense lawyers, ordered that the trial of the seven men charged with the Watergate bugging
incident begin on November 15, 1972. But the *Post* added, "Lawyers for the
defendants indicated after the two-hour hearing that they would seek a postponement from the U.S. Court of Appeals."[32] That afternoon, in a meeting
that included Ehrlichman, Haldeman reported to Nixon that Teddy Kennedy had changed his mind and was now going to investigate Segretti's activities. This led to a discussion of a *New York Times* story reporting that
twenty-eight phone calls had been made by Segretti to the White House,
meaning either to Chapin or to Hunt, but because the recipients of the calls
had not been identified, the piece was heavy on innuendo.[33] Ehrlichman
noted that the *Post* was "equating Chapin with Ellsberg," which was beyond
a stretch by both Ehrlichman, if he could justify his conclusion, which I
cannot, and the *Post*. He added that the *Times* was busy building up Chapin's

authority, making him responsible for "key decisions." Both Haldeman and
Ehrlichman remarked that the *Times* had him dealing with the president on
a daily basis, although Haldeman had checked and found that "he was in
here [the president's office] once, but I think it was over a year ago." The
president could recall only a single visit in the previous four years.

While Haldeman and Ehrlichman were with the president, I was meeting
with Henry Petersen at the Department of Justice to discuss the congressional investigations of Watergate. During that visit Petersen told me in the
strictest confidence—because he believed the White House should know—
that Mark Felt was the source of any number of FBI leaks. Petersen said he
had not informed Pat Gray or Dick Kleindienst because he feared they might
overreact, and Felt on the loose could cause even more serious problems.
Petersen, who had once been an FBI agent, had known Felt for years and did
not hold him in high esteem; he told me that Felt was known by his colleagues as "the white rat" because of his prematurely white hair and his inclination to talk to the press. When I asked Petersen how he knew Felt was
leaking, he assured me that he had rock-solid evidence. An attorney whom
Petersen had promised not to name represented one of the publications to
which Felt had been leaking, and he had confided in Petersen because he was
worried that they were receiving grand jury information and wanted to protect his client.[34]

Because of Haldeman's schedule, I did not meet with him until the following afternoon, October 19, in his office, and shortly after our session
ended the president called him to his EOB office. Their conversation began
with a discussion of Nixon's planned reorganization of the executive branch
during his second term, and only when the president raised the possibility
of a leak at the FBI did Haldeman reveal that he had learned who the leaker
was.[35] "You know, if there is a leak down at the FBI, why the hell can't Gray
tell us?" Nixon asked. "What the hell is left? You know what I mean?" Haldeman commented, "We know what's left. And we know what's leaked, and we
know who leaked it. The FBI doesn't know they have a leak. Gray doesn't
know who's leaking, and it's pretty high up."

"Somebody next to Gray?" Nixon asked, and Haldeman minced no
words: "Mark Felt." Nixon, annoyed, wondered, "Now, why the hell would
he do this?" Without attempting to account for Felt's motive, Haldeman
warned, "You can't say anything about this, because it will screw up our
source, and there's a real concern. Mitchell is the only one that knows this,

and he feels very strongly that we better not do anything, because if we move on him, then he'll go out and unload everything. He knows everything that's to be known in the FBI." Nixon agreed, as Haldeman continued to insist, "Can't do anything! Never!"

Haldeman again warned, "He has access to absolutely everything. Ehrlichman doesn't know this yet. I just got this information. I was going to tell Ehrlichman without telling him the source." Nixon agreed, "Don't tell him, don't tell him the source," and they discussed whether or not to tell Pat Gray, thinking they should at least warn him, even if not revealing precisely what they knew. Haldeman said that the last bombshell that Felt might leak would be the information about Jeb Magruder and Bart Porter funding Liddy's operation. As the conversation continued, he explained, although *Time* magazine already had some of this information, he believed the reelection committee could explain those few facts.

"What would you do with Felt, Bob?" the president asked. "Well, I asked Dean on that," Haldeman replied. Nixon pressed, "What the hell would he do?" "He says you can't prosecute him," Haldeman reported, which Nixon did not understand, so Haldeman explained, "He hasn't committed any [crime]." When the president suggested that they would have to "live with it," Haldeman proposed having him transferred to "Ottumwa, Iowa," but Nixon worried that he might then go out and write a book.

"You know what I'd do with him," Nixon said: "Ambassador." Both fell silent to consider this option (which Nixon would later use as a way to dispose of CIA director Richard Helms), until Haldeman quietly agreed, "Something like that, yeah." The president asked how Haldeman had learned about Felt, and he explained that it had come to "a guy" at the Justice Department whom Haldeman did not name. "The guy at Justice told John Dean," Haldeman continued. "And he has not told anybody else, including Kleindienst or Pat Gray, because he's afraid that either of them might react in such a way as to do more harm than good."[36] Nixon concluded, "It's better to say nothing." A surprised Haldeman asked, "Say nothing?" "Absolutely," Nixon instantly affirmed.

The following morning, October 20, the president told Haldeman that he had thought further about Felt and the potential dangers of removing him.[37] While he had concluded that they should not inform Gray, he noted, "Now, the other thing that concerns me is Ehrlichman's relationship with this fellow. He says that this fellow has handled a lot of problems for him. I don't

know what they are. Will you check with him and find out?" Haldeman said
he would do so. Nixon continued, "Well, I think you better tell him what the
situation is. But also, he's got to see what kinds of games this fellow, what he
knew, he may not. But I think Ehrlichman said that he is the man that did
[things]; I'm not aware of anything." Haldeman did not know either, but
offered, "Ehrlichman said he had been involved in a lot of things with the
FBI," though he did not know specifically what those thing might have involved. "[Felt's] his contact. See, that's the thing I'm concerned with," the
president repeated, to make his point, and Haldeman assured him that he
would speak with Ehrlichman but would not tell Gray anything.[38]

### October 24, 1972, the White House

During an Oval Office conversation Haldeman advised the president that
both Chuck Colson and John Ehrlichman were concerned about a CBS News
story by Daniel Schorr that had been picked up by the *Post*.[39] The paper reported that "President Nixon has ordered a reopening of a White House
investigation into the June 17 Watergate bugging incident, CBS News said
last night." The report stated, "According to Schorr, the inquiry was resumed,
'after President Nixon was cautioned by acting FBI director L. Patrick Gray
that the agency had established more serious direct links to the White House
than the President might know about." The piece added that I, "who had
conducted the original Watergate inquiry for President Nixon, was said by
CBS to have interviewed Dwight Chapin and Donald Segretti." The *Post*
wire-service story said that Schorr had not specified if I would be inquiring
into "alleged sabotage and spying activities."[40]

The president wanted to know if this was bad. Haldeman thought not,
although, he noted, "the Schorr thing is a complete lie." All this talk of my
investigations resulted in Haldeman's asking me to gather the facts relating
to the Segretti-Strachan-Chapin situation. When Haldeman mentioned this
to the president later that morning, Nixon observed, "I just don't see how we
can do anything but lose by trying to come out in a white paper."[41] Nonetheless, Haldeman wanted me to prepare one, "just because we ought to have
one anyway" and to see "what it looks like." In the early afternoon Colson
told the president that the public thought the McGovern campaign was ha-
rassing Nixon with Watergate and Segretti, which was why it was having no
impact on him in the polls.[42]

*October 25–26, 1972, the White House*

As Election Day approached the *Post* fired one last big volley, at Haldeman, which was as close to the president as they could get: an October 25 front-page story, along with a smiling albeit oversized picture of "H.R. (Bob) Haldeman," with the banner headline: TESTIMONY TIES TOP NIXON AIDE TO SECRET FUND. This was the biggest Watergate story the *Post* had run, and its opening paragraph reported that the president's chief of staff "was one of five high-ranking presidential associates authorized to approve payments from a secret Nixon campaign cash fund, according to federal investigators and accounts of sworn testimony before the Watergate grand jury."[43] The implication was obvious: The president's top aide was connected to Watergate. There was, however, a fundamental problem with the account: It stated that Hugh Sloan had given this sworn testimony naming Haldeman, when, in fact, he had not, nor had Haldeman been interviewed by the FBI. Haldeman had denied the charges against him through White House deputy press secretary Gerald Warren when the *Post* sought a comment the preceding evening.

Not before this story, nor afterward, did Ron Ziegler so aggressively attack any news organization as he did the *Post* that morning—which itself became a front-page story the following day, quoting him denouncing the paper's reporting as "political" and "the shoddiest type of journalism." Even after learning that Sloan's lawyer had informed the *Post* of its error, Ben Bradlee issued a statement saying, "We stand by our story."[44] Woodward and Bernstein later admitted that they "had assumed too much" and been persuaded "by their own deductions." Even Mark Felt, meeting with Woodward at Deep Throat's favorite underground garage, chastised them, calling their story "the worst possible setback," because they had "people feeling sorry for Haldeman," something Felt had not believed possible.[45]

In truth, and notwithstanding Ziegler's highly staged furor, beyond the press room the story barely sent a ripple though the Nixon White House. A few wisecracks were made at the 8:15 A.M. staff meeting during the discussion of how to handle it, and all agreed it should be addressed aggressively, since the *Post* was oblivious to simple denials. The president, who was in a prescheduled appointment with Henry Kissinger regarding a prospective peace settlement in Vietnam, phoned Ziegler, who stepped out of the staff meeting, and in the course of their conversation mentioned the Haldeman

story, which the president had not bothered to read.[46] Ziegler told Nixon it
was an opportunity to hit the *Post,* because the story was filled with errors,
and that they were working on the response. The president, however, was
more concerned about how they handled Vietnam.

This matter was not taken up with the president again until Haldeman
met with him in the EOB office later that morning.[47] "Anything about Watergate?" the president asked. Haldeman said the *Post* did not mention the
Watergate break-in per se and proceeded to summarize the serious errors in
the piece. There was a brief discussion of who would respond, and Haldeman
was happy to have Ziegler handle it.

The story was still being discussed the next morning, October 26, only
because it had made front-page news in a number of newspapers. During a
morning meeting in the Oval Office with Ehrlichman, Nixon mentioned and
asked for his view on the fact that the *Post* had done stories on both Colson
and Haldeman, but said, "[T]his whole business about sabotage is ridiculous," because it was part of the normal presidential election process.[48] Citing
Democratic demonstrations conspicuously planned to disrupt some of his
appearances, Nixon was troubled by the hypocrisy of refusing to call those
efforts sabotage while accusing his own campaign of engaging in it. "What
I've always told the people here, for Christ sake, let's find out what the other
side is doing, so that we can have intelligence," the president asserted, though
he did worry that Chapin had gotten carried away with Segretti.

"Actually, as near as I can tell, what Dean's checking shows, Chapin never
programmed this guy," Ehrlichman reported. "He recruited him, he sent
him over to do this kind of thing, to do disruption, but Dwight never programmed him. He never told him what to do, never told him where to go,
only took reports from him a couple of times, and then in kind of a humorous offhand way, because Segretti just didn't report to him."*

The president's takeaway from the *Post* attack on Haldeman remains difficult to understand, based on the recorded conversations, as his reactions
appear to be buried in the personal material withdrawn by NARA from the
public. When dictating to his diary on October 25, however, he noted,
"Haldeman spoke rather darkly of the fact that there was a clique in the
White House that were out to get him. I trust he is not getting a persecution

---

*On November 5, 1972, Dwight Chapin would provide me (and John Ehrlichman) with much more
detailed information about his interactions with Segretti, and they were more extensive than first
outlined. See *U.S. v. Chapin* (trial transcript, Criminal Court, No. 990-73), April 3, 1974, 422–31.

complex." The president added (although there is no record of the call in the president's daily diary) that he phoned Haldeman from the residence to reassure him: "We were going to have to take some heat in the next two weeks, but that we would sail through and not be knocked off balance."[49]

## *October 28, 1972, the White House*

On October 27 CBS News televised a special Watergate report based largely on *Washington Post* coverage. The president, who had not watched it, read a detailed report about it in his news summary on October 28, which prompted him to ask Haldeman if he had viewed it as soon as he arrived in the Oval Office that morning.[50] Haldeman said CBS had planned a one-hour special but had cut it back to only fifteen minutes. "Well, this is very damaging," the president observed. Haldeman could see the president was reading the news summary's report of the broadcast, so he explained that Mort Allin, Pat Buchanan's assistant who had prepared it, had gotten very excited about it, but in fact there had been no new news in it. Haldeman also reported that Colson had called Frank Stanton, the president of the network, and learned that they were going to run more of it that night, programming that Haldeman dismissed as "despicable." Colson was then summoned to the Oval Office and instructed to deal with CBS, to go "kick 'em in the ass."

As the final week of the 1972 presidential campaign arrived, the president was preoccupied with his efforts to reach an acceptable peace accord with North Vietnam, and the record shows that neither Watergate nor his reelection campaign were given much consideration. Clearly he was already thinking ahead to his second term.

# Reelection, Reorganization, a Dean Report Considered, Chapin's Departure and Dorothy Hunt's Death

*November 1–7, 1972, the White House and the Campaign Trail*

Although Watergate had effectively become a nonissue as of the week before the 1972 presidential election, in an EOB office meeting during the early afternoon of November 1, Ehrlichman suggested that the president or the White House mention "a tentative investigation" on all the Chapin and other recent allegations. This, he said, would "set the stage for somebody, Dean or me, or somebody, to then make ourselves available, and say, Okay, here's what we found out. Chapin did this and this, Segretti did this and this," based on affidavits that would be gathered.[1] Ehrlichman suggested an "investigative group in the White House [of] Dean, Dick Moore, who is an attorney and who has been in on this right from the beginning, and me." The work would be completed "about the first of December, or sooner, if necessary." The president approved of the idea.

In a rambling late-afternoon conversation on November 2 with Haldeman, in the EOB office, a frustrated Nixon pushed his chief of staff so he could better understand how the Segretti and Watergate debacles had come about. Haldeman had concluded that the core of all these problems was Liddy, which he summed up as "If you want to get right down to what went wrong."[2] The president added that he felt "Martha and John is what went wrong," but Haldeman explained that it had all started even before Mitchell went over to the CRP: What had happened was that they had Jeb Magruder, who hadn't known what he was doing, and it was now clear that Liddy hadn't either. (It is unfortunate that this conversation is not more audible, for at one point Haldeman takes Nixon back to the origins of the plan to gather intelligence during the 1972 campaign—the idea of using Jack Caulfield—and that Mitchell had rejected that plan, called Operation Sandwedge.)

Shortly before noon on Friday, November 3, the president, joined by the First Lady, headed on a last campaign swing, flying to Chicago, Tulsa and Providence and calling supporters in the U.S. Senate from Air Force One as he moved about the country. On November 4, before leaving for another campaign flight, he met with Haldeman, and at one point in their EOB office conversation the president announced, "I have done some thinking in terms of Watergate."[3] That thinking concerned how he was going to keep himself above the fray and defend himself, namely by repeating the following: He had been "shocked to learn of the break-in"; he had "read the riot act to everybody in the White House"; he had made "Dean responsible"; and he had "told Clark MacGregor he was responsible to investigate." None of this happened to be true, as the record shows, but Nixon was constantly refining his defense.

After that meeting the president headed for his helicopter on the South Grounds of the White House, and then to Andrews Air Force Base and his final campaign trip, to Winston-Salem, Albuquerque and on to Ontario, California, which was followed by a short helicopter trip to his San Clemente compound. He continued campaigning via telephone and recorded television messages until he voted in San Clemente at 7:00 A.M. on Tuesday, November 7, before flying back to the nation's capital at ten that morning.

Nixon's reelection victory was a massive landslide in which he carried every state but Massachusetts, and the District of Columbia, by significant margins. When the votes were all tallied he had received 60.67 percent of the popular vote and 538 electoral votes, or 96.65 percent of the Electoral College, placing him just behind Franklin Roosevelt and Lyndon Johnson in historic wins. Nixon, however, failed to carry Congress, which was the only hope—a quiet but not unspoken White House staff hope—to bring an end to Watergate. Nixon had not bothered to campaign for congressional candidates or to make any real effort to win GOP control, and he did not have sufficient coattails to give the Republicans control of either the Senate or the House of Representatives, which meant that Watergate would not end with the trial of the Watergate seven.

To most all who saw Nixon on election night it was clear that his victory had not really boosted his spirits. He was in a terrible mood, depressed and barely able to even pretend he was a winner, later writing that he was "at a loss to explain the melancholy that settled over [him] on that victorious night." He did suggest in his memoirs that to "some extent the marring effects of Watergate" weighed on him. He clearly understood that his failure to win Congress meant Watergate would loom large in the coming days and months.[4*]

### November 8, 1972, the White House

To the absolute surprise of nearly every member of the White House staff, the cabinet and the subcabinet, they were all fired. After the president attended the morning staff meeting to thank the group for its help in his re-election, and to request their assistance in reorganizing the executive branch for the second term, Haldeman took over the meeting and asked for everyone's resignation. From there the president went to a cabinet meeting in which he gave a similar talk, and was again followed by Haldeman requesting everyone's resignation, along with instructions to obtain the resignations of all the presidential appointees within their departments or agencies as well. The process was handled brutally, and everyone was confused, if not angry. During my meeting with the president on September 15 I had become privy to these plans, and Haldeman had told me that, because of Watergate, I would be asked to remain on staff. He had also requested that I check on several legal issues before the mass resignation requests were issued. (Haldeman also submitted his resignation, along with Ehrlichman's, when flying back to Washington from San Clemente on Election Day, but the president rejected both.[5])

By midmorning on November 8 it occurred to me that the White House would not want to upset Assistant Attorney General Henry Petersen, who was in charge of the Watergate investigation, so I called Haldeman to get his approval to assure Petersen he would not lose his job as the head of the Criminal Division. Both Haldeman and Petersen appreciated that I had taken care of this detail before I flew off to California to meet with Donald Segretti to pull together a quick investigation of what, in fact, he had done for and with people in the Nixon White House. The president, meanwhile,

---

*The Watergate cover-up activity grew in intensity after the election, and there were countless conversations and meetings in which I exchanged information and received directions from Haldeman, Ehrlichman and Mitchell. But either because Nixon was spending significant time out of the White House, or because Haldeman and Ehrlichman were not discussing the subject with him, there is relatively little activity recorded by Nixon in either his tapes or his diary during this period other than that noted through the end of the year.

accompanied by Haldeman and Ehrlichman, headed to Florida to focus in earnest on the task of reorganizing the executive branch with new personnel (including shifting some tested people to new jobs) as he sought to reinvigorate his administration. In the coming weeks it was clear that Nixon and his senior staff had created a remarkable amount of ill will in Washington with their postelection ingratitude, a problem that would soon return to haunt his presidency.

## November 10-12, 1972, Key Biscayne

No sooner had I completed an extended interview with Segretti in Palm Springs on November 10 than I was summoned to Key Biscayne. On November 11, I met with Haldeman and Ehrlichman at the guest house in the presidential compound so that they could listen to the recording of my session with Segretti (which was made with his consent). As usual, Haldeman made detailed notes, and then went to the president's home to report what Segretti had revealed. While not sinister, his actions were political pranks in the extreme.

On November 12 Haldeman told me I should return to Washington with the president when he and his staff departed on Air Force One that evening. During the flight Nixon came back to the guest compartment to meet my wife, and he warned her, "We're going to keep your husband damn busy."[6] My role had changed. With Watergate I had been simply picking up tidbits of information from Liddy, Magruder, Mitchell, Mardian and Kalmbach, as well as from the lawyers hired to represent the reelection committee, and became a go-between for Haldeman and Ehrlichman with Mitchell. Now I was responsible for directly investigating Segretti's relationship to the White House, a project on which I worked, along with my many other assignments in the counsel's office, until early December.

## November 13-14, 1972, Camp David

After his postelection respite in Florida, the president headed for Camp David on Monday morning, November 13, where he remained based for much of the rest of the month, with Haldeman and Ehrlichman joining him for lengthy stays. It was there they worked on the fundamental reorganization of the executive branch of the government, creating presidential counselors who would have jurisdiction over various departments and agencies while reporting directly to the president or his senior staff. Along with the restructuring of the lines of authority, the three men were busy deciding who would actually run the government. The president decided to keep Kleindienst as attorney general for a year, and said to Ehrlichman on November 14, in a discussion of the Department of Justice, that he would tell Kleindienst, "We can't make an exception of your department, Dick. We're cleaning up all the departments, so they're going to go."[7] But then, remembering Watergate, the president remarked, "We can't start making exceptions, with the possible exception of Petersen." Then he said to Ehrlichman, "I understand you want to keep him." Ehrlichman chuckled, sarcastically responding, "I don't necessarily want to, but we've got to, he's got the—" The president interrupted, saying, "He knows too much." And Ehrlichman kept talking, explaining, "He's got the keys to the can."

Another Watergate-sensitive appointment that arose during this conversation was the director of the FBI. The president wanted a cop at the FBI, and liked Jerry Wilson, who was the head of the DC Metropolitan Police, as long as Ehrlichman was "sure he's a ballplayer." "I just don't want Gray to have to go up for confirmation," Nixon added. "That's the problem with Gray." He liked the idea of appointing Gray as undersecretary of state, seemingly forgetting that this, too, was a post that would require confirmation.

### November 24, 1972, the White House

The subject of Henry Petersen arose again when the president returned to the White House for a day. Nixon complained to Ehrlichman during a morning meeting in the Oval Office: He was annoyed that the Justice Department had yet to prosecute anyone regarding Watergate.[8] Still, the president told Ehrlichman, he wanted to give an appearance of change, although he acknowledged that "Petersen has got to be kept." Ehrlichman agreed and said he had confirmed that after further checking, and added, "He's adequate, and when this thing is over, we'll find a nice judgeship for him, and he can go out."

During a brief meeting before heading to New York City that afternoon, the president explained to Haldeman that he had been doing further thinking about Watergate:[9] "I had thought that what ought to happen, I been doing some more reading about the Watergate thing, and so forth. Why the hell don't you get Mitchell and John Ehrlichman, you and Dean and sit down and thrash the damn thing out?"

"Ehrlichman, Dean and I are going to do that right now. Let us go one round first before we get into—"

"Here's what I would like to do with it, and right here, maybe Dean will have to say something," he began telling Haldeman. "The main thing that we've got to do is to protect the presidency, and on that, we need a simple, clear statement, and we need it early, which simply says again what we've already said, by Dean, and in the form of a report to the president." He began describing what my report should say: "'Pursuant to your request, I have made an investigation in regard, for the so-called Watergate incident now, [and] I have found that there is no present member of the White House staff who was, who had knowledge of it, or was involved in the, da da da, Watergate matter.'" He then explained, "You see, I have said that publicly, and I want him to say it again." But the president wanted even more, although he was not clear on how it would be phrased: "Ah, [then, I would] go on to say, I've also found that ah, that ah, ah, that ah, neither ah, neither ah, ah," but when he could not clarify his thoughts he fell silent for a moment, until he finally continued. "If he can, you ought to use the opportunity to clear Stans, and the finance committee, you know what I mean? Just say that they were not involved. As far as your campaign committee, if they're not cut out, they're, it is because, you should just say they're going on with the investigation, but, but, I conducted, my investigation indicates that ah, that, that, at least Stans, I mean, maybe you can get that out of the way, such, so that I can, so you say, that Secretary Stans had no knowledge, nothing to do with it, and Attorney General Mitchell, former attorney general Mitchell. Don't go any further than that, don't go any further. Don't go down to Magruder or people like that, because you're going to get your ass caught."

Then he said, "Now, with regard to the Segretti thing, he should just say that, ah, maybe that statement has to come a little later, but it should be one. We get all the business about, as John [Ehrlichman] says, letting it all hang out. Let's find some sort of a peace. But in the end, there may not be that flat, categorical statement. And I think it's got to come from Dean, that I conducted an investigation pursuant to your direction. I have found that, and then maybe this will fix everything, if he names names. For example, he should tick them off: that Mr. Haldeman was involved. Untrue. Mr. Colson was involved. Untrue. That, ah, as far as Mr. Chapin was concerned, he recommended, and so forth."

He soon continued, "I think that kind of statement is needed from the standpoint of the presidency. Now, I don't want to do anything that will harm other individuals if we can avoid it, but you see, by that you get the very simple statement that that's what it was about. That's the kind of thing, you see, that will, that we can stand on. As Ziegler says, there's the statement that we stand on. And now John Ehrlichman's view probably will be, and Dean's as a lawyer, we'll let it all come out, and it will be clear that the president's not involved." But he did not want to wait on the legal process, telling Haldeman, "This is a public relations exercise as much as anything else. Dean has got to report that pursuant to my directions he has conducted a thoroughgoing investigation of this and has found that so forth. See what I mean?"

Haldeman, who had been making notes, responded, "Yep, he has to draw that conclusion, or else you'll be—" Nixon interrupted, "There was no White House participant." He explained how the report could state that Chapin had not directed Segretti, but Haldeman cautioned him that this was "shady ground." As their conversation about Chapin, and also Strachan, continued, the president asked, "Well, what is your view, Bob, about Chapin, what we could do with him? Don't forget, now is the time we've got to do something there." Haldeman, without missing a beat, replied, "Well, I think he's got to move out," to which Nixon said, "No question about that."

"And, I mean, out of government. I don't think he should just move out of the White House," Haldeman clarified, noting, "I think if he stays around somewhere else, you got a problem. But don't rush him out." The president suggested having him work for his foundation, but Haldeman thought not; rather, they might assist in placing him with the Marriott Corporation, which sponsored special events, a subject of interest to Chapin. As for Strachan, they would place him elsewhere in government. "Well, we've got to clean the skirts," the president said, to sum up.

While Nixon was in New York, dropping by his former law firm, Mudge, Rose, Guthrie and Alexander, to say hello, Haldeman called for a meeting with Ehrlichman and me, and we gathered in Ehrlichman's office for a lengthy afternoon session at which Haldeman reported on his conversation with the president. That evening Haldeman noted the outcome of our meeting in his diary: "Decided we'd have to follow the full-disclosure route on Segretti, and that we can't do anything much on Watergate because of the court case."[10] It was agreed that I should prepare a report on Segretti.

*December 5, 1972, the White House*

Although the president's schedule, as well as his thinking, was dominated by his efforts to negotiate a peace settlement in Vietnam, Haldeman continued to share incidental matters of interest, such as the fact that Teddy Kennedy's Senate subcommittee was undertaking an investigation of Segretti.[11] In passing, the president asked about the Dean report, and Haldeman said, "Yeah, I should have it today, his draft."

*December 9, 1972, Camp David*

On Saturday the president slept late, had breakfast at 10:30 A.M. and started making calls from his Aspen Lodge study. At 12:30 P.M. he phoned Chuck Colson, who gave him information that would have a significant impact on the handling of Watergate:[12] "I just got a terribly tragic bit of news. That plane crash," Colson said, referring to the widely reported crash of United Flight Number 553 the preceding Friday afternoon, December 8, at Chicago's Midway International Airport. "Howard, Howard Hunt's wife was on it, and it's—" Nixon cut him off, "His wife is dead?" Colson, depressed and shaken, answered, "Yes, sir. She was killed in that plane crash in Chicago." "Oh, my God," Nixon replied. Colson understood that the loss of Dorothy Hunt— who he told the president was an extraordinary woman, brilliant, charming, polylingual and the mother of four beautiful children—would be devastating for her husband.

*December 10, 1972, the White House*

On Sunday morning Haldeman spoke with the president about the Chicago airline crash.[13] "That was a tragedy, wasn't it?" Haldeman said, when Nixon raised the subject. "Oh, Christ! I don't care what the hell he ever did or anything like that," the president replied, and mentioned that he was going to send a condolence note to Howard Hunt. But when he learned more details on the aftermath of the crash, he decided against it. Haldeman informed the president that ten thousand dollars in cash, in hundred-dollar bills, had been found in Dorothy Hunt's purse, which had been recovered from the plane's wreckage. When Haldeman said that they would probably be tracking the serial numbers on the bills, the stunned president asked hopefully, "Who gave 'em to him? We didn't?" Haldeman did not know where the money had come from: "You know, whether it's theirs, or there's payoff money involved in it, it could be some of it, a lot of bills."* Of course, if it was indeed payoff money, it could present a very serious new problem. When the president said he had not seen that information in the press reports, Haldeman reported that he had read about it in a wire service story.

When Nixon remarked that he hoped Hunt would be able to explain the cash, Haldeman pointed out that they "may not be able to track it, he may have been smart enough to wash it," making it untraceable. "Suppose, incidentally, this money is tracked back, who is it tracked to?" Nixon asked, clearly concerned that it might be traced back to someone close to him. Haldeman did not think that was a problem, and explained, "They put together some cash to take care of these people. I don't know where it came from. I assume they were smart enough to do it [so] that it was not traceable cash, as the other stuff," Haldeman noted, referring to the money found earlier in Barker's account.

Later in the conversation the president returned to Watergate: "Oh, incidentally, on the PR side, I thought of something else. I don't like the White House staff getting bad PR, or bad raps; we need to look at that." He didn't want his "God damn good staff" getting smeared on "Watergate and Segretti," spelling out his real point: "I want to get myself cleaned up." He thought it important that Haldeman and Ehrlichman be cleaned up as well, because "you fellows carry out my orders."

Further conversation about payoff money made it difficult to address the president's wish to make Watergate disappear, so at one point Nixon began asking for more information, somewhat indirectly and softy confronting Haldeman: "I know the situation, what the hell? You had to know a little about it. Ah, Chapin knew a little about it, ah et cetera, et cetera. You know what I mean—" "Chapin doesn't know anything about [Watergate], all he knows is Segretti," Haldeman answered, avoiding the question of his own knowledge of Watergate.

"Yeah. What I might have, you had to know that something—" Nixon pressed. "I knew that something was going on," Haldeman admitted. "You knew there was [a bug], bugging," the president said, although these words

---

*It was extremely rare for Haldeman to speak so bluntly and honestly about the money going to the Watergate defendants, and he would later claim—unsuccessfully—that the money given to these men was not to pay them off.

were slurred. He added, "You knew we were getting some information." Haldeman acknowledged that he did, responding, "That's right." "But we didn't know such a stupid thing was included, was going on," the president continued, regarding the Watergate operation. "That's right. I didn't know we were bugging people," Haldeman added but did not further clarify his knowledge, other than to concede vaguely, "I knew we were bugging the other side." To this comment Nixon added, "Perfectly legitimate."* Following a confused exchange about what White House aide Jack Caulfield was or was not doing, the president wondered if he had known of the Watergate operation, since Haldeman had earlier told him of Caulfield's proposed Operation Sandwedge, which Mitchell had turned down. "Well, I'm not sure he did," Haldeman said, "but I think what happened, obviously what happened, Mitchell set this apparatus up, did not stay in very close contact with him. We did talk about an early issue, and that was doing it out of New York versus doing it out of our own campaign offices. John pulled that back, pulled it out, set it up over there [at the campaign]. Then we started pushing and, and this is really, this is the point where what a lack of information there was, we weren't getting the right kind of—" Haldeman continued without responding to a question from the president, who was concerned to know if he had done something to provoke it. "—we weren't getting, the obvious stuff. When I asked, can we have tape recordings of not, ah, bugged stuff, of a public speech or this press conference—"

"Well, I asked about that. I asked for that God damn stuff all the time," Nixon added, then talking over Haldeman, who continued, saying he wanted a record of what Humphrey and McGovern had said. Nixon then remembered that he had added Scoop Jackson to the list. Haldeman said, "And I pushed hard on that, but they weren't getting it. Now what I'm told is, Magruder didn't know much about this other apparatus," referring to Liddy's operation. "He knew that it was in place. He didn't know what it did. He kept pushing them." Haldeman explained that this occurred because the White House was seeking more information. "And Liddy's story is that the reason he was bugging is, Magruder was lashing him so mercilessly on getting information, and then Liddy moved out and did it." But that was not the whole

---

*The audio is very difficult on this conversation and Haldeman may have been explaining, as he did in later conversations, that he urged the CRP intelligence-gathering operation to record public speeches with recording equipment. But I discount this potential explanation of this conversation because Haldeman knew that was not "bugging," as did Nixon.

story, for after the arrests Haldeman had learned more, so he added, "Now I know there is another factor, in which they very much laid low, because Mitchell was pushing on using them, there was this, ah—"

"Paper," Nixon injected.

"Secret papers, and financial data that O'Brien had, that he was going to get. I didn't even know about that, so we weren't pushing on that.* But we were pushing on trying to get this external information, which would not have required bugging at all, but just maybe as simple as holding a tape recorder at a press conference, or something like that, and getting pictures and words." Nixon, still wondering if he were somehow complicit, asked in a barely audible rhetorical fashion, "Do you remember I used to talk to you sometimes, loosely, I [always said], Jesus Christ, they bugged us [unclear]. I personally [unclear] now fight back!" Haldeman responded that O'Brien had been the wrong person to bug.

After a brief pause in the conversation, the president expressed concern that Ehrlichman had concluded that nothing could really be done to deal with the situation, but Haldeman corrected him: "[Ehrlichman] wanted to strengthen the Dean report stuff, because there was some other things we could do on it," but I was concerned about how far to go with it, "because the FBI knows a lot of stuff." This prompted Nixon to ask what he should do about the FBI. Haldeman thought maybe Nixon should put Lou Nichols, an old friend and former FBI agent, back in and in charge of the agency, but the president rejected that idea, as he did Henry Petersen, who, he told Haldeman, "isn't worth a shit." Haldeman remarked that they might have to live with Gray's getting torn up at a confirmation hearing. Still seeking information about Watergate, Nixon changed the subject to ask, "You don't think Colson knew about the bugging?"

"No, not the Watergate bugging, anyway. But I think he knew about other things, and it's awful close to Hunt, that's my problem," Haldeman noted. "That's fine," Nixon said. This exchange indicates that Haldeman and Ehrlichman had told the president that they wanted to get Colson off the staff. As Haldeman proceeded he again hinted at problems he was not sharing with the president about Hunt and Colson, if Haldeman actually knew—namely, the Ellsberg break-in, which involved Ehrlichman far more deeply than Colson. "That's the one area that you have to watch it," Haldeman said, referring

*See Appendix A.

to the Hunt and Colson relationship. "If you look at all the possible problems on this, you've got to assume that one, or some of them, are going to evolve, and some aren't." Haldeman did warn that things could start to unravel. If the Cubans broke, for example, it could lead to other problems. With this comment Haldeman yawned loudly, very unconcerned, and changed the subject. He observed that Chapin would be a bad witness, because he was such a nice person, but Strachan, who "knew everything that was going on," would be a good witness, because he could not remember anything. Regarding Strachan, the president asked, "Does he know about Watergate?" Haldeman said, "I don't think he knows it was being done in advance, but I don't know. I don't know. I don't know how much he knew, but he may have known they were gathering information." The president believed the odds were that Strachan did know, but Haldeman remained uncertain. Then the president said confidently, "Mitchell had to know this," with which Haldeman agreed.

*December 11, 1972, the White House*

The president had a four-hour Oval Office conversation with Haldeman, with occasional drop-ins by Ziegler and Ehrlichman.[14] While the subject was primarily postelection politics, Watergate wound its way through the discussion, beginning when Haldeman reported that Pat Buchanan had had a session with "Dean, Ehrlichman and Ziegler this morning," and all had concluded that the White House should not "reescalate Watergate, we shouldn't put out a Dean report until we have to or unless we have to." Haldeman told the president that I had completed a report (he did not mention it concerned only Segretti), but given the fact that both the *Post* and Capitol Hill seemed to be pulling back a bit, it was not timely to do anything. The president returned to this subject later but first had a question about Dorothy Hunt: "Have they found anything on the traceability for the ten thousand dollars found in her bag?"

Haldeman reported that I had spent most of the weekend on that matter and been told that Mrs. Hunt had traveled to Chicago with the money to make an investment in a Howard Johnson restaurant with other members of her family, who had a pattern of dealing in cash. The money was still in the hands of the Chicago police, who would be turning it over to Howard Hunt. Haldeman added, "John [Dean] doesn't know whether it's traceable or not. He's not particularly concerned, but he doesn't think it is."

The president returned to the matter of issuing a report, concerned that his entire administration had "sort of an aura of corruption," and that he had not cleaned it up or answered questions about it. Haldeman explained the problem raised in the Buchanan, Ziegler, Ehrlichman and Dean session: "No matter what you say, you've raised more questions than you've answered, and you bring the thing back up to a level of public attention. And it's a strategic question, not a tactical one. It's whether you close it off better from the president by opening it one more time and trying to box it or by letting time fade it away." Haldeman said there were unsatisfactory aspects to both approaches, and it bothered him that the Segretti matter had become tied to Watergate. But once you separated them and dealt with Segretti, where could you go with Watergate other than to repeat "nobody presently on the White House staff had any involvement?" Haldeman advised the president that the judge, without stating his name, handling the Watergate case—he was referring to Judge John Sirica—may prove to be a problem, because he seemed to be tying Segretti to Watergate, which brought them back to the question of a need for a statement. Again, nothing was resolved.

Haldeman told the president that, because of the death of his wife, Howard Hunt was moving for "a severance, or whatever the legal term is." He considered this a positive development, because it would weaken the case against Liddy: "They can make a case on Hunt. They have a very tough time on the evidence making a case against Liddy, except by tying him to Hunt. If they separate the cases, and try them separately, Liddy's case will collapse, which is very much to our interest, of course." But Haldeman acknowledged that this did not solve the president's problem of distancing himself from Watergate.

When Ehrlichman joined the conversation they soon returned to Watergate. Nixon said he felt he should say something sooner rather than later, but Ehrlichman counseled, "I don't think there's anything to add to what you've already said." Then Haldeman ran out a prospective scenario on the Segretti matter as it related to Strachan and Chapin—"a second Dean investigation." I had actually undertaken this investigation, and my key finding had been that it had nothing to do with Watergate, that Segretti was "pretty much an unguided missile," as Ehrlichman described him. Ehrlichman did mention that I had found that some of Segretti's activities may have been illegal, such as "sending out some flyers without identifying the source, but that's a misdemeanor-type [offense.]" As the president continued to press on his need to make a statement, Ehrlichman said he did not think it was "as much a question of not having anything to say, or whether or not something should be said, but it's a question of when it should be said and by whom." He added, "It obviously can help a lot if we draw the poison off the thing before you have to see the press, so Ziegler or somebody else, not Dean, in my opinion, because Dean has to keep it pure, but Ziegler or somebody can give the conclusions of what Dean said." The president agreed, but there was no consensus of who should do it, or when, or whether it should be leaked. Clearly the president wanted to absolve himself and his staff and to document how his campaign had been subject to sabotage.

## December 12, 1972, the White House

During an afternoon conversation in the Oval Office, Haldeman summarized a memorandum Pat Buchanan had sent the president explaining why it was unwise to say anything at the time about Watergate or Segretti.[15] He was certain that Watergate was going to come back into the news with the trial of the seven defendants the following month regardless of what the president said, and although it was "quiescent for the moment" on Segretti, its remaining so would depend on whether Teddy Kennedy pursued an investigation with his Senate subcommittee.

## December 13–20, 1972, the White House

Woodward and Bernstein had a *Washington Post* story buried in the front section that caused some concern at the White House. It reported that a private telephone had been installed in the plumbers' EOB offices in the name of their secretary, Kathleen Chenow; she was billed for the phone at her Alexandria, Virginia, apartment and in turn took the bills to John Ehrlichman's office to be paid.* Woodward and Bernstein had interviewed Chenow for over an hour and learned that the telephone had been used exclusively by Howard Hunt, who received calls there from Bernard Barker. They reported that the telephone had been installed from August 1971 to March 15, 1972, well before the first Watergate entry on May 28. The *Post*

---

*Hunt and Liddy had requested this nontraceable telephone to communicate with their operatives, one of whom was Bernard Barker. And, like all their activities, it left conspicuous tracks. When Ron Ziegler was asked about the telephone he pleaded ignorance but assured the press corps that John Ehrlichman had no knowledge of it. Ziegler news conference, briefing #1620, 11:10 A.M., December 12, 1972, Nixon library, National Archives and Records Administration.

also had more about Dorothy Hunt: an Associated Press wire-service story revealed that she had purchased a maximum flight insurance policy (either $200,000 or $250,000), while Woodward and Bernstein reported that Howard Hunt had given an interview about his wife's plan to use the large amount of cash she was carrying to invest in a motel with other family members living in Chicago. They further reported that the FBI was investigating the source of the money although the Chicago police had reported that it was not associated with the money earlier found in Bernard Barker's Miami bank account.[16]

Late that afternoon the president met with Haldeman and Ehrlichman in his EOB office and told them in an agitated tone, "I had a handwritten note delivered to me through Rose's office from Kleindienst today asking to talk with me about the FBI director before I made a decision on it."[17] The president said he didn't mind "these God dang end-runs," but clearly he did. Kleindienst had had a mutual friend slip the note to Rose, fully aware that he was ignoring the standing protocol for all appointments with Nixon, for unless the president sought specifically to see someone, all such meetings for White House staff, cabinet members, outsiders and even the First Family went through Haldeman. While Haldeman pulled him up short for the breach, Nixon granted Kleindienst a meeting to make his case that Pat Gray should be selected, the president remained noncommittal.[18]

On December 28, Joseph Kraft, one of the president's least favorite syndicated columnists, wrote in the *Post* of "an extraordinary thing" taking place at the FBI, as middle-level agents were "frantically trying to signal to the outside world that their boss, Acting Director L. Patrick Gray III, is a rotten apple."[19] In fact, J. Edgar Hoover's bureaucracy, led by Mark Felt, was quietly working to undercut Gray, or any outsider, from taking charge, as they too had many secrets to hide, enabling Felt to enlist the assistance of others.[20] As the president made clear to his staff and to Kleindienst, his only problem with appointing Gray was the almost certain bloodiness of the confirmation battle that would ensue, which would keep Watergate in the news for months—exactly what he did not want or need. Yet in the coming weeks and months, if a wrong decision could be made about how to deal with this still festering problem, Nixon managed to make it.

# PART III

# UNRAVELING

*January to March 23, 1973*

For months Richard Nixon had been frustrated that Watergate had not only been deflecting his attention from more serious matters of governance but tarnishing his presidency. He had particular difficulty understanding why his advisers had been unable to come up with a defense that insulated him and his presidency from Watergate's potential damage, whatever it might turn out to be. In fact, as his new term commenced, the situation was far worse than he could begin to imagine. This was because he had remained largely uninformed of the facts, partly through his own design but also partly because of the reluctance of Haldeman, Ehrlichman and Mitchell to inform him of precisely what had gone on and how matters were or were not being addressed. Within thirty days of the beginning of his second term the president decided that he must take charge of his Watergate defense himself to protect his high office. However, it was already too late for such action, and he would instead proceed step by step to destroy his presidency.

Nixon spent the Christmas holiday with the First Lady at their home in Key Biscayne and returned to the White House on December 26, where he could better monitor the escalated bombing he had ordered of the Hanoi-Haiphong area in an effort to get the North Vietnamese back to the negotiating table in Paris.[1] On December 27, at the president's insistence, Bob Haldeman headed for California and a much needed vacation. John

Ehrlichman was with his family in Sun Valley, Idaho, for a skiing holiday. Because the president was at odds with his national security staff regarding the bombing strategy, he missed the solace he usually found in conversations with Haldeman, and so frequently telephoned or met with Chuck Colson as the new year began.

*January 1973*

# Keeping Magruder Happy,
# Giving Hunt Assurances,
# and the Watergate Break-in Trial

*January 1-2, 1973, the White House*

Concerned that Henry Kissinger might be undercutting his bombing policy in Vietnam with the news media, Nixon had embraced Colson's idea of monitoring the call records of Kissinger's staff, looking particularly for calls to *New York Times* columnists and the paper's Washington bureau chief, Scotty Reston. Nixon told Colson during an Oval Office conversation that Kissinger was having a good time in California, adding that Henry needed constant praise and reassurance, because he had to feel he was "the indispensable man."[1] It was Kissinger's deputy, Al Haig, who was a true soldier, Nixon noted; he managed to get the job done without hand-holding. When Colson reported that he had made no progress on monitoring Kissinger's telephones, the conversation turned to a favorite theme of the president's: how to punish his enemies and reward his friends during his second term. Nixon said he planned to issue instructions to members of his staff and cabinet to cut off all access to the *New York Times* and *The Washington Post* and give favorable treatment to the *Washington Star*, the *Chicago Sun-Times*, the *Detroit News* and "even the *Los Angeles Times*." He requested an updated list of all contributors who had given one hundred thousand dollars or more to the campaign, as well as friendly editors, publishers, business and labor leaders and top law firms. To enforce discipline at the White House, the president announced, he planned to "fire a few asses around here," just to make the point.

The president said he was pleased that Colson was going to have a couple of Jews as law partners at the firm he was joining in Washington, DC. "I don't know if I will be able to live with them," Colson confessed. "Oh, they're awful," the president agreed. He added, "I hope you're not putting blacks in there. Don't go that far." After discussing the president's proposed Kitchen Cabinet, which would include Colson, and a discussion of the proposed Vietnam war settlement,* Nixon returned to his "political enemies." He thought the success of the election had undermined them, though he was sure they would be after him again soon. "Now is the time to really, really clamp down, just not let them get up off the ground," Nixon said, bringing his fist down on his desk to make the point.

"I really want to go after that *Post*," Colson said, and explained that he hoped to tap into Mellon heir Richard Scaife's money and boredom, not to mention his publishing holdings.† In the short term Colson planned to harass the parent company via its television broadcasting licenses and stockholder litigation. Once they had Colson's man George Webster heading the IRS, the possibilities would be endless. Colson said nothing to the president about the letter he had received from Howard Hunt, dated December 31 and hand delivered to his office. Hunt wanted Colson to contact his attorney, Bill Bittman, who had been calling and trying unsuccessfully to arrange a meeting. Hunt had written: "My wife's death, the imminent trial, my present mental depression, all contribute to a sense of abandonment by friends on whom I had in good faith relied." He closed with an implicit threat: "There is a limit to the endurance of any man trapped in a hostile situation and mine was reached on December 8th"—the date of his wife's death. Colson held the letter for a couple of days, and on January 2, as I was returning to Washington, he sent it to my office with a routing slip asking: "Now what the hell do I do?"[2]

## January 2, 1973, the White House

After spending the holidays in California, I flew back to Washington on January 2 with Haldeman in the president's new Boeing 707, which was still being tested before becoming Air Force One. During the flight I mentioned to Haldeman that new problems had arisen with both James McCord and

---

*Kissinger will initial an agreement with the North Vietnamese on Janury 23, 1973, and secretary of state William Rogers will sign the formal settlement agreement in Paris on January 27, 1973.

†Because of Watergate, Colson never developed his plans to attack the *Post* with Scaife, who had given Richard Nixon $1 million for the 1972 campaign. Later, however, Scaife did become a financier of right-wing attacks on the Clinton presidency. See, e.g., Judy Keen, "First Critic: Richard Scaife Is THORN IN CLINTON'S SIDE," *USA Today*, MAY 28, 1998, A-1.

Howard Hunt, and he, in turn, revealed that Jeb Magruder, through Larry Higby, was pressing him for a meeting. Did I know what it was about? I did not, but I told Haldeman that Magruder was very worried that he was going to have to repeat his perjurious testimony at the coming Watergate break-in trial. From our conversation, I was not at all certain that Haldeman would meet with Magruder.

As we neared Washington air space, Nixon was meeting again in the Oval Office with Colson, who was elaborating on the group he had assembled to attempt to wrest away The Washington Post Company's Florida television station licenses.[3] While the odds were slim of winning them, Colson said, his group was willing to spend big money "to raise hell with the Post," appreciating that it would cost the company a fortune to defend its licenses. This pleased the president. As this conversation continued, Nixon remarked that the only problem for his last campaign and now for his presidency was "the Watergate and Segretti business." Nixon confided that "Haldeman slipped a bit" with Segretti's operation, for he shouldn't have had Chapin involved in it. "My point," the president said, "is that's too God damn close. You know what I mean? That kind of operation should be on the outside."

The president was hopeful that Colson could attack the administration's enemies effectively from outside the White House but advised that it should not be done from his law firm. Colson said he would have a small public relations group take on the task, which he had already discussed with Haldeman. This was fine with Nixon, and to reassure the president of his reliability, Colson added, "I did a hell of lot of things on the outside, and you never read about it. The things you read about were the things I didn't do, Watergate and Segretti." Nixon said he wanted somebody to carry out dirty deeds but complained that people like his new favorite, George Bush, would not do them: "Bush will never do it. He'll do positive things, but that's all."

Colson then confided how he wanted Nixon to believe he operated: "The key to it, if I may say so, is to be damn sure that the things you do are done in such a way that they don't bounce back. In other words, the Watergate, whoever finally approved that, and I don't know who it was and I don't want to know, was just plain stupid, Mr. President. I would never, if I had known about that, I would have fallen down in the doorway to block somebody from doing it, because inevitably you get caught. You can't put five men into that God damn building without getting caught." He continued, "Segretti, in a way, the same thing. The only way you can handle Segretti-type activities is with somebody far removed from us who sets it up." Nixon agreed that not only was Segretti too close to his staff, but having Kalmbach finance him was too close to him personally. To drive home the impression he wanted to give of the strength of his skills in this area, Colson said, "But you see, I did things out of Boston, we did some blackmail and—"

"My God," the president interrupted, and Colson quickly explained, "I'll go to my grave before I ever disclose it. But we did a hell of a lot of things and never got caught. Things that—" Colson stopped himself before he said too much.*

## January 3, 1973, the White House

Haldeman did in fact meet with Magruder the next morning and had their first conversation about Watergate since the arrests at the DNC. Magruder did not know precisely how much information Haldeman had, as he was unaware that Mitchell and I had kept both Haldeman and Ehrlichman fully informed about his testimony. However, only Haldeman and Ehrlichman knew the president had also been kept fully informed and that Magruder's perjury had Nixon's tacit approval. Magruder did not want Haldeman to forget that he had given perjured testimony not only to save himself but Mitchell as well from being charged for the Watergate break-in, and in the process he felt he had saved the president's reelection. Now he was going to have to repeat that false testimony to protect the presidency.[4] Clearly, and understandably, he wanted some assurance from Haldeman that he would be taken care of if a problem arose.

When Haldeman arrived in the Oval Office later that morning, Watergate was discussed only briefly, when the president suggested that they might request Colson remain at the White House for a few additional months.[5] Haldeman, having just learned new information from Magruder about Colson, said he thought Colson should go. "I found out some things," he told the president, without revealing his source. "Even though he's going to be missed," Haldeman warned, "there's more to his involvement in some of the stuff than I realized." Nixon was not happy to hear this, for he saw Colson as a direct link to himself. Haldeman explained that not only was Colson

---

*I once had a similar conversation with Colson, in which he boasted to me that he had done things for which he could go to jail. That would never happen, he said, because there was no way anyone would ever discover them. He did take these secret activities to his grave, just as he promised.

aware of Watergate, but he had advocated it through Liddy and Magruder.[6] Nixon asked if Colson was aware of Haldeman's knowledge, to which Haldeman responded that he did not think so, and then the president inquired if Colson was involved through Hunt.

"Yeah, through Hunt—and Liddy," Haldeman added with emphasis. "And if Liddy decides to pull the cork, Colson could be in some real soup." The reason, Haldeman explained, was that "Colson is in a position of having perjured himself. Colson and Mitchell have both perjured themselves under oath already." "You mean Colson was aware of Watergate?" Nixon asked. Before Haldeman could answer, the president said, "That's hard for me to believe." Haldeman continued, "Not only was he aware of it, but he was pushing very hard for results from it, and it's very specifically that and—" Nixon interrupted again, "Who was he pushing?" "Magruder and Liddy, and that's why we got to be awful careful to take—" Haldeman stopped, backtracking to clarify, "Liddy we're taking care of in one way," he said, without mentioning money, and then picked up where he left off. "And we got to be very careful they're taking care of Magruder the right way, in the other way." The president seemed to understand the distinction and asked, "How do you think, how are you going to do that?"

"I don't know. But I just . . ." Haldeman began, and was apparently about to say that he had just met with Magruder but checked his words. He had clearly decided not to reveal that conversation, possibly because he was uncertain how the president might react to his assurances to Magruder that he would be taken care of if he continued perjuring himself. Rather he told Nixon, "I'm going to make sure he has the feeling that he's—" But Haldeman declined to finish this sentence, either. While not an attorney, he understood that what he was doing with Magruder was criminal, so he changed the subject. "John Dean's been doing a superb job of just having, you know, getting all the facets together—"

But the president, well aware of Magruder's earlier perjury, wanted to know more: "What does he need, a job of some sort, or what?" "Well," Haldeman answered, "either a job or ample recognition, so he can go out into something outside. He doesn't know what he wants to do. He doesn't know what he should do. And this partly depends on how [it] bounces this year. But the main thing is, he's got to feel in his own mind, in his own heart, that we're on his side." Nixon agreed, and, Haldeman further reported, without mentioning the president's blessing, that he had, in fact, assured Magruder he would support and assist him. The president asked, "He's working on inauguration?" "Oh yes, he's the director of the inaugural," Haldeman assured him, "and he's running that thing, so that gives him an ongoing base through the twentieth."

The president returned to Colson. "Does Mitchell know that Colson was involved? Does Colson know that Mitchell was involved?" "I think the answer is yes to both of those," Haldeman answered. "Although I'm sure Colson assumes that Mitchell is involved if he doesn't know it directly as a fact, and I'm not positive that Mitchell knows that Colson was involved. See, Mitchell's involvement was early, and then he backed out, and—"

The president was having trouble believing this information, apparently suspecting it was another instance of Haldeman's occasional efforts to dilute Colson's influence, while Haldeman's account was in fact accurate. "I can see Mitchell doing it, but I can't see Colson getting into the Democratic [Committee]," Nixon said, as they talked over each other. And then he asked, as he had before, "What the Christ was he looking for?"

"They were looking for stuff on two things. One on financial stuff, and the other on stuff that they thought they had on what they were going to do at Miami, to screw us up, which apparently was, ah—" and as Haldeman paused to gather his thoughts, Nixon injected, "Democratic plot," to which Haldeman then added, "—that they thought they had uncovered."* "Colson was salivating with glee at the thought of what he might be able to do with it," Haldeman explained. "And the investigator types were reluctant to go in there; they were put under tremendous pressure [that] they had to get this stuff." When the president replied with a skeptical, "Hmm," Haldeman pulled back a little, saying, "None of this, I don't know any of this firsthand. I can't prove any of it. Really, I don't want to know, because if I ever get involved in it, I want to be ignorant, which I am." "But," he continued, not only was Liddy a potential problem for Colson, but by implication Magruder and Mitchell might be problems for Colson as well. He further noted that "Hunt also knows. See, on Hunt's side of it, he could really screw Colson, but apparently there's no real danger of that." Nixon remarked, "There doesn't appear to be any great danger of Liddy [either]." Haldeman agreed, and he resumed, "And I think we're okay on Magruder. The other one that's a problem is Sloan, and he doesn't know enough, apparently, to matter, although he suspects a lot."

*See Appendix A.

"What can we do to take care of him?" the president inquired. While giving no specifics, Haldeman indicated that they were already trying. After a pause to absorb this, Nixon asked, "What is Magruder going to do?" As Nixon was posing this, Haldeman was telling him again, "Give John Dean a lot of credit for being a damn effective operator on this one without bothering anybody with the details, just sort of living with it hour by hour—" Nixon, speaking sotto voce, agreed, "Very appreciative, we'll remember, we'll remember." Haldeman then vaguely shared a concern I had mentioned on the flight back to Washington: I had unwittingly gotten myself on the wrong side of the law, though I was not certain if I was in trouble. "Now he's got interest in it, he's in it in a sense himself because of what he's trying to do about it," Haldeman explained.

Nixon, his mind elsewhere, asked, "What about [doing something] with Magruder? What can we do there? Is there anything?" Haldeman reported that Magruder was interested in the Bicentennial Commission, but the problem was that it was a very "politically visible spot," which prompted the president to immediately reject it. Haldeman said that Magruder did not really want anything, a fact that surprised and pleased Nixon, "And wouldn't consider anything until after the trial. He doesn't want to be thought of for anything."

"What's the present plan for the trial?" Nixon asked, wanting to know "whether they're going to plead guilty or go to trial or what?" Haldeman said some would plead, but they were still making motions. Nixon wanted them all to plead guilty. They discussed whether Congress would go forward with the trial under way (Nixon thought not), and Haldeman reported that Kennedy's staff investigation of Segretti had largely faded away. Then, thinking of the toll this had taken so far, Haldeman added, it was "too damn bad," because Colson was "a substantial loss, there's no question." So, too, was Chapin "a substantial loss."

Colson, Nixon said, would "find a way to be back in and out of the White House. He said that there's only one thing he's asking for is, at the end, he would like to take a trip, a little trade fair or something." Haldeman knew about this and indicated that they were looking for a nice junket for him.

Nixon said he recognized that "these fellows" involved in Watergate had thought they were part of "a good cause," but he was still not clear on who had been pushing whom and said he "thought it was Mitchell" who had pushed.

"Mitchell did not push them, apparently," Haldeman said, and then offered his interpretation, employing somewhat obtuse metaphors and descriptions that Nixon apparently understood: "Mitchell's thing really was an awareness of machinery rather than an initiative. Mitchell, at the point that was going on, Mitchell was not taking a very active role at all." After a long pause the president asked, "But Colson was? Colson's pushing Magruder, is that what it was?" Haldeman answered, "And Liddy," a fact the president was not pleased to hear. Haldeman continued, "Yeah, and it gets down to undeniable specifics. I mean, there's specific needs, times and places and that sort of thing, and—" The president, thinking like the lawyer he was, raised an important distinction: "Yet the point is whether he was pushing to receive information on that, the question of perjury and so forth, whether he was pushing to get information, or whether he was pushing to get information through bugging, you know?" Haldeman reported that Colson's push was "very specific" and a "venture" known to "the committee."

While Haldeman was meeting with the president I received an urgent call from Paul O'Brien. Hunt was at the breaking point, I was told, as his criminal trial was about to begin. Colson was refusing to take calls from Bittman, who wanted to discuss executive clemency for Hunt. Soon after my discussion with O'Brien, Colson called me to ask if I had seen the letter from Hunt. I had not, but fished it out of my inbox and told Colson I wanted to speak to Ehrlichman about the situation, which I did at noon. Ehrlichman felt that Colson should listen to Bittman's proposal.[7]

That evening I joined Ehrlichman in his office to meet with Colson after his conversation with Bittman. Colson arrived uncharacteristically shaken; whatever Bittman had told him obviously troubled him, and he now said he felt it was imperative that Hunt be given an assurance of clemency. Ehrlichman said he wanted to think about the situation and instructed Colson to not discuss the matter with the president. Two days later, with no word from Ehrlichman, Colson ignored his injunction.

### January 5, 1973, the White House

Neither Ehrlichman nor Colson mentioned the Hunt situation when they spoke with Nixon on January 4, but when Colson met with the president on the following day in his EOB office, he raised it. The audio on this recording is extremely poor, virtually impossible to transcribe,[8] but the National Archives Subject Log indicates, as did I, that they also heard the discussion of clemency during this exchange.[9] The president made a contemporaneous note in his diary: "Colson told me on Friday [January 5] that he had tried to do everything he could to keep Hunt from turning state's evidence. After what happened to Hunt's wife, etc., I think we have a very good case for showing some clemency."[10]

Although Nixon also interpreted the information from Colson during their January 5 conversation as more finger-pointing among his subordinates, the truth was that his staff was slowly (and finally) giving him the basic facts about what had actually occurred—while not really explaining their own roles in the affair. On this point, Nixon recorded in his diary: "It was Colson's view apparently that either Haldeman or Ehrlichman or both might have been more deeply involved than has been indicated. Of course, it is all hearsay. Colson's point is that Magruder is a name dropper and that Magruder may have mentioned the names of Haldeman and Ehrlichman and telling the Watergate people to get information. Apparently, according to Colson, too, some of the meetings took place in Mitchell's office at the Justice Department (since he would not move to the CRP until March 1972). This would be hard for me to believe but then again during the campaign people are not as rational or responsible as they normally would be. This, I know, must be a great burden for Haldeman and Ehrlichman during this past tough week and I could see that something was eating them without knowing what."[11]

*January 7, 1973, Camp David*

The president met at Birch Lodge with Haldeman, on January 7, which Haldeman later reported involved in part "fill[ing] him in on all the [Watergate] coverage in the paper today, and the fact that it's building up."[12] The *New York Times* had a story—7 GO TO TRIAL TOMORROW IN BREAK-IN AT DEMOCRATIC OFFICES—that identified the defendants and noted that Judge Sirica had "repeatedly prodded the Government to take up the reasons behind the break-in." *The Washington Post* had two front-page stories: WATERGATE JURORS FACE GUARDED LIFE, which described the Spartan living conditions the jurors would encounter while being sequestered for an estimated "six weeks to three months" during the trial, and MANSFIELD ASKS PROBE OF WATERGATE, which reported that Senate majority leader Mike Mansfield (D-MT) had sent a letter to Senator Sam J. Ervin (D-NC) requesting he undertake an investigation of Watergate and "other insidious campaign practices." It appears this news resulted in a discussion about how those associated with the president should handle their testimony, for as Haldeman noted in his diary, the president felt "our people should take the Fifth Amendment rather than getting trapped into testifying."[13]

## January 8, 1973, the White House

In an Oval Office conversation Ron Ziegler raised the fact that the Watergate trial was starting, and Nixon instructed that there should be no comment from the White House during the proceedings.[14] Ziegler agreed, and it was understood that the Justice Department would handle all responses and reactions. Nixon was pleased to learn that Clifton Daniel* was coming to Washington to head the New York Times bureau. Ziegler believed they could develop a good working relationship with him; the president observed that their doing so was a good way to stick it to the Post. Haldeman arrived as Ziegler departed, followed shortly by Ehrlichman.[15]

Ehrlichman relayed the details of his appearance the previous day on Meet the Press, where he had been questioned about Watergate by Time magazine columnist Hugh Sidey: Did he know the facts of Watergate? No. Did the president know? No. Sidey asked why the White House had not investigated, and Ehrlichman replied that the FBI had conducted the biggest investigation since the Kennedy assassination, and literally dozens of witnesses would be called in the forthcoming trial. He added that the White House had conducted its own investigation, and no one in the administration was found to be involved. Anything beyond that, Ehrlichman told Sidey, he was not prepared to discuss, nor did he know the motive behind Watergate or the inception of the plan.

Haldeman reported that "the way it appears now, Hunt is going to take a guilty plea on three counts," after the opening statement. "They will ask him, presumably, whether there were any higher-ups involved, after he takes his guilty plea, and he'll say no." Rothblatt, the lawyer representing the Cubans, was a zealot who wanted to fight; Liddy was not going to plead but rather go to trial hoping for a reversible error by the judge or prosecutors; he believed he could

---

*Daniel had served as bureau chief for the Times in London and Moscow, and was married to Margaret Truman, the daughter of former president Harry Truman.

"screw something up somewhere." Haldeman assured the president, "They all will sit mute. None of them will testify, none of them will take the stand, except McCord, who does intend to take the stand, but McCord has no firsthand knowledge of any involvement of other people. Therefore, Dean's not too worried about his taking the stand." Haldeman added that, if convicted, which he presumed they would be, they could be immunized by Congress, but they would "take contempt of Congress charges rather than testifying before Congress. At least, that's their present position." Ehrlichman explained that both the grand jury and Congress could immunize them to obtain their testimony.

A little later Ehrlichman asked, "Did you see the Marty Schram story over the weekend?" The *Post* had run a story from *Newsday* that reported: "The Watergate burglary and espionage mission at Democratic Party headquarters was part of a widespread project in which documents were photographed in the Embassy of Chile and several liberal Democratic senators were kept under electronic surveillance, according to a source close to the defendants."[16] Neither the president nor Haldeman had seen the piece, so Ehrlichman offered his own version of it: "There's a story to the effect that a CIA agent has bagged a lot of embassies here, including the Chilean embassy. That's been kicking around now for two or three weeks. *Newsday* finally ran it as a story, and they assert that there is a CIA project officer who is around this unit, and they've been in existence for some time." Haldeman thought this account might be part of the defense the Watergate burglars were developing.

After a brief discussion of the bugging of the Nixon campaign plane in 1968, Ehrlichman returned to the Watergate trial and shared new information he had picked up: "I was going to say, one of the witnesses in the Watergate case is going to be a kid that Hunt recruited who was in the Muskie headquarters and then in the McGovern headquarters.* And—" The president

*The kid to whom Ehrlichman was referring was a college student at Brigham Young University, Thomas Gregory, recruited by Howard Hunt, and who had taken a semester off to work for Hunt. Gregory had been referred by the nephew of Hunt's boss Robert Bennett at Mullen & Company, the public relations firm Hunt worked for when not consulting at the White House or assisting Liddy with his nefarious undertakings. Ehrlichman obtained this information from Attorney General Dick Kleindienst, who was giving Ehrlichman periodic heads-up. Gregory did testify but this information did not become public until January 11, 1973, at the trial. Gregory, who had unwittingly gotten himself deep into the illegal operations of the Hunt/Liddy schemes, was given immunity by the prosecutors and became the key witness in the case against Liddy and McCord. Gregory was involved in the unsuccessful efforts to bug McGovern's headquarters on May 15 and 28, 1972, but quit before June 17, 1972, the last planned but never executed entry and bugging of the McGovern headquarters. See testimony of Thomas Gregory, *U.S. v. Liddy* (Jan. 11, 1973) and Senate Watergate Committee, *Final Report*, 27-28, 196-197. Sam Dash, chief counsel of the Senate Watergate committee, told me he wanted to call Gregory as a witness, but Senator Wallace Bennett (father of Robert Bennett) intervened with Chairman Ervin, and blocked calling Gregory since they could get the information from others.

interrupted to ask, "Worked for Hunt?" Ehrlichman confirmed he did and continued, "Was paid thirty-five hundred dollars, and finally broke off with Hunt because he refused to bug Gary Hart's telephone over at the McGovern headquarters. That's going to reopen and re-escalate this whole political sabotage business, I would guess. And that would come fairly early in the trial, I would think, because it's part of the conspiracy." Ehrlichman began speculating, "Now, if Hunt pleads and is sentenced maybe they won't call that guy. I don't know whether Liddy—"

"But what about the Congress, though?" the president asked. Nixon said he did not have a problem with this kid's having been planted in a candidate's headquarters: "That, believe me, doesn't bother me too much. Good God, there are people planted in headquarters all the time." "And bugging," Haldeman added. "So they can say that he was in the headquarters, and that Hunt recruited him, he was in the Muskie headquarters." Nixon later continued, "What did the guy do in the headquarters? I mean, he just worked there?"

"Oh, he'd send down schedules and collect papers, and just whatever he could lay his hands on, I guess," Ehrlichman answered. "And he didn't mind doing that, but when they asked him to plant a bug, [that's] why he bailed out." There was some confusion over the timing, which neither Haldeman nor Ehrlichman were able to correct, and the president eventually complained, "Well, I've heard pieces of the story. That's how it always is."

In a meeting with Colson that afternoon, in his EOB office, the president said, "Incidentally, Haldeman told me that apparently that Hunt is going to [plead guilty to every one of his counts]. And very definitely, I think it's the right thing for him to do, Chuck."[17] Colson informed Nixon, "He's doing it on my urging." After a brief discussion about Hunt's college student operative, the president sat silently for a moment, and then said, "Well, don't let it get you down."

"Oh, hell no," Colson reassured him. "I know it's tough for all of you," Nixon said. "For you, Bob, John and the rest. We're just not going to let it get us down. This is a battle, it's a fight." He noted that it was a fight they should undertake knowing "[w]e'll cut them down one of these days. Don't you agree?" Colson said he thought it good that Liddy was going to trial, as "a hell of a lot of stuff has come out" already. The president felt that as long as the trial was in progress, Congress would have to keep its "God-damn cotton-picking hands off." The president sought some clarity as they discussed the trial procedures and then reminded Colson, "But, you know, Chuck, it's something they all undertook knowing the risks. Right? What did they think?" Colson said he did not think they appreciated the risks. "They didn't think they'd get caught?" the president asked, and then he suggested that they might have believed that the Democrats would drop the matter after the election. Colson offered this analysis: "I think they figured that these were all guys who were CIA. They all were taking orders from people like Liddy, acting on behalf of John Mitchell and others. You know what I mean?"

"Mitchell would take care of them?" Nixon asked, a bit incredulous. "How could he?" Colson did not have an answer but changed the subject. He instead explained that Hunt's lawyer had told him that Hunt had objected to the Watergate operation because of the way Liddy was handling it; Hunt had recognized the problems and risks. "I think where there's a question of clemency, Hunt is a simple case," Nixon said. "I mean, after all, the man's wife is dead, was killed; he's got one child that has—"

"—brain damage from an automobile accident," Colson finished.

"That's right," the president said, and he was soon envisioning how they would manage it: "We'll build that son of a bitch up like nobody's business. We'll have [conservative columnist William F.] Buckley write a column and say, you know, that he should have clemency, if you've given eighteen years of service," referring to Hunt's CIA tenure. "That's what we'll do. That's it, it's on the merits."

But noting that Hunt had not been involved in Watergate alone, Nixon added, "I would have difficulty with some of the others."

"Oh, yeah," Colson agreed, "the vulnerabilities are different with the others also." Nixon wanted to know why he thought that was the case. "Well, because Hunt and Liddy did the work," Colson began. "The others didn't know anything direct, that is, they didn't have to do it." Colson might have stated the matter more directly—namely, that Hunt and Liddy could cause Colson and the White House problems—but Nixon understood his point, and replied, "Well, I agree with you." Colson added, "I don't give a damn if [the others] spend five years in jail in the interim," which led Nixon to protest, "[That's not] a good attitude."

"But that means they can't hurt us," Colson countered. "Hunt and Liddy were direct guardians of the meetings, and all those discussions are very incriminating for us," which prompted Nixon to again seek assurance that Liddy was tough. "Yeah, he is, apparently one of these guys who's a masochist, he enjoys punishing himself," Colson explained. "That's okay, as long as he remains stable. I think he's tough. He's an ideologue." Nixon liked this, and the conversation moved to other matters, including the fact that Mike Mansfield had gotten Teddy Kennedy off the hook on Watergate by passing it on to Senator Sam Ervin.

"There's lots at stake," the president observed, "and, incidentally, we'll survive it." Nixon said Watergate was like ITT: People would eventually tire of it unless the investigators got "a big name," the most likely candidate being John Mitchell. But he noted: So far Mitchell's involvement was only hearsay; at least Mitchell himself was smart; and "he was close to it but not in it directly." Colson begged to differ and suggested that Mitchell may have committed perjury. "Perjury, that's a damn hard rap to prove," Nixon reminded him, and said that, while Alger Hiss had been found guilty of perjury, "they haven't got that kind of evidence on Mitchell. Or anybody else, have they?" Colson did not think they did, but he was concerned about a congressional inquiry. He mentioned that if Hunt was forced to plead to all the counts of his indictment, he could also be forced to testify before Congress, and there he could not take the Fifth Amendment.

After the conversation moved on to other matters, the president returned to congressional investigations and said that if "the Watergate thing goes too far," he was ready to counter with the fact that he had been bugged by the FBI at President Johnson's request for the final two weeks of his 1968 campaign. He knew this because the person who had done it for Johnson was Deke DeLoach, who had told Mitchell, and J. Edgar Hoover had also told Nixon. The president thought this information could be a powerful way to turn off the Watergate investigation, because it could involve former vice president Hubert Humphrey as well. "Yeah, we've got a few cards to put out," Nixon boasted, to which Colson agreed, "Let's do it."[18]

## January 12–18, 1973, Key Biscayne

The president headed for Key Biscayne for six days to relax and work on his inaugural address. Hunt pled guilty on January 11, and Barker, Martinez, Gonzales and Sturgis would follow suit on January 15. It was during this period that Seymour Hersh of the *New York Times* began writing some of the most troubling stories that would be reported about Watergate. Woodward and Bernstein had been focused on who was responsible for the break-in and on portraying it as part of a larger espionage and sabotage effort. If that operation existed in any organized form, I did not (and do not) know who was behind it, and even four decades later I have never found evidence for its existence; it seems, instead, to have been a fantasy scenario apparently advanced by their Deep Throat source, Mark Felt. Hersh, in contrast, suspected that a cover-up was in progress, and it was there that he focused his considerable energies and ability.

On Saturday, January 12, I called Haldeman, who was in Florida with the president, to warn him about a troubling Hersh *Times* story, as well as on an ongoing problem with McCord. As Haldeman later noted in his diary: "I had a report this afternoon from Dean on the Watergate. Apparently there is going to be a Hersh story in *The New York Times* saying that the Cubans told them [referring to the *Times*] that they're all on salary, that there's a $900,000 fund at the Reelection Committee for them, and that they dropped bugs all over town. The chain of command went from Barker to Hunt to Liddy to Colson to Mitchell." Haldeman also noted that CRP spokesperson DeVan Shumway, as well as Colson and Mitchell, had all given flat denials on this. Additionally, the Cubans had sent a letter to the judge saying they wanted to dismiss Rothblatt, because they wanted to plead guilty. He included that I had also reported, "McCord is off the reservation now," but that I thought the CRP lawyers could get him back, because McCord had "a plan regarding calls he made in September and October [to foreign embassies]. He thinks he can get a tainted evidence thing on it, because the calls were bugged by the government. He's playing a blackmail game where if I (McCord) fall, all fall, but he has no hard evidence. That won't be settled for a while, but Dean thinks he can settle it. Apparently McCord was distressed at the judge's severity. The Cubans plead on Monday [January 15]."[19]

*January 19–30, 1973, the White House*

Other than an occasional back channel report from the CRP attorneys, who were talking with the lawyers representing the Watergate defendants, the Nixon White House largely followed the Watergate trial from the front-page coverage in *The Washington Post*, which often featured two stories about the proceedings. Nixon could follow the trial by merely scanning the headlines of the *Post* on his breakfast table each morning, since he had largely stopped reading the full stories.[20] On January 30 McCord and Liddy were found guilty on all counts of burglary and bugging, after the jury deliberated for ninety minutes. If Nixon did read any of the paper's accounts of the trial, he asked no questions during recorded conversations. The trial seemed to have only two impacts on him: He increased the pressure on his staff for information about the 1968 bugging of his campaign plane; and he complained—since everyone in Washington, including Judge Sirica, openly suspected there was a cover-up under way—about being accused of a cover-up. The fact that five defendants had pled guilty and two had been convicted by a jury certainly suggested one.

*February 3 to 23, 1973*

# Senate Watergate Committee
# and Gray's Nomination

*February 3, 1973, the White House*

During the bail hearing for the seven convicted Watergate defendants, newspapers and wire services reported Judge Sirica's comment that he wanted the government to continue investigating Watergate. He said he did not believe the testimony given by the government's key witnesses during the trial, and he hoped that the Senate investigation would "get to the bottom" of what had occurred.[1]

When Nixon met with Colson in the Oval Office that morning, a clearly annoyed president said, "You know, here's the judge saying I did this. His God damn conduct is shocking as a judge. He's not being a judge for me. Is he young enough to look for an appointment with the Democrats in four years after me?"[2]

"No, no, no, no, no," Colson began. "Sirica is a tough, hard-boiled, law-and-order judge. He's a Republican. I know him pretty well. I've been with him at various social events. Very decent guy. And dedicated to you, and to Eisenhower. I can't understand what John's doing. He's been ill. The only thing I can figure is that he didn't need this. This case just got under his craw for some reason, and he's a hot-headed Italian, and he blew on it. You know, he's handled himself terribly. Awful. Refusing to accept the Hunt plea [which the government had agreed to accept, but Sirica had made Hunt plead to all charges]. And of course, the odd thing about it, Mr. President, is that the [assistant] U.S. attorney who has been prosecuting this case is not our guy. I mean, I would imagine he's a Democrat. He's been there since 1964 at the

U.S. Attorney's Office.* But I think Sirica figures that what he's doing has been totally in the right."

Nixon found no comfort in Colson's analysis. "Yeah, I mean, my point is that now what's happened is that he's trying to prod the Senate into conducting a big investigation," the president complained. He was convinced that Ervin's Watergate inquiry would be partisan. He started looking for a counteroffensive and asked, "Well, what, if anything, have we heard is being done or can be done on the counterattacks, et cetera? Are any of the charges against our Democrat friends being investigated? Have they been? And will they be? Or you just don't know?"

When Colson reported that they did not have anything to balance against Watergate, and no one was on the attack, the president replied, "Well, let me suggest one other thing. This Brewster thing, according to Bobby Baker, runs a hell of a lot deeper, and runs to a number of Democratic senators.† Now what are we doing about having an investigation, calling in Spiegel, putting him under oath at FBI, and [asking] what other senators [are involved], go right down the list. What are we doing about that?" Colson loved the idea, and after a lengthy discussion about it, Nixon wondered how this could actually be used as leverage against Ervin, to force him to back off Watergate. "But my point is, how do we get after his colleagues so that they'll tell Ervin to lay off? That's my point. And when are we going to do it? Christ, I don't understand what the Christ is the matter around here, Chuck, that this has got to really be pushed. I don't want you to be in a position where you're just the bad guy pushing it, but Haldeman, I think, is too busy on some of this stuff, and somebody has got to get at it. Ehrlichman's busy. Dean is a gunfighter." "Dean is good," Colson reassured the president, but he then clarified

---

*Colson appears to be referring to Seymour Glanzer, one of three assistant U.S. attorneys on the case, along with Don Campbell, and the lead assistant, Earl Silbert, who handled the Watergate break-in investigation and prosecutions.

†The morning news had been filled with reports regarding former senator Daniel Brewster (D-MD). In 1969 he had been indicted by the Nixon Justice Department (although the investigation had started well before Nixon was elected) for solicitation and acceptance of bribes. The case arose from campaign contributions from a lobbyist for Spiegel, a mail-order firm that was seeking favorable mail rates. The U.S. District Court for the District of Columbia had dismissed the indictment against Brewster under the "speech and debate" clause of the Constitution (which immunizes members of Congress from liability for their legislative actions), but the Justice Department appealed directly to the U.S. Supreme Court, which in June 1972 overturned the District Court by a 6 to 3 vote, explaining an illegal bribe was not protected by the Constitution's speech and debate clause. The case was reinstated, Brewster had been convicted, and the February 3, 1973, front-page *Washington Post* headline reported: BREWSTER GETS 6-YEAR TERM, $30,000 FINE. (Note: Brewster's conviction was later overturned because the judge had instructed the jury improperly. In 1975 Brewster pled no contest to a misdemeanor charge of accepting an illegal gratuity.)

the line of authority relating to Watergate: "Ehrlichman has been sort of in charge of this, but maybe get John Dean more deeply into it." Again trying to reassure Nixon, Colson said, "John is good."

Returning to Watergate, Nixon yet again returned to his frustration at not knowing precisely the extent of his staff's participation in the affair, and he began gently probing Colson for the truth. "I assume that it must lead to Mitchell. That's what bothers Haldeman. Do you?" When Colson said he knew that it led to Mitchell, the president asked, "Are you sure?" Colson said he was, and Nixon noted this was a problem.[3] He insisted, "We can't let Mitchell get involved. It just can't be done. We need to protect him, and, of course, we've also got to be sure that Haldeman's not involved. We've got to be sure that they don't piss around on you. You know what I mean? Or Ehrlichman, anybody. But the point is that, sure, this kind of thing happens."

Colson agreed, "I mean, the Watergate issue has never been a public issue. It is a Washington issue. It is a way to get at us. It's a way the Democrats think they can use to embarrass us and keep us on the defensive and keep us worried, and keep us from doing other things. And that's why they've kept it alive. I don't think it's worth a damn in the country, Mr. President."

"Well, my whole point here is this, and don't take this now as a directive to go out and raise hell with Ehrlichman and Dean," Nixon instructed Colson, who assured the president this matter would remain between them. Colson again spoke of my "great capacity for work" and noted that I had been "consumed in the delicacies of this case," which the president, in turn, stated a bit more bluntly: "He's keeping it from blowing." Colson added, "Which, by the way, he's done a spectacularly good job on." Just as Colson started to alert the president to my potential problems, Nixon interrupted to ask when Sirica was going to sentence the Watergate defendants. Colson did not know but mistakenly suggested that he might not sentence Liddy and McCord while they appealed their convictions. Colson also mistakenly (but not without good reason) thought Sirica might be reversed for his conduct during the trial. The discussion turned to keeping members of the presidential staff from testifying before the Senate, based on the constitutional doctrine of separation of powers, under which presidents had refused to allow Congress to intrude into executive operations—long called "executive privilege." Colson reminded the president that all the Watergate defendants were going to be summoned as witnesses before the grand jury, where none of them had the protection of the Fifth Amendment.

*February 6, 1973, the White House*

In a morning meeting that included Haldeman, Ehrlichman brought the president up to date on the efforts to weaken the Senate's investigation of Watergate.[4] Ehrlichman reported that he was going to have "a meeting with Mitchell and all the shakers and movers" that morning* to figure out how "to throw sand in their eyes to frustrate the damn thing," by getting the authorizing resolution for a Watergate investigation amended to apply to other political campaigns, such as John Kennedy's of 1960. But Ehrlichman was skeptical about such efforts. When Haldeman returned to the Oval Office in the early afternoon the president said he wanted John Mitchell involved in dealing with the Senate's Watergate inquiry, because "it's going to be right on his back."[5] Haldeman assured him that Mitchell was involved and had attended the meeting earlier that day.

The president asked who would appoint the Republicans to the Senate Watergate committee, and when Haldeman said it was the minority leader, Hugh Scott, Nixon said he wanted to have "a couple sons of bitches on our side." After further discussion of the committee, Nixon asked, "Has anybody followed up on my suggestion that the FBI immediately [investigate], because of what Senator Brewster said, Bob?" He repeated what Brewster had said after his sentencing: "'There might be [other] members of the Senate involved in this, you know; I just got caught.'" Nixon explained that Colson said he had information about others, and complained, "God damn it, the FBI should investigate on that. What is the present thinking, Bob, with regard to the FBI? Do we go with Gray?" Haldeman said they were running name checks on another suggestion from Ehrlichman, and they were still considering EPA director William Ruckelshaus.

*February 7, 1973, the White House*

While Haldeman and Ehrlichman were meeting with the president that morning in the Oval Office, The U.S. Senate debated the Watergate investigation.[6] None of the actions taken by the Senate surprised the White House.[7] Based on reports from its congressional relations staff, Haldeman informed

---

*The meeting was held later that morning in Ehrlichman's office at ten, with Haldeman, Bryce Harlow (who had been in charge of congressional relations at the outset of the Nixon presidency), John Mitchell, Dick Moore, Bill Timmons and me.

the president, all the proposed Republican amendments to include Democratic presidential campaigns in the inquiry, or to give Republicans equal power on the committee, would fail. The president asked Ehrlichman, "What is your opinion, John, about now proceeding with the leakage on the [National Security Council] staff?" David Young, the last member of the plumbers unit, had been gathering information on national security information leaks of varying degrees of seriousness throughout the government.

"Oh, I'd like to wait until after the Pentagon Papers trial before we move on any of this stuff," Ehrlichman responded. "We have a five-year statute of limitations on all that kind of stuff. We have the other one hanging on, which is Neil Sheehan at the *Times*, and I've got both of them on a tickler system to come out regularly."* When the president asked about the trial of Daniel Ellsberg and his accomplice, Anthony Russo, in Los Angeles federal court for the theft of the Pentagon Papers, Ehrlichman said, "Well, the Pentagon Papers trial will be over, I would guess, in another ten days, two weeks, something of that kind. It may go longer than that, but I don't think much longer."

"They're not going to convict anybody?" the president asked. "I doubt it. I would be very surprised," Ehrlichman admitted. "You never thought they would," Haldeman noted, directing his comment to Ehrlichman. "I never thought they would. No," Ehrlichman agreed. Referring to the motion to stay the proceedings approved by Justice William O. Douglas, Ehrlichman again told the president that this had been a happy turn of events, because Ellsberg had been unable to use his trial as a platform before the election. Ehrlichman reminded him that they were not finished prosecuting those involved in publishing leaked national security information, for he had not only Sheehan but also Jack Anderson in his sights.

Ziegler arrived toward the end of this meeting, seeking guidance on how to handle the Senate's actions regarding Watergate. The president said he should say nothing other than that the White House would cooperate with any investigation. After a lengthy discussion, the only real guidance Ziegler received was that the president would soon issue a statement of executive privilege regarding whether or not his aides would testify, and that that would be handled on an individual basis.[8]

After Ziegler had departed, the president said, "Incidentally, I read this

---

*A tickler filing system results in an aide or secretary asking a designated person or persons to be reminded at a future date or dates how some matter in the file should be resolved or addressed.

remarkable piece [in] the *New York Times* by that left-wing son of a bitch Seymour Hersh. It said that Strachan called Liddy about Segretti. I thought that was out about eight months ago, or three or four months." Haldeman clarified, "It was four months ago, five months." Nixon was annoyed that the *Times* was recycling old news as new revelations, which he thought made clear why Ziegler should ignore the Senate's proceedings.

*February 8–11, 1972, the Western White House*

On the afternoon of February 8 the president headed for San Clemente, and I was summoned there at the president's request on Friday, February 9, with Dick Moore, for two days of discussions regarding how the White House should deal with the Senate's Watergate hearings.[9] Moore and I stayed at the La Costa Resort & Spa hotel, where we met for extended sessions with Haldeman and Ehrlichman in a large suite on both Saturday and Sunday. The president did not participate in our meetings. Haldeman's notes (recorded in his diary) reflect what he undoubtedly told the president, which boiled down to keeping an outward appearance of cooperation while doing everything possible to obstruct the Senate's proceedings.[10] Haldeman did not record that John Ehrlichman suggested that Dick Moore, when he reported on this meeting to John Mitchell, should get Mitchell to raise more money for the Watergate defendants—and Moore did so.

*February 13, 1973, the White House*

When the president returned to the Oval Office on Tuesday morning, he met with Colson, who was about to leave on his junket to Russia and Romania.[11] The president still needed to select a new FBI director, and he asked, "Would you keep Gray?" Colson thought Gray would be fine if he had a strong deputy, such as former assistant FBI director Bill Sullivan, who had been helpful to the Nixon White House by spiriting wiretaps records out of the bureau so Hoover could not use them as leverage against the president. These wiretaps had been placed on White House aides working for the National Security Council and reporters to try to identify leakers; the names of the targets had been transmitted to Sullivan at the FBI by Haig. Colson continued, "Al Haig called me yesterday and said, Jesus, get Sullivan back in there. Haig is very high on Sullivan. I don't know Sullivan, but I know of so many people who do think highly of him." Assured by Colson that Gray was loyal to him, Nixon remarked, "Totally. Oh, God, I wish we had more Pat Grays."

When Nixon expressed concern that Watergate was threatening to become an even worse nuisance than ITT, Colson said the only way to prevent that was to be "very, very hard-nosed with that committee. And if they want Haldeman, Ehrlichman, me, [and] I'm sure they will, [they had] to limit the areas that they're going to go into." While the president was not concerned about lower-level people, he was troubled about anyone with whom he spoke appearing before the Senate: "I'm afraid that that gives an appearance of a total cover-up, which would bother me a bit, you know."

Colson, however, had been thinking about a larger problem, one that he wanted to discuss before he departed on his trip: "If whoever did order Watergate was going to come out in the hearings, for God sakes, let it out now. At least get rid of it now. Take our losses." Nixon agreed and asked, "Well, who the hell do you think did this? Mitchell? He can't do it, he'll perjure himself, so he won't admit that. Now that's the problem. Magruder?" "I know Magruder knows," Colson reported. Nixon, who knew more than he told Colson, said flatly: "Well, then he's perjured himself, hasn't he?" Colson answered, "Probably." Nixon then said, "Alright, what would you say then? Let's take our losses. Who the hell's going to step forward and say it? See my point? Liddy, of course, he directed Watergate. But who do you have in mind? I mean, I'm afraid I can't risk it, Chuck, unless you have somebody in mind." When Colson did not, the president continued, "My point is, would you suggest that Mitchell go in and say, this must've occurred? I did not realize it at the time, but Mitchell seems to have stonewalled it up to this point."

The president felt he could rely on the FBI's "tremendous investigation," at least "unless one of the seven [Watergate defendants] begins to talk. That's the problem." This thought prompted Nixon to ask, "as far as the seven" were concerned, as he understood it "the only ones that really know" what had happened and why would be Hunt and Liddy. But was McCord also knowledgeable? "Probably," Colson surmised. He said that his future law partner, David Shapiro, who knew Sirica very well, thought Sirica would call in the seven Watergate defendants and offer them no jail if they told him everything. In short, "Make a deal with them, before he sentences them." When Nixon asked if any would accept this, Colson repeated, "Would they accept it?" and drew a deep breath as he collected his thoughts. "I don't think Hunt would. He's too much of a believer. On the other hand, who knows?

He's lost his wife, which was a great source of strength to him. He's got four kids."

Colson told the president he was not worried about the Senate's investigation, as the only thing they might find would be "some technical violations of the statute, a few mailings that were done by different committees outside of here. Those were technical violations of the statute" that would be hard to make into "capital cases." The problem would be "if they could get Ehrlichman, Haldeman or me to say under oath that we were aware of anything that was a violation of the statute, then they've got a circus on their hands." To deal with that, Colson added, "either you have to have a John Mitchell–type memory," which caused him to chuckle, "or not appear."

That afternoon, when meeting in the EOB, the president told Haldeman that Colson "sure as hell doesn't want to go down there and testify."[12] Yet the president thought Colson had made a good point in suggesting that whoever was involved needed to come forward now. Haldeman revealed that Colson had made the same argument to him, saying, "Mitchell was going to get hung on this anyway. Why doesn't he come out now and say, 'I'm tired of allowing this farce to go on.'" The president said Mitchell should say it without really saying it, and they discussed different ways he might do so. Nixon still had trouble accepting that Mitchell was involved: "This is an amazing damn thing. It's hard for me to believe that, but it's possible, I guess, that Mitchell could have approved these activities. What in the name of God? Mitchell is a lawyer. He knows about these things." Haldeman offered some clarification, based on his conversation with Magruder. "But the one thing apparently Mitchell didn't know was that McCord was involved in it, because it was all supposed to be getting done by only five people. I think it was kind of weird that McCord was in there, too."

The president's concern about Mitchell continued throughout the conversation, and toward the end they discussed the possibility that Mitchell could be disbarred, if not sent to jail, unless a judge suspended the sentence. Nixon sounded genuinely distressed at the prospect of potential jail sentences for those involved in Watergate. He told Haldeman that he certainly knew his campaign was gathering political intelligence. He said he knew they were getting "information from Chapman's friend," the reporters they had planted with their potential Democratic opponents, and that "Colson was trying to get stuff on Kennedy, and all that other shit."

*February 14, 1973, the White House*

On a brief visit to the Oval Office to say farewell,[13] Colson reported that during a long conversation with Haldeman the day before, and in a conversation with his new law partner David Shapiro, he had developed some additional thoughts on executive privilege: "The president cannot have immediate advisers and a confidential relationship unless he is assured that that confidentiality can be preserved, like a law clerk with a judge or congressional aide." He was writing these ideas up and would send them to me to review with Shapiro while he was gone.

"Good, bring him over and get him to it," replied the president, who was concerned about the charge of stonewalling. That would suggest a cover-up, which could be worse than waiving executive privilege and allowing testimony. "I always go back, of course, to my own experience in the Hiss case. The Hiss case, of course, the [Truman] administration was doubly guilty." Not only was Hiss himself guilty, but "what really creamed them was the charge that the administration was trying to cover it up." Nixon said the Justice Department had tried to drop the case against Hiss, but his congressional committee showed that Hiss was "the red herring," so they killed the cover-up. "It was the cover-up that hurt, not the fact that Hiss was guilty. Get my point?" Colson's concern was a Senate fishing expedition, with the Senate getting into other matters. The president agreed: "Today, for example, like the story in the *Post* this morning commented that Liddy had the FBI doing internal security taps. But I can't believe that's true. I mean, I don't know what they're talking about."* "That could have been true," Colson advised. "They had that security unit set up in the basement of the EOB which Bud Krogh ran." Feigning ignorance, Nixon said, "Oh, I see." Colson continued, "And that was perfectly legitimate. That's the kind of thing they were hired to do. Investigating the authenticity of the Dita Beard letter was a perfectly legitimate thing. And, I told the FBI about that. There wasn't anything to hide." Colson cleared this throat, and added, "The thing you can't do is, you can't get partway pregnant. You can't start talking about one aspect of a relationship with a White House employee and not another."

---

*See Bob Woodward and Carl Bernstein, "Data from Security Taps Reported Given Liddy, Hunt," *The Washington Post*, February 14, 1973, A-1. (The White House press office had denied the story.)

"What does Shapiro think?" Nixon asked. "Shapiro believes that if Mitchell was indeed responsible that he should step forward now and take the heat, and—" Cutting Colson off, the president rhetorically rejected the consequences: "Not go to jail? He can't go to jail." Colson continued, "Well, his point is that he's going to, anyway. Shapiro's point is, if he was guilty, and if it's going to come out in the hearings, then don't let it come out in the hearings, take our own losses ourselves." The president observed that that was easy to say but not so easy to do, and wondered how it could be handled. "It depends on what John knew," Colson answered. "I don't know what he knew firsthand."

"Right." In jumbled syntax Nixon asked if Mitchell was "aware about Hunt and all that sort of thing, is that correct? Is that what's going to come out? That hasn't yet." Colson answered, "That's right. But you see, John doesn't have any privilege. John doesn't have an immediate relationship to you. He was a cabinet officer, and he did have." He continued, "Well, Shapiro's only analysis is just as a cold-blooded analytical lawyer. If you're going to have a big explosion on national television and let goddamn Magruder—"

"Magruder," the president interrupted. "Those are the two, I guess, that are really a problem." When Colson said to the president that he would have the same problem if Magruder knew about it, Nixon quickly added, "Oh, he did." Colson concurred, "I'm sure he did," knowledge Colson had based either on his own conversation with Magruder or on information Bittman had given him when the latter was pressing Hunt's case. "How about Mitchell? Do you think he did?" Nixon asked. Colson could only say he admired Mitchell's convenient memory. "Yeah, yeah," Nixon remarked, and nothing more needed to be said on the subject, so he moved on. "But the point is, after you're gone, you mean that this concern about Hunt cracking, which you expressed, is that incorrect? I suppose if the judge calls him in, do you think that Hunt might just say, 'Well, I'll tell my whole story.' My view is that he won't tell the whole story. My view is that he'd say, 'Alright, I will tell what it is.' But what he would do, frankly, is would be to tell about Mitchell. Do you think that's what he would tell them? Or Magruder? My view is that he would limit the losses, but he wouldn't go all the way." Before he left Colson told the president that working for him during his first term was "really, the proudest thing I've ever done in my life, sir." Nixon reminded him, "Well, you're not leaving, you're just going across the street." "Half a block away," Colson said. "I'm at your service for anything, anytime."

Early that evening Nixon discussed Gray's nomination with Ehrlichman in the Oval Office.[14] "I've been doing a lot of thinking about it. I think we had better take a known quantity with weaknesses that we're aware of in this particular area than to try to take somebody else. Gray is loyal. I realize he's weak in some areas. I realize there'll be some confirmation problem, but let's look at that for just a moment. Maybe it's just as well to have Gray get up there and have them beat him over the head about Watergate, and have him say what the hell he's done."

"Well, he's prepared to do that. I've been over this today with John Dean to see what he says the problems will be. He says it will be a very long, very tough confirmation, and will be an opportunity for a different set of senators to get into the Watergate than the Ervin group.[15] It'll be the Tunneys and the Kennedys and the Bayhs, and so on," Ehrlichman reported, mentioning some of the most aggressive Democrats in the U.S. Senate at the time: John Tunney of California, Teddy Kennedy of Massachusetts and Birch Bayh of Indiana—all lawyers and members of the Senate Judiciary Committee. Ehrlichman added, "But recognizing that, Gray tells a very good story."

The president thought, incorrectly, that sending Gray up would close the door on cover-up charges: "You see, if you kick him upstairs to the circuit court, they'll say that we're afraid of something. There's no way we'll get around it. It'll look like a cover-up. He does not get a different set [of senators]" for a judicial confirmation. Rather, "He gets Kennedy, and Tunney and the rest." As the president saw it, they would go after Gray on any post requiring confirmation. "Gray, it seems to me, makes a rather good impression. I don't know, I haven't seen him on television. Does he?" Nixon asked. "He's very earnest," Ehrlichman replied. "He's very square corners, you know, kind of the retired navy captain." Then, sharing my assessment, Ehrlichman added, "He's vulnerable, according to John's analysis, on two counts. One is whether or not he handled Watergate adequately, and John says, 'I think he'll acquit himself very nicely there.' The other is his stewardship of the Bureau over the period of the last eight months. There, John says, the established bureaucracy of the Bureau will be feeding all kinds of garbage to the committee, and Gray will be on the defensive. So, he says, we're liable to be in for a few surprises, on the handling of other matters or things of that kind that are incalculable right now. But he said he doesn't think that he is in serious jeopardy, and on balance, he thinks Gray is, as you say, is a known quantity,'" This was, in fact, a far stronger endorsement than I had given Ehrlichman.

"He is a guy we can tell to do things, and he will do them," Ehrlichman concluded about Gray. The president protested that Gray had actually been "a little weak on that," but Ehrlichman pointed out that that was because he hoped to face a confirmation. Ehrlichman had also discussed Gray with John Mitchell, who had said that, once confirmed, Gray would be compliant. Citing Mitchell as his authority, Ehrlichman proposed that the president call Gray in and explain: "Pat, I had an arrangement with J. Edgar Hoover that up until now I have not had with you, and I have missed it. Once you're confirmed, I want it understood that we go back to a personal relationship." Nixon added, "Without the attorney general," to whom the Bureau director reports for management purposes, being directly involved. Ehrlichman continued, "'That when I call, you respond, and that we have to have an absolutely tight relationship.'" The president did not wish to make such calls, however, but rather wanted Ehrlichman to do so. "Well, then you could delegate that and go from there," Ehrlichman replied. He added, "As it is now, John [Mitchell] says we made a mistake in the inception in not tying him down tight enough. But we did it for a number of reasons. He was contingent, and we had this [Watergate] thing hanging up, and he's tracked reasonably well. Now he has some guilty knowledge in connection with the Watergate, that only Dean and I know about, and that has to do with Hunt. We turned some stuff over to Gray to get it out of here. That'll never come out. He'll never testify to that, there isn't any way that he could testify to that." When the president wanted to know more, Ehrlichman explained, "Well, it just isn't necessary. There's no way for anybody to know. And that he understands that that set of circumstances never happened, and it's never, never appeared, and never come out."

"If Gray's got them, where are the files?" Nixon asked. Ehrlichman answered, "I don't know where he's got them, but he's got them. We felt that we wanted to be in a position to say we had turned everything over to the FBI, so I called him up to my office one day, and we said, 'Pat, here's a big fat envelope.'" Nixon asked, "What is this—stuff that Hunt did on that case in California?"*

"Well, no, it's other stuff, and Dean's never told me what was in the en-

---

*This appears to be a reference to the Ellsberg break-in, which Ehrlichman claims he told the president about on July 8, 1972, when they took their long walk down Red Beach in California. Nixon would later deny in a sworn statement that he knew of the Ellsberg break-in before March 17, 1973, when I told him about it during a conversation.

velope," Ehrlichman answered. Nixon said he did not know what Hunt dealt with at the White House, but speculated, "Well, he must have been in a hell of a lot of stuff. He did some things for Chuck, apparently, that he made record of." The president wanted to know if that material was in the envelope, and Ehrlichman said it was: "Well, we opened [Hunt's] safe. See, Dean took everything out of his safe, and we turned everything over to FBI agents who came for it, except this envelope full of stuff. And then I called Gray to my office. Dean came in. I said, 'Pat, here's an envelope. We want to be in a position to say we've turned everything over to the FBI, so we're giving it to you. I don't care what you do with it, as long as it never appears.'" The passing of Hunt's file to Gray troubled the president, but Ehrlichman doubted that Gray had ever opened the envelope, and added, "If he was smart, he didn't."

Ehrlichman continued, "Bob or I or John Dean or somebody ought to give you the rundown on how this Ervin hearing is going to go, the kinds of things that are liable to come smoking up, so you're not surprised. But, we think that there's a reasonably good possibility of coming through it very much like we've come through the trial, with a certain amount of day-to-day flak and evening television stuff but no lasting results." Ehrlichman's report was, in fact, far more sanguine than our discussions had been. Nixon noted, "But really the problem is that if one of these guys could crack," to which Ehrlichman agreed. The president continued, "The one that could crack that would really hurt would be Hunt." Ehrlichman agreed again but noted, "Magruder could really hurt in a different direction." "Well, Magruder, if he cracks, he goes to prison," Nixon said, though Ehrlichman cautioned, "Well, unless he takes immunity." Nixon wanted to know if he would do so. "Possibly, possibly," Ehrlichman surmised. "There are several of those guys that we're relying on. Sloan is not a problem," Ehrlichman observed, and Nixon understood that Sloan really did not know anything. "But Magruder is a problem of, ah—" Ehrlichman acknowledged. Nixon interrupted, saying, "Magruder knows a hell of a lot," and added rhetorically, "Let's face it, didn't Magruder perjure himself?"

"Yep," Ehrlichman quickly answered, at which Nixon feigned surprise, asking, "Or did he? I don't know." Ehrlichman flatly reassured him: "Sure did." Nixon admitted that he thought that had been the case, and added, "From what I've heard, he must have," and then pretended to speculate about Magruder, asking: "He said he was not involved, he didn't have the knowledge, and he did. Is that right?" "Basically, that's it, yeah," Ehrlichman confirmed, though Nixon had more questions. "But beyond that, I mean, beyond Magruder, who the hell else perjured himself? Did Mitchell?" Ehrlichman said, without actually knowing, that he assumed that was the case.

After exploring potential vulnerabilities, the president returned to the selection of an FBI director. Ehrlichman mentioned that another "prime candidate is Henry Petersen," but he added that, as the man who had handled the Watergate investigation, he had problems similar to those of Gray. "Oh, Christ, yes," Nixon agreed, plus, he felt, "he wouldn't care what happened to us." Ehrlichman raised and Nixon dismissed other candidates: Bill Ruckelshaus and Vernon Acree, the head of Customs, who Ehrlichman noted was Jack Caulfield's friend and suggestion. The president, unhappy that there was not "a strong man, a loyalist" available for the post, began warming to the idea that Gray could sell the Senate on the completeness of the investigation they had conducted on Watergate. "Well, for example, they'll ask, 'Did you investigate, did you get it straight from Haldeman?' He didn't," the president said, answering his own question, and then asked Ehrlichman, "But did they get one [a statement] from you?"

"Oh, they got two from me," Ehrlichman said,* and reported that the FBI also had taken a statement from Colson, but because no leads pointed to Haldeman, he was never questioned. The assurance that there had been no links to the White House gave the president the comfort he needed with Gray, so he told Ehrlichman, "I think I'd send him up. Okay?"

With that decision made, the conversation turned to the Woodward and Bernstein article in the *Post* that morning about the plumbers unit, which Hunt and Liddy were part of, and the president expressed surprise that national security wiretaps had become available to Howard Hunt. "They didn't," Ehrlichman said, explaining that they had been available only to David Young in his leak investigations. Although Hunt had worked with the plumbers unit, Ehrlichman rather significantly downplayed his involvement in the Ellsberg break-in. "He was taking all those leaks and matching them up to see where the commonality among them was to try and determine which documents they came from." Ehrlichman then clarified, "Oh, Dave Young never got any of this domestic tap stuff," referring to the wiretaps on

---

*The FBI's records show that Ehrlichman was only interviewed on one occasion, July 21, 1973, at which time he told the agents all he knew about Watergate was what he had read in the newspaper, a false statement for which he would be indicted on March 1, 1974.

newsmen and White House staff authorized by the president in the spring of 1969. "Who the hell did?" Nixon asked. "Well," Ehrlichman said, "I got some of it, Bob got a lot of it. Bob got most of it, I think. I'm not aware that anybody else ever did." (The National Archives has redacted the material about who was wiretapped and what was reported.) Later in the conversation, the president was instructing Ehrlichman to express "outrage" if asked about these wiretaps, since the Nixon administration had cut back on the intelligence operations of its predecessors and taken the U.S. Army out of domestic spying. Returning to Pat Gray, the president confirmed, "I'm inclined to think that we just better go with Gray, because I think at the present time we have the worst of both worlds. We can't leave it uncertain." Ehrlichman said he would arrange for Nixon to meet with Gray, but they would not put it on the president's publicly announced schedule, and Nixon could tell Gray that he wanted a back channel if he was nominated for the post.

## February 16, 1973, the White House

The president met with Gray and Ehrlichman in the Oval Office.[16] While they had never been close, Nixon had known Gray since his freshman term in the U.S. House of Representatives in 1947, when Gray was a career navy officer studying law at George Washington University. After working on Nixon's unsuccessful 1960 campaign, Gray had gone into private law practice in Connecticut, returning to the government when Nixon was elected in 1968.

Nixon told Gray he had talked with John Mitchell about his nomination, and it was obvious it was going to open up the Watergate investigation before a committee other than Sam Ervin's. "Now the question is whether you feel that you can handle it, whether that's a good thing, bad thing and so forth," Nixon said, and he expressed his concern that the person nominated for FBI director would be badgered, and whether it was good for us to have the Watergate investigation under the scrutiny of two committees.

They speculated about the kinds of questions Gray might be asked and answers he might give. And the president warned Gray not to make Mark Felt his deputy, given his leaks, which Gray did not want to believe.* "But what

---

*Gray did not live long enough to fully appreciate the extent of Mark Felt's betrayal, but he did get a sense of it when Felt and Ed Miller, an assistant director, were later indicted for authorizing FBI burglars to get information on the Weather Underground while Gray was acting director. They claimed

I've got to do is, and which I'm in the process of doing, is come up with an overall plan to submit to you," Gray said. "And you and I should discuss that plan." Nixon was not ready to drop Felt from the discussion, and he warned Gray, "The only problem you have on Felt is that the lines [for leaks] lead very directly to him." When Gray disputed this, Ehrlichman chimed in, "Well, you know we've tried to trap him. The trap is set to see if we can turn something up." Nixon suggested, "Well, why don't you get in the fellow that's made the charge, then?" Ehrlichman thought that a good idea, and the president reported, "Of course he's not a newsman; on the other hand. He's a lawyer for *Time*." Gray said he knew who had made the charge, and noted "I must say it to you, those people over there are like little old ladies in tennis shoes, and they've got some of the most vicious vendettas going on in their gossip mill."

"It would be very, very difficult to have a Felt in that position without having that charge cleared up," Nixon affirmed, which Gray acknowledged, and then the president added, "And, incidentally, let me say this, and this is also a directive, you should take a lie detector test on him. It leads right to him now."

Nixon said that he had never known of a leak occurring when Hoover was running the FBI, and added, "I could talk to him in this office about everything" without its leaking. Nixon said it was not because FBI agents loved Hoover; rather, it was because "they feared him." Hoover had given lie detector tests to everyone, even his loyalists. "You've got to play it exactly that way. You've got to be brutal, tough and respected, because we can't have any kind of a relationship with the Bureau, which is necessary, unless we can trust it. I used to have, and I would expect, with the director in the future, to have a relationship. With Hoover, he'd come in about every month. He'd be here at breakfast or he'd come in here. He'd come in alone, not with the attorney general. I'd talk about things." Nixon said Hoover might raise hell about other parts of the government, but "it was extremely valuable, and it never leaked out of here; you know that he was giving me the stuff that he had. And he talked with Ehrlichman, he was my contact. Ehrlichman will be yours in the future, you've got to have one man that will not talk. I could

_____

to have used a secret communications system and, falsely, that Gray had authorized the activity. Gray's attorney, Alan Baron, investigated the charges and found the government had no case against his client, and the charges against Gray were dismissed. Ironically, former president Richard Nixon testified in Felt's defense at his criminal trial when he was convicted. President Ronald Reagan then pardoned Felt, a truly cunning operator and undoubtedly one of the most Machiavellian characters in government.

use Dean, but he's too busy on other things." Nixon proceeded to explain to Gray that the relationship between the FBI director and the president was like the relationship of the president and the chairman of the Joint Chiefs. "Now, having said that, though, we can't do it unless there's total communication security and total discipline in the Bureau. I think you've got to do it like they did in World War II: [If] the Germans went through these towns, and then a sniper hit one of [their soldiers], they'd line up the whole goddamned town and say, unless you talk, you're all getting shot. I really think that's what has to be done. I mean, I don't think you can be Mr. Nice Guy over there." Gray assured Nixon he had not been.

Nixon then told Gray that the media would be against him, as would academics, and even Congress, for "it's a hard damn fight." He wanted a director who would "tail people, you know, from time to time," such as "some jackass in the State Department, some assistant to the secretary" who the president thought might be "a little off." Gray again assured the president he would be up to the job. "I'd say, as far as the Watergate, I'd rather put it all out there and not be defensive," the president concluded, and if the Ervin committee called Gray, he and Ehrlichman should work that out. With that, Nixon told Gray he had the job.

### February 21, 1973, the White House

In their midday Oval Office meetings, Haldeman reported he had learned that Sam Ervin was trying "a slick move" to get former Republican senator Ken Keating—a Harvard Law School graduate who represented New York from 1959 to 1964 and became a New York Court of Appeals judge before Nixon appointed him ambassador to Israel—to serve as chief counsel to his Watergate committee.[17] Keating turned down the offer. As Haldeman was relaying this the Senate was announcing that Sam Ervin would chair the Senate Select Committee on Presidential Campaign Activities (SSC, or Senate Watergate committee) to investigate Watergate, and that Howard Baker would serve as vice chairman. It was also announced that Ervin had selected the Georgetown University Law Center's top criminal law professor, Samuel Dash, a former Philadelphia prosecutor, to serve as chief counsel. John Ehrlichman, unaware of these developments, was making belated suggestions to the president about who should serve as Ervin's chief counsel, not that the White House could have influenced the selection in any event.[18]

*February 22, 1973, the White House*

Only minutes into a long afternoon session with Haldeman in the EOB office,[19] the president asked, "Anything new from Dean and his outfit that you heard," adding, regarding the selection of Sam Dash, "I see they got the Jew for the lawyer, huh?" When Haldeman did not have a good response, the president continued, "Why didn't our boys fight?" Haldeman did not think they could do so, given that the Democrats controlled the Senate, so the discussion turned to who Howard Baker would select as the minority counsel. Haldeman reported that Baker was talking about hiring a thirty-year-old former assistant U.S. attorney from Tennessee, news that was greeted with a long sigh by the president. Bill Timmons, who was from Tennessee, had talked to this potential candidate, Fred Thompson, and thought he "would be so totally dazzled by being brought into Washington that he'd be completely lost," Haldeman said. "Howard Baker has asked to meet privately with you on an unannounced basis on the Watergate thing. He wants guidance. And Timmons passes it along, saying it's our call, and he can't even make a recommendation." Haldeman reported that Ehrlichman and I thought the president should meet with Baker, who he assured the president would be discreet.

Haldeman then mentioned the "next" problem on his list, Jeb Magruder, which led to another sigh from Nixon. "We've got a problem there in that we've got to keep him on an even keel," Haldeman explained, "but he is just totally determined to get back into government work somewhere. He thinks he's completely cleared himself, which he did. He did a hell of a job at the thing," referring to Magruder's perjured testimony at the Liddy and McCord trial. "And," Haldeman added, "he's going to do a hell of a job at the Senate hearings. But Dean is very concerned about keeping him on balance." Magruder wanted a top staff post at the Bicentennial Commission and Haldeman said, "What we've come up with as an idea is to make him a consultant of the bicentennial project on an interim basis." He would not be on the White House staff, and it was "a fairly natural transition from [his job at the inaugural committee]." Nixon immediately said to hire him, and then asked, "Could Magruder hang Mitchell on his testimony?" Haldeman replied obliquely, "I don't think he would."

"The question is the perjury charge," Nixon said. "That's what I'm concerned about Magruder." Haldeman explained that the bicentennial job was "a way to keep him happy."

The discussion turned to the Senate's Watergate investigation and consideration of whether Pat Buchanan or Ken Clawson should be an "observer
spokesman" for any Watergate hearings. The president did not want Buchanan but he had no reaction to Clawson.

Haldeman continued through his agenda: "Then the other question
which Dean feels is very serious, and Mitchell does also, is getting Attorney
General Kleindienst back on the reservation. The problem is that Kleindienst, as I think I've mentioned to you, is biding his time looking for a job,
getting ready to go out. But he has total loyalty to you. And [the thought is
that] you asked him to stay in office one full year. In other words, until the
hearings are past. [He shouldn't leave] before, because the hearings may well
result in a request for additional action by the Justice Department, and there
shouldn't be a new attorney general in there. And you can get Henry Petersen to handle the sensitive problems, because Petersen has total loyalty to
Kleindienst, and has done a superb job and knows all this stuff. We can't
afford bitterness in the Justice Department. We can't just get a new attorney
general trying to get into these problems; rather, we need to keep him on a
while." Nixon agreed but wondered if Kleindienst would remain. To help
deal with the problem, the president thought he should tell Kleindienst he
had total confidence in me. Kleindienst typically dealt with Ehrlichman, the
senior staff man, and rather than lowering the attorney general's status with
a switch to a middle-level staffer like me, he was giving me more authority
to take some of the load off Ehrlichman. They would bring Kleindienst in
for a chat.

"Actually, Bob, the hearing thing, I think the Watergate thing will become extremely tiresome," the president said. He also thought the committee would have a problem, given that the Watergate defendants were
appealing their convictions. The president thought maybe "the Segretti
thing" would become the focus. "Oddly enough, they're not doing any investigation of Segretti," Haldeman reported. "That means no one is working
the Segretti thing at this point, which Dean can't figure out, because we all
had the same feeling that that's what they were going to play on." With
concern in his voice, Nixon asked, "You mean they're just sticking to
Watergate?"

"Right," Haldeman reported. "Well, it's really a damn shame this Watergate thing goes on and on and on," the president noted. Haldeman called it
"sort of a permanent cross" of embarrassment. When the president said the
hearings were expected to go on for a year, Haldeman explained that the

Senate had called for the committee's report "no later than February of next year," so he did not think the hearings could go that long.

In the course of other items on his list, Haldeman suddenly remembered, "Oh, Baker's appointed Fred Thompson to minority counsel."

"Oh, shit. That kid?" the president asked. "Well, we seem to lose them all here, don't we?" "Well, that's why they felt you ought to see Baker," Haldeman replied. The president wondered if it was now too late, but Haldeman thought not, and they discussed making White House staff available to Baker.

Haldeman now called me regarding a talking paper I had prepared for a meeting between Nixon and Baker, and wanted to know why it did not include all the actions the Democrats had taken to undermine Nixon's campaign, such as using communist money to underwrite violent demonstrations. "Bob," I told him, "we haven't developed much hard information yet regarding the communist money. We have no documentation of that sort of money ever having been involved."[20]

When their conversation resumed, Haldeman explained to Nixon that they were still trying to develop a strategy to delay the Senate proceedings as long as they could. Although the president thought they should get them over with as quickly as possible, the White House, in fact, had absolutely no control over the situation.

That afternoon, Howard Baker was slipped into the Executive Office Building from West Executive Drive by Bill Timmons and taken to the president's office.[21] Baker managed to seat himself about as far away from the microphones buried in the president's desk as possible, resulting in a mostly inaudible recording. While the president's official record of the meeting indicates it lasted approximately forty minutes, the recording runs only eight and a half minutes. This visit might well have continued in Nixon's outer office, which would not have been recorded. Notwithstanding the poor audio, the gist of the recorded conversation can be heard, and Nixon later mentioned matters they had discussed.

Pleasantries were brief, and almost immediately Baker told the president, "Nobody knows I'm here, except Bill Timmons." Baker wanted to keep his visit secret.* It is not clear what "guidance" Baker was seeking, but what he

---

*To this day this meeting will not be found in the president's daily diary. It was set up so that, immediately afterward, Baker would attend a reception in the State Dining Room for members of Congress who had supported the president's Vietnam policies. Shortly after their meeting ended the president

got were protestations of innocence from the president, with Nixon domi-
nating the conversation. Baker may have been concerned that he was inadvertently assisting in developing a case that would destroy a Republican
presidency, so he wanted to see if he could read any problem signs, and later
use this private meeting to protect his own ambitious career. Early in the
conversation Baker stressed that he did not want the committee conducting
"a fishing expedition." Nixon's only real complaint was that he did not like
the idea of Haldeman's and Ehrlichman's being hauled up to the committee
and put on television, but he agreed with Baker that they should get the
hearing over with as quickly as possible. The president said he had made an
investigation, and Watergate would fall on Mitchell's shoulders.

"Who is Dash?" the president asked. "Sam Dash was Dick Kleindienst's
classmate at Harvard [Law]," Baker reported. "Who is Thompson?" the president asked. "Fred Thompson is an [assistant] U.S. attorney for Tennessee,"
Baker responded. The president expressed concern about Dash's getting
"awfully partisan," and whether Thompson could "go in there" and handle
him. Baker said Thompson was tough, six feet six inches tall, "a big, mean
fella." "Smart?" Nixon asked. "Terribly," Baker assured him. The president
reported that he was going to ask Kleindienst to stay on through the hearings, and while Baker found Kleindienst "a little flamboyant, a little unpre-
dictable," he thought he would be fine in this case. After about six minutes
of bouncing matters around without much direction, Baker said, "I'm really
sorry to trouble you with this." The president said it was no problem, adding,
"In the meantime, I know you'll do a good job. You're exactly right. The main
thing is to have no damn cover-up, that's the worst thing that could happen."
He added, "If it does get rough, then I think you may have to, at a certain
time, turn and get out, get away from it." Baker agreed, and the meeting
ended.

*February 23, 1973, the White House*

Talking with John Ehrlichman the next morning, the president reported,
"Baker's line is about what you'd expect. He would like to have his contact

---

went up to the residence to freshen up, while Timmons guided Baker to the reception, which included
thirty senators (including two other members of the Senate Watergate committee: Chairman Sam
Ervin and Edward Gurney [R-FL], and over 140 members of the House of Representatives. It was a
perfect cover for Baker's private session.

be Kleindienst. He and Ervin met with Kleindienst."[22] The president asked if that was okay with Ehrlichman, who replied that it was fine. "Kleindienst has a kind of metaphysical attachment to John Mitchell," Ehrlichman observed. The president said, "I must have scared him to death. I put it very hard to Baker about Mitchell. Because Baker was hinting about the White House staff and all that, and I said, well, I checked them all over, and I said, unless somebody's lying, my main concern [is Mitchell.]" But the president told Ehrlichman that was not quite true, because "the thing I'm concerned about [is] the Magruder thing, [because] Bob and that Magruder is just awfully close. I don't think Magruder would say something. But he might."

"If he did, he would implicate Mitchell. He would protect Bob, I suspect. I think that's the way now [it would fall]," Ehrlichman surmised. Nixon solicited Ehrlichman's view regarding Colson's role, whose exposure Nixon assumed was Hunt. Ehrlichman agreed, adding, "And Magruder." The president was confused, and asked, "Did Magruder work with Colson?" Ehrlichman explained, "Magruder claims to Dean, and Magruder's playing a game, he's telling different people different things, apparently, and I've not talked to him. But the impression I have is that Magruder's peddling the line that Colson is the guy who put the unmitigated pressure on him."

"To change the bug?" the president asked. "To do this," Ehrlichman said flatly. "To bug?" Nixon asked again, and Ehrlichman responded with a matter-of-fact "yep." The president reported, "Well, you see, Colson denies that completely," which Ehrlichman said he knew. The president continued, "But I've asked both Bob and Colson. Well, I don't know, I can't—" This information troubled the president. He added, "I have really got to know whether or not, because, mainly because—" His thoughts were not clear as he stuttered a bit, but he said, if they were involved, "then I'll deny that I ever heard it." Ehrlichman said he understood, and Nixon declared, "I've got to know whether Bob knew about it, and I've got to know whether Colson knew about it." No one had ever laid it all out for him, even when he had asked. He added, "If they both, if they did, then we're going to play our games," clearly meaning to cover it up. "That's right," Ehrlichman agreed. The president explained that it was important for him to know this before issuing a statement on executive privilege.

Nixon then continued his report on the meeting with Baker, telling Ehrlichman, "I gave him a good lecture about how the Hiss case was handled," saying he told Baker, "We ruled out hearsay. We ruled out guilt by association and innuendo and so forth. You ought to really insist on that."

The president went on: "He wanted me to issue a statement to the effect that we would cooperate with the committee. I said, I'm going to have a press conference one of these days, and I'll so say. I've always stated that. I mean, I'm not going to put out any written statement to the effect." The president then told Ehrlichman that Baker explained the way the committee's inquiry was going to proceed, which he did not like: They would first call "a lot of pipsqueak witnesses, little shit-asses over periods of weeks to build it up, the pressure, so they would have to call Colson, you got to call Haldeman, you got to call Ehrlichman and Chapin, whoever the hell, sorry, they'll have called Chapin, anyway." Nixon said Baker's strategy was to conduct their own private investigation, confront Ervin, and cut off the inquiry, whether or not it went higher than the seven already convicted. Baker wanted to "call the big men right away. Prick the boil." After that, Baker felt, everybody would get bored to death. Nixon said he liked the strategy.

The president reported that Baker wanted to sit down with Ervin and place a "total limitation as to the subjects." The president added that he had told Baker he did not like having his top aides "dragged up." Again Nixon pressed Ehrlichman: The real question was, whose testimony were they afraid of, and therefore needed to cover on executive privilege? He wanted to know if it should be Haldeman or Colson, but when he addressed Ehrlichman, he said, "I don't think you have a problem." Ehrlichman, who would be convicted of more crimes than anyone save Liddy, flatly told the president, "I don't have the problem." Nixon pressed, "You worked with Hunt." Ehrlichman repeated, "I don't have the problem."

Ehrlichman noted that those he thought did have a problem—Mitchell, Stans, Colson and Kalmbach—were all out of the White House, so without any potential privilege, and the real concern was who had approved the money for the operation. "And those chips are going to have to pretty much fall where they may, as I see it." "What are they going to say? They raised the money?" Nixon asked. Ehrlichman noted, "There's a hell of a lot of money, and it floated around, and there weren't receipts, and there was funny book-keeping, and there was a lot of hanky-panky, and money went to Mexico and back, and there were just a hell of a lot of odds and ends of stuff over there. Now, Stans says he's clean, and I suspect he is. I think he can tell a damn good story."

"Knowing Stans, yes," the president agreed. "So Mitchell was going to end up being the fall guy in that," Ehrlichman noted. "What'll Mitchell say?" the president asked. Ehrlichman replied, "I don't know what he'll say. I just don't know what he'll say. He's been puffing his pipe and looking at the ceiling and saying, 'You guys got a problem.' And we're beginning to get to him a little bit. Dean's been hammering away on him to impress on him that he's got a problem here." They speculated about what Mitchell might say, agreeing that his best defense was to claim he simply failed to keep close controls on the distribution of the money. "It's his only defense, and it may be correct," the president said.

Ehrlichman replied, "I think he knew, and I think LaRue was sort of his agent, and he kept him posted." This was a new player in the Watergate story. "LaRue?" the president asked, for it was the first time anyone had mentioned the former Nixon White House aide and Mississippi oilman being connected with these illegal activities. "Oh, yeah, LaRue's in this thing up to his ass," Ehrlichman assured the president. "Has he been called?" Nixon asked. "LaRue's a mysterious, shadowy figure that hasn't been called," Ehrlichman said. "But he was into it?" the president said with dismay. "Oh, yeah," Ehrlichman again assured the president, and then decided to give him a bit more information about Haldeman: "Now, Bob had what we call constructive knowledge." Nixon asked, "How did he get that?"

"Through a fellow named Gordon Strachan. Gordon Strachan's job here was Bob's liaison with the campaign." Ehrlichman had the president's full attention with this information, for while Nixon knew of Strachan's role in the Segretti matter, he had not been aware that Strachan had somehow been involved in, or connected to, Watergate, other than a fleeting hint by Haldeman during their December 10, 1972, morning conversation. Ehrlichman continued, "Gordon Strachan kept the most meticulous attention to the details. But very little of it was actually imparted to Bob. Strachan was a sort of a data bank, so that if Bob needed to know something, he'd pick up the phone and say, 'Gordon, what about this or that?' and he knew."

"My point is, did Bob know that information was coming from tapped sources?" Nixon asked. "No, but I suspect Strachan did," Ehrlichman surmised, leading Nixon to suggest, "Strachan's just the message guy." Ehrlichman continued, "Well, Strachan probably never comes into it, because Strachan's job was not to direct anybody to do anything. He was just to keep informed." This was less than a full characterization of Strachan's role, which involved carrying messages for Haldeman and taking part in certain actions when requested to by him.

"Information manager," the president said, which Ehrlichman affirmed, and continued, "Now, on Colson you have two diametrically opposite stories. You have his and you have Dean's conclusions born of a lot of odds and ends of circumstantial evidence that he's putting together. Dean tells me privately that he thinks that Colson was in fact in meetings and that Colson probably was the effective cause of Magruder doing this tap work. Now, that's his conclusion, based on circumstantial evidence," which Ehrlichman did not mention had come to me from Magruder, Mitchell and Colson. After a few false starts the president reacted to this information, as he had when Haldeman had given him similar information earlier: "I believe Colson's totally capable of it, but I would doubt if Colson would be that unintelligent, that's all." Ehrlichman, however, quickly called Colson's intelligence into play, reminding Nixon, "Well, let me tell you, the Hunt trip to [interview] Dita Beard was a bonehead play."

"Oh, it was. Silliest thing I ever heard of," Nixon agreed. Ehrlichman noted that was a "Colson operation from beginning to end, so I have to assume that Hunt was kind of intrigued with—" Nixon interrupted to note that Colson "very possibly might be behind this whole thing," and Ehrlichman continued, "—I think he was. I think he was, because Hunt's a cops-and-robbers type. Now, I'm not going to tell you with any degree of assurance that Chuck's involved, but what's important to know about this is that there are circumstances which diligent counsel could put together in the same way as John [Dean] did." Nixon did not disagree with any of Ehrlichman's analysis, and it brought him back to the issue of executive privilege, which was the first thing they needed to decide. Nixon thought he might talk with Kleindienst about it, when he called him to get him to stay on, suggesting they start with written interrogatories as the opening negotiating point.

As they probed this topic, the president finally said he was worried about Colson, who out of the White House could not be protected by executive privilege. But Ehrlichman was not concerned. "Colson will handle himself beautifully. He's righteously indignant. He's been on the Elizabeth Drew show. He's taken the *Today Show* questions, and he says, hell, I haven't anything to hide, and I'm fine, I'm clean and all the rest of it."

"Right, right, right," Nixon said, and added, "Except he'll perjure himself." But Ehrlichman was not sure it was perjury, and the president harkened back to the Hiss case, and then noted, "Whether it's against Mitchell or Colson, it's a hell of a hard rap to prove. Don't you agree? As a trial lawyer?"

When Ehrlichman described their situation as "very circumstantial," Nixon added, "I don't believe you can convict a person on circumstantial evidence of perjury. I don't believe it can be done." Ehrlichman posed a hypothetical: "Let's suppose we said, as a matter of long-standing policy back seven generations, the president's immediate staff does not testify, regardless of what the matter is. And so in effect we take the Fifth Amendment, and we sit here, and we just sit it out. Is that worse?"

"Yeah, it's a cover-up. It's a cover-up, and I think that's worse than what'll come out, in my opinion," the president said. "Well, I think so, too," Ehrlichman agreed. "I'd like to do that from a personal standpoint," Nixon said, "but believe me, I've been through this. The cover-up is worse than whatever comes out. It really is. Unless somebody is going to go to jail. I'm not going to let anybody go to jail. That, I promise you. That is the worst." The conversation that followed did not resolve what kind of executive privilege statement might be appropriate nor was there additional discussion about who might go to jail because of Watergate. As Ehrlichman left the Oval Office, Attorney General Dick Kleindienst was ushered in.

At the outset of their conversation the president offered his attorney general advice about big-time law firms, which he knew well.[23] He had spoken the day before with John Connally, who wanted to hire Kleindienst. "First, you should not go with Mitchell. You must not do that," Nixon stated adamantly, without explaining why. Kleindienst had, in fact, already reached that same conclusion. "Second, you should not go with former [Florida Democratic senator George] Smathers, because [of the type of practice, although] you'd make twice as much money at Smathers, but you had to deal with a lot of Jews and other people that Smathers said [are] bad people. Third, Connally's a decent man and, and, I've had business with his firm. Since he would make you one of the managers of the firm, it's a big firm, you'd have your voice in things. And since he would not be pushing you to get in business, it means you wouldn't have to sell your soul, very few get that as well. You'd be tremendously valuable to them. He likes you, that's the key for the guys who are running that firm. You'd make a hell of a lot of money. And you'd live in Washington and, if you want to go the law way, that's infinitely better than New York firms. New York firms are selfish, horrible bastards. Texans would be selfish, too, but there is decency about them, and Connally would be good. Connally also is going to be in on a lot of good international stuff, and you could have a lot of fun with, if you want to do it, you know, you'd enjoy moving around the world and so forth. You'd be a very good asset to him, which I told him, and I think you could, you have something to bring to him that you can't bring to Mitchell."

Adjusting his position in his chair, the president continued. "The other possibility you have in law is to go in for yourself. The difficulty with that is that then everybody's going to be coming to you, frankly, for influence peddling. See, the Connally firm is big, established. They've got clients already, and they wouldn't say, well, they came because of [your arrival]. The main thing I found when I went into a firm in New York, they were very nice about it, but I felt an obligation to get out and try to hustle some business for them, and of course, people did come to us. God, in the long range, it was embarrassing. You should never be out feeling that you've got a rod in your back to get out and, you know, to hustle business. You'll do it anyway, but you must always be in a position, Dick, to be able to turn down something that doesn't smell good. There it is. How does it sound? Now, you just think about it." Kleindienst, somewhat overwhelmed by the president's thoughtful analysis and candid counseling, replied only, "My goodness."

Nixon raised a few more points, based on his chat with Connally, while Kleindienst reminded him that federal law prohibited him, while in office, from negotiating for a job outside government. So he was not having any conversations with the Connally folks. They discussed the practice of law for a while, until the president turned to the reason he wanted to visit.

"Now, the other thing I wanted to get into, obviously, is Watergate, and I want to talk to you candidly about it, and this affects your plans. You were talking about staying on through July or August or something like that," the president began. "I'll stay on as long as you want," Kleindienst volunteered. "I'd like to ask you to stay, and I want you to tell Connally this, until [the Watergate committee issues its] reports." The president estimated that would be through the year. "You'll lose a hundred thousand dollars, let's face it, but if you could stay through the year, I would appreciate it." "I want to stay there as long as you want me, Mr. President," Kleindienst repeated.

Nixon now wanted to be sure the attorney general was onboard to assist with the Senate's Watergate investigation hearings. The president reported that he had met with Baker but wanted Kleindienst to deal with me at the White House. "Very bright young fellow," my former boss at the Justice Department added, and the president continued, "I would like for you to use him exclusively on Watergate. Now, I don't want you to talk to anybody else,

okay? I don't want you to talk to Ehrlichman. I don't want you to talk to
Haldeman. I don't want you talking to Colson, or anybody else, just Dean.
Fair enough?" Kleindienst said it was, but he thought that only he should
deal with Baker.

Nixon agreed, but mentioned that Baker had it all wrong on Maury Stans,
so Kleindienst should correct that misinformation. "Now that brings us,
however, to the fellow that I really think is the greatest problem, and that is
Mitchell. Now, on Mitchell, he has laid the line, you know. I've forgotten, so
let me tell you what I understand." After a brief recounting of his experience
with perjury on the Hiss case, Nixon said, "Now, John [Mitchell], I don't
know this, but I can't help but believe, [so I] assume that John must have
known about these activities." Kleindienst agreed.[24]

The president continued, "The point is that John has denied it categorically, and so what I'm concerned about is the perjury." Then the president
said, "But now, with that in mind," he raised the situation with Baker, who
he told to cross-examine Mitchell and to bring out the facts about his "horrible domestic problem. I said, Martha, you know, is very sick. And John
wasn't paying any attention, and these kids ran away with it. Now that's the
line I've taken, and that's the one I want you to take. John Mitchell is a pure,
bright guy who would have never done such a thing, but the kids ran away
with it. And if John did lie, it was simply because he'd forgotten. Now,
whether that will wash or not, I don't know, but I just want you to know that
[is what] I consider the Mitchell problem." Nixon thought Mitchell would
survive. "But I can't have John run the possibility of a charge of perjury."

Kleindienst agreed, and the president proceeded. "Alright. Now, let's
come to the White House staff. I think you should know about it. Dean is
conducting an investigation. I figure, Gray is conducting an investigation
and so forth. And I'm thinking of putting Gray's name up [for nomination]."
The president paused to tell Kleindienst, "When they ask about Watergate,
Gray can say that he conducted a hell of an investigation," and then he continued, "Ehrlichman didn't know a God damned thing, that's for sure." Colson worked with Hunt on the ITT matter, which created an inference, but
"Colson totally denies it. Now, the other is Haldeman. The problem with
Haldeman's case, frankly, is Magruder. Magruder did work for Haldeman."
Kleindienst now interrupted, revealing more knowledge of the matter than
might be expected, given that he had let Henry Petersen run the investigation: "Magruder's got the same problem Mitchell has. It's possible that he

and Mitchell both might have known." Nixon pulled back slightly, "Well, that's what people assume. Now, with Magruder you've got the problem that if you go to him, he's not a very strong personality, and Magruder—" The president stopped midsentence and simply said, "I don't know." Again, Kleindienst clearly read the situation, noting, "I think he probably knows." Nixon completed the speculation, noting, "Magruder will probably turn on Mitchell rather than Haldeman, that's my guess. He's Haldeman's man."

"I don't think he'll turn on anybody," Kleindienst offered. "You don't?" Nixon asked, surprised. "No, I think he's [that sensitive]." When the president expressed doubt, Kleindienst affirmed, "I really do."

This rather frank exchange was followed by Nixon's raising his favorite potential defense, the allegation that his campaign plane had been bugged in 1968. Kleindienst candidly told the president that he did not think it would make any difference whatsoever in the Senate's Watergate investigation. This was true but was not what Nixon wanted to hear. The president then explained Baker's suggested strategy of calling the major players early and asked whether the Watergate committee should be given raw FBI files, and Kleindienst said, summaries only. The remainder of the conversation was largely a bull session, but the president had accomplished what he set out to do. Kleindienst would remain in place and be the liaison to the Senate Watergate committee, and he was sensitized to Mitchell's and Magruder's situations, not to mention the problems of the Watergate investigation's embarrassing the president.

# Nixon Discovers His White House Counsel, and Gray Puts Me in the Spotlight

A
s February was coming to an end, with Magruder still content and under control at a high-level appointment in the Department of Commerce, none of the Watergate investigators were content or under control. Nonetheless, Nixon was ready to risk Gray's nomination, based on the logic that Gray would be forced to testify about the FBI's Watergate investigation whether or not he was sent up for confirmation. To lighten the load on Ehrlichman and Haldeman, who were still very busy with the organization and staffing of the second administration, the president decided to deal with me directly, so I could deal with others for him.

Eight months after the arrests at the DNC's offices I had become what I later described as the "desk officer" of the cover-up, in which role I monitored ongoing activities and passed information from Haldeman and Ehrlichman to Mitchell, and vice versa, occasionally adding my thoughts. I spoke regularly to the Justice Department and the lawyers representing the reelection committee, who in turn collected information from the lawyers representing the Watergate defendants. Contrary to the president's statement to Kleindienst, and at his August 29, 1972, press conference, I had never investigated anything relating to the Watergate break-in other than the Segretti matter, which I first reported on verbally to Haldeman and Ehrlichman and later in a written summary and which Haldeman had reported to Nixon. On February 27, quite unexpectedly, my secretary, Jane Thomas, told me that the president wanted to see me immediately in the Oval Office. It was the first of what would become almost daily meetings that would continue from the end of February through two thirds of March, as the Watergate cover-up largely unraveled.

From having almost no contact whatsoever, I was now seeing or hearing from the president several times a day, about Watergate. The historical record shows that I had a total of thirty-seven Watergate-related talks with Nixon, of which thirty-one were recorded, starting with the first, on September 15, 1972 (when the Watergate indictments had been handed down) and the remainder beginning on February 27, 1973; the last occurred on April 16, 1973.[1] When I wrote *Blind Ambition* in 1975 I had access to transcripts of ten of those discussions.[2] My description of those meetings in my earlier book remains valid: "Three themes dominated my conversation with the President until mid-March: his desire to launch a counter-scandal against the Democrats, his reminiscence of the Hiss case, and his determination to find a strategy to handle the upcoming Ervin hearings."[3] To this depiction I would add that these early conversations were about process rather than the substance; considerations of who had done what and why arose only later. In this book I have not repeated my earlier characterizations from *Blind Ambition* of those conversations, but only added insights after hearing them in context or upon learning new information.

When later appearing before the Senate, I testified I thought I had been taped during an April 15 conversation, and suspected that may also have been the case during other discussions, but that I did not really know for certain. I tried to remember the gist of all the talks, and any specific details I could recall. But I certainly appreciated how imperfect our memories are in reconstructing actual conversations.[4] When the tapes later became available I discovered I had been unable to separate events from one day to the next, and I conflated events or put one event I thought had occurred on one date on another day. Our memories are not date-stamped, a fact I tried to make clear when testifying. While I felt I did (and blessedly still do) have a good memory, I made clear to the Senate that it was not perfect.[5]

### February 27–28, 1973, the White House

During my Oval Office conversation on the afternoon of February 27 the president instructed me to step forward and start dealing with Kleindienst regarding the Senate's Watergate hearings.[6] I mentioned my doubts about Baker's selection of Fred Thompson as his minority counsel: "Well. I can't knock age, he's thirty years of age (only two year younger than me), but he doesn't know a thing about Washington." When the president wanted to know how much detail I had given Kleindienst, I explained, "I've braced Kleindienst in the past about, you know, the potential implications of what this whole investigation the Bureau conducted, what the U.S. Attorney's Office was doing. Things I thought could haunt us if it gets out of hand. I didn't want to get into a lot of specifics. At our last meeting, I just sat with him and said, 'Dick, I don't think I ought to brief you on everything I know. I don't think that's the way to proceed. But if I see you going down the wrong track, I'm going to have to tell you why.'" Nixon approved, and wanted to know Kleindienst's reaction. "He said, 'I agree, that's the way it should stand.'"

We discussed the president's executive privilege statement, my thoughts on its timing, and whether he should issue it separately versus making a statement during a press conference. We talked about the recent *Time* magazine leak of national security wiretaps and my conversations with Bill Sullivan, who had given me information about how Lyndon Johnson had used the FBI. At one point the president asked me about Mark Felt's leaking: "Do you believe the *Time* magazine lawyer? Is Felt up to it, is he capable of this sort of thing?" Rather than sharing my misgivings about Felt, I explained I had received this information about Felt from Henry Petersen. I also reported that Kleindienst thought, if the leaker was Felt and they pushed him out, it would only create more problems, given his knowledge.

"You take the responsibility for Kleindienst, I'm going to keep Ehrlichman and Haldeman out of any relationship with Kleindienst. You should have it only, but you've got to watch him and brace him," Nixon instructed. The conversation turned to Pat Gray's confirmation hearings, and I gave him my thoughts about Gray. The president already sensed that he had made a mistake in nominating him, telling me, "Pat Gray is a little naive." When Haldeman arrived, this twenty-five-minute meeting came to an end, and Nixon requested that I keep him posted on executive privilege and Kleindienst. That evening he dictated for his diary, "The talk with John Dean was very worthwhile. He is an enormously capable man. Dean went through quite an amazing recitation as to how Johnson had used the FBI. Apparently he had the FBI to bugging or at least intelligence work on even the New Jersey Democratic convention [in 1964]."[7]

The next morning, February 28, I was summoned back to the Oval Office for a conversation that ran over an hour.[8] It had not proceeded very far before I realized it was not unlike our September 15 discussion, and was more of a rambling bull session than anything else. Soon I found myself sharing stories about Lyndon Johnson's White House, and we further speculated on Mark Felt's leaking, with the president considering his removal. He did not think Felt could leave and reveal what he knew: "He couldn't do it unless he had a guarantee from somebody like *Time* magazine saying, 'Look we'll give you a job for life.' Then what do they do? They put him in a job for life, and everybody would treat him like a pariah. He's in a very dangerous situation. These guys, you know, the informers. Look what it did to Chambers," he said regarding his key witness in the Hiss case. "Chambers informed because he didn't give a God damn. But then, one of the most brilliant writers according to Jim [*unclear*] we've ever seen in this country, probably the best writer in this century. They finished him. Either way, the informer is not wanted in our society. Either way, that's the one thing people do sort of line up against. They say, well that son of a bitch informed, I don't want him around. We wouldn't want him around, would we?" Never conceiving that one day I would find myself in that very role, I agreed, "That's right."

"What is the situation, incidentally, with regard to the sentencing of our people, the seven? When the hell is that going to occur?" When I answered most likely in a week or so, he asked, "Why has it been delayed so long?" I responded that I understood the judge was awaiting a presentence report, based on background reviews by probation officers. More pointedly, the president wanted to know if Judge Sirica was "trying to work on them to break them." which he believed was the case. "Well, there's some of that," I replied, and told the president we had learned (from Hunt's lawyer, who had informed the CRP attorneys) that Judge Sirica was using the court's probation office for more than a normal probation report, since they were undertaking a mini-Watergate investigation for Sirica.

"You know, when they talk about a thirty-five year sentence," the president began, with a tone of outrage in his voice, thinking about how Sirica was treating the Watergate defendants, "here's something that does not involve weapons, right? There were no injuries, right? There was no success—" then corrected himself "—well, success maybe, I don't know." He paused, and then continued, saying what was being done to the Watergate defendants was ridiculous when compared to "these blacks, you know, who goes in and holds up a store with a God damned gun, and, they give him two years and then probation after six months." I added, "And they let him out on bond during the time that he is considering his case. These fellows cannot get out—"

"Aren't they out? Have they been in jail?" All but one was in jail, I explained. "Hunt made the bond. Everybody else is in jail. They've got a
hundred-thousand-dollar surety bond, which means they have to put up
actual collateral, but none of these people have a hundred thousand dollars.
The Court of Appeals has been sitting for two weeks, or better now, on a
review of the bond issue. They're not even letting these people out to prepare
their case for appeal."

My mention of the U.S. Court of Appeals for the District of Columbia
Circuit touched a nerve with Nixon, and he spoke of how he wanted to turn
that court from its far-left leanings. This discussion, in turn, led to one about
the U.S. Supreme Court, where the president had appointed Chief Justice
Warren Burger (1969) along with three associate justices: Harry Blackmun
(1970), Lewis Powell (1971) and William Rehnquist (1971).* He was hoping
for additional vacancies, and we shared rumors about the health of the five
Democratic appointees still sitting on the Court. Nixon was aware of the fact
that Justice William Douglas had a pacemaker. He asked me if William Brennan was in good health, and I said he was, as far as I was aware, but when
the president said Brennan was over seventy, I corrected him, for at the time
Brennan was only sixty-seven. "Thurgood Marshall?" the president asked.
"Marshall's in bad health," I reported. "Well, they say that, but is he really?"
I shared the information I had gotten from a former Supreme Court law clerk
now working in my office, who had told me that Marshall was in conspicuously bad shape, a "weak man and not in good health." The president added,
"Marshall, of course, is a black." Nixon added caustically, "He is so God
damn dumb. We can get one that is as bad as he is." He continued: "Well, I
was thinking, for example, if we take this fellow [William H.] Brown,† the
one at the Equal Opportunities thing," for the president thought "he'd be
very good. The other [black], of course, is taking Jewel over here," he said,
referring to Jewel Lafontant. "Why not kill two birds with one stone, get a
black woman."‡ "Make it an historic appointment," I noted with enthusiasm.

---

*This part of my conversation was redacted for decades. Until writing this book I had never listened
to it, but when I did I understood why Nixon had suppressed it.

†Nixon had named Brown chairman of the U.S. Equal Employment Opportunities Commission in
1969. Brown (born in 1928) is now a Philadelphia-based attorney and, as Nixon recognized, an able
attorney.

‡Jewel S. Lafontant was the first African American woman to graduate from the University of Chicago
Law School; she had been an assistant U.S. attorney (1955–58) and a delegate to the 1960 GOP convention, who gave a seconding speech for Nixon. In 1963 she was the first black woman to argue a case
before the U.S. Supreme Court, and she had run unsuccessfully for judicial office in Illinois. In 1972

Nixon continued, "She's a good woman. When they say she isn't a tower-ing figure, well, who the hell is a towering figure on that Court? I've don't have to say that Douglas hasn't got a brain; Brennan's a boob; Thurgood Marshall's a boob; Whizzer White is better than ordinary, and he's above average; Potter Stewart is a weak man, Potter's a nice fellow but weak and not strong, for something's happened to him since he's been here. Our own people, Blackmun is slightly above average; Burger is way above average, because of his administrative abilities; Powell is way above average. And that's the bulk of it." He had missed one, so I asked, "And Rehnquist?" Nixon quickly declared, "Rehnquist is the top."

The president told me he was reading, and recommended, "a fascinating little book, not well written, by Malcolm Smith, Jr., on Kennedy's thirteen great mistakes," which critiqued his foreign and domestic policy practices. "They are great mistakes," Nixon added, "and one of them had to do with the Bay of Pigs." As the conversation progressed, Nixon turned philosophi-cal about the Watergate defendants, and he spoke about the cover-up as if he were very aware of what was happening.

"Well, you can follow these characters to their Gethsemane. I feel for those poor guys in jail, I mean, I don't know—" He hesitated for a mo-ment, then said, "Particularly for Hunt. Hunt with his wife dead. It's a tough thing." "There is every indication that they're hanging in tough right now," I reported. Then the president asked, "What the hell do they expect, though? Do they expect to get clemency within a reasonable time?" I answered can-didly, "I think they do." He asked, "What would you say? What would you advise on that?" I was noncommittal, wondering about how he was feeling, "I think it's one of those things we'll have to watch very closely." He then said, "You couldn't do it, say, in six months?" I said, "No." "No," the president echoed, wistfully. "No, you couldn't. This thing may become so political as a result of these hearings that it is more—" I was about to tell him he might never be able to employ clemency when he asked, as I was looking for a way to express it, "—a vendetta?" I could not disagree with his assessment. "Yeah, it's a vendetta. This judge may go off the deep end in sentencing and make it so absurd that it's clearly an injustice," I submitted. Nixon asked, "Is there any kind of appeal left?" I responded that Liddy and McCord, who had

---

Nixon appointed her as a U.S. representative to the United Nations, and later Nixon made her the first-ever African American woman deputy solicitor general at the Department of Justice.

gone through the trial, were both appealing. "And there is no telling how long that will last. I think this is one of these things we'll just have to watch," I said.

"My view is, say nothing about the event on the ground that the matter is still in the courts and on appeal," the president said. I agreed, and he continued. "That's my position. Second, my view is to say nothing about the hearings at this point, except that I trust that they will be conducted in the proper way, and I will not comment on the hearings while they are in process. And then, of course, if they break through, if they get lucky—" This thought seemed too unpleasant to pursue, so the president told me, "But you see, it's best not to elevate, and I'll get Ziegler to do the same, it's best not to elevate that thing here in the White House, because I don't want the White House gabbing around about the God damned thing." Briefly the president surmised what his detractors might say, yet this did not change his thinking. "But the president should not be commenting on this case. Do you agree to that?" I told him I did.

When the conversation turned to investigating Donald Segretti, it raised the matter of Herb Kalmbach's records, since it had been he who had paid Segretti. The president observed, "Kalmbach is a decent fellow. He'll make a good witness. He's smart." I agreed, and I told the president Kalmbach had been taking a hammering in the Los Angeles press, much to the displeasure of his law partners. "Oh, well, it'll be hard for him, because it'll get out about Hunt. I suppose the big thing is the financing transaction they'll go after. How did the money get to the Bank of Mexico and so forth? What'll he say?"

Mention of the Mexican money, which had come up at the outset of the Watergate investigation, indicated that the president had certainly been informed at that point. "That, it can all be explained," I assured Nixon. The president, surprised, appears to have well recalled that this was the reason that Haldeman had wanted to call in the CIA to get the FBI to back off, and he and Haldeman had used it in an effort to get the FBI to end the Watergate investigation of Hunt, as well. I answered, "Yes, indeed. Yes, sir. They're going to be disappointed with a lot of the answers they get when they actually get the facts, because the *Times* and the *Post* had such fun with innuendo," I reported. (Indeed, on this matter they *were* disappointed, for the Mexican money was neither an illegal campaign contribution nor had it financed Liddy's Watergate-related activities.)

After Nixon told me that Howard Baker should run the Watergate investigation as he had run the Hiss investigation, I replied, "Well, you know, we've gone a long road on this thing now. I had thought it was an impossible task to hold it together until after the election as things just started squirting out, but we've made it this far, and I'm convinced we're going to make it the whole road and put this thing in the funny pages of the history books rather than anything serious. We've got to. It's got to be that way."

"Well, anyway, it'll be somewhat serious. But," the president added, "the main thing, of course, is also the isolation of the presidency from this." "Absolutely," I agreed. "Because that, fortunately, is totally true," Nixon noted. "I know that, sir," I assured him.

"Good God almighty. I mean, of course, I'm not dumb, and I will never forget when I heard about this God damned thing [in Florida, I thought], Jesus Christ, what in the hell is this? What's the matter with these people? Are they crazy? I thought they were nuts. You know that it was a prank. But it wasn't. It was really something. I think that our Democratic friends know that's true, too. They know what the hell this was. I mean, they know that we then wouldn't be involved in such—" He did not finish the point he had already made, that it was a stupid thing. "They'd think others were capable of it, however. I think they are correct. They think Colson would do anything." The president chuckled. "Well, anyway, have a little fun. And now, I will not talk to you again until you have something to report to me."

He repeated that I should speak with Kleindienst and suggested I tell him, "Look, for Christ sakes, Colson's got brass balls and so forth." The point he wanted me to make with Kleindienst was the fact that "this was not done by the White House. This was done by the Committee to Re-elect, and Mitchell was the chairman, correct?" I said that was correct, and Nixon added, "So, I would think that it would be that Kleindienst owes Mitchell everything. Mitchell wanted him for attorney general, he wanted him for deputy, and here he is. And God damn it, Baker's got to realize this, and that if he allows this thing to get out [of hand], he's going to potentially ruin John Mitchell. He won't. I mean, Mitchell won't allow himself to be ruined. He's too clever. He'll put on his big stone-face act, but I hope to Christ he does. The point is that, as you well know, that's the fish they're after. But the [Senate Watergate] committee is after somebody in the White House. They'd like to get Haldeman, Colson or Ehrlichman." I added, "Or possibly Dean." I hoped he might ask why I thought that, because I was not clear how much he did or did not know about my role in the cover-up. So I added, "Anybody they can. I'm a small fish, but—" He cut me off, and continued, "Anybody in the White House they would, but in your case I think they realize you're a lawyer, and they know you didn't have a God damned thing to do with the campaign." When I agreed less than wholeheartedly, the president read my tone and remarked, "That's what I think. Well, we'll see."

That evening he wrote in his diary: "I had another very good talk with John Dean. I am very impressed by him. He shows enormous strength, great intelligence, and great subtlety. He went back and read not only *Six Crises* but particularly the speech I made in the Congress and it made the very points I'm trying to get across here—that the Truman administration had put up a stonewall when we tried to conduct an investigation. They wouldn't allow the FBI or the Justice Department or any agencies of the government to cooperate with us and they were supported totally by the press at that time. I'm glad that I am talking to Dean now rather than going through Haldeman and Ehrlichman. I think I have made a mistake in going through the others, when there is a man with the capabilities of Dean I can talk to directly."[9]

### March 1, 1973, the White House

Despite his instruction not to report back to him until I had new information, the next day the president wanted to meet first thing in the morning, and then an hour later and again shortly after lunch. His concerns were provoked by Gray's confirmation hearing. When I was summoned to the Oval Office, he asked if I had spoken with Kleindienst, and I reported that the attorney general was taking the position that he could not speak for the White House, but he personally thought that presidential aides should be unavailable, as a general rule, unless there was some exceptional circumstance that would have to be examined at that time.[10] Nixon's real concern, though, was the report in the morning papers that Pat Gray had told members of the Senate Judiciary Committee that he would turn over raw FBI investigative files relating to Watergate. In doing so he effectively shattered the FBI's long precedent regarding providing such information to Congress.[11] Everyone had been stunned, including me.

"What's the matter with him?" Nixon growled. "For Christ's sakes, I mean, he must be out of his mind." The president wanted me to remind Kleindienst that during the Hiss case the FBI had not cooperated with him at all, and the Department of Justice would not even allow Hoover to talk with him. "God damn it, that's the line he's got to realize," the president insisted. I mentioned that I had learned they were pushing Gray as well on whether Segretti had been given FBI reports by the White House, as claimed by *The Washington Post*. I assured the president that that had not happened and added, "Kleindienst is going to pull him up short on it, and say he didn't clear the position with the attorney general." Kleindienst had told me he was upset with Gray, and while he was willing to provide summaries, only in a worst-case scenario would he allow the committee counsel, but not the senators, to look at raw FBI reports.

"Why wasn't he prepared, John, in advance of this? He should have gone over this with Kleindienst," the president said. "Jesus Christ, is he a little dumb?" I answered as diplomatically as I could, suggesting that Gray was "a little bull-headed," but I noted that this was "a bad slip on his part" and that he was going to return to the hearings and testify that he "didn't have authority to say that," which seemed to satisfy the president.

I told the president that the FBI agents who Gray was volunteering to the Senate would likely say that they had been very unhappy that I had sat in on their interviews of White House staff, which I had done at Ehrlichman's instruction. "Why, of course," the president replied. "You are counsel for them, aren't you?" I said I was, and Nixon asked, "Who else did they want—outside counsel? Jesus, in the White House they're entitled to their counsel." Then he suggested how to handle the standing policy of the FBI that no one should be present when they conducted investigative interviews: "[Tell them] you're conducting your investigation for the president." Although I had not done so, I agreed, since Nixon had said on August 29, 1972, that I had undertaken such an investigation. He thought Gray should say the same, although I never passed that directive on to him.

Nixon observed that "Gray has demonstrated in his first day's hearing he's got a weakness" and added that that was "the reason I was very hesitant about appointing him. There's too much bravado there. He's a big, strong navy guy, you know, everything is great, boy, let's go." Then, with a more reflective tone, he noted, "A guy that has that much outward self-confidence doesn't have much inward self-confidence." I found that an interesting observation and said so. Nixon continued, "It's like a poker player, you know, the guy that's got the cards; with a good poker player you never know either way, if he's got the cards or whether he doesn't, Christ, you'll never know."

But with a bad player, "when he doesn't have them he's a little loud, he talks too much." As the conversation progressed Nixon said that if Gray did too much pandering to the Senate, he would simply remove him as the nominee. "I have no compunctions about that," he added, and while he understood that Gray was "frightened and all that," he felt that under Gray the FBI had not been adequately managed, especially as regards the Watergate investigation.

The president mentioned that Pat Gray had called him on July 6, 1972, while he was in San Clemente to warn him about his aides. He thought Gray was being an alarmist. At the time of this conversation with Nixon, I was only vaguely aware of the June 23, 1972, meeting of Ehrlichman and Haldeman with Helms and Walters, which had resulted in Walters going to Gray to get the FBI off the investigation of the Mexican money. I told Nixon what I thought had prompted Gray's call: "[We] had been leaning on Gray to stay on top of the investigation," I explained, which was a fact. "And Pat was out making a lot of speeches, and we kept telling him, Pat, you ought to sit on top of this investigation and keep an eye on it." Although I did not go into detail, Gray had literally been campaigning for the job of FBI director by visiting virtually every FBI field office in the United States, where he would give a boilerplate speech to a mandatory standing ovation from the agents. Ehrlichman had been livid that Gray was never in Washington and out of touch with the Watergate investigation, other than the periodic briefings he got from Mark Felt.

I had not been back in my office for an hour when I was summoned back to the Oval Office.[12] Nixon wanted to know if I had talked with Kleindienst, since Kleindienst was trying to call him. I had indeed spoken with Kleindienst, who said he had discussed the FBI files with Gray. The president wanted to know if Kleindienst had read about the Hiss case, and I reported that I was sending that chapter to him from my copy of Six Crises. "God damn it, tell him to get the book and read it," Nixon insisted.

We briefly discussed executive privilege, and before I knew it, the president was reading to me, unable to hide his glee, from Malcolm Smith's John F. Kennedy's Thirteen Great Mistakes in the White House to make the point he had raised in our earlier conversation:

In the spring, there occurred between Kennedy and business leaders a dramatic battle with congressional overtones. At three o'clock on an

April morning a ringing telephone bell wakened an Associated Press reporter. The man on the other end of the line introduced himself as an agent of the Federal Bureau of Investigation and told the AP man to expect an early visit from the FBI. One hour later FBI agents rang his doorbell. Two hours after that, a reporter from the *Wall Street Journal* was rooted out of bed by other FBI agents. At 6:30 A.M. a newsman working for the Wilmington, Delaware, *Evening Journal*, found FBI men waiting at his office door. The special early-morning attentions of the FBI were given as well two major executives of large steel operations which have announced price increases. These invasions of privacy were at the order of the president's brother, Robert Kennedy. As attorney general he misused his authority.

"There it is," the president said, with a tone of satisfaction. It appeared that he had called me back just to make this point, so that I might appreciate that his predecessor had played hardball and gotten away with it. I told him I thought this was excellent information and, given the often exaggerated charges of abuse being brought against his administration, should be made known. "The records are full of this sort of thing," he assured me. Nixon requested that I bring him the speech he had made in the House of Representatives on the Hiss case. As it happened, and he noted in his diary, I had pulled, read and copied this almost-eleven-thousand-word speech from the January 26, 1950, *Congressional Record*, so I sent it over with a draft of the executive privilege statement when I returned to my office.

While I was gathering and sending that material to the president, he was talking to Kleindienst, asking him if he had read the Hiss material yet.[13] Kleindienst had, and they discussed this history at some length. When Kleindienst reported that he had been meeting with Pat Gray two or three times each day, Nixon indicated that he wanted Gray to be "totally forthcoming," for he had to "establish his image as a lawman, but on the other hand don't go to the point where he wins bravados in the newspapers, and the columns, and the editorials of the Eastern press. If you go that far, then you've lost, because they do not want you to do the right thing. They want you to do the wrong thing, see?" Kleindienst could only laugh, notwithstanding the fact that the president was serious. It was the kind of impossibly nuanced instruction Nixon often gave, and would soon be giving me.

Nixon closed by again placing me front and center. "But let me say that

I'm deliberately limiting my communication only with Dean, because you have confidence in him." When Kleindienst agreed, the president added, "And he never opens his mouth." Nixon then addressed my receipt of FBI files, which he suspected might surface in the Gray hearings. "I have ordered Dean to conduct an investigation. Good God, if Gray's going to make the files available to Congress, can he do it for the president?" Kleindienst said that he and Gray had discussed that during their morning conversation.

Shortly after lunch the president called me back to the Oval Office once again, for another short visit, to tell me he had spoken with Kleindienst.[14] He had received the copy of his Hiss speech, the draft regarding executive privilege and the background material. While making notes on the draft, I assured him he was not withholding information, unlike Truman had in the Hiss case. The president said Kleindienst had a vested interest in the Watergate investigation, because he was "enormously indebted to Mitchell, and loves him like a father." He wanted me to remind Kleindienst that Mitchell was "the most vulnerable" and added, "You talk about the White House staff. They might have known something. I don't think they did. But in Mitchell's case, my presumption is he did. Get my point?"

*March 2, 1973, The White House*

Ziegler arrived at the Oval Office late in the morning to usher the president to the press room for a press conference.[15] He alerted Nixon to growing interest in the false story that I had shown Segretti copies of his FBI interview, but the president assured him that he was up to speed on that matter if it arose. The president arrived in the press room shortly after 11 A.M., and after announcing his forthcoming meeting in California with South Vietnamese president Thieu, he took questions. In the ninth question former Nixon White House aide and longtime *Des Moines Register and Tribune* reporter Clark Mollenhoff asked if Gray had been recruited by the Nixon people to give political speeches during the 1972 campaign.[16] The question was weak, and the president had no information that anyone had recruited Gray for political purposes. Nixon said the FBI director should be nonpartisan, and the Senate had every right to question him about such matters. Mollenhoff followed up with an equally poor question from the Gray hearings, about the FBI's not questioning Martha Mitchell, but Nixon said he would not comment on Gray's testimony.

Six questions later he got two Watergate questions: "Mr. President, now that the Watergate case is over, the trial is over, could you give us your view on the verdict and what implications you see in the verdict on public confidence in the political system?" Nixon answered: "No, it would not be proper for me to comment on the case when it not only is not over, but particularly when it is also on appeal." Then he mentioned my mythical investigation again, actually supplying a date for this supposed inquiry, to protect Gray on the matter of turning over the FBI reports to the White House: "I will simply say with regard to the Watergate case what I have said previously, that the investigation conducted by Mr. Dean, the White House counsel, in which, incidentally, he had access to the FBI records on this particular matter, because I directed him to conduct this investigation, indicates that no one on the White House staff, at the time he conducted the investigation—that was last July and August—was involved or had knowledge of the Watergate matter. And, as far as the balance of the case is concerned, it is now under investigation by a congressional committee, and that committee should go forward, conduct its investigation in an evenhanded way, going into charges made against both candidates, both political parties. And if it does, as Senator Ervin has indicated it will, we will, of course, cooperate with the committee just as we cooperated with the grand jury."

"Mr. President, yesterday at the Gray hearings, Senator Tunney suggested he might ask the committee to ask for John Dean to appear before that hearing to talk about the Watergate case and the FBI–White House relationship. Would you object to that?" "Of course," Nixon responded, but then he was asked why. This question had not been anticipated, so the president had to wing it, but it gave him the opportunity to bring up his position on executive privilege, just as he had wanted, without having to do so via a formal statement. "Well, because it is executive privilege. I mean you can't, of course, no president could ever agree to allow the counsel to the president to go down and testify before a committee. On the other hand, as far as any committee of the Congress is concerned, where information is requested that a member of the White House staff may have, we will make arrangements to provide that information, but members of the White House staff, in that position at least, cannot be brought before a congressional committee in a formal hearing for testimony. I stand on the same position there that every president has stood on."

Frank Cormier, the senior Associate Press reporter in the White House press corps, thanked the president, signaling the end of the session, but Clark Mollenhoff, always something of a bull-in-a-china-shop sort with his booming voice, asked another question. The president could have walked out without responding, given that Cormier had formally ended the conference, but after hearing its gist, Nixon decided he wanted to take the question. Mollenhoff had shouted, "Mr. President, on that particular point, if the counsel was involved, if the counsel was involved in an illegal or improper act and the prima facie case came to light, then would you change the rules relative to the White House counsel?" Nixon answered: "I do not expect that to happen, and if it should happen, I would have to answer that question at that point," and then, a bit annoyed with Mollenhoff, he continued. "Let me say, too, that I know that, since you are on your feet, Clark, that you had asked about the executive privilege statement, and we will have that available toward the end of next week or the first of the following week, for sure, because obviously, the Ervin committee is interested in that statement, and that will answer, I think, some of the questions with regard to how information can be obtained from a member of the White House staff, but consistent with executive privilege."*

Back in the Oval Office, Ziegler told the president he thought the Watergate material would be buried in any story about the press conference.[17] Ziegler was mostly correct, although the *Post* did feature a page-three story by its legal reporter, John MacKenzie, noting that the president would not permit me to testify at the Gray hearings. MacKenzie further reported that the chairman of the Senate Judiciary Committee, James Eastland (D-MI), did not believe a majority of the committee would vote to call me during the Gray hearings.[18] But I was very uncomfortable at being thrust further into the limelight, for I was already certain that public attention regarding anyone connected with Watergate was not good, and Gray, in testifying he had given me FBI reports, had pulled me into the fray.[19]

In the early afternoon of March 2 Haldeman told Nixon that he had been talking with John Mitchell, who brought up a delicate matter of some significance regarding the convicted Watergate defendants still awaiting sen-

---

*After the press conference that morning, Clark Mollenhoff called me to apologize, saying he did not intend to impugn me in any way but wanted to flush out the issue. Clark, who was an attorney, and I had a good working relationship, and we had spoken the evening before about executive privilege in an off-the-record conversation. Clark did, however, despise Haldeman and Ehrlichman and could be tough on Nixon. See Dean telephone memorandum, March 1 and 2, 1973, National Archives and Records Administration (NARA).

tencing.[20] "Mitchell raised, which I don't think he raised with anybody else, I don't know if John Dean's filled you in on one of the major problems on the business John's [referring to me] working on, is the question of continuing financial activity in order to keep those people on base. And the way he's working on that is via Mitchell to Tom Pappas," Haldeman reported. Pappas, a longtime Nixon supporter and fundraiser, was a wealthy Greek-American businessman.[21] The president indicated he understood, so Haldeman added, "Wh[o] is the best source we've got for that kind of a thing. Pappas is extremely anxious that [Ambassador] Tasca stay in Greece." Nixon answered immediately, "Let him stay." Haldeman continued, "And our plan, you know, was to move him and put someone else in Greece, but Mitchell says it would be a very useful thing to just not disrupt that."

"Good. Let him stay. No problem. Pappas has raised the money thing for this other activity, or whatever it is? How does he do it?" Haldeman said that Pappas had sold his oil company and was now "just sort of one of the unknown John Paul Gettys of the world, or something." Nixon replied, in a thoughtful manner, "I'm just glad for him." More important, Haldeman explained, "and he's able to deal in cash." With that comment, this remarkable exchange ended, the conversation moving on to other matters before returning to Watergate, and me. Nixon told Haldeman, "Hell, I'm convinced that Dean is really a gem. I've talked to him two or three times about—" Talking over the president, Haldeman said, "He's a real cool cookie, isn't he?" Nixon continued, "He might be cool, but he's awfully smart. God damn, there's judgment there, you know. He thinks things through [and all that]. He's really not cocky. You see, the trouble with a cocky guy who'll come in and have a lot of bravado, but God damn it, he won't check his facts." Haldeman agreed, saying, "But not Dean. He's just the other way. He hasn't always checked his facts, but he never covers up if he hasn't. He just says he doesn't know. And God, he's been through the wringer in trying to keep all this pieced together, you know, as everything's straying out from under him in every direction. The great thing is, he's been [great dealing with] Mitchell, in dealing with people. Because all this is a people game, trying to keep these people on an even keel and not having someone break and go rattling on. And all these God damn Watergate seven guys, he's had to nursemaid all these months."

The president sighed, and asked, "What are we going to do?" Rather than respond, Haldeman continued offering his assessment of how I handled problems, as with a chuckle in his voice he said, "Because he is a character. I think he takes out all his frustrations in just pure, raw, animal, unadulterated sex." "Is that right? Is he quite a—" the president began to ask, as he and Haldeman talked over each other. Haldeman continued, "I guess he just solves all of his hang-ups that way. And then he can nail all the rest of this with real finesse." Nixon asked, "He just got married pretty early, didn't he?" Haldeman thought not, saying, "I think he was living with her for two years before he married her." That was fine with Nixon, who said, "Fair enough, he knew who was he was getting." Haldeman added, "He's completely in love with her, makes no bones about it."

"Well, I must say, I'm impressed by him," the president added, instructing Haldeman to have Colson speak to me about any Watergate-related matter in the future rather than with Haldeman, Ehrlichman or him. "I think it's very important we get to Chuck funneled into Dean's shop, don't you agree?" Haldeman said that was already occurring. Then the president added, "It's just better, Bob, that, for example, I have not talked to anybody but Dean. Do you agree on this? He's a lawyer, and all that." Haldeman agreed, because he felt that the president would keep getting all the information from a centralized place instead of in bits and pieces.

## March 3, 1973, the White House

On Saturday morning, when meeting with Haldeman in the Oval Office, Gray was still on the president's mind: "So what's your judgment as to how Gray is handling himself?"[22] Haldeman instead gave the president my take, "Dean said he's not doing well. He's letting too much out. Gray's line is that this is all a tactic, that he's doing it on purpose. For instance, his offer to let them look at the raw files, he's doing it because he's convinced that [Sam] Ervin won't allow that to happen, and that this is all a clever thing, and that Gray then turns it all off on Tuesday [March 6, , when the Gray confirmation hearing was scheduled to end]." Haldeman reported that while Chairman Eastland was sure he had the votes to move Gray's nomination to the Senate floor, Senator Robert Byrd (D-WVA) was taking such a strong anti-Gray position that Haldeman himself was less certain. Haldeman also noted, "And Eastland's advice to us on tactics has been almost as wrong as Mitchell's, and Mitchell's has, of course, always been based on Eastland." Neither Haldeman nor the president had confidence in Kleindienst, Mitchell or Eastland, for they had been consistently wrong on confirmation proceedings in

Eastland's Judiciary Committee, from Supreme Court nominations to those of attorneys general.

That afternoon Ron Ziegler dropped by the Oval Office and announced that "the Dean-Watergate thing" had come up in a press inquiry, with follow-up questions about the president's position of not allowing his counsel to testify. Ziegler wanted to know if he could say that, if it was appropriate, I would cooperate. Nixon reminded Ziegler that Harry Truman had cut him off from the Justice Department and FBI during the Hiss investigation. "We are doing exactly the opposite," Nixon stressed. "We're saying we will cooperate with them. The FBI will cooperate, and the White House staff will cooperate. We'll furnish any information," he said, when it was relevant, "But we will not agree to the appearance of White House staff members before a congressional committee's informal sessions." Nixon then clarified, "Basically, what we want to do here is to keep the position, but we're not covering up. We should constantly say, 'We're ready to cooperate, but we cannot cooperate on their terms. And we're not withholding. We're not covering up. We're ready to [assist]. If they want to ask anything, ask it." The president said this was "a great departure" from the policies of his predecessors.[23]


## March 6, 1973, the White House

Back from two days at Camp David, the president scanned the front-page of *The Washington Post* while eating breakfast, and he read that Pat Gray had provided the Senate Judiciary Committee with a July 21, 1972, letter to me summarizing the FBI's investigation, which included the fact that Nixon's reelection committee had been less than cooperative.[24] I was not surprised when I was summoned to the Oval Office later that morning and asked by the president how we were doing with Pat Gray.[25] I had not yet received a report from Capitol Hill, where Gray was in his second day of testimony before the Senate Judiciary Committee, but I did report that I had spoken with him maybe four or five times since his first day of testimony, on March 1: "His policy had been one to cooperate all the way with the committee up to this point. He's turned over for the record everything that was requested, including the things that hit the papers this morning, which I think he should have deferred on. Kleindienst told me that Gray isn't touching base with him, despite his efforts to get him to explain the timing on when he's turned things over."

I shared with the president Gray's theory, which was to cooperate right down the line, to this point. "Today, when he goes up, draw the line. He'll talk about, you know, he's infringing upon the rights of individuals. He's not going to open sensitive files that have not been groomed for public consumption, if they're going to be put in the public forum, they'll harm innocent people, and really close the store down today. That's what he's supposed to do. Now, he mentioned it to me, he said, 'I know my nomination can be withdrawn.'" This caught Nixon by surprise, and I rephrased it: "Gray said to me, when I talked to him on Friday, 'John,' he said, 'I appreciate the fact that my nomination can be withdrawn at any point in time if you all see what I'm doing as improper.'" The president seemed pleased that Gray had not forgotten this fact, and I continued with my report. "Kleindienst talked to Eastland this morning," who had signaled he still had the votes, and that Senators Hart, Bayh, Kennedy and Tunney had indicated they did not plan to prolong the hearings until the Watergate investigation had been completed. I reported, "Now, Ervin gave an interview this morning with WTOP, the local station out here, saying that he would support the request of Tunney that I appear before they proceed with Gray," although Ervin, also a member of the Judiciary Committee, did not say how far he would push this issue.

Senator Ervin had used the analogy of White House aide Peter Flanagan, who had been forced to testify during the Kleindienst confirmation hearings, and intimated that I might be the hostage for Gray as Flanagan had been for Kleindienst. "I've already answered that, though," the president said, referring to his press conference statement. "We're not going to give an inch on that. We're not going to give an inch," he repeated.

The conversation later turned to the *Post* story. It reported that people at the reelection committee had been mentioned in the FBI's summary reported as complaining to the FBI that they had felt intimidated about talking to them with the committee's lawyer present during the interviews, and it had caught the president's attention. He wanted to know who. I explained, "It was a girl by the name of Penny Gleason," the daughter of a Republican Montgomery County government official. The president asked, "So, so what happened? What does she know? Who'd she work for?" When I reported, "She worked for McCord," Nixon asked, "She wanted to talk?" "She wanted to talk. Didn't know anything, but she wanted to talk, and it was all hearsay. Her statements were her own impressions." Nixon wanted to know why Gray had not addressed such matters in his opening statement to make them a nonissue. Before I could respond that Gray was refusing to take advice from anyone, Nixon answered his question with "stupid ass." We discussed how raw FBI reports were less than accurate, and how Gray's continuing to drag me into his confirmation was also dragging the White House into Watergate. I made the point that we only wanted him to withhold information he should properly withhold, and Nixon said no nominee should be "confirmed at the expense of everybody here" in the White House, adding, "Oh, no. That can't be done." He felt the threat to call me to Gray's hearings had not been fair, and boasted, "Well, you noticed the way I kicked the little bitch in the ass" at the press conference. As our discussion continued, the president said he wondered if "Gray's smart enough. I'm just not sure. I hope he is." I said we would know by week's end, because Gray was scheduled to testify for two more days. He was making his second appearance today, March 6, and then he would appear again on March 7 and 8.

### March 7, 1973, the White House

Gray's testimony of the previous day—claiming that he had not been happy that I had sat in on FBI interviews of White House staff, although he also said that I had in no way hindered the FBI's questioning[26]—had once again landed me on the front page of *The Washington Post*. The president called me to the Oval Office early that morning, and when I arrived, he was writing out questions.[27] When he finished he asked me who was on our team supporting Gray on the Senate Judiciary Committee. I reported that the two Republicans being most helpful were Senators Roman Hruska (R-NE) and Edward Gurney (R-FL). The president said he wanted to have a question planted with a friendly senator, who would ask Gray if he had investigated whether or not presidential candidate Richard Nixon had been bugged in 1968. He wanted the sort of questions posed that would reflect on the material he had read to me about Kennedy's White House mistakes and that I had gathered from Sullivan about Democratic presidents who had abused the FBI. "It does not make any difference whether this material is hearsay or not. The game is not played according to the rules. It's played according to the headlines and the rest. You understand?" he asked.

After discussing with whom the questions might be planted, and the questions themselves, he said he wanted to put it to Gray: "I'm going to make him lie, because I think Gray's not handling himself well. What he said yesterday with regard to the fact that this 'jolly well' bullshit, and all that sort of thing, that it was highly improper for you to be present [during the FBI interviews]. Now, God damn it, we're not going to let him get away with that." I explained that I was reading the daily transcripts of Gray's hearings, and he had falsely claimed he had objected to my sitting in on the FBI's interviews. I told the president that in fact Gray had had no objection whatsoever when Ehrlichman told him he wanted me present at White House interviews. At that time he had said it was not a problem.*

"Well, now we're going to put it to him," Nixon said. "He will know he's lying, when he does, because he knows I told him that Hoover bugged us, that Hoover had told me. He knows that he's been told that, because I told Gray specifically. I said, 'I want you to go back and check it.' He hasn't done it." The president then said, "Now, you see, what I'm trying to get at here is Gray, and mind you, it probably has come to the point, it's probably not in our interest to let him get in," so he was "looking for a way to disqualify Gray from the job, surreptitiously." Nixon noted, "We thought yesterday was the day of truth. And now he turns out worse yesterday than the day before."

"I want all communication with Gray cut off. That's it," Nixon ordered. "It doesn't do any good to talk to him. Agree?" I reported, "He called here last night. He talked to Ehrlichman rather than me, because I have just been pulling him up short every time he talks to me." Referring to our days together at Mitchell's Justice Department, I said, "I have known Pat for a long time," and the only time I had ever come down hard on the FBI was after the leaks started. "And then I insisted before they came over here that they tell me what they wanted, who they wanted it from, why they wanted it and what protection they would take on the information they were given." The leaks had been excessive and unprecedented.[28]

Nixon returned to his scheme to disqualify Gray by planting questions he was sure that Gray would dissemble over. He would then summon Gray and confront him: "You didn't tell the truth there," the president would say, and he thought Gray would respond, "I agree. Now, I'll withdraw." Again Nixon asked me if I understood. I did, and I understood that his repeating this question effectively communicated that he felt it was very important.

When Haldeman arrived in the Oval Office, as I was leaving, the presi-

---

*Ehrlichman publicly stated that he had requested I be present at his FBI interview. See, e.g., John M. Crewdson, "Nixon Aide Tells of Talk to FBI," *New York Times*, March 10, 1973, 13. Gray dared not invoke Ehrlichman, who had made the arrangements he was complaining about, but he had no compunction about blaming the situation on me.

dent began by sharing his assessment of his nominee to head the FBI: "You know, Gray is a bit of a pompous ass, isn't he?"[29] Haldeman said, "Well, yeah. I know Dean's on top of it, but the son of a bitch Gray said, you know, 'This is all fine. We're going to close the curtain down on Tuesday.' Well, he didn't close it down at all. He lifted it up a little higher." Haldeman said he felt that the Gray nomination had been a mistake, and that while he and Ehrlichman had been against Gray from the outset, it had been Mitchell who had argued for him. "He's trying to sell himself at the expense of everybody else, which is exactly what Kleindienst did," Haldeman said of Gray.

The preceding evening (March 6) the president had held a private White House dinner for "business and community leaders," which included the major contributors to Nixon's 1972 campaign. During the evening he had mixed and mingled with his guests in the East Room, and then in the State Dining Room. At some point he chatted with Tom Pappas, who told Nixon he would like to visit with him. The president quickly scheduled him for the next morning. Five days earlier Haldeman had told the president that Pappas was cash rich, after having sold his oil company, and that he had been helping with the "continuing financial activity in order to keep those people"— referring to the Watergate defendants—"on base." Haldeman had also informed Nixon that this was a quid pro quo understanding, for Pappas wanted to keep Henry Tasca, his friend, as ambassador to Greece. Nixon had agreed to do so. On the morning of March 7, when the president told Haldeman that Pappas was coming in, he began to refresh his recollection of exactly who had told him that Pappas was helping out, or as he said to Haldeman, "somebody said he's financing people." Haldeman confirmed that it had been he who had told the president this, and suggested, "You might as well get your chits out of him" by telling him that Tasca could remain in Greece.

When Pappas arrived, the funding of the Watergate defendants was handled discreetly and obliquely in a little over a minute of their eight-minute conversation. They spoke briefly and generally about Ambassador Tasca, then about a coming state visit by Greek prime minister George Papadopoulos and Nixon's family friend Frank Birch, who had once run a gas station in Whittier, before the president turned to the darker business of Watergate.[30] "Let me say one other thing," the president began, lowering his tone. "I want you to know what I was mentioning last night, I am aware of what you're doing to help out on some of these things that Maury's people and others are involved in. I won't say anything further, but it's very seldom that you find a friend like that. Believe me. And frankly, let me say, Maury is innocent—"

Speaking in a raspy whisper, Pappas injected softly, "I know." And Nixon continued, "Mitchell is innocent," and then added, "A few pipsqueaks down the line did some silly things—" which Pappas understood, saying reassuringly, "Sure, sure" "But it's down the line they're all guilty, you know that," Nixon added, without indicating that these were in fact the people to whom Pappas's money was being directed. "But nobody in the White House is involved," Nixon asserted. "It's just stupid, it's just stupid," Pappas said. Nixon agreed that bugging the Democratic National Committee was useless, adding, "I always thought it was the most stupid thing. But you know, a lot of them are amateurs." The president declared, "That's what it is. Amateurs, believe me." After a bit of idle chatting, the conversation ended with everyone happy: Tasca would stay, and Mitchell had a solution to his cash needs for the Watergate defendants.[31]

### March 8, 1973, the White House

I was called to the Oval Office for a midmorning visit,[32] and it was clear Nixon was in a hurry, as he asked, "I was curious about the big play that the Segretti thing got in the *Post* this morning," he began, wondering if this was a new story. It was a large headline, accompanied by oversized pictures of Dwight Chapin, Herb Kalmbach and Donald Segretti, that caught the president's attention.[33] I told him it was not, but rather a matter of Gray's testimony adding to the record. I suspected the real reason he wanted to see me was that he wanted to know if I had planted his questions with a friendly senator, as instructed, and I assured him that that had been done. (To make certain the questions were not attributed to the White House I had given them to Senator Hruska's daughter to pass along to her father, with the permission of John Ehrlichman, for whom she worked as a private secretary, along with careful instructions. Senator Hruska, however, never posed the questions, maybe because it was already clear that Gray was not going to be confirmed.)

### March 9–13, 1973, the White House

By now Gray's confirmation hearing had effectively morphed into a mini-Watergate hearing, with the Democrats using select items plucked from the raw FBI material and other information offered by Gray. What Gray had provided was being used not only to discredit him as a potential FBI director but to drag others who were defenseless into the fray. Remarkably. Gray just kept digging himself a deeper hole, and by thrusting me into his hearings, he provided the Democrats with sufficient leverage to kill his nomination: They asserted that if I did not appear as a witness, they would not confirm him. By the time I spoke with the president for twenty minutes, on Saturday, March 10, in a nonrecorded telephone call from Camp David, I had become totally disenchanted with Pat Gray. So had Nixon. When the president spoke with Pat Buchanan on Sunday afternoon, March 11, he told Buchanan he was not going to give Gray a lifeline by responding to any press questions about either Gray or Watergate.[34] He would not defend his nominee. A few hours later, when talking with Colson, they commiserated over what a lousy witness Gray had been proven himself and the damage he had done to the FBI.[35]

On March 13 Haldeman observed when meeting with the president shortly before noon, "It is almost like we have a death wish and never learn" in sending a nominee like Gray up to the Senate, for he had proven even more a nightmare that Kleindienst had been in early 1972.[36] Haldeman noted, "Gray, just like Kleindienst, would not listen to anyone," insisting on screwing it up his own way. By then Gray had pulled me so deeply into his hearing that Haldeman advised the president that even a Nixon loyalist like Judiciary Committee chairman Jim Eastland was "going to vote for calling Dean up."

That afternoon I was asked to join the president and Haldeman in the Oval Office. Haldeman soon departed and I spent over an hour discussing Watergate-related matters with Nixon.[37] While we principally considered procedural and process matters, we briefly wandered into who was and was not involved. The conversation touched on a range of matters: having Colson serve as a White House consultant, to give him executive privilege protection; the drafting of a speech for Senator Barry Goldwater, to raise the fact that Congress was ignoring all of the things that had been done to the Nixon reelection campaign; my advising the president to expect a lot of Watergate questions at a press conference he was considering, because of Gray's hearings; and matters relating to Chapin, Kalmbach, Segretti and myself. We also ran through the kinds of questions he was likely to be asked, and he tested responses; I updated him on what Bill Sullivan had and had not reported;

whether Sullivan could or could not change the direction of the Gray hearings by opening old FBI misdeeds; and Sullivan's motives. Nixon wondered if Sullivan knew about the bugging of Martin Luther King, which I reported he did, and that he would testify about it if called upon.

I reported that the Senate Judiciary Committee was voting, either as we spoke or that afternoon, on whether I should be asked to testify, and based on my information, I had no doubt that they would send me a letter inviting me, but not a subpoena. I told the president that, given the issues which had arisen, I would have no problem answering any point Gray had raised. "Would you respond under oath?" the president asked. "Heck, I would be willing to, yes," I assured him.

The president liked my response, explaining that he was preparing for his press conference, where he planned to make a comment to that effect. As the conversation proceeded, I answered Nixon's questions about the Senate's holding up Gray for my testimony being a purely political matter and Eastland claiming that, in fact, he had the votes to get Gray's nomination out of the Judiciary Committee to the Senate floor. But because Senator Byrd was opposing Gray, it was not clear if he could win confirmation. To my surprise Nixon said, "Gray, in my opinion, should not be the head of the FBI. Not because of any character or other flaws, or thoughtless flaws, but because he is going to be much like Kleindienst. After going through the hell of the hearings, he will not be a good director."

"What happened to this Texas guy that took his money back?" the president asked. The Mexican money had once again caught Nixon's attention via an Associated Press story that had appeared on the front page of *The Washington Post* on Saturday, March 10, while he was at Camp David. The story recounted how Robert H. Allen, a Texas oilman who had given $89,000 that was later traced to the bank account of Bernard Barker, had requested and received back the entire $100,000 contribution he had given to the reelection committee.[38] The Justice Department was investigating the legality of the contribution, which had come to the Nixon committee in the form of four checks from a Mexico City lawyer.

I shared what I had learned from the reelection committee lawyers: "All hell broke loose for Allen for this reason: His money apparently originally came out of a subsidiary of one of Allen's corporations down in Mexico. It went to a lawyer in Mexico, who put it down as a fee billed to the subsidiary. Then the Mexican lawyer sent it back into the States, and it came back up here. But the weakness of it is the Mexican lawyer: One, didn't have a legitimate fee; and two, it could be a corporate contribution. Allen had personally put a note up with the corporation to cover it. But Allen is meanwhile having problems with his wife, and a divorce is pending, and tax problems. So he requested the refund."

The president said he thought the problem with the money was that "it was being used for Watergate." I clarified this, explaining, "It wasn't used for the Watergate. That's the interesting thing. What happened is, these Mexican checks came in. They were given to Gordon Liddy,* who said, 'What do we do, why don't you get these cashed?' Gordon Liddy, in turn, took them down to this fellow Barker in Florida, and said, 'Would you cash these Mexican checks?' So that's how they went through Barker's bank account [and came] back here. They could have been just as easily cashed at the Riggs Bank. There was nothing wrong with the checks. Why all that rigmarole? It's just like a lot of other things that happened over there. God knows why it was all done. It was totally unnecessary, and it was money that was not directly involved in the Watergate. It wasn't a wash operation to get money back in to Liddy, and the like."

The president wanted to discuss who would be good and poor witnesses before the Ervin committee. We both thought Sloan would not be effective but that Kalmbach would be a solid witness. The president was not happy that Kalmbach was referred to as his lawyer. "Well, what I meant is this. I don't care about that, it's just the fact that it's played that way, as if he's in and that he's talking to me all the time. I don't talk to him about anything. I don't know, I see Herb once a year when he brings the income tax returns. I'm sure that he handles that San Clemente property and all the rest, but he isn't a lawyer in the sense that most people have a lawyer."

After we speculated on the skills of those likely to be called by the Senate regarding Watergate, the president asked when Judge Sirica was going to sentence. I said we thought it was going to happen the previous Friday, March 9. Liddy was already serving his sentence at Danbury, Connecticut, because he wanted to get it over with and gain good time, and Hunt was out on bail. Liddy and McCord were appealing, but I noted that, given Sirica's "zeal to be a special prosecutor," Liddy and McCord might have a case for a new trial.

---

*I misspoke, for I meant Hugh Sloan, who asked Liddy what to do and how to get the checks cashed. See G. Gordon Liddy, *Will: The Autobiography of G. Gordon Liddy* (New York: St. Martin's Press, 1997), 222.

"Well, some of those statements from the bench," the president found "incredible." He asked about the Cubans, and I said I had no idea. When I added, "Sirica's known as a hanging judge," Nixon remarked, "That's the kind that I want," which struck me as so strange a comment that I laughed, but he was serious. He asked about the Senate's Watergate investigation, and I reported that Kleindienst had finally scheduled a meeting with Ervin. I told the president the hearings would start in early May, and we speculated about how long they might last and what kind of public attention they might attract. Nixon was sure new information would emerge from the hearings: "Oh, yes, there'll be the revelations in Watergate." He said the Senate wanted to find out who was involved: "Is there a higher up? They're really, let's face it, after Haldeman." "Haldeman and Mitchell," I added. "Mitchell, I mean," the president corrected himself. "Colson is not a big enough name for them. He really isn't." I added, "Or I bet they'd take Ehrlichman if they could drag him in, but they've been unable to drag him in, in any way." I was not sure if the president understood that the effort driving the cover-up included Ehrlichman. He did not respond.

"Ultimately, Haldeman's problem is Chapin, isn't it? Bob's problem is circumstantial," I said, unaware that Ehrlichman had similarly described Haldeman's situation to the president. "Bob didn't know any of those people, like the Hunts and all that bunch," Nixon explained. "Colson did. But Bob, Bob did know Chapin. Now, however the hell much Chapin knew, I'll be God damned, I don't know." "Well, Chapin didn't know anything about the Watergate," I assured him, "and—" The president cut me off. "You don't think so?" "No," I replied, "absolutely not."

"Did Strachan?" the president asked. "Yes," I responded. "He knew?" Nixon was surprised. "Yes," I repeated. "About the Watergate?" he asked for clarification. "Yes," I answered, referring to the fact that Liddy had broken into and bugged the DNC's Watergate offices. It was not clear to me then, nor is it clear today, the precise details of Strachan's knowledge. I do not believe he had advance knowledge of the Watergate bugging and break-in. Strachan later testified that he was not given nor did he review information obtained by the bug in the DNC, but he was aware of Liddy's "electronic surveillance plans" being approved by Mitchell.[39] Liddy later claimed he specifically told Strachan he was going to reenter the Watergate offices of the DNC to repair the defective bugging equipment, but Liddy's account may be confused.[40]

"Well, then, Bob knew. He probably told Bob, then. He may not have. He may not have," the president speculated aloud. I reported that Strachan was judicious in what he relayed, and that he was as tough as nails. "What'll he say? Just go in and say he didn't know?" Nixon asked. I speculated, "He'll go in and stonewall it and say, 'I don't know anything about what you are talking about.' He has already done it twice, as you know, in interviews." I did not consider Strachan to be a natural liar but rather, by personality and disposition he said what needed to be said, nothing more, and he did not trust his own memory. When the president probed, I also added that Strachan was personally loyal to Haldeman.

"But he knew? He knew about Watergate? Strachan did?" I gave a loose affirmative, "uh huh," and the president responded, "I'll be damned. Well, that's the problem in Bob's case, isn't it? It's not Chapin then, but Strachan. Because Strachan worked for him." I agreed, but noted, "They would have one hell of a time proving that Strachan had knowledge of it, though."

"Who knew better? Magruder?" the president asked. "Well, Magruder and Liddy," I answered. "Ah, I see. The other weak link for Bob is Magruder, too. He having hired him and so forth," the president observed. "That applies to Mitchell, too," I added, since the president seemed both interested in and surprisingly unaware of the facts. "Now, where do you see Colson coming into it? Do you think he knew quite a bit, I can't, I can't—" the president caught his own thought with another about Colson. "Yet he could know a great deal about a lot of other things and not a hell of a lot about this, but I don't know."

"Well, I've never—" as the president cut me off I was about to say that I had never pressed anyone about any of this information; rather, I only knew what had been volunteered to me. Nixon continued, "He sure as hell knows Hunt. That we know. And was very close to him." "Chuck has told me that he had no knowledge, specific knowledge, of the Watergate incident before it occurred," I said. "There have been tidbits that I have raised with Chuck. I have not played any games with him, I said, 'Chuck, I have indications—'"

"Don't play games," the president advised. "I don't," I assured him. "You've got to be the lawyer [who] has got to know everything," he insisted. I agreed, and continued with my explanation. "And I said, 'Chuck, people have said that you were involved in this, involved in that.' And he said, 'That's not true,' and so on and so forth. I don't—" I had misspoken, so I started again, "I think that Chuck had knowledge that something was going on over there. A lot of people around here had knowledge that something was going on over there. They didn't have any knowledge of the details, of the specifics of the whole thing."

The president addressed my information. "You know, that must be an indication, though, of the fact that they had God damn poor pickings.

Because naturally, anybody, either Chuck or Bob, was always reporting to me about what was going on. If they ever got any information, they would certainly have told me that we got some information, but they never had a God damn thing to report." Nixon said this with a chuckle signaling irony. "What was the matter? Did they never get anything out of the damn thing?"

"No. I don't think they ever got anything," I answered. "It was a dry hole, huh?" he asked. "That's right," I answered. "Jesus Christ," Nixon said with disgust. "Well, they were just really getting started," I noted. "Yeah. Yeah," the president said, gathering his thoughts, and then explaining, "But Bob one time said something about the fact we got some information about this or that or the other, but I think it was about the convention, what they were planning,* I said they're [unclear]. So I assume that must have been MacGregor, I mean, not MacGregor, but Segretti—"

"No," I corrected the president, and he finished his thought, "Bob must have known about Segretti." This was a very different matter, I reported, still unclear of what he did and did not know. "Well, Segretti really wasn't involved in the intelligence gathering to speak of at all," I explained. Before I could continue, the president asked, "Who the hell was gathering intelligence?" As is clear now, the president was portraying himself as being almost totally uninformed, when in fact he knew the answers to the questions he was raising, probably either as a way of testing my knowledge or of protecting himself, if not both. But I answered his queries.

"That was Liddy and his outfit," I reported. "I see. Apart from Watergate?" Nixon asked.

"That's, well, that's right," I answered. "That was part of their whole—" I began, then cut to the point, "Watergate was part of intelligence gathering, and this—"

"Well, that's a perfectly legitimate thing," the president interrupted. "I guess that's what it was."

"What happened is they—" I started again to explain, but he again cut me off. "What a stupid thing. Pointless. That was the stupid thing." When I agreed, the president continued, "To think that Mitchell and Bob would have allowed this kind of operation to be in the committee." I defended Haldeman, saying, "I don't think he knew it was there." But the president misunderstood, "Are you kidding? You don't think Mitchell knew about this thing?"

"Oh, no, no, no. Don't misunderstand." I realized the president and I were

*See Appendix A.

talking about different matters, so I rephrased: "I think he knew that Liddy was out intelligence gathering. I don't think he knew that Liddy would use a fellow like McCord, for God's sake, who worked for the committee. I can't believe that." The president had more questions, for we never had discussed the details of Watergate before. Nixon asked, "Hunt? Did Mitchell know Hunt?" I did not think Mitchell knew Hunt. "So Mitchell's thing is [then to say], 'Gee, and I hired this fellow and I told him to gather intelligence for the committee [*unclear*].'" I agreed. "Magruder could say the same thing," the president noted. I said, "Magruder says that, as he did in the trial, he said, it was—" I stopped, because I was not sure if we were talking about what had actually occurred or the cover-up line, not to mention the fact that my name had now been reported in connection with Liddy. I continued, "Well, of course, my name has been dragged in as the guy who sent Liddy over there, which is an interesting thing," and which I proceeded to explain. "What happened is, Magruder asked for a lawyer [at the reelection committee, and] he wanted to hire my deputy over there for general counsel, and I said, 'No way. I can't give him up.'" Nixon asked, "Was Liddy your deputy?"

"No, Liddy never worked for me. A fellow named Fred Fielding, who works for me. And I said, I can't give him up. Magruder said, 'Will you find me a lawyer?' I said, 'I will be happy to look around.' I checked around the White House, and [Bud] Krogh said, 'Liddy might be the man to do it, to go over there. He would be a hell of a good lawyer. He has written some wonderful legal opinions over here for me, and I think he is a good lawyer.' So I relayed that to Magruder."

"Right, yeah," the president said, indicating with his tone that this was old news, and he changed the subject. "How the hell does Liddy stand up so well?" the president asked. "He's a strange man, Mr. President," I answered. "Strange or strong, or both?" the president asked, seeming not to be clear on what I had said. "Strange and strong," I responded. "Good," Nixon said flatly. "His loyalty, I think, is just beyond the pale. He's just—" I began. "He hates the other side, too," the president observed. "Oh, absolutely, he's strong. He really is," I said, confident Liddy would not crack, if based on no other reason than my brief meeting with him on June 19, 1972, after the arrests of his men at the Watergate, when he demonstrated that he was humiliated by the disaster he had almost single-handedly created.

"Is it too late to, frankly, go the hang-out road? Yes, it is." He answered his own question as quickly as he posed it. I agreed, but before I could get a word in, he continued, "The hang-out road's going to have to be rejected. I understand it was rejected by somebody." I said it had been kicked around. Nixon was aware that Ehrlichman had been an early proponent of the hang-out route, but not that he wanted to hang out everyone except Ehrlichman.

"Well, I think I convinced him why he wouldn't want to hang out either," I told the president, inviting him to ask me why, but he did not. Not knowing what else I should tell Nixon, I was as vague as Haldeman and Ehrlichman when I explained, "There is a certain domino situation here. If some things start going, a lot of other things are going to start going, and there are going to be a lot of problems if everything starts falling. So there are dangers, Mr. President. I'd be less than candid if I didn't tell you there are. There's a reason for us not, not everyone, going up and testifying."

"I see," he noted, then protested, "Oh, no, no, no, no, no. I didn't mean go up and have them testifying. I mean putting the story out to PR buddies somewhere. Here's the story, the true story about Watergate." In short, the president was talking about a PR story versus the real story of what had occurred. "They would never believe it," I protested, which was not to say that a true—albeit incomplete—version of Watergate could not be prepared, which was implicit in my tone and the following exchange we had. I suggested, for example, that while it was in fact the truth, the news media would never accept that there was no direct White House involvement in the Watergate break-in, referring specifically to "that incident that occurred over in the Democratic National Committee headquarters." I explained, "People, here, did not know that that was going to be done. I think there are some people who saw the fruits of it, but that's another story. I am talking about the criminal conspiracy to go in there. The other thing is that the Segretti thing. You hang that out, they wouldn't believe that. They wouldn't believe that Chapin acted on his own to put his old friend Donald Segretti in to be a Dick Tuck on somebody else's campaign. They would have to paint it into something more sinister, something more involved, a part of a general plan."

"Shit, it's not sinister. None of it is," the president protested. "No," I agreed, and suggested that some of Segretti's actions were humorous. "As a matter of fact, it's just a bunch of crap," Nixon said. Nixon summed up his take on the entire Watergate-Segretti scandal as the last gasp of his partisan opponents: "They've just got to have something to squeal about." He observed that they "got the hell kicked out of them in the election" and that "the Establishment" was dying. He felt they were using Watergate to smear his foreign policy and election successes. So he wondered if we could not find some dirt on the Democratic presidents, and one in particular: "If you get Kennedy in it, too, I'd be a little more pleased."

I explained that if, when investigating Segretti, the Senate went into Kalmbach's bank records, it could backfire and surface the private investigation that Kalmbach had also funded of the events in the island town of Chappaquiddick, where Teddy Kennedy had been involved in the death of Mary Jo Kopechne, a passenger in his car.[41] The president feigned ignorance, but it is now clear from other conversations, with Haldeman, that he was fully aware of the investigation by Jack Caulfield and Tony Ulasewicz. I explained it to him in some detail in this conversation, although I had only hearsay information, since it had all taken place before I arrived at the White House. I only knew the first name of the private investigator: Tony.[42] Caulfield also had made Tony Ulasewicz available to assist in paying the hush money then being provided to the Watergate defendants.

"Now, how will Kalmbach explain that he'd hired this [fellow to investigate] Chappaquiddick? Out of what type of funds?" the president asked. "He had money left over from preconvention—" I started to explain, but the president understood. "Are they going to investigate those funds, too?" Nixon asked. "There's nothing illegal with those funds," I answered. "How can they investigate them?" he asked. "They can't," I said. "Huh," the president grunted, pleased. I explained, "What could happen is, they could stumble into this in going back to, say, '71, on Kalmbach's bank records. They've already asked for a lot of his bank records in connection with Segretti, as to how he paid Segretti." Nixon asked, "Are they going to go back as far as Chappaquiddick?" Referring to Tony's investigation, I noted, "This fellow worked into '71 on this. He was up there. He talked to everybody in that town. He's the one who caused a lot of embarrassment for Kennedy already. He went up there as a newspaperman [and asked questions like], 'So why aren't you checking this? Why aren't you looking there?' And pointing the press's attention to things. Gosh, the guy did a masterful job. [Although], I have never had the full report."

*March 14, 1973, the White House*

Again I found myself on the front page of *The Washington Post* because the Senate Judiciary Committee had voted unanimously to invite me to testify in the Gray confirmation hearings. Gray had trapped himself by unnecessarily drawing me into the matter, and Nixon had made it clear that "no president could ever agree to allow the counsel to the president to go down and testify before a committee."[43]

When Nixon called me that morning he wanted to discuss the situation in preparation for a press conference.[44] I told him I had received a formal invitation letter from the Senate Judiciary Committee and read my draft response, declining to appear pursuant to the president's statement of March 12 but offering to assist and provide information to their questions about the Gray confirmation, consistent with the president's statement (which effectively meant replying to any written questions). When the president asked if I should volunteer to provide sworn answers, I suggested we wait and have the committee call for such responses, thus keeping all our options open. The president wanted me to circulate my response among other members of the staff excluding Haldeman and Ehrlichman, as "I don't want to get Haldeman or Ehrlichman in the thing, because they're both parties in interest." Nixon suggested Ziegler, and then offered that he himself could make "a rather cool decision about it" and what ought to be done. He instructed me to come over whenever I was ready.

Accordingly, Ziegler, Moore and I met in the president's EOB office later that morning. The recording of this conversation is of particularly poor quality, although the gist of the conversation can be determined.[45] We discussed written responses, and the president suggested, "Just give them a lot of gobblegoop, that's all. Then let them squeal. They're never going to be satisfied with any answers." When the discussion turned to Segretti's activities, Ziegler noted, "We've made it very clear that no one in the White House directed espionage and sabotage." Nixon then explained to Ziegler, "Espionage and sabotage is not illegal. Do you understand? That's the point that I'm making: Espionage and sabotage is illegal only if it's against the government. Hell, you can espionage and sabotage all you want, unless you use illegal means." The president did indicate, however, that he would, of course, say he did not condone such activity. In passing, he mentioned the report I was suppose to have prepared, noting that it related to Watergate, not the Segretti "crap." I reminded the president that the FBI had never investigated Segretti's activities, only Segretti's relationship to Hunt and Liddy, which had been unrelated to the Watergate break-in. Although the president noted that Americans did not want their "president spending his time horsing around with all this crap," we continued to discuss it, until he concluded that nobody was going to say anything, because any answers that were provided would only led to more questions.

When our session ended, Ziegler went off to respond to the press and the president headed for the Oval Office, where he soon met with Haldeman.[46] They speculated about media interest in a Senate Watergate investigation, and Haldeman suggested it would not last long. Nixon again expressed disgust with Pat Gray's performance ("Gray is so cocky, and not the smartest guy in the world"), while Haldeman pointed out that FBI guys were now going after Gray, former Hoover supervisors whom Gray had removed. As this conversation was ending Nixon observed that he did not seem to have any real support on Capitol Hill for dealing with Watergate even from fellow Republicans.

After lunch the president had Dick Moore and me back in his EOB office to rehash events,[47] and he called me later that afternoon to ask if I knew of "any other instance where raw files of the FBI had been turned over to committees of Congress."[48] I did not but said I would check to make certain. "You call the FBI and tell them I want [an answer] in three minutes," Nixon instructed sternly and said if they did not have an answer by then, "I'll fire the whole God damn Bureau." I burst out with a spontaneous laugh, but the president did not join me. "I mean that," he said. "You get right ahold of them." While I was getting an answer, Nixon conferred with Ziegler, until he realized that he had not heard back from me and phoned again.[49]

While the operator was placing the call, the recording captures the president telling Ziegler, "You get action around here if you kick 'em in the ass. These agencies taking two or three days to get a response to a simple little question like that," he complained. When the president came on the line, I told him, "Unless I get counterinformation upon further checking, the answer is no—there had been no formal submissions of FBI material like this ever before." However, I explained, there had been informal situations in which Hoover had provided raw FBI files, e.g., to Senate committees investigating organized crime and for the Harry Dexter White case, with which Nixon was very familiar.* "What I'm going to say is that it was always Mr. Hoover's practice never to turn over [raw files] formally to a committee," Nixon declared, and Hoover only did it "on a basis of total security for the

---

*In 1948 the former Treasury Department official was accused by the House Un-American Activities Committee of being a Soviet spy. He died of a heart attack three days after he testified before the committee. History had largely confirmed that, in fact, he was a Soviet spy, not because he was a communist but rather because he was a sympathizer with the Soviet experiment.

purpose of conducting investigations and so forth and so on. And there's never been a leak of those of those things before." I confirmed the response, and the president, satisfied, said, "Okay. Well, keep 'em scared over there."

## March 15, 1973, the White House

The president, sensing correctly that in the wake of Pat Gray's Senate testimony his press conference would be dominated by Watergate, started the day in his EOB office going over additional press conference questions and responses with Ziegler. Nixon called me with a series of process questions, including whether White House aides (namely, Colson) had given civil depositions, in the DNC's Watergate lawsuit.[50] At 11:22 A.M. he and Ziegler headed for the White House press room.

The first question of the conference set the tone: "Mr. President, do you plan to stick by your decision not to allow Mr. Dean to testify before the Congress, even if it means the defeat of Mr. Gray's nomination?"[51] The president's answer was one of the longest of any press conference during his entire presidency, summarized here. He did not believe any "responsible" senator would hold Gray hostage to my testifying, and he had it made very clear at his last press conference that "Mr. Dean is counsel to the White House. He is also one who was counsel to a number of people on the White House staff. He has, in effect, what I would call a double privilege, the lawyer-client relationship as well as the presidential privilege." Nixon then compared his cooperation in Watergate to Truman's noncooperation during his Hiss inquiry. He closed his lengthy response by announcing that "Mr. Dean will furnish information when any of it is requested, provided it is pertinent to the investigation."

The follow-up question pressed the point further: "Mr. President, would you then be willing to have Mr. Dean sit down informally and let some of the senators question him, as they have with Dr. Kissinger?" "No, that is quite a different thing," Nixon replied, which he proceeded to explain. When asked if he thought the FBI's Watergate investigation had in any way been compromised by Pat Gray's giving information to me or talking with John Ehrlichman or others, the president answered with an emphatic, "No, I am not concerned about that" and then flipped the question to declare that he was far more concerned about FBI leaks. He also said that Hoover had regularly showed him raw FBI files, and he informally did the same for some members of Congress, such as Chairman Eastland.

When asked about Gray's revelation that Kalmbach had paid Segretti forty thousand dollars, Nixon dodged the question, saying he would not comment on such individual situations being investigated by the Senate but gave a lengthy response about how the White House would cooperate with them. He also elaborated on his executive privilege statement, explaining, "Members of the White House staff will not appear before a committee of Congress in any formal session. We will furnish information under the proper circumstances. We will consider each matter on a case-by-case basis." He invited the U.S. Senate to take him to court if they disagreed: "We would welcome it. Perhaps this is the time to have the highest court of this land make a definitive decision with regard to this matter. I am not suggesting that we are asking for it. But I would suggest that if the members of the Senate, in their wisdom, decide that they want to test this matter in the courts, we will, of course, present our side of the case. And we think that the Supreme Court will uphold, as it always usually has, the great constitutional principle of separation of powers rather than to uphold the Senate."

Another Watergate-related question followed: "Mr. President, isn't there an essential difference really between your investigation of the Hiss case and the request of this subcommittee to Mr. Dean to appear? In the former, foreign affairs was involved, and possibly security matters, where here they only wish to question Mr. Dean about the breaking into the Watergate?" The president responded, "Yes, I would say the difference is very significant." He explained that when a committee of Congress was investigating espionage against the government of this country, that committee should have had complete cooperation from at least the executive branch of the government. All he had requested during the Hiss case "was to get the report that we knew they had already made of their investigation. Now, this investigation does not involve espionage against the United States. It is, as we know, espionage by one political organization against another." When asked about his responsibility for the Committee to Re-Elect the President, John Mitchell and other people who were working for them, Nixon said that Mitchell and Stans would take responsibility, and in due time respond, for they had no privilege or basis to refuse to testify, adding, "I am sure they will give very good accounts of themselves, as they have in the court matters that they have been asked to."

Back in the Oval Office just before noon, Ziegler assured Nixon he had done a good job.[52] Nixon was pleased as well, and told Ziegler, "Well, there wasn't anything we didn't anticipate." The president mentioned that he brought up Hiss because "they hate that case," and Ziegler agreed: "It drives them up the wall." As they reviewed the questions and the president's responses, Nixon noted, "They are obsessed with that Watergate. It's the strangest thing." Kissinger, who had watched the press conference from the doorway, dropped by the Oval Office and praised the president's performance: "I thought it was very good. I thought your form was very good, too. I mean, you were relaxed and confident and strong."[53] Kissinger, too, was struck by the amount of press attention to Watergate. Later that afternoon, Haldeman met with the president in the Oval Office, and the president asked him what he thought of the press conference.[54] He had not attended it but had read the stenographer's record, and he told Nixon he found the questions "unbelievable," and he was amazed that the first question had been about my testifying at the Gray hearings.

That evening the president asked Dick Moore and me to come to the Oval Office.[55] As we were seating ourselves Nixon said, "So the first question was about Watergate, or Dean, or something like that, and to think that they're really [not] shamed with [their] irresponsibility in the press corps, so they put forth forty minutes of haranguing, I mean, badgering." He added with disgust, "The bastards never asked one question about the most important subject," referring to his peace efforts in Vietnam. I told the president I was still reading the transcript when he called, but I had feedback from the Senate, which was "in a tizzy trying to figure out what they're going to do." The president asked what I thought they would do, and I said they had again backed off issuing me a subpoena. The president asked Moore, "I invited them to have a court test. Do you think that's good, Dick?" Moore admitted that when the president had first raised the possibility the day before, he had had doubts, but the way Nixon had handled the matter had dissolved his doubts.

*March 16 to 20, 1973*

# Return of the Dean Report, the Ellsberg Break-in and Hunt's Blackmail

*March 16, 1973, the White House*

After providing me with clarification for Kleindienst on raw FBI files, the president said in a meeting that morning, "Oh, incidentally, you raised the question yesterday," referring to the meeting with Moore and I, "that there had been no follow-up during the press conference, because he had not been asked, 'Will you give us a copy of the Dean report?'"[1] Dick Moore had noted the failure of the press to ask this question. This provided me an opportunity to make sure the president understood that this was a nonexistent report. So I reminded him, "There was no report involved." While he ignored my response, he did recognize the problem and suggested how he might have answered: "I would say that it was purely an oral thing, that there's no written report, but he'd be glad to give you're a summary of his findings." Not sure where the president was going with this, I responded noncommittally as he continued. "That's what we're going to say in that case, if that question is raised. Be sure that Ziegler has that, of course, that's what you said," the president added, clearly eager that Ziegler maintain the position that the White House was cooperating.

Nixon solicited my thoughts on how information supporting this posture might be made available. I explained that on the Segretti matter I had gathered affidavits from the key figures and then drafted a summary report based on them that Ziegler might use. The president wanted to know why it had not been released, and I explained, "Well, there are some questions you can't answer. Or if you do, ah—" He finished my statement, "—you get people in trouble." Nonetheless, Nixon still thought "There's much to be said for a presidential, or White House statement, not presidential." I did not disagree but had no idea how that could be done. The president suggested that if I went off to Camp David with Dick Moore, we could come up with something; Mitchell might also join us, he added, although he acknowledged that Mitchell's judgment "has been very bad on things like Carswell, Kleindienst and Gray."* "The main point, as I said," Nixon noted, "we cannot have the White House or the presidency in the position of covering up."

When Ziegler joined the conversation, Nixon began proposing and answering hypothetical questions for Ziegler's guidance, and he posed question one about Gray's report and on whether Gray had prepared one, which he had not. I could not resist tossing in the question he had not been asked but that we had been discussing: "How about the Dean report?" Nixon responded, "No, Dean didn't make a report. There's no written report here." Then turning to me, he asked, "Do you want to say that? Because I would say that?" I responded, "I think you've already said the report was oral," but I was not sure. If that was the case, the president said, he would respond, "'His report was oral, but he will furnish all the information and answer all questions pertinent to the investigation.' Is that fair enough?" he asked. I did not respond directly but instead added, "Consistent with the policy statement on March 12, 1973," which meant written interrogatories only.

When I departed, the president acknowledged to Ziegler that I had "a terribly difficult job," and after discussing more likely follow-up questions Ziegler might get that morning, Nixon instructed him on Watergate: "The president is directing complete cooperation with the Ervin committee, but consistent with the March twelfth statement. And Mr. Dean will answer, and so forth." What the president wanted was in fact impossible: Namely, to give the appearance of cooperation while in fact doing nothing that would present any risk to the White House. Because he wanted Ziegler to appear confident that no problems lurked, he told him, "Our problem is not the substance of Watergate and Segretti"—which, in a very limited sense, was true—"Our problem is the cover-up. The main person we have to protect is the president, and the White House." Then he raised the matter of how information would be provided, and explained, "It will be written interrogatories, and so forth," a process that would be worked out with the Ervin

---

*As noted earlier, Harrold Carswell was Mitchell's disastrous recommendation for the U.S. Supreme Court, who was rejected by the Senate. In fact, Carswell had been recommended by Chief Justice Warren Burger to Mitchell.

committee counsel. As all attorneys appreciate, written interrogatories are almost useless for gathering facts and determining what has or has not happened, a fact well understood by the president. But he obviously hoped the general public did not have that knowledge.

Ziegler left the Oval Office as Haldeman arrived.[2] The president told Haldeman he was urging me to get John Mitchell more involved, along with Dick Moore, in writing a statement. Nixon also reported, "Howard Baker has got a character flaw," so they should not count on him for much in the coming inquiry. Haldeman said they still needed a way to respond to key Nixon supporters and friends on Watergate, people who "think if we just clear it up, then everything will be fine, and that [the president] is being misguided by [his] White House staff." Both Nixon and Haldeman felt some sort of written document on Watergate would take the heat off of everyone. "I think the trouble is that Dean said that he's examined that," the president reported, "and I said you can't push that out. You can't make it a statement, because it leaves too many holes in it." Nixon said he told me to bear in mind that a cover-up could be worse than the underlying problem, because a cover-up could hurt the president.

Haldeman explained that my problems with issuing any kind of report—a subject he had discussed with me at length on two occasions—was that it would involve everyone. He told Nixon I had taken a crack at writing it but had given up; he did not explain that my reason for doing so was that he, Ehrlichman and Mitchell would be the central players in any accurate account, and that an honest explanation, or even a half explanation, would inevitably lead back to them. What he did relay was that, while a Segretti report would be feasible, since it would not incriminate the White House, a Watergate report could raise questions of criminal responsibility, and "then you have a problem," Haldeman noted. "And if you start pushing people, you've got people who've got to decide whether they stay with what they've said or change their story, and then we get into a real mess. That's why Dean's put this scheme of containment on the line. But I just wonder if it isn't a losing game."

"Well, that's sort of my feeling. I mean, it has been for a while," the president said. "I don't know, but the problem is, [it gets a little complicated for everyone that's involved in this]. But you see, I think it's going to happen anyway. You better have it [sooner rather than later]. That's always been my theory." Haldeman agreed, "It would be a lot better now to lob it all out now and get it done than to have them squeeze it out," Haldeman began, "The problem is—" And Nixon interrupted, "—the cover-up." Nixon's interruption acknowledged not only the problem, but the unfortunate reality that an ongoing cover-up was a fact of life in the Nixon White House, even if the president was pretending otherwise. Haldeman, however, played it down. "Yeah, but his argument, the other one, is that you don't know how far they're going to get. And he thinks we can succeed or they can succeed, [and then people will forget. And that's probably where they already are]," Haldeman said, describing an argument I have no recollection of ever having made. As this conversation continued, Watergate and the Senate investigation flowed in and out; they assessed potential witnesses, answered concerns of their GOP supporters and noted that the underlying offenses were not being covered up, since seven people had already been convicted for the activity.

"But they're not satisfied with that," Haldeman pointed out, and added, "They've got to know who directed it." The president agreed, though even at this late date, he was still trying to understand precisely what had happened on that night in June. "[Well], we clearly established that you haven't anything to be concerned about," Haldeman assured him. "Mr. Jeb Stuart Magruder was not my man. Magruder worked for me when he was here, but when he went over to the committee, he was working for John Mitchell, and I didn't see Magruder twice in a year. So I have no problem." Nixon clarified, "What I meant is, I speak from a circumstantial point. They can say, just like Chapin, like Segretti was not Chapin's man." Haldeman said he understood, yet clearly he was still not giving the president basic information that investigators would later uncover about his role leading up to the Watergate break-ins. As the conversation continued, the president could merely speculate about who knew what, in order to assess his exposure.

This conversation was interrupted for two photo opportunities on the president's schedule, but Haldeman returned to resume the conversation when those were completed.[3] The president again mentioned a Dean report, which at that time he still vaguely called "some sort of white paper" that would be issued by the White House. Nixon was concerned that the message that would be taken from his press conference was that he was essentially saying to the Congress, "Screw you. I will not let Dean testify," which would effectively be interpreted as a cover-up. Haldeman mentioned the difficulties such a report might create for lower-level staff, without explaining the problems it would raise for his top aides, so it was not surprising that the president returned to the subject with Ehrlichman, with whom he spent the next two hours.

He met with Ehrlichman in his EOB office midafternoon[4] and they later walked to the Oval Office.[5] "I've been deliberately trying to keep Bob and you out of this further, as much as possible, out of the conversations with Dean," Nixon told Ehrlichman, who was pleased with the arrangement, cheerfully noting, "That's worked pretty well, I think." Nixon was concerned that Haldeman felt hurt by being excluded, but Ehrlichman assured him that that was not the case; as for himself, he said, "Well, I've actually, I've appreciated that."

"I've tried to keep you out for other reasons," the president continued. "Because you have been, well, because your reason—" he hesitated, seemingly about to mention Ehrlichman's involvement with Liddy and Hunt but, realizing that was too blunt, did so obliquely. "And I've, actually, Colson's involved in that, and I want to keep him out of it because he's involved, too. The problem, as I see it, getting into it for this first time, which I, of course, would attempt to answer the questions. You obviously see what I'm trying to do," he said, explaining that he was attempting to answer questions without appearing to refuse to cooperate, which was why he had said, "We're proud of our record with that. We have furnished information. We have, and then we will continue to cooperate in a proper investigation," envisioning his White House doing what they should be doing, but, in fact, were not.

Nixon was unhappy to learn from Ehrlichman that Howard Baker was claiming that the president had agreed to send top staff to the Watergate hearings, and he observed that maybe Baker was so "double-faced he doesn't know" what he was or was not informed about: "I know exactly what I told him, and I also told Dean to tell [Baker] I had a record of the conversation."[6] Ehrlichman was aware that Kleindienst was trying to "smoke him out today." After Nixon dismissed Baker as being "not very strong," and as someone who was never going to "go anywhere in life," he turned a Dean report. Nixon recalled that, when they were out in California, Ehrlichman had not supported the idea of "having some definitive statement made at some point." The president indicated that he was discussing this matter with me, and I had said "there are some things we can't cover." He continued, "Now, I don't know what the hell he's talking about, but I'll find out."

Ehrlichman reported that Kalmbach had "lined up five beautiful jobs" for Segretti, who was checking out the opportunities. They also talked about a problem Nixon wanted to understand: "Apparently, Sloan is pissed off at Magruder." Nixon said that Sloan was angry that Magruder had lied about directing Sloan to pay money "to a certain person"—namely, Liddy—and that Magruder had been given a government job. Ehrlichman, well aware Magruder had lied, did not know if that was the case, although he was aware of a longtime jealousy between the two men that dated back to their days working at the White House. The president, worried about Magruder's stability, told Ehrlichman that he "may not be aware of the fact that he can't change his story now." Ehrlichman assured Nixon that Magruder "feels that he is committed to a story which was totally successful, it worked." Neither thought that Magruder would "rat on" Haldeman.

The president wanted more information. Did Ehrlichman believe Magruder and Liddy had worked together to develop "the whole stupid thing"? Or was it "more possible that Mitchell was in on it, or possibly that Colson was in on it?" Then he added, "I don't think that Haldeman could have been in on it." Ehrlichman said he did not have all the facts. Nixon described his situation: "The reason, if I know the facts, then I have an idea of what could come out." While he had once avoided the facts, it was now apparent he needed them. He added, "The people who have to be protected here would be Mitchell and Haldeman, above all. Colson, you know, too." But most important, Nixon said, somewhat awkwardly, "It's very important that not a thing gets Mitchell and Haldeman."

Ehrlichman provided Nixon his well-informed "theory of the case," weaving fact with his considered speculation, and while there were some gaps in his knowledge, his theory was actually very close to the truth of the matter as it was documented by later investigations. Ehrlichman started with Colson, who he felt had acted either through Magruder or Mitchell to put pressure on Magruder for information but had not necessarily pushed them (CPR) to bug Larry O'Brien and the DNC; his approach had been, rather, I don't care how you do it, just do it. When the president asked when and why, Ehrlichman thought Colson had acted "between ITT and the time Mitchell went over there," which the president would have understood to mean between late February 1972 (when Jack Anderson broke the ITT story) and March-April 1972 (when Mitchell took full control of the reelection operation). Ehrlichman then suggested the possible motive: "There was a period of time when we were wrapping up San Diego"—referring to moving the

GOP convention to Miami, which was announced on May 6, 1972[7]—"And there was a lot of fear that the Democrats were going to use demonstrators." Then, most revealingly, Ehrlichman recalled, "And there was also that [rumor] that the Democrats had entered into an illegal alliance with [Florida governor Reubin] Askew for the financing of their convention in Florida." This prompted Nixon to ask, more in a tone of seeking confirmation than asking a question,* "So, they were just trying to find that out." Ehrlichman continued, "And there were a lot of things floating around that particular job." Ehrlichman described how the pressure built up on Magruder, who probably called Liddy in and said, "I'm getting unbelievable shit from the White House," so he needed to do something. Liddy, in turn, said he would take care of it, but he needed "a hundred grand or whatever." Magruder sent Liddy to Sloan, who wanted to know if the money had been approved by Mitchell. Magruder then called Mitchell, and said, "Listen, you've got to call Sloan and clear this." Ehrlichman reminded the president he was speculating, and then continued: Likely Magruder said to Mitchell, "John, you've got to call Sloan for me and clear the expenditure of a hundred thousand dollars cash." And Mitchell said, "Well, what's it for?" "Well," he said, "Gordon Liddy is going to undertake to get that information that I keep getting badgered about from the White House." The president added, "About the Democratic convention," again, in a tone that was more rhetorical than inquisitive.

Ehrlichman continued with his account: Mitchell now said to Magruder, "Are you sure you can do it?" Jeb said, "Yeah, I think Liddy can pull it off." And Mitchell said, "Okay, I'll call him." So Mitchell called Sloan and said, "Just go ahead and give Liddy the money." Ehrlichman observed, "This was that kind of an almost casual to begin with," but having left Hunt out of his account so far, he continued, "undertaking and then Liddy, being a kind of a nut, sat down with Hunt and said, 'Okay, how are we going to pull this operation off?' And Hunt said, 'Listen, I know five Cubans that'll come up here for that kind of dough, and they'll crack the United States Treasury for that.' So they had to call McCord for equipment, since the security director does that. And they said, 'Well, we need some walkie-talkies, and we need tools, and we need this and we need that.' And McCord says, 'What the hell are you guys up to?' And they told him, and they tied him into the operation. And that's how she went."

*See Appendix A.

Nixon, rather stunned, only remarked, "Gosh," and then asked, "That's where they were getting the reports on?" Ehrlichman confirmed, "They were getting reports. Liddy was getting the reports, and my hunch is that he was sharing them with Magruder, Colson and probably Mitchell." The president added, "And Strachan." Ehrlichman confirmed Strachan, and continued. "And there's some pretty juicy stuff in there," indicating that he had become privy to what was overheard in the DNC. (The National Archives has withdrawn approximately forty-seven seconds of material here, based on privacy, because it was obtained using an illegal wiretap.) "What else?" the president asked. "I don't know," Ehrlichman answered, adding, "That's the only occasion I've had to find out what was in it, when that [interview] thing cropped up." Clearly Ehrlichman had his own channels for obtaining information, and before hearing this I was unaware that he had been privy to the contents of the bugged DNC conversations. Although he did not explain how he had obtained all of this information, a good clue came with his next comment: "But I suspect, without knowing, that Mitchell probably advised himself of the general parameters of the operation through Fred LaRue; he's sort of Mitchell's eyes and ears. Fred told me about—" Ehrlichman started to say, but cross talking makes this section of the tape inaudible. LaRue, however, would undoubtedly have known the contents of the overheard conversations from either Magruder or Liddy. Ehrlichman told the president that LaRue was "going to be a witness in this," whom Ehrlichman noted that Senator Jim Eastland would look after. "But Fred will be up there," Ehrlichman assured the president. "So that's how I can see it unraveling. If you want to lay it all out, that's the way you're going to have it."

Thinking aloud, Nixon was still considering how he might issue a report in light of this information. "If Mitchell was involved," he said, "we can't put it all out." Thus, as far as Watergate was concerned, he thought they might "simply state flatly that these seven were involved," which was true, and then declare, "there was nobody else involved—period." On Segretti, "we just put the facts out." The report he envisioned was basically intended for "our friends," who needed to be reassured. "Well, God damn it, as I've often said it, John, if the facts are going to come out, let us help get them out." How to do that was the question. Ehrlichman agreed and said: "Supposing you were to look at it this way, and I've thought a lot about this. Supposing you were to say Mitchell's future, Colson's future, Ehrlichman's future, whoever, is not as important as the integrity of the presidency." Nixon liked that thought a lot, and firmly repeated, "The integrity of the presidency." Ehrlichman continued, "Now, if you accept that premise, then there is really nothing at all that you can't say. And let the chips fall where they may." "I believe that," Nixon said, but then added a qualifier. "I believe that, except for Haldeman."

That remark reopened the entire discussion, and Ehrlichman opened the door to another dark passageway: "It comes back to Bob in another way that I've never mentioned to him, but for some time, we had [Frank Lane or Frank Raines]* on the payroll." Nixon, surprised, asked, "Frank was?" knowing exactly to whom Ehrlichman was referring. Ehrlichman reported, "He was supposed to be doing odd jobs on various task forces in Southern California for [unclear]. He was a bagman. He was delivering money. He was in contact with people. He was paying our sleuths." The president wondered if such records were kept, and Ehrlichman said they were kept forever. He told Nixon that Haldeman was not in direct contact with this bagman, and Nixon instructed Ehrlichman to tell Haldeman about this business. The upshot of the exchange was that, notwithstanding Ehrlichman's earlier call to "let it all hang out," they both came to the conclusion that lines would have to be drawn on what could be revealed.

Still the president wanted a Dean report. It would not be sworn. Ehrlichman, however, warned Nixon, "Well, it's almost impossible to draw that document. To make it the whole truth, to make it consistent with the extensive facts and have it hold together without going all the way. I mean, you'd have to incriminate Mitchell to some extent, you know, and so on." The president had an answer for that, "Oh, I already handled Mitchell. He approved it but didn't know what it was used for." Ehrlichman surmised I could draft such a document, "But you don't answer every question." That was not the president's goal, however; he merely wanted to say *something*—"The president has spoken about the God damn thing"—which, in his view, would remove him from the cover-up. "We've been over this a number of times," Ehrlichman explained, "and every time we've decided, no, that we can't do it, because there's no way to do an effective job of disclosure and tie up all the loose ends in this thing: the nagging loose ends, the little inconsistent facts, the unassailable piece of evidence that wasn't included. It is always the

---

*Neither my transcriber nor I were able to further transcribe the name of this person. Nor was I able to indentify someone fitting the description provided by Ehrlichman, but I found the information of potential importance so I have included it, with the thought that someone might recognize either the person or the description.

little thing that bites you in the end and, and makes you worry about it." As Ehrlichman was talking, the president sighed and said, "I know. I know," finally suggesting, "He can make it more general."

"You have to make it general, and when you make it general, then it's a cover-up. It's a ridiculous thing," Ehrlichman said, noting the ultimate impossibility of the task. Conversations like this were remarkably inconclusive, because Haldeman, Ehrlichman and the president were not telling one another all they knew, and this lack of candor continued to the end, until investigators and prosecutors finally established facts and liabilities beyond a reasonable doubt. Ehrlichman thought maybe Dick Moore should be given the assignment of writing a report, explaining, "Dean's not as artful as Dick" and noting that Moore had had experience as a writer. "Dick could write it more from the standpoint of where everybody gets a copy."

That evening the president called Colson, simply to commiserate,[8] and then phoned me.[9] Nixon requested updates on a number of matters, but the real reason for his call was to press me to write a report. "Well, you should go forward and work with Dick Moore, and others with regard to the matter of getting sort of a general statement that might be prepared, I mean, to be given to me after the court directs sentences, you see," he instructed. "I don't know whether w-w-w-we will want to use it or not," he stuttered, seemingly signaling his awareness of the impossibility of the task, and adding, "but in order to know, we've got to see what it could be, you see?" For the moment I simply reported, "I just learned late this afternoon that Sirica is going to definitely sentence on Friday next, a week from today [March 23]. He plans to give a speech from the bench at that time. The government is recommending no specific term in years for any of the defendants; rather, prison sentences for all of them."

After answering his questions about sentencing, I addressed the matter of the Dean report: "I had a long conversation with Dick Moore, just this evening. Dick and I really have been talking all this time about this whole thing, and there is a degree of impossibility in writing a sort of let's-hang-it-all-out report without creating problems that would open up a new grand jury, without creating problems that would cause difficulty for some who've already testified. I've caveated some of these to Dick. Dick doesn't possess all the knowledge I have. So it's a particularly difficult assignment for Dick," at which Nixon chuckled. "Yeah," I continued, "and, in fact, I told him, I said, 'It might be to your advantage, Dick, to write from your basic lack of knowledge." I indicated that we would work on it further, and Nixon made it clear he wanted it set forth "in the most general terms, just virtually saying what I might even say in answer to a press conference question, but in more general terms that an investigation has been conducted, and this, and that, and the other thing, and whack. Just like that, do you see what I mean? Rather than going into the specifics of who did what to whom. Do you see what I mean?" When I did not respond, he kept talking, only vaguely explaining what he wanted, circling back to "general terms." Then he added, "I realize the problems of getting too specific, because then you do open up the possibility of, 'Well, why didn't you say that? Why didn't you say that?' But you just put it in very general terms, you see? I don't know. Do you think that's possible?"

"It's going to be tough, but I think it's a—" I grabbed for a thought, because one does not turn down the president of the United States when he makes such a request, so I said, "I think it's a good exercise, and a drill that is absolutely essential we do." "Yeah. That's the point," the president said appreciatively. "The exercise is important." Looking for an upside to the undertaking, I added, "It sharpens thinking, and as I've—" Nixon cut me off, adding, "To find out what our vulnerabilities are, and where we are, and so forth and so on." He was making a good point, which I wondered if he fully appreciated, but because I was not certain he actually wanted a written document identifying our weaknesses, I raised another approach. With a chuckle, I suggested, "Maybe there'll be some time when I should possibly report a little fuller than I really have, so you can appreciate the full sum of the vulnerable points and where they lead to." When the president agreed, I continued, "I don't think that should be a written document right now." "Oh, by no means," he said flatly. "No, I don't want any damn written document about any of that. I'm just speaking of a document that is put out—" "A public document," I said, and he clarified, "—[the] sort of a report perhaps which then we could deliver it to Ervin, you know?" Now he was making the task even more difficult, so I began groping, "That might, ah," but then spoke more frankly, "It's going to be tough, but I say it's certainly worth the effort."

The president offered me a summary of his request, which I quote here verbatim to demonstrate the difficultly of fulfilling it and his confused thinking on the topic: "Yeah. And just sort of a general thing, and very general, very general, you know? Put, put out, ah, but by all means, laying off of all the—Don't, don't get into the, well, we investigated this, we investigated that, we saw this, we deny this, we support this and so forth. Lay off of all that. I have in mind just sort—Basically, so that it can be said that, ah, something was presented that I have seen or that, you know what I mean? So that they, so that, ah, my reiterated statements from time to time that, well, no one in the White House staff was involved will have some basis, you see?"

What was clear was that the president wanted support for the initial claim he had made within days of the arrests, based on his conversations with Haldeman. I had certainly confirmed it months later and still believed it was technically true based on all I knew. He said just having that in writing would be helpful, yet he was clearly asking for me to say more than nobody in the White House (with the possible exception of Strachan) was aware of Liddy's activities. I would do what I could, but it was really an impossible assignment to carry out truthfully. More important to me was the fact that I had made the point that we needed to talk, so I could explain the vulnerabilities, for I increasingly believed he really did not understand what was actually happening. I felt that if I could describe these to him, as I had to Haldeman and Ehrlichman (who clearly had not discussed them with the president), that he, too, would back away from the notion of issuing a Dean report, as they had every time this matter had been previously suggested.

### March 17, 1973, the White House

It was Saturday and St. Patrick's Day, so the White House was very quiet. Shortly after his late morning briefing, Ron Ziegler went to the Oval Office to report to the president,[10] "The Senate's simmering down a little bit on this separation of powers and executive privilege [matter]." Dick Moore joined me in my office to see what we could come up with to meet Nixon's request for a report. The president, learning I was in my office, asked me to come to the Oval Office. When I arrived early in the afternoon I told him what Moore and I were working on, and he mentioned that if I needed some peace and quiet, I could go to Camp David.[11] I told him I had been talking with Mitchell, and "we probably need a good sit-down, kick-this-thing-around session." We discussed the latest from *The Washington Post*, and the need to get ready for the Ervin hearings, and how it was likely to be a public spectacle. Nixon reminisced about his handling of Hiss in executive session, and the president turned again to a written report. He wondered aloud if Moore and I, even with Mitchell, could collectively write one. He again explained what he wanted in vague terms: "What I'm getting at is that the moment that you get it too specific, and I realize that they're going to say why did you withhold something, that you could simply say these are conclusions that we have reached based on your evaluation of the information that came to your attention. They got a chance to look at all the evidence, and we want to be as helpful as we can. Here's what we've concluded, and we welcome you to review it."

I started to fill him in on background: "Well, the interesting thing is, in the sequence of the way things occurred, and I don't know if anyone has ever taken you through this, but the last involvement to my knowledge of the White House was when I came back from a meeting—" I began to describe the meetings in Mitchell's office I had reported to Haldeman when Nixon cut me off. He wanted me to say I knew nothing about Watergate, but as I clearly did, I said, "Right, well, ah—" and began again, but he was still telling me how to respond. "'I've stayed miles away from it, so I didn't know even if there was a White House involvement,'" he said, seemingly speaking for me as well as himself.

"Well, but there was, you know, there was a preliminary discussion of setting up an intelligence operation, and the last—" at which point the president again interrupted, but I continued to give him information I believed he needed. "—and the last was when I came back from a meeting with Mitchell, Magruder and Liddy, and after telling them that they couldn't discuss this in front of the attorney general of the United States, I came back and told Bob that if there's something like that going on, we've got to stay ten miles away from it, because it just is not right, and we can't have any part of it. Bob said, 'I agree, and we'll have no part of it.'"

"Hmm," the president groaned softly, acknowledging this account, which I did not know whether Ehrlichman or Haldeman had actually ever imparted to him. I continued, "And that was where I thought it was turned off, and the next thing I heard was that was this break-in on June seventeenth, which was six months later." While I was still talking the president asked, "You heard discussion of that, but you didn't hear any discussion of bugging, did you, in that, your meetings? Or did you?"

"Yeah, I did. That's what distressed me quite a bit," I responded. "Oh, you did?" he asked, which I affirmed, and the president continued, "Who raised it? Liddy?" When I confirmed that fact he asked, "Liddy at that point said we ought to do some bugging?" "That's right," I said, "and Mitchell just sat there with his pipe and puffed and said nothing. He didn't agree to it, and I, at the end of the meeting—"

"Well, you don't need to say in your statement about the bugging," the president instructed, to which I agreed. "You could say that they were going to engage in intelligence operations, you said the main thing is that it must be totally legal, and that the laws and ethics and so forth and so on. And so you came back, and Bob says no, so you can answer. You know what I mean?" The president suggested I could "make some self-serving God damn affidavits." When I pointed out that "the embarrassment point would be that the White House knew that there was an intelligence operation going," the president countered, "Why should I get embarrassed?" He felt everybody knows that such operation are undertaken. The president also thought it could be explained, and we discussed a hypothetical justification that was not totally inaccurate: namely, that Liddy's operation was believed, as the president stated it, to be "totally necessary because of the violence, the demonstrations, the kind of activities that we knew were threatened against us at our convention and in our campaign and in all of our appearances. We had to have intelligence and about what they were going to do that we could, in turn, issue instructions to our group to go around and find out what they're doing, and, something like that."

"This is another point on not using the FBI for political purposes, either," I explained, which in fact was one of the reasons Liddy had been given intelligence responsibilities (though it was not the only reason). The president liked that approach, observing, "You see, I've been thinking. I should say, for example, the matter was discussed as to whether or not that agents in the Bureau should be [involved], it was pointed out that in the 1964 elections, the Bureau was used. I said that [they] couldn't be involved. Do you get my point? And then Haldeman said, under no circumstances, or Haldeman never mentioned it to any of the agents. It all had to be done privately, because the Bureau should not be involved in a partisan contest. We did not use the Bureau in this. We did use them against demonstrations, but when they're political in character, the Bureau was never used. Which is true." I acknowledged this, and the president added, "The Secret Service was used, but that's their job." The president then offered more vague examples, "Frankly, they've got to say, 'I did this, this, this and this,' and Chapin would have to tell them the truth. Agreed? And he would say I had this and da, da, da, da, da, but I had nothing to do with this or that other thing."

Our conversation was interrupted by Haldeman, who had scheduling and other issues the president needed to address, but as he worked Nixon continued to return to the proposed contents of the report. He liked the idea of everyone giving me sworn affidavits, as did I, for the document would then reflect what I had been told rather than what I had learned (often by accident), although I suspected no one was going to be willing to sign a sworn affidavit that accounted honestly for his role, or even a sworn flat denial. But the president understood the broader problems, and after Haldeman departed we went even deeper into these problems: "Now, you were saying, too, where this thing leads, I mean in terms of the vulnerabilities and so forth. It's your view the vulnerables are basically Mitchell, Colson, Haldeman indirectly, possibly directly, and of course, the second level is, as far as the White House is concerned, Chapin. Right?" I added, "And I'd say Dean to a degree," being as candid as possible. "You?" he asked with a tone of surprise. "Why?"

"Well, because I've been all over this thing like a blanket," I explained, referring to my activities in the cover-up. "I know, I know," he said, "But you know all about it, but you didn't, you were in it after the deed was done." "That's correct," I assured him. "I had no foreknowledge." It was there that Nixon remained focused: who knew what about the break-in, while totally ignoring the criminal implications of the cover-up. The president continued: "Here's the whole point. My point is that your problem, I don't think you do have a problem. All the others that have participated in the God damned thing, and therefore are potentially subject to criminal liability. You're not. That's the difference. And on that score, of course, we have to know where we are. Everybody that was in there. Magruder, as I understand, knows, told some people that Haldeman knows, and told other people that Colson knows," Nixon noted, and I pointed out, "Oh, Jeb is a good man, but if Jeb ever sees himself sinking, he will reach out to grab everybody he can get hold of. I think the unfortunate thing is, in this whole thing, is [that] Jeb is the most responsible man for the whole incident." "Really?" Nixon said, and by this point I knew when he was truly surprised.

"Well, let me tell you, after it happened, and on Monday," I began, referring to June 19, 1972, "it didn't take me very long to put the pieces together, what had occurred. I got ahold of Liddy, and I said, 'Gordon, I want to know who in the White House is involved in this.' And he said, 'John, nobody was involved or has knowledge, that I know of, that we were going in or the like, with one exception, and it was a lower-level person."

"Strachan," the president injected, and I continued, "Strachan. He said, 'I don't really know how much he knew.' And I said, 'Well, why in the hell did this happen?' And he said, 'Magruder pushed me without mercy to go in there. Magruder said I had to go in there.' He had to do this."* Nixon, understanding the players and pecking order, asked, "Who pushed Magruder?" Then he asked, "Colson?" "That's what Jeb—" I began to respond, when the president cut me off, asking, "Colson could, Colson push Magruder, though?" I answered giving the president both sides of what I had learned, explaining, "No, that's why there's two stories." "That's my point," Nixon responded. "I don't, I think Colson can push, but he didn't know Magruder that well. And had very damn little confidence in him. So maybe that must have come from here. Is that the point? Did Haldeman push him?"

"Well, I think what happened is that, on sort of a tickler—" I began to explain how Haldeman's staff often got an assignment in their suspension/ tickler file and felt pushed to address it, assuming everything possible had be done if it had been requested. And they pushed in Haldeman's name, so others on the staff never knew who really wanted the information, or how important it might be to the president. "I can't believe Haldeman would push Magruder," Nixon observed. Nor did I, in fact, but I wanted him to understand the way the tickler system worked. So I explained, "No, I think Strachan did. Because Strachan just had it on his tickler, he knew they were supposed to be gathering intelligence and talking to Jeb and saying, 'Where is it?' and 'Why isn't it coming in?' 'You haven't produced it.'" (In fact, years later Strachan's records suggest that was indeed the case.) Nixon asked, "Intelligence problems? What were they worried about?" Nixon continued, "They worried about, as I understand it, the San Diego demonstrations. I'm not too sure about this, but I guess everybody around here except me worried about it." "Well, I don't know," I replied, for I personally thought much of the intelligence gathering was silly. "What else?" Nixon asked, but before I could answer, he said that he thought Mitchell was concerned about a secret ten-million-dollar fund the Democrats had, but then added, "What the hell difference did that make?"

I gave the president my take: "I cannot understand why they decided to go in the DNC. That absolutely mystifies me as to what—Anybody who's walked around a national committee knows that there's nothing there." The president, evidencing more knowledge than I had, explained, "Well, the point is, they're trying to see what they could develop in terms of the—" he did not

---

*While this was what Liddy told me, today I better understand his highly manipulative personality, and the ease with which he falsely pointed the finger at others. So he was no doubt making something of an overstatement.

finish what appears to have been the description of a fishing expedition.* Instead he said, "And now Magruder puts the heat on somebody else. The point is, the way you see things could be, as I understand it, is that possibly [*unclear*], that Sloan starts pissing on Magruder, and then Magruder starts pissing on, who? Even Haldeman?"

"No, no, if somebody out of here were to start saying, 'Alright, Jeb, you're going to take the heat on this one—'" I began to explain, when again the president cut me off with, "Nobody down here's going to say that." "We can't do that." I agreed. "I think what you've got to do, to the extent that you can, John," Nixon said, "is to cut it off at the pass. And you cut off at the pass, and Liddy and his bunch just did this as part of their job." This was a rather clear instruction to create a bogus report, and he then elaborated on how he wanted it written.

The conversation turned to Segretti, and we both agreed that that was not a big problem to explain. I then turned to a more serious consideration: "The other potential problem is Ehrlichman's, and that is his connection with Hunt and Liddy both." "They worked for him?" the president asked, and I explained the issue as I saw it: "These fellows had to be some idiots, as we've learned after the fact. They went out and went into Dr. Ellsberg's doctor's office, and they were geared up with all this CIA equipment, cameras and the like. Well, they turned the stuff back in to the CIA at some point in time and left film in the camera. The CIA has not put this together, and they don't know what it all means right now, but it wouldn't take a very sharp investigator very long, because you've got pictures in the CIA files that they had to turn over to Justice." "What in the world?" Nixon asked. "What in the name of God would Ehrlichman have somebody get close to Ellsberg?"†

"They were trying to—this was a part of an operation in connection with the Pentagon Papers. They wanted to get Ellsberg's psychiatric records for some reason," I reported. When Nixon asked, "Why?" at that time I could only answer, "I don't know." (Today we know they wanted to use that information to discredit Ellsberg.) Sounding surprised, Nixon said, "This is the first I ever heard of this. I [didn't] care about, Ellsberg was not our problem. Jesus Christ." Until this conversation I had figured the Ellsberg break-in had

---

*See Appendix A.

†While Nixon would later claim this was the first he had learned of this activity, the fact that he has Ehrlichman responsible suggests that Ehrlichman had, in fact, made some mention of this operation during the July 8, 1972, walk on Red Beach, as Ehrlichman later claimed.

been a national security operation. While I did not know a lot about such operations, I did know they required personal presidential approval. I had advised Ehrlichman I learned of the break-in from Liddy on June 19, 1972, when he reported having used two of the same men at the Watergate to break into Ellsberg's doctor's office, and they were in jail. The two, Bernard Barker and Eugenio Martinez, who had pled guilty, were then awaiting sentencing for the Watergate break-in and bugging.

Since Nixon had volunteered and acknowledged Ehrlichman's role, I confirmed it based on the information I had received: "Well, anyway, it was under an Ehrlichman structure. Maybe John didn't ever know. I've never asked him if he knew. I didn't want to know." But this was no small fact, for it had been driving much of the cover-up. I had learned from Bud Krogh that after the failed effort to break into Ellsberg's psychiatrist's office, Liddy and Hunt had requested permission to try again, but Ehrlichman and Krogh had refused. Inexplicably, although Liddy and Hunt had far exceeded their authority, they had never been reprimanded; and Liddy was then given a promotion and sent to the reelection committee with Ehrlichman's approval and blessing. Mitchell, who had learned about Liddy's White House activities in a post–DNC arrest debriefing, had used the fact that Ehrlichman had run this illicit operation not too subtly to keep Ehrlichman's cooperation in the cover-up. (It is unclear, even from the recorded conversation, precisely how much Ehrlichman had told Haldeman, who had only made the vaguest references to this activity.)

Nixon, clearly, did not want this matter addressed, "I can't see that getting into this," he insisted, but as I explained, that was easier said than done: "Well, look, here's the way it can come up. In the CIA's files, which the Senate Watergate committee is asking for, in the material they turned over to the Department of Justice, there are all the materials relating to Hunt. In there are these pictures which the CIA developed, and they've got Gordon Liddy standing proud as punch outside this doctor's office with his name on it. And it's not going to take very long for an investigator to go back and say, why would somebody be at the doctor's office, and they'd find out that there was a break-in at that doctor's office, and then you'd find Liddy on the [White House] staff, and then you'd start working it back. I don't think they'll ever reach that point," I said, hopefully.

"Can't be. It's irrelevant," Nixon the lawyer said. "It's irrelevant. Right," I agreed, thinking strictly in terms of the Watergate break-in. Nixon noted,

"That's the point. That's where Ervin's rules of relevancy [have] got [to be enforced]. Now, what the hell has this got to do with it?" The president continued, "And, of course, Colson apparently was working with Hunt on that ITT, that silly woman out of there," he said, referring to Dita Beard. "Hunt went out as a disguised doctor or something." I added, "He had [a] red wig on, and funny glasses and went out and interviewed her."

"Jesus Christ," the president declared with disgust, then noted, "But that's nothing. You know, there's nothing illegal there." I continued with other matters that could come up that related to Ehrlichman. "It's not illegal," I began. "In fact, it's kind of interesting, if it ever occurred. Right after Chappaquiddick, John had a man dispatched up there, this New York City detective—" I said, repeating the Tony Ulasewicz story I had learned from Caulfield. "Oh, yeah, I heard about that," the president said, for I had mentioned it obliquely, as had Ehrlichman when discussing Kalmbach's bank accounts. I continued, "Two years he was on this thing, and he knows more about how Teddy Kennedy lied his way through that and closed that down than any living human being." And we discussed how this information might be uncovered from Kalmbach's bank records.

To wrap up the session, the president returned to the Dean report. "Now, I'd simply say, 'Look, I required from every member of my staff a sworn statement, here's one from here, here's one from here, here, here.' Now, so we know that's the basis of my statement. Now go to it. If you've got something else you want to find out, get searching," the president said. "That's good. That's great," I responded. I had gone into the meeting feeling concerned that I would be carrying the load almost singlehandedly, but the fact that the president had clearly authorized me to get sworn statements that I could use as the basis for the report eased my mind considerably. The burden would be placed on those who made the statements to explain their knowledge. They would either provide the basis for a report or effectively kill the project. I had tried this approach earlier, but understandably, no one wanted to commit to sworn statements. Now, however, I had been given direction to do so by the president. The president liked this approach better, as he explained. "The sworn statement, John, is much better, rather than giving a statement by Dean," he said, and went over a few hypothetical examples. "Run that by Moore, will you?" he asked, and then sent me on my way with a friendly, "See you later."

*March 18–19, 1973, the White House*

On Sunday, March 18, Senator Sam Ervin appeared on CBS News's *Face the Nation*, where he stated that if President Nixon's aides refused to testify before his Watergate committee, he was going to have them arrested and jailed at the Capitol by the sergeant at arms. On Monday morning, March 19, Ervin's remarks elicited waves of laughter at several White House staff meetings, and in the Oval Office, where Haldeman met with the president, and Ziegler stopped by for guidance before his press briefing.[12] The president thought Ziegler should ignore Ervin's remarks and stress the point that the president was cooperating. "Nothing excites the president's staff more than everyone in the White House being shipped off to jail," Haldeman cracked. "They're totally enthused with that."

Late that afternoon the president requested that Dick Moore and I join him in his EOB office for a progress update on a Dean report.[13] We had been at it for hours, and Moore explained, "At the moment, I don't think we're prepared to let it all hang out until we know much better where we're going." The president said, "I don't want it to hang out." I suggested, "Let part of it hang out in a way that doesn't create more problems," to which Nixon responded, "There are problems, but I'd like part of it to hang out." In fact, this continued the impossible discussion, because no one wanted to acknowledge the need to arbitrarily draw lines releasing some but not all the information. Nixon was calling for half truths when only whole truths would solve the problems.

On March 19, in the afternoon, CRP lawyer Paul O'Brien appeared in my office, a visit that, as I later testified (and described in *Blind Ambition*[14]), was a game-changing event.[15] Only years later would I understand that it was the impetus that provoked me to face the reality of the situation confronting the president and all of us in the White House engaged in the cover-up. Before the meeting with Paul O'Brien I had been hoping against hope that, because of the power of the presidency, the inherent influence of his high office and the inclination of most people to want to believe a president, we could survive. But O'Brien's blunt message to me after his meeting with Howard Hunt changed all that. Here is how I wrote about it in 1976:

> "And I've come with Howard Hunt's message for you, John," O'Brien continued. "He said, 'You tell John Dean that I need seventy-two thousand dollars for support and fifty thousand for attorney's fees—'"

"Why me?" I shouted as my head shot around toward O'Brien. "Why the hell did he send the goddamn message to *me*?"

O'Brien gave me a helpless look. "I don't know, John. I asked him the same question, and he just said, 'You tell Dean I need the money by the close of business Wednesday. And if I don't get it, I'm going to have to reconsider my options. And I'll have some seamy things to say about what I did for John Ehrlichman while I was at the White House.' And that's the message."[16]

O'Brien, who was very aware of how difficult it was to raise money for the Watergate defendants, had asked me what I was going to do. When I said I was going to do nothing and I was out of the money business, he was taken aback. What O'Brien did not know was that it had been Hunt's call to Colson after the election demanding money that had first led me to check the law, to understand that what we were doing was wrong. When Colson had involved Ehrlichman and me, not to mention the president, in Hunt's demands for clemency, I had been terribly uncomfortable. I had agonized over Mitchell's request that McCord be given the same clemency assurance Hunt had been given.[17] Now Hunt was in effect attempting to extort Ehrlichman, not to mention Bud Krogh and the president, through me to pay him more, and more, and more. I had become involved in the Watergate cover-up at the request of Haldeman and Ehrlichman, serving at first as something of a messenger between them and Mitchell. As time passed, however, after they set the policy during the first days following the arrests, more and more problems had been delegated to me to deal with, problems others had created and wanted to avoid. I had become as much a fool as I was a victim. And now the president was pushing me to write some sort of quick-fix, all-purpose document that would get him out from under it all, based on a purported investigation of Watergate that I had never conducted.

During the early evening of March 19, after I had gone home, the president called Colson, then the leading member of his yet-to-be-formed Kitchen Cabinet and someone with whom he could comfortably test his ideas.[18] In this conversation neither man exchanged new information but merely provided support for each other's thinking. When Colson spoke about "the battering" the media had given the Nixon White House over Watergate, the president said he thought "it's rather good they're making Dean the issue, because Dean is the one guy, you know, he's not involved at all." Colson added that I had "a double privilege," referring to attorney-client as well as executive privilege. But Colson appropriately alerted the president to the fact of my "involvement in some of the subsequent activities, which are sensitive," though he thought I was "totally covered, because he's been acting in the capacity as counsel." Colson added, "I just think that Dean, if they're going to make a test case, he's their weakest case." When the president asked Colson if he should stand firm on me, he said, "Absolutely. I think it would be a terrible mistake now to back off on that issue, Mr. President."

When this conversation later turned to Pat Gray, who was in limbo, since the Judiciary Committee was refusing to act on his confirmation unless I testified, Nixon said he was just as happy having Gray "out there." Both men thought Gray had botched his own confirmation, and Colson counseled, "I think letting him be hostage [is] fine." Or as Ehrlichman infamously instructed me earlier on the Pat Gray situation, "Let him hang there; let him twist slowly, slowly in the wind."[19]

### March 20, 1973, the White House

While John Ehrlichman briefed the Republican leadership of Congress in the Cabinet Room on domestic policy issues, the president met with the Senate and House Republican minority leaders, Hugh Scott and Leslie Arends, in the Oval Office.[20] The most significant matter discussed was a comment made by Scott about Watergate, which reinforced the president's belief that he had to have a Watergate report. When he was discussing why my testifying at Pat Gray's confirmation hearing was very different than President, when Sherman Adams, Eisenhower's chief of staff, testified before the Senate to address an accusation that he had accepted a bribe, Scott made the point that the Republicans in Congress did not feel the president was cooperating on the Watergate investigation, which troubled them. The president insisted he was cooperating, and reflexively brought up the Hiss case and the Truman administration as an example of noncooperation. But Scott's remark stung. Scott reported that the Senate did not have the votes to subpoena me to appear at Gray's confirmation proceedings, but there was serious "grumbling" among loyal Republicans about the president's handling of Watergate. "See, this administration has nothing to conceal," Nixon protested. "The White House has nothing to conceal. We are ready to cooperate fully, and we have cooperated, but it has to be cooperation on the basis that it does not violate the separation of powers."

When the meeting ended the president called me to ask, "Do you have that statement, or did you plan to make it what you think the—" The president did not finish his point, but I understood what he was asking.[21] Dick Moore and I had been working on a follow-up statement to my March 14, 1973, letter declining the invitation to appear before the Senate Judiciary Committee in connection with Gray's confirmation—a sort of short-form Dean report. I told the president we were "stomping and honing" the draft statement, and it was five to ten minutes away from completion. He requested I send it to him when it was completed.

As he was ending his call with me, Haldeman entered the Oval Office, and Nixon turned to the issue Scott had raised.[22] "I think what really should be done is, the leadership needs to be briefed on the Watergate thing. Just at least our own friends have got to have a feeling that everything is okay. Do you understand?" The president reported that Moore and I were working on the matter, and added, "You see, Bob, our own people have got to have some assurance they are not going to get out there on a God damn limb." Haldeman felt that if the GOP leadership was to be briefed, so should the GOP members of the Ervin Committee be as well. The president agreed. When Ehrlichman joined the last half hour of the conversation, the president made it clear he wanted some kind of Watergate statement issued, and he did not much care what kind of statement it was. He then complained that nobody was in charge.

Following the president's meeting with Soviet Union scientists, Haldeman returned to the Oval Office, and the president telephoned me again, asking a less than subtle, "Well, anything you want to take up?"[23] I told him we had a draft statement that he was welcome to read, although Dick Moore was still working on it. He instructed us to wait until we had it ready, and requested we bring it to his office, which we did that afternoon, although the subsequent conversation reached no conclusion about the draft we submitted.[24] By now the president had moved on from the sworn statement approach, preferring instead that the report be laced with broad, self-serving, unequivocal denials: "Never at any time were they any discussions that had anything to do with intelligence-gathering operations." I warned the president that flat statements would not be accurate; the draft we had prepared in fact contained carefully worded responses to questions raised by Senator Sam Ervin on his March 18 *Face the Nation* appearance and by Senator Robert Byrd's March 14 speech on the Senate floor.[25] Clearly, this first effort by Moore and I was not what he had in mind, and I was not sure whether he was asking me to lie or simply refusing to acknowledge what had actually transpired.

During his next Oval Office meeting, which included Governor William Cahill (R-NJ), Governor Linwood Holton (R-VA), and Republican National Committee chairman George Bush, the president received more information about the public's reaction to Watergate.[26] Bush reported that they were getting negative readings because the White House was viewed as not assisting in the Watergate inquires. Nixon suggested how they should answer the questions, and state that the White House was in fact fully cooperating.

Ehrlichman arrived as this meeting was ending, and after the GOP officials had departed, he and Nixon got into a discussion of Watergate that occupied the next hour and a half. [27] When I first began to listen to this conversation, I wondered if Ehrlichman would notify the president of Hunt's blackmail attempt involving him, since I had just informed Ehrlichman about it.* Notwithstanding direct questioning by the president about his potential vulnerabilities, Ehrlichman did not mention a word about Hunt's demand.

Nixon tested on Ehrlichman his idea of giving a confidential briefing to Republicans in Congress, and he suggested I should be the one to do it. When Ehrlichman responded that they needed to decide the content of any such a briefing, Nixon explained that his concern was that GOP leaders such as Hugh Scott did not want to "get caught with their pants down." Ehrlichman advised, "You shouldn't ever tell Scott anything you don't want used against you," and Nixon noted, "That is true not only for Scott, but true for all." Nixon said he wanted the report Moore and I were working on to state that Haldeman and Ehrlichman were not involved; as for Chapin and Strachan, well, he "would try to ignore that as much a possible." Where Colson was concerned, he would put out some facts, but not all. "You had nothing to do with Hunt in the campaign or Watergate?" Nixon asked Ehrlichman, who answered, "No." While this was literally true, it was a remarkably incomplete statement from someone who was now the subject of an attempted blackmail by Hunt.[28]

Ehrlichman began a lengthy discussion about how they might deal with

---

*Ehrlichman's appointment calendar shows our meeting occurred at 3:30 P.M. in his office; he went to the Oval Office at 4:00 P.M.

a Senate subpoena, but they needed to have the Justice Department prepare guidance for the White House about how to contest it in court. When Nixon made it clear he was more interested in attacking the Senate, Ehrlichman cautioned, "You're in a situation now where I don't think a counterattack would be credible or effective. It would escalate this thing." The president wanted to speak out on Watergate, for he did not want to give the impression he did not care about the matter. "Now, the problem I see is that apparently [Dean and Moore] fear that if they put out that statement, it is going to open up a lot of other questions. But let's suppose it does?" Nixon's solution was simple: "It's a PR exercise. The whole thing is a PR exercise. So you put that out, and then they attack. Is that necessarily bad? I mean, the point is, we can say that we are being forthcoming, but they are never going to let us off the hook by letting us submit our written interrogatories. My point is, why not give them the written interrogatories, give them the information, volunteer it, and say, 'Alright, you've got it here.' Now, what you're doing is simply wanting to exploit the issue rather than get the information. What more information do you want?" And soon they were rehashing hypothetical scenarios.

As the conversation continued, Nixon told Ehrlichman he had to assist me with Watergate. He pointed out that as soon as one problem was resolved, a new one erupted. As Ehrlichman described the situation: "Well, it's just the steady dripping on the stone, you know? Every day it's something new, some other damn loose end comes loose. But," Ehrlichman noted, "oh, well, I think the fact that you've been spending some time with him, whether it's been productive for you, has been very good in buttressing him." The president felt I could handle the situation for the time being, but he told Ehrlichman, "I think, when the time comes and there's some decisions to be made, and some calls, some options and proposals, then that's time enough for you to get into it." Nonetheless, the president wanted to know how Ehrlichman was leaning about releasing a statement.

"I want to reserve my view until I see what Dick [Moore] comes up with, because I haven't seen the draft, so I don't know whether it has any hope or not. My inclination is to flush it if there's a way to do it," Ehrlichman said. "Flush what?" the president asked. "The whole, the whole scene," Ehrlichman answered. "Oh," the president replied, surprised, and then asked, "How?" Ehrlichman explained, "Somehow, I don't know how, and that's what I'm groping with. Get it over with, leave you standing aside looking at it, saying,

'My God, I never had realized that that was what was going on over there, or here, or wherever it is.' And then pick up and go forward. Now, maybe the flushing goes on in the Ervin committee, maybe it goes on in a statement, maybe it goes on in a grand jury. I don't know how it goes on, but to my way of thinking, we're not any longer in a situation where you can successfully trim your losses, as we've been for a year." The president agreed, adding, "Well, we had to trim them before the election." Ehrlichman concurred, "Why, sure. Of course."

"That was the purpose. We knew that," the president said, acknowledging the cover-up. "But afterwards, it seems to me that preferably sooner." "Well, it's a question of figuring out how to do it without it splashing on you, and in the tying up the corners of it," Ehrlichman replied. "And I must say, I don't know how to do that at the moment, but I'm satisfied that that's a safer direction in the long haul than trying to contrive a defense for the hearing, or to counterattack the hearing, or somehow or another to hope that the hearings will go, you know, lightly, and so on. They won't." They discussed different ideas, but nothing appeared very realistic. "You know, there are all kinds of things you can think about. But I just don't have any way to direct you at the moment," Ehrlichman admitted. "I just don't know how to handle it. There's a little puzzle on it." This conversation was not unlike most Watergate conversations that involved Ehrlichman and Haldeman, and increasingly me, which always became circular, because while telling the truth was not an acceptable approach, everything short of the truth raised serious problems.

After the conversation took a tangent into Mitchell's problems with Robert Vesco,* the president returned again to the possibility of the White House issuing a Watergate statement. "Even if the statement does raise other questions, it is a statement," the president began. "And they've all get it. And everybody says, 'Well, my God, the president has got a statement, and so forth.' And I think, let's face it, as far as presidential liability for getting caught in terms of the White House staff, there's no problem with you," he said to Ehrlichman, fishing for a response. When none was forthcoming,

---

*A fugitive American financier who had contributed to the Nixon reelection campaign (his contribution was later returned). Vesco, always looking for an angle, had hired President Nixon's nephew, Donald Nixon, Jr. Ehrlichman had been charged by the president to keep an eye on "Donny." Mitchell and Maurice Stans had become entangled in the Vesco web, and were being investigated by the office of the U.S. Attorney for the Southern District of New York, which had originally sought to indict Vesco before he fled the United States.

Nixon continued, "There's no problem involving Haldeman, I mean, the people from here." Nixon acknowledged that Magruder might "blow," but he was not sure about the consequences should that happen. "Who knows what the hell he could do?" the president asked. Ehrlichman counseled, "Well, but you can't clutch him to your bosom in any case." The president said he was concerned about Magruder's perjury, but Ehrlichman was not and explained that if McCord or someone else said he gave "all this stuff"— referring to the products of the bugging of the DNC—to Magruder, they could discredit McCord. Ehrlichman elaborated, "See, you've got a convicted felon, McCord, saying this, and Magruder probably goes out to the cameras and says, 'That crazy man, I don't know what he's talking about.' And so then you've got an ambiguous situation."

"Magruder is not the brightest guy in the world," the president noted, "but I think that he's slick." Ehrlichman added, "He must be quite an actor, from what they tell me," alluding to Magruder's performance before the grand jury and during the trial. "Yeah, I hear you," the president said. Reassured about Magruder, the president moved on to Colson. "He can handle himself, I would think," Ehrlichman said, and Nixon noted, "He's certainly been involved in a lot of things, but he's not at the present involved in this," referring to Watergate. "As far as you know," Ehrlichman added.

The president wanted to know whom the Democrats and their media supporters were really after. Ehrlichman thought himself and Haldeman, but Nixon saw it slightly differently. "Well, not so much you," he said, but rather he thought they were after Haldeman, Colson and Mitchell. Ehrlichman broadened the targets to include anybody who could be tied to the president, not to mention smearing the White House itself by mere association. Nixon said, "We cannot let it harm you guys. That's the whole point. We cannot let it."

Nixon returned the White House taking action. "Have Dean brief the cabinet and the Republican leaders," Nixon suggested, and added, "He's quite persuasive, don't you think?" Ehrlichman liked the idea but added, "I want to sit down and figure out what he would say, where it would take us, what kind of questions it would lead to, because once you start this, then he's got to be very artful about turning away questions that he doesn't want to answer." Nixon offered, "Just say that I haven't got any information," an approach Ehrlichman liked. "He can get away with it with our own people," Nixon said, pointing out, "You don't have to be as artful before your own people, John, as you do before the press." Ehrlichman agreed, and together they rehearsed the kind of evasive answers I might give.

They began discussing how to explain why no one from the White House would testify about Watergate but had no good rationalization. Nixon wanted to examine the worst-case potential, which for the president meant to assume that Magruder would say, "Yes, Haldeman knew about this and told me to do it, and knew I was going to do it, and I furnished information to him." "Alright," Nixon asked, "what problem is that for Haldeman?" Ehrlichman, who had no real knowledge of or experience with criminal law, explained, "Well, he's an accessory at that point," broadly describing a person who aids or contributes to the commission of a crime. A more accurate description would have been "coconspirator," but Ehrlichman would not learn about the crime of conspiracy until he was later charged. The analysis that Ehrlichman provided the president had no relationship to reality whatsoever, so the president had no accurate sense of Haldeman's criminal exposure nor of anyone else's. But it did bring the conversation to the fact that the Watergate seven were scheduled for sentencing that coming Friday, three days hence. "So, we'll see how that goes," Ehrlichman said, and he anticipated the judge would "undoubtedly be very hard on them [and] probably berate them." Nixon asked if he would berate the prosecutors as well, by which he meant his administration. "Probably," Ehrlichman replied, noting, "He'll say a number of things from the bench about his own view of the evidence. He'll sentence them to jail with no suspended sentences. He may revoke the bail of McCord, who's on appeal, and jail him pending his appeal. And so it'll be a rough deal. And then see how it goes through the weekend to see what happens to McCord, who has a hang-up about jail."

"He doesn't want to go?" the president asked, unable to understand how McCord, who had participated in the Watergate burglary with its obvious risks, could be "overly" sensitive to the fact that he might have to go to jail. "He didn't like it when he was in there at all. And then we'll see what happens," Ehrlichman reported. He thought that if Sirica sent McCord to jail, it would be a problem. When the president questioned what McCord might do, Ehrlichman, with remarkable prescience, saw what was coming: McCord would tell Judge Sirica he wanted to talk.

When Ehrlichman departed, after a few telephone calls and some paperwork, the president buzzed for Haldeman to come to the Oval Office.[29] "I think John is pretty much out of touch, as I am now," Haldeman said of

Ehrlichman when Nixon recounted their conversation, explaining, "We've kind of stayed away from it." When Nixon mentioned McCord's concern about going to jail, Haldeman offered that McCord would "have a lot on Mitchell." This brought the president back to his concern. "You can't, Bob, just sit here thinking everybody is shutting up," he said. They discussed the problem of the seeming impossibility of writing a statement that would serve any useful purpose and not sink the White House further if it was wrong. The president said he was also thinking about my making an oral report to the cabinet, or, as he explained it (verbatim): "Lay a few things to rest. I didn't do this, I didn't do that, da, da, da, da, da, da, da, Haldeman didn't do this, Ehrlichman didn't do that, Colson didn't do that. You get my point, see?" If Haldeman understood, he did not say so, as Nixon said the cabinet needed to be told what he had been told—although he had in fact been told only the gist of matters, that should have raised more questions.

When the subject turned to the Senate's Watergate inquiry, the president fully anticipated, and Haldeman concurred, that it would be a "daily spectacle with television cameras and press." What would make it a major story, the president noted, would be getting "a big fish up there," as had been the case in the McCarthy hearings. Haldeman added, "And you never know what any of the big fish will do when they get up there, and then we all said we want to go up and all that, but if they lob one in you're not expecting, you don't know how good a witness he'll be." The president thought it was "a tough god damned thing" and was particularly worried about perjury. Haldeman, in turn, pointed out that the "people who are going to go for perjury already have and will do it again and are going to be up there anyway."

"You mean like Magruder?" the president asked, whom he quickly denounced as "that son of a bitch." This led to a discussion of who was and who was not covered by executive privilege: Chapin, Colson, Dean and Strachan, they agreed, were covered, while Magruder, Hunt and Liddy were not. Haldeman thought Strachan had no criminal exposure, because he did not direct anything. Haldeman described Strachan's only job as being "to keep on top of everything" and to know what was going on. They speculated that Magruder might testify to what Strachan knew. "But only that he knew, not that he had any authority," Haldeman clarified. "No participation. He was an observer." They sat silently for a moment, and then Haldeman added, "The danger you got there is that he probably, and I possibly, got reports on some of that stuff." Nixon said, "Sure. I'm aware of that." Haldeman continued, "And if I did, I didn't know it. But Strachan did know, because he gave me stuff that thick," as Haldeman undoubtedly gestured, and added, "And I never looked at it. On all campaigns, budgets, personnel things and everything else." The president again warned, "The main thing is, don't get anybody up there on perjury where they can prove [it]."

It was when listening to this conversation between Haldeman and the president, directly after hearing the one with Ehrlichman, that I realized how compartmentalized everything had become at the Nixon White House regarding Watergate. While Mitchell, Ehrlichman and Haldeman had once discussed the problem among themselves in the early days, they now communicated almost exclusively through me, although Ehrlichman and Haldeman did exchange some information.[30] No one was sharing anything with anyone else, nor with the president, who even at this late date had no real idea of his exposure. What became conspicuous to me as I prepared this book was at the time something I only sensed, but sensed clearly enough to realize I had to take some form of action by being a bit more blunt with the president, now that I was getting comfortable dealing with him. So when the president called me at home the evening of March 20, I decided to make certain that he had the information I felt he needed to make realistic decisions about a report.

"You're having rather long days these days, aren't you?" the president asked, opening the conversation.[31] Chuckling, I replied that I thought they would soon get even longer. He requested an update on the Gray confirmation proceedings, which I told him were being played politically, as if the president had already abandoned Gray. "What's your feeling, though, John, about Gray? Are you just as comfortable to let him go down? Which do you want? I mean, we can put some pressures on, and I just wonder."

"I don't think it's worth saving, sir. I really don't," I offered, putting it as charitably as I could, and suggested that it would take Gray several years to get control of the FBI. Actually, I doubted Gray could ever do that, given that the existing chain of command in the Bureau held him in near contempt. I gave the president the vote count in the Judiciary Committee, where it appeared that Gray would have trouble getting voted out.

At an opening in the conversation I decided to breach scheduling protocol of requesting a meeting with the president through Haldeman and raised what was foremost on my mind: "I had a conversation with John Ehrlichman this afternoon before he came down to visit you. And I think that one thing we have to continually do, and particularly right now, is to examine the broadest implications of this whole thing, maybe about thirty minutes of just my recitation to you of the facts so that you operate from the same facts that everybody else has." When he replied with a noncommittal, "Right," I continued, explaining, "We've never really done that. It's been sort of bits and pieces. Just paint the whole picture for you, the soft spots, the potential problem areas and the like, so that, you know, when you make judgments, you'll have all that information." Now sounding interested, the president said, "Would you like to do that, when?" I answered whenever worked for him, and we arranged a meeting for ten o'clock the following morning. He agreed it would be better with nobody else there. When he asked if I was coming down in favor of just stonewalling, rather than issuing a report, I answered, "A stonewall with lots of noises that we're always willing to cooperate." Notwithstanding my response, he asked if I could give an oral report to the cabinet and the leaders, and I told him I could but suggested he wait until we had met. He agreed, saying: "No, I want to know. I want to know where all the bodies are first." I said that after he had the facts, it could be programmed any way he wanted, although my thinking was, if I laid out the situation objectively and honestly, the president would understand the next move had to be to end the cover-up. Finally he brought the conversation to a close, telling me jokingly to "take the evening off." I agreed to do so, and did.

# A Cancer on the Presidency
# and Nixon's Response

*March 21, 1973, the White House*

At 8:40 A.M. I spoke on the telephone with Haldeman to explain that I had asked to meet with the president because I felt I needed to walk him though all the pertinent facts of Watergate. Haldeman felt it a good idea. I had hoped to make some notes to be sure I covered everything but hadn't had the time to do so. As I was walking to the Oval Office midmorning, the president was meeting with Haldeman and Ehrlichman on scheduling matters and Pat Gray's decision to stop talking about Watergate.[1] Ehrlichman still revealed nothing about Hunt's blackmail demand. Haldeman was leaving the office as I entered.[2] My conversation with Nixon would run an hour and forty minutes, with Haldeman returning for the last forty minutes.

Today I understand that much of what I explained to Nixon in this conversation had already been told to him by Haldeman or Ehrlichman, but they had often been both vague and remarkably untroubled by the conspicuous criminality of our activity. I had hoped that when I laid out the facts the president would demand the cover-up end immediately. But I did not really know Nixon, although I certainly understood him better after this conversation. After a brief discussion of Gray's hearing, I explained why I had requested the meeting:[3] "The reason I thought we ought to talk this morning is because, in our conversations, I have the impression that you don't know everything I know, and it makes it very difficult for you to make judgments that only you can make on some of these things, and I thought that—" Nixon then finished my thought: "I've got to know why you feel that something, that we shouldn't unravel something," he said, thinking about a report. And I continued, "Well, let me give you my overall first," I said, for my concerns extended far beyond what might merely unravel.

"In other words, your judgment as to where it stands, and where we're going to go," the president said, getting the gist of where I was headed. To make sure I had his full attention, I stated, "I think there's no doubt about the seriousness of the problem we've got. We have a cancer, within, close to the presidency that's growing. It's growing daily. It's compounding, it grows geometrically now, because it compounds itself. That'll be clear as I explain some of the details of why it is, and it, basically it's because, one, we're being blackmailed, [and] two, people are going to start perjuring themselves very quickly that have not had to perjure themselves already to protect other people and the like. And there is no assurance—"

"That it won't bust?" the president interrupted. I continued, "So let me give you the sort of basic facts, talking first about the Watergate, and then about Segretti, and then about some of the peripheral items that have come up. First of all, on the Watergate: How did it all start? Where did it start? It started with an instruction to me from Bob Haldeman to see if we couldn't set up a perfectly legitimate campaign intelligence operation over at the reelection committee. Not being in this business, I turned to somebody who had been in this business, Jack Caulfield. I don't know if you remember Jack or not. He was your original bodyguard, before they had candidate protection, [a former] New York City policeman."

"Right, I know him," the president said.

"Jack had worked for John [Ehrlichman] and then was transferred to my office. And I said, 'Jack, come up with a plan that, you know, is a normal infiltration, I mean, you know, buying information from secretaries and all that sort of thing.' He did. He put together a plan. It was kicked around, and I went to Ehrlichman with it. I went to Mitchell with it. And the consensus was that Caulfield wasn't the man to do this. In retrospect, that might have been a bad call, because he is an incredibly cautious person and, and wouldn't have put the situation where it is today."

"Yeah," the president acknowledged.

"But after rejecting [him] they said, 'We still need something.' So, I was told to look around for somebody that could go over to 1701 and do this. And that's when I came up with Gordon Liddy. They needed a lawyer. Gordon had an intelligence background from his FBI service. I was aware of the fact that he had done some extremely sensitive things for the White House while he'd been at the White House, and he had apparently done them well. Going out into Ellsberg's doctor's office," I added, which I had told him about. "Oh, yeah," the president recalled, and I continued. "And things like this. He'd worked with leaks. He, you know, tracked these things down. And so the report that I got from Krogh was that he was a hell of a good man and, and not only that, a good lawyer, and [he] could set up a proper operation. So we talked to Liddy," I said, referring to Krogh and myself. "Liddy was interested in doing it. Took Liddy over to meet Mitchell. Mitchell thought highly of him because, apparently, Mitchell was partially involved in his coming to the White House to work for Krogh. Liddy had been at the Treasury before that. Then Liddy was told to put together his plan, you know, how he would run an intelligence operation. And this was after he was hired over there at the committee. Magruder called me in January and said, 'I'd like to have you come over and see Liddy's plan.'" The president sought clarification, "January of '72?"

I confirmed that was correct and continued with the story, and Magruder's request. "'You come over to Mitchell's office and sit in on a meeting where Liddy's going to lay his plan out.' I said, 'Well, I don't really know as I'm the man, but if you want me there, I'll be happy to.' So I [went] over, and Liddy laid out a million-dollar plan that was the most incredible thing I have ever laid my eyes on: All in codes, and involved black-bag operations, kidnapping, providing prostitutes to weaken the opposition, bugging, mugging teams. It was just an incredible thing." The president wanted to know if that had been approved, and I told him it had not. I explained, "Mitchell just virtually sat there puffing [on his pipe] and laughing. I could tell, because after Liddy left the office, I said, 'That's the most incredible thing I've ever seen.' He said, 'I agree.' And so [Liddy] was told to go back to the drawing board and come up with something realistic. So there was a second meeting. They asked me to come over to that. I came into the tail end of the meeting. I wasn't there for the first part of it. I don't know how long the meeting lasted. At this point they were discussing again bugging, kidnapping and the like. And at this point I said, right in front of everybody, very clearly, I said, 'These are not the sort of things that are ever to be discussed in the office of the attorney general of the United States,' where he still was, 'and I am personally incensed.' I was trying to get Mitchell off the hook, because he's a nice person, doesn't like to say no to people he's going to have to work with."

"That's right," the president agreed.

"So, I let it be known. I said, 'You all pack that stuff up and get it the hell out of here, because you just can't talk this way in this office, and you shouldn't, you should reexamine your whole thinking.' I came back—" Nixon interrupted to ask, "Who else was present besides you?" I responded, "It was Magruder, Mitchell, Liddy and myself." I then continued: "—I came back right after the meeting and told Bob [Haldeman], I said, 'Bob, we've got a growing disaster on our hands if they're thinking this way,' and I said, 'The White House has got to stay out of this, and I, frankly, am not going to be involved in it.' He said, 'I agree, John.' And I thought at that point the thing was turned off.[4] That's the last I heard of it, when I thought it was turned off, because it was an absurd proposal." The president agreed, so I proceeded. "Liddy, I did have dealings with him afterward. We never talked about it. Now, that would be hard to believe for some people, but we never did. Just the fact of the matter," I reported. The president accepted this, and I noted, "We had so many other things." The president said he was aware that I worked with Liddy on campaign law matters, as Haldeman had informed him of that, and I continued. "Now, so Liddy went back after that and was over at 1701 with the committee, and this is where I [have to] put the pieces together after the fact as to what I can put together of what happened. Liddy sat over there and tried to come up with another plan that he could sell. They were talking, saying to him he was asking for too much money, and I don't think they were discounting the illegal points at this [time]. You know, Jeb is not a lawyer. He didn't know whether this was the way the game was played or not, and what it was all about. They [i.e., Liddy and Hunt] came up with, apparently, another plan, but they couldn't get it approved by anybody over there. So Liddy and Hunt apparently came to see Chuck Colson, and Chuck Colson picked up the telephone and called Magruder and said, 'You all either fish or cut bait. This is absurd to have these guys over there and not using them, and if you're not going to use them, I may use them.' And things of this nature."

"When was this?" the president asked. "This was apparently in February of '72," I answered. "That could be. Did Colson know what they were talking about?" the president inquired. "I can only assume," I said, "because of his close relationship with Hunt, he had a damn good idea of what they were talking about. A damn good idea. He would probably deny it, deny it today and probably get away with denying it." The president and I agreed that would likely be the case unless Hunt said otherwise, with the president adding, "But then Hunt isn't enough. It takes two [witnesses], doesn't it?" He was referring to successfully prosecuting perjury, so I said, "Probably," a bit surprised by the comment. I added that there were in fact two people present: "Liddy was there also, and if Liddy were to blow—" Nixon said, "Then you've got a problem. I was thinking of the criminal liability in the White House. Okay."

"I'll go back over that, and tell you where I think the soft spots are," I advised, hoping to continue with my narrative, but the president continued to interrupt. "Was that Colson?" he asked. "Colson, you think, was the was the person who pushed?" I answered, "I think he helped to get the thing off the dime. Now, something else occurred, though." But Nixon interrupted again: "Did Colson, had he talked to anybody here. Did he talk to Haldeman?" I told him I did not think so, and pushed on. "But here's the other thing, where the next thing comes in the chain. I think that Bob was assuming that they had something that was proper over there, some intelligence-gathering operation that Liddy was operating. And through Strachan, who was his tickler, he started pushing them to get something, to get some information, and they took that as a signal, Magruder took that as a signal to probably go to Mitchell and say, 'They're pushing us like crazy for this from the White House.' And so Mitchell probably puffed on his pipe and said, 'Go ahead.' And never really reflected on what it was all about. So they had some plan that obviously had, I gather, different targets they were going to go after. They were going to infiltrate, and bug, and do all this sort of things to a lot of these targets. This is knowledge I have after the fact. And, apparently, after they had initially broken in and bugged the Democratic National Committee, they were getting information. The information was coming over here to Strachan. Some of it was given to Haldeman. There's no doubt about it."

Nixon now asked, "Did he know what it was coming from?" I said I did not know, and agreed with the president's assessment of "not necessarily." I also agreed with him when he said, "Strachan knew what it was from," but as I explained, "I have never wanted to press these people on these points, because it hurts them to give up that next inch, so I had to piece things together.[5] Alright, so Strachan was aware of receiving information, reporting to Bob. At one point Bob even gave instructions to change [Liddy's] capabilities from Muskie to McGovern, and had passed this back through Strachan to Magruder, and apparently to Liddy. And Liddy was starting to make arrangements to go in and bug the McGovern operation. They had done prelim—" Nixon interrupted to ask, "They had never bugged Muskie, though, did they?"

"No, they hadn't, but they had infiltrated it by a secretary and a chauffeur. There's nothing illegal about that." The president agreed, and I continued. "Now, so the information was coming over here, and then the next point in time where I became aware of anything was on June seventeenth,* when I got the word that there had been this break-in at the Democratic National Committee, and somebody from our committee had been caught in the DNC. And I said, 'Oh, my God, that, I can only—' you know, I essentially, putting the pieces together—" Nixon rhetorically finished my sentence: "You knew what it was?" I confirmed, "I knew what it was. So I called Liddy on that Monday morning, and I said, 'Gordon,' I said, 'first, I want to know if anybody in the White House was involved in this.' And he said, 'No, they weren't.' I said, 'Well, I want to know how in God's name this happened.' And he said, 'Well, I was pushed without mercy by Magruder to get in there, get more information, and the information, it was not satisfactory. Magruder said the White House is not happy with what we're getting.'"

"The White House?" the president asked, startled. "The White House. Yeah," I reported, and Nixon asked, "Who do you think was pushing him?" I told him I did not know. What I did know was the way things worked at the Nixon White House, so I explained that "probably Strachan" thought Haldeman wanted information, because I had seen times when things had gotten into Haldeman's staff's tickler system and they pushed and pushed on matters they deemed important that in fact were not. The president noted that the Democrats had just nominated McGovern, which he suggested might have been the impetus. At the time of this conversation I was not aware that on June 17, 1972, Liddy's prime target had been McGovern's headquarters, where they were headed after they stopped by the DNC's Watergate offices to fix the malfunctioning bug they had installed earlier and take a few pictures from the files while there, so I told the president, "I don't know, other than the fact that they might have been looking for information about—"

"The convention," he injected, and I copied what he asserted was the target at the DNC: "The convention." He affirmed that to be his understanding,

---

*I misspoke, for it was not on June 17, when I was in Manila, Philippines, rather June 19, after I returned.

"Well, that's right."* And I provided the information I had: "Because, I understand, also, after the fact, that there was a plan to bug Larry O'Brien's suite down in Florida." I added, "Liddy told me that this is what had happened, and this is why it had happened." The president sought clarification: "Liddy told you he was planning, where did you learn there was such a plan? From whom?" I was not sure what the president was asking, so he clarified his question. "Where did you learn of the plans to bug Larry O'Brien's suite?" I answered, "From Magruder, long after the fact."

"Oh, Magruder, he knows?" the president said, clearly feigning surprise. "Yeah, Magruder is totally knowledgeable on the whole thing. Alright, now, we've gone through the trial. I don't know if Mitchell has perjured himself in the grand jury or not. I don't know how much knowledge [Mitchell] actually had. I know that Magruder has perjured himself in the grand jury. I know that Porter has perjured himself in the grand jury." Again, it is not clear if Nixon had a memory problem regarding Bart Porter or he was affecting ignorance for my benefit when he asked, "Porter?" I answered, "He's one of Magruder's deputies. They set up this scenario, which they ran by me. They said, 'How about this?' I said, 'Look, I don't know. If this is what you are going to hang on, fine.' But they—" The president cut me off, uninterested in my role in the Magruder and Porter perjury. "What did they say before the grand jury?" he asked. "They said, before the trial and the grand jury, that Liddy had come over as a counsel, and we knew he had these capacities to do legitimate intelligence. We had no idea what he was doing. He was given an authorization of $250,000 to collect information, because our surrogates were out on the road. They had no protection. We had information that there were going to be demonstrations against them, that we had to have a plan to get information as to what liabilities they were going to be confronted with. And Liddy was charged with doing this. We had no knowledge that he was going to bug the DNC."

"Well, the point is, that's not true," Nixon acknowledged. "Magruder did know that." I informed the president that his involvement was far more direct: "Magruder specifically instructed him to go back in the DNC." Nixon, acting surprised, asked, "He did?" Since Magruder himself had admitted this to me, I said, "Yes." Nixon asked, "You know that? Yeah. I see." Clearly troubled, the president said, "Okay," so I added, "I honestly believe that no

*See Appendix A.

one over here knew that. I know, as God is my maker, I had no knowledge that they were going to do this." Nixon added, "Bob didn't, either," and then added, "They know you're not the issue. Bob could have known." "Bob," I replied, "I don't believe specifically knew they were going in there." The president agreed, and I said, "I think he knew there was a capacity do this, but he wasn't giving it specific direction."

"Strachan, did he know?" the president asked again. "I think Strachan did know," I repeated, based on information Magruder had given me and Strachan's reaction in the aftermath of the arrests at the DNC.[6] I continued, "Alright, so those people are in trouble as a result of the grand jury and the trial. Mitchell, of course, was never called during the trial. Now—" The president had a question: "Mitchell has given a sworn statement?" I said Mitchell had effectively testified to the grand jury, via an arrangement whereby he actually testified at the Department of Justice and that was read to the grand jury. And the reason he had been called was that the grand jurors wanted him. The president thought that good. "I don't know what he said," I added. "I've never seen a transcript of the grand jury." I paused, sighing, for I had a long way I wanted to go and was not making much progress with my narrative.

"Now, what has happened post–June seventeenth? Well, it was—" I stopped and shifted ground, because I wanted to remind the president that his talk about my supposed investigation was baseless. But I was not about to call him a liar, since for all I knew, Haldeman or Ehrlichman may have told him I had indeed undertaken such an inquiry. Instead, I simply noted diplomatically, "I was under pretty clear instructions—" I chuckled nervously "—not really to investigate this. That this was something that just could have been disastrous on the election if it had been investigated, and all hell had broken loose, and I worked on a theory of containment to try to hold it right where it was." The president said he understood, and I added, "There is no doubt that I was totally aware what the Bureau was doing at all times. I was totally aware of what the grand jury was doing. I knew what witnesses were going to be called. I knew what they were going to be asked, and I had to. There was just—" The president interrupted, and in doing so indicated he knew how I had stayed informed, "Why did Petersen play the game so straight with us?" Nixon clearly understood that Petersen had been my source of information.

"Because Petersen's a soldier," I answered. "He kept me informed. He told me when we had problems, and the like. He believes in you. He believes in this administration. This administration has made him. I don't think he's done anything improper, but he did make sure the investigation was narrowed down to the very, very fine criminal things, which was a break for us. There's no doubt about it." Nixon asked, regarding Petersen: "He honestly feels that he did an adequate job?" I answered, "They ran that investigation out to the fullest extent they could follow [they followed the leads], and that was it." But the president saw a problem: "But the point is, that's where I suppose he could be criticized for not doing an adequate job is, why didn't he call Haldeman? Why didn't he get a statement from Colson?" Then the president remembered, "Oh, they did get Colson." I confirmed that and explained, "But see, the thing is, based on their FBI interviews, there was no reason to follow up. There were no leads there. Colson said, 'I have no knowledge of this' to the FBI. Strachan said, 'I have no knowledge of—'" I stopped to correct the path of my statement. "You know, they didn't ask Strachan any Watergate questions. They asked him about Segretti. They said, 'What's your connection with Liddy?' and he just said, 'Well, I, you know, I just met him over there,' and they never really pressed him. They didn't, you know, so Strachan appeared, as a result of some coaching, he could be the dumbest paper pusher in the bowels of the White House," I said, since all witnesses had been advised they only needed to answer the questions asked. "Right," the president said.

I began: "Alright. Now, post–June seventeenth," I began, then remembered, and was struck by the irony, that a member of my staff had accompanied Liddy to a meeting at Henry Petersen's office on campaign law matters on Friday, June 16, which I mentioned in passing to the president, and then continued, "After the incident, [Liddy] ran Kleindienst down at the Burning Tree Country Club and told him that 'you've got to get my men out of jail,' which was kind of a [shocker]. Kleindienst said, 'Now, you get the hell out of here, kid. And whatever you've got to say, just say to somebody else. Don't bother me.' And this has never come up," I noted, but I wanted the president to be aware that his attorney general had understood what was going on from the day after the arrests at the DNC.

"Yeah," the president said. When he left it there, I continued, "Liddy said that they all got counsel instantly and said that 'we'll ride this thing out.' Alright, then they started making demands that 'we've got to have attorneys' fees. We don't have any money ourselves, and if you're asking us to take this through the election.' Alright, so arrangements were made through Mitchell, initiating it in discussions, and I was present, that these guys had to be taken care of. Their attorneys' fees had to be done. Kalmbach was brought in. Kalmbach raised some cash. They were obv—" Nixon interrupted, indicating he was aware of this activity, saying, "They put that under the cover of the Cuban committee." Although I had heard a passing reference to a Cuban committee, I did not really know anything about it.[7] In fact, not until writing this book did I understand that on June 20, 1972, Nixon had suggested the creation of a Cuban committee to Haldeman to take care of those involved in Watergate. I replied, "Yeah, they had a Cuban committee, and they had—" at which point I stopped, as I did not know what I was talking about, so I returned to what I did know. "Some of it was given to Hunt's lawyer, who in turn passed it out. This, you know, was when Hunt's wife was flying to Chicago with ten thousand; she was actually, I understand after the fact now, was going to pass that money to one of the Cubans, to meet him in Chicago and pass it to somebody there." I had been given this information after the initial reports that she had been carrying the cash for a family investment.

"Maybe—" the president began, then restarted, "Well, maybe it's too late to do anything about it, but I would certainly keep that—" he chuckled nervously "—that cover for whatever it's worth. Keep the [Cuban] committee." I was talking as the president was sharing his thinking, which caught me off guard, so I decided to make it clear to him that this activity was criminal: "Well, that, that's the most troublesome post thing, because, one, Bob is involved in that; John is involved in that; I am involved in that; Mitchell is involved in that. And that's an obstruction of justice."

"In other words, the fact that you're taking care of witnesses?" the president asked. "That's right," I said. "How was Bob involved?" the president asked. "Well, they ran out of money over there. Bob had $350,000 in a safe over here that was really set aside for polling purposes. And there was no other source of money, so they came over here and said, 'You all have got to give us some money.' I had to go to Bob and say, 'Bob, they need some money over there.' And he said, 'What for?' And so I had to tell him what it was for, because he wasn't about to just send money over there willy-nilly. And John was involved in those discussions, and we decided that there was no price too high to pay to let this thing blow up in front of the election."

"I think you should handle that one pretty fast. That issue, I mean, that the three-fifty went back to him," the president said, pushing back and wanting this issue to disappear. I both pulled back and pushed forward by informing him that this problem continued: "But here's what's happening right now. What sort of brings matters to the [moment]. This is the one that's going to be a continual blackmail operation by Hunt and Liddy and the Cubans. No doubt about it. And McCord, who is another one involved. Mc-Cord has asked for nothing. McCord did ask to meet with somebody, and it was Jack Caulfield, who is his old friend who'd gotten him hired over there. And when Caulfield had him hired he was a perfectly legitimate security man. And [McCord] wanted to talk about commutation and things like that. And as you know, Colson has talked to, indirectly, to Hunt about commutation. All these things are bad in that they are problems, they are promises, they are commitments, and the very sort of thing that the Senate's going to be looking for," I said, but I did not want to sound threatening to the president, so I again pulled back, adding, "I don't think they can find them, frankly."

"It's pretty hard," the president agreed. I repeated, "Pretty hard. Damn hard. It's all cash." "Well, I mean, pretty hard as far as the witnesses are concerned," the president observed. "That's right," I agreed. But the problems were ongoing and increasingly unsolvable, so I pushed forward. "Now, the blackmail is continuing. Hunt called one of the lawyers from the reelection committee on last Friday to meet with him, over the weekend. The guy came in to see me to get a message directly from Hunt to me, for the first time," I said, reporting Paul O'Brien's visit on March 19. "Is Hunt out on bail?" the president asked. I confirmed this and continued, "Hunt now is demanding another seventy-two thousand dollars for his own personal expenses; another fifty thousand dollars to pay his attorneys' fees. A hundred and twenty-some thousand dollars. Wants it, wanted it by the close of business yesterday. Because, he says, 'I'm going to be sentenced on Friday, and I've got to be able to get my financial affairs in order.' I told this fellow O'Brien, 'You came to the wrong man, fellow. I'm not involved in the money. I don't know a thing about it, can't help you.' I said, 'You better scramble around elsewhere.' Now, O'Brien is a ball player. He's been, he's carried tremendous water for us."

"He isn't Hunt's lawyer?" the president asked. "No. He is our lawyer at the reelection committee," I clarified. "I see. Good," he replied. Reacting to the president's concern, I assured him, "So he's safe. There's no problem there." Again, though, I had to continue to give him bad news. "But it raises the whole question of, Hunt now has made a direct threat against Ehrlich-man, as a result of this. This is his blackmail. He says, 'I will bring John Ehrlichman down to his knees and put him in jail. I have done enough seamy things for him and Krogh that they'll never survive it.'"

"What's that, on Ellsberg?" the president asked. "Ellsberg and, apparently, some other things. I don't know the full extent of it," I answered. "I don't know about anything else," the president said, professing his own innocence. I told him, "I don't know either," and then, with an uncomfortable chuckle, added, "and I almost hate to learn some of these things." I then resumed my narrative: "So that's that situation. Now, where are the soft points? How many people know about this? Well, let me go one step further in this whole thing. The Cubans that were used in the Watergate were also the same Cu-bans that Hunt and Liddy used for this California Ellsberg thing, for the break-in out there. So they're aware of that. How high their knowledge [goes] is something else. Hunt and Liddy, of course, are totally aware of it, and the fact that it was right out of the White House."

"I don't know what the hell he did that for," the president declared, fur-ther undercutting in my mind any claim that this Ehrlichman-Krogh-Young-Colson-Liddy-Hunt operation was based on national security needs. When I had no answer, the president asked with a tone of frustration, "What in the name of God, did that—" As the president was expressing his displea-sure, I interjected, "Mr. President, there's been a couple of things around here that I have gotten wind of. There was at one time a desire to do a second-story job on the Brookings Institute, where they had the Pentagon Papers. So I flew to California, because I was told that John [Ehrlichman] had instructed it, and he said, 'I really hadn't. It's a misimpression, but for Christ sakes, turn it off.' And I did. I came back and turned it off." Something in the president's reaction caused me to pull back; at the time I was not aware that it had been Nixon who had personally ordered the Brookings break-ins.* So I added, "Because, you know, if the risk is minimal and the gain is fantastic, it's some-thing else. But with a low [I misspoke; I meant to say "high"] risk and no gain, gee, it's just not worth it."

After instinctively softening the blow because of Nixon's reaction to this

---

*After the release of the Pentagon Papers Nixon ordered break-ins at the Brookings Institution on four occasions to retrieve classified material he believed they held: On June 30, 1971, in Conversation No. 533-1; on July 1, 1971, in Conversation No. 534-2; on July 1, 1971, in Conversation No. 534-5; and on July 2, 1971, in Conversation No. 537-2. See also, Stanley I. Kutler, *Abuse of Power: The New Nixon Tapes* (New York: Free Press, 1997), pp. 3, 6, 8, 10, 13, and 17.

tangential matter, I resumed my Watergate narrative: "Well, who knows about this all now? Alright, you've got the Cubans' lawyer, a man by the name of Rothblatt, who is a no-good, publicity-seeking, son of a bitch, to be very frank about it. He has had to be turned down and turned off. He was canned by his own people because they didn't trust him. They were trying to run a different route than he wanted to run. He didn't want them to plead guilty. He wants to represent them before the Senate. So F. Lee Bailey, who was the partner of one of the men representing McCord, got in and cooled Rothblatt down. So that means that Lee Bailey's got knowledge. Hunt's lawyer, a man by the name of Bittman, who's an excellent criminal lawyer from the Democratic era of Bobby Kennedy, he's got knowledge." "Do you think that he's got some? How much?" the president asked, undoubtedly thinking of his clemency conversations with Colson.

But I could only speculate, conservatively, and did: "All the direct knowledge that Hunt and Liddy have, as well as all the hearsay they have." The president made an unclear comment as I continued. "You've got the two lawyers over at the reelection committee, who did an investigation to find out the facts. Slowly, they have gotten the whole picture. They're, now, they're solid, but they're—" Nixon made my point that they were knowledgeable, so I continued to suggest that, not only did all the principals know, but their wives likely did as well, and as an example I used Dorothy Hunt: "Mrs. Hunt was the savviest woman in the world. She had the whole picture together. Apparently she was the pillar of strength in that family before the death."

"Great sadness," the president said. "As a matter of fact, there was some discussion over here with somebody about Hunt's problems after his wife died, and I said, of course, commutation could be considered on the basis of his wife, and that is the only discussion I ever had in that light." I affirmed that I was aware of those conversations and proceeded: "So that's it. That's the extent of the knowledge," I said, referring to people outside the White House. "Now, where are the soft spots on this? Well, first of all, there's the problem of the continued blackmail, which will not only go on now, it'll go on when these people are in prison, and it will compound the obstruction of justice situation. It'll cost money. It's dangerous. And I think people around here are not pros at this sort of thing. And this is the sort of thing Mafia people can do—washing money, getting clean money and things like that. We just don't know about those things, because we're not used to, you know, we're not criminals and not used to dealing in that business," I said, with a uneasy chuckle. "It's a tough thing to know how to do."

"That's right," the president said, adding, "Maybe we can't even do that." "That's right," I agreed, jumping on the president's comment. Because I had gotten no response from him when I explained that this was an obstruction of justice, I decided to raise the practical difficulties involved: "It's a real problem as to whether we could even do it. Plus, there's a real problem in raising money. Mitchell has been working on raising some money, feeling, you know, he's one of the ones with the most to lose. But there's no denying the fact that the White House, and Ehrlichman, Haldeman and Dean, are involved in some of the early money decisions." Then the president stunned me. "How much money do you need?" he asked, which was not a question I had expected, nor a matter to which I had given any serious thought. I paused for an instant and reached for what I thought would be a sizable number, making it all more difficult. "I would say these people are going to cost a million dollars over the next two years."

"We could get that," the president responded. I replied with an unenthusiastic "um, hmm," which he ignored, saying, "You, on the money, if you need the money, I mean, you could get the money. Let's say—" I tried to interrupt him, but he continued, "What I meant is, you could, you could get a million dollars, and you could get it in cash. I know where it could be gotten. I mean, it's not easy, but it could be done. But the question is, who the hell would handle it? Any ideas on that?"

"Well, I would think that would be something that Mitchell ought to be charged with," I said, trying to keep the White House away from it. "I would think so, too," the president agreed. I further suggested, "And get pros to help him," since Mitchell always seemed to come back to the White House for assistance. Nixon added, "Let me say, there shouldn't be a lot of people running around getting money. We should set up a little—" the president started to explain, but I stopped him so I could describe how Mitchell was operating.

"Well, he's got one person doing it who I'm not sure is—" I began. "Who is that?" the president asked. "He's got Fred LaRue doing it. Now, Fred started out going out trying to solicit money from all kinds of people. And I learned about that, and I said, 'No.'" The president agreed. "He's apparently talked to Tom Pappas," I added. "I know," the president said, which went by me so fast that it did not register. Instead, I reported, "And Pappas has agreed to come up with a sizable amount, I gather, from Mitchell." I had no idea that Nixon had personally engaged in this fund-raising undertaking for the Watergate defendants when he asked, "Yeah. Well, what do you think? You don't need a million right away, but you need a million, is that right?"

"That's right," I said, a bit dismayed, since I had not brought this information to the president's attention to raise money; rather, I had hoped telling him of Hunt's demand would have the opposite effect, that he would direct this business be stopped. Instead, he continued: "You've got to do it in cash, I'm sure. If you want to put that through, would you put that through—" The president said he was "thinking out loud here for a moment," and then asked, "—Would you put that through the Cuban committee?" Since I did not know about the Cuban committee, I said, "No." Still thinking aloud, the president shared several half thoughts, with his bottom line being how this information would be handled if it ever became public. Specifically, he asked, "Is the Cuban committee an obstruction of justice if they want to help?" Because I was not certain such an entity even existed, and because I did not think we should be in this business, I could only stutter and sputter[8] until the president finally clarified, "Would you like to put, I mean, would that, would that give a little bit of a cover, for example?"

"That would give some for the Cubans, and possibly Hunt," I responded meekly, then thought of a problem it would not solve. "Then you've got Liddy and McCord, [who are] not accepting any money." Regarding McCord, I added, "So he's not a bought man right now." The president now urged me, "Continue a little bit here now." Realizing I had not managed to convey the urgency of the situation, I decided to try to paint an even grimmer picture: "When I say this is a growing cancer, I say it for reasons like this. Bud Krogh, in his testimony before the grand jury, was forced to perjure himself. He is haunted by it. Bud said, 'I haven't had a pleasant day on the job.' He said to me, 'I told my wife all about this'; he said, 'The curtain may ring down one of these days, and I may have to face the music, which I'm perfectly willing to do.'" Nixon asked, "What did he perjure himself on, John?" Bud and I had never really discussed it in any detail, but as best I could recall, he had said he had testified that he did not know the Cubans involved in Watergate, when, in fact, he did know two of them. The president wanted to know if Bud had denied knowing them, and I said, "That's right. They didn't press him hard on this."[9] The president made his point. "Perjury's an awful hard rap to prove. He could say that I—Well, go ahead," he instructed.

"Well, so that's one perjury. Now, Mitchell and Magruder are potential perjuries. There's always the possibility of any one of these individuals blowing: Hunt, Liddy. Liddy's in jail right now. He's trying to get good time right now. I think Liddy is probably, in his own bizarre way, the strongest of all of them. So there's that possibility," I explained. The president noted, "Well, your major guy to keep under control is Hunt, I think. Because he knows about a lot of other things." I agreed, "Right," and added, "He could sink Chuck Colson. Apparently he is quite distressed with Colson. He thinks Colson's abandoned him. Colson was to meet with him when he was out of here, now that he's left the White House. He met with him through his lawyer. Hunt raised the question. He wanted money. Colson's lawyer told him that Colson wasn't doing anything with money, and Hunt took offense with that immediately, that Colson had abandoned him."

"Don't you, just looking at the immediate problem, don't you have to handle Hunt's financial situation? Damn soon?" the president pressed, and I had to admit that that was an immediate problem, saying I had talked with Mitchell about it. "Might as well," the president said. "May have [to do it], you've got to keep the cap on the bottle that much in order to have any options." I could not disagree. Then the president raised the key question, "Either that or let it all blow right now."

"Well, that, you know, that's the question," I said, and the president requested I continue. I had presented what I viewed as the key issue, but there were other less serious ones to consider. I told him of the Kalmbach situation—that he had controlled almost two million dollars in cash, and that Herb felt it would be difficult to account for much of this money, because it would open up other White House activities. Unaware that Ehrlichman had discussed this very topic with Nixon, I was surprised to find the president did not feel this posed serious problems, and I assumed he knew much more than I did about these funds. I informed him that four hundred thousand dollars had been sent somewhere in the South, which Nixon thought had been to Governor George Wallace. I continued: "He has maintained a man, who I only know by the name of 'Tony,' who is the fellow who did the Chappaquiddick study and other odd jobs like that. Nothing illegal" that I was then aware of. "I heard about that," the president said. I added, "I don't know of anything that Herb has done that is illegal, other than the fact that he doesn't want to blow the whistle on a lot of people, and may find himself in a perjury situation." I explained that this was a problem if Kalmbach was asked about the money, and about how he paid Segretti. That they would seek Kalmbach's bank records. Nixon asked, "How would you handle that then, John? For example, would you just have him put the whole thing out?" The president said he was not bothered by any of Kalmbach's earlier activities, and other than that Kalmbach himself was worried, I had no further information to impart.

When the president asked me about other vulnerabilities unwinding because of Watergate, I reported what I knew about the grand jury in the Southern District of New York that was investigating Mitchell and Vesco. Then there was the Segretti matter, which Haldeman had told me he had discussed with the president but was not of great concern to anyone, although there was a very remote possibility the Justice Department might claim Segretti's actions had violated a federal civil rights statute prohibiting interference with a candidate for national office, which was a felony. The president felt that the Segretti matter would be primarily a public relations problem, which could be made so confusing no one would understand it.

I returned again to what troubled me most: possible criminal charges against Haldeman, Ehrlichman, Mitchell and Dean for our involvement in obstruction of justice. The only idea I had was that we should all meet and see if we could come up with a way to deal with the situation, since we had never attempted to do that, and also figure out how it could be "carved away" from the presidency. I explained that one of the reasons I was no longer effective in dealing with the problems was that Pat Gray had brought me into the public eye. In addition, everyone was now moving into a protective mode to save himself. I had earlier recommended to Ehrlichman, who liked the idea, that we all go to the grand jury. I now put this suggestion to Nixon, who also initially favored it, until I told him "some people are going to have to go to jail. That's the long and short of it." He wanted to know who, and I told him I could be one of those affected. While I had hinted at my legal vulnerability earlier, I now bluntly stated I was troubled by the obstruction of justice. "I don't see it," Nixon said, and I explained that the relevant issue was my role as a conduit of information in taking care of the defendants.

"Oh, you mean like the blackmail?" the president asked. I acknowledged that was the problem, and he added, "Well, I wonder if that part of it doesn't have to be continued. Let me put it this way: Let us suppose you could get the million bucks, and you get the proper way to handle it, and you could hold that side. It would seem to me that would be worthwhile." I did not know a proper way to handle hush money, so I reminded the president that all those already convicted would want clemency. The president acknowledged that this was a problem where Hunt was concerned, and I told him it would be an issue with the others as well. When Nixon remarked that he did not think he could offer clemency until after the 1974 midterm elections, I advised him that he should not even consider it, for it would involve him in a way he should not be involved.

"There've been some bad judgments made, there've been some necessary judgments made, before the election," I explained, but he should not have this burden weighing on his second term. "It is not going to go away, sir." The president agreed and wanted to know my other concerns, adding that he felt I "[might] be overplaying" my feelings about my role in obstructing justice. I told him that Ehrlichman had potential criminal liability for the conspiracy to burglarize the offices of Ellsberg's doctor if Hunt made good on his threat. Then I recalled that I had not mentioned all the White House and reelection committee secretaries who had varying degrees of knowledge of illicit activities who could also be targeted by the Senate investigation. I told the president I did not have a plan to solve all these problems, but I knew that Haldeman and Ehrlichman had stopped talking to Mitchell about them, and suggested again that we should have "a real down and out with everyone" who had the most to lose.

"I think Bob has a potential criminal liability, frankly," I added. The president then said, "Suppose the worst, that Bob is indicted and Ehrlichman is indicted. I must say, maybe we just better then try to tough it through. Do you get my point?" I did, and he continued, "If, for example, say we cut our losses and [pay] no more blackmail and all the rest, and the thing blows, and they indict Bob and the rest. Jesus, you'd never recover from that, John. It's better to fight it out instead, and not let people testify, and so forth and so on. Now, on the other hand, we realize that we have these weaknesses in terms of blackmail."

I agreed that there were two alternatives: Either to figure out how to cut the losses and minimize the human impact in a manner that would not undermine the Nixon presidency or to "just hunker down," fight all the way, not let people testify, keep it all buried and hope we could make the right decisions. After making that observation I was surprised when the president said, "I do want you to still consider my scheme of having you brief the cabinet, just in very general terms, and the leaders, in very general terms, and some general statement with regard to my investigation. Answer questions. Report Haldeman was not involved. Ehrlichman—"

"Well, I can, you know, if we go that route, sir, I can give a show," I began, but because I had just told him there had been no investigation, and that

Haldeman and Ehrlichman were deeply and criminally involved, I could not resist adding a cynical comment: "We can sell it, you know, just like we were selling Wheaties." The tone of my remark seemed to pull the president back to the seriousness of the situation, my mention of the "mine fields down the road," the fact that "the guys are going to jail," the fact that "we're not going to be able to give them clemency." Nixon was stunned when I informed him that the Watergate defendants conceivably could get as much as fifty-year sentences, given the comments that Judge Sirica had been making and that he had hiked their bails bonds up beyond their ability to pay while letting a man charged with shooting Senator John Stennis out on the street with virtually no bond.

The president buzzed for Haldeman to come to his office so that a meeting could be set up with Mitchell, Ehrlichman, Haldeman and myself as soon as possible. When Haldeman arrived, the president summarized the high points of our meeting and said he wanted me to give the others the same information I had given him, including the potential criminal liabilities. In fact, over the preceding eight months I had already given them that information, and not unlike the president, they had paid little attention to it, addressing instead whatever was then the current problem. Haldeman, however, did not mention this, and I did not feel it my place to raise it. What was particularly striking about this meeting was that, when the president mentioned matters I had already discussed with Haldeman on repeated occasions, he reacted as if they were all news to him. For example, when the president remarked that Colson had called Magruder, which had triggered Magruder to get Liddy's plans approved by Mitchell, Haldeman acted surprised, as if hearing it for the first time.* These were the types of games the president's men were playing with one another, and with the president. From the distance of four decades it appears that while both men were occasionally conscious that their conversations were being recorded, Haldeman may have been more sensitive to this than Nixon, not to mention more cunning.

When the president asked if I thought Colson should also attend the meeting with Mitchell, Ehrlichman, Haldeman and myself, I said no. I reported that Colson's lawyer had become a chatterbox; he had discussed Hunt's demands with members of my staff, a matter about which they had

---

*During Nixon and Haldeman's conversation of January 3, 1973, immediately after Haldeman met with Magruder in his office, Haldeman described these events to Nixon, so clearly they were well known to him.

no knowledge. Haldeman asked, "Who's Colson's lawyer? That Jew in his law firm?" I said it was David Shapiro. "That's where your danger lies," Haldeman told the president. "It is in all these stupid human errors developing."

The next forty minutes of conversation fell within what had already become the template for discussing this subject, both during the months that led to this juncture and those that would follow: Problems were raised, but solutions could not be found, because no one wanted to truly face the terrible reality: We had become something of a criminal cabal, weighing the risks of further criminal action to prevent the worst while hoping something might unexpectedly occur that would resolve the problems. Watergate conversations had become like the devil's merry-go-round, with the same basic tune played over and over while various people climbed on and off. The lever controlling it all was in the hands of Richard Nixon, who from our March 21, 1973, conversation until the end of his presidency would engage in these increasingly protracted exchanges searching for less than truthful solutions to ever-growing problems.

Two instructions emerged from this meeting, one to me and one to Haldeman. I had suggested we might gain some time to deal with Hunt's demand if Kleindienst called Judge Sirica and said the government had new information that could influence his sentencing decision; might he delay sentencing for a week? The president wanted me to follow up on this (though when I discussed it hypothetically with Henry Petersen he advised against it). Haldeman was to convene a meeting with Mitchell, Ehrlichman and me as soon as possible to explore our options, which he did. Once we decided on the plan we would discuss it further. Nixon said to me, "You had the right plan, let me say, I have no doubts about it, the right plan before the election. And you handled it just right. You contained it. Now, after the election, we've got to have another plan, because we can't have, for four years, we can't have this thing" that would eat away at his presidency. I had gone from being the intermediary and communications link between and among all these people to the president's designated fixer.

"Well, there's been a change in the mood," I noted for Haldeman and the president, and I was talking not only about Capitol Hill, the anti-Nixon media and the president's legions of detractors, but about Haldeman, Ehrlichman, Mitchell, Colson, Magruder and everyone else involved in the Watergate affair, including myself. I was willing to soldier on, for I still believed the president and my colleagues would do the right thing, although I was beginning to have my doubts. "John's point is exactly right," Haldeman noted, and explained to the president "that the erosion here now is going to you, and that is the thing that we've got to turn off at whatever the cost. We've got to figure out where to turn it off at the lowest cost we can, but at whatever cost it takes." I agreed, "That's what we have to do." The president observed, "Well, the erosion is inevitably going to come here, apart from anything, you know, people saying that Watergate isn't a major concern. It isn't. But it will be. It's bound to be." I volunteered, "We cannot let you be tarnished by that situation," still believing I had laid the basic diagnosis before the president before the prognosis became terminal. And the meeting ended.

The president had a full schedule that morning, but when back in his office that afternoon he asked Rose Woods to come in.[10] About three minutes into this meeting the president said, "Let me ask you something. I'm just doing a little checking. We, at the present time, may have the need for some substantial cash for personal purposes for some things that are outside, political things and so forth and so on. Approximately how much do you have at this point?" he asked, regarding a secret fund she maintained. Rose was not exactly sure but said, "I know we still have that four hundred." She reported that nobody was aware of this four hundred thousand dollars other than the president.

Shortly after 3:00 P.M. the president asked Haldeman to come to his EOB Office.[11] When Haldeman arrived he reported that he would be meeting with Ehrlichman and me, and the president said the first matter that needed to be considered was "what we're going to do about Hunt. I think we've obviously overloaded Dean, who's been carrying this thing. Everybody says, 'Well, that's Dean's job,' you know." But the president said it was time for others to step in.

"Well, we've been backing him up pretty well," Haldeman explained, but he noted the difficulty of keeping everything together. As for dealing with Hunt, the president saw the problem as the lack of available funds. Haldeman pointed out that it was not only Hunt, but "it's Liddy and that other guy, McCord, and the Cubans." He reported that Fred LaRue had been trying to raise money but was not very good at it: "LaRue isn't a very dynamic guy." Haldeman said this had resulted in the need to go back to Mitchell with the money problem, explaining that "guys in the White House" couldn't handle this. Kalmbach had withdrawn from this risky money-raising business. The president acknowledged the problem, pointing out, "It's a dangerous thing they're going to do, going around getting money." Haldeman said that I should be the one to convince Mitchell to do this, observing, "You can't have a fund-raising drive and give everybody certificates and gold pens."

When Nixon mentioned my concern that this activity involved an obstruction of justice, Haldeman responded, "Well, see, I hadn't really thought of that." The president said, "I hadn't thought of it, either," and added that he was not sure if that was actually the case. As the conversation continued the president revealed that he did in fact have access to money, and they would have to risk using it, if necessary. Haldeman warned, "It better be washed," and then explained that there were ways to do it, referring to what I had been told about taking the money to Vegas or going through a bookmaker in New York. When Haldeman said that Mitchell and LaRue should still have some of the $350,000, the president remarked it "could take a hell of a lot more than that."

Again trying to assess whom Hunt might cause problems for, the president suggested that Colson might be able to deal with him regarding his threat against Ehrlichman. "Ehrlichman said he didn't seem a bit concerned about it," Haldeman said, which surprised Nixon; Haldeman added, "He thinks he's three times removed. That there's no problem, but I don't know where that leaves John."* Even Haldeman suspected that Ehrlichman was more vulnerable than he was admitting.[12] The president, however, recognized the seriousness of Ehrlichman's position and asked next, "What about Krogh?" for Krogh posed a potential problem for Ehrlichman. Haldeman said he was still making inquiries about Krogh and had spoken with me about his perjury problem. The president also remained concerned about Colson, not only regarding Hunt, but as he told Haldeman, "You had indicated the pressures [that were put] on Magruder. Dean said that all came from Colson. With Hunt and Liddy in his office, he called Magruder and said, 'Now, look, get off your ass and start working. We've got to get [intelligence on] this or that.'" The president said I had concluded that Colson's call

---

*Ehrlichman would later be indicted both by California, for conspiracy in the burglary of Ellsberg's doctor's office, and the Watergate special prosecutor, for conspiracy to violate the constitutional rights of an American citizen (also in the burglary of Dr. Fielding's office), for making false statements to the FBI, and for making false statements to the grand jury. When the federal government indicted him, California agreed to drop their charges. Howard Hunt, Bud Krogh and David Young testified for the government against Ehrlichman, who had personally authorized the covert Fielding operation in writing. He was convicted on all counts. See *U.S. v. Ehrlichman*, 546 F2d 910 (1976).

probably caused Mitchell and Magruder to take action, and Nixon was concerned that he might have provoked Colson's actions. "Yeah, I know that there was a scheme," Haldeman conceded, now that I was not present. "With bugging, kidnapping and [mugging]," the president noted. "There was all kinds of stuff," Haldeman agreed. The president noted, "Now, the point that I make is if, for example, Liddy and Hunt were in the office when Colson called Magruder, then Colson directed it. He knows God damn well what it was about."

Haldeman volunteered that he might have, inadvertently, been responsible for Magruder's decisions. "It's another implication thing," he said, "I had horrendous pressure on Magruder, at one point, on the basis that [he] didn't have people covering the Democratic candidates and taping their speeches. And their press conferences, and their Q and As. Remember, you got into it. You asked for some stuff on it. And I thought Buchanan had the stuff, and he wasn't getting anything." The president recalled, and thought it innocuous. Haldeman continued, "Alright, but see, Magruder could say he was under enormous pressure from me to cover on that. He was. It wasn't to bug anybody. It was to carry a tape recorder openly. I mean, I didn't give a shit what they did with it, I just wanted the tape. So we could prove that Humphrey said what he said about McGovern." The president added they had also pushed for "their schedules" as well, adding, "all that's perfectly legitimate." This discussion of Watergate ended with the president, pursuing my suggestion, asking Haldeman to discuss, when he met with Ehrlichman and me, White House staff going to the grand jury. Haldeman liked the idea of the grand jury as well, because unlike the Senate, where there would be "no limitation," there were rules—although Haldeman did not yet realize that those rules did not particularly favor those testifying before it.

At 5:20 P.M. on the afternoon of March 21, Haldeman, Ehrlichman and I were asked to come to the president's EOB office, following our meeting in Ehrlichman's office at 3:45. The president was anxious to hear what we had to report, and Ehrlichman took the lead in explaining. "Well, you go round and round and you come up with all questions and no answers," he reported, in short. "Back up where you were at when you started."[13] We had considered both the grand jury and a special investigative-type panel, which might immunize from prosecution all involved to get to the truth, but neither alternative was realistic to provide everyone protection. "Well, let's take the grand jury without immunity, what about that?" the president asked. "Yeah, well,

I think that is still a possibility," Ehrlichman replied. "It leads to some very drastic results. Counsel over here reads the statutes," he said, referring to me, "and there are awful opportunities for indictment, and so you end up with people in and out of the White House indicted for various offenses." I had in our meeting earlier that day in Ehrlichman's office raised the fact that it appeared we had been violating Sections 371 (the federal conspiracy statute) and 1503 (the federal obstruction of justice statute) of Title 18 of the U.S. Code. While I conceded that I was not a criminal lawyer, based on the cases annotating those statutes, I thought Mitchell and Magruder had potential criminal liability both for the Watergate break-in and bugging and for their activities following the June 17, 1972, arrests, as did Dean, Haldeman and Ehrlichman for our post–June 17 activities. When I first raised these criminal issues, months earlier, Ehrlichman had rejected them out of hand. When I brought them up again during our meeting earlier that afternoon, and was more explicit about their ramifications, Ehrlichman had tried again to dismiss them. But now, while speaking to the president, he seemed to acknowledge the problems were real.

Given the disadvantages of the grand jury option, Ehrlichman continued, "the other route would be two papers, or possibly three, and these papers would say, 'Mr. President, you asked me about this thing. Here's my review of the facts.' And I think we disagree as to whether or not that's a viable option or not. I think you could get out a fairly credible document that would stand up, and that will have the effect of trimming the scope, and would have the effect of maybe becoming the battleground on a reduced scope, which I think is important." Ehrlichman said he felt the "big danger in the Ervin hearings" would be their running out "leads into areas that it would be better not to have to get into."

"But does anybody really think we should do nothing?" Nixon asked. "That's the other option, period. Keep fighting it out on this ground, if it takes all summer?" Haldeman assured everyone it would indeed take all summer. "That's the other thing, whether we're going to contain the thing," Ehrlichman noted, and reported that we had considered all these possibilities, including "playing the odds, keep trying to put out fires here and there. The problem of the Hunt thing, and possibly McCord, and some of these other people breaking, there is no sign-off ever. It just goes on and on and on." Then the president asked Ehrlichman, "Well, if that's the case, then what is your view as to what we should do now about Hunt, and so forth?" "Well, my view is that Hunt's interests lie in getting a pardon if he can. That ought to be, somehow or another, one of the options that he is most particularly concerned about. His indirect contacts with John," referring to the blackmail demands, "don't contemplate it at all." Ehrlichman surmised that "they think that that's already understood."

"I mean, he's got to get that by Christmastime," the president added, referring to Hunt's clemency. The president asked me how Hunt's confessing everything could help him, wondering if he could "get clemency from the court." I explained how Hunt might appeal to Judge Sirica, saying he would cooperate with the government, and the judge might respond to the plea for leniency. The discussion turned to paying off Hunt, and I reported that, while I had not spoken to either Mitchell or LaRue, I understood they were "in a position to do something." This information caused the president to lament to us all, "It's a long road, isn't it?" I then raised more vulnerabilities that I had touched on only lightly during my morning session with the president, like the remarkable number of secretaries who had varying degrees of knowledge. I reported that the DNC's legal team was planning a rather "intense civil discovery" in the coming weeks and appeared to be coordinating with the Senate's inquiry. And finally, while discussing the matter in general terms (though the fact that I was speaking to the president with Ehrlichman present did not escape my notice), I added, "And the other thing I must say I've noticed is, there is an attitude that has grown amongst all the people that have been involved in this thing to protect their own behinds. And they're going to start hiring counsel. Dwight [Chapin], for example, now wants a lawyer. Kalmbach has hired himself a lawyer. Colson has retained a lawyer."

Picking the right moment in our circular conversation, Ehrlichman asked, "Or is there another way? Like the Dean statements, where the president then makes a full disclosure of everything which he then has. And [then the president] is in a position, if it does collapse at a later time, to say, 'Jesus, I had the FBI, and the grand jury, and I had my own counsel. I turned over every rock I could find. And I rested my confidence in these people in good faith, and it's obvious now . . .'" Ehrlichman trailed off, having made his point. He was flat-out stating that I should write a bogus report behind which the president could hide, and when it fell apart he could blame me. Ehrlichman was effectively volunteering me to fall on my sword, an offer I declined to take.

Slowly the president reembraced the scheme he had formulated when he first thrust me forward on August 29, 1972, with my nonexistent investigation clearing everyone. I listened as he explained how we had been around and around on this matter, and he finally said, "If you, as White House counsel, John, on direction, I asked for a written report, which is very general, understand." He nervously chuckled as he continued, now knowing what I knew, "I don't want to get all that God damned specific. I'm thinking now in far more general terms, having in mind the fact that the problem with a specific report is that this proves this one and that one and that one, and you just prove something that you didn't do at all." I did not have a clue what he was saying, but I listened. "But if you make it quite general in terms of your investigation, [which] indicates this man did not do it, this man did not do it, this man did do that." Then he added that he wanted me to address the Segretti-Chapin thing, which I answered with a noncommittal, "Um hmm." When the president asked if this was possible, Ehrlichman jumped back into the discussion and suggested, "To give some weight to that, could you attach as an appendix a list of the FBI reports to which you had access: interview with Kalmbach; interview with Segretti; interview with Chapin; and Magruder; and whoever; Dean; the whole business. So that the president at some later time is in a position to say, 'I relied—'"

"Not on Dean alone but on corroborated evidence," I said, interrupting. "That's right," Ehrlichman added, and he elaborated further on using the FBI reports, with the president largely repeating Ehrlichman's argument. Looking for a way out of this conspicuous deception, I said that because of the Gray hearings, which had called into question my credibility, I might not be the best party to undertake this task, and that someone else should assume responsibility for it. In response, Ehrlichman made the absurd claim: "This will rehabilitate you, though." The president added that he did not believe my credibility was in question but rather that they merely wanted me to testify. This discussion went on for some time, with Ehrlichman even suggesting I simply whitewash the Ellsberg break-in. I said nothing until I finally pointed out the obvious: "Well, I still see in this conversation the things that we've thought of before, we've talked about before, but they do not ultimately solve what I see as the grave problem of a cancer growing around the presidency, and that cancer is going to continue to grow. This is just another thing that gives a problem. It does not clean the problem out."

Ehrlichman asked, "Doesn't it permit the president to clean it out at such time as it does come up, by saying, I relied on it. And now, this later thing turns up, and I don't condone that. And if I'd known about that before, obviously I wouldn't have done it. And I'm going to move on it now." The president turned to me, and asked, "Your point is, you really think you've got to clean the cancer out now, right?" I answered, "Yes, sir." He then asked, "And how would you do that?" clearly wanting an answer that did not result in a breakdown of executive privilege. "You have to do it to get the credit for it," I explained, "that gets you above it. As I see it, I see people getting hurt, and I hope we can find an answer to that problem." I was, in effect, telling the president to take action on the information he now possessed.

Ehrlichman again jumped in with an idea. "Alright, suppose we did this? Supposing you tender a report to the president on everything you know about this. And the president then fires some people, step one. Step two, send the report over to the Justice Department that says, 'I've been diligently at work on this. My counsel's been diligently at work. Here are his findings.'" While I said nothing, I thought Ehrlichman's idea had merit, for at least now we were discussing an honest Dean report, much as I had outlined to the president that morning. The president immediately recognized the problem with this approach, however, and asked, "Where would you stop it?" "Christ," Ehrlichman responded, "I don't know where it stops." Again, no agreement could be reached about where to stop, because once you did so, it became a further cover-up. At one point I facetiously suggested that the president could draw names from a hat to decide "who gets hurt and who doesn't," which would be about as fair a process as any. Once again, an honest report to the Justice Department by me was ultimately dismissed, because it would hurt too many people. Consideration was given, but rejected, to confiding in Henry Petersen. And when the conversation came back to me writing some sort of statement, I said, "The idea was a temporary answer," with which the president agreed but said he would settle for a temporary answer.

I raised the very real problem looming over our conversation: namely, that when Sirica sentenced the convicted Watergate defendants on Friday, it would likely change the dimensions of everything. Although I had no special knowledge other than what I had read in news accounts and gathered from conversations with the CRP lawyers, it did not take much foresight to imagine what was likely to occur in the coming days and weeks.* "I think [it] will

---

*Although I was unaware of it at the time, Ehrlichman had reached the same conclusion in his earlier conversation with the president.

prompt new problems," I said, and added, "I think he will charge that he cannot believe the trial was conducted by the government presenting a limited case, that he is not convinced the case represents the full situation." I noted that, if that happened, "It'll have a dramatic impact on the day of sentence with Sirica from the bench, because he'll charge that there are higher-ups involved in this. He may take some dramatic action, like appointing a special prosecutor. Who knows?" When Nixon asked if he could do that, I answered, "Sure, I think he could."* I explained that the prosecutors were going to take all the people who had been sentenced back before the grand jury and question them. "Sirica may, you know, give them provisional sentences. And say if they are helpful to the government back before the grand jury, he'll reconsider the sentences." And I suspected, as I said, that he would give them "horrendous sentences." (This, of course, was exactly what happened.) The meeting again ended with no answers.

Later that evening the president called Chuck Colson.[14] During the course of this conversation, when the president mentioned in passing that I had done a superb job of keeping all the fires out, Colson warned Nixon, "Yeah, well, Dean has a problem also, Mr. President. I didn't want to say this to you Monday night when you mentioned him to me. Dean has done a spectacular job. I don't think anybody could do as good a job as John has done," Colson began. "The thing that worries me is the possibility of somebody charging an obstruction of justice problem. In other words, the subsequent actions would worry me more than anything, and that's where John has, you know, he's done all the things that had to be done, but that makes him a little more of a participant than you would like. He's the fellow that has to coordinate it all." Colson noted that I had a double privilege, but still he was concerned. "The subsequent developments would be the only ones that would worry me. I don't worry about how Watergate came about." Notwithstanding the fact that I had already acknowledged to the president that I could go to jail, he dismissed Colson's concern. "Of course, that was what had to be done," he said. "Hell, yes," Colson agreed. He laughed lightly, as he said, "I know, I know. No second thoughts. That's not the point." Colson was also trying to warn him that someone new from outside should be brought in to handle the mess.

That evening the president dictated a long entry to his diary: "As far as

---

*While I made this comment to underscore the severity of the problems we faced, on reflection, I am sure that without statutory authority (which did not exist), no federal judge could appoint a federal prosecutor, which was purely an executive function.

the day was concerned it was relatively uneventful except for the talk with Dean, who really, in effect, let it all hang out when he said there was a cancerous growth around the president [that] is simply going to continue to grow and that we had probably to cut it out now rather than let it grow and destroy us later. He obviously is very depressed and doesn't really see anything, other course of action, but to move to let the facts out." Nixon concluded that "Hunt seems to be a real problem" and added, "I don't think that certainly Haldeman or Ehrlichman had any idea about bugging. I, of course, know Dean didn't. He, in fact, pointed out that when Liddy first presented this scheme, it was so wild Mitchell sat puffing on his pipe chuckling all the while. Then came the real cruncher. Apparently what happened is that Colson, with Liddy and Hunt in his office, called Magruder and told him in February to get off his ass and start doing something about setting up some kind of operation." He acknowledged, however, that Colson may not have known that what he was urging would result in an illegal operation.

Nixon added, "I learned for the first time that Ehrlichman apparently sent Hunt and his crew out to check into Ellsberg, to see something about his psychiatric problem with his doctor or something like that. That seemed to me to be a very curious junket for Ehrlichman to be involved in. Ehrlichman says that he was three or four steps away from it, but apparently Krogh has a problem here because Krogh did answer one question to the effect he did not know the Cubans which, of course, puts him in a straight position of perjury. This, of course, would be a terrible tragedy because Krogh was involved in national security work at the time that had nothing whatsoever to do with Watergate and the whole Ellsberg business." As for my concern about Haldeman's role with the $350,000 being sent back to the reelection committee and used to pay Hunt and others, which I described as an obstruction of justice, the president noted, "I don't think that this is the problem that Dean seems to think it is, but of course he has to warn against every loose end might come out, particularly in view of some of the things that have come up to this point. They're going to meet with Mitchell in the morning and I hope that Mitchell will really put his mind to this thing and perhaps part of it all can come some sort of course of action we can follow. It seems to me just to hunker down without making any kind of statement is really too dangerous," the president added, and then he fell silent for fifty-nine seconds, with his cassette recorder continuing to run, before he dictated, "I got to go over to the house, it's quite late." [15]

## March 22, 1973, the White House

The president arrived at the fourth-floor EOB auditorium at 8:44 A.M. to make an appearance at the foreign and domestic policy briefing for his sub-cabinet and all commissioned White House staff members. Haldeman, Ehrlichman and all the key staff were present, including me, but I departed with Haldeman after the president made some brief remarks. Haldeman said that Mitchell was on his way to Washington, and we would meet in his office when Mitchell arrived. Haldeman then accompanied the president to his first-floor EOB office for another Watergate-related conversation.[16] When the president asked who was advising Pat Gray, Haldeman said no one, since he refused to take advice, and reported, "I think that we've just got a loose gun that rolls back and forth on the deck there."

Nixon said that, following our meeting with Mitchell, he wanted to see all of us, as well as have a private talk with Mitchell. Haldeman advised, "It wouldn't hurt for you to express to Mitchell some concern that Kleindienst doesn't seem to be stepping up and running things here." When Nixon indicated that he was troubled by my telling him that I felt I had participated in obstruction of justice when I passed messages about taking care of the defendants, Haldeman replied, "We, John and I, worked on that with him. Perhaps he thinks I'm tied into that, too, because of this, in a sense, was my fund that he was taking." Haldeman seemed to be testing the president, for he was well aware that I thought he had a problem, which we had discussed as recently as the day before in front of the president. Haldeman explained in some detail how Mitchell and LaRue had needed money to pay the Watergate defendants and requested that I ask Haldeman for money from his $350,000 fund. He said it had been after the election, and rather than continue to take "X thousand" dollars each time, he sent all the money back to LaRue. He told the president that Strachan had handled the money, but "Strachan had no knowledge of what that was for. He was carrying out Dean's instructions, that Dean was carrying out instructions from me, and he got approval from me."

While Haldeman and Ehrlichman did not like my analysis, the president noted, "Dean is very good this way. He saw how the next question would be, quack, quack, quack, quack." But Haldeman thought my quacks overwrought and told the president I was "inordinately worried about" obstruction because I was involved. He said that I had suggested placing "wagons around the White House, [since] the White House literally doesn't have any problem prior to the Watergate break-in." When I made this statement to Haldeman I was not aware of Ehrlichman's personal approval of the Ellsberg break-in, so the only place the White House was culpable on a criminal basis, as I saw it, was "the potential charge of obstruction of justice after the fact, that we have no problem with the crime itself." But Haldeman protested, "Why is that obstruction of justice, anyway?" The president did not have an answer, but said, "Well, particularly when it's not to sip champagne."

Nixon began examining the "weak reeds in the situation," with Magruder topping everyone's list, but he noted that Ehrlichman's weak reed was Hunt, on the Ellsberg matter. Haldeman thought David Young was a weaker reed than Bud Krogh for Ehrlichman. Nixon raised the matter of Krogh's perjury: "Now how does he get out of that? Has anybody thought of that?" Haldeman answered, "Well, Ehrlichman's view of it—which kind of surprises me—is to be cold-blooded.* Yesterday he said, 'When Krogh gets finished with his lying.'" Ehrlichman apparently wasn't worried about what Krogh might say about him. They moved on to discuss potential obstructions of justice, and both the president and Haldeman rejected this as a salient concern. "I don't think Dean had anything to do with the obstruction," the president said emphatically. "He didn't deliver the money. That's the point. I think what really set him off was when Hunt's lawyer said Hunt needs a $120,000. Well, that was a shot across the bow," the president correctly perceived. Soon they turned to Magruder, who, I had told the president, had committed perjury, which certainly was not news. The president did not want Magruder appointed to anything in government, and Haldeman explained that that was why they had gone the route they had taken, to keep Magruder on an even keel. "He's not a Liddy type. He's exactly the opposite," Haldeman explained. The president wanted to know what would happen if they "decided to throw him to the wolves"—whom would Magruder hurt? The president worried that it might be Colson. Then they both remembered Strachan. But Haldeman was not concerned. "Gordon [Strachan] is a guy I wouldn't worry about, but Magruder is a guy I would, because Magruder is loaded with ego, personal pride [and] political ambition."

The president returned to Ehrlichman and the Ellsberg break-in. "How does John answer the Ellsberg thing?" the president asked. Haldeman re-

---

*Krogh had worked in Ehrlichman's Seattle law firm, and Ehrlichman had brought him to Washington as his associate counsel when he entered the White House in 1969. He was Krogh's mentor and long-time family friend.

ported, "He says, 'I didn't know anything about it.'" The president pressed
him on the matter, and Haldeman again emphasized Ehrlichman's lack of
knowledge of it, but when Nixon said he was "rather curious" to know what
this operation had been all about, Haldeman responded, "Well, you better
ask John, because I don't really know."[17] Haldeman did, however, explain
what he did know: Hunt and the Cubans had broken into Ellsberg's "psychiatrist's office to get a report on Ellsberg's mental analysis or something, and
they bungled the break-in. They didn't get what they were supposed to get, and
then they came back and said could they go back again, and that request got
to Ehrlichman, and he said, 'Absolutely not,' he said, and they didn't, apparently." The president asked what had been the purpose. "To discredit Ellsberg, make a spy out of him," Haldeman explained. With this information,
the president and Haldeman concocted a "national security" explanation to
deal with the fact that neither the CIA nor FBI had been employed, because
they couldn't be trusted not to leak. "I don't know whether that'll hold up,"
Haldeman admitted.

They discussed what would happen if my advice to not pay Hunt was
followed, and neither knew the answer nor liked the implications. The president also rejected my recommendation regarding a Dean statement, as he
clearly wanted something he could release publicly. "It's better to have something rather than nothing," he told Haldeman. Later in this lengthy conversation Haldeman reported, "Dean feels very strongly, and John Ehrlichman
seems to concur, that we do need the advice of somebody who knows more
about the criminal [law] than we do." The president said, "We can't go to
Henry Petersen," and Haldeman responded that there had been a discussion
of my going to Petersen on "a totally confidential, outside-of-school" basis.
But that was dismissed as unrealistic.

When the discussion turned to my cancer analogy, and to cutting it out,
the president said, "The question is whether we really can." Wondering if the
patient could survive, he admitted he did not know, but he was concerned
about the institution of the presidency. "I don't think it's as bad as John
[Dean] is concerned that it is," Haldeman offered. "On the other side of the
cancer analogy is that you go in and cut out all of what you think is cancerous and discover that it wasn't malignant." So Haldeman advised caution
lest the president cut off body parts that were critical. My suggestion that
people be fired raised the question of who, and Haldeman stated, "There's
nobody in the White House that's fireable."

Haldeman departed for his office and the meeting with Mitchell,

Ehrlichman and me. About all that resulted from what I thought would be a Mitchell-versus-Ehrlichman showdown was a coded report that Howard Hunt's demands had been taken care of by Mitchell.[18] Following that meeting and lunch (for which each went his own way), we gathered at the president's EOB office, shortly before two o'clock, to report that effectively nothing had transpired, nor been resolved. That meeting, with all the players holding their cards close to their chests and wearing their best poker faces, lasted almost two hours and included a remarkable private session between Mitchell and Nixon.[19]

I arrived at the meeting annoyed because I had just come from the press office, where I learned that Pat Gray, ever the loose cannon, had implicated me yet again, when Senator Byrd took him through a series of leading questions based on misinformation. Haldeman, aware of the problem, explained it to the president: "Gray is the symbol of wisdom. Today, he accused your counsel of being a liar." I observed, "He may be dead, because I may shoot him," which caused everyone to laugh. "How is that?" the president asked. Haldeman continued, "[Gray] said, 'Yes,' he thinks John Dean did lie to the FBI when he said he wasn't sure whether Howard Hunt had an office in the White House." As I explained, "When the agents asked me if they could see [Hunt's] office, the way it occurred was right after [Colson's FBI] interview. And I said I would have to check that out. And now it's been interpreted that I was lying to the FBI about the fact of whether he had an office or didn't have an office here." Haldeman noted, "It wasn't the question."* Haldeman also correctly noted that tomorrow's headline would undoubtedly be: "Gray Says Dean Lied."

After everyone but Mitchell had departed, he and Nixon had a private conversation in which they soon got to the heart of the matter. "Now let me make this clear," Nixon said. He was not going to proceed with his staff the way Eisenhower had with his chief of staff, Sherman Adams.† "I don't want it to happen with Watergate," the president said emphatically. Nixon felt

---

*When I later spoke with Pat Gray, he admitted he had "screwed up" and made a mistake, which he said he would correct when he made submissions for the record. He never bothered to do so. Nor did the matter ever arise again in connection with the Watergate investigations.

†Sherman Adams, a former governor of New Hampshire, was President Dwight Eisenhower's White House chief of staff. He ruled the White House with an iron hand and, other than Cabinet officers and National Security Counsel members, controlled who had access to Eisenhower. When it was discovered that Bernard Goldfine, a testile manufacturer under investigation by the Federal Trade Commission, had given Adams an expensive vicuna overcoat, he was soon forced to resign. In later years Nixon claimed Eisenhower had him remove Adams, but this is not supported by the record. Nonetheless, Nixon long believed that Eisenhower had been thoughtless in removing Adams, for no wrongdoing was ever established.

Eisenhower had made a mistake with Adams, who should not have been sacked. "And for that reason, I am perfectly willing to—" he started to say, but then decided to state it much more bluntly to his friend: "I don't give a shit what happens. I want you all to stonewall it, let them plead the Fifth Amendment, cover up or anything else, if it'll save it, save the plan. That's the whole point." But Nixon had to be realistic, too, so he gave the other side. "And I would particularly prefer to do it that other way, if it's going to come out that way anyway. And that's my view, that with the number of jackass people that they've got that they can call, they're going to—" The president rephrased his thought. "The story they'll get out, through leaks, charges, and so forth, innuendo, will be a hell of a lot worse than the story they're going to get out by just letting it out there."

"Well—" Mitchell began, but the president continued. "I don't know. But up to this point, the whole theory has been containment, as you know, John. And now we're shifting. As far as I'm concerned, actually, from a personal standpoint, if you weren't making a personal sacrifice, it's unfair." He referred again to Eisenhower's handling not only of Adams but of Nixon himself, when he was accused during their 1956 reelection campaign of having a secret slush fund from wealthy businessmen. Eisenhower was concerned that he was "clean," Nixon said, "but I don't look at it that way. That's the thing I am really concerned with: We're going to protect our people, if we can." While this was probably comforting to Mitchell, who was a realist and a staunch believer in the Nixon presidency, he also said, "Well, the important thing is to get you up above it for this first operation," referring to Watergate. "And then to see where the chips fall and get through this grand jury thing up here, then the committee is another question."

### March 23, 1973, Key Biscayne

As anticipated, I again made the *Post*'s headline: GRAY CONCEDES DEAN "PROBABLY" LIED TO FBI. Local and national television producers were now staking out key Watergate figures, so a sizable cluster of reporters had gathered outside my home in the early morning hours. With the president and Haldeman in Florida, and Ehrlichman departing for the West Coast at noon, I decided to work at home. Judge Sirica was sentencing the Watergate seven that morning, which meant I would be doing a great deal of telephoning, which could be handled from home.

I was not surprised to learn that morning that James McCord had sent a letter to Judge Sirica claiming: Political pressure had been applied to the Watergate defendants to plead guilty and remain silent (not true); perjury had occurred during the Watergate break-in trial (true, but not related to McCord); others involved in the Watergate operation had not been identified during the trial and should have testified (true, but again not related to McCord); and the Watergate operation was not a CIA operation, which McCord claimed the Cubans had been misled to believe was the case (no one had claimed it was a CIA operation, including the Cubans).[20] Judge Sirica accordingly delayed sentencing McCord but gave all the others the maximum: Liddy was given twenty years and a forty-thousand-dollar fine; the Cubans were each sentenced to forty years; and Hunt was given thirty-five years. Sirica told all the defendants except Liddy that their sentences were provisional, and he would review them in three months, based on their cooperation with the Senate's Watergate investigation and the grand jury. To this day Sirica's sentencing remains a hallmark of judicial extortion.[21]

Ehrlichman had already learned of Sirica's decision from the press office, and when Haldeman called, I told him I was stuck at home. The president called to ask my reaction to the events in Sirica's courtroom. He recalled that I had warned him someone would break, and he thought McCord was a hell of a lot better than Hunt. I agreed and explained that, while McCord could create a lot of bad publicity, he would have little foreseeable legal impact. We had long expected McCord to break and had determined he only knew what hearsay he had from Liddy. The president suggested I go up to Camp David, where I could escape the press and take a little vacation. I declined the offer, but then agreed and headed for the presidential retreat after the press surrounding the house departed. Had I known Haldeman would call after I arrived to instruct me to write a Dean report, I would have gone to my office to work. But as it turned out, both the brief vacation away from the chaos and McCord's letter proved to a blessing, although not for the president.

# PART IV

# THE NIXON DEFENSE

*March 23 to July 16, 1973*

Richard Nixon viewed himself as something of an expert on political crises.[1] While he had missed the early signs relating to Watergate, Nixon found that McCord's letter forced him to face the reality that the matter had become a fast-developing potential presidential catastrophe. "The easiest period in a crisis situation is actually the battle itself," Nixon had written in his vice-presidential memoir, *Six Crises*, adding, "The most difficult is the period of indecision—whether to fight or run away."[2]

At the time I myself was uncertain how the president would resolve his dilemma. I had tried, during our conversation on March 21, to alert him to the serious dangers he faced, hoping that by informing him of my own criminal liability it would be a catalyst for action. McCord's letter, however, forced him to act sooner than he might have wished, because it thrust Judge John Sirica into the resolution of Watergate along with the Senate Watergate committee and the U.S. Attorney's Office, which had resumed its grand jury investigation.

These events dramatically increased the president's attention to Watergate, and as a result, the final part of this account includes more than twice as many recorded conversations than all the earlier discussions combined. (The material in this section is based on more than six hundred conversations while there were only some three hundred Watergate-related conversations prior to this date.) Not only were there more conversations, but many were substantially longer than the earlier ones, which has required greater condensation (hopefully without loss of substance). Nixon's face-to-face meetings after March 21 reveal—near exhaustingly—his propensity for engaging in highly repetitive conversations, day after day. Almost three hundred of the tapes were recordings of telephone calls, which were typically brief, and most contained little new or critical information.

Notwithstanding the fact that the president had available his electronic recordings of his Watergate-related conversations, a detailed schedule of his activities prepared by his staff, his personally dictated diary entries relating to many of these matters, as well as the notes of his meetings made by Haldeman and Ehrlichman, this remarkably comprehensive factual record was almost totally ignored by Nixon as he constructed his final defense. With the exception of having Haldeman listen to his March 21 conversation with me and returning to report its gist to him, and Nixon himself listening to a few of his other conversations with me, the president relied on self-serving and deeply flawed memories of events up to and including March 21, and then twisted our March 21 conversation to fit his needs. Nixon did not want anyone other than Haldeman to know about the secret recordings, so he prepared his final defense and implemented it by simply ignoring the actual facts he could easily have checked. This proved a fatal mistake.

Nixon later explained he "tried to grapple with the facts only to find that they were not like the pieces of a puzzle that could be assembled into one true picture. They were more like the parts of a kaleidoscope: at one moment, arranged one way, they seemed to form a perfect design, complete in every detail. But the simple shift of one conjecture could unlock them all and they would move into a completely different pattern."[3] While there is some truth to this metaphor—when you twisted the facts, the picture did change—the fact remains that he should not have twisted the facts, nor engaged in "conjecture," rather pressed for the truth, which he never did. In fact Nixon knew if the twisting stopped, his top aides would become involved in an obstruction of justice. More troubling is the fact that he knew that *he* had been, as well, although he was unwilling to acknowledge it, other than hypothetically. Accordingly, his conversations during late March and throughout all of April reveal that not only did he know he needed to remove Haldeman, Ehrlichman, and me, but he had to do so in a way that he was least likely to incriminate himself and his presidency, not to mention minimizing any blowback from our leaving. Nixon would accordingly create a new conspiracy—in effect a cover-up of the cover-up—which began in late March 1973 and became fully formed in May and June of 1973, operating until his presidency ended on August 9, 1974.

# Options and Indecision

*March 23–27, 1973, Key Biscayne*

When Haldeman arrived at the president's compound on Friday afternoon, March 23, he found Nixon fully immersed in Watergate, and they spent most of the next five hours going over it,[1] the first of many such protracted sessions. There were similar conversations on Saturday, Sunday and Monday, March 24 to 26, with Haldeman calling Colson, Mitchell and me to flush out the details. Nixon also turned to former attorney general Bill Rogers for advice. What emerges from this Key Biscayne Watergate marathon was a new Nixon concern about his own involvement. He had Haldeman press Colson for exactly what Colson had said to Bill Bittman about clemency for Hunt, and Colson assured him that he had not mentioned discussing the matter with Nixon. He conceded, however, "that what Bittman inferred from his comments might be different from what was actually said."[2] Nixon suggested that if anyone on the White House staff was charged with criminal conduct he take a leave of absence, and was surprised when Haldeman noted, "Well, that's exactly, of course, what they want. To drive someone in the top command out of office and indicate that the whole White House is shot through with corruption." Nixon agreed, adding, "We have to find a way to cut this thing off at the pass before it reaches that point, because there's no question in my mind that neither Haldeman or Ehrlichman are guilty."[3] As for Colson, the president was not certain. It had to have become clear to Nixon after this weekend that his problem was not what had occurred before June 17, 1972, but rather, afterward.[4]

On Sunday, March 25, the *Los Angeles Times* notified the White House press office that it was planning to run a story that James McCord was claiming Magruder and I had both had advance knowledge of the Watergate break-in. Liddy had told McCord that I had attended a meeting in Mitchell's office where he presented his plans, but McCord was not aware that I had tried to kill them. I denied the charge, as did the press office, and I hired a lawyer—a Georgetown Law classmate, Tom Hogan, who in time would become chief judge of the U.S. District Court for the District of Columbia—who placed the *Los Angeles Times* on notice.[5] The bogus story died, however, when the president sent Ziegler out to assert that I had no advance knowledge of the Watergate bugging and to express "absolute and total confidence" in me.[6]

## March 27, 1973, the White House

"Well, what is the situation today as to what Ziegler's going to say?" Nixon asked when Haldeman arrived in the Oval Office.[7] "We've had some new developments, and it keeps bouncing," Haldeman replied; he reported that I was still at Camp David working on my "paper," but I had learned that "Liddy spent yesterday at the grand jury. He took the Fifth Amendment all day." Haldeman said Sirica was going to immunize Liddy to force him to talk, but Haldeman had been told "Liddy will still stonewall it and take contempt." There was troubling news, too: "Bittman has now informed [the CRP lawyers] that Hunt is ready to fold and is now going to pull the plug. Curiously enough, Bittman is now very disturbed about that, because he's the guy that gave Hunt the money," Haldeman said, chuckling. "So he's now an accessory." The Hunt threat was still being "evaluated," but even more problematic was the fact that "Magruder has sort of crumbled at the seams." Because McCord had claimed I was aware of the Watergate break-in, I would be called to the grand jury, and my testimony would not jibe with Magruder's. As a result, Magruder had told the CRP lawyers, aware they would tell others, that he had a new version of "what really happened on the Watergate." He was claiming that the plan had been cooked up at the White House, that it was triggered when Gordon Strachan told him, "Haldeman has said that you cannot delay getting this operation started any longer. The president had ordered you to go ahead immediately, and you are not to stall anymore. You're to get it done." Haldeman reminded Nixon that Magruder was a good liar: "He's a hell of a convincing guy, as evidenced by how he got off on the Sirica trial."

"Well, Bob, let's look at the actual facts there. Could that have happened?" the president asked. "No," Haldeman assured him flatly. "Never?" the president quizzed. "I don't believe so," Haldeman responded. He said that Magruder wanted to meet with him and Mitchell and that I thought it a good idea, "to keep him on balance, but not rush right into having it." Haldeman mentioned my concern about when "one guy blows and everybody starts to. Hunt's going to lob all his stuff out. Magruder's going to change his story and try to sell them on some other line, and we don't know what—" When the president interrupted Haldeman to say he was surprised that Magruder was throwing it to the White House rather than to Mitchell, Haldeman explained that if he claimed Mitchell was involved, he could be incriminating himself and admitting to perjury. "How would he get out of that?" the president asked. Haldeman had no answer other than to suggest the possibility of Magruder's being given immunity by Sirica to nail "the big boys." Haldeman thought Sirica just might do it.

Haldeman said he had not spoken with Mitchell about Magruder but felt he should come to Washington, and that they ought to meet with Magruder to "find out what the guy really is up to." The president agreed. Haldeman added, "I mean, Magruder talked to Dean earlier yesterday, before [he talked to] the lawyers. At that time he was taking a totally different line, which convinces Dean that Magruder is a little psycho, or something. I mean, he's playing a strange game, at least, because he said to Dean, 'Geez, John, it's a shame that that son of a bitch McCord has hauled you into this, because you and I both know you had absolutely nothing to do with it.'"[8] Magruder then turned around and not only pulled Haldeman into the Watergate break-in and bugging, but Strachan and the president as well. An alarmed Nixon asked, "Well, Jesus Christ. So suppose that charge is locked in there, then what does that mean? What would you say? What do we say about all that? Totally untrue?" Haldeman agreed, and added, "But this is the thing Dean has warned about, you know? He said, 'You just got to face the fact that untrue charges are going to [be made]. And you may be able to defend yourself, but in the public eye, you may not.'"

Haldeman then raised the issue of the president's taking the initiative in dealing with Watergate, explaining, "Ehrlichman raised the point: if you do this, then at the same time you should take some specific steps yourself. You should suspend John Dean, because he's been named. Simply say that obviously he is, with no implication of guilt—" Nixon interrupted, "I'd ask him to take a leave of absence?" Haldeman affirmed that, and reported that Ehrlichman also suggested suspending Pat Gray, whom over the weekend the president had decided to cut loose, and have Ehrlichman tell Gray to request his nomination be withdrawn. But the president did not like this thinking.

"I'm not going to suspend anybody," he injected, but acknowledged the problem. As the conversation came to a close, Haldeman also reported that "Rogers will argue you also ought to get rid of Kleindienst in that process." This surprised the president.

Nixon spent over two hours that morning and into the afternoon in the EOB office with Haldeman and Ehrlichman discussing Watergate, with Ron Ziegler briefly taking part.[9] Ehrlichman said Watergate had become both debilitating and time consuming, not to mention difficult, because it involved "people we know." The president noted that "whatever they did [was] with the best of intentions," which he felt was "the sad thing about" Watergate. He added, "I don't want people on the staff to divide up and say, 'Well, it's this guy that did it, or this guy that didn't.' The point is, what's done is done." Ehrlichman agreed but counseled that it was time to cut losses.

Ziegler arrived seeking guidance for dealing with the question of White House staff going to the grand jury. The decision was made that he should continue to say the White House was prepared to cooperate but nothing more.

Haldeman now reported information I had given him from Paul O'Brien, who was "very distressed with Mitchell," because he felt Mitchell "could cut this whole thing off if he would just step forward." Haldeman explained, "As far as O'Brien can determine, Mitchell did sign off on this thing, and Dean believes that to be the case also," although neither thought they could prove it. O'Brien was concerned because others were getting "whacked around" to protect Mitchell. Haldeman repeated for Ehrlichman's benefit Magruder's latest, that Liddy's "superintelligence operation was put together by the White House, by Haldeman, Dean and others." Being finally candid, Haldeman admitted, "Now, there's some semblance of validity to the point, that I did talk, not with Dean but with Mitchell, about the need for intelligence activity and—" Nixon added, "—and that Dean recommended Liddy?" Haldeman answered, "Yeah, but not for intelligence. Dean recommended Liddy as the general counsel." Then reading from his notes of his conversation with me, Haldeman reported in detail Magruder's latest claim that the president had been aware of it all, and then continued: "I didn't realize it, but [bugging] was also in the Sandwedge [the operation proposed by Jack Caulfield] going way back, the early plan. That, incidentally, is a potential source of fascinating problems in that it involved Mike Acree, who's now the customs commissioner, and [Rose Woods's brother] Joe Woods, and a few other people." Nixon injected, "Nothing happened," as he knew from our March 21 conversation.

Haldeman agreed, and continuing to read from his notes, reported that I had explained when screening Liddy to be general counsel that political intelligence would merely be incidental, although the campaign did need information on demonstrations (because the White House could not share the classified information we received). Then Haldeman told the president for the first time what had occurred at and after the second meeting in Mitchell's office. "Dean came into the [second] meeting late, [and] he could see that they were still on the same kind of thing. And he said, in effect, I got Mitchell off the hook because I took the initiative in saying, 'You know, it's an impossible proposal and we can't, we shouldn't even be discussing this in the attorney general's office.' Mitchell agreed, and Dean came [back] and told me that he had seen this wrap-up on it, that they shouldn't be doing it, that we shouldn't be involved in it in any way, you know, drop the whole thing. And then Dean said, 'I saw a problem there, and I thought they had turned it off, and in any event, I wanted to stay ten miles away from it, and did.'"

Ehrlichman wanted to know how Liddy got the money, "since only Mitchell or Stans" could authorize the amounts Liddy had been given. Haldeman felt Mitchell had in fact signed off on it. As they proceeded Nixon asked if the lawyers O'Brien and Parkinson were involved, and Haldeman said only after June 17, 1972: "Dean has asked through O'Brien to see Maroulis, Liddy's lawyer, for Liddy to provide a private statement saying that Dean knew nothing in advance on the Watergate, which Liddy knows to be the case. Dean would like to have that statement in his pocket and has asked Liddy's lawyer to ask Liddy for such a statement, which he feels Liddy would want to give him."* Haldeman said he had put the question to me of whether I had any knowledge of Liddy's operation, and I had answered, "Absolutely nothing." Nixon noted, "I would totally agree with that. I would believe Dean there, [because we asked him when there was no reason to lie] to us about that. But I would believe for another reason: That he thought it was a stupid God damned idea." Ehrlichman added, "There just isn't a scintilla of hint that Dean knew about this," explaining "Dean was pretty good all through that period of time in sharing things, and he was tracking with a number of us on it."

---

*Liddy's attorney advised him not to give such a statement, because it could waive his Fifth Amendment rights. But O'Brien, who prepared a memo of my conversation with Maroulis that I later provided to the Senate Watergate committee, said after talking to Liddy's lawyer that he also said "Liddy did wish to convey that his reasons for not providing such a statement was not because he disagreed with the facts but because of the advice of counsel." Dean testimony, 3 Senate Select Committee on Presidential Campaign Activities (SSC) 1005.

The president did not think Colson knew in advance, because he was dealing with Colson extensively at the time, and "I think he would have said, 'Look, we've gotten some information,' but never a word." Nor did Nixon have any indication that Haldeman or Ehrlichman had known. Nixon turned to the Ellsberg break-in and said, "I didn't even know, frankly, that the, ah, the Ellsberg thing." He then added to Ehrlichman, "And I guess there you deliberately didn't tell me?" Ehrlichman responded, "Well, sir, I didn't know," and claimed he had not learned about it until after it had taken place. "And I told you afterwards we stopped it from happening again in that setting, but, ah—" When the president asked if it was national security, Ehrlichman confirmed, "That was in the national security."*

They next went through an interrogationlike drill with hypothetical questions about lines of defense, awareness of wiretapping, Hunt's involvement with the Pentagon Papers—with Ehrlichman again denying knowledge of the Ellsberg break-in but adding a new detail from after he turned down the Liddy and Hunt proposal for another entry attempt in California: "Interestingly enough, Colson called me several times and remonstrated with me and tried to persuade me that they should go back in, and I said no." He also reported, "Young and Krogh operated that whole operation. From the beginning, as a matter of fact, with the other leaks, and Krogh is very frank in saying, 'I authorized this operation in Los Angeles, no two ways about it.' He says, 'If I am asked,' he says, 'that's what I'll say, and I'll resign and leave the Department of Transportation and get out of town.' He said, 'I thought at the time we were doing the right thing and so forth.' I don't think he'll have to. Number one, I don't think Hunt will strike, but if he did," Ehrlichman recommended, "I would put the national security tent over this whole operation." Nixon agreed.

Haldeman returned to Magruder and summed up the problem: McCord had flatly accused him of perjury, and accused me of complicity. "Magruder knows as a fact that Dean wasn't involved, so he knows that Dean is clean, he knows when Dean goes down and can testify as an honest man. Dean will

---

*Based on written documents and the testimony of Bud Krogh and David Young, Ehrlichman was convicted of approving Hunt and Liddy's "covert operation" at Ellsberg's psychiatrist office "[i]f done under your assurance that it is not traceable," which Ehrlichman added when approving the operation. Colson, who raised the money for this California operation, was also indicted, as a coconspirator. During pretrial motions U.S. District Court Judge Gerhard Gesell ruled that President Nixon lacked the authority to authorize such an undertaking for national security reasons, not to mention that he had, in fact, never delegated such authority to Ehrlichman, nor could he. See *U.S. v. Ehrlichman*, 376 F. Supp. 29 (1974).

not finger Magruder but Dean can't defend Magruder. Magruder says, 'Okay, Dean goes down to the grand jury and clears himself, there's no evidence against him except McCord's statement, which won't hold up, because it isn't true. Now, I go down to the grand jury, because obviously they're going to call me back, and I go to defend myself against McCord's statement, which I know is true. Now, I've a little tougher problem than Dean has, and you're saying to me, don't make up a new lie to cover up the old lie. What would you recommend that I do? Stay with the old lie and hope I would come out or clean myself up and go to jail?'" "What would you advise him to do?" Nixon asked. Haldeman replied, "I'd advise him to go down and clean it up. Say, 'I lied'" and try to get immunity. "If he can *get* immunity," Ehrlichman added about such a dubious prospect.

Haldeman noted, "Going to jail for Jeb will be very, very, very difficult." The conversation continued to circle the issues, and it was decided only that Haldeman should meet with Mitchell and Magruder. Haldeman called Mitchell from the president's telephone, which was recorded.[10] Magruder was with Mitchell in New York City, and they agreed to meet the next afternoon. Mitchell raised one issue: Bart Porter, whom Magruder had recruited to corroborate his false testimony, was supposed to get a job at the Department of Housing and Urban Development, which was being held up. Mitchell asked Haldeman to see what he could do, and Haldeman reassured him, "Okay, I'll take care of it."

Later that afternoon Nixon met with Bill Rogers in his EOB office to discuss Watergate.[11] Haldeman had briefed Rogers, and Nixon asked for his judgment. "Well, Mr. President, I think you and I are probably in the same position. I think neither of us really know a lot about it." "Well, we know the facts," Nixon reminded him, and he assured Rogers he had "personally questioned" Haldeman, Ehrlichman and me. The president said he was looking at his options, "but none of them good." Rogers saw few concerns for the White House regarding the break-in itself but recognized that the real issue was "the aftermath": "They took some real chances, probably unknowingly, chances which could be construed as obstruction of justice." Nixon agreed that that was the problem. Rogers was not sure what he would recommend, for "no course will be attractive." He did not like the idea of a commission or panel, or of the president's talking with Judge Sirica about a special prosecutor.

The president conceded that I had never actually conducted an investigation for him, or questioned people on the White House staff, but rather that I had sought out and discovered information informally. And as for the congressional investigation: "A committee of Congress is a double weapon. It destroys a man's reputation in public. And if it turns its files over to the Department of Justice for prosecution, they will prosecute the poor bastards. We did it to two people. I did it to Hiss. We did it to the Five Percenters." Nixon wanted to argue that the proper place for a criminal action was in the judicial system and the grand jury, unlike he had done with Alger Hiss and his congressional investigation of Hiss's perjury, with which Rogers agreed.

When Rogers departed, the president asked Haldeman to return.[12] Haldeman said he had spoken with me at Camp David, and I had reported my conversation with Mitchell, who had told me to "stiffen up"; he warned that if my testimony contradicted his false statements before the grand jury, or elsewhere, no one would believe me: It would be my word against Mitchell's and Magruder's. While it was not a threatening warning, I had said to Haldeman, Mitchell was in effect telling me to lie, which he reported to the president, who had no comment.

Haldeman had not yet spoken to Colson, so the president instructed Haldeman to call him immediately.

Haldeman shared some of the suggestions that had been made to the president to take action on Watergate.[13] Colson felt they were all an overreaction to McCord's letter and his hearsay. He did not like the idea of a commission to investigate Watergate "under any circumstances, and God, I would not appoint a special prosecutor. I'd never make that offer to Sirica, because he'd take you up on that immediately." Colson did not want to discuss on the telephone his adamant opposition to a special prosecutor, and Haldeman suggested he come to Haldeman's office immediately.

Haldeman met with Colson from 5:15 to 5:45 P.M. and then returned to Nixon's EOB office.[14] Paraphrasing Colson from his notes, Haldeman reported, "The problem is that there is a very clear case for conspiracy to commit perjury, and a very clear case for conspiracy to obstruct justice. Both those cases can be made, and they can be sustained, and if you put in a special prosecutor, or go to a Warren Commission, you would ensure indictment and almost certainly ensure convictions on those counts for a number of people." Colson also expressed concern about "a runaway grand jury," adding that "the best thing we've done up until now was the superb handling of the grand jury." Haldeman continued: "And he says the problem on the obstruction thing is that everyone in the White House, maybe not everyone, but a hell of a lot of people are participants in one way or another. And here's what he said: except himself." Colson's recommendation was that the president obtain an experienced criminal trial attorney. He believed the president should give the impression of cooperation but remain firm and not give up anything."

After going over Colson's key points with Haldeman, even Nixon recognized his conversations were going nowhere, and in a weary let's-be-honest moment, he observed, "Well, I have [done a] full circle today," all of his ideas having now been shot down. Nixon wanted a better understanding of who had criminal exposure in the cover-up. He realized it touched Colson, and told Haldeman, "It might touch you. It might touch Ehrlichman, correct?" Haldeman said nothing. "And it might touch Dean." Haldeman observed that if it touched me, it would then go to others. "Strachan?" the president wondered. "Well, yeah, I guess so," Haldeman agreed. "Who else?" the president asked, "Outside of the White House, do you think it hits Mitchell?" Haldeman did, and added, "And LaRue, and Mardian, and Parkinson, and O'Brien."

"Those, too?" the president asked with surprise, and then added, "I just know Dean is going to have to end up taking the rap. He won't do it, will he?" Haldeman responded, "Well, he's part of [the thing]." When the president speculated about others, Haldeman said: "I'm not sure the rest of us are involved. I sure as hell don't think I am on the basis of the money." Nixon asked about Colson's involvement with the money for the Watergate defendants. "Colson, I don't know whether he was," Haldeman said, and added, "Ehrlichman is, in the sense of getting involved in the operations thing." Like Haldeman, the president was thinking of his personal exposure and admitted, "Yeah, but I had Colson, who turned over a promise of the clemency thing. Well, what do you think that does? He's concerned about the clemency thing. That is the point here. Or is he [hung]?" When Haldeman agreed it was the clemency matter that concerned Colson, the president continued, "And the perjury, the perjury involving—" Haldeman interrupted, "That all hangs on Magruder." "Magruder is the only person that has committed perjury," Nixon confirmed, but before Haldeman could fully answer, Nixon began opining once again that the cover-up was worse than the crime, and he wondered whether to let it all hang out, as Ehrlichman had once suggested, or whether in the end we would get hung anyway. Haldeman responded that Colson did not think they should let it all hang out but rather assume the worst, live with it, and not get bogged down worrying about it.

The president brought the conversation back to Colson and said, "With Colson, I've got to let you know that I never promised anybody, that nobody promised them clemency."*

When the president broached the subject of the calls in Congress to "get rid of Haldeman and Ehrlichman," Haldeman quickly added, "and Dean," noting that Nixon had already gotten rid of Colson. Nixon asked Haldeman for his "feeling on that," and Haldeman urged caution, explaining, "The danger of throwing any baby to the wolves is, you always just make the wolves more hungry and prove to them that you've got some more babies."

As this conversation wound down, they returned to Colson's recommendation that they get a criminal lawyer on staff or assigned as a special counsel to the White House. It was a recommendation I had first made to Ehrlichman on June 19, 1972, which no one had ever raised with the president. But Nixon did not want a special criminal counsel: "I've already spent an enormous amount of time on it, worrying about the son of a bitch, and I won't be able to do anything about it. What I need to do is to rely on other people to go talk to the special counsel, you know?"

### March 28, 1973, the White House

When summoned to Nixon's EOB office at 8:45 A.M., Haldeman had already been meeting with John Mitchell for a half hour; thus, their conversation was very brief.[15] "I don't want to be in the position to ask [Mitchell] what the hell happened," Nixon said and, apparently still thinking about Haldeman's conversation with Colson, wanted Haldeman to raise the obstruction of justice and perjury matters with Mitchell. Haldeman asked Nixon if he had read the Jules Witcover story that morning in *The Washington Post* "on the front page. He surveyed everybody he could find, across the country, in the way of the Republican state chairmen and Senate campaign committee leaders and the ticket sellers for the dinners and all that, and all those people say, absolutely no problem. Nobody has any interest in Watergate. He talked to the pollsters, like Oliver Quayle, who says nobody gives a damn about the Watergate. And [pollster] Sindlinger says, during the election it was only about 10 percent, the highest it ever got. Now Watergate's 2 or 3 percent. He said, we just can't find anybody who's interested."

---

*Literally, this was probably true, for Nixon had not given Colson a commitment, although he had certainly all but done so. Nor had Colson told Bittman that he had been made such a promise, although Bittman and Hunt were given the impression Colson could deliver clemency around Christmas.

Nixon said his only concern was any appearance that the White House was not cooperating. As far as public relations were concerned, "John Ehrlichman's reactions are not good," so he wanted Haldeman to take the lead regarding Watergate. "I'm not looking for something that is sort of a big play in order to settle this thing. That isn't going to settle it. They're going to be crapping on and on for a long time. But I'm looking for something that this time, and once and for all, the president can get out and have press conferences and say, we are cooperating." As this conversation proceeded, he said, "We've got to get out some sort of Dean report. I just think we have to, don't you think so?"

"Well, I don't know," Haldeman replied. "I am not sure we do. I used to think we did." Haldeman felt that I had been tainted by Gray's and McCord's false charges, and the president had already said he had the Dean report.

With that Haldeman returned to his meeting with Mitchell; they were later joined by Magruder. When they broke for lunch, Haldeman called me at Camp David requesting that I return, as Mitchell and Magruder wanted to meet with me. I told Haldeman that I did not wish to have such a meeting, but he insisted. As I later testified, this was a clear sign to me that Haldeman was not going to come forward and help end this problem but rather was beginning to protect himself. For this reason I decided to stop my efforts to write a report that would cause no one any serious problem.[16]

Four decades later, when I listened to Haldeman's report to the president of his meetings that day with Mitchell, Magruder and me, I learned that my sixth sense had been correct, but Haldeman had been more subtle. Mitchell and Magruder, in an effort to get me to lie to support their false testimony, claimed I had invented that testimony and had agreed to support it, if necessary. Although they apparently convinced Haldeman of this account (as evidenced by his later report to Nixon), they later dropped the story when I refused to support their perjury, which I had not even been aware of.

As I was en route from Camp David, Haldeman returned to the president's EOB Office where, as he seated himself, said, "It gets so dull," referring to Watergate. "Round and round on the same old thing." But he did have some new information: Mitchell had pressed Magruder, before their meeting, to tell him what, in fact, had occurred. Reconstructing from his notes, Haldeman summarized the report: Magruder had said, "The whole intelligence plan was hatched here at the White House by Hunt, Liddy and Colson. And Colson called Jeb twice to tell him to get going on this thing, and he specifically referred to the Larry O'Brien information, was hard on that. And

Jeb says Hunt and Liddy were in Colson's office, and LaRue was in Jeb's office on that phone call."

When the president asked about Larry O'Brien, Haldeman responded, "Well, that is what they're bugging the Watergate for." The president wanted to know why O'Brien, and Haldeman said, "Information regarding the Florida convention stuff, down there."* Nixon interrupted with a question: "Well, that would be Colson. Right?"

"Liddy," Haldeman answered, then added, "Colson or Liddy. Liddy was in Colson's office when that took place," confirming earlier reports to the president. Magruder had also told Mitchell that "Gordon Strachan probably had a lot of direct dealings with Liddy." Haldeman confirmed, "We know that he had some," but he did not elaborate, and continued, "[Magruder] says a copy of the output of the Watergate project, what happened there, is, this guy Baldwin made notes of what was gathered, the facts, and he wrote those up, gave them to McCord. [Then] McCord gave them to Liddy. And Liddy made two copies. One copy was delivered to Magruder. And one copy was delivered to the White House."

"By Liddy?" the president asked. Haldeman again confirmed, and then clarified, "This is what Magruder said, that Liddy [did it]; he doesn't think that McCord knows this. Because McCord doesn't know what happened after Liddy. But [Mitchell] said Jeb got a copy, and the White House got a copy. And [Magruder] doesn't know where the White House copy went, whether it went to Strachan or Colson. He felt sure it went to Strachan, and maybe, or probably, it went to Colson. And Gordon Strachan told [Magruder] that I had approved the plan. [Magruder] told Mitchell that the president had approved it." With disgust in his voice, Nixon said, "Well, he's a liar." During this conversation Mitchell gave ambiguous information regarding his own role in approving Liddy's operation, although in their subsequent conversation later that day, he would soon clarify it.

Haldeman continued his Mitchell report: "[Magruder] says that there were four people in the White House who had full knowledge of the Watergate operation: Colson; Dick Howard, who worked for Colson; Gordon Strachan; and Haldeman. How does he think that those four people had knowledge of that? He said Colson had knowledge because of the phone call."

"And Howard?" the president asked. Haldeman answered, "Howard had knowledge because of conversations he had with [Magruder]." Nixon asked,

*See Appendix A.

"Okay. And what about Strachan?" Haldeman replied, "Gordon Strachan, he knows that he had knowledge because he got copies of the reports Liddy had." Nixon then inquired, "And you?" Haldeman answered, "And Haldeman, because Gordon Strachan told [Magruder] that I approved the plan. Now, Gordon Strachan says flatly and absolutely that he did not tell Magruder that, that I did approve the plan." "And you didn't approve the plan at the Watergate?" Nixon asked, to which Haldeman assured him, "No, sir. I did not."

Magruder was going to stay with his false story, Haldeman continued, because he had to, yet he was worried that White House witnesses—namely, Colson, Strachan and me—would impeach him. Magruder implored Haldeman or Mitchell to speak to me to get me onboard. Magruder was worried about his family should all this fall apart, and Haldeman explained that Magruder was "very afraid of jail, but not physically afraid of it." He was fearful for "a very interesting reason. He's a good-looking guy. He's afraid no one will talk to him."

Haldeman continued, "[Hunt] knows that Colson was involved in Watergate. Colson told them to get going and get him the stuff on O'Brien," although Colson "still claims he didn't know about the Watergate." And he added, "Now, that's a big technicality, but what he was imparting was the objective, not the means."

Haldeman departed and returned to speak with the president later that afternoon, following his session with Mitchell, Magruder and me. It was a brief conversation, as the president was working on a television speech he would deliver on March 29 on Vietnam and economic issues.[17] "They had their session," Haldeman reported. "Dean recognizes the problem," but he added that I had refused to lie for Mitchell and Magruder. Haldeman said he suggested to me that "the best solution appears to be a very strict calculation of privilege." I would "only answer questions regarding [my] own participation in specific Watergate-related activities," meaning the planning and break-in but not the aftermath, and not testify about Mitchell or Magruder. After Nixon protested the unfairness of the entire situation, and they rehashed their earlier conversations, Haldeman departed for Capitol Hill, where he was the featured guest at the Wednesday Club, an organization of Republican members of the House of Representatives.

That evening the president called Haldeman at home to find out how his session on the Hill had gone.[18] "You had a hell of a hard day," Nixon said, and reported that daughters Tricia and Julie had come home, because "you know, they're low." Watergate was getting to his family, so he told Haldeman what he shared with his daughters: "Well, this has been a hard day, but what the hell, we've had harder ones. Let's face it, that December bombing [in Vietnam], what could have been harder than that, you know, really?" Later that night the president returned to his EOB office to work and called Haldeman for an update.[19] Haldeman reported that Hunt had spent four hours with the grand jury, and "according to the report, he created no problems with anything he said." He continued, "Dean says he can't do what Mitchell and Magruder want him to. So he's trying to figure that one out." Haldeman also mentioned to the president that I had hired a criminal lawyer, which Haldeman thought a good idea. Nixon said, "Well, yeah, I suppose so," and then added, "Well, then, I guess the problem we've got there, Bob, is really, too, with Dean now, isn't it?" Haldeman answered, "That's one of them." Nixon asked if I wanted to go "all the way, in other words, on all. I mean on the stuff afterwards and so forth and so on, which does involve the White House staff." Haldeman said I was "trying to untangle that."

When Haldeman added that I was trying to figure out how much trouble I might actually be in, Nixon responded that he hoped I was alright. He thought the Hunt problem was under control and McCord had only "a lot of hearsay." As far as the differences with my potential testimony versus that of Mitchell and Magruder, Nixon thought the latter two each had to say they had made a mistake. Haldeman suggested just saying that there was a disagreement. "Do you think it'll come out in any event?" the president asked. When Haldeman replied that it inevitably would, the president questioned how Mitchell and Magruder would handle it. Haldeman said he had talked to Mitchell after his meeting with me, and "[Mitchell] seemed to think [Dean] understood what his problem was, too, and that Dean could work something out." Haldeman said he had asked me, and I said that I did not know how it could be resolved, but I was going to work on it. Nixon assured Haldeman, "We'll stand by him all the way on that, just say that's privileged and he can deny any knowledge himself. But, in effect, Mitchell and Magruder, they want Dean's recollection to be the same as theirs?" Haldeman said they did. "That's a problem. Oh, well, he can't do that," Nixon replied.

When Nixon repeated that he would stand behind my claiming privilege, Haldeman pointed out that if I took the Fifth Amendment and refused to testify, Nixon would have to fire me. "Maybe that has to be done," Nixon said, and asked, "Then the question is about the others, huh?" When Haldeman had second thoughts about undercutting me, Nixon said, "Oh, Christ,

I wouldn't think of undercutting him. Never. He's been a hero thus far, you know? Really. He's been sturdy, like a giant. No, no, no, no, no. I mean, I'm just thinking out loud, if rather than take the Fifth, he says, I'm not guilty of anything, but I'm not going to get into that, because it's such a fuzzy area, you know, the lawyer-client and so forth and so on, but I'm just not going to talk about it. It won't look bad. But you'll keep in touch with him with that situation tomorrow, will you?" Haldeman said he would. "Be sure that he knows that he's backed to the hilt, doesn't he?"

"Oh, yeah. He's in good shape," Haldeman reassured him. In fact, Haldeman was sending me opposite signals, which I had seen happen before in the Nixon White House, when others were about to be sacrificed. At my meeting with Magruder and Mitchell I had posed a question to Mitchell that I had never before directly asked him: Had he, in fact, approved Liddy's plans? Mitchell admitted that, much to his chagrin, he had. I reported this exchange to Haldeman and later testified about it.[20] Years later I discovered Haldeman's diary entry for March 28: "Mitchell and Magruder both told [Dean] that they had both signed off on the [Liddy] project, which Mitchell told me, also. Dean feels it's imperative that we get a criminal lawyer and suggested maybe he should hire one. Then he could consult with him on the whole thing, which is a good idea."[21] That evening I called my civil attorney, Tom Hogan, and asked him if he could arrange a meeting with Charles Norman Shaffer, a former federal prosecutor and a skilled criminal defense attorney, whom I had met previously on a number of occasions.[*]

## March 29, 1973, the White House

In a meeting at the EOB office Haldeman reported that McCord's closed-session testimony before the Senate had leaked out.[22] "Senators have refused to tell us what was said," Haldeman explained, but they wanted it to become public so some would rather leak than report. Howard Baker had called Vice President Agnew, who in turn called Haldeman to warn him that Baker felt the president's "stand on executive privilege [was] very unwise in a public relations sense." Other than more rehashing of events, nothing was resolved. Haldeman said he and Ehrlichman were available for further conversation, and they agreed to meet back at the EOB office later for what turned out to

---

*For a full account of my relationship with Shaffer see *Blind Ambition: The White House Years* (New York: Simon & Schuster, 1976), chapt. 8ff.

be a less than productive session.[23] Ehrlichman suggested releasing a statement through Ron Ziegler's office regarding White House cooperation with the grand jury investigation and the Senate inquiry, and added, "Dean doesn't care what it says as long as it indicates that he's volunteered to do it." Ziegler joined the conversation for about a half hour, and they began to draft the statement, placing calls to Mitchell, Howard Baker and me. They would work on it all day and in subsequent conversations.[24] The final product mentioned no one by name but reassured the press that the White House was cooperating.

This conversation on March 29 included an odd note, with the president advising Ehrlichman, "Get your criminal lawyer. Remember, don't get him because you like him."[25] Ehrlichman said, "Don't worry," and Nixon instructed, "I want the worst son of a bitch." Ehrlichman said he understood. "You get him," the president repeated, but Ehrlichman did nothing about it.


*March 30, 1973, the White House*

Following a busy morning schedule, Haldeman arrived in the Oval Office in the early afternoon.[26] Nixon asked if he ought to meet with anyone before he headed to California for a week, and Haldeman suggested he might speak with me, as "it's going to buck him up, not that he needs it." Haldeman informed the president that, based on his latest information, it did not appear that anyone from the White House would be called to the grand jury.

Because Senator Lowell Weicker was attacking the White House, the president and Haldeman discussed him at some length, particularly how they might embarrass him for having accepted a hefty cash contribution to his last campaign that had been arranged by the White House. They believed he had not reported it and were trying to get confirmation from "the bagman" who was supposed to pass him the money that it happened. Public records would show if it had or had not been reported. Haldeman then reported the latest leaks from the Senate Watergate committee, which involved vague accusations about Haldeman that he characterized as "a prime example of the phony stuff." McCord had purportedly written a memo to Haldeman regarding White House staff security precautions at the GOP's Miami convention but had never spoken to or had any other communications with him. Yet the *Baltimore Sun* was running a headline McCORD NAMES HALDEMAN.

Returning to the discussion of whether the president should meet with me before departing for California, Haldeman now said, "But I don't know what you'd cover with Dean." Nixon added, "We haven't got a damn thing to cover, can we say that?" Before Haldeman answered, Nixon suggested, "We might get his views."

"You get this funny, boy, this raw human stuff keeps [coming out] as you grind people against the wall," Haldeman observed, explaining, "That's why I was not so sure you ought to have Ehrlichman in with Dean. And I don't know whether this is true, but Mitchell says that Dean doesn't trust Ehrlichman, because Ehrlichman is maneuvering to sink him. And Dean thinks that Mitchell and Magruder [were] maneuvering to sink him, [but] I don't think he does anymore."

When Nixon protested, "I don't think Ehrlichman's maneuvering to sink anybody," Haldeman agreed, "No, I think Ehrlichman will maneuver to keep himself clear," and while they agreed he should, neither man thought he would "do it at the expense of somebody else." When the president said everyone should protect himself, Haldeman chuckled and replied, "Dean's moving hard in trying to protect himself on that damn meeting thing, which is still going to come up. Because he was just talking to me and reminding me that I knew about the meeting, and if I'm called I'm going to have to testify that there was a meeting. I knew about it. And that's hearsay, because I wasn't there, and I can't prove there was [one], but I was told there was one."

"Now, it isn't going to get any better on Watergate," the president told Haldeman after a brief interruption by Ziegler. "It's going to get worse, you know what I mean? It's going to go on and on and on and on." While Haldeman was not as pessimistic, he agreed. The president expected the Senate Watergate committee hearings to go on every day "with Segretti and the plumbing operation." As they contemplated this unpleasantness, the president added, "I guess we'll just go on and do our job and take the heat and so on and so forth."

Haldeman felt they needed to create some sort of "mechanism to deal with the Senate" to respond to the charges. "We can't just let them throw whatever they're pushing to throw at you." They discussed this and felt it should be handled as if they were in campaign mode, but they were uncertain who should handle this operation. "I don't see, when you add it all up, that you have anybody who can run the Watergate, except John [Ehrlichman]." When the president agreed Haldeman added, "The problem is, he's a personal factor in it, and it's bound to crunch him at some point," and he was not sure how Ehrlichman could deal with it. "Well, you're a factor, because you'll be constantly named because of your positions, basically," the president reminded Haldeman. The president closed this conversation by emphasizing he wanted Haldeman to follow up and get something on Lowell Weicker.

That evening, Haldeman recorded in his diary that Nixon was concerned now about "the damage to the presidency and his ability to govern and feels that we have to take action to clear this up because of that. He's getting a lot of heat from the likes of Goldwater, etc., who have a real concern and are expressing it to him via letters, etc." He also noted that Ehrlichman had met with Nixon about Watergate, and that Ehrlichman later told Haldeman that the president "comes down that the thing to do is put it to Magruder and try to draw the line there. There's a question whether that's possible."[27]

## April 1-8, 1973, the Western White House

The week in San Clemente brought no relief from Watergate despite Nixon's attempts to detach himself, telling Haldeman he would have no further conversations on the topic with Mitchell, Moore, Colson, George Bush, Agnew or me.[28] Instead Ehrlichman "must get the confidence of all [these] people and handle the matter for the president." Nixon insisted that there was to be "no falling-out amongst our people" with everyone going off in "all different directions. No one's going to flush anybody. and they must understand that." These instructions, however, were never shared with anyone other than Haldeman and Ehrlichman, who were isolating themselves with the president.

Haldeman's notes and diary for this period indicated that I was keeping him informed of my activities—namely, that I had hired a criminal defense attorney, who was talking with the assistant U.S. attorneys handling the Watergate investigation and had advised me not to discuss my testimony with either Mitchell or Magruder. It was during this period that Ehrlichman decided he would conduct his own investigation, and he began meeting with or telephoning (while secretly recording) people.* On April 5 and 7 I reported to Haldeman that my attorney had learned in conversations with

---

*For example, on April 5, 1973, Ehrlichman met with CRP attorney Paul O'Brien at his Western White House office, which Ehrlichman testified later he orally reported to the president on April 14, 1973. Senate testimony of John Ehrlichman, 7 Senate Select Committee on Presidential Campaign Activities (SSC), 2731–33.

prosecutors Earl Silbert, Seymour Glanzer and Don Campbell that Liddy had, as Haldeman later described it, "told them everything he knows," although not even Liddy's own lawyer was aware of his doing so. While witnesses could be sent to jail for lying to federal investigators, there were no restrictions on federal investigators' lying, and this information about Liddy turned out to be totally false.

On Sunday, April 8, I had my first "off-the-record" meeting with the prosecutors. When I informed Haldeman beforehand of the meeting, he asked me to hold off, offering the memorable metaphor: "Just remember that once the toothpaste is out of the tube it's going to be very tough to get back in." But Shaffer had set up the meeting in his office, so it was too late to change it. One of the first things I said to Earl Silbert, whom I had known at the Justice Department, was that I was surprised but pleased that Liddy had talked to them. When I learned a few days later that the purported Liddy confession had not in fact taken place, it gave me pause in dealing with them. It was also one of the factors that soon caused me to stop dealing with them altogether: They then breached the agreement they had made with Shaffer that anything and everything I told them would go no further than their office, and particularly not to the Justice Department. I knew if what I said made its way to Henry Petersen, their superior, it would then go to Kleindienst, and from there to the White House—where Haldeman and Ehrlichman would start covering themselves. Based on Shaffer's good advice, however, I did not give them very much information.[29] After I met with the prosecutors, Ehrlichman requested I meet with him and Haldeman at the White House, which I did.[30]

During the first two weeks of April, I effectively had one foot in the White House and one foot outside it, trying to deal with problems far larger than my own while being fair to others. I had Shaffer call Jeb Magruder's lawyer, James Bierbower, on April 7 to advise him to get Magruder to the prosecutors' office quickly, because I was dealing with them, which would create a problem for Magruder.[31] I likewise refused the entreaties of the prosecutor to wear a hidden device to record my colleagues. At this point I had not even discussed the president or many of the grim details of the cover-up with Shaffer.[32] While events were moving quickly, and I was taking steps to encourage that movement, I still hoped that Haldeman and Mitchell would do the right thing: step forward and take responsibility for their actions. But it became increasingly clear that that was not likely to happen.

Back at the White House, on the evening of April 8 Ehrlichman telephoned the president after our meeting, reporting that I would not appear before the grand jury until I had a chance to talk to Mitchell and to pass word to Magruder through his lawyer about my grand jury appearance.[33] Ehrlichman added that I was speculating that Liddy had "pulled the plug on Magruder," because there was "no love lost" between them. The president responded, "Mitchell has got to decide whether he is going to tell John Dean, 'Look here, I don't think you want to say a word, and you've got to go down and lie.'" "[Dean] says John Mitchell is sort of living in a dream world right now," Ehrlichman replied. "He thinks this is all going to go away. For instance, he hasn't bothered to obtain counsel. He hasn't really done much about preparing himself or anything of that kind." When Nixon asked what my take on the overall situation was, Ehrlichman reported, "Well, Dean says it isn't going to go away. It's right on top of us, and the smartest thing he, Dean, could do is go down there and appear cooperative." When the president asked about Magruder, Ehrlichman said that he remained "highly volatile," adding, "But Dean's very strong feeling is that this is the time when you just have to let it flow."

"I tend to agree with him, you know. Do you?" the president asked. Ehrlichman did agree, and he reported how out of fairness I was going to inform Mitchell and Magruder of what I was doing, just as I had Ehrlichman and Haldeman.


*April 9, 1973, the White House*

The morning conversation with Haldeman in the Oval Office rehashed familiar Watergate subjects, along with their disgust at Colson's having passed a lie-detector test about the break-in.[34] "Oh, God, it's all such a tawdry damn thing," Nixon said. Haldeman reported on the meeting he and Ehrlichman had with me the preceding evening, and that I had pointed out the danger for the president with everyone's having his own lawyer: Those lawyers would have no interest in protecting the president or the presidency, because their responsibilities were to their clients. After a long silence, Nixon raised a matter that was seriously troubling him.

"You know, with regard to recording what goes on here in the room. I feel uneasy about that, not uneasy in terms of anybody else seeing it, because we'll control it, but uneasy because of the fact it's even done." This concern provoked a twenty-minute discussion of the secret recording system and other record-keeping methods. When Nixon asked about how notes were made of his meetings, Haldeman explained, "I keep notes, and later I'll write a book. [So] I dictate a thing each night that just covers what was covered during that day. It summarizes the developments." He said it did not cover all meetings but "really covers an awful lot." White House staff members attending other meetings also wrote memoranda of them for the president's files. "Some are good, and some are lousy, and some don't ever get done," he added. Haldeman felt there was limited value in the taping system. "The only value of the tapes would be," he suggested, "if you, in your notes, find something, you know, where you're working on it and you say, I don't remember that. You can get into exactly what, who said [what], and then you can go back and run it. The problem with them, and I've wondered about that, [is] you've got just an unbelievable [number] of hours of tape."

The president said he could not allow "anybody else [to] look at them," and Haldeman agreed that that was a problem limiting their usefulness. "I'm never going to want to read all that crap," Nixon said of his tapes. "I never will." They discussed who might listen to them, and the president said he did not want Rose Woods doing so, only he and Haldeman. "What I would like to do is this," the president said. "I think we should take all that we've got and destroy them." Making a note, Haldeman said, "Okay, I understand," and the president continued. "We should, I think we should stop them." Nixon then asked how the Secret Service handled them, and Haldeman explained that Alex Butterfield had set up the system, which was now being overseen by Steve Bull, who had taken over Butterfield's responsibilities; Haldeman himself had "stayed away from" it. Nixon asked if there were copies, and Haldeman assured him that none had been made. "I thought about this in San Clemente, when we were there last week," the president explained. "I'd like you to stop it now. And second, I think we should destroy them, because I have so much material right now in my own files that I'll never be able to [get through it], you know what I mean? There's just so much."

Haldeman now questioned the wisdom of destroying everything, as well as closing down the system itself. He reminded Nixon that they had historically important material relating to the decision to go to China, as well as other key national security decisions, where often Kissinger was the only other person discussing matters with the president. They both knew that Kissinger made notes of his conversations and worried that Henry might recount this history from his point of view. The president agreed they must not destroy the key national security conversations, and liked Haldeman's suggestion of having a little hidden switch he could use to record select conversations, which was what Ehrlichman did in his own office. Accordingly, they decided they would go through the president's daily schedule to decide what to record. "Rather than maintaining a full record," Haldeman repeated to clarify his instructions, they would maintain only a select one. "I will feel much better about it if we do that," the president said, adding, "I don't want to have in the record the discussions we've had in this room about Watergate." Nor did he want to keep recordings with his often negative comments on Kissinger and Bill Rogers. When the president asked if Haldeman agreed, Haldeman reminded him, "Those are supervaluable, in some ways." Nixon acknowledged that fact but noted that they could not use them, saying, "And we'll remember enough."*

At 2:05 P.M. Haldeman returned to the president's EOB office and, before Ehrlichman arrived, reviewed their policy on the secret taping system.[35] Haldeman explained how the system worked: The Secret Service locator signal, which tracked the president's whereabouts in the White House, activated the recording system. "So that it only works in this office when you're in it, or in another office when you're in it." The president's telephones in his EOB and Oval offices, and maybe the Lincoln Sitting Room as well, all recorded automatically. Haldeman reminded Nixon that there was a similar system at Camp David and assured him that nobody was monitoring his calls: "This is all done automatically." Haldeman noted again that others in the White House—Colson, Ehrlichman and himself—had devices that enabled them to record telephone calls selectively, which, he noted, was "perfectly legal." Nixon, however, remained uncertain about what he wanted to do regarding the recording of his telephone conversations, and the matter was not resolved.

When Ehrlichman joined the conversation he had just returned from a lunch with Kleindienst, who was about to testify before Congress on executive privilege. "Basically what he will testify to is that this is entirely up to the president, and if you don't like it, lump it." Ehrlichman reported that he had also spoken with me, but I had not talked with Mitchell, because I

---

*The president would again instruct Haldeman to destroy the tapes that afternoon, and on April 18, 1973, in Conversation No. 900-4. Needless to say, and for reasons never fully explained, Haldeman did not carry out the president's instructions. It appears that Haldeman became overwhelmed himself by Watergate, and in later recorded conversations with the president he incorrectly believed that the tapes might somehow protect the president. Had Haldeman followed Nixon's instruction, there is no doubt that Watergate would have had a very different outcome, and it is most unlikely Nixon would have been forced to resign. National Archives and Records Administration (NARA).

wanted to meet face-to-face to explain the situation. This prompted the president to wonder if he was having enough contact with Mitchell, "in terms of reassuring him," and then asked, "Who the hell is Mitchell talking to?" Ehrlichman reported that he was talking with Paul O'Brien and Dick Moore. "Well, I'll get back to John," the president said, for he did not want his former partner to feel he was deserting him. Nixon assured Ehrlichman that, if necessary, he would take care of Mitchell, so long as the president came out unscathed. Ehrlichman recommended that Nixon give Mitchell a general reassurance of his undying friendship, but not become more involved, or discuss the details of the case.

Len Garment, a former law partner of Nixon's and White House staff member from the outset of the Nixon presidency, who was working with Ehrlichman to establish the rules of the Senate's Watergate hearings, was asked to join the meeting. The president told Garment he did not want him getting deeply involved, and as regards John Mitchell, a former partner of both of them, Nixon explained, "Let me say this: I have never asked him about it. I don't ever want to be in a position that John tells me [something that isn't true]." The president said, "I do not know." Nixon continued, saying that, based on what he had learned from me and others, no one at the White House had approved the Watergate operation. "Not from Colson, not from Haldeman, that I know. That's one of the reasons we were all God damn surprised when it came out." He added, "That's why Ziegler called it a third-rate burglary." Nixon claimed I had checked it out and learned it had been hatched at the reelection committee. Then, putting "the most favorable light on it," Nixon said he thought Mitchell had approved a "security operation," but "he did not have knowledge of or approve the Watergate operation. That's what I get. Where his vulnerability is, whether or not he's gone overboard in [what he told the grand jury]," which Nixon said he did not know. He added, "You and I, at this point, have to believe John." But he again cautioned Garment not to get involved in trying to figure out who did what; rather, he should let the grand jury take care of that.

That evening Ehrlichman reported to Nixon by telephone about his off-the-record meeting with Senate Watergate committee chairman Sam Ervin and vice chairman Howard Baker at the Blair House, the residence across the street from the White House for guests of the president.[36] The visit was "very cordial, very friendly. Ervin's attitude was very, very good." They would meet again Wednesday, April 11. Ehrlichman noted, "We spent most of our time talking about John Dean," which did not surprise the president. Garment and the committee's counsel would get together "and try and work out a system by which Dean's information can be taken without violating executive privilege." Ehrlichman had assured Ervin and Baker that, contrary to press reports, I had not "showed FBI reports to Segretti," so they could get such information by written interrogatories, and the charges against me were hearsay twice removed, which would be the equlivant to my giving sworn testimony without my having to appear before the committee. Ehrlichman said the hearings would begin "right after the recess" in late April, and "McCord is locked in as the first witness." He further reported, "And television [coverage], interestingly enough, is discretionary." If a witness objected, "then it will be in the discretion of the committee."

Shortly after this telephone conversation ended, the president called Ehrlichman back to be sure he had told Garment to take a very hard line, "that we cannot give on Dean going down" to testify at the hearings.[37] "In other words, we've got to hold on something, and so I think we should hold on Dean. That we will answer anything on him in written interrogatories." Ehrlichman agreed.

### April 10, 1973, the White House

During an early morning Oval Office conversation, when discussing the payments to the Watergate defendants, Haldeman explained how I had become involved in passing messages from Mitchell to Haldeman and Ehrlichman: I had not volunteered but had been drafted by necessity, for "no one else would do it." Haldeman said, "Mitchell just kind of laughed and said, 'You got to start doing something,'" and reminded the president, "I mentioned this to you at the time."[38] In the early afternoon Ehrlichman came to the Oval Office and reported that Mitchell was in town, and that Haldeman and I were going to meet separately with him.[39] Ehrlichman said I would tell Mitchell I was talking to the prosecutors and would not lie for Mitchell and Magruder, and Haldeman would tell Mitchell he could not support his contention that he was not running the president's campaign operation—as Mitchell had testified under oath—while he was still attorney general. Ehrlichman further reported I had informed him that I expected to be asked about the "hush money" to the defendants when I appeared before the grand jury. The president responded, "Well, they've got to go into that, because, because we've got Hersh," referring to the series of stories in the *New York Times* by Seymour Hersh regarding payments to the Watergate defendants.[40]

This prompted a conversation about the money paid to the defendants and speculation about who might say what and how. They rehearsed potential testimony for Mitchell, Haldeman and me, until Nixon asked, "What in the name of God is [Mitchell] going to say about the money, then?" If Mitchell was pressed, and confronted with the true testimony of others, Ehrlichman said, he did not know what Mitchell would say. Ehrlichman then admitted that the reelection committee "sent me a message through Dean that they needed help in raising money for these poor souls. And I sent word back through Dean that I just did not know how to go about it." The president asked, "But you did have such a conversation?" Ehrlichman affirmed he had.

"He had that conversation with Haldeman, too?" the president continued. "Yep," Ehrlichman replied, adding that Haldeman had said he did not know how to help, either. "So then they sent a message to Kalmbach through Dean, whether that'll come out or not, I don't know." After passing over Kalmbach, they discussed the $350,000 cash fund that Haldeman controlled being sent back to the CRP for payments to the defendants. Ehrlichman reported that he was working with Haldeman to make him a better witness, because "he tends to be very intellectual in his answers," and Ehrlichman felt he could be selling his position better. "And I asked Kleindienst, when I saw him again yesterday, to get me a reading on what's happening at the grand jury, which he promised to do." The best news that Ehrlichman had for the president was that lead Watergate prosecutor Earl Silbert had told Kleindienst that they had no interest in calling Haldeman or Ehrlichman or Colson, but rather were only interested in Strachan, Dwight Chapin and me. But both men realized that, with the Senate Watergate committee paying careful attention, the prosecutors were undertaking "a very full and completely thorough investigation." After the president gave passing consideration to a "special adviser" on Watergate, like a retired Supreme Court justice or federal judge, the conversation ended with Nixon's concluding that, while he was not being "Pollyannaish," he felt the situation was under control.

## April 11, 1973, the White House

Shortly before noon, Ehrlichman reported during an Oval Office conversation that Mitchell had called to say that Robert Strauss, the new chairman of the Democratic National Committee, was ready to settle their civil lawsuit against the reelection committee, having received approval to do so from

Senate majority leader Mike Mansfield, Speaker of the House Carl Albert, and the chairman of the Senate's Watergate committee, Sam Ervin.[41] Mitchell said they could settle if Maury Stans would agree, but that this might require a nudge from the White House. The president instructed Ehrlichman to tell Mitchell to do as he thought best and to have Len Garment do the nudging of Stans. (The lawsuit was ultimately settled for $775,000.[42]) Discussion of the suit prompted the president to complain about Sam Ervin's "pissy-ass game" regarding the rules for White House witnesses at his hearings: "This old fart is trying to screw us."

Ehrlichman said he was going to pass the word to Howard Baker "that they really don't want to get into Kalmbach's records," because "there's going to be some senators and congressmen on both sides of the aisle that really wouldn't like to open that whole can of worms." Nixon, however, was unclear about what he was referring to. "Well," Ehrlichman explained, "you get into the [Teddy] Kennedy investigation, for one thing."* Apparently Kalmbach had also arranged payments of campagin contributions to favored conservative Democratic congressional candidates. Most of this conversation focused on their concern about the reports Liddy had prepared for the reelection committee and the White House about information he was overhearing at the DNC, which he dictated to his secretary, Sally Harmony, based on the material gathered by Alfred Baldwin.† It appeared that these documents had been given to Gordon Strachan, which probably meant Haldeman was involved. Notwithstanding Haldeman's denials, the president remained concerned about him.

At 12:34 P.M. Ehrlichman was back in the Oval Office conversation to report on his talk with Mitchell about the DNC lawsuit; he agreed he would arrange to settle it.[43] More important Ehrlichman said he had tried to brace Mitchell for what lay ahead, encouraging him to "focus" on the potential problems. Mitchell said he had retained Paul O'Brien to represent him. Ehrlichman thought this was a good development, "because we can use O'Brien now as a conduit to Mitchell in a way I didn't think we could before," suggesting that such information might now be protected by attorney-client privilege.

---

*It appears that Ehrlichman did pass the word and the Senate never did open that "whole can of worms."

†No recordings were made of the DNC-intercepted conversations because McCord could not get his radio receiver connected to his tape recorder. So Liddy cleaned up Baldwin's notes on the overheard conversations. G. Gordon Liddy, *Will* (New York: St. Martin's Press), 235.

The president made it clear he did not want Mitchell testifying in a way that appeared that either he or the White House was covering up. It was the potential criminal exposure that most troubled the president: "I don't give a damn if the Ervin committee comes out and condemns us. That does not worry me," although he proceeded to make it clear that he did not want Ervin to have a free ride: He wanted a strong minority report by the Republicans on the committee. Ehrlichman explained that that was not going to be all that easy for Baker and the other Republicans were "not about to endorse anybody at this point," and Baker himself had become "very standoffish."

Ehrlichman wanted Nixon's views on my testifying before the Senate, because the committee wanted to subpoena me, which could "get the litigation started," if that was going to be necessary. The committee felt it could get its request for subpoeaned information to the U.S. Supreme Court by summer. This was fine with the president, but Ehrlichman, who was meeting with Ervin and Baker again that evening at Blair House, said he would keep it an open question: "I'd rather not give them a definite no on Dean at this point." Ehrlichman appeared both comfortable with my testifying and with a court test on my not testifying.

Repeatedly, throughout this conversation, Ehrlichman mentioned how unhappy the Senate committee was with McCord as a witness, because of the weakness in his information and its crediblity. The president said that a result of Sirica's delaying McCord's sentence, to see how he could help the Senate was to give McCord high incentive for fabricating testimony or, as Nixon described it, "producing a bunch of God damn crap." Accordingly, the president told Ehrlichman he wanted attention devoted to the "destruction of McCord." Given Ehrlichman's meeting that evening, the discussion of the Ervin committee's proceeding remained at the forefront of this discussion. "John, let's face it," Nixon said, the proceeding was not going to end until they got "some big fish and fry them, and then they'll go away. Not until then." No big fish concerned Nixon more than Haldeman and Ehrlichman, and he wanted to know what would happen if Magruder, with his "apple-cheeked credibility and all that," were to blow." Nixon believed that merely calling him a liar would not solve a potentially "uncontrollable" situation. Nixon was also concerned about me, and asked, "Is Dean now trying to be subpoenaed? Is that right?" Ehrlichman reported I was "still waiting" and had "not yet heard." The president understood that both Dwight Chapin and Gordon Strachan had already been to the prosecutors' office.

Most everything Ehrlichman had discussed with the president earlier in the day was revisited, to varying degrees, during midafternoon Oval Office conversation with Ehrlichman, Haldeman and Ziegler.[44] Ziegler attended to considering appropriate public statements about a situation that Ehrlichman sardonically described as "We're getting bombed because [the president] appears to lack candor, forthrightness, [and] responsiveness to the needs of the nation in cleaning out a festering corruption." The president observed that whatever statement was made, it should be made strongly."

Regarding the Senate's likely Watergate hearings and the grand jury's investigation, Ehrlichman felt all the White House witnesses would be strong, but the "weak witnesses would be Mitchell, LaRue, Mardian, folks of that kind" from the campaign. Nixon agreed, then noted, "Haldeman is the man we have to think about here. I don't know what you do in the Dean thing. It's tough." There followed a lengthy and indecisive discussion about whether or not I should testify before the grand jury, but it was unanimously agreed that I should not appear before the Senate committee. At most I should provide written answers to questions, or possibly take part in an informal meeting with the committee members. It was presumed that Haldeman would testify before the Senate, and he was working on a statement. Although Ziegler had been dealing with Watergate since its inception, he was relatively new to these process discussions, and he suggested that enough information be released "to draw a circle around the president, around the White House, to give the presidency and the White House something to stand on."

"How do you do that, Ron?" Ehrlichman asked. Ziegler, who became frustrated and annoyed when Ehrlichman pushed, replied, "I don't have the solution, John." "Well, I've got the itch. I don't know how to scratch it. That's my problem," Ehrlichman said, dismissing Ziegler.

Haldeman was concerned that if I did not appear before the Senate it would be claimed "that Dean was the mastermind that ran this whole thing." The problem with that argument was that it would come back to either Mitchell or Haldeman, since it was well known I did not have that kind of power. The president liked the idea of claiming that, as the lawyer, I had conducted an investigation, although he understood I had not done so, because my undertaking was protected by privilege. They plotted and speculated about what might have occurred during the planning stages that produced the break-in, and then in the aftermath, and Ehrlichman ran out several scenarios of my testimony, all of which absolved everyone but me.

Ehrlichman suggested, for example, how I might testify I had learned about the hush money demands: "I continued to attend meetings at the committee to reelect," Ehrlichman, playing the role of Dean, began, "principally for the purpose of counseling on election laws, to make sure that the White House didn't get off on the wrong foot, and so forth. At those meetings the question of the care and feeding of the defendants kept arising, and people kept turning to me, particularly John Mitchell, saying, 'You've got to help us get the money to keep these fellows from starving and to keep their attorneys going and so forth.' And so, on several occasions I came back to the White House and communicated John Mitchell's message to various people in the White House. On one occasion, I contacted Herb Kalmbach to see if he could raise money for John Mitchell. On other occasions, I communicated with people outside of the White House with regard to this matter, and I became a participant in the process of raising and trying to send any money to the defendants." The president, confused by Ehrlichman's proposed fictional account, asked, "Did he raise money?" Ehrlichman answered, "He was in the process. But he didn't personally put an arm on anybody."

"But you didn't help [him]?" the president asked Ehrlichman. "No, but Herb did," Ehrlichman answered, failing to acknowledge that Kalmbach had done so at Ehrlichman's direct request. "So, in other words, he did raise some money?" the president further pressed. "He was instrumental, I would say," Ehrlichman suggested. "Really?" Haldeman asked with an incredulous tone at this new account. Ehrlichman began to back off when Haldeman, who was aware of the true facts of the matter, said, "It seems to me he was instrumental in passing information along to those who could raise the money. But not that he was instrumental in raising it. He didn't contact anyone." "That's what I said," Ehrlichman protested. "That's a semantic, Bob." "No, but he knew," the president added. "The point is, [he had knowledge]."

"He was in the process," Ehrlichman repeated, and they continued to fashion my testimony for me, including, at one point, Ehrlichman's more accurately noting that I was "merely a connection, you know, that there are people at both ends involved." But those people at both ends—Mitchell, Magruder, LaRue, O'Brien and Parkinson at one and Ehrlichman, Haldeman and the president at the other—remained unmentioned. Ehrlichman noted, "If this were a dead-end road that nobody would go down unless Dean said something, then you don't have a problem. But it isn't." Haldeman pointed out, "People at both ends have an overriding interest in not saying anything."

At the end of this ultimately inconclusive meeting, Nixon flew off to

Camp David to continue to search for a solution that would keep these problems a safe distance from his presidency.

### April 12, 1973, the White House

The *New York Times* reported that Dwight Chapin and Gordon Strachan, along with Donald Segretti, James McCord and Robert Reisner, a former Magruder assistant who kept his schedule, had all appeared before the grand jury the day before.[45] As Nixon was now relying exclusively on John Ehrlichman to deal with Watergate, he summoned him to report to the Oval Office early that morning. Ehrlichman said that Reisner's appearance meant the prosecutors were looking at Mitchell's meetings with Magruder, Liddy and me.[46] Ehrlichman said he would call Kleindienst later that morning to "get some feel" for the grand jury testimony now being presented, although he was confident that Strachan and Chapin were describing Segretti's activities, which was of little concern. The only real unease that morning was whether Strachan would be asked about receiving reports from Liddy's Watergate-bugging operation. Ehrlichman did not believe, however, that McCord had that information, so he doubted the subject had arisen. He did have new information concerning the Senate's hearings, which had been postponed until May 1.

Strachan and Chapin's grand jury testimony was still on the president's mind when Haldeman arrived later in the morning at the Oval Office.[47] Haldeman had talked with Strachan, who said that Watergate prosecutor Earl Silbert had spoken with him after his appearance; he "sounded apologetic" and told him that "there's clearly no criminal problem" with Segretti, and "there's nothing for us to go after." Haldeman added, "Strachan says it's incredible; you walk into the grand jury room, and there's twenty people in there, of whom three are white; all the rest are black, several of whom are asleep." "Jeezzz," Nixon replied, and Haldeman went on to explain that federal prosecutor Seymour Glanzer played the bad cop, with Silbert playing the good one. The president and Haldeman ultimately found nothing of concern in the Chapin and Strachan appearances other than the need for Haldeman to release a statement before his role could be leaked from the grand jury.

Following a brief photo opportunity on his schedule, the president asked Ziegler to remain in the Oval Office to discuss the White House staff's providing affidavits or statements regarding their roles—or lack thereof—in various Watergate-related activities.[48] Ziegler did not like the idea unless such documents went considerably further than the denials he had heard. Ziegler had been collecting his thoughts in a series of notes he now produced. He wanted to draw a protective circle around the White House, which he had discussed with Ehrlichman. He was not opposed to a Haldeman statement, but like affidavits, it, too, had a risk. Ziegler knew the players, and was trying to protect everyone without telling the president he thought some might lie, which would hurt both them and the president. So he cast the problem as later-developing information that would make earlier statements appear incorrect, or worse, part of a cover-up. Ziegler felt there was a Washington fixation with Watergate but that outside of Washington it still was not a big story.

"You don't want Haldeman to make a statement. You don't want sworn statements to be put out. You know, that's right," the president said, for then there would only be calls for more information, claiming what had been offered was incomplete. "Then don't do anything," the president advised. He did, however, want Ziegler's media-sensitive reaction to the outstanding problems, based on Ziegler's incomplete knowledge. "You don't think Dean can be saved, do you?" the president asked, and Ziegler said he did not, based on what he knew. "Do you think Haldeman can be saved?" the president asked of the man who had recruited Ziegler. Ziegler did not think he could be saved either, and even offered, "I'd say it is a 60 percent chance that he cannot be saved."

Ziegler suggested options, including issuing a preemptive complete and truthful statement, one that would not crumble under the weight of testimony. He conceded that this would be very difficult to do, but a recognition by the White House that there had been "bad judgment, or a better word—" Nixon interrupted, "Admit it?" Ziegler continued, "—and possible wrongdoing, without saying it was wrongdoing, and let the chips fall. In other words, draw a circle around the White House. That puts the president in the position of saying, I have found out—which is true—in recent weeks, on my own, moving quietly, not making a big public thing about it, that indeed there was more to be told, and I have instructed the men to tell it, making the point in the complete statement [regarding] the Segretti activity on the part of Haldeman, and the other activity is separate and not illegal, and he stays. In other words, nothing that he has done, despite what the scope of the impression. Dean, I would think, and this is not final, would not be canned, but could resign. Now, he could be transferred to somewhere else. I don't know."

"No, no," the president replied. "He should, he could resign on the basis that, because of the charges that have been made and so forth. He's innocent of the charges, but he's seriously jeopardized his ability to carry on these functions that he's assigned, and therefore, he resigns." The president liked this option, of a complete statement, and felt they should test the water on that, and they tried to flesh it out a bit as the conversation continued: "Rather than just let the son of a bitch be dragged out. The problem that I'm concerned with is Bob," the president said. He told Ziegler he believed they were going to get Mitchell, and asked Ziegler if he thought a complete statement might save Haldeman. Ziegler, who at that time was unaware of Haldeman's Watergate-related activities, felt a complete statement regarding his Segretti connection would be the best chance of saving him. When the president pushed on Mitchell, Ziegler described Mitchell, from his limited information, as having no knowledge whatsoever of illegal activity, and that a complete statement would not affect Mitchell any differently than any other option.

After speculating on testimony, Nixon said, "I think the complete statement thing appeals to me, from the standpoint that the president has, we've conducted an investigation, and here's a complete statement for those that have been named, since we know that the committee is going to delay it, and it's time for the air to be cleared now." Then the president came back to the recurring problem: "The trouble, the problem there, we've talked about complete statements before, Ron. Every time anybody tries to write one, they can't write it." Since Ziegler had not been privy to these discussions, they soon inevitably concluded it was difficult to do so, and Ziegler was coming to the conclusion that any statement less than "complete"—that is, as honest and as accurate as possible—would simply not work.

Ehrlichman reported back to the EOB Office that afternoon.[49] "We seem to have a lot of business these days, don't we?" the president asked, as Ehrlichman seated himself. After Nixon highlighted his earlier discussion with Ziegler, he added, "I think Ron's views are pretty much worth considering." Ehrlichman agreed, and then asked, "Remember we were worried about [Liddy's secretary] Sally, what's her name, was going to testify—?" Nixon provided the name, "Harmony," revealing his retention of details. Ehrlichman reported that, in fact, there were no such memos sent to the White

House. "They came to Strachan."* Ehrlichman explained, "They were not in the form of dialogue, or taps," but rather like FBI reports from surveillance based on "'a usually reliable source,' or 'a source beyond impeachment,' that sort of thing." Ehrlichman paused, then added, "They were very unspectacular." Strachan reported that there had been three of them. "They don't have them now, though," the president rhetorically offered, but Ehrlichman continued without responding. "On one occasion [Strachan] sent Bob one of them, with a cover memo, which referred to this, among many other items, there were probably eight or ten tabs, and said, politically sophisticated sources report, so and so, see tab L or H or [whatever]. Now that's very tough, to my way of thinking. I think that's very, very [hard to take]," Ehrlichman said, obviously concerned about this bit of evidence that tied the White House to the first Watergate break-in.

The president asked anxiously, "Has he testified to that?" Ehrlichman assured him that he had not but explained that Strachan had another problem arising out of his grand jury appearance the day before. It was, Ehrlichman said, a ludicrous situation: Strachan realized he had mistakenly testified before the grand jury about returning the $350,000 to the reelection committee when the amount actually had been $328,000. He reported that he had spent two hours sorting it all out and advised Strachan to inform the prosecutors and correct his testimony.[50]

After taking the president through this Strachan "emergency," Ehrlichman continued with his report about the White House receipt of the fruits of the Watergate bugging. "So anyway, I said, 'Gordon, while you're here, just answer a question for me, will you? To your knowledge, did they prepare White House [copies]?' 'Yes.' 'Where'd they go?' 'Well, I got some.' I said, 'How many were involved?' He said, 'Three.' And that would have been between May and June, obviously, at the time that it happened. I said, 'Did Colson know about it?' He said, 'I don't know.' 'Did you ever give Colson copies?' 'No, if Colson got copies it wasn't from me.'" Ehrlichman noted that, therefore, if Colson had received copies, they had to have come from the reelection committee, adding, "So, if the testimony is that only one copy came to the White House, we know that it came to Strachan. Colson's alright. So there's that."

---

*According to his office calendar Ehrlichman had just come from a meeting with Strachan and Haldeman in his office.

This was still bad news, so the president asked for more specifics. He said, "Well, now let's go on to Haldeman, [and] this business of the use of the term, John, 'politically sophisticated' stuff, good God, ah—"

"Oh, I can put a good face on this," Ehrlichman reassured the president, as could Nixon: "Bob has just got to say that he got all sorts of information, never had anything that, that—" he began to suggest, but then realized, "—but he's got to admit it." Ehrlichman offered his own approach: "But you got to think about the bad things that are going to be put on this. Styles Bridges, at this point." (Ehrlichman was alluding to the fact that when Bridges, one of the putatively poorest members of the U.S. Senate, died in 1961, shortly after being reelected, his widow discovered he had left her an enormous amount of cash, by various accounts not less than $120,000 nor more than $2 million. Ehrlichman's point was that there were no good explanations for the money.)

"If they have a copy?" the president pressed. "If they have a copy of the thing from Strachan?" Ehrlichman said they did not. Strachan had no doubt told Ehrlichman what he had told me: Namely, he had destroyed all such incriminating documents in his files at Haldeman's request.[51] "I know," the president said. "Strachan doesn't have any of his stuff, which is just as good then." They speculated about whether anyone would have known that Haldeman had received the bugging summaries,[52] and why this had not arisen earlier; Ehrlichman suggested blaming me. "But Dean did not know there were two copies handed over," Nixon reminded him. "I think we'd better not say that Dean didn't tell us." Ehrlichman still liked the idea of claiming "the Dean report was inadequate." But at this point the president was not yet prepared to throw me under the bus, and thinking of our March 21, 1973, conversation, he told Ehrlichman, "Dean made a perfectly conscientious report."

When the conversation again turned to casting blame, the president said, "Let's talk about Dean for a moment. Dean's probably thought about this. He's a God damn decent guy, you know. Remember, whether he served us well," Ehrlichman began to interrupt, but Nixon continued talking, "it is not a moral question; he was doing what he was supposed to do." Ehrlichman conceded, "I've already said I think he did serve you well, for a fact. And he did. He did a Herculean job, under tremendous pressure." Ehrlichman did not, however, volunteer in this conversation that I was in fact implementing his policy, often at his direct instructions. The president continued, "He did it all by himself, didn't have any help, Mitchell wasn't helping him as much as he should, Mitchell was then out, of course. God damn, Mitchell was the guy that really let us down in that period, John. It couldn't be done by MacGregor. It couldn't be done by the committee. But Jesus Christ, blaming poor John Dean, that's the reasoning the committee doesn't have a [*unclear*]," the president said.

"Now what I was trying to spin out on Dean, here, was Ziegler's hypothetical to me," Ehrlichman said, backpedaling. "He says, it now appears inevitable that Dean's going to be badly bruised, if not totally destroyed by this, inevitably in the long haul, that even if you interpose and exert your executive privilege on behalf of Dean, surrounding him, the damage will be severe." The president and Ehrlichman worried that the same problems would arise for Colson and Haldeman, and then discussed my taking a leave of absence, as well as the once-forbidden topic of Haldeman's taking a leave of absence.

The president lamented this problem. "Just at a time when we got Bob out of scheduling, and we got him out of all the East Wing crap,* and we got him out of the line of fire there, and we've got him so that he can concentrate basically on the big plays, the things that I say he ought to do, now we've got this thing. But let's face it. The amount of time that he's having to spend on this at the present time is tearing him up, and it will tear me up. There's your problem, John." Ehrlichman raised the obvious question of also letting Haldeman go: "Well, what do you think about that?" Nixon acknowledged, "We've got to think the unthinkable sometimes." Ehrlichman replied, with perhaps a bit too much encouragement in his voice, "Yeah, yeah. Well, I just, I don't find that unthinkable. I see a lot of advantages to it," but then more evenly remarked, "I've got to think about that. That's a pretty big medicine. But as I say, I certainly don't reject it out of hand."

Nixon turned to "the effectiveness of the presidency" and suggested that all the "things coming up with the economy and the summit with the Russians, and there are some pretty God damn big plays, [could] lower the decibels" of Watergate, and might enable the president "to screw that [Ervin] committee." He noted that as long as they had a target in the White House they would pursue it. "Just trying to think it through," Nixon mused, "I don't know of anything that we could do that would be more disappointing to

---

*This is a reference to the First Lady's scheduling and activities operation, which was located in the East Wing of the White House.

Ervin than to have Haldeman take a leave." Ehrlichman agreed, and Nixon continued, "You know, Ervin would like to bring the president to his knees and have him forced to fire [Haldeman] as a result," the president began, and imitating Ervin's Southern accent, said, "As a result of my committee's investigation, it is clear that Mr. Haldeman has to go." Ehrlichman joined in with his own Ervin impersonation: "I don't want to inflict any hardship on the president."

This conversation ended with the president's observing that they had to consider Haldeman's leaving, and Nixon instructed Ehrlichman not to discuss this matter with others.[53] But because actions in the tight-knit White House always spoke louder than words, the mere fact of Haldeman's diminishing time with the president and Ehrlichman's increased presence spread quickly through the grapevine. It was during this period that I began to hear talk of Ehrlichman's becoming chief of staff, not to mention rumors that he was slowly turning the knife not merely in Haldeman's back but in Mitchell's, Colson's and mine as well—even though those rumors were more damning of Ehrlichman than the actual conversations behind closed doors would justify.

A few hours after Ehrlichman's departure, the president called Colson in Boston, where he had given a speech.[54] After agreeing that "madman" John Sirica was causing everyone to panic, the president asked Colson if he would "just sort of write your précis as to what the hell, how you see this thing unfolding and how we should handle it. I'm sure you've thought about it, because, you see, with everybody going off in his own direction, that's not good." The president said he was concerned that everyone was getting "so obsessed with it that we think it's the only story in town."

"My view is that we should decide on what the plan ought to be," Colson said. "Everybody follow it, and whatever it is." "I think there's a tendency for everybody to get upset with Watergate as being, that this is the thing that's going to destroy the presidency, you know," Nixon said. "This is sort of the view of Ray Price, and that kind of group," he said, referring to one of his top speechwriters. Although the president said this dismissively, he quickly added, "They may be right." Colson, who was well aware that Nixon often sought sympathy, reassured the president that Watergate was not going to end his presidency. With that resolved the president wanted to know if Colson had left material in his files that could be used to attack the Democrats, a project he had assigned to Pat Buchanan; he believed it was "terribly important" and of the "highest priority" to get out a "white paper" going after the Democrats and McGovern for their campaign tactics.

## April 13, 1973, the White House

On this day Nixon had nine Watergate-related conversations: five just with Ehrlichman;[55] one with Ehrlichman and Haldeman together;[56] and three brief discussions with Haldeman alone.[57] Ehrlichman updated Nixon on what was happening at the grand jury, based on reports from Kleindienst (Segretti took the Fifth; Dean hasn't testified) and explained the principle of obstruction of justice, as he understood it, with an example given to him by Kleindienst: "If you gave a man money to plead guilty, that is not a crime if he's guilty. If you give a man money not to testify, that's a crime." Kleindienst had also said, "This is a very tough offense to establish." [58] Nixon asked if Ehrlichman had told them not to testify, referring to the Watergate defendants. He said those making the payment had not, speaking broadly regarding his understanding. "They said they were going to plead guilty," Ehrlichman explained, "and we felt sorry for them." He was offering a hypothical rationale for why the payment had been made. Both men had little doubt that McCord would claim "he was given money to shut up," as the president stated it.

Nixon raised again my taking a leave of absence and who might replace me as White House counsel. He also wondered how I might testify without revealing everything. Ehrlichman replied that he was going to have a "heart-to-heart" talk with me. He said that, based on his understanding of its current direction, "nothing has stirred up this grand jury so far, so that he, Dean, will be the operating efficient cause of the change in direction in this thing." Ehrlichman then said matter-of-factly, "Now I have to assume that that isn't going to make any difference to Dean." He continued, "He's prepared to go down and just tell the truth. To tell what he knows. Not to reach out—" The president interrupted to clarify, "To tell them in a very, shall we say, limited way," and they proceeded to surmise how I might answer some questions but dodge others.

After further discussion of the White House and Mitchell's liabilities, the president mentioned to Ehrlichman that he had told Colson to get a white paper together on the Democrats, adding, "John, I want you to kick the asses around like they haven't been kicked." There was more discussion of both

Haldeman's and my taking leaves of absence, with the conversation ending on a discussion of whether, in fact, Liddy had been talking, as the prosecutors had claimed. The president thought not, but Ehrlichman was not sure.

The Haldeman Oval Office conversation at 11:22 A.M was brief and repetitive, with Haldeman assuring the president that he had gone over Strachan's testimony with him before he appeared before the grand jury.[59] Ehrlichman returned to the Oval Office just before one o'clock for his second session, with troubling news from the first of his two meetings with Colson that day.[60] Colson claimed he had a taped conversation of Magruder (apparently talking with a newsperson) in which Magruder claimed that both Colson and Haldeman had encouraged him to engage in electronic eavesdropping. Magruder had also now claimed that "Haldeman knew of the plan to bug the Watergate in advance," and it was clear to Ehrlichman that he was trying to turn it "from Mitchell to the White House." Ehrlichman reported that Colson was now recommending that "Dean ought to be fired, [because] Dean will be seriously implicated in the obstruction of justice thing, which [Colson] sees as probably the most serious exposure right now."

The president absorbed this news with little reaction, but what did get his attention was Colson's claim that the prosecutors "will attempt to prove a conspiracy to obstruct justice, which will involve a lot of people who were not direct actors, and, he said, will lead to the door of the Oval Office." When the president asked whom Colson was talking about, Ehrlichman answered, "I can't imagine what he means. I don't know." The president speculated that he might be referring to Haldeman, and Ehrlichman said he had asked Colson about that. Colson had replied, "I know that you and Bob were both talking to Dean about this," but Ehrlichman had deflected that observation. Ehrlichman observed that Colson's "obviously got his own fish to fry, and he has decided that Mitchell ought to be sunk." He later added, "If Colson is out sowing the seeds of Magruder and Mitchell's destruction, he'll know how to do it very effectively. And I think that he is obviously not under control, Colson isn't." Ehrlichman surmised that Colson's strategy was to keep the matter out of the White House and over at the reelection committee.

Nixon wanted Ehrlichman to pin Colson down on whom he was referring to that could take the obstruction of justice problem to the door of the Oval Office. "What the hell would we talk about? There has been no discussions of obstruction of justice in this office," the president insisted. Ehrlichman, who had no knowledge of my conversations with Nixon, assured him,

"I haven't any idea of what he is talking about. I didn't ask him." Ehrlichman said he had requested that Colson give him a written scenario and also told Nixon that he wanted Haldeman to listen to the tape Colson said he claimed to have.

"By all means, by all means," the president agreed, and noted how everything was breaking fast. When Ehrlichman reported he would be meeting with me that afternoon, the president said, "I don't think we should fire Dean" as Colson had suggested, and Ehrlichman agreed. Neither the president nor Ehrlichman had any doubt about why Colson was going after Mitchell, for, as Nixon pointed out, "Mitchell always hated Chuck, and Chuck has never liked Mitchell." But neither could understand why Magruder might be talking to the press. Ehrlichman thought Mitchell might be manipulating Magruder, but he was not overly concerned about the matter, as Magruder could be shown to be a liar. They briefly discussed whether I had suborned Magruder's perjury, but whether cross-examination could destroy Magruder was not clear. "I'm told he is an adroit witness and very credible," Ehrlichman noted. "Well, if you want to destroy a witness, John, you have to have the cooperation of the press," the president noted. "In this instance, the press will want to believe Magruder, just like they will want to believe McCord."

Noting his concern about Haldeman and Colson, the president soon returned to the taped Magruder conversation. After confirming the latest Magruder charges, Ehrlichman said, the tape also had Colson forcing Magruder to hire Hunt at the reelection committee, "which Colson says is not the truth."* Magruder's latest volley also caused the president to speculate that someone was leading him to think he might be granted immunity. Ehrlichman, however, said that could not happen. "Why can't he?" the president asked. "Suppose he rats on people that are higher up, doesn't that get him immunity?"

"I discussed this with Dick [Kleindienst]," Ehrlichman said, "and he says, well, if a little guy came in and delivered to the U.S. attorney ten big guys, yes. But if one of the ten big guys came in who had already testified and said, okay, now I'm going to change my testimony and come clean on five of my colleagues, he says we'd say, go jump in the lake, fellow." Ehrlichman was

---

*Literally Colson was correct, for it was a member of his staff, Richard "Dick" Howard, who had called Magruder to lean on him to hire Hunt. See Jeb Stuart Magruder, *An American Life: One Man's Road to Watergate* (New York: Atheneum, 1974), 181.

equating Magruder with a big guy who would be told to go jump in the lake. This conversation came to a close with the president again instructing Ehrlichman to "pin Colson down when he says this thing goes to the Oval Office." Ehrlichman assured the president he would. Then, thinking that Colson was talking about clemency for Hunt, the president told Ehrlichman the only time that subject had ever come up was "the time you and I walked on the beach," although the president did vaguely recall Colson's talking about meeting with Hunt.

Haldeman met with the president in his EOB Office in the late afternoon, and they were joined by Ehrlichman for the latter part of what was another wide-ranging Watergate conversation.[61] Haldeman and Ehrlichman had been busy collecting information, which they shared with each other and the president.

Haldeman had some information from Strachan, who claimed that he did not know that the documents he received from the reelection committee were Watergate bugging reports; Haldeman explained that there was no way to tell. He said that Magruder needed to be told by an authority figure what to do and where he now stood and he'd react properly; he was a lost soul. Magruder thought he was doing what he was supposed to do, and he was on his way to jail. Haldeman felt the president should not listen to the Higby tape of Magruder, which had been made earlier at Haldeman's request to get as truthful an account of Magruder's knowledge as possible.

This wide-ranging conversation included more speculation about my testimony and when I might appear before the grand jury. The president asked why Colson wanted me fired, and Ehrlichman thought it was because he saw me aligned with Mitchell. Nixon wanted to know who was going to talk to Magruder, but no one volunteered. Ehrlichman said, incorrectly, that federal rules of criminal procedure precluded discussion of testimony with any other witness before the grand jury. Nixon instructed: "Dean is to go to the grand jury under the strictest rules. And the most limited testimony he can possibly give, John. Now that has just got to be." The president added emphatically, "And he's not to talk to anybody, no PR, and so forth." After a discussion of the Ervin committee the president instructed, "It's best for the people in the White House not to say a God damn word." They explored other approaches during the conversation until Ehrlichman grounded it by saying, if he were Mitchell, he would deny everything, take the Fifth Amendment, and make it difficult every step of the way. Haldeman said that the worst thing they could do would be to hang Mitchell and added, "The worst thing we can do is keep getting ourselves in the middle of it. I think we've ruined the career of John Dean, probably." The president agreed. They reminisced about perceived missed opportunities to have put an end to Watergate, although all were wishful-thinking scenarios that would have involved half truths, and on close analysis, ended with all but Ehrlichman's falling on their swords for the president.

The day the Watergate review was not yet over, however. After appearing at a reception, the president called Haldeman late in the afternoon to ask about Ehrlichman's meeting with Colson and his partner, David Shapiro. Ehrlichman was still in that meeting, so they discussed Magruder, as he had just listened to Higby's secret recording of him, and reporting that Magruder now felt he might be facing 100 to 125 years of jail time for his perjury.[62] While Nixon was eating dinner alone in the Lincoln Sitting Room, Ehrlichman called with a brief report on his meeting with Colson and Shapiro.[63] "Well, they have quite a tale of horrors to tell," Ehrlichman began, starting with what undoubtedly struck him as the most important detail: Colson had learned—Hunt's lawyer, Bill Bittman, had told his lawyer, David Shapiro— that "Hunt has decided to tell all to the grand jury Monday at two o'clock." Ehrlichman surmised that "Bittman made a deal with the government so that Bittman does not get caught in this obstruction of justice business." He said that Hunt would implicate CRP lawyers Paul O'Brien and Ken Parkinson "as the bagmen and the transmitters of money through Hunt to the Cubans and to Hunt for Mrs. Hunt for other people, and so on and so forth."

Nixon asked, "Why will Hunt do this, do they say?" "They think simply because he has no incentive to stand mute now," Ehrlichman explained. "He sees the whole thing going up in smoke, and he just doesn't want to be the only guy holding the bag. I think Bittman is the guy who's getting something out of it. Of course, Hunt purges himself of contempt when he does this. So he gets a little something out of it." Ehrlichman characterized his session with Colson and Shapiro as a "'sink Mitchell' operation," to which Nixon took offense, saying, "Well I hope you laid into them a little, John." Ehrlichman assured him that he had and added, "For what it's worth, I have Colson's commitment that he will do nothing, say nothing, make no move, without prior approval at this point." Ehrlichman reported that Colson and Shapiro had learned there were two other grand juries at work on cases that involved Mitchell: the Vesco grand jury in New York City and one in Washington,

DC, looking at a tax evasion matter regarding someone's getting government contracts in exchange for campaign contributions. "Jesus Christ, I can't fathom that," the president said; neither could Ehrlichman.

Based on his meeting with Colson and Shapiro, Ehrlichman also reported that Hunt had thought Liddy's Watergate plans were a "screwball operation," and that Hunt had not wanted to go forward, but Liddy insisted that Mitchell had specifically instructed him to proceed; that Liddy was sitting silently in jail because he had "a blood oath from Mitchell" that he would be pardoned; that Hunt had testified I had ordered him to leave town (though Ehrlichman did not know if I actually had); and Colson and Shapiro recommended Nixon beat everyone to the punch by getting Liddy to talk and unravel Watergate. Ehrlichman reported that Shapiro thought Mitchell should plead insanity, based on his life with Martha, as his criminal defense, but this was dismisssed out of hand by Nixon.

Colson was most distressed over McCord's story, leaked to the press by Senate investigators, that Liddy and Hunt had concocted another harebrained scheme to fly to Las Vegas, leave the airplane running, break into publisher Hank Greenspun's safe, and jump back into the airplane and head off—a plan McCord claimed Colson had masterminded but Colson vehemently denied.[64] On top of all this, Ehrlichman said, he had forgotten to raise with Colson what he meant about getting to the door of the Oval Office, because Shapiro was there Colson had not raised it, making it apparently confidential, but he would get back to Colson and the answer.

After finishing dinner the president called Haldeman for his "analysis of Chuck's latest," but neither Haldeman nor Ehrlichman, who was still with him, could figure it out.[65] Nixon thought he understood it, and explained, "Every individual here, or course, is trying quite naturally to save his own position." Nixon further observed, "The second thing, one thing that is a most absurd suggestion, [is] that Mitchell should go in and plead insanity, you know. I mean, what the hell, that's just unbelievable that they would suggest such a thing. That shows you how desperate." Haldeman said he found Shapiro "a rather slimy fellow." The president asked if Colson had produced the transcript of the purported Magruder conversation, and Haldeman said Shapiro told him they would never get it, but that they "swear up one side and down the other that it's absolutely true." Nixon asked, "You think he's lying? Chuck is lying?" Haldeman responded, "I find it very hard to believe that he's telling the truth." The president said he thought Ehrlichman felt the same. Nixon added that Ehrlichman also felt that Magruder was "ready to crack" and tell all. "No question," Haldeman affirmed. "He obviously has crossed the bridge that he's not going to lie anymore." The president, sounding worn down by it all, asked if they had analyzed "the Colson thing." Haldeman said they had not, so the president asked them to "take a half hour, and call me back."

"Well, we've been chewing this thing over and chewing it over, and I can't say that we are at any conclusion," Ehrlichman reported in the follow-up call.[66] "We'd like a chance to go to dinner and talk about this instead, and we could just mull it tonight, and hit it. We'll be in early in the morning and be ready to talk to you at about ten thirty or eleven, I would guess." This was fine with the president. Ehrlichman then reported. "We've got some new input that will be coming in from John Dean tonight that we want to add to it. His folks are in touch with the U.S. attorney tonight." Ehrlichman confirmed the president's recollection that Hunt was scheduled to testify at two o'clock on Monday, "Unless we do something that would force that calendar to change, and we've been working with some ideas about that."

When the president asked, "What can you do on that, though, John?" Ehrlichman responded, "Well, we could do several things to move that up—if there were a more attractive witness, or a more conclusive witness, or something of that kind, or if we drew the U.S. attorney off to do something else."

Sounding resigned and philosophical about it all, the president said, "Well, you know, on the plus side, this is the problem, and so forth, in a sense, John, the best thing is to get the God damn thing [over], and to prick the boil. There's no question about it. And no use to try to deal with this. And I think if Liddy's going to testify, if Hunt is going to testify, and Magruder is going to testify, that's the ball game. That's the game. And—" the president said with a chuckle in his voice, "—that will screw the Ervin committee, at least." With that the conversation ended, and the president headed over to the White House bowling alley in the basement of the EOB to enjoy his favorite exercise for about half an hour.

# Pricking the Boil and Cleaning House

I t was inevitable that the unraveling cover-up would sooner or later simply collapse. On March 21 I had made my best effort to attempt to convince the president that Haldeman, Ehrlichman and I all had serious problems with respect to the cover-up, and to warn him, so that he did not become personally enmeshed. Over three weeks had passed since both that disappointing conversation and the meetings I had had with Haldeman and Ehrlichman on the same day. I had brought my colleagues copies of sections 371 (the federal conspiracy statute) and 1503 (the federal obstruction of justice statute) from an annotated edition of Title 18 of the U.S. Code, and as the president requested, I had minced no words with them about why we were in trouble. On April 8, when I hired Charles Shaffer to talk to the Watergate prosecutors, I had urged Haldeman and Ehrlichman to likewise hire criminal defense attorneys. By mid-April, any hope I had that we could end the cover-up was fading fast. I had not spoken to Shaffer about the president, and to the prosecutors I mentioned only vague problems that suggested a cover-up, as I hoped Haldeman and Ehrlichman would admit to our mistakes as well, and if we all honestly explained what had happened, the Nixon presidency would survive.

Nixon's recorded conversations reveal that the April 14–15 weekend was a fateful turning point, when the cover-up finally collapsed. The president had immersed himself in his problems and sorted through his options. He later told Ron Ziegler that it was on April 13 that he made "the terrible decision we had to make" to remove Haldeman and Ehrlichman from the White House.[1] Over the course of that weekend, Haldeman, Ehrlichman, Mitchell, Colson and Nixon would all realize that new battle lines had to be drawn, for it had become clear to them that I was unwilling to lie or fall on my sword. It was also during this weekend that I realized my mistake in thinking that by stepping forward myself and openly going to the prosecutors, others would follow. I had encouraged Jeb Magruder and Fred LaRue to do so as well, and they had. On Friday evening, April 13, I learned that the assistant U.S. attorneys with whom my attorney had been dealing had been forced by their superiors to breach our confidentiality agreement, ending my informal working relationship with them. I still decided to make one last attempt to encourage Haldeman and Ehrlichman to admit having made serious mistakes. Thus began the process by which I was transformed from a friend and trusted staff person into a bitter enemy of my colleagues and the president. In a White House that maintained a list of its enemies, I would soon make my way to its top.

*April 14, 1973, the White House*

The president began the day with a trip to his dentist but was back in his EOB office by 8:44 A.M., and he requested that Ehrlichman and Haldeman join him.[2] This hour-and-a-half-long conversation revealed Nixon in a far more commanding, take-charge state. He clearly understood his situation and his options. He asked his top aides, when both had arrived, if they had reached any conclusions or had any recommendations. Ehrlichman said they had arrived at no conclusions, but that they did have recommendations, and they felt the president should be personally involved in unraveling Watergate. Nixon first wanted to hear again about Ehrlichman's conversation with Colson and Shapiro. In response to leading questions, Ehrlichman repeated much of what he had said earlier, adding again that Hunt had apparently decided there was no longer any point in remaining silent since others were testifying. Colson and Shapiro thought the president should get busy and nail Mitchell. "So what does Colson want us to do?" Nixon asked. Several things, Ehrlichman explained, and specified, "He wants you to persuade Liddy to talk."

"Me?" Nixon asked. "Yes sir," Ehrlichman said. Nixon said he did not recall Ehrlichman mentioning this detail previously, but Ehrlichman said he thought he had. (Nixon was correct; Ehrlichman had only referred to "the president's man" going to Liddy.) Colson wanted the president to be able to say that it was he who had cracked the case. He felt that "the next forty-eight hours are the last chance for the White House to get out in front of this, and that once Hunt goes on, then that's the ball game." Nixon needed to take "provable, identifiable steps which can be referred to later as having been the proximate cause."

The conversation turned to Magruder and what he was or was not telling reporters. Haldeman doubted Colson's account. He said Magruder claimed he had run into former White House aide Danny Hofgren at a bar in the Bahamas (where Magruder had flown to hire his lawyer) and told him, "Everybody's involved, Mitchell, Haldeman, Colson, Dean, the president." The president wondered if Magruder really believed this, but Ehrlichman assured him that Higby's tape of Magruder would "beat the socks off him if he ever gets off the reservation." Ehrlichman, who like Higby had taped conversations, said that while the practice was illegal, Higby could serve as a witness. Haldeman pointed out that it was not, in fact, illegal in the District of Columbia, where it was only necessary to have the consent of one party to secretly record telephone conversations.

After discussing Colson's motives and Magruder's perjury, the president asked Ehrlichman if Hunt would testify that he had been promised clemency. Though Ehrlichman thought not, Nixon was clearly concerned about his vulnerability: "You see, the only possible involvement of the president in this is [the clemency issue]. Now apparently, John, either you or Bob or Dean, somebody told Colson not to discuss it with me." Ehrlichman said he had, and the president wanted to know when it had happened, but not letting Ehrlichman get a word in edgewise, he continued, recalling his conversation about clemency for Hunt with Colson. "I remember a conversation, it was about five thirty or six o'clock, Colson only dropped it in sort of parenthetically. He said, 'I had a little problem today,' and we were talking about the [Watergate] defendants, and I sought to reassure him, you know, and so forth. And I said, [when he told me about the death of Hunt's wife], 'It's a terrible thing,' and I said, 'Obviously we'll do just that, we will take that into consideration.' And that was the total conversation," the president explained, putting his best spin on it.

Ehrlichman explained that Hunt had written Colson "a very 'I've-been-abandoned' kind of letter" after the election, which Colson has brought to Ehrlichman's attention. Ehrlichman said he advised Colson to talk to Hunt (which the president thought had been "good advice") but not to say "anything about clemency or a pardon," and he warned Colson that "under no circumstances should this ever be raised with the president." The president reported, "Well, he raised it, in a tangential way. Now he denies that, as I understand it, that [he told Hunt] he'd be out by Christmas." The president accurately described how Colson had dealt with Bittman, giving him that impression but avoiding "any commitment" and simply allowing Bittman to draw the conclusion he wanted.

Nixon next wanted to know how Hunt might testify regarding Colson's pressuring Magruder on Liddy's plans: "Does Colson realize his vulnerability there?" Ehrlichman said Colson felt he had no vulnerability, because Hunt and Liddy had talked only "in general terms about intelligence, and when they said intelligence, he meant one thing, and apparently they meant another." Nixon understood, noted the weakness of Colson's defense, and pushed forward: "Question: Is Hunt preparing to talk on other activities that he engaged in?" This question raised unstated matters, such as the Ellsberg break-in, which directly involved Ehrlichman, who responded he "couldn't derive that" from his conversations. When the president asked, "The U.S. attorney, I would assume, would not be pressing these things?" Ehrlichman agreed, saying, "Ordinarily not." This led to a discussion of the Greenspun operation, which Ehrlichman thought they had undertaken successfully, speculating that it had been done at the request of Hunt's employer Robert Bennett (son of a Utah U.S. senator and later himself a Utah U.S. senator), who represented a faction of the divided Howard Hughes organization.

Nixon, remaining very much in charge, said, "Hunt's testimony on payoff, of course, would be very important." Ehrlichman, who was unaware of the president roles with the money and his particular interest, thought Hunt would likely implicate the reelection committee lawyers, Paul O'Brien and Ken Parkinson. When the president pressed, Ehrlichman said Hunt would "hang them on obstruction of justice." Nixon asked if this would implicate Kalmbach as well, but Ehrlichman thought not.

"What did Dean call Kalmbach about?" the president asked. "He said we have to raise some money in connection with the aftermath, and I don't know how he described it to Herb," Ehrlichman answered, to which Haldeman added, somewhat misleadingly, "Dean says very flatly that Kalmbach did not know the purpose for the money and has no problem." Obviously Kalmbach did know that the money was going to those involved with the Watergate break-in, but little more than that. (I did, in fact, think that Kalmbach had a problem, as I would explain to both Haldeman and Ehrlichman that afternoon.) "So basically, then, Hunt will testify that it was so-called hush money, right?" Nixon asked. "I think so," Ehrlichman agreed, with the caveat, "Now again, my water can't rise any higher than its source."

They next discussed how Hunt's testimony might help him get a reduced sentence. Haldeman thought Hunt could also help himself by not calling it hush money but simply saying that he wanted to help out the families of the men he had recruited. The president liked that: "That's what it ought to be, and that's got to be the story that will be the defense of these people [involved with the money], right?" Ehrlichman acknowledged it was the only defense. Haldeman added, "That was the line that they used around here. That we've got to have money for their legal fees and family support, to support them." The president admitted, "Well, I heard something about that at a much later time. And frankly, not knowing much about obstruction of justice, I thought it was perfectly proper. Would it be proper?"

"Well, it's like the defense of the Chicago Seven," Ehrlichman said,[3] and Haldeman added, "They had a defense fund for everybody." Nixon continued, "Not only a defense fund, Christ, they took care of living expense, too. You remember the Scottsboro case? Christ, the communist front raised a million dollars for the Scottsboro people, nine hundred thousand went into the pockets of the communists."[4] As Haldeman laughed, Nixon asserted, "So it's common practice. Nevertheless, that's Hunt then, [probably] saying it was payoffs."

The president proceeded through a mental checklist, methodically moving to each item but, as was his style, returning to topics discussed the preceding evening or even earlier in the same conversation. "I think I've got the larger picture," he announced, as this conversation progressed, but what he needed to figure out was how to get credit for breaking the case—perhaps for having gotten Magruder to testify, or maybe Mitchell and Liddy. Ehrlichman, however, had been trying to position himself as the catalyst for having broken the case. He had been meeting with Magruder, Strachan, O'Brien, Haldeman and me, so he asked the president to step back and imagine how it might unravel from the point of view of a week, if not a month or so, later. "I'm trying to write the news magazine story for next Monday, a week. And if the grand jury indicts Mitchell." Ehrlichman had two versions of this imagined account. Adjusting his voice as if reading an actual news story, he offered the first version: "'The White House's main effort to cover up finally collapsed last week when the grand jury indicted John Mitchell and Jeb Magruder. Cracking the case was the testimony of a number of peripheral witnesses, each of whom contributed to developing a cross-triangulation and permitted the grand jury to analyze it,' and so on and so forth. And then, 'The final straw that broke the camel's back was an investigator's discovery of this and that and the other thing.' That's one set of facts. And then the tag on that is, 'The White House press secretary, Ron Ziegler, said the White House would have no comment.'"

Nixon groaned with displeasure at this possible turn of events, and Ehrlichman continued with the story he felt they should develop, based on information he had obtained: "The other one goes, 'Events moved swiftly last week, after the president was presented with a report indicating for the first time that suspicion of John Mitchell and Jeb Magruder as ringleaders in the Watergate break-in were in fact substantiated by considerable evidence. The president then dispatched so and so to do this and that and it'—maybe to see Mitchell or something of that kind—'and these efforts resulted in Mitchell going to the U.S. Attorney's Office on Monday morning at nine o'clock and asking to testify before the grand jury. Charges of cover up by the White House were materially dispelled by the diligent efforts of the president and his aides in moving on evidence which came to their hands in the closing days of the previous week." "I'd buy that," Nixon said, and he indicated he was ready to talk tactics.

"'Now,'" continued Ehrlichman, taking on the role of Nixon in his scenario, "'I've been concerned because, since the end of March, I have turned up a fair amount of hearsay evidence that points at this guy. Now, just take—'" Nixon interrupted, "And so did Dean, so did Dean." Ehrlichman, who was not aware of my March 21 conversation with the president, added, "'And so did John.'" But the president wanted to make clear that we really did not know if Mitchell was or was not guilty. Ehrlichman conceded that he only had hearsay but that he had listened to Higby's recording of Magruder, who "flat-out" said on the tape that he and Mitchell were guilty. So, Ehrlichman continued, "'I said to myself, "My God! I'm, you know, a United States citizen. I'm standing here listening to this, what is my duty?"'" Nixon answered, "Well, the point is, you've now told me. That's the problem." He clarified, "The problem of my position up to this time has been, quite frankly, nobody ever told me a God damn thing, that Mitchell was guilty."

"That's right," Ehrlichman agreed. "Well, we still don't know," Haldeman pointed out. "I will still argue that I think the scenario that was spun out by Dean on Mitchell is basically the right one. I don't think Mitchell did order the Watergate bugging, and I don't think he was specifically aware of the Watergate bugging at the time it was instituted." The president added, "For your information, here's what [Mitchell] told Rebozo, who he knows very well." This conversation occurred either "right after [Mitchell had testified before the grand jury] or a month ago," Nixon reported. "He told Rebozo, 'I may have perjured myself on the ITT matter but I sure didn't on this God damn thing.' Well, there you go." And Haldeman agreed that "technically that may be correct." Ehrlichman added that that was what he had told Dick Moore as well. They discussed who should confront Mitchell, and Nixon thought it should be Ehrlichman, who knew the case, rather than Rogers, whom Mitchell did not like and could "wind him around his finger."

But the president knew the relationship between Ehrlichman and Mitchell was strained, at best, so he asked Ehrlichman to explain the situation, as he saw it. "Let me put it in a setting," he began. "Mitchell has felt from the days of Haynsworth and Carswell—" referring to Mitchell's rejected recommendations while attorney general for seats on the U.S. Supreme Court, which led Nixon to interrupt, "That you were out to get him." Ehrlichman ignored the president's characterization and continued, "—that I disapproved of him, And that it fell to my lot to second-guess his operation at the Justice Department, day after day." In fact, the problem was far deeper and had real consequences, but the fact Ehrlichman acknowledged that it existed was enough to satisfy Nixon.[5]

The president told Ehrlichman, "You know the case. You've conducted the investigation for me. You have reported to me, and I have asked you to go up and lay it on the ground to Mitchell, and to tell Mitchell, look, there is only one thing that could save him. I think John's got to hear that kind of talk, and I think he's got to hear it from somebody that doesn't have—" The president caught himself from absolving Ehrlichman from any involvement, but not missing a beat, continued, "I was thinking of bringing Rogers in and telling him all this stuff, but God damn it, Mitchell will wind him around his finger."

Ehrlichman said he would do it if Nixon wanted it done but noted, "Bob has a pretty good feel of Mitchell's attitude toward me that I don't have." Haldeman said nothing in response, and after further conversation and speculation about the testimony and problems of others, Nixon returned to the subject of Mitchell. "I don't think there's anybody that can talk to Mitchell except somebody that knows this case. Now there's one or two people, I mean, I've versed myself in it enough to know the God damn thing. But I'm not sure that I want to personally know. I want to say to Mitchell, Now look, I think that the attorney for the committee, O'Brien, found out this, and I found out that, and the grand jury's going to do this.' I just don't know. They talk about my going out [and doing it], but really, I am not trying to duck it. I don't mind, I've done unpleasant things, and I'll take this in one minute. The thing, John, is that there's nobody really that can do it except you. And I know how Mitchell feels. But you conducted this investigation. The way I would do it—Bob, you critique this—is, I'd go up and I'd say, 'The president's asked me to see you.' That you have come in today with this report. These are the cold facts indicating, of course, that this does not indicate [guilt], but the grand jury is moving swiftly, Magruder will be indicted, you think. Under the circumstances, time is of the essence." The president proceeded to outline Mitchell's problem, suggesting that Ehrlichman point out that the president had assumed responsibility, and nobody in the White House is involved. He then added to the pitch for Ehrlichman to present: "'We did try to help these defendants afterward, yes.' [Mitchell] probably would not deny that, anyway. He probably was not asked that at an earlier time. But, just as any, the defendants are entitled to that sort of—"

"Well, now you're glossing it," Ehrlichman protested, as it was getting into what he was calling the aftermath, which he did not think he should bring up. The president, understanding, backed off and asked Ehrlichman for his version of his confrontation speech to Mitchell. Ehrlichman's points were a bit more blunt: The jig is up. Magruder's going to blow. It's now time to rethink what best serves the president. You are not going to escape indictment. It would be better if you were prosecuted on an "information" [a voluntary plea] rather than an "indictment [from the grand jury] by fifteen blacks and three whites." Mitchell would get credit for stepping forward, and it would serve the president's interests. Both Haldeman and the president occasionally added suggestions to this approach, and when Ehrlichman finished, they all speculated about how Mitchell might or might not react.

When inquiring about when I might be going to the grand jury, the president obviously recalled our March 21 conversation. "How does Dean, incidentally, what is the liability, or Hunt, or I'm thinking of the payoff thing, in this business," he began, juggling his thoughts over how much information he wanted to share; the following passage is reprinted verbatim to indicate Nixon's concern about this subject: "Dean, Dean, ah, Dean asked, told me about the problem of Hunt's lawyer wanted, had gotten, this was a few weeks ago, needed sixty thousand or forty thousand dollars or something like that. You remember? He asked me about it, and I said I don't know where you can get it. I said I would, I mean, I frankly felt he might try to get it, but I didn't know where. And then he left it up with Mitchell, and Mitchell then said it was taken care of, am I correct? Is my recollection?" Ehrlichman answered, "Yes, sir." Nixon asked Ehrlichman, "Is that approximately correct? Did he talk to you about that?" Ehrlichman answered, "He talked to me about it. I said, John, I wouldn't have the vaguest notion where to get it. I saw Mitchell later in the day, Wednesday, [I think]," Ehrlichman recalled.* "What happened?" Nixon asked. "And he just said, it's taken care of," Ehrlichman reported.

Haldeman added his own recollection: "Mitchell raised the topic. He turned to Dean and said, 'What have you done about that other problem?' And Dean kind of looked at us and then said, 'Well, you know, I don't know.' And Mitchell said, 'Oh, I guess that's been taken care of.'" Haldeman then reported I had told them later that it had been taken care of by LaRue, who, I advised them, was going to cooperate with the prosecutors. Haldeman added, "Oh, Dean told us he had a long talk with LaRue, and LaRue said, 'This whole thing is ridiculous now,' and [added] 'If I were in charge of this now, what I would do is, I'd get a large bus, and I'd put the president at the wheel, and I'd throw everybody we've got around here in it, and I'd drive up to the Senate, and I'd have the president open the door, and I'd say, you all get out and tell everything you know, and I'll be back to pick you up when you're through.' He said, 'It's all out now, and there's nothing we can do about it.' And LaRue also said, you know, 'I can't figure out how I got into this to begin with, but it seems to me all of us have been drawn in here in trying to cover up for John.'"

"For Mitchell?" the president asked. "Yeah, which is exactly what's happened," Haldeman added. The discussion of LaRue ended when Haldeman pointed out that LaRue was going to tell the truth and take responsibility for his actions: "I think LaRue's figured that the jig is up."

After the president clarified that no one had ever discussed clemency for Liddy, or for anyone other than Hunt, with him, he returned to the hush money and offered his version of our March 21 conversation: "Dean told me an interesting thing; when I said [to] Dean, 'John, where's it all lead?' I said, 'What's it going to cost, if you continue on this course? He said about a mil-

---

*In fact, it was Thursday morning, March 22, 1973, at 11:00 A.M. in Haldeman's office, as Ehrlichman's desk calendar reveals.

lion dollars. I said facetiously, '[That's a lot]. I know where you can get that.' That's the point. That's the foul-up in the whole Mitchell argument. Unless I could just up and say, 'Look, fellows, it's too bad,' and I could give you executive clemency, like tomorrow, what the hell do you think, Dean, I mean, do you think Hunt and the Cubans are going to sit on their ass in jail for four years and their families not [be] taken care of? That's the point. Now where the hell do you get the money for that? That's the reason this whole thing falls. I mean, that astonishes me about Mitchell and the rest. It's not only improbable, there's no way to get the money, is there? Who was it, Tom Pappas they had to see me?"

Haldeman confirmed that it was Pappas but remained very vague. The president recalled that Haldeman had told him that Pappas "was helping on the money," but Haldeman reminded the president that he was seeing a number of contributors, and Pappas "was Mitchell's contact." The president recalled that he was careful with "good old Tom" when thanking him for raising money "for the purpose of helping the poor bastards through the jail." But when Nixon asked Ehrlichman how long this financial support could be provided, Ehrlichman said he had no idea, although he and the president acknowledged that the Berrigan brothers had funds.

They briefly discussed how long I should remain at the White House, and when the president said he was ready to let me go, Ehrlichman cautioned that that might not be the right decision. He said he felt that I might receive better treatment by the grand jury and the U.S. attorney if I were kept on, which he thought important. Haldeman concurred that they would treat me differently as "the dismissed president's counsel" and Ehrlichman added that dismissal was "a very heavy psychological factor." The president agreed to keep me on, since there was no reason not to do so, and noted, "Dean is not like Mitchell now, let's face it. Dean is not like Mitchell in the sense that Dean only tried to do what he could to pick up the God damn pieces, and everybody else around here knew it had to be done."

They next discussed my involvement in "the aftermath," the now-accepted euphemism for the cover-up. Haldeman noted, "The known involvement in the aftermath was for what was understood here to be the proper purpose." The president said, "The question of motive." "That's number one," Ehrlichman said, and his second reason was based on his investigation. "There were eight or ten people around here who knew about this, knew it was going on," Ehrlichman said, regarding the aftermath. "Bob knew, I knew, all kinds of people knew." Nixon added, "Well, I knew it, I knew it." Realizing what he had just confessed, and possibly realizing that it had been recorded, the president immediately tried, rather awkwardly to retract it. "I knew, I must say though, I didn't know it. But I must have assumed it, though, but, you know, fortunately, and I thank you both for arranging it that way, and it does show why the isolation of the president is a bad position to be in." Ehrlichman, apparently unable to contain his disbelief at Nixon's sudden reversal and claims of ignorance, punctuated the president's comments with several guttural "humpf" sounds. These seemed to invoke a bit of candor from Nixon; he continued: "But the first time that I knew that they had to have money was the time when Dean told me that they needed forty thousand dollars." Nixon then gave a confused description of what he did not know and added, "But others did know."

"The point is," Ehrlichman said, "that if the wrongdoing which justifies Dean's dismissal is his knowledge that that operation was going on, then you can't stop with him. You've got to go through this whole place wholesale." This got the president's attention: "Fire the whole staff?" "That's right," Ehrlichman answered. "It's a question of motive. It's a question of role, and I don't think Dean's role in the aftermath, at least from the facts that I know now, achieves a level of wrongdoing that requires you terminate him." Nixon thought that a powerful point and added, "You can be pragmatic and say, well, Christ, cut your losses and get rid of him. I mean, give them an hors d'oeuvre, and maybe they won't come back for the main course. Go out, John Dean. On the other hand, it is true others did know." The president instructed Ehrlichman to have a talk with me, particularly about motive. He said he had, and explained that I became involved because Mitchell had kept turning to me for help, and I would come back to Ehrlichman and Haldeman at his request. Mitchell would send the message, "These guys, Hunt's getting jittery, and says that he's got to have umpty-ump thousand dollars, and Mitchell's terribly worried about it, and it was never expressed, but it was certainly understood." When the president pressed as to whether I had ever discussed the motive, Ehrlichman could not recall, although both he and Haldeman did remember that they had referred me to Kalmbach to raise money, which soon led into another discussion of the $350,000 being returned to the reelection committee.*

---

*While it is possible they had forgotten during this conversation, later they simply denied that I had come to Camp David after the election with an audiocassette of Hunt's conversation with Colson, demanding money from him, that made it very clear that the Watergate defendants expected to be paid for their silence. Dean Senate testimony, 3 Senate Select Committee on Presidential Campaign Activities (SSC) 969.

This conversation ended with Ehrlichman's again selling the president on his investigation, which was supposedly broader than my nonexistent report. He said he had examined the full picture of what had happened while I had only probed to determine if there was any White House involvement. When the subject turned to bracing Magruder, the president said that Ehrlichman should start by telling him "of the president's own great affection for" him and his family. Haldeman recommended taking the same stance with Mitchell, and the president agreed. The president said he was doing to Ehrlichman what President Eisenhower had done to him as vice president when he sent Nixon to deal with Eisenhower's chief of staff, Sherman Adams.[6] When referring to the impact of my testimony on Mitchell, not to mention others, Haldeman noted, "If Dean testifies, it's going to unscramble the whole omelet." And after further discussion about Mitchell and Magruder, Haldeman and Ehrlichman departed for Ehrlichman's office, with the president requesting they report when they had further information.

I had spent Saturday morning in my office with my attorney, Charles Shaffer. Over the prior week I had given him general information about the cover-up, still excluding any discussion of the president's role. I had only incidentally described Mitchell's, Haldeman's and Ehrlichman's roles in the affair, as it had been necessary to do so to explain my own actions. Shaffer had little doubt that those who would likely be indicted for what we called "pre" activities (relating to the planning and execution of the Watergate break-in) would include at least, in addition to the original defendants, Mitchell and Magruder, but we placed a question mark by Strachan. I took out a yellow note pad, and we added those for whom we thought my testimony might result in "post" indictments for what I called the "post" activities—the events after the arrests on June 17, 1972. For the post candidates I listed: "H" (Haldeman), "E" (Ehrlichman), "JWD" (me), "LaRue," "Mardian?" "O'Brien," "Parkinson?" "Colson?" "Bittman?" "Kalmbach/Tony (Ulasewicz)?/source [thinking of Pappas and others who had provided funds]" and "Stans?" Beside the names of those on this later list I added the statutes and their penalties: "Potential O/J" (obstruction of justice), "§371 5/$10" (five years and ten-thousand-dollar fine) and "§1503 5/$5" (five years and five-thousand-dollar fine).[7]

Shortly after noon, with my list in hand, I went to Ehrlichman's office. Just as I knew he was going to tell Mitchell that the time for resolution had come, I was trying to do the same with Haldeman and Ehrlichman. I told them I had considered the exposure of everyone involved with my attorney, and we had prepared a list of who might be indicted for conspiracy to obstruct justice. More important, I told them that Shaffer had learned that they were now targets of the grand jury, just as was I. My new information momentarily startled both men, because it conflicted with reassurances Ehrlichman had received from Kleindienst only days earlier. Ehrlichman, however, dismissed my warning as pure speculation. While I had discussed the facts with them in a similar conversation on March 21, I reminded them that what I was sharing with them today were the opinions of a seasoned criminal attorney. Shaffer had counseled me to share only conclusions and not get into details. Given the fact that Ehrlichman was busy secretly taping his conversations, it was good advice.[8] While the tone of the meeting was friendly, for they recognized that I was trying to help both the president and them, it was very clear that neither of them was going to acknowledge that he had done anything wrong. As Ehrlichman said to me, "I think something putrid has gotten into your drinking water over there in Old Town, where you live."

Haldeman left the session in Ehrlichman's office to meet with Magruder, and at 1:55 P.M. returned to the Oval Office to report on that discussion. Meanwhile Mitchell had arrived and was still meeting with Ehrlichman.[9] Haldeman told Nixon that Magruder had decided the night before to tell all, and "his lawyers met with Silbert today." He was not requesting immunity, "because he didn't feel entitled to it." Magruder had made his decision after realizing that the matter had reached an endpoint: "They've got witnesses on witnesses now, and there's no reason for [him] to be quiet," Magruder had said, and related that the only thing Magruder hoped to get out of coming forward was a lighter sentence. He told Haldeman he was guilty "on six or eight counts of perjury, two counts of conspiracy and two counts of obstruction of justice [with possible] sentences of 135 to 160 years in jail," though his lawyers had yet to make a deal. "He told me that whole thing in an unbroken voice and showed more strength than I thought he had, to be perfectly frank," Haldeman said. Magruder also had advised Haldeman that others involved at the reelection committee—Fred LaRue and Bart Porter— were going to cooperate with the prosecutors, although Mitchell was not. Haldeman had had this conversation with Magruder just as Mitchell was arriving, so he was able to share the gist of it with Ehrlichman. The president asked about "the aftermath," but Haldeman did not believe Magruder knew anything about it. Haldeman surmised that Magruder's testimony would hurt both Strachan and me.

Ehrlichman arrived in the Oval Office with Haldeman accompanying him at 2:24 P.M. to report on his meeting with Mitchell.[10] "He is an innocent man in his heart, and in his mind, and he does not intend to move off that position," Ehrlichman said. When the president said he wanted "chapter and verse," Ehrlichman proceeded to recount their exchange in greater detail, as best he could recall it. Mitchell's position was "You know, these characters pulled this thing off without my knowledge." He claimed, contrary to Magruder, "I never saw Liddy for months at a time. I didn't know what they were up to. Nobody was more surprised than I was." When Ehrlichman pointed out that Mitchell had "lobbed mud balls at the White House at every opportunity," Mitchell claimed that "the origin, of course, was in the White House, where Bob Haldeman and [Mitchell] talked about something called the Operation Sandwedge. That was really the grandfather of this whole thing. And, of course, that was never put together because we couldn't get the right people to do it. They were talking about Joe Woods and people of that kind, so it never happened."

Ehrlichman said he played Mitchell "with kid gloves" and, more specifically, he explained, "In fact, I never asked him to tell me anything. He just came forward with all this stuff." Ehrlichman said they speculated on my and Magruder's testimony and that Mitchell's "characterization of all this is that he was a very busy man, and he wasn't keeping track of what was going on at the committee, that this was engendered as a result of Hunt and Liddy coming to Colson's office and getting Colson to make a phone call to Magruder, and that he, Mitchell, was not aware that all that had happened until [a committee aide, Van Shumway] brought Liddy into Mitchell's office sometime in June, and that's the first knowledge he had of it."

Haldeman asked if that was before or after the arrests, and Ehrlichman did not know but said that it could be checked, because he had taped the conversation. Ehrlichman said he raised with Mitchell Magruder's account of bringing him a memo with targets, and his checking off those he wanted pursued, but Mitchell denied it (although he had admitted it to Haldeman on March 28, which he had recorded in his diary). Haldeman interrupted to clarify that, while he had not checked off anything, Mitchell had approved Liddy's operation.[11] Mitchell also told Ehrlichman that a lot of his problems with Liddy were that Liddy was a name-dropper. Mitchell indicated that he planned to defend himself every way he could, but he understood he could never get a fair trial in Washington, D.C. He regretted that so much was going to redound on the White House.

Ehrlichman reported that they discussed the money, particularly the $350,000 that had come from the White House. As he went through Mitchell's recollections, Haldeman corroborated most of Mitchell's account, and the president wanted Strachan informed so that he would get his own testimony correct. Mitchell said he was not aware of anyone's going to the defendants and telling them not to testify, and Ehrlichman quoted him as saying, "I wasn't really worried about what they testified to. I was worried about what they'd say to the press." Haldeman noted, "That, somehow, Dean doesn't see that, that way," nor would anyone else when this claim was made to justify the payments. "Oh," Ehrlichman remembered, "I told him that the only way that I knew that he was mentioned, insofar as the aftermath was concerned, was that from time to time he would send Dean over saying, 'Hey, we need money for this,' and [Mitchell] said, 'Who told you that?'" Haldeman jumped in with "John Dean." Ehrlichman, taking Haldeman's statement as his own, continued, "And I said [to Mitchell], 'John, that's common knowledge. And Dean, among others, has told me that.'" Then, unaware that I had personally told Mitchell that I was talking to the prosecutors, Ehrlichman said that I had not been subpoenaed, which was true, nor had I testified, which was also true, but then said, "The way they are proceeding down there [at the U.S. Attorney's Office], it looks like they are losing interest in [Dean]." When the president corrected him, Ehrlichman admitted that he had been spinning the facts, because he did not want Mitchell to think they were "jobbing him." When Ehrlichman reported that Mitchell was claiming that it was the fault of the White House, because, in effect, Haldeman, Colson and Dean, working through Magruder, had frozen him out, Haldeman said, "He's got an impossible problem with that." To which Ehrlichman added, "The poor guy is punting." (Ehrlichman failed to mention to the president—or had lumped it into "mud throwing by Mitchell"—a fact captured on Ehrlichman's recording of their meeting: Namely, Mitchell thought the cover-up had been necessary because of Hunt's and Liddy's activities while they worked at the White House, which Mitchell had felt more serious threats to the president's reelection than Watergate.[12])

Ehrlichman and Haldeman discussed Mitchell's tremor, which Ehrlichman thought worse than usual, and the president broke the silence that followed. "You've done your duty today. What's the next question?" Haldeman responded that it was whether Ehrlichman should see Magruder at four o'clock. Ehrlichman thought there was no longer any purpose, and Haldeman remarked that Magruder would do as Mitchell wanted. But the president, thinking ahead, said he thought the purpose was to make a record, since Ehrlichman was secretly recording these sessions. "For that purpose, maybe I should," Ehrlichman conceded. After discussing what they should and should not say to Magruder, the discussion turned again to me.

"I think we owe it to ourselves," the president said, "to find out about John Dean, for example, what he now understands, what he thinks." Ehrlichman agreed, saying, "This is probably a golden opportunity, in a way." The president was blunt. "[W]ell, let me put it this way: We've got to find out what the hell he's going to say." Not as anxious about this matter as the president, Ehrlichman and Haldeman let the conversation drift back to Magruder and Mitchell, until Ehrlichman injected a point I had made to him regarding those on my indictable list: "Dean argues that in a conspiracy, such as they are trying to build, they may not have to prove the same kind of animus as to some of the participants, but only that they were in [the conspiracy]. I would have to read the cases. I just don't know what the law is."

Soon Ehrlichman brought up our earlier meeting, at which I had gone over the indictable list with him and Haldeman. After speculation about the possibility of Colson's being indicted, Ehrlichman sighed and said, "Dean seems to think everybody in the place is going to get indicted," which produced nervous laughter. "What Dean said is just looking at the worst possible side of the coin," Haldeman offered. "That you could make a list of everybody who in some way is technically indictable in the cover-up operation. And that list includes, in addition to Mitchell, Haldeman, Ehrlichman, Colson, Dean, Strachan, Kalmbach, Kalmbach's go-between, Kalmbach's source, LaRue, Mardian, O'Brien, Parkinson, Hunt and, you know, just keep wandering through the impossible. He said maybe the route is for everybody on that list to take a guilty plea and get immediate, what do you call it, clemency," he said after being prompted by Ehrlichman. "That shows you the somewhat unclear state," he chuckled, "of John Dean's analytical thinking."[13]

The president wanted to know if he had requested an independent investigation at the time McCord sent his letter. "I was ready to report to you my tentative conclusions, and you wanted it turned over to the Department of

Justice," Ehrlichman explained, as they concocted a new potential scenario. "If Mitchell is indicted, you think he's going to be convicted?" the president asked. Ehrlichman did, particularly since Magruder had gone to the prosecutors. "But that's only one man," Nixon protested, and Ehrlichman assured him that that was sufficient. As Ehrlichman headed off to meet with Magruder, the president said, "Be sure you convey my warm sentiments."

Haldeman and the president sat silently for a minute, until Haldeman said, "I think I ought to get Strachan squared away," adding, "The only sticky wicket on that is Dean. I can't understand, because it's in his interest too, as well as everyone else's, to see the [money] motive for what it was"—that is, for purportedly humanitarian reasons. After several more lengthy pauses, with each man deep in his own thoughts, Haldeman departed.

Late that afternonn, Ehrlichman and Haldeman went to the EOB office to report on the meeting with Magruder and his lawyers, who Ehrlichman reported had just come from an informal conference with the U.S. attorney.[14] Haldeman, who had discussed the matter with Ehrlichman on the way, described it as the "same old sticky wickets, but no new one," and noted that it was "much rougher on Dean." Ehrlichman took the president through Magruder's latest account.[15] A few interesting details were featured, particularly that Colson was pushing for information on Larry O'Brien at the time he called Magruder to encourage approval of the Liddy projects.* Magruder said that only he received a copy of the results of Liddy's bugging at the DNC, which he then showed to Mitchell, who "thought it was a lot of junk, too." He described the pictures taken by Liddy's team inside the DNC as being of the "the kind of papers you'd find lying around a campaign." He also said that Mitchell had found this information so useless that "he picked up the phone and called Liddy and chewed him out." (There can be little doubt that Liddy, embarrassed by this call, used it as a pretext for returning to the DNC on June 17, 1972, later telling McCord and Hunt that they were proceeding on direct orders from Mitchell.) Magruder said the June 17 scheme "was entirely on Liddy's own motion [and that] neither Mitchell or Magruder knew that another break-in was contemplated." (Based on Magruder's consistent account of this second break-in, Liddy's own later account appears invented after the fact.[16])

"As I listened to this the second time around, let me tell you what my

---

*See Appendix A.

concerns are," Haldeman said of Magruder's session with Ehrlichman. "I think when he got down to it, he told the truth. And when he is talking to us, at least, he is bringing us into it. He will, for instance, want to elaborate on Sandwedge and say I was involved in it. Now to the extent that I listened to a presentation, I was. But I, at the time, said, 'This is something I don't want to be involved in, and something that should not be handled in here. Don't come to me any more with it,' and they didn't. And then they'll say I was also involved in the meetings. But [Dean] came to me after that second meeting and said, 'They came up with, you know, with the plans, a preposterous plan. And I told him that it can't be done. They shouldn't even be talking about it in the attorney general's office.' I said, 'John, get out of it. You stay out of it, too.' And he did. He said he would stay out of it from then on, and I suspect he did. But they'll tie me in that way, by indirection. Maybe that sounds like everybody goes down with the ship, but when it comes to this cover-up business, expanding on the three fifty, I have not felt uncomfortable with that, but Dean is extremely uncomfortable with it."

Ehrlichman thought he should speak with Kleindienst, with which the president agreed, and the call was recorded on the president's telephone.[17] After rehearsing what he would say with the president, Ehrlichman told Kleindienst that Magruder had paid a visit to the U.S. Attorney's Office, had changed his testimony, and had implicated Mitchell and others. "Christ almighty," Kleindienst responded. Magruder's attorneys had been alarmed that Charles Shaffer seemed to have obtained secret information from the grand jury, a concern Magruder had undoubtedly stoked because I had told him he would not be indicted after his first grand jury experience. I did have inside information from Henry Petersen, and Shaffer's source was Sy Glanzer, so nothing was improper. But Ehrlichman and Kleindienst speculated about it, and Kleindienst warned Ehrlichman to be careful with the information he now possessed.

After Ehrlichman completed his call, Haldeman got down to very serious business: a discussion of his resignation. In earlier conversations the president had dismissed such an idea, but now he was willing to entertain it. Haldeman was not offering his resignation outright but was effectively forcing the president to ask for it. "You've got a really crunchy decision," he told the president, "which is whether you want me to resign or whether you don't. That's one you've got to figure out. The problem with that is, if I go on the basis of the Segretti matter, you got to let Dean go on the basis of his implication, which is far worse." He noted that Strachan had left the White House, so he was not dealing with a member of his staff, which he felt relieved him of responsibility as well as liability. But, Haldeman added, "if they waited awhile, and Ehrlichman's brought in, you then are going to have to let him go." Nixon said nothing as he pondered these matters.

Ehrlichman returned to the conversation I had had with them earlier, when I told him that he and Haldeman were indictable. He told the president, without getting into details, that he was unconcerned about his dealings with Kalmbach (although my analysis would later prove correct, and Kalmbach would be a devastating witness against him). "Dean's got sort of a hypothesis that he's developing in our conversation that referring him to Kalmbach was almost, was actionable. As a matter of fact, I didn't refer him to Kalmbach. He came to me and said, 'May I go to Kalmbach?'" Haldeman jumped in and said, "He did the same thing to me." Nixon posed a key question: "Go to Kalmbach for the purpose of?" "For the purpose of getting Herb to raise some money," Ehrlichman replied. "For the purpose of paying the defendants. For the purpose of keeping them, quote, on the reservation, unquote." The president repeated the concern I had raised with Ehrlichman and Haldeman: "With that they could try to tie you and Bob in a conspiracy to obstruct justice." "That's his theory," Ehrlichman replied. But it was not a theory on my part, rather an effort to convince them that we had all unwittingly walked into a conspiracy to obstruct justice, and that the best way to deal with the situation was to be truthful. The president recognized that Ehrlichman had just effectively admitted that he and Haldeman were part of a conspiracy to obstruct justice.[18] But when it became clear to him that neither man was conceding this point, he asked Ehrlichman what he and Haldeman would say their motive was in the aftermath. "Well, as far as I can reconstruct it," Ehrlichman began, and conceding that "I may be putting it favorably," he said their concern was not what the defendants would testify to before the grand jury, which was secret, but whether they would go out and sell their stories to the *Saturday Evening Post* or *Life* magazine. "We weren't protecting anybody," Haldeman declared. The president added a footnote to this discussion, saying, "I wish we could keep Dean away from that."

That evening, before heading to the White House Correspondents' Association dinner, the president dictated a long entry for his diary.*[19] Because

*See Appendix A.

of the events that followed, his April 14 diary entry was the last he would make for fourteen months, until June 1974, when his presidency was rapidly disintegrating. While Nixon, Haldeman, Ehrlichman and Kleindienst were attending the dinner, at the U.S. Department of Justice the assistant U.S. attorneys running the Watergate investigation, based on what they had learned from Magruder the day before and me earlier, believed they had basically broken the case. They had been calling their boss, Henry Petersen, all day, and when they finally reached him that evening they told him it was urgent that they meet with him immediately.[20] In his office that evening they shared the facts they had obtained from Magruder, and off-the-record—and inadmissible against anyone—from me. The reason I had insisted on confidentiality was to prevent this information from being used to further the cover-up at the White House, which is exactly what happened. That night Petersen, joined by Silbert and Titus, went to see Kleindienst at his home when he returned from the correspondents' dinner to brief him on the fast-developing Watergate case.

When the president returned to the White House after the dinner he changed from his formal attire and settled into the Lincoln Sitting Room. At 11:02 P.M. he spoke with Haldeman, who praised his remarks at the event.[21] The president said he had told Bebe Rebozo about Mitchell, so he would not be surprised, then added, "One thing that occurs to me, Bob, is this, as I reflect a little on Magruder's stuff. I'll be damned if I don't think that some of that could be, you know, exaggeration. But, I just don't know. He's obviously flailing around like a wild man at the present time." They both doubted Magruder actually knew the truth and had speculated about others as well. This brief conversation ended with Nixon wrapping himself in his presidency for his loyal chief of staff. The White House correspondents had awarded him a silver globe as a "peace award" for his accomplishments as president. Nixon said, "Rather interesting to me tonight that, you know, when you really think of, what the hell, here we are, it's really quite true, without being melodramatic. The hopes for peace in this damn world do depend on this office right now, in the next four years and, God damn it, we've got to be sure that that isn't compromised by anything that indicates any lack of confidence in the president, isn't that what it gets down to?"

Six minutes later the president called Ehrlichman to inquire about his plans for the following day.[22] Ehrlichman said he had calls coming from Kalmbach's attorney and wanted to "see Dean in the morning also." He also hoped to see Kleindienst, and Nixon told him to brief Colson on Magruder's testimony. As the conversation progressed, the president said, "You know, I was just thinking tonight as I was making up my notes for this little talk," referring again to the White House correspondents' dinner. "You know, what the hell, I mean, it is a little melodramatic, but it's totally true that what happens in this office in these next four years will probably determine whether there is a chance for some sort of uneasy peace for the next twenty-five years. And that's my, whatever legacy we had, hell, it isn't going to be in getting a cesspool for Winnetka. It's going to be there."

When the conversation turned back to Magruder, the president bluntly dismissed him as "a very facile liar." Ehrlichman agreed, saying, "Believes his own stories" but pointed out, "He comes across very sincere, very earnest and very believable." They speculated on how Magruder would impact Mitchell and whom Mitchell would hire to represent him. The president assured Ehrlichman that he was not going to allow the Congress or the country to force Haldeman out of his job if he was innocent.

"Well, John, you've had a hell of a week, two weeks and, of course, Bob is going through the tortures of the damned." Ehrlichman agreed that Haldeman's "family thing is rough."* But that was not what the president meant. "Here's a guy that, Christ, has just given his life, hours and hour and hours, you know, totally selfless and honest and decent. That's another thing, God damn it to hell," he began, and in a stuttering, emotional sentence said he could not fire someone just because charges were made. "Jesus Christ, I mean, you can't do that, John. Or am I wrong? I don't know." Ehrlichman assured him his judgment was correct, but the president pushed him further. "But, how do you feel, honestly? I mean, apart from the personal feelings we both have for Bob. You know, I raised this myself. I said, well, one way out is, say, 'Well, look, as long as all these guys have been charged, out they go, and then they can fight this battle, and they can return when they get cleared.' Not good, is it?" Ehrlichman replied, "I don't think that's any way to run a railroad."

The president said he was thinking of drawing a line and asked, "You're going to talk to Dean. What are you going to say to him?" "Well, I'm going to try and get him around a bit, but it's going to be delicate," Ehrlichman ex-

---

*Haldeman's youngest son, Peter, had just been expelled from Sidwell Friends, a private school in Washington. As Peter later wrote, these were very difficult years for him. Peter Haldeman, "Growing Up Haldeman," *New York Times Magazine*, April 3, 1994.

plained. Nixon questioned, "Get him around in what way?" "Well," Ehrlichman answered, "to get off this passing-the-buck business. It's a little touchy,
and I don't know how far I can go." Nixon effectively wanted Ehrlichman to
tell me that giving complete testimony was not going to help me, and he said:
"Look, he's got to look down the road to one point. But there's only one man
that could restore him to the ability to practice law in the case things still go
wrong. Now he's got to have that in the back of his mind. And he's got to know
that'll happen," the president said, but he instructed Ehrlichman not to make
any such veiled offer of clemency to me. Not only did he want me to toe a line
that would not cause him problems, he wanted Ehrlichman to make sure
everyone had a consistent account. The president noted, "I think you thought
I was sort of being facetious about saying, get everybody, all these people, and
this includes LaRue, and Mardian, and of course, Kalmbach, they've got to
have it, and Dean, too. They've got to have a straight damn line that of course
we raised money. Be very honest about it. But we raised money for a purpose
that we thought was perfectly proper. But we didn't want to shut them up.
These men were guilty. Right?" Again Ehrlichman agreed.

"And we weren't trying to shut them up; we just didn't want them to talk
to the press. That's perfectly legitimate, isn't it? Or is it?" "I think it is," Ehrlichman hedged. "I don't have a perfect understanding of the law on that,"
he conceded.

"The president is calling the signals," Nixon declared and told Ehrlichman, "You can say that the president, because of the charges that have
been made, wanted an independent investigation made, and he ordered,
directed you to make it. You've made an independent investigation of the
situation, because the president wants, if there's anybody who is guilty in
this thing, he must, through the judicial process, be brought to the bar. Is that
what you'd say?" They rehearsed it all, including how Ehrlichman would try
to bring me around.

"Well, with Dean, I think you could talk to him in confidence about a
thing like that, don't you?" the president asked. "I'm not sure. I just don't
know how much to lean on that reed at the moment. But I'll sound it out,"
Ehrlichman assured the president. They further rehearsed what Ehrlichman
would say to me and how far he could push. "Well, get a good night's sleep,"
Nixon finally said. "It's painful, and I just feel better about getting the God
damn thing done. And after all, it's my job, and I don't want the presidency
tarnished, but also, I, I, I'm a law enforcement man."

Meanwhile, a few miles away, Kleindienst was still meeting with Petersen, Titus and Silbert. They all agreed that Kleindienst should meet with the president alone, without Haldeman and Ehrlichman present—and that Kleindienst needed to get to the president without tipping off either man.

## April 15, 1973, the White House

Because the president had stayed up late talking with Bebe, he slept in on Sunday morning. When Kleindienst tried to phone him at 8:41 A.M., Steve Bull took the call and the attorney general's message that he needed to speak with the president. Bull relayed this information to Ehrlichman, who said he should go ahead and pass it on to the president, which he did while Nixon was having breakfast in at 9:45 A.M. *The Washington Post* had a glaring front-page headline—"NEW MAJORITY" GROWING DISILLUSIONED WITH NIXON—above a highly negative story by seasoned political reporters Haynes Johnson and Jules Witcover.[23] At 10:13 A.M. the president called Kleindienst from a residence telephone not connected to the recording system. Kleindienst requested an urgent meeting without either Haldeman or Ehrlichman present, and the president told him to come to the church service at the White House at eleven o'clock that morning, and they could then meet in his EOB office, after the services and reception.

At 10:35 A.M. the president asked Ehrlichman to join him in the Oval Office, where they spoke for forty-five minutes, putting Ehrlichman's in-progress meeting with Strachan on hold. Nixon informed Ehrlichman about the call from the attorney general and asked, "Kleindienst said he had been up most of the night with Titus. Who is Titus?" Ehrlichman told him Titus was the U.S. attorney for the District of Columbia. The president assumed they wanted to discuss "this special prosecutor thing" and asked what line he should take. Ehrlichman did not have a firm position, but the president did: The "problem with the special prosecutor, as I see it, it just puts another loose cannon right there rolling around the deck. Tear the hell out of the place. I think we've had enough of the damn thing myself, now I'll have to hard-line it. Dick [Kleindienst] has not been, let's face it, very helpful throughout this thing."

Nixon said he had been "cogitating last night" about the situation and thought the main problem was "on the obstruction of justice thing." They discussed who knew about that who might be a problem and came up with the names of the attorneys: Rothblatt and Bittman. "Bittman was an instigator of the whole thing," Ehrlichman explained. "He was concerned about his fees. So he was one of the active promoters of that, as near as I can tell." The president asked him to spell it out on "the obstruction thing": "What was involved? I mean just from our side, from our guys?"

Ehrlichman had come up on the learning curve regarding obstruction, so he gave a perfectly legal explanation of the motives: "Well, you had defendants who were concerned about their families, and that's understandable. You had lawyers who were concerned about their fees, and that's less understandable. You have, well, I mean in terms of the end result, you had a campaign organization that was concerned about the success of its campaign and didn't want these fellows to say anything in public that would disrupt the campaign." "Is that legitimate to want people not to say it out in public?" the president asked. Ehrlichman thought it was but admitted, "Alright, but at the same time, a lot of those same people who had that legitimate motive had an illegitimate motive, because they were involved in protecting their own culpability, and here we're talking about LaRue, Magruder, Mitchell possibly." "[You mean] they wanted the defendants to shut up in court?" the president asked bluntly. "Certainly," Ehrlichman replied.

"Let's take Dean as a case in point," Nixon said, wanting to know if, in the framework of Ehrlichman's analysis, I could get out of it somehow. Ehrlichman, who had yet to grasp the full implication of the conspiracy law, replied, "Well, see, Dean's problem is that he was in touch with these committee people who could to Dean express a benign motive and at the same time have had a corrupt motive. If I were Dean I would develop a defense that I was being manipulated by people who had a corrupt motive for ostensibly a benign motive." As for himself, he was only concerned that Hunt had written forty books, and he could see "Hunt writing an inside exposé of how he broke into the Democratic National Headquarters at the request of the Committee to Re-elect the President." Ehrlichman assured the president, "Oh, I didn't care what Howard Hunt said to the prosecutors. He could have said anything he wanted to the prosecutors in a secret session, that didn't hurt us. The grand jury was secret." Ehrlichman soon added, "I can say in truth and candor that Dean never explained to me that there was any kind of a deal to get these guys to lie or change their stories or refuse to testify to the trial of the action or anything of that kind. That was just never discussed. So I don't feel too uncomfortable with this."[24]

Following the White House church service, the president had Kleindienst ushered to his EOB office for a meeting that lasted a little over an hour.[25] While much of what Kleindienst and Petersen had learned from their U.S. attorneys had left them startled and unsettled, it came as no news to Nixon. The president later noted that "Kleindienst was highly emotional, and his voice choked periodically," and "his eyes were red with fatigue and tears."[26] Although Kleindienst was surprised that I was talking to the U.S. Attorney's Office, I had told my colleagues that I was doing so, so it did not surprise Nixon. Kleindienst did report that what my lawyer and I were telling the prosecutors was off-the-record unless we made a deal and that my lawyer was seeking immunity for me. Kleindienst also informed the president that I had, off the record, implicated Haldeman and Ehrlichman in the cover-up. When the president told Kleindienst that he had asked Haldeman and Ehrlichman if they had any complicity, and they denied it, Kleindienst soft-pedaled the little information I had received from the prosecutors, suggesting it was about merely moral indiscretions, not crimes. Nonetheless, he said both should resign.

They then had a broad, if not confused, discussion of obstruction of justice, with Kleindienst explaining that it all depended on motive.[27] When the president pressed for information on what I had told the U.S. attorney, Kleindienst replied that I had reported to Haldeman on the meetings in Mitchell's office with Magruder and Liddy and thought that I had turned it off. He also mentioned my discussion of the $350,000 being used to pay defendants as it related to Haldeman. As for Ehrlichman, Kleindienst told Nixon that I had said that Ehrlichman had instructed me to tell Hunt to get out of the country on June 19, 1972, which I had done, although I had quickly retracted the message I had sent Hunt through Liddy, who was not sure he could reverse it. In addition, Ehrlichman had told me to "deep six" the material found in Hunt's safe, which I had refused to do. This information about Ehrlichman was new to the president.

Approximately fifty-one minutes into this conversation with Kleindienst the tape abruptly ends, and the last nineteen minutes are missing. In fact, the rest of the day's conversations in the EOB office are missing. The next reel on the recording machine was supposed to have automatically started when the first machine had recorded for six hours, but that did not happen. Although this was one of the more dramatic Watergate days at the White House, it went largely unrecorded. Shortly after two o'clock on the afternoon of April 15, 1973, the EOB office recording system stopped working,* which was a far more important loss than the infamous 18½-minute gap of June 20, 1972. If there was ever any day for which Nixon, and Haldeman in particular, might want the recordings to disappear, it was this day, and that was exactly what happened: They simply disappeared.[28] Nonetheless, the highlights of this day can be reconstructed, and the telephone recording system, which continued to function, provides a few additional clues as to what transpired.

When Kleindienst departed, Ehrlichman was summoned to the EOB office. It is not clear how much of Kleindienst's report the president shared— he initially told Haldeman little when he called him after this meeting with Ehrlichman. This telephone call was recorded,[29] and it was well into the conversation before Nixon even mentioned Kleindienst's visit. Nixon reported that the attorney general thought it would take four or five years to sort out John Mitchell's guilt, because Mitchell would fight it all the way to the Supreme Court. Nixon then turned to the Johnson/Witcover piece in *The Washington Post*, characterizing it by noting, "We are so low now we can't go any lower. What do you think of that?" Haldeman did not know, but the mention of Kleindienst had not slipped by him. "So what does Kleindienst think now?" Haldeman asked.

Rather than tell Haldeman that Kleindienst had called for his and Ehrlichman's resignations, the president answered, "Well, he's for a special prosecutor." Nixon added that he had come to that conclusion as well. While he would leave Silbert in charge of running the case, he would place a special prosecutor in the U.S. Attorney's Office to supervise it all, avoiding any charge of a cover-up, and to sort out who was and who was not guilty of criminal offenses. The president did report that "Kleindienst also comes in with the idea that I should, he thinks, sometime I've got to go out and make a Checkers Speech at nine o'clock at night."†

"Oh, Jesus," Haldeman said, and Nixon told him that he had rejected the

---

*Approximately six hours of Watergate-related discussions are missing, which would have been one reel of recordings. Haldeman made notes and diary entries of matters that he found of interest during the meetings where he was present.

†This was an emotional speech vice presidential candidate Nixon gave during the 1952 presidential race in which he pleaded that he not be removed from the ticket with presidential candidate Dwight Eisenhower because of a fund that had been created for him during his time in the U.S. Senate by prominent businessmen. He ended the speech by saying a man in Texas had sent his daughters a cocker spaniel they had named "Checkers, [and] the kids loved that dog, [so] regardless of what they say about it, we're going to keep it." It worked, and Eisenhower dared not remove him.

suggestion, for that would only elevate Watergate in the public conscious-ness. Haldeman agreed, and the president continued. "But when the shit hits the fan I'm going to have to say it's correct [to handle it] in the judicial sys-tem. The special prosecutor thing helps in another way, that it gets one per-son between me and the whole thing." The president noted that his nonexistent Dean report was now discredited, which caused him to chuckle, since I was taking the hit in the press rather than he.

At 4:00 P.M. Kleindienst returned to the EOB office with Henry Petersen in tow, whom he had found cleaning his boat. Petersen, still wearing a dirty T-shirt, jeans and sneakers, was making his first command performance before the man who had appointed a Democrat and career Justice Depart-ment employee to head the Criminal Division. Petersen repeated the loose charges I had made about Haldeman and Ehrlichman and said that he also thought they should resign. The president said he would defend them, be-cause he did not have proof of their guilt. According to Nixon, Petersen re-sponded, "What you have said, Mr. President, speaks very well of you as a man. It does not speak well of you as a president."[30]

After trying unsuccessfully to reach Ehrlichman, who had gone home, the president joined Bebe Rebozo, who had come up from Florida, for a drive to the Washington Navy Yard and then a dinner cruise on the *Sequoia* down the Potomac. During dinner the president asked Bebe how much money he had in his savings at his bank, because he was thinking of giving it to Halde-man and Ehrlichman to help with their legal expenses. Rebozo rejected this notion and said that he and Bob Abplanalp could raise two or three hundred thousand for them in cash. Nixon said he dreaded going back to the White House because of the growing problems.[31] He returned there at 7:40 P.M. and went directly to his EOB office to meet with Haldeman and Ehrlichman, who had come at his request.

During this unrecorded meeting, which ran almost an hour and a half, the president told Haldeman and Ehrlichman of his meeting with Petersen, and that I was "in all day" with the prosecutors. (Petersen would give Nixon a report the following day, April 16, on what I had told them.) Petersen had said that the combined testimony of Dean and Magruder meant that both Haldeman and Ehrlichman would be going to the grand jury. "They told Dean," the president reported, referring to the prosecutors, that they "would do the best they could for him," offering me their "good offices if I cooper-ated." The president said to Ehrlichman and Haldeman that I had told the prosecutors that: Ehrlichman had instructed me to "deep six" material from Hunt's safe; he had ordered Hunt out of the country; and he had given the material from Hunt's safe to Pat Gray. Kleindienst had reported that Liddy had not talked, contrary to the information Shaffer and I had been given by the prosecutors. They had nothing on Colson. The president thought "Petersen was crusading."

Ehrlichman said that he had been trying to reach me all day. (When Shaffer and I learned the prosecutors had broken their confidentiality agreement, he strongly urged me not to continue to talk to Ehrlichman or Haldeman. I did, however, pass word to the president that I would speak with him if he wished.) At 8:15 P.M., while still meeting with Haldeman and Ehrlichman, the president called Petersen for an update, but Petersen had no additional information. Petersen liked the idea, which had been suggested by Colson and Ehrlichman, of the president's sending Liddy a signal that he wanted Liddy to talk. At 8:25 P.M. the president received the note from me indicating my willingness to speak with him.[32] Soon I received a message from Nixon that he would like to meet me at 9:15 P.M., and I headed for the White House. When Nixon ended this meeting just minutes befor my arrival by telling Haldeman and Ehrlichman that both Kleindienst and Petersen felt they should resign, they "were stunned."[33]

My meeting with the president in his EOB office lasted for just under an hour. I explained to him that I had been quietly but actively trying to end the cover-up without destroying his presidency. Naive as it seems now, at the time I really believed that my going to the prosecutors, plus having Shaffer encourage Magruder's attorney to have him speak to them as well, would result in Mitchell, Ehrlichman, Haldeman and Colson joining us in admitting the errors that had been made, and the affair would finally come to an end with the president left standing. I had no idea at that time that the president himself had been so deeply involved in the cover-up, principally through Haldeman, but not without Ehrlichman from time to time, as was clearly revealed by the conversations that began on June 20, 1972.

This conversation is not important so much for what was said as for the way it was said, and for what I learned. From the outset Nixon seemed different than he had been in our previous conversations. Clearly he had been drinking, and while not drunk, he seemed exhausted, slurring his words and looking remarkably rumpled in contrast to his usual crisp appearance. Three things made the conversation unforgettable. First, he took me though a series of leading questions involving distorted facts about Haldeman, Ehrlichman or himself. But they made me wonder (as I later testified) if he was recording me.[34] Second, he was clearly and deeply concerned about his own actions with regard to our March 21 conversation, because at one point he asked me if I recalled his mentioning that it would be no problem to raise a million dollars for the Watergate defendants. When I told him that I did, he said that he had of course been joking. He then got out of his easy chair, crossed the office and asked me in hushed tones about his conversations with Colson about clemency for Hunt, telegraphing not only his concern with personally being involved in obstruction, but that he did not want his question recorded. Third, I had to muster considerable fortitude to advise the president of the United States that I was concerned that if he did not handle this problem correctly it could result in his impeachment. He assured me he would do so.[35]

When I departed, Haldeman and Ehrlichman returned, and the president repeated almost everything I had told him about their activities while it was fresh in his memory. Based on Haldeman's notes summarizing the key points of that meeting, Nixon told them that I had "no knowledge of the bugging, [but] on obstruction, both Haldeman and Ehrlichman are involved." I had described their involvement in the obstruction as a "conspiracy by circumstances, whether or not intended." I did not think Kalmbach "knew the reason for [the] money," which was followed by some of the details about when and how the money was transmitted. I reported that I had "briefed Ehrlichman and Haldeman every inch of the way." Then Nixon asked me about Petersen's providing grand jury information to me, and I felt he had not given me anything "improper." I had told the prosecutors of meeting with Ehrlichman and Colson regarding clemency for Hunt, and that Ehrlichman had told Colson to "make no commitments." Haldeman's notes end with Ehrlichman's calling Pat Gray to inform him that I had told the prosecutors we had given him materials found in Hunt's safe rather than hand them over to the FBI agents. Gray at first said he would deny receiving them. Ehrlichman called him back and told him it would be best for him to tell the truth, because Ehrlichman knew better. Gray then admitted he had destroyed the material.[36]

In an earlier conversation, Nixon had told Haldeman and Ehrlichman that Bill Rogers believed he should fire me, because I was discussing a plea deal with the prosecutors, but Henry Petersen had objected, since I had come in voluntarily and they had breached our understanding.[37] I told Nixon that evening that I was prepared to leave whenever he wished me to do so, but I thought my departure would not begin to solve his problems with Haldeman and Ehrlichman, who had either instructed or approved my every move, making them equally culpable. Kleindienst had made clear that he was withdrawing from any involvement and Henry Petersen was now in charge of any prosecutions. But Nixon saw this as an opportunity for he wanted to claim that he was now directing the investigation.[38]

### April 16, 1973, the White House

Haldeman and Ehrlichman arrived in the Oval Office at 9:50 A.M. carrying two letters that Ehrlichman had prepared at the president's request.[39] They quickly went over the documents, the first of which read: "As a result of my involvement in the Watergate matter, which we discussed last night and today, I tender to you my resignation effective at once." The second announced that I was taking a leave of absence because of "my increasing involvement in the Watergate matter [and] my impending appearance before the grand jury and the probability of its action."[40] Ehrlichman told the president to have me sign them both, and he could decide later which he preferred to use. Nixon next asked what I had been talking about the night before when I mentioned "other bugs." Ehrlichman speculated that they were the FBI bugs that had been placed on journalists when the White House had been looking for leakers. (Actually my reference was to bugs placed both on White House staffers and on the president's brother, which Ehrlichman had ordered.)

The president told his aides that that he wanted to develop "a scenario" with regard to his role in Watergate: "When the president began to find out about this, what he did." He said that he remembered calling me in and saying he wanted a report and that he sent me to Camp David to work on it. "[Dean] came back and said he couldn't," Nixon recalled, so he planned to ask me about that when we met that morning. Steve Bull came into the Oval Office and said I had arrived, in response to the president's summons. Nixon told him it would be five more minutes, during which they discussed Petersen's wanting the president to send a signal to Liddy. Haldeman said that I had told them that Liddy was talking but Kleindienst claimed he wasn't. "Petersen's either lying to you, or Dean is lying to us," Haldeman said. The president, however, had figured it out: "The U.S. attorney gave [Dean] a snow job and said that Liddy has talked."

Ehrlichman said that Ziegler "wants to get out the fact that Dean disserved you, that the Dean report was inadequate, it didn't go far enough, that several weeks ago you reinstituted an examination—" The president interrupted here, stating in a very formal tone, "I began my personal investigation of the case," and they began laying out a scenario for the president's personal investigation, although to give Ehrlichman part of the action, he added that he had delegated some of it to Ehrlichman. They agreed that they could not allow the Justice Department to take credit for cracking the case, but rather Nixon would say he had been assisted by Henry Petersen.

"Ask him," Ehrlichman said, referring to me, "what you should say publicly about the Dean report." Nixon replied that I had told him the previous night that there was no Dean report (which, in fact, I had already told him on several occasions). "I think it was an oral report," Nixon said, and he went through whether he had asked me if anyone in the White House was involved, and I had said that, as best I knew, nobody was involved.

At 9:59 A.M. Haldeman and Ehrlichman exited as I entered the Oval Office, and I could hear them laughing as they departed from a doorway across the office. I met with the president for forty minutes, and he asked me if I recalled discussing my resignation the night before. I told him I did. He asked me for my "feeling on that." Based on our prior conversation, I sought clarification: "Are we talking Dean or are we talking Dean, Ehrlichman and Haldeman?"[41] He said Dean, for the moment. Then, indicating he had had letters prepared, slid them across his desk to me and asked my advice. I scanned the documents, which read like open-ended confessions, and told him my advice was that he should have Haldeman's and Ehrlichman's resignations as well. "Well," he quickly replied, "as a matter of fact, they both suggested it for themselves. So I've already done that with them."

Nixon had never been a particularly good dissembler, and I sensed that this was not true, as he seemed embarrassed by it all. But as he elaborated that he did not want to press me, or anyone, I agreed that my leaving was a good idea, but if I did so, so should the others: "I think you have problems with the others, too, Mr. President." Looking again at the documents he had given me, and thinking that Ehrlichman had no doubt drafted them, I said, "What I would like to do is to draft up for you an alternative letter, with both alternatives, just short and sweet." This was acceptable to him, and he again made the point he had made the preceding evening: "Understand, I don't want [the letter to] put anything out. Because I don't want to jeopardize your position at all." Then doing a bit of stroking, he said, "You've carried a hell of a load here," but not wanting to continue down that road, he added, "and I just feel that, since what you said last night—" But this thought did not go anywhere. Instead he explained that he had to do the same with Haldeman and Ehrlichman: "I have leave of absences from them, which, however, I will not use until I get the word from Petersen on corroboration."

"Let me, let me summarize this specific point again, because I need to know—" he continued. He noted parenthetically, "We know there was no Dean report," and added, "Ziegler has always said it was oral." I agreed, thinking of our March conversations. But Nixon wanted to discover if I still thought that no one on the White House staff had been involved with Watergate, and I said, "I have no knowledge." Then he turned to "the aftermath," and the "obstruction of justice thing," the difficulty of proving it in court, again going over the money for Hunt and his own situation. He reminded me, "The only time I ever heard any discussion of this supporting of the defendants," he began, but recognizing his own dissembling, partially corrected himself, "and I must say I guess I should have assumed somebody was helping them, I must have assumed it, but, and I must say people were good in a way," suggesting no one had ever told him. He wanted to know again how that had been handled, so I repeated how Paul O'Brien had brought me Hunt's message for Ehrlichman, who asked if I had talked to Mitchell, who later said the problem was solved. "In other words, that was done at the Mitchell level?" the president asked, which I confirmed. "But you had knowledge. Haldeman had a lot of knowledge. And Ehrlichman had knowledge." Again, I confirmed. "And I suppose I did," he admitted. "I mean, I am planning to assume some culpability on that, right?" Before I could explain that I had not acted on anything he had said during that conversation on March 21, he interrupted, saying he was going to "be tough on myself" adding, "though I must say I didn't really give it a thought at the time, because I didn't know—"

"No one gave it a thought," I interrupted, reminding him that on March 21 I had told him that paying Hunt was an obstruction of justice. Again we both tried to remember what had and had not been said during that earlier conversation. When he again pressed me regarding telling him that no one in the White House had been involved, I told him I could not testify that I had reported that information at the time he maintained I had done so, although I had indirectly passed such information as I acquired through Haldeman and Ehrlichman. When the president tried to recall how many discussions we'd had regarding Watergate, he said, "We had three conversations, to my recollection." "Oh, sir, I think we had more than that," I corrected him, and I reminded him that the National Archives kept a record of his schedule. Then, thinking again about our March 21 conversation, he claimed a bit of an epiphany: "You see, I, that's when I became, frankly, interested in the case, and I said, 'Now, God damn it, I want to find out the score.' And I set in motion Ehrlichman, Mitchell and a few of, not Mitchell, but others. Okay?" Clearly the president was starting to develop a new defense: He would say he first learned of the serious nature of the problems on March 21, which was true. (His later claim that he first learned of the cover-up on March 21, however, was not.)

Next he instructed me that I could not talk about "the electronic stuff" in "the leak area, national security area," which he consider privileged. He asked, "Have you informed your lawyer about that?" I said I had not, and I agreed it was privileged. But still thinking of his defense, and given that the Justice Department and Henry Petersen were quickly unraveling Watergate, he said, "We triggered this whole thing. You know what I mean? Don't you agree?" As I started to respond, he added, "You helped trigger it." I told him, "When history is written, and you put the pieces back together, you'll see why it happened. It's because I triggered it. I put everybody's feet to the fire, because it just had to stop. And I still continue to feel that—" The president interrupted and said, "That's right. You put Magruder's feet to the fire?" I responded, "Yes, I did." Nixon asked, "What got Magruder to talk? I would like to take the credit." As I explained how I had refused to agree to support Mitchell's and Magruder's false testimonies, the president backed off this idea of his assuming credit, but instead he told me to tell the truth, which I assured him I would do. He then recalled that Alger Hiss would not have gone to jail if he had not lied about his communist activities.

"The truth always emerges," I told the president, a sentiment with which he agreed. Before I headed off to rewrite my resignation letter, the president reminded me that I was still White House counsel, so he wanted my general advice on how to proceed, just as he did from Haldeman and Ehrlichman. I told him that there was still something of a mythical belief held by Haldeman and Ehrlichman "that they don't have a problem, Mr. President. And I am not really sure that you are convinced they do. But I'm telling you, they do." I was not accustomed to lecturing the president but was being as firm and certain as I could, for I knew how deeply both men were involved. "There's no question about it," Nixon said, assuring me that he understood. While we agreed that these were not easy cases to prove, he told me he had reached a conclusion: "Both Ehrlichman and Haldeman are in on the obstruction. And that's the point." "That's right," I said and added, "I think it'd be a very good idea if they had counsel." Nixon said, "I told them last night to get lawyers, so I'm one step ahead of you there. Is there anything else you think I should do?" And before I could respond, he said, "Shit, I'm not going to let the Justice Department break this case, John."

"I understand. You've got to break it. You are breaking it, in a sense," I noted. We discussed in vague terms how he had been trying to get to the bottom of Watergate since I had spoken with him on March 21. In fact, I knew it was McCord's letter, and the threat of Hunt's and Magruder's damning testimonies, that had forced his hand, but I wanted to encourage him to follow through with Haldeman and Ehrlichman, so I was still willing to agree with his version of events. There was a bit more rehashing regarding Colson, who I felt was clean, but like all of us who had been tainted by the cover-up, he had what at the time I called "technical problems." I used this term because it struck me that, with the exception of Magruder's perjuring himself, which Jeb had too enthusiastically volunteered to do to save himself and Mitchell, if not Nixon's reelection, everyone else who had crossed the near-invisible lines onto the wrong side of the law had done so out of ignorance. But ignorance was not a defense.

I had scarcely left the Oval Office before Haldeman and Ehrlichman returned.[42] Haldeman asked if the scenario they had planned for me had worked out. "Yeah, it did. Let me fill you in briefly here," Nixon said, and first explained that I would not testify about national security matters. He explained that when he raised the resignation/leave of absence letters with me, I had asked, "What about Haldeman and Ehrlichman?" Nixon told them he said to me that he already had theirs, a statement with which neither disagreed.

They began rehashing the by now standard agenda of topics, with Nixon at one point noting, "Let me say this: I don't think it's gaining us anything by pissing on the Dean report as such." Reluctantly Ehrlichman agreed, for he had another idea: "Remember, you had John Dean go to Camp David and write it up, and when he came down he said, 'I can't.' That's the tip-off, and right then you started to move." "That's right," Nixon said. "He could not write it." Haldeman added, "Then you realized there was more to this than you'd been led to believe." But Nixon raised a concern: "Then how do I get credit for getting Magruder to the stand?" Ehrlichman suggested that the president could simply state that, because Dean himself had been involved in the case, he had been taken off it, and Nixon assigned it to Ehrlichman instead. Thoughts of how the president would defend himself were already forming, as were the first efforts at spinning recent events and reconfiguring the facts to suit their needs. Nixon was working with the two men whom he had only minutes earlier acknowledged were deeply involved in obstruction of justice, but he was placating Haldeman and Ehrlichman, just as he had me, while trying to obtain what information he could.

When Haldeman returned to the Oval Office at noon Nixon asked, "You have any further thoughts about how we stage this damn thing, in the first stage?"[43] In a typical rambling Watergate discussion, Haldeman reported that Ziegler had been working on a plan with a group of advisers: Len Garment, Dick Moore and Chappie Rose,an attorney in private practice whom Nixon had met when he was vice president, although Rose had limited criminal law experience. Haldeman read a sample of his own public relations press statement, which claimed that he had only acted on the advice of the White House counsel, John Dean. The president disliked that approach and suggested that Haldeman not take the position of trying to hang someone else—to which Haldeman countered that he would have already hung himself by the time he issued his statement.

Ziegler came to the Oval Office shortly before one o'clock to encourage Nixon to visit with Garment, but the president wanted to wait until he had visited with Bill Rogers.[44] Ziegler also had some gossip to share: At the White House correspondents' dinner, Harry Rosenfeld, Woodward and Bernstein's metropolitan editor at the *Post*, had spoken with Ray Price, who had once worked for Rosenfeld at the *New York Herald-Tribune*. Rosenfeld told Price that everything they had on Watergate was solidly documented, and that they were not printing everything they knew. They were now working on a story that "will hurt the presidency, the current president and the office." Price told Ziegler that Rosenfeld was one of the few conscientious people at the *Post*. Speechwriter David Gergen, who had been at Yale with Woodward, had spoken with him at the same dinner and had learned from him as well that they had much more than they had reported so far. Gergen told Ziegler that he felt Woodward was into something bigger than he could handle. Ziegler observedthat the *Post* seemed to be "hovering on the outer fringes," waiting to see what the White House did next.

Ziegler then tried to outline the public relations issues the president would need to address: he had learned new information from the attorney general; the situation with me; and the accuracy of the Dean report. He said, "Well, the facts that the president has been told, as at least I understand it in terms of Dean, is that you were forced to make judgments based on only 32 percent of the information that he had available to him. I'm talking now about what will come out later." (This appears to be based on my having told Ziegler that neither Ehrlichman nor Mitchell was providing the rest of the information about what had provoked the White House cover-up and its operation.) But the president was not concerned about the Dean report and told him that everything had been turned over to the attorney general, and the statement that nobody at the White House was involved in the break-in remained valid. Ziegler, who did not know about my conversations with the president, said his point was that because Nixon was now aware of posttrial information, "which has just now come to your attention," he had to take "decisive action." Nixon asked how he should do that, as "making Dean the scapegoat is only going to make things worse." Before Ziegler departed, Nixon advised him of Petersen's new role, and he highlighted what Petersen had been told so far.

Henry Petersen himself came to the president's EOB office early that afternoon." Over the next few weeks they would have a total of seven personal meetings and twenty telephone conversations,[45] during which Nixon would shamelessly attempt to manipulate him, using insider prosecutorial information from Petersen to protect Haldeman, Ehrlichman and himself.[46] In this session the president was intent on impressing upon Petersen that he had taken charge. After discussing whether John Mitchell could get a fair trial in Washington (neither thought he could, particular if the Senate proceeded), the president again emphasized his instructions to Petersen: "You understand now, you're talking only to me, and there's not going to be anyone else on the White House staff. In other words, I am acting counsel and everything else."

"I [need to deal with] Dean, what do we do about him?" the president asked, reporting that he had demanded my resignation that morning. Petersen said that this was a president decision; he did not want to be in a position in which the prosecutors were forcing my resignation, and explained that they were negotiating with Shaffer about what I would do. When Ziegler briefly joined them, the president asked, "How does Dean come out on this thing?" "The decision isn't made," Petersen reported. "His counsel says they want a deal. His man was an agent. This man didn't do anything but what Haldeman—" Nixon finished the sentence: "—Haldeman and Ehrlichman told him to do." Petersen added, "And Mitchell. And if you insist on trying him, in defense, we're going to try Ehrlichman, Haldeman, Nixon and this administration. That's going to be our defense." With some alarm Nixon asked, "He'd try the president, too?" Petersen answered, "It's a God damn poker game. Yes, sir."

After Ziegler departed, Nixon returned to the question of whether the negotiations with me were still open or if I was pleading guilty. Petersen said we were negotiating, and Nixon wanted to understand my argument of having been an agent of Haldeman, Ehrlichman and Mitchell. Petersen explained that it was a tactical defense, that a jury would not convict a person they believed was "the fall guy." When Nixon argued that the Cubans had been agents as well, Petersen replied that my position was "much more sympathetic. Dean has performed neutral acts which, in the circumstances they were performed, take on the trace of criminality, and he excuses that with, one, he wasn't fully informed; two, he was only an agent; and three, he didn't have enough authority to countermand Mitchell, and Haldeman didn't countermand. Dean was impotent in the circumstances. That will be his defense."

"Also he told you that unless you grant him immunity, he's going to attack everybody, including the president. Is that right?" Nixon asked. Petersen confirmed that and cautioned Nixon: "But you can't use that." When the president asked why, Petersen said, "Because Dean didn't tell us that. His lawyer said it in the course of negotiations. And he doesn't say that as a threat. He says, this is what I am going to do. This is my defense. You're taking unfair advantage of this man." Nixon then claimed, "I [didn't] see Dean until a month ago, never even saw him." Later in the discussion Nixon, trying to ascertain that they had not made a deal with me yet, asked, "But you are trying to make a deal, aren't you?" Petersen confirmed that they were trying. My negotiations came up several more times, and Nixon finally admitted, "I'm a little concerned about Dean's or his lawyer's, that he's going to attack the president and so forth. Other than that, I mean, Dean above all else—"

"Well, I don't think the president personally, the presidency as an office of the administration," Petersen clarified. "Because of Ehrlichman and Haldeman." He added, "That statement [was] made in the heat of argument. Charlie Shaffer's a very committed, emotional, able lawyer. He stands up and says, 'God damn it, I'm not going to plead him. If I have to do this, I do this in return.'"

The other major thread running through this discussion was the president's probing for information relating to Haldeman and Ehrlichman. Responding to his earlier request, Petersen gave the president a written document summarizing the charges against the two aides as of that date, based on the information I had provided in my off-the-record conversations with the prosecutors:[47] Gray's having been given material from Hunt's safe; Ehrlichman's instructing me to "deep six" material found there; Ehrlichman's ordering Hunt out of the country;* Haldeman's having been informed of my meetings with Mitchell and Liddy, during which I had rejected Liddy's plan and Haldeman had agreed. But, Petersen noted, Haldeman had done nothing to "discontinue" Liddy's activities, and Magruder had told the prosecutors he had delivered to Strachan for Haldeman copies of information from "intercepted telephone conversations." Nixon, who had far more information about all this than Petersen, began to probe for the weaknesses in his cases against Haldeman and Ehrlichman. He pressed Petersen on his recommendation that they resign, but Petersen did not back down. The president also discussed the material in Hunt's safe at some length but did not inform Petersen that he knew Gray had destroyed it.[48]

Two minutes after Petersen departed, Ehrlichman appeared and had barely seated himself when Nixon blurted out, "Gray denied to Petersen that he ever got the bundle. Oh, he's a dumb son of a bitch."[49] Nixon handed Ehrlichman the document Petersen had brought summarizing the charges

---

*Ehrlichman would deny that he told me to "deep six" the material from Hunt's safe. But I had been so stunned by his instruction at the outset of the cover-up that I mentioned it to my assistant, Fred Fielding, when it happened, and Fielding was later called as a witness to corroborate my testimony. See testimony of Fred Fielding, *U.S. v. Mitchell et al.*, November 5 and 21, 1974. Ehrlichman secretly recorded a confused Colson, who had been present when Ehrlichman ordered Hunt out of the country, and Colson thought that had happened in his office and Ehrlichman had not been present. So Ehrlichman used the information from Petersen after getting Colson to corroborate for him that it had not happened as I claimed to protect himself on that minor detail.

against him, all of which Ehrlichman denied. They then focused on Gray's denial. The president wanted to know what I would say, and Ehrlichman repeated that I had indeed carried the material to his office for Gray, but as far as what was inside the envelope, Ehrlichman said he only knew what I had told him—that it had come from Hunt's safe. Ehrlichman said that if Gray claimed he did "not receive a big manila envelope from Dean, then I'm going to have to dispute that."

Ehrlichman then returned to Petersen's summary: "Dean doesn't give them much. Well, gee, did Hunt go out of the country. No." Ziegler returned and again asked the president if he wanted to see Garment. He did not, and Ehrlichman added—not surprisingly, since Garment wanted him and Haldeman to resign—"I agree totally." Then, chuckling, he added, "I mean, it's therapy for Garment, is the reason you see [him]." The president instructed Ziegler to give Garment "a little bullshit" to pacify him.

Shortly after Ziegler and Ehrlichman departed, the president called and requested that I come to his EOB office. I arrived late that afternoon with my revised resignation letter and material for a draft statement being developed for Nixon by Dick Moore, Len Garment and the speechwriters.[50] I had spoken with Dick Moore and given them adjustments to one key paragraph, indicating the president had accepted the resignations of Haldeman, Ehrlichman and myself. The president now asked that I speak with Garment about the draft statement and requested that I read him my letter: "You have informed me that Bob Haldeman and John Ehrlichman have verbally tendered their request to be given an immediate and indefinite leave of absence from your staff. By this letter I wish to confirm my similar request that I be given such a leave of absence from the staff." "You don't want to go if they stay?" he asked. I was not interested in being "the scapegoat," I replied, to which Nixon replied, "Like Magruder's been a scapegoat for Mitchell." I agreed with that assessment.

The president did not appear to disagree with my letter, with his most serious comment being grammatical—namely, that "you" was not a polite word to use with reference to the president. He was still preoccupied with Petersen's charge that Haldeman should have taken action after I returned from the second Magruder/Liddy meeting in Mitchell's office. The president said that because I gave Haldeman this information, Petersen's point was "that actually Haldeman, then, did know." I told him I disagreed with that interpretation and assured the president that Haldeman had also told me he did not know. What had happened, I explained, was that both Haldeman and I had assumed Mitchell would never approve Liddy's reckless plan. I had told Haldeman, "They're talking about bugging, they're talking about kidnapping, they're talking about mugging squads, taking people down from San Diego south of the border." Nixon asked, "You told Bob this? Wanting to know what he said?" "He said, 'Absolutely no,'" I answered. "So you will so testify, then?" I assured him that I would.

I explained that Haldeman had told me to not do anything: "Just stay away from it, don't talk to them," and I had not. Nixon wanted to know what happened next, and I told him that I had no direct knowledge. I said Haldeman and I had been over this, and he recalled my coming into his office and telling him "about this crazy scheme that's being cooked up." Rogers was coming over, the president said, noting, "Everybody's in the middle of this, John." "All I'm trying to think is how to get you out in front," I told him. We discussed the possible timing for the release of a statement, and I departed. It was my last personal meeting with Richard Nixon.

When Rogers arrived in the EOB office, he and the president sat at a considerable distance from the recording microphones, so only the gist of their conversation can be discerned.[51] Nixon, however, was being less than candid with his old friend, spinning facts and distorting what he had been told. For example, rather than telling Rogers what Petersen had actually said, he used me as a foil, telling Rogers what I thought Petersen believed. When discussing the payment of money to the Watergate defendants, Nixon reported that no one was told not to talk. This recording is not sufficiently audible to know what advice, if any, Rogers offered, but it is remarkable that Nixon solicited Rogers's advice based on information the president knew was distorted.

Shortly before nine o'clock that evening, still working in his EOB office, Nixon called Henry Petersen to ask if there were any developments he should know about.[52] Petersen reported that Fred LaRue had come in and "admits to participating in the coordination and obstruction of justice." LaRue had provided information about using the $350,000 White House fund to pay the defendants. He said that he had been present with Mitchell [and Magruder] at a third meeting, in Florida, when Liddy's plan was approved, and while reluctant to say whether electronic surveillance had been discussed, Petersen thought he was coming around. LaRue did tell them that Liddy's plan could not have been approved without Mitchell. Petersen said LaRue had hired one of Colson's law partners to represent him, but the prosecutors objected, and got Sirica to toss the lawyer off the case for having a conflict. So LaRue had to find another lawyer and would be back in the morning.

When Petersen reported, "Liddy confessed to Dean on June 19, and Dean then told Ehrlichman," the president said nothing, but he later returned to this point and said that Dean should've told him this fact, but had not. (In fact, I had informed him that I had spoken to Liddy on June 19, and Ehrlichman had told him I was reporting on a regular basis.) Petersen further reported that I had said Colson had been present in Ehrlichman's office when Hunt was told to get out of town, and that I had been asked by Mitchell to "activate Kalmbach," but lacking the necessary authority, I had gone to Haldeman, who authorized it. So Kalmbach was now to be called before the grand jury. Petersen said the prosecutor still did not have a deal with Magruder, because Magruder was worried the Judge Sirica would throw him in jail, and he did not want to go to jail before the others if he confessed. So they were working with the judge see what they could do.

Last, Petersen informed Nixon that they were wrestling with whether or not they could, based on the information they had so far, name Haldeman and Ehrlichman as unindicted coconspirators. He said they were reluctant to do so for fear of being accused of further covering up, since it would appear that they were escaping any indictment and likely punishment. Peterson noted, however, that anybody named as an unindicted coconspirator at this early stage would likely later be indicted as a conspirator. When the president asked about my status, Petersen said they were still negotiating, trying to get the facts nailed down.

After speaking with Petersen, the president went to the White House residence, where he called Ehrlichman from a telephone that was not attached to the recording system. They talked for twenty minutes, probably about the latest information that Petersen had shared regarding Ehrlichman, who had been carefully reconstructing his participation in the cover-up. He was now claiming, for example, that his calendar indicated that he had virtually never met with me regarding Watergate—and he was sure that when we did meet it related to topics like the president's estate plan and leaks. In addition, he had a tape recording disproving Chuck Colson's erroneous memory that the instruction to get Hunt out of town had taken place in Ehrlichman's office. He also enlisted Colson to say that he had never heard Ehrlichman order me to "deep six" anything.

*April 17, 1973, the White House*

The president's morning schedule was filled with an arrival ceremony for the Italian prime minister and then an extended meeting with him in the Oval Office, so I was surprised when he phoned me at 9:19 A.M. He was then very diligently attempting to hold the trust of everyone on his staff who had been involved in Watergate.[53] This would be my last recorded conversation with Richard Nixon, and I was struck at the time by how insincere he sounded. (My last conversation with Nixon was another conciliatory call on April 22 that he made from Key Biscayne on Easter Sunday morning, which was unrecorded.) He asked if I had looked at the executive privilege statement being prepared, and I replied that Len Garment's draft was fine. He said he would call again that afternoon, after he had read Garment's draft, but he did not, nor was I surprised when he did not. He said he could not believe "some guy down in the U.S. Attorney's Office would say the president blew the case in order to get publicity." I was not sure what he was talking about, so I told him I would get him some additional information. He was surprised that Judge Sirica was quizzing those who had pled guilty in open court and wondered if others named might not raise constitutional questions. "Give me a little feeling on that," he requested, adding, "Don't let them know I'm checking on that. But give me your, do a little rundown." The president's request struck me as a make-work project, and given the events later that day, I never pursued the matter. He repeated that he would call me back, and then said, "I hope you got a good night's sleep, as well as you can these days. But let me say, like I told the other boys, I said, God, you know, it's tough for everybody, John. All of you are good friends and, I said, you have fought the good fight, and you'll live to fight another one. That's the important thing."

"No problem here," I assured the president, wondering what had prompted that sign-off. While Nixon was speaking with me, Len Garment was on his way to the Oval Office.[54] It was a meeting intended to placate Garment, in which he was offered excuses for why they had not met earlier. Nixon listened quietly as Garment tried to appeal to his better nature, unaware of how deeply the president had been involved in the cover-up. Garment asked him to "act preemptively and sweep away all this petty detail and rationalizations and baloney that will be in the interest of all the persons involved." Garment said the clock was running out. "And the key thing," he continued, "the single issue overriding all of this, is that the American people believe you when you say that you had no knowledge of this." Garment argued that all involved had to be suspended until the investigation had run its course.

"What do you think about Dean? How does he feel about it?" the president asked, and Garment reported that we had spoken and that I was ready to resign, though Garment thought suspensions were better. Garment talked, and Nixon listened, but Garment did not have the facts, and the president did not tell him to get those facts from me. In fact, quite the opposite. "Incidentally, don't discuss it any further with Dean," he instructed. Garment agreed, but later that day he did not hesitate to contact me when he saw that Ehrlichman and the president had undertaken a blatant effort to shut down my attempts to cooperate with the prosecutors. While Garment was unquestionably loyal to Nixon, he had no tolerance for dirty play.

After Garment departed the president called Haldeman in for a quick visit before the arrival ceremony on the South Grounds.[55] The president went over several matters in Petersen's report, including the fact that I had told Ehrlichman of Liddy's confession on June 19, 1972. The president wanted them to "get a line" on that situation.* He also wanted Haldeman and Ehrlichman to "sit down and do some hard thinking about what kind of strategy [they were] going to have with the money." He said he thought their line regarding not wanting the defendants to talk to the press was weak. He remained concerned about Hunt's last payment, since it involved him, but Haldeman assured him that Mitchell had taken care of the matter without the help of anyone in the White House. Finally Nixon instructed, "Ah, look, you've got to call Kalmbach," given the fact that Petersen had informed him that Kalmbach was being called to the grand jury. "I've been trying to find out from Dean what the hell he is going to say he told Kalmbach. What did Kalmbach say that Dean told him? They wanted money for this support purpose?" Haldeman had no answer but reported that Ehrlichman was talking with Kalmbach. The president reported that LaRue was now "a broken man" who was talking very freely.

When the president's schedule opened later that day he asked Haldeman

---

*Because I had gone from my walk down Seventeenth Street with Liddy (where we had been seen by Jack Caulfield as we headed back toward the White House just before noon) directly to Ehrlichman's office, and met with him at twelve o'clock, Ehrlichman had trouble denying I had reported to him just after meeting with Liddy. Since Ehrlichman had lied to the FBI about having any knowledge of Liddy's activities after the Watergate break-in, he simply claimed he had no memory of my mentioning Liddy on June 19, 1972.

and Ehrlichman to join him in the Oval Office for a discussion that lasted almost two hours.[56] Ehrlichman indicated that the proposed executive privilege statement was ready but required the president to make some decisions about it. "I just finished an hour with Colson," Ehrlichman continued, "who came over very concerned, and said that he had to see you." Colson's message, which he had explained at length, was that "Dean had to be dealt with summarily. [Colson's] partner has a tie with the U.S. Attorney's Office, and they seem to know what's going on there.* Very simply put, I think his argument will be that the city of Washington generally knows that Dean had little or no access to you. That Haldeman, Colson and Ehrlichman had a lot of access to you." Nixon agreed, "True, that's quite right. Dean was just a messenger." Ehrlichman continued, "That knowledge imputed to us is knowledge imputed to you, and if Dean is credible and testifies that he imputed great quantities of knowledge to us, and is allowed to get away with that, that will seriously impair the presidency ultimately. Because it will be very easy to argue that all you have to do is read Dean's testimony, look at the previous relationships, and there she goes! So [Colson] says, the key to this is that Dean should not get immunity. That's what he wants to tell you."

"Well, he told me that, and I couldn't agree more," the president said. Ehrlichman continued, "Now, he says you have total and complete control over whether Dean gets immunity through Petersen." Nixon was not certain of that, yet he did not want Colson coming in to tell it to him. Nixon thought granting immunity to me would be paying the smallest price, but Ehrlichman had a different view: "Well, the price that he'll pay, the quid pro quo for the immunity, is to reach one of the three of us, or all of us." When Nixon did not disagree, Ehrlichman continued, "Colson argues that if he is not given immunity, then he has even more incentive to go light on his own malefactions, and he will have to clam up, and he will have to defend himself." The next half hour focused on the pros and cons of this matter, or as Nixon put it, "I think you got to figure what the hell does Dean know." Then, more bluntly: "What kind of blackmail does he have?"

Ehrlichman's action plan was to remove me from the staff, with the president instructing Petersen that I was not to receive immunity. His press plan was to publicly claim that the Dean report had been inadequate, and when

---

*Years later Colson told me that his law partner, David I. Shapiro, was close to assistant U.S. attorney Seymour Glanzer, who later joined his Washington law firm, Dickstein Shapiro. Presumably, Glanzer was the source of this information, since few were privy to it.

I could not write it up, it had been a sign to the president that I was much more deeply involved than he had previously known. So I was taken off the matter, and working through Ehrlichman, the president began his own investigation. Ehrlichman explained his rationale for removing me from the White House: "You've got Dean coming in saying to you, 'I've talked to the U.S. attorney, and I've told him a lot of things that I did wrong.' So you put him on leave." "I asked him that," Nixon explained, "and he said, I'll go on leave with Haldeman and Ehrlichman." Ehrlichman, bristling, replied, "Well, he's not in any position to bargain with you on that." Nixon countered that Petersen's informing him that he had evidence that both Haldeman and Ehrlichman should resign placed him in a difficult position. "Well, that takes me to my next step," Ehrlichman said, "which is my continuing misgivings about Petersen. And I'm sorry to be put in the position of having to raise this question, in light of his having said that about me," referring to Petersen's calling for Ehrlichman to resign, "because it makes it a very doubtful kind of statement, but just from a personal, selfish standpoint, I would rather the case were in the control of somebody who would call them right down the middle. Rather than some guy that I know has egg on his face from his previous working with Dean. And I know that out of Dean's mouth."

Haldeman added, sounding increasingly angry as he spoke, "If you have any doubt about that and want it from an unbiased source, call Dick Moore and ask him, because there is no question that Petersen is up to his ass with Dean in violation of the law." Then, somewhat threateningly, he told Nixon, "And you have knowledge of that now, too."[57] Ehrlichman continued, "Now I cannot sit by quietly. If I take a leave, and I go out of here, I am going to very vigorously defend myself. And one of the first things I am going to do is sink Petersen." After Haldeman added his view—"The first thing is Dean; the second is Petersen"—Ehrlichman continued, "Well, Dean sunk himself, as far as I'm concerned, but I will not have Petersen left in a position to make the prosecutorial decisions, because just as sure as I'm sitting here, I promise you that he will indict me." Nixon, surprised, asked, "Oh, he will?" Ehrlichman said, "Yes, sir, he will, whether there's any evidence or not. He will indict me, because it is very much to his interest to do so," without elaborating on why Petersen might want to do so. "God damn it, why was he put in charge of the case?" Nixon asked. Ehrlichman said he thought it was only a temporary thing, then added, "I just want to say to you in the strongest kind of terms that I will have no choice in this matter. And I'll do it by fair means or foul."

When they returned to the discussion of Ehrlichman's action plan, the president said he was not certain that my removal from the staff would make any difference in whether I was given immunity, because I was the witness they needed to make their cases. He asked his aides if they had "given any thought to what the line out to be, I don't mean lie but line, on raising the money for these defendants. Because both of you were aware of that, right?" After they acknowledged that they had been, Nixon said, "You can't go in and say, I didn't know what in hell he wanted the three fifty for." When Haldeman said he had prepared a statement, the president explained, in a tone of disbelief, "I'm concerned about the legal thing, Bob. You say that our purpose was to keep them from talking to the press?" "Well, that was *my* purpose," Ehrlichman said. "And before I get too far out on that, I want to talk to an attorney and find out what the law is, which I have not yet done." Haldeman indicated that he, too, wanted to check with an attorney, and said his statement was merely a draft.

The president, noting that other people were involved, wanted to know what Kalmbach had been told. "Mr. President," Ehrlichman told him, "when the truth and fact of this is known, that building next door is full of people who knew that money was being raised for these people." Nixon, incredulous, asked, "EOB?" Ehrlichman assured him that was the case. Nixon could understand that many people might have been aware of the situation but doubted that many of them were actually involved in it: "In other words, there's a difference between actors and observers." Ehrlichman, however, thought otherwise: "Well, apparently not, because I'm not an actor," he asserted, with Haldeman agreeing, "Neither am I." Ehrlichman, who now began lecturing the president, said, "I want you to think very critically about the difference here between knowledge of the general transactions going on, on the one hand, and being an affirmative actor on the other, because that's the difference between Dean and me."*

Ehrlichman, realizing he was not swaying Nixon, tried another approach. "Now, on this business of whether Dean should have immunity, I think you

---

*Ehrlichman was apparently casting aside his knowledge of the law of agency, for he surely understood that a principal is liable for the actions of his agent, not to mention the law of conspiracy, in which all the coconspirators are accountable for the actions of the others when in furtherance of the conspiracy, even if they have no specific awareness of those actions.

have to ask yourself, really, the basic question: whether anybody in the White House who does wrong ought to get immunity, no matter how many other people he implicates." When the president asked whether that would be true for Strachan, Ehrlichman insisted, "Anybody," and continued, "I just question whether, in the orderly administration of justice, if it looks right for anybody in the White House to get immunity." Over the course of the next hour Ehrlichman succeeding in convincing the president, who finally agreed to privately inform Petersen that he wanted no immunity granted to anyone at the Dean level of the White House and above (which meant former White House aide Strachan was not included but anyone at Magruder's level, the president noted of his former middle-level aide, who had been at a similar level to me, would be).[58]

Notwithstanding a sustained effort (asserting that I was a direct pipeline to the U.S. Attorney's Office and had removed documents from the White House, neither of which was true), however, Ehrlichman could not convince the president to fire me just yet. Nixon was apprehensive about the consequences of such a decision, though Ehrlichman claimed he had not the slightest concern. Although I had reminded Ehrlichman of the parts he had played—in everything from the decision to not hire a lawyer with criminal experience to his role in activating Kalmbach to his involvement in the Ellsberg operation—none of it fazed him. As he described these charges to the president: "He's brought in a bunch of silly garbage about me which doesn't add up to a nickel's worth of a lawsuit. He's come in and told you that he's been involved in all kinds of stuff. It seems to me a very different qualitative kind of problem." As the discussion continued, he resumed his case for denying me immunity: "Dean getting immunity, or anybody in the White House getting immunity, is in itself treatable as a cover-up. And obviously, if we are put in a position of defending ourselves, the things that I'm going to have to say about Dean are that basically Dean was the sole proprietor of this project. And he reported to the president. He reported to me only incidentally."

"Reported to the president?" Nixon asked. Ehrlichman replied that he would have to say that, but before he could explain, the president asked, "When?" Ehrlichman did not know, and again the president cut him off. "The problem you've got there is that Dean," the president began, and then turned to a new thought. "Dean does have a point there, which you've got to realize. He didn't see me when he came out to California [referring to the

August 29, 1972, announcement of the Dean report]. He didn't see me until the day you said, 'I think you ought to talk to John Dean.'"

Ehrlichman agreed, adding, "But the point is that basically he was in charge of this project." The president countered, "He'll say he reports to the president through other people." This was Ehrlichman's argument, as he explained: "Then you see what you've got there is an imputation." The president did not like this situation, so he asked Ehrlichman, "Who the hell did he report to?" Notwithstanding the fact that Ehrlichman and Haldeman had been telling the president I was reporting to them, Ehrlichman now asserted, "Well, he in many cases, to no one. He just went ahead and did things." Haldeman again chimed in, confirming, "That's right."

At one point, deep in this conversation, as Ehrlichman was urging the president to instruct Petersen and, in turn, Silbert to "not go into matters of national security importance," he explained that Colson had raised the question of "this caper in California, for instance." When the president asked which caper he was referring to, Ehrlichman replied, "This thing of Hunt out there, the national security thing connected [with] Ellsberg." The president agreed that "anything in the leak thing, the plumbing thing, was national security."

The press plan for the executive privilege statement was coming down to blaming everything on me, effectively elevating me from a message carrier to the mastermind of the cover-up. Because I was asking others what they remembered, Haldeman thought I was now "playing the Magruder game, flying from flower to flower, planting [my] pollen." He described me as "an unbelievable disaster for us" and tried to understand my motivation: "He's not un-American and anti-Nixon. I'll tell you what he did, I'll tell you during that period he busted his ass trying to work this out, and it wore him to a frazzle, and I think it probably wore him past the point of rationality. I think he may now be in a mental state that's causing him to do things that, when he sobers up, he's going to be very disturbed about with himself."

"Also, he's probably got a very, very clever new lawyer named Shaffer. I think that's part of the problem," the president observed. "Could very well be," Haldeman agreed. "But John, I can't believe is a basically dishonorable guy. I think there's no question John is a strong self-promoter, self-motivated guy for his own good."

They now turned to an attempt to rewrite my conversations with the president, and later Haldeman, on March 21, with Haldeman claiming the president had never said it would not be a problem to raise a million dollars for the defendant. Instead, the president had said it was blackmail by Hunt, and it was wrong. The meeting ended with the president asking if he should call me into his office to say that he was issuing a statement but that it would make no mention of me. Ehrlichman thought it a good idea, but Nixon never followed up on it.

Shortly after this conversation ended, it was so unclear exactly what had and had not been agreed upon that the president called Ehrlichman to clarify matters before he met again with Henry Petersen.[59] "I just wanted to be sure to check the points you want [raised] with Petersen. He'll be [here] in five to ten minutes. So one, no immunity from any of the top three?" Ehrlichman confirmed that and, gathering his notes, told the president the points he had written down were, first, that he would issue a statement regarding his policy on suspension and firing: Anyone indicted would be suspended and anyone convicted would be fired. Ehrlichman said that that would be in the statement he was drafting, and Nixon told him he wanted Ehrlichman to brief the press on this point; he would privately inform Petersen that there would be no immunity for "any top person, like Dean or up."

Petersen arrived in the Oval Office at 2:40 P.M. and remained for an hour.[60] "Anything new I need to know?" Nixon asked after a few friendly quips. "No, sir," Petersen replied. Obviously still thinking about Haldeman and Ehrlichman's attack on Petersen, not to mention the concern that Petersen might be a friend of mine who had violated the law somehow in passing me information, the president said, "I don't want you really to tell me anything out of the grand jury unless you think I need to know it." Being very careful, the president added, "I guess it would be legal for me to know?" Sounding less than certain, Petersen replied, "Well, yes, I think it is legal for you to know."

After establishing that Petersen admired Bill Rogers, Nixon told Petersen that Rogers's "views are somewhat different from yours." The president continued, "I think you have to know that Dean has talked very freely to Mitchell. Whether he has talked to others about [Watergate], I do not know." When Petersen said he was aware of my relationship with Mitchell, Nixon explained that the point was that I was sharing information with Mitchell, which I had obviously received from Petersen and "from the grand jury." Nixon assured him that he did not want "the Department of Justice, and you particularly, to get embarrassed," but Petersen was not worried about that. Nixon pressed, saying Rogers "was greatly concerned about the leaks from the grand jury" during the preceding summer, "during June, July, August, September and so forth, that is the point."* Without stating it directly, the president was referring to the period during which Petersen was keeping me advised of the grand jury's activities. Again, Petersen dismissed his argument: "I don't think that is critical." But before he could explain his position, the president told him that he didn't want the case to fall apart "after all this agony," because the man he was now "relying on"—meaning Petersen—might find himself in some untenable position. "Mr. President," Petersen protested, "I don't want to be in that position." Again Nixon continued the offensive: "Well, now, you've got your life and career ahead." And again Petersen did not back down. Nixon finally put forward the ultimate potential threat for Petersen, telling him that Rogers "is recommending a special counsel. He's very much afraid that anybody who has been handling this damn thing up to this point" was going to have problems. "How do you feel about that?"

No one ever said Richard Nixon was not clever, and at that point he had Petersen in a position where he had to defend himself and the ability of the Department of Justice to continue with the Watergate case. Petersen claimed his conversation with me had "touched on three things: One, leaks," which he said he did not take very seriously, for they were part and parcel of Washington business; "second was Dean's personal involvement," relating to the handling of the records from Hunt's safe; and "third was status reports."†

Petersen was vague enough about those status reports to cause the president to ask if this was a potential problem area. "No, sir," Petersen responded. "I can disclose to an attorney for the government in the course of my work. Dean was, in addition to counsel to the president, obviously an attorney for the government, and there is nothing improper in that." The president was pleased to hear this remarkably broad interpretation of Rule

---

*Because of Nixon's propensity to put words in the mouths of those he used to make points, I searched his recorded conversation with Rogers for the information he shared with Petersen. I can find no such statements by Rogers during any of the recorded conversations, and it does not appear Nixon had any unrecorded conversations with Rogers, although that certainly could have occurred.

†As Haleman's notes of my conversations with Petersen document, he was giving me far more than status reports. In addition, Petersen overlooked perhaps the two most important of our conversations: when we met on June 20, 1972; and on November 8, 1972, after Nixon called for the resignation of all presidential appointees. When I spoke with Petersen to tell him he was safe in his post I had found him remarkably angry and very upset. He told me "he had gone above and beyond the call of duty [and] acted at some risk" in restraining the Watergate investigation, which was still ongoing, yet had been asked for his resignation. But as noted earlier, I had anticipated his concern and taken care to keep him in place.

6(e) of the Federal Rules of Criminal Procedure. But then Petersen raised the real-world consequences: "Now, politically, if someone wants to say, as they said to Pat Gray, you shouldn't have been talking to John Dean, well, there's no way out of that." But Petersen effectively dismissed such potential claims as "demagoguery," which he did not take seriously.

When the president turned to what he called "a basic command decision with regard to what you do about the White House people," he began giving Petersen a spin on the facts that made both Haldeman and Ehrlichman appear less culpable, which Petersen, who did not have a firm grasp on the situation, accepted without questions. Nixon then returned to his chief objective, which was to make certain I did not receive immunity. He claimed Bill Rogers had told him that immunity could not be given to "the guy that sunk Pat Gray." Petersen accepted this interpretation of Gray's failure to be confirmed and told Nixon that he, too, did not want me to have immunity. When Petersen asked if the president had decided to accept my resignation, Nixon replied that no, he was going to treat everyone the same, an approach Petersen supported. At another point in the conversation the president offered what he claimed were his motives: "Let me say I am not, I guess my point on Dean is a matter of principle, it is a question of the fact that I am not trying to do Dean in. I would like to see him save himself, but I think find a way to do it without, if you're going the immunity route, I think we are going to catch holy hell for it." Since the public thought I was a major figure, Nixon argued, this was appropriate. "Well, what the hell, he can talk without any immunity can't he?" Then, in the next breath, he answered his own question, "Oh, I guess if he is a defendant, he wouldn't talk to you?" "That's right," Petersen replied.

This conversation included a lengthy discussion of "unindicted coconspirators," a term that refers to an individual who was part of a conspiracy but has not been indicted, usually because the government wants him to testify. "Let me ask you this, Mr. President," Petersen said. "What would you do if we filed an indictment against Magruder, hypothetically, and—" The president hastened to add "or Dean," but Petersen kept to Magruder and continued, "—to which he's going to plead guilty, and we name as unindicted coconspirators everybody but Haldeman and Ehrlichman." The president interrupted again to ask about Colson, but Petersen felt he was peripheral. When the president questioned if he would name "Dean, for example?" Petersen said he would name everyone but Haldeman and Ehrlichman: "Now one of the things we had thought about leaving them out was to give you time and room to maneuver with respect to the two of them." Nixon reacted, "Let me ask you, can I ask you, talking in the president's office," Nixon began, and after a brief interruption to sign some papers, continued, "You mean if Haldeman and Ehrlichman leave, you will not indict them?"

"No sir, I didn't say that," Petersen stated clearly. "That would be a strange [thing to do]," the president noted. "No, it was not a question of that," Petersen explained. "It was a question of whether or not they were publicly identified in that pleading at that time. And, well, for example, as a scenario that comes out, and you say, this is a shocking revelation, as a consequence of that I have consulted and I have just decided to clear out everybody here who might have [been involved], and as a consequence Mr. Ehrlichman and Mr. Haldeman are going. Thereafter, we would proceed with the evidence wherever it took us. That's what we were thinking about, to be perfectly honest with you."

"Well, you really ought to include them [*unclear*], if you include the others," the president acknowledged, and then quickly added, "Oh, you don't want names in the indictment of Magruder." "That's right," Petersen confirmed, "unless we were able to go forward." Petersen then added, "Well, I don't want to belabor the point. I have made it clear that, in my view, that I think they have made you very, very vulnerable. I think they have made you wittingly or unwittingly very vulnerable to rather severe criticism because of their actions, at least in public forums, they've eroded confidence in the office of the presidency by their actions."

They then discussed the difficulty that Judge Sirica was causing by acting as both prosecutor and judge with his unwillingness to accept pleas that the government was willing to accept, which was now affecting Magruder and others who were hesitant to plead before Sirica, given the outrageous sentences he was handing down. Petersen reported that LaRue had broken down and cried when he came in to testify about John Mitchell, which prompted the president to proclaim that, as president, he was "just trying to do the right thing," to which Petersen responded, "Mr. President, if I didn't have confidence in you, I wouldn't be here."

"Did we do any good on the Liddy call?" Nixon asked. Petersen said that Liddy's lawyer, Peter Maroulis, had flown down from New York, and they arranged for Liddy to be transported to the cell block of the D.C. Court to meet with him. But Petersen did not know the results of that meeting. "I am sure Liddy is thinking it over, but we'll see. That man is a mental case," Petersen said.[61]

They now turned to Ehrlichman's draft on executive privilege, with the president reading key parts aloud. Petersen indicated that he did not like the language in the draft regarding immunity, which read: "No person in past or present positions of importance can be given immunity from prosecution." "I don't think you ought to say that, Mr. President," Petersen said and, explaining that he was effectively nullifying the immunity statute and giving potential defendants the right to invoke the Fifth Amendment, which could deny the prosecutors the use of their testimony. "Even if we never utilize immunity," Petersen said, "the fact that it is there and can be used to strip them of the Fifth Amendment rights is a terribly important tactic to have available. That phrase in there takes that tactic away from us." While Nixon could not say it, if he could silence everybody behind the Fifth Amendment, it would solve many of his problems. He accordingly suggested modifying the language: "Say 'major government employees,' how'd that be?" "I would prefer that we not say it," Petersen persisted. "Well, I'm just trying to cover my tracks on the Dean thing," Nixon finally admitted. They tried various phrases that might silence me while not making a nullity of the immunity statute, should they wish to use it.

Finally Petersen, whom Nixon had already convinced for his own good that I should not have immunity, offered language he could accept. The president could say, "I have expressed my hope to the appropriate authorities that it would not be necessary to immunize any major official in order to develop a prosecutable case." After a bit more back and forth, the president said, "Okay, I've got it." He moved the conversation back toward his efforts to paint the facts in a light he felt more favorable while getting Petersen's insights into the strengths and weaknesses of the government case, whom they might indict, and when.

As the conversation was winding down, the president urged Petersen to have the Justice Department get the prosecution and Watergate over as soon as possible. Petersen in turn presciently advised him: "You know, there is another dimension, Mr. President. These fellows, Magruder, Dean, have talked to us. They'd be less than human if they didn't watch to see if the system was surviving the test, so there is another reason for their delay. Conceivably they'll say, 'Well, this may be too strong for the Department of Justice or the president, or the White House; they're not going to have the courage to face up to this, [so] let's wait and see what happens.' So if we don't see some movement, then our bargaining position will become increasingly tougher day by day by day." This, of course, is exactly what would happen, and Petersen was repeating almost verbatim what Shaffer had told his team of prosecutors. In fact, I did not believe the Justice Department could handle the case and had moved on to work with the Senate Watergate committee, which was on a constitutional parallel with the presidency.

But Nixon ignored Petersen's warning. "Yeah, well, keep in my mind I'd like to get the God damn thing over with, and I know the trials of Mitchell and all these people will take a long time," he responded, noting, "Mitchell will never plead guilty, never. [He'll] fight it all the way down the line." Then he asked, "What would you do if you were Mitchell?" "I think I would probably go to Saudi Arabia, to tell you the truth," Petersen replied. Petersen, who had been elevated to his post by Mitchell, added, "When I think the former attorney general of the United States being subject to criminal trial, it is just terrible." Nixon added, "For obstruction of justice." The president clarified, "Not the bugging, the obstruction of justice," and he ended the session.

Within a minute of Petersen's departure, Haldeman and Ehrlichman were back in the Oval Office, for what became a forty-five-minute session to polish the executive privilege statement, which the president himself would take to the press room to read before the cameras and White House press corps.[62] As they gathered at the president's desk, he said that the first part of the statement regarding the Senate Watergate committee was fine, but they needed to work on the second announcement. After interruptions to advise Senator Sam Ervin regarding the section of the statement relating to his committee and to bring Ziegler up to speed, Nixon gave Haldeman and Ehrlichman the highlights of his conversation with Petersen and told them that a few changes would have to be made to the immunity language of the statement. Nixon said that Petersen was considering indicting Magruder and naming a list of others as unindicted coconspirators. As he related the conversation: "They're going to include everybody on that list. I said, 'Is Dean going to be on that list?' He said yes. He said, 'Frankly, to be quite candid, that we ought not to include Haldeman and Ehrlichman on that list. Which gives you an option.'" Nixon claimed that this hypothetical of Petersen's represented the current thinking of the Justice Department, and then continued: "I said, 'Are you telling me that if Haldeman and Ehrlichman decide to take leave that you will not then proceed with the prosecution? And leave them there?' 'No,' he said, 'I don't mean that.' He said, 'What I mean is that they are not going to appear on that list, and they will appear before the grand jury and make a case there to determine whether they should be indicted.' So there's that the gun up ahead."

Ehrlichman hastened to ask, "Well, whether we take leave or not doesn't affect the list that they read off?" Nixon said, to the contrary, it did, although Petersen had stated just the opposite. "Oh, it does?" Ehrlichman said with alarm in his voice. "Yes," the president replied softly. "They will put us on the list if we don't take leave?" Ehrlichman asked again, for clarification. "That's what he was saying," the president told them. "Well, the bastard," Ehrlichman declared. Using Petersen as his foil, Nixon explained, "Yes, because otherwise, he says, Sirica is going to question Magruder, and he's going to question him about Haldeman, and it will appear that they were involved in this." As this all sank in there was a brief pause, and the president said the question now was whether he should go forward with an announcement today. Ehrlichman thought he had to do so or the matter would get away from him. But the key issue still hung over the conversation, and after further discussion, Nixon again mischaracterized what Petersen said, telling his aides that unless they left the White House, they would be named as unindicted coconspirators in Magruder's case yet still remain exposed to prosecution.*

They then proceeded line by line through the draft statement, editing a word here and a phrase there. Needing to explain why Nixon had personally become interested in Watergate, they tested several vague statements, until the president suggested, "Why don't we say on—Shall we set a date? March twenty-first? That sounds a hell of a lot stronger if we set a date." Because it did sound stronger, Nixon selected our March 21 conversation as his turning point. In fact, during a candid moment with Henry Petersen, Nixon had told him that it had been the McCord letter that gotten him seriously focused on Watergate, which the record shows was true. Of course, he knew exactly

---

*Haldeman can be heard making notes on the president's desk during this difficult to hear recorded conversation. Based on those notes, Haldeman later dictated to his diary his understanding of what Nixon was reporting from Petersen regarding the Magruder case: "They'll say he's named certain people, and that other people are non-indicted co-conspirators that will be named as a group. This will include Dean, but Petersen will not include Ehrlichman and Haldeman if they take a leave. The P said are you saying if Haldeman and Ehrlichman take a leave you won't prosecute them? He said no, it just means they aren't on the list. They'll still appear at the grand jury and I'll have to make their case there." Haldeman further noted the president as saying, "Petersen's really saying that we'll be on the list unless we decide to take a leave." H. R. Haldeman, *The Haldeman Diaries: Inside the Nixon White House* (New York: G. P. Putnam's, 1993), 645.

what he was doing in selecting March 21 as the key date: That conversation was a serious liability for him, so he would turn it into an asset. He was building his defense, which no one else would understand, but March 21 would have him taking action before McCord's letter rather than reacting to it. Nor would anyone understand the reference to immunity in this statement.

For a passing minute the president had second thoughts about including an immunity paragraph, telling Ehrlichman, "I don't want to put the immunity thing in publicly. As I said privately to [Petersen], I don't think there's a hell of a lot to be gained by saying it publicly." Ehrlichman quickly persuaded the president otherwise, for it sent a message to Congress. The president conceded the point, and after about twenty minutes of discussing the draft, the statement was completed, and Ehrlichman took it to a secretary to prepare a final draft in a larger-font copy for the president to read before the press. While that was being done, Haldeman told the president more about how the prosecutors were continuing to lean on Gordon Strachan, making conspicuously false statements to him. The president thought he understood why they were doing this: "You see, they think it is worse than it is. They think he is covering up and they're wrong. That's what it really gets down to."

"They are trying to confuse him," Haldeman said. "That's what got him bothered. The poor guy. You see, what's really worried him is that he's covered everything with Dean, every step of the way. Everything he has done, he's talked with Dean about over the last year, and he's scared to death Dean will make up something or take something that is partly right and twist it, which is what Dean is doing, and hang him on it."[63] Haldeman also told the president that he and Ehrlichman, who had both retained the same attorney, had had a first meeting with their lawyer.

When the statement was completed, Ehrlichman returned (the Oval Office recording tape was in the process of being changed and so there is no recording) and presumably the president read it over before heading to the White House press room, where he read the following statement, with two announcements, but refused to answer any questions. First he reported the agreement with the Senate Watergate committee, then said he had an announcement regarding Watergate:

> On March 21, as a result of serious charges which came to my attention, some of which were publicly reported, I began intensive new inquiries into this whole matter. Last Sunday afternoon, the attorney general,

Assistant Attorney General Petersen and I met at length in the EOB to review the facts which had come to me in my investigation and also to review the progress of the Department of Justice investigation. I can report today that there have been major developments in the case concerning which it would be improper to be more specific now, except to say that real progress has been made in finding the truth.

He proceeded to read the statement that declared that if anyone was indicted he would be suspended, and if convicted, "automatically discharged." Next he read his new position on immunity: "I have expressed to the appropriate authorities my view that no individual holding, in the past or at present, a position of major importance in the administration should be given immunity from prosecution." There was no doubt in my mind that this was intended as a message to me, and an effort to block me from ending the cover-up. What Nixon and my colleagues did not know was that I had already decided to testify before the Senate with or without immunity, and had given up on the federal prosecutors. Charles Shaffer had wisely insisted that if I wanted him to represent me, we follow this course of action.

Following the president's statement, Ziegler met with him briefly in the Oval Office, seeking guidance before he returned to the press room to answer questions.[64] Ziegler said he had been asked why I had not attended the meeting with the attorney general and Petersen. Nixon told him to say, "He decided it was necessary to initiate an independent investigation, and Mr. Dean agreed." Ziegler said he had also been asked if the August 29 statement was still operative? Nixon instructed Ziegler to say his "August twenty-ninth statement was based on an important investigation Mr. Dean conducted, and it would be improper to comment further on matters at the present." Ziegler was told to respond to almost every question with a nonanswer: namely, that he did not want to prejudice either the prosecution or the rights of innocent people.

"I want to get into a little snow job with some of these [reporters] on background," Ziegler said, to explain privately to them how Nixon had been working behind the scenes to break the case, an idea that Nixon liked. "Well, you're going to have a very rough time in the next two or three months on this," the president said, "because they're going to name Mitchell and Magruder, very likely [also] name Haldeman and Ehrlichman as coconspirators, certainly Dean." He added, "Dean is likely to blow his stack, piss on the

White House, I don't know. His attorney's threatening to." "Well, Dean's decimated anyway," Ziegler replied. "Dean can say whatever he wants. Any man who goes for nine months, who has been lying to the president, which [will be] the impression if he is indicted, or if he is involved in this, is discredited. Anytime this becomes public, he's a bad fellow, automatically." Nixon was not convinced, and said I had a lot of information regarding Watergate and Ehrlichman, regarding leaks and the Ellsberg matter, and bugging other than the FBI's. Ziegler, however, remained confident: "He's still discredited. Discredited in anything he says. The fact of the matter is, everyone has a stake in Dean, the press has a stake in Dean, the White House has a stake in Dean. If it happens that Dean was guilty of misleading, lying, not providing the full story, he's destroyed."

After the president spoke generally about potential problems, and they discussed the Senate's Watergate investigation, Ziegler said, "I think I'll call Dean and tell him what I'm going to say, should I?" The president agreed, and added, "And I'd try to take his temperature. He might be a little shaken by that statement I made." Nixon suggested that Ziegler should reassure me that the president was treating everyone equally, and as the press secretary was leaving, Nixon again urged that he call me and added, "But remind him the president said to be sure to protect the president."

At the press briefing Ziegler was hammered with a flurry of questions: What prompted the president's statement? What had happened on March 21? Was the Dean report still the operative statement about the White House? Did the "major developments" apply not only to Watergate but also to the alleged espionage and sabotage? Who asked for the meeting with Petersen? Did the president still have confidence in Dean? Was anyone resigning? Why didn't Mitchell meet with the president when he was here? How long was Ziegler going to continue to not answer questions? Did Ziegler stand by his March 26, 1973, statement that Dean did not have prior knowledge of the Watergate matter? Was Ehrlichman involved in the new investigation? Ziegler answered most of these questions by referring to the new April 17, 1972, presidential statement as the operative policy, about which he refused to elaborate because he did not want to prejudice either the prosecutor or innocent people.

After dealing with paperwork in the Oval Office, Nixon moved in the late afternoon to his EOB office, where he met for almost two hours with Bill Rogers, and they were later joined by Haldeman and Ehrlichman.[65] Rogers told Nixon that he thought his statement was appropriate, and Nixon brought Rogers up to date on recent information, such as Pat Gray's admission that he had destroyed the material from Hunt's safe, though he claimed he had been instructed to do so, a contention that both Rogers and Nixon found absurd. Nixon shared his latest information about the Justice Department's handling of the case and explained how he had added the no-immunity language in his statement to deal with me. He told Rogers the prosecutors handling the case "were hot on trying to give" me immunity because "they want to get Haldeman and Ehrlichman, frankly."

Nixon gave Rogers another version of Haldeman and Ehrlichman being named as unindicted coconspirators, which Rogers had difficulty understanding, insisting they were "not guilty of a God damn thing." After agreeing on their innocence, Nixon complained that Watergate was consuming all his time, and it was destroying Haldeman, Ehrlichman and Dean. He asked Rogers to help by advising Haldeman and Ehrlichman. The president then claimed that he had met with me only three times before he had started his own investigation on March 21. He told Rogers that he had sent me to Camp David to write a report, but that I had ultimately demurred, explaining, "I really can't write a statement that you can put out." Nixon said he was insisting the White House "let it all hang out" but that Haldeman and Ehrlichman were not going to tolerate any charges against them, which he had told them about that morning: "[They're] going to fight, discredit Dean, discredit the prosecutor." Nixon warned it was going to be a real fight and added, "Dean's pissed off."

Haldeman and Ehrlichman arrived from a first meeting with their new attorney, John J. Wilson, whom Rogers had recommended. He was seventy-two, and they found him sharp and knowledgeable. Wilson had advised them, in the event they went to trial, that he had a heart condition. Nixon interrupted their account to insist, "You don't need a trial lawyer," and Haldeman agreed that what they needed was brains. Best of all, Ehrlichman said, Wilson knew the entire cast of chargers at the Justice Department, specifically, Henry Petersen and Seymour Glanzer, and he "despises them," Haldeman added. Nixon said, "I am not going to talk to Petersen anymore. That's done, except to suck all the information I can get from him, you know what I mean."

Ehrlichman said Wilson had explained to them what would happen when Magruder pleaded: "In this district it is customary for the judge to interrogate if he wished" when there is a guilty plea and the government files "a statement of the case, in the nature of an information." They had discussed with Wilson at some length what Nixon had falsely told them about Petersen's intention to proceed against Haldeman and Ehrlichman if they refused to take leaves of absence. Rogers agreed that to do as Nixon claimed Petersen was planning was "a perversion of the system, for it allowed prosecutors to ruin anyone without their day in court."

Ehrlichman revealed that they had also discussed with Wilson another way to block my testimony—namely, that he and Haldeman were my two conduits to the president, who was my client, and under the attorney-client privilege I could not discuss these matters. Ehrlichman felt their relationship to me as such conduits entitled them to the same privilege. Accordingly he suggested, "What I said to Dean and what Dean said to me in private conversation with no third party present could be a [matter] of privilege." He gave an example: "Dean's conversation where he says he came in and told me that Liddy had confessed." "Well," he noted, "the only reason to tell me was not for me as me, but because I was one of the two conduits that he had to his boss. The organizational setup was that way." Ehrlichman asserted that if this strategy was correct, and the president did not waive his privilege, it would silence me. "I'll take a look," the president said, and asked Rogers what he thought. But Rogers offered no opinion, or was being polite, because the proposal was so fundamentally farfetched.[66]

When Bill Rogers departed the conversation became a bit less restrained. Nixon was pleased that his aides had procured an attorney, because they were all in a fight. Haldeman reported that Wilson said, "Glanzer is a bad operator. He knows him well. He doesn't know Silbert." They discussed the latest media coverage. Nixon thought I was leaking, while Haldeman sensed that *The Washington Post* was keeping a lower profile, playing for the longer game. "As a matter of fact," Ehrlichman added, "you might have to turn on the [television] set some day and watch your White House counsel crap for the glorious television [audience]." Ehrlichman urged the president to "immediately approve a new White House counsel," and he had a candidate in mind: Jim Thompson, the former U.S. attorney who tried Illinois governor Otto Kerner. Thompson had visited the White House, and Ehrlichman noted, "He's tough, bright, dedicated to public service, attractive [and] clean." Nixon wondered if he would be loyal, and Ehrlichman said he thought he would.

"I know you don't think it's important," Haldeman told Nixon, "but the White House counsel *is* important. [The job] is important if it goes wrong, and it's totally insignificant as long as it goes right." Nixon did not disagree but noted, "Now let's face it, face up to this thing: Dean handled a lot of stuff well." Haldeman agreed, and as Nixon felt the discussion of a new counsel was premature, the conversation moved forward.

Ehrlichman reported that their new lawyer, Wilson, was going to talk to the U.S. attorneys and warn them that if Haldeman and Ehrlichman were placed on some list of conspirators, it could ruin innocent men. Ehrlichman said Wilson "has quite a close relationship with Titus," the U.S. attorney, and he was going to tell them not to make some sort of side deal with me, granting me informal immunity, in which they would simply tell me I was a witness and not a defendant. As the conversation proceeded, a minor problem was identified: I was, in fact, only a middle-level staffer at the Nixon White House, which was why the president had worded his no-immunity statement so broadly. Yet, as Nixon observed, that statement was now a problem for the prosecutors, because "Dean is the only one who can sink Haldeman and Ehrlichman." Ehrlichman said I could not be viewed as some "little clerk," notwithstanding the fact that he had generally viewed me that way since my arrival at the White House. But for purposes of preventing me from obtaining immunity, Ehrlichman would elevate me even in his perception of my place on the staff.

"I have no intention to see Dean again," Nixon told them, "unless it's useful. I don't think you can control him; he's fanatic. If you feel it would be useful, let me know." Ehrlichman said, "I will tell you, what is lurking in the back of my mind is that, based on the chain of circumstances, Dean may be provoked to make a public statement which is slanderous and hostile." Ehrlichman was hoping I might do so, as they could then file libel lawsuits if they were defamed. Nixon agreed, and they speculated about who else they might sue, but reached no conclusions. They agreed that in the coming days they had to "maintain the façade of normal operations." If they were not tied up with their attorneys, Ehrlichman suggested they go to Florida with the president for the weekend. Ehrlichman also asked, if they were forced to take a leave, if the president might consider their "use of Camp David occasionally." Nixon, dodging the request, said he wanted them to go forward so they could "beat the rap, at all costs, beat the God damn rap."

Curious if Wilson had explained the legal issues in question to them,

Nixon asked, "What the hell is the law on obstruction of justice?" Haldeman said they had not had a full discussion on that yet, and Ehrlichman added that they would be briefed on it that evening. Haldeman reported that Wilson had characterized obstruction of justice as "damn tough, loose." He also had told them that Glanzer was "the major, leading authority on it. He uses it like a bludgeon." Haldeman further cited Wilson as saying that the obstruction law was" broad, and cases go all different ways."

Though he now had legal representation, however, Ehrlichman's mood was sinking. Even if they "beat the rap," he felt they were still "damaged goods." They were not to Nixon, he told them, and he said he wanted them to work for his postpresidential foundation. Ehrlichman, looking at the larger picture, noted, "But I think we've just about had it. I think the odds are against it." Nixon interrupted this discussion to ask if they had spoken with Kalmbach regarding the money. They had not, and Ehrlichman, being less than candid, said I had only told Kalmbach that the fund-raising was an urgent situation.[67] Which brought the president back to the plight of his two top aides. He again offered them money for their legal fees, but Ehrlichman said, "Let's wait and see if it's necessary." Nixon assured them the money would not be his—Bebe had some funds that could be used. Ehrlichman said, "I'll tell you, my feeling on this is that, I may be an optimist, I'm just not willing to believe that the process will result in an indictment. I just can't accept that." Haldeman, too, had not given up hope, adding, "You've got to have faith that the system works." The president, assessing the situation more realistically, said they should not forget that there would be an effort to get them and to get Nixon, and that "Glanzer is a great obstruction of justice man." Ehrlichman observed that "Glanzer can't do this all by himself," counting on Wilson's putting up a block with Glanzer's boss, Harold Titus. Haldeman said they must "keep some face." Ehrlichman reported that he was handing over many of his daily duties to his top assistant, Ken Cole, informing him that he was going to have to carry a heavier load. Ehrlichman mentioned that he had passed Kissinger in the hallway, "And I could have sworn I had a spot of leprosy," adding that Henry really did not know how to handle what was happening.

Nixon asked, "Where do we put Garment at this point?" "I think he's eligible for a trip," offered Ehrlichman, to mildly disparage the president's former law partner who was considered the White House liberal, and added, "I think maybe you ought to send him to Ceylon or someplace." They agreed that a decision about Garment, who was threatening to resign, could be deferred. The president was more concerned about finding a new FBI director and a new attorney general. And he somewhat surprised them both when he asked, "Bob and John, if you have to be replaced, who the hell would we put in your spot?" No viable suggestions emerged, and when the president again offered them money for legal fees, Ehrlichman said, "If we get into a trial phase, I would go out of town and hire the best God damn trial lawyer in the world, bring him in here, and load him up, and really put on a show. So that'll cost plenty, you know." Haldeman asked who he had in mind. "Somebody like Bill Frates down in Miami, or somebody of that kind. He's very skillful and very tough."

Before Nixon returned to the residence to change for a state dinner, he made a quick call to Ziegler. "Did you get Dean?" he asked.[68] Ziegler reported, "Yes, I did, and outlined the position to him, and he sounded fine, and a copy of the statement [is] being sent over to him." He then described to the president the types of questions he had gotten at his briefing, which he said he had dodged by refusing to talk about any individual. "Very good, Ron," the president said.

Following the dinner the president returned to the Lincoln Sitting Room and called Henry Kissinger.[69] Nixon confided that he could not look at his problem in "the detached way [he] really should," because those involved in Watergate were "good men." So he was rejecting Garment's approach of firing Haldeman, Ehrlichman and Dean "without waiting until" they got to the real culprit, John Mitchell. "I'm not going to fire a guy on the basis of a charge made by Dean, who basically is trying to save his ass and get immunity, you see. That's why I had that phrase in there that no immunity should be granted to a top person. He has no right to do that," Nixon declared, and Kissinger agreed.

Nixon was essentially testing his new and developing defense on Kissinger, and explained, "Some of these people will even piss on the president if they think it will help them. It's pretty bad. I'm the only one, frankly, of the whole bunch who really didn't know a God damn thing about it until March, when finally Dean came in and said, well, here's where it is, which he should have done months ago." "Well," Kissinger observed, "they were in over their heads, and they tried to, instead of stepping back and assessing where they were, got in deeper and deeper." "Maybe we'll even consider the possibility of, frankly, just throwing myself on the sword, and letting Agnew take it," the president rather dramatically declared, again testing Kissinger. Kissinger's reaction was instant, and he sounded horrified: "That is out of the question, with all due respect, Mr. President. That cannot be considered." But he was not finished: "His personality, what it would do to the presidency. And the historical injustice of it. Why should you do it, and what good would it do? Whom would it help? It wouldn't help the country. It wouldn't help any individuals involved. With all respect, I don't think the president has the right to sacrifice himself for an individual. And it would, of course, be personally unjust." With a long sigh, Nixon told Kissinger that the dinner that evening "was a hard one for me to get through," and then he added," I don't think the audience sensed it." "No one sensed it," Kissinger assured him. "No one. In fact, I didn't know you had made a statement [until] one of my dinner partners said, 'Isn't it astonishing how the president is behaving, given what he's done today?' 'Yes,' I said, 'he had a tough meeting in the morning, but he does that all the time.' She said, 'No, the statement.' So it was an astonishing performance."

The president said he wanted Kissinger to talk off-the-record to people about how difficult all this was for him, if it might help. Kissinger assured the president he would do so, and that it would help, adding, "It's impermissible to touch the president. That cannot be permitted, at whatever price. And I'm sure that Bob wouldn't want that." The president confided, "Bob and John are willing to throw themselves on the sword over there. When they do, they're going to fight like hell." "But one of them ought to stay," Kissinger insisted, candidly, "I would hope so," Nixon said, "but I'm afraid it can't be Haldeman. I'm afraid the only one that possibly could be saved would be Ehrlichman, and that's tough, too."

Kissinger was not in the dark about what was at stake and told him, "Well, Garment wants you to fire Haldeman [and] Dean." And Ehrlichman as well, Nixon added, but Kissinger questioned that, saying, "I don't know whether he wants you to fire Ehrlichman, too." The president pointed out that the evidence was changing, and Kissinger offered that they should resign on the grounds that their usefulness had been impaired, and that they had to be "like Caesar's wife." The president said he was considering his alternatives and told Kissinger not to get discouraged, and to do his job. "You, two or three of us," Nixon said, "have to stick around, try to hold the God damn fort." Seeking to bolster Nixon, Kissinger said, "You have saved this country, Mr. President. The history books will show that, when no one will know what

Watergate means." Nixon was doubtful, however, and Kissinger noted, "It's a human tragedy for Haldeman and Dean and a few of those fellows."

"Dean is the real, the fellow that's really going to be the loose cannon," Nixon said, and explained again that I was the reason for the no-immunity directive in his statement: "And that's going to burn his ass, because then he'll thrash out about everything you can imagine. Although Ziegler has made an interesting point. He has God damn little credulity; after all, he was making the report. He was the one that said there was no involvement, and that's what we relied on. And it took him until February, or March, until he finally came in and said, here it is. A little damn late, isn't it?"

"I'd just fire him as soon as it comes out and let him scream from the outside," Kissinger advised. The president was silent for a moment, then said he guessed he would have to do that when the time came, adding, "Well, you know, nobody really will know what they put a president through on a thing like this." "Well," Kissinger agreed, "it's inhuman, Mr. President. These bastards know damn well that you couldn't have known about it, if one considers all the things you had to go through. You couldn't be a police judge, too. You're running the government, you're doing all the negotiating, you're carrying a bigger load than any president has." The president mentioned his trips to Russia and China and ending the war but wondered if he should have spent more time on his campaign, rather than on Vietnam. "If you can't rely on your own people to tell you the facts, then it's rather difficult." Kissinger added, "Exactly. If you had done that, we might still be in the war." Nixon found Kissinger's assurances comforting, and told him, "And in the meantime, put your arm around Haldeman and Ehrlichman."

"You can count on it, Mr. President. I've been standing by Haldeman. I didn't know Ehrlichman was in trouble, too. Now you can count on the fact that I'll stand by them. But the major person to stand by now is you," Kissinger said. The conversation ended with a discussion of the state dinner and how "old Frank Sinatra," who had entertained that night, had given everyone a lift.

After saying good night to Kissinger shortly after midnight, Nixon called Haldeman and told him: "I just wanted to say, keep the faith."[70] Haldeman said that he and Ehrlichman had reviewed the worst-case scenario and "what's in between," and "the thing now is just play it as it lies, day by day, and see where we come out." The president asked if Strachan had been to the grand jury, but Haldeman did not think that had happened, and Nixon told him he wanted to meet in the morning to discuss who was vulnerable, for he thought I would probably be given immunity notwithstanding his statement.

"One thing we've got to do, Bob, is get some kind of line with regard to this whole business of helping the defendants. I just feel some way that ought to be able to be done, you know what I mean? I don't know whether there is any way, though, is there?" Haldeman felt they could only keep stressing the point that the money had been intended for fees and support and that was it. Nixon again reviewed how Hunt had been taken care of by Mitchell, with Haldeman, Ehrlichman and me being told the next day, and asked if there was some way Ehrlichman could be separated out. "You see," Nixon noted, "the vulnerabilities of a lawyer here is enormous, because it's a destruction of his career." Haldeman thought there was a long way to go before Ehrlichman would face that possibility, and Nixon backed off this idea.

Despite the statement he had issued only a few hour earlier, Nixon was now privately claiming that it was Ehrlichman who had triggered his interest in the Watergate matter. "Ehrlichman's own investigation was, it's very important that we get that, you know, that is what really triggered it, rather than what Dean said, see my point?" Haldeman responded with a noncommittal, "Mmm, hmm," and the president continued. "That makes sense," Nixon said, suggesting they discuss it, and then got to his point: "We've really got to think how to save what there is left of the president, the presidency." He now thought an Ehrlichman report worked better because "Ehrlichman did call the attorney general and say look, here it is, and after that call, Magruder cracked, so let's put it all down. Do you think that's a good idea?" The president asked Haldeman who in addition to Strachan at the White House had any problems; he asked specifically about Larry Higby, who would slip through the cracks notwithstanding his intimate connections with all things Haldeman: "It doesn't touch our trust in Higby, does it? Or?" Haldeman answered Nixon's hanging question softly, "Yeah," indicating that Higby was indeed touched, though Haldeman added that he had not been subpoenaed.

Nixon remained most concerned about me. If I was indicted, the president was convinced, "then, of course, he'll says he's going to destroy the president, too. Isn't that what he's threatened? He's been threatening all the time, isn't he, even you? Isn't he?" Checking the president's anxiety, Haldeman assured him, "No, no, he never did." Nixon began trying to provoke Haldeman into saying that he and Ehrlichman had been pushing to let it all hang out, but I had somehow blocked them. When Haldeman did not react as hoped, Nixon suggested the tragedy was Mitchell, and his refusal to step up. After a pause the president offered an example—Mitchell's request to activate Kalmbach. "Who said that, Mitchell said it, didn't he?" Nixon asked twice, and Haldeman answered twice that Mitchell had requested that I go to Ehrlichman, but he did not recall that I had come to him as well; rather, I had only "alluded" to his agreement. "Well, make him prove it, okay John, Bob, Bob, bye."

## April 18, 1973, the White House

Before going to the bipartisan leadership meeting in the Cabinet Room to discuss energy issues, the president spoke to Ziegler in the Oval Office.[71] Ziegler had drafted an explanation of why Nixon had taken action based on new Watergate information, which was presented as the president's response to newspaper reports, grand jury information and the Gray hearings. Nixon listened as Ziegler read the document, and while the president added a few thoughts, he was not seriously considering Ziegler's suggestions. At 8:11 A.M. Haldeman arrived in the Oval Office for a brief chat.[72]

Nixon had been thinking about his secret recording system. "I would like you to take all these tapes, if you wouldn't mind," Nixon began. "In other words, there is some material in there that's probably worth keeping, [but] most of [them are] worth destroying. Would you do that?" "Sure," Haldeman said, and the president added that he thought some of the material might go to the future Nixon library.

Haldeman proceeded to tell the president that he had been thinking the night before about the Hunt threat on March 21, a date Haldeman said he did not recall but had looked up. He now felt that the Hunt money matter actually had nothing to do with Watergate but rather was a national security matter. Nixon recognized that Haldeman was reaching beyond reality, so he did not pursue the topic. Rather they speculated again what I would do with, or without, immunity. Ziegler, who was the only link to me at the time and was stepping in and out of this meeting, reported on our conversation of the preceding evening: "When Dean called me last night, he said, 'You know what the twenty-first was, don't you?' And I said, 'No, as a matter of fact, I don't.' He said, 'That's when I went in and gave the president my "cancer on the presidency" speech, which brought the president out of his chair.' And—"

The president affirmed this, saying, "That's right, he did." When Ziegler brought up the matter of my failure to provide the president with a written Dean report, Nixon said, "In fairness, it wasn't that he couldn't put it on paper." The president explained, "We were trying to make a public statement," and my report "would have criminally implicated others." He felt I was turning on other people now to save myself, and he wanted Ziegler to talk to me. Ziegler said he would.

Haldeman reported that the media reaction to his April 17 statement showed that news people were still focused on who had ordered the Watergate break-in rather than any possible cover-up. Nixon wondered if the press was interpreting his new statement as a repudiation of his prior one, in which he asserted that no one in the White House had been involved in the break-in. When Ziegler asked if he was referring to the August 29, 1972, statement, Nixon confirmed that he was and urged Ziegler to call me and assure me he was not now claiming anything different, notwithstanding news media misinterpretations to the contrary.

While Ziegler left the president and Haldeman again sorted through their recollections, particularly of Hunt's demand and the president's involvement. Haldeman recalled that money was paid to the Watergate defendants "to keep them, as they say, keep them on the reservation." Haldeman again suggested that Hunt's demand could be considered as "a national security threat" and then offered another rather extreme suggestion: "I haven't really thought it out, but there is another route. Which would be, throw the entire prosecution, the entire Justice Department, out." Given that the president would later fire a special prosecutor and allow his attorney general and deputy attorney general to resign after they refused to do so themselves, Haldeman's suggestion may well not have sounded excessive to Nixon, but this line of discussion ended when Ziegler returned to report on his conversation with me.

Ziegler had found me at home, my house still surrounded by a crowd of television cameras and reporters, and as he reported our conversation: "I said, 'I wanted to check in with you this morning following the briefing and so forth, and to let you know that in the news I saw someone make references to the fact that the Dean report was full of holes. We're not characterizing this in any way on specific instructions from the president. We are not going to focus on any individual; this is not fair to any individual to do that. And as my briefing yesterday showed, we did not do that.' And then I went through with him what I propose I'll say again in the briefing, which is, I'm not going to comment. He said, 'I understand that.' And he said, 'The thing to keep in mind is that the Dean report also involved the [March] twenty-first conversation with the president, the oral discussion with the president.' I said, 'I don't think there is any question about that, John.'"

Nixon noted that the "Dean report" was not false, and Ziegler continued, sharing what I had reported: "He said, 'Ron, look, I understand the position you're in.' He said, 'The important thing is that we now have the president out in front.'" My comment provoked Nixon to interrupt and ask if I said Haldeman and Ehrlichman should go. "No, that's all he said," Ziegler responded. This conversation gave the president little comfort, for he had told Haldeman and Ziegler he was confident that, if I did not get immunity, I would launch an attack on the White House.

The president's schedule was full throughout the morning and early afternoon. A camera crew in the Oval Office was packing up after Nixon had filmed his message on energy for the evening news, so Nixon stepped into his private office to call Henry Petersen shortly before three o'clock for a quick conversation.[73] Petersen told him there had been no significant developments, although he thought Gordon Strachan was coming by, and that he was being represented by Fred Vinson, a former assistant attorney general and Petersen predecessor in running the Criminal Division, for the Johnson administration. Petersen said they had not "finished with Magruder," and when Nixon asked about me, Petersen said, "Dean's, well, we've backed off of him for a while. His lawyers want time to think." The president said he was treating me "like everybody else because" to do otherwise would be unfair.

After talking to Petersen Nixon returned to the Oval Office and requested a meeting with Ehrlichman.[74] He again raised the question of whether or not I should have immunity, and after a long sigh, Ehrlichman answered, "If he has immunity, he's got to deliver." As Ehrlichman saw it, immunity would only give me incentive to deliver against him and Haldeman; without immunity my incentive would be to deliver against the president. "Bob and I parsed out pretty carefully what Bob's recollection of the meeting you had with Dean was, the blackmail/Bittman stuff. And it's Bob's recollection that there's nothing in that meeting, even if it were tape-recorded and published, that could harm you in the sense of you appearing to obstruct justice."

Nixon, who knew that Haldeman had been present only at the end of the March 21 meeting, did not feel as certain. Ehrlichman continued, reporting that they had been going through the president's schedule and found that he had had some eight or nine meetings with me, more than Nixon had thought.* Ehrlichman said that while he had no way of knowing what was said in those meetings, he was not concerned, as he did not believe that I would seek to damage the presidency if I did not receive immunity: "I just don't think he's made that way, but assuming he did, you would have to ask yourself what took place in those private meetings that might have given him any ammunition." Nixon countered that, even though I might not be inclined to attack the president, my lawyers would be. The president wanted to know when Ehrlichman had started his Watergate investigation, and Ehrlichman replied, March 30, explaining that he had chosen that date because of McCord's letter, and that when Pat Gray had called me a liar, I had removed myself from Watergate matters. The president wanted to know if Ehrlichman acted before or after Magruder talked, and he said before.

The president told Ehrlichman, speaking rather elliptically at first, that if the Ellsberg break-in came up, it should be explained as a national security matter: "On that we just have to be stonewalling, of course." In short, Nixon would simply say that any investigation was out of bounds if it involved national security. Ehrlichman agreed, saying, "That's in the laps of the gods, as I see it." He said he had been going through his old files and had more information. "The way that project was finally represented to me was that it was a covert look at some files, which could be read to be that they walked in when the nurse wasn't looking, and they flipped through the file. It wasn't until much later that we learned that they had actually conducted a burglary."

"What about the other thing, the wiretapping?" Nixon asked, since he knew I was aware of it. "The wiretapping, in most cases," Ehrlichman explained, "was conducted under the statute by leave of the attorney general with the Bureau." With regard to the private wiretapping, "Dean had told me he thought it was done," Ehrlichman said. "The only private one that I know of that was not actually conducted by the Bureau under proper sanction was one that was going to be attempted in Georgetown, and they were never able to do it."[75] Incorrectly Nixon assumed, "That's pretty good. Should I get Dean in sometime and talk to him about my various [concerns]?"

Ehrlichman suggested Ziegler voice them instead: "I tell you, Ziegler's got

---

*In fact, I had a total of thirty-seven Watergate conversations with Nixon in the form of either meetings or telephone calls.

a pretty good thing going with him. And they talk, and Ron seems to keep him calmed down." He went on to explain that the operations of the counsel's office had come to a halt; he was offering them no guidance, and I was not coming into the office. Ehrlichman was also busy spinning the facts, claiming we had not really talked about Watergate, using his calendar as evidence to establish that we had met infrequently. (He excluded our frequent telephone conversations.) To deal with the problem of the Ellsberg break-in, he wanted the president to get Henry Petersen to advise him about how to invoke executive privilege or national security to keep that information from surfacing. The conversation ended when the president said he was going to go to Camp David "and try to see if I can break my sleeping pattern," and he invited Ehrlichman and Haldeman to join him to get "a little rest." He considered inviting Kissinger as well, but then, on second thought, said Henry was "a pain in the ass."

As the president and his aides flew to the Catoctin Mountain retreat, the Watergate story was bursting at the seams: *The Washington Post* was ready to break a story that somehow involved Magruder, Mitchell and me, not to mention Paul O'Brien and Bill Bittman. Carl Bernstein was pressing Henry Petersen for information about when he was going to indict Mitchell and me. Petersen spoke with the president in the early evening, but the conversation was not recorded, because Nixon had requested that all the recording equipment at Camp David be removed. From later recorded conversations back at the White House, we know that Nixon got quite angry with Petersen and scolded him about investigating matters he considered "national security," like the activities of the plumbers.* From Haldeman's diary, we also know that he and the president discussed the *Post* piece. [76] The *Post* had called the press office to get confirmation but because much of their information was wrong, it was not confirmed so they were holding back on the story. When talking to Petersen, Nixon told him that I had claimed I had been granted immunity by the prosecutors (which I not), and the president chided Petersen for granting it. When Petersen denied the charge, Nixon said he had a tape-recording that proved I was making this assertion. [77] Haldeman also noted that the president warned Petersen specifically to stay out of the Ellsberg break-in, which Petersen said he had already learned about from me. [78]

---

*See pages 566 and 567.

At 6:30 P.M. the president met with Haldeman and Ehrlichman, which became a meal that lasted until almost eight o'clock. Haldeman later described the session as "a painful sort of farewell dinner"—"painful" because the president got into "the whole problem of whether John and I should go." Haldeman said Nixon made three points they needed to consider: one, that Magruder would accuse them in open court; two, if they left would it buy off an indictment; and three, the risk of being destroyed by constant assaults if they remained at the White House. Nixon felt they should move on and devise another strategy: "Get out and fight like hell," as Haldeman wrote, although the president told them he had not yet made a final decision. Haldeman also noted that Nixon claimed he was not being emotional about all this, when, in fact, Haldeman thought he had been overly emotional. They returned to the White House the next morning.[79]

### April 19, 1973, the White House

After arriving on the South Grounds at 9:28 A.M., Haldeman, Ehrlichman and the president went directly to the Oval Office.[80] After discussing but reaching no conclusion about my replacement as White House counsel, Ehrlichman reminded the president that they had become involved in the Ellsberg investigation because J. Edgar Hoover had restrained the FBI's own inquiry. He conceded, however, that the Liddy and Hunt operation was "apparently in excess."

Nixon again brought up the subject of Haldeman's and Ehrlichman's leaving the White House. Haldeman said that Kissinger had called to counsel him not leave "until you're totally convinced" that a criminal proceeding was inevitable, and then to move to stay ahead of any criminal actions. Haldeman said he thought they had been badly served by a number of people, and though he was not certain who all of them were, he volunteered Mitchell and myself as likely suspects. "I don't know today," Haldeman said, "and I don't believe you do, really, what happened in the Watergate case." Nixon agreed.

Ehrlichman pointed out that when the president expressed his public confidence in people, it helped boost their morale, and their reputations, so he hoped that Nixon would be very slow in eroding that confidence. He added, "That's why I say I think we ought to wait and see what develops here. See what Petersen says this morning." With that the president requested

Petersen come to his office, but he was concerned about their delaying. Nixon felt they were in a "horrible mess." It all had been extremely hard on him, but "I hope, I think, I will see it through. I can sweat it out," while still dealing with other problems that confront the president. "[On the] other hand," he stressed, Haldeman and Ehrlichman had to "face the fact" that there needed to be some way to insulate him. His "official family" was no different that his personal family, so the impact of Watergate was ultimately personal. Add in all his other responsibilities as president, and "the wear and effect of this is enormous, and it may be destructive, it may be fatal."* He told them, "I think you should be aware of that, so I was not really kidding about Agnew," referring to allowing his vice president to take over the presidency. Nixon continued, "I wonder if this whole thing, whether you stayed or not, is not so destructive that our ability to govern will be totally destroyed."

Ehrlichman was the first to respond, saying coldly, "I think that depends on how you handle yourself in the next few months. If you take occasions to separate yourself from this, take occasions to condemn the wrongdoers in a way that's not faultily [sic], if you communicate your sentiments in some way or other, as backgrounders or otherwise, I think you can come through this rough water very nicely." "Absolutely," Haldeman agreed. "I don't think it even remotely approaches being fatal." Nixon had "to hang tough and rise above it, as you do it."

Ehrlichman shifted the discussion to *New York Times* columnist James Reston's interesting piece on Mitchell, wondering why Mitchell had not come forward and taken responsibility. Yet Ehrlichman felt Nixon should refrain from reading such stories, spend a week in Florida and delegate calls to others: "Hell, they can't wreck the country in a week." Nixon assured them he did not read the newspapers, nor did Bebe give him such information when he was in Florida.

Ehrlichman continued, "But if you could just detach yourself for a week, and then come back from the mountains, so to speak, with a fresh perspective on this, and sit in the sun and listen to some good music, and see some shows, and just take a week off, I just think you'll come back with an entirely different view of this." "That's probably the best advice you've gotten," Halde-

---

*Nixon had mentioned resigning to Haldeman on previous occasions as the collapse of the Watergate cover-up made it increasingly difficult for the president to focus on government business. Haldeman dismissed Nixon's threats to resign as moments of self-pity, but as April progressed there were times when Nixon sounded as if he were seriously considering this option. But then his mood shifts, and he is ready to fight to the bitter end.

man concurred, and he reminded Nixon that in the past he had dealt with problems by pulling back, stepping away from them, and thinking them through. "We're assuming a set of events that we don't know [are] going to take place. We've got to be prepared." Haldeman also reminded the president that Kissinger had argued strongly that he had to cancel the Soviet summit before he started bombing Vietnam, lest the Soviets cancel in response; Nixon had argued the opposite position and had proven to be correct. "Whatever we do," Nixon replied, "the only man, the only problem we've got here is what we do with regard to John Dean, and I think maybe John Dean is going to do it anyway." The president felt the most powerful force to prevent me from doing anything was to make certain I "did not get immunity and had to look [to Nixon] for amnesty." Ehrlichman asked if he wanted that leaked to the news magazines, and the president said sure.

When Henry Petersen arrived later that morning, Haldeman and Ehrlichman went up to Ehrlichman's office for a five-hour session with their attorneys, John Wilson and his partner Frank Strickler. In the Oval Office Nixon got directly to the point with Petersen: "Well, the problem is this, with the Ellsberg case," he began. He reported that their "dear, departed friend Edgar Hoover" had refused to investigate Ellsberg, who was married to the daughter of a close friend of Hoover's.[81] "Under the circumstances, Henry, an investigation was undertaken with a very, very small crew at the White House." Nixon explained that that was "the Hunt group" and quickly added, "Nothing in terms of break-ins or anything was approved. But seeing what these crazy bastards have done since," the president suggested, they had acted on their own. "They didn't do a damn bit of good. I mean, all they got was what appeared in the [news]papers, that Ellsberg had psychiatric problems," which they learned from Henry Kissinger, who had once had Ellsberg as a student. None of what they obtained in the break-in would help win in the prosecution of Ellsberg. "Then, after that, Hoover got into it," the president said. "Now when Hoover got into it, you should know he wiretapped." But Nixon was confused and there had never been an order to wiretap Ellsberg; rather, Ellsberg had been picked up accidentally when wiretapping a former member of Kissinger's national security council staff, Morton Halpern, when Ellsberg had been a house guest at the Halpern home.

The president explained that his reason for informing Petersen about "the Hunt thing" was "simply to say it was a national security investigation. It is not related in any way to the Watergate thing," which was untrue for it had both informed Liddy and Hunt about activities that Nixon's top aides felt were acceptable and driven the White House's interest in the cover-up. Petersen understood and asked if there was anything else, because "I can't stay away from that which I don't know." He explained that he did not want to inadvertently get into such matters through Hunt. "Yes, you could get into other things," the president warned him. "For example, Hunt [was] involved in bugging, apparently. He tried, for example, on one occasion, it was basically during this whole Ellsberg period, this place was leaking like a sieve, and you remember Kissinger's national security people?" Petersen did, but Nixon did not elaborate any further. Petersen mentioned to the president that the Internal Security Division of the Justice Department had been moved under him, into the Criminal Division, and explained that authority for national security undertakings "runs from you to the attorney general."

"In the case of the Hunt thing, you should know that when he was at the White House, and he was working in the field of drugs, he worked on this particular activity, and Liddy worked with him, as I understand. But frankly, I really didn't know this myself until this case came out. I said, 'What in the name of God is Hunt doing?' I understand [now] what he was doing, and I would have approved at the time, because we had nothing that we could get out of Hoover." Nixon added, "I want you to understand that I have never used the word 'national security' unless it is." He assured Petersen that he wanted no stone left unturned regarding Watergate, and proceeded to another matter of importance: "In terms of privilege, any conversations with the president are obviously privileged." "Yes, sir," Petersen assured him, "I understand that," and with his privileges—national security and presidential conversations—firmly established, he moved on.

Pumped for further information, Petersen said they were assessing the credibility of Magruder and Strachan, given the conflicts in their testimony, and they were contemplating giving them both lie detector tests. Strachan had claimed that Haldeman did not get the budget for Liddy's activities nor the intercepts from the DNC; Magruder said Haldeman received both.

Nixon decided to give Petersen a preemptive version of his March 21 conversation with me, which he introduced as a by-the-way bit of information. He claimed he had asked me what it would cost to support these men, and when I said a million dollars, he was outraged. Nixon said he told me, "You can't go down this road, John," and said I'd added that Bittman was demanding attorney's fees. The president was extremely adept at reading people, and realizing he had stunned Petersen with this disclosure, he quickly and awkwardly said, "Forget what I just told you." He then proceeded to personally vouch for Ehrlichman and Haldeman, insisting that neither of them was a liar, but having opened the topic of money for the defendants, the president felt it needed to be given context.

"Now let me say that Ehrlichman, [and] everybody around here, had to be aware of the fact, everybody in town, of the stories to the effect that these defendants were getting something. You know, that they were getting attorneys' fees, the Mrs. Hunt stories and so forth, when she died. And Dean, on one occasion, did apparently talk to Ehrlichman about the need for that. And Ehrlichman said, frankly, being a very good lawyer, 'I can't have anything to do with it.' That's a problem you'll have to work out with the lawyer." Nixon next told Petersen that Ehrlichman had been the antagonist on all this, for it was he who wanted to let it all hang out. He then described Mitchell as the key figure in the affair. While Nixon said he had never spoken to Mitchell about it, "never asked him, what should have happened after this was that Mitchell should have stepped forward and taken responsibility, say he was not minding the store, and watching these jackasses, and I am very sorry, and pleaded, and get on with the campaign."

"It would have been much better, Mr. President," Petersen agreed, at which Nixon noted, "But it's too late now. There started the tragedy."

Nixon changed the subject to seek further clarification of the differences in Strachan's and Magruder's accounts regarding Haldeman. Nixon said that, as he understood it, Magruder was claiming that Haldeman got the results of the bug, but Strachan was saying they did not recognize them as such. "Awfully hard to make a case on that," the president observed. "One man against the other, which one do you believe?" He then raised the matter of the money Haldeman had available, which, Petersen said, "may turn out to be the toughest issue." Nixon mused that John Wilson would have to sort the money matters out.

"Dean's position is that he was a conduit?" the president asked, after briefly covering a number of other concerns. Petersen responded that my position was that I was an agent and information gatherer, and he judged that it was going to be a very difficult case to prove, because it would be all testimonial, with very little documentary evidence. The president acknowledged that it was Petersen's call regarding immunity for me, and Petersen said nothing was happening on the decision. My lawyer was patiently letting events play out, which was part of the bargaining process. Meanwhile they were gathering evidence before the grand jury. The president noted that they obviously had evidence on me—in fact, Nixon asserted, I had come in and confessed my involvement to him. The president asked if I had knowledge that Liddy's plans had gone forward, and Petersen said I did not. Nixon next said that I had been involved in subornation of Magruder's perjury—was I claiming to be an agent on that? This was a matter beyond Petersen's knowledge, but the president gave him his take on the case against me, speculating on facts that, in fact, did not exist.

"How far away are you?" the president questioned. Petersen said it was hard to say, since it was a terribly complex jigsaw puzzle. Nixon wanted Petersen's advice on the case against Ehrlichman and Haldeman, and he reviewed what was known about both, trying to downplay the facts regarding each. Petersen explained that for the break-in they were developing "a conspiracy case, in which all the pieces will fit together. But in such a conspiracy case, the fact—assuming it were true, and we still have a question on the credibility of Magruder—that Haldeman was given a budget, which he had the power to veto, which included operation Gemstone, which he knew to be an electronic-intercept operation, would be a tremendously important fact." Nixon asked, "That's Magruder versus Strachan?" Petersen confirmed and continued, "When you add to that the receipt of the product of the illegal intercepts in identifiable form, coupled with the conspiracy, and his relationship with Mitchell, and his position of authority, I have no doubt whatsoever that we could include him in a conspiracy. The question is one of credibility, which we're trying to resolve. But even if that were to fail, on a question of proof, well, then you come into the secondary aspect of it, that even if you have not found him guilty beyond a reasonable doubt, rather by a preponderance of the evidence, you have—" The president interrupted and said he understood, meaning there was the consideration of the morality of the situation.

Petersen agreed that there was no case against Ehrlichman for the break-in and only a thin case for obstruction of justice. As the conversation continued, Petersen began telling the president everything he knew, while Nixon offered nothing. To end this sorry manipulation, Nixon could not resist one last appeal to Petersen's ego: Would he like to be director of the FBI? Petersen replied that while he would never seek the job, if the president appointed him director, that would be fine; if he did not, that was fine, too. Nixon closed by saying, "Let's take Easter off."[82]

Following Petersen's departure, Ziegler returned to the Oval Office to report, "John Dean issued this statement, just a short time ago," and placed a copy on the president's desk.[83] I had had my office dictate it to the press office immediately after the statement was read by my secretary to the wire services, *The Washington Post* and the *Washington Evening-Star*. In short it was a message I sent to Nixon, Haldeman and Ehrlichman, since they had become incommunicado, to inform them that I was not willing to become the Watergate "scapegoat."[84] Nixon read the statement silently, and as he was finishing, Ziegler read the last paragraph aloud and asked whether or not the White House should respond. He did not think they should but expected to be quizzed heavily about it at his morning briefing. The president told Ziegler to say, "No, there won't be a statement" but wanted to know if I had informed Ziegler I was going to issue my own statement. When Ziegler said I hadn't, Nixon asked, "Do you think you can communicate with him?" Ziegler said he could, but he had wanted to consult with the president first.

Appreciating that the president was not reading the newspaper coverage of Watergate, Ziegler continued, "The Christopher Lydon piece in the *New York Times* today was moved by [Dean's] former brother-in-law, I do know that. And the basic thought of that is that"—here Ziegler read the subheading of the story—White House Counsel Described as Alone but Confident as He Prepares to Face Senate and Grand Jury Inquiries. Ziegler continued, "Goes on to say that Mr. Dean has intimated he can show his own innocence of wrongdoing and guide investigators to other members of the president's inner circle." Then, paraphrasing from the story: "According to close friends of Mr. Dean, there never was a full written report to the president, which Ziegler said was 'not disputed.'" Nixon asked if he had indeed said that, and Ziegler replied, "Yes sir, we've never said the Dean report was written." Then, continuing to paraphrase: "On Mr. Dean's investigation, the same sources said that Mr. Dean never met with Mr. Nixon to talk about the Watergate case until last month, shortly before the president came upon 'serious charges' and started the new investigation he reported yesterday." "So then," Ziegler ended, "there were some paragraphs of differences."*

Nixon felt that they should not make any comment but, rather, requested that Ziegler call me immediately—"No, no, no, don't tell him you are in my

---

*Ziegler chose not to tell the president that the article implicated others as well: Colson, Mitchell, Magruder, Strachan, Chapin, Mardian and Stans. See Christopher Lydon, "Key Figures in Watergate Are Silent or Unavailable," *New York Times*, April 19, 1973, 34.

office"—to tell me what he planned to say at the press briefing. The conversation lasted about a minute.[85] Ziegler said he had seen my statement. I asked if he had any problem with it, and he said he didn't think so. I said that since Ziegler was in a position such that he could not issue anything, I had done so myself. Ziegler told me the president's statement on April 17 was not intended to identify a scapegoat but rather to ascertain the truth. We signed off, and after Ziegler repeated our conversation to the president, the two speculated about my intentions.

Ehrlichman stepped away from the meeting with the lawyers to go to the Oval Office early in the afternoon.[86] As he seated himself Nixon said, "I guess Dean has really been shot across the bow, claiming he's the scapegoat." Ehrlichman asked if I had made a deal, and Nixon said I had not, and that Ziegler would not respond to my statement. Nixon proceeded to give Ehrlichman the gist of his discussion with Henry Petersen; he reported that he had alerted Petersen to Hunt's national security activities and instructed Petersen that the Justice Department should not investigate them (meaning the Ellsberg break-in), as well as nothing involving eavesdropping (meaning the 1969–70 electronic surveillance of newsmen and NSC staffers conducted by the FBI at the request of the Nixon White House and with the approval of attorney general John Mitchell*). Ehrlichman (falsely) assured Nixon he had done no bugging. Nixon indicated that he had instructed Petersen about not giving me immunity, and Ehrlichman said his own attorneys were going to "talk with Glanzer and see what's going on" with respect to the immunity question. Nixon then informed Ehrlichman that Petersen was developing a conspiracy case against him, regarding "Dean going to Ehrlichman with regard for the need for funds for the defendants." Ehrlichman conceded that he had told me "it was all right to call Kalmbach" about raising money, and while they were reviewing that situation with the attorneys, Ehrlichman did not think his actions with respect to Kalmbach were illegal, as he elaborated: "See, the reason [Dean] had come to me in order to call Kalmbach is that Kalmbach didn't want to work for Stans anymore. And we used a pretext that Kalmbach was going to be under Bob and my aegis from now on to do special projects, so he couldn't be a fund-raiser anymore. It was effective the sixth of April." Nixon understood but asked if this still might not constitute a conspiracy, to which Ehrlichman admitted, "Well, that's arguable. These

*This activity, along with the Ellsberg break-in, will become headlines in May 1973.

fellows seem to think that there's a legitimate defense, in that it doesn't get up to the level of being an actor in a conspiracy."

Nixon laid out the Strachan-versus-Magruder conflict concerning Haldeman's receiving Liddy's budget for illegal activities and the fruits of his illegal surveillance of the DNC, as well as Haldeman's rehiring Liddy after Magruder fired him. When the president mentioned that the prosecutors were investigating the $350,000 used to pay the defendants, Ehrlichman said, "We've got into that in elaborate detail with the lawyers this morning. John Wilson says, 'There's nothing illegal about what you did, Mr. Haldeman.'" Ehrlichman added, "[Haldeman] was attempting only to get rid of money that he had that didn't belong to him, and what the recipient did with it, he didn't have any control, intent or design." Nixon, not finding this credible, pointed out, "Bob knew that it was going to the defendants," but Ehrlichman countered, "Not of a certainty" and reported that Wilson had cross-examined him on the matter and noted, "This old boy is good; he's quite something."*

They now turned to Hunt's demand for $120,000 and his threat to "blow the whistle, right?" Ehrlichman carefully qualified Nixon's characterization: "Blow the whistle on the national security operation, that was the threat. And you'll remember our response to that was, you cannot defend blackmail in that kind of a situation, and that's all that is, pure blackmail. And we said, 'No dice,' and I could be just as flat-out on that, as that's the honest-to-God truth." This account was, of course, only Ehrlichman's latest version of the events, as Nixon well knew, since he had been involved in this particular matter, which may have prompted the president's follow-up: "Now let me put one other question to you. Very painful, I know, it's very painful for you to think of this, and it is for me, too, but anyway, I think it would be helpful," he began. He wanted his aides to think about "the separation problem," his less-harsh term for their leaving the White House, which he felt "has to be considered." He wanted them to "look very coldly in terms of Bob, in terms of the presidency." He said he did not know how others were involved with me, but "the son of a bitch is unsafe. I don't know what you do with Dean; he's obviously very upset. He's just lashing out. God damn it, I don't know

---

*During his trial testimony, Haldeman acknowledged that he was aware the money was returned to the reelection committee to pay the defendants, but he believed it was for attorneys' fees and support, or for humanitarian reasons. The jury rejected this defense. See testimony of H. R. Haldeman, *U.S. v. Mitchell et al.*, November 25, 1974, 8500ff.

what we've been told. Frankly, I'm at a loss. We were all talking frankly. That God damn Dean."

Ehrlichman again advised him to simply say that he was merely trying to probe my thought processes, and it paid off, because he sent me off to Camp David to write a report, and I couldn't write it, and that was when I was uncovered. Although he had already been using this explanation, Nixon acknowledged, "I suppose that really isn't true." Ehrlichman argued that I would have been able to construct "some kind of artful evasion" had I not "been so pervasively involved," and added, "I just had a mental image of the guy sitting there with big piles of paper saying, 'I've just written a confession and I would be nuts to deliver this to anybody.'"

"Well, that's what we have to say," Nixon agreed. Ehrlichman wanted Nixon to find some way he could exert privilege to prevent me from talking anywhere and offered a suggestion: "I'd send a fellow around to talk to Dean and say, 'Look here, you are going to be separately liable for breach of confidentiality.'" When Nixon asked for clarification, Ehrlichman continued, "Well, I think you ought to get Petersen to advise you on this, but there certainly is a statutory protection, and I think you could invoke it." Did Ehrlichman think there was a law covering breach of confidentiality with the president? Nixon asked. "Well, no, not as such," he replied, but he did think there might be on "various national security bases. I'm just not that familiar with the statutes. I don't know what all you have in the way of statutory protection, but you remember our CIA case, where the guy was enjoined by the court, we fell back on that body of law."*

Discussion of the Hunt demand, and Ehrlichman's memory of it, was featured throughout this conversation, but Ehrlichman did not believe that either Bittman or Hunt was likely to talk about it. As the talk was concluding, Ehrlichman appreciated the information the president had "sucked"—to use his earlier description—from Petersen, which he said would fit right into the discussions they were having with their lawyers. "If you don't mind, I will take John Wilson aside and talk to him about this separation business. He's very wise."

---

*There was (and still is) no statute of the nature Ehrlichman describes. The CIA case to which he was referring was a situation in which CIA director Richard Helms requested the president's support and assistance with the Justice Department in blocking the publication of a tell-all book by former CIA operative Victor Marchetti in the spring of 1972. The CIA wanted the Justice Department to prevent publication of the book by enforcing the confidentiality agreement Marchetti (and others) had signed when he joined the CIA. At the White House's request, the Justice Department went to court and got a federal judge to enforce the contract. White House staff did not sign such confidentiality agreements.

After placing the blame on Mitchell, neither man had trouble doing so with Haldeman as well. "The Dean argument will be that he told me all these things about Haldeman and that I didn't move on it. Correct?" Nixon asked. "Sure," Ehrlichman replied. "And that Dean's being made a scapegoat." "And then," Nixon said, "so all this about Haldeman comes out. Haldeman would probably have to go, wouldn't he? To be quite candid." That was how Ehrlichman saw it, explaining, "Yeah, because actually they'd drive him out."

Ehrlichman continued, "You've given me some stuff here, as a worry for him that we didn't have before, that may add to this." Nixon, surprised, asked, "Like what?" "Oh, this business about the dispute between Strachan and Magruder," Ehrlichman replied. They contemplated how Haldeman might fight the charges, and Ehrlichman mentioned that they had discussed the issue at breakfast, and "Haldeman said, 'I'm going to get *Six Crises* and I'm going to read the chapter about the fund,' and he said, 'That's going to be my guide.'" Nixon ignored this remark and said they had to consider Haldeman's "separability," because the evidence being gathered by the U.S. attorney created "a very strong possibility that Haldeman will be indicted. Do you agree with that?" the president pressed. "Well, they seem to think so," Ehrlichman said, referring to their attorneys. Nixon asked if Haldeman would be convicted of conspiracy, and based on what they knew so far, Ehrlichman explained, the attorneys had not reached that conclusion, but "they're being very guarded, obviously, because we're just now giving them the facts, and they haven't tested what we're telling them."

In midafternoon on April 19, Nixon met with Dick Moore for what turned out to be a surprisingly informative meeting.[87] The conversation began as an effort to probe Moore for what he knew about my thinking and actions, for the president was aware that we had worked together on a Watergate report. Although Dick Moore was anything but long-winded, Nixon, who often impatiently completed the sentences of others, did not really want to hear what he thought but to make it clear to Moore what he *should* be thinking and remembering. Deep into this rambling conversation, a new fact slipped out about paying the Watergate defendants. "Well, let me tell you what was said about that," Moore remarked, referring to the money, "at the La Costa meeting. Did John Ehrlichman talk to you about the La Costa meeting?" "Yeah, yeah, yeah, yeah, yeah, that's right, in California," Nixon replied, so Moore continued. "Just the background. Let me give you the focus or perspective." Nixon interrupted to ask, "Dean was there?" "Yes," Moore confirmed. "Dean and I got sent for on a Friday afternoon, the day after the Senate passed the resolution for the Select committee [on Water-gate]. Could we come out for the weekend to talk about the Watergate? We got on the airplane."

"At our initiative, wasn't it?" the president asked, and Moore said it was. "I ordered that," the president added. "So you went to La Costa, so what happened?" Moore explained that we had two meetings, one on Saturday and one on Sunday, each lasting several hours. The president asked if we had seen him, and Moore said no—these were "brainstorming" sessions. Moore described how we discussed the Senate's investigation, and there was a con-sensus that Mitchell had to get more involved. And Moore said he was told, "Well, Dick, will you, after this meeting, would you go up and see [Mitchell] and fill him in on this whole damn thing and get him to hire some people [to work on it]?" On the second day, Moore recalled, the issue of the defen-dants arose as a "by the way, they need more money for those fellows. I am just paraphrasing the thing. I don't know how it came up. But maybe it's Mitchell turn, maybe he can do some of it." Moore's memory was not clear, but he thought Ehrlichman or Haldeman had raised it, in the context of, 'Can't LaRue handle it, or something of that sort?'" Moore continued, "And it came up as to whether maybe John Mitchell" ought to raise the money. "Someone, I think John [Ehrlichman], and this was facetious, he said, 'Maybe Rockefeller can get us some money. Oh, [Mitchell] could get all he wants from Rockefeller, all he has to do is ask Rockefeller.'"

"Money for what?" the president pressed. Moore said, "I presumed that they needed more money for attorneys' fees or what have you." Nixon wanted to know if it was payoff money. "No, you wouldn't say it about that," Moore replied, explaining that, obviously, the question was what Ehrlichman and Haldeman, who were sending him on this mission, understood the purpose of the funds to be. The president said that if it was for attorneys' fees, there was no problem; if it was to replenish a fund to compensate these fellows for withholding or altering their testimony, it was a problem. Subtly, Nixon was shaping Moore's memory. Nixon told Moore he had never heard of the money discussions at "the La Costa thing" until their conversation.

Moore had additional information about money discussions regarding the Watergate defendants: He recalled that he and I had spoken on March 19 within hours of Howard Hunt's sending his money demand to me through Paul O'Brien with the threat that, if it was not forthcoming, he would have things to say about his work for Ehrlichman. I had been angered by the threat and informed Moore of it, since he had become privy to the fund-raising for the defendants during our La Costa visit. As Moore now told Nixon, "This was the first time I got the direct notion that they were appealing through Dean for money for silence; it was about a week before sentencing." Startled, Nixon soon provided an account of our million-dollar discussion, when he had asked me how much money and how long, claiming he had told me, "You can't do that." Moore said that when he and I had discussed Hunt's blackmail attempt, he had told me about a former client who had been blackmailed and nearly killed. Paying blackmail was a no-win situation. "Well, Dean, to his credit, said that when he was with me," Nixon reported, and he told Moore that he understood the money for Hunt was raised, apparently, by Mitchell.

During his conversation with the president Moore also reported that he had seen the list my lawyer and I had prepared of those we thought indictable. This list did not interest the president, who wanted to discuss Hunt's demands, and his latest new problem, the La Costa meeting. Nixon suggested Moore talk with me, but Moore cautioned that he was on his way to the grand jury, and the first question they might ask could be about with whom he had discussed his testimony. So the president continued probing, asking Moore's thoughts about immunity for me and my relationship with Henry Petersen, searching for light in all this darkness.

When Moore departed, Nixon summoned Ehrlichman to the EOB Office, where they discussed Moore's account of the La Costa meeting.[88] "I hope he recalls it better than I do," Ehrlichman said, and the president took him through the conversation. "Well, I don't recall the Rockefeller [comment]," Ehrlichman said, but he did not deny that Moore had been asked to raise money from Mitchell for the defendants. Nixon also reported that Moore was aware of Hunt's blackmail demands.

"Well, if I could suggest a point of view on La Costa," Ehrlichman said. "Our inability to do what you asked us to do at La Costa, which was to draft a public statement which could be put out as such, led in quick succession to your long talks with Dean." Ehrlichman claimed I had told them that they could not put out a statement at La Costa, which resulted in the president's sending me to Camp David, "and then that eventually led to cracking him."

Ehrlichman then said that he and Haldeman hoped the president might be agreeable to meeting with their "avidly loyal" lawyer, John Wilson. He described Wilson as having the president's "interest at heart" and as "trying to approach this from your standpoint, rather than ours." Nixon agreed to see Wilson that evening when he returned from a cruise on the Potomac. Ehrlichman repeated the information that Wilson and his parter knew Silbert, Glanzer and Titus and would be visiting them soon: "So they'll find out, I think, quite a lot."

When Nixon asked if he had told the lawyers about La Costa, Ehrlichman said he had not, and the president noted, "That's a new element." Ehrlichman then offered a general explanation of how the money issue was approached: "This subject came up in Dean's conversations, he would ask me for advice, what to do, and almost invariably, I had no response for him. I was helpless in that situation. The one time I did respond was when he specifically asked if they could use Kalmbach. And that was the only time. I've never been able, other than the Bittman thing, where I said, 'Hell no,' I've just never been able to help him. And so it doesn't surprise me if I said, you know, 'Get somebody else to help you, John.'" Ehrlichman continued, "John was getting increasingly desperate as time went on." "Dean was trying to keep the lid on," Nixon noted. To which Ehrlichman agreed, "Trying to keep the lid on, and I could never help him."[89]

After once again reviewing Magruder's role—with both men agreeing he was a liar—Ehrlichman turned to the question of resigning, reporting that their lawyers had reached a "very preliminary" recommendation that "they both try to look at it from your standpoint." Their conclusion was "that Bob's leaving would hurt you more than help you." They believed "it would look like you were overreacting, number one. That the facts known were not sufficient to justify it, so there must be other facts hidden that you're not expressing." "Oh, I see," Nixon replied, and the subject was dropped.

The president inquired if they had considered the possibility of their being named as unindicted coconspirators. Ehrlichman said that had indeed gotten the attention of their lawyers, who had gone to see the prosecutors. "Just to find out what that's all about. Because they say that's just not proper procedure."

After Ehrlichman left, the president departed his office for his limousine for the drive to the Washington Navy Yard, where he boarded the *Sequoia* and dined alone on the presidential yacht as it slowly cruised down to Mount Vernon and then back to the shipyard. By 8:26 P.M. he was back in his EOB office, where he greeted Haldeman and Ehrlichman's new legal team, John J. Wilson and Frank H. Strickler, partners in the Washington law firm White-ford, Hart, Carmody and Wilson. After they exchanged pleasantries, Wilson, who would do most of the talking, said to Nixon, "We admire you so much, we both are dyed-in-the-wool Republicans. I was just telling Bob Haldeman that when I joined the party years ago, I said, 'No sign of beating Calvin Coolidge with a liberal.'" After the laughs died down, Wilson continued, "We've had three days, three different daily sessions, with Bob and John" and visited the district attorney's office. "We want to first go over Bob's situation. He's written a memo of things which boils down the sensitive areas, boils down to the matter of the $350,000. He said that Dean had come to him and told him of the need of this money." Nixon asked, "For what purpose?" "To alleviate families, and legal counsel, of the Watergate people," Wilson replied. "And that was one occasion. Later on, when the money was transferred over to the committee, he just wanted to be rid of it. And he had no intention as to where it might go. And that's that. Now we said to them that 'We don't doubt that about the truthfulness.'" But Wilson explained that they told Haldeman, "Circumstantially, it would be wrong to have done this. A jury might think he did it with [improper intentions]."

"When you put it to a jury, it looks like, it's just very questionable?" the president asked, after a passing bit of confusion. "Yes, yes," Wilson concurred, and Strickler added, "Depending upon how the testimony comes out [with] various people, it could become an issue." Wilson explained that it was potentially wrong: "Well, by a fair stretch, this might be something of an accessory after the fact to a conspiracy at the Watergate. This, Mr. President—" Nixon did not understand, because the point had been jumbled, and asked, "Accessory? For what? For the purpose of?" "Of sort of aiding the consequences," Wilson said, and he offered as an example Dr. Mudd's assistance to John Wilkes Booth after President Lincoln's assassination. "I just got that pardon [request]," the president noted, albeit over a century after the fact. Wilson continued, "Yes, I pointed out that [Mudd] didn't commit the crime but he did so to aid the thing afterward."[90]

As the conversation continued, Wilson acknowledged that there was a good chance Haldeman would be indicted, not because he felt the evidence justified it but because of the particular prosecutors assigned to the case: "Bear in mind that we've got a group of zealots, particularly in Seymour Glanzer, who is a fire-eating prosecutor, and zealots always shoot for the top."

"You think you might be able to defend him?" the president asked. Responding almost simultaneously, Strickler said, "On the evidence we now have, yes," and Wilson added, "Yes, that's our feeling," although he acknowledged, "You know we are guessing at this, Mr. President." When Wilson continued to hedge, the president assured them, regarding both Haldeman and Ehrlichman, "They don't lie."[91]

Wilson now turned to an assessment of Ehrlichman's situation. He was not concerned with Ehrlichman's telling me to "deep six" material from Hunt's safe and giving materials to Pat Gray, who destroyed them. (When Henry Petersen's name was mentioned, Wilson said, "I must give you an aside. I don't trust him, myself." Wilson then talked vaguely about another case he had with the Justice Department in which Petersen had divulged information about Wilson's client to a former Justice Department employee. He added, "I don't go around maligning everyone. He's on my list of people I don't trust.") As far as Ehrlichman's connection with the money for the Watergate defendants was concerned, "He didn't know about the three fifty," the president maintained, but Wilson disagreed. "Oh, I think he knew about it; he must have according to the—" Nixon interrupted to explain, "Well, what I mean is, it wasn't in his field," and then continued with a leading question: "Dean says, 'Can I talk to Kalmbach?' And [Ehrlichman] said, 'Yes.'"

"And Kalmbach went out and did raise the money," Wilson said, and added, "Now these matters involving John alarm us even less, if I can make a comparison, than Bob's do." The president asked he if was referring to "the criminal side," and Wilson confirmed that he was, and said that he saw Ehrlichman as even further removed from "the release of the money." When, however, they lined up both cases, "Well, frankly, our judgment is that neither one can be successfully prosecuted."*

Wilson and Strickler did not have to argue that Haldeman and Ehrlichman should not take leaves of absence, as Nixon relieved them of the responsibility, saying "I don't want to do anything that would jeopardize their cases." The president summed up their position: "Let me ask: In other words, your advice at the present time is to stand firm with these men, because basically, if you flush them now, it's going to probably hurt. Let me put it this way, it will hurt their case, wouldn't it?" The lawyers agreed and departed at 9:32 P.M., and five minutes later the president called Haldeman to report on

---

*While this judgment proved very wrong, in fairness to these attorneys, they were given less than all the facts by Haldeman and Ehrlichman, who at that time could not conceive of the possibility that much of the actual record of their conduct would become available in Nixon's recordings, which would convict them with their own words.

the meeting. "Couple of characters, aren't they?" Haldeman asked. "Very useful, very interesting," Nixon agreed, and noted, "They only had a half hour with the U.S. attorneys, and they say, stand firm." Haldeman mentioned that the prosecutors had had a busy day with Hunt, but he had been unable to learn what Hunt had told them.

Haldeman said the *Post* had called the White House for confirmation or reaction to a story from "an associate of John Dean's, who is seeking to make John Dean's version of the whole thing public," saying that "Dean, in his testimony before the grand jury, will implicate people above and below himself, and will state that Haldeman engineered a cover-up." Haldeman, paraphrasing from notes from his talk with the press office, continued: "One close associate said that Dean is prepared to tell whatever role he might have played in the Watergate case came as a result of orders from superiors in the White House. Despite the allegations [to the contrary], Dean had no advance knowledge of the bugging. That the truth is long and broad and it goes up and down, higher and lower, and that they can't make a case that this was just Mitchell and Dean. Dean will welcome the opportunity to tell his side to the grand jury. He's not going to go down in flames for the activities of others."

"Oh, boy," Nixon exclaimed, as Haldeman added that the *Post* was trying to reach Haldeman for comment. Haldeman said that Ziegler had called me about the story, and "Dean's first comment was, 'Oh, fuck.' And then he said, 'I have a pretty good suspicion who it is, and he's got things scrambled. I never mentioned Haldeman. I just said "higher up," and he drew that conclusion, apparently.' And he [Dean] said [to Ron], 'Why don't you call the *Post* and tell them the story's not true before they run it.' Dean said, 'Well, Ron, there's some fact and some fiction in it,'" which was followed by a discussion between Ron and me about how to get the story corrected.

Haldeman told Nixon that Ron was trying to reach the *Post* to inform them that the story was not accurate. "Ron's afraid that Dean cleverly waited until nine-thirty to tell him that so that it would be too late to change the story," he added. As they discussed this situation, Haldeman said, "Dean's obviously got other people playing his game now, people who are tougher than he intends." Nixon speculated that it was my lawyer, and Haldeman agreed. The discussion turned to plans for the upcoming Easter weekend. "What we might do, if it's okay, is go up to Camp David for a day or two. We've got reporters camping on the door here now," Haldeman said, referring to his home. The president thought it was an "excellent idea," adding, "Oh, Christ, yes, go up to Camp David, Bob."

The president reminded Haldeman to be sure to attend the cabinet meeting the following morning, and when Nixon suggested he come to Haldeman's defense at the meeting, Haldeman advised, "I don't think you should. Look, there are so many weird bounces in this, if one of us gets a bad bounce at some point," it could redound on the president.

*April 20, 1973, the White House*

When Haldeman arrived in the Oval Office for his first meeting, at 8:15 A.M., Nixon expressed concern about his morale, which Haldeman assured him was fine. Nixon asked if the Dean story in the *Post* had run as predicted. "He's saying there were higher-ups and lower-downs also included," Haldeman reported, adding, "He's determined he's not going to be alone. The *Post* modified the story. Originally they were saying Haldeman engineered the cover-up. Now they said Haldeman and others in the White House were involved in the cover-up, which at least is not quite as [bad]." This discussion did not proceed very far before Nixon said, "Let me ask you about one conversation. The only thing that troubles me about this is my own recollection of a conversation with Dean, where you were with him, when he said that Bittman had stated that he needed money for [Hunt's] attorney fees." More specifically, the president wanted to know if Haldeman remembered the million-dollar conversation and whether he had encouraged me to get the money. Haldeman said he could not find any notes for that meeting, which he incorrectly thought had occurred in the evening, and though he did recall being present, he did not remember my saying we had to get the money. Haldeman did think, however, that the president had said, "We ought to be able to get the money." Haldeman characterized the conversation as Nixon's "running out the string." In response to further questions from Nixon, Haldeman explained how Mitchell had later reported the money for Hunt had been paid.

Haldeman had by now adopted Ehrlichman's view of this conversation, assuring Nixon, "I don't see that you have any problem at all." As he now misrepresented the situation, "In the first place, at the time you were investigating the case. You were probing, you know, all directions with everybody you could, and everything you could get, with no obligation to move in any fixed time, only an obligation to work this thing out. The other factor is that what was clearly, distinctly a threat was relayed, [and it] was related to national security. Because Hunt specifically said he needed this or he was going to spill the beans on the stuff he did for Ehrlichman, and that, as you instantly knew, anything he did for Ehrlichman was involved in the national security project over here." "And we couldn't pay blackmail for that," Nixon added, to which Haldeman replied, "And we didn't."

They speculated about whether this conversation would ever come up. "I don't think Dean's going to do that," Haldeman said. "I don't think it's going to come out at all. It's a privileged conversation, that's for sure." Nixon agreed, and Haldeman continued, "Whatever was done, it was done by Mitchell." They proceeded to agree again that Nixon had been investigating, and "at that point had no reason to believe" anything I had told him, "because, you now have found, he was lying on various things." Haldeman was pushing the new defense beyond credibility even for Nixon, who noted, "Well, we say he was lying, [but] in our fairness to him, we have to say [it was] for us that he was doing it. Because I had told him on several occasions, 'You've sure done a hell of a job here. You've done a good job.'" But Haldeman had an answer for this: "But now you point out that he was playing a double game, apparently."

"Let's get a line on this money thing," Nixon urged. "I'd rather be on the offensive on that. Say, if you can, just say, 'Yes, money was raised.' Obviously the money was raised, so why did they put it on the doorstep? 'Well, that's the way it was given to Mrs. Hunt. That was the way she handled it. Raised the cash for that purpose.'" Haldeman said they had to separate authorizing Kalmbach from the $350,000 itself; they would claim that they did not know what Kalmbach was doing and merely wanted to return the $350,000 to the reelection committee.

They rehashed Mitchell's problems, which could become their problems as well, and the fact that he had attended three meetings regarding Liddy's plans, and while he could claim nothing was approved during the first two, Haldeman noted that "Magruder still has that story of going down to Key Biscayne." He thought, though, that Mitchell might be able to deal with that meeting, because "Dean wasn't at [it]." He then enthusiastically added, "See, they had Liddy over there yesterday, and he wouldn't talk." The president, surprised, asked, "Is that right?" and Haldeman replied, "In spite of your signal." Cynically Nixon added, "I did my job. And that's why Dean wanted me to get [Liddy] to talk. I did my job, and the U.S. attorneys know. I'm glad I did."[92] This conversation ended with Haldeman assuring the president that they would figure out how to handle the money and "get out ahead of it, get a line on it."

The cabinet meeting that morning focused on energy and its influence on foreign affairs, and not a word was said about Watergate.[93] After it ended, George Bush, chairman of the Republican National Committee, asked the president if he might have a minute with him, and they spoke for twenty minutes in the Oval Office.[94] Bush had just returned from a trip to California, where he had met with Governor Ronald Reagan. It was Bush who raised Watergate, telling the president, "I'm feelin' for ya on this other stuff." Bush had raised Watergate because he said he had his own problem: a fellow named Ken Rietz, who had been involved in the Nixon campaign and been sent up to the RNC, where he had "worked in the dirty trick department," doing some "espionage on Muskie and stuff like that." Bush had told Rietz they had to figure out how to get him out of the RNC without jeopardizing any of his rights, and Nixon agreed that if there was a problem, Rietz should be let go. Bush said that if he could help Nixon in some way other than by wringing his hands, he was willing to do so. Nixon urged him to just keep saying that the president has taken charge, and as he walked Bush to the door, assured him it would soon pass.

When Bush departed, Nixon requested that Haldeman return to the Oval Office, where he told Haldeman the gist of the conversation with Bush.[95] Haldeman thought the situation had arisen because Magruder was still "lashing out" and pulling others in to get a better deal for himself. But Haldeman cautioned that people like Rietz had to be careful, because Magruder had exaggerated his activities.

Nixon, sounding relaxed and thoughtful, wanted to consider Haldeman's problems again, and he pointed out that whatever they decided, it would not be sufficient for some people. Haldeman gave an example: "One of the columns this morning made the point that they're not going to settle for scapegoats. You can't get away with trying to blame this on Magruder and Dean, which I think is probably true. And then they said you have to move it up to Haldeman, and they totally ignore Mitchell. And because you have to move to someone who was high enough to have had the responsibility, that's the dilemma that you have. If you move to Haldeman, then there's no way the president escapes responsibility."

"Wonder when will Dean start crashing on Ehrlichman?" the president soon asked. Haldeman thought maybe I had effectively done so in the information given the *Post* regarding "people higher up" and "people lower down" being involved without actually having named names. He reported that Ziegler said I had been totally surprised by the *Post* story. In addition, he also speculated that Ehrlichman had more problems with me than he did, for I had met with Ehrlichman on Watergate more often than I had with Haldeman. He added that the president had no problem with me, because he had been investigating at that time, and he had given me no orders to do anything. Nixon corrected him—the million-dollar conversation was now weighing heavily on his mind, and he recalled telling me, "I guess we can get that." But Haldeman, although he had not been present, claimed he had warned that they dared not start down that track, and the president had agreed. "You agreed that, you know, you won't get anywhere. That doesn't accomplish anything." The president wanted to know who had called Mitchell to come down. "I don't know. I don't have any idea. I don't know that anybody did," Haldeman replied.* He said that he did not think Ehrlichman had made the call because "John Ehrlichman wasn't the least bit concerned about [Hunt's threat]."†

When Haldeman departed, Nixon called Henry Petersen, and after a brief chat about leaks got to the reason for his call—the latest update.[96] You have Mitchell today?" Nixon asked. "Yes sir, he's in the grand jury now," Petersen replied, and said he thought Mitchell would be out today. He also reported that Magruder had taken a lie-detector test successfully, and that Strachan was scheduled to follow. "How about Dean?" the president asked. Petersen said they were "still in arm's-length negotiations," noting that I hadn't "really decided to be a witness yet."[97] The president sought Petersen's assurance that my conversations, as well as Haldeman's and Ehrlichman's, with the president were privileged, as well as subject to "national security." "I understand," Petersen tacitly agreed. He also reported that Kleindienst had talked with Jeb Magruder's new boss, the secretary of commerce, after

---

*Haldeman's telephone log showed that he made the call to Mitchell at 12:30 P.M. on March 21, 1973, and he would later be forced to admit that he requested Mitchell come to Washington, where Mitchell would report that money had been paid to Hunt. Testimony of H. R. Haldeman, *U.S. v. Mitchell et al.*, December 2, 1974, 8586–87.

†Bud Krogh would put the lie to Ehrlichman's seeming public indifference toward Hunt's blackmail, for privately he was very concerned. Testimony of Egil Krogh, *U.S. v. Mitchell et al.* November 22, 1974, 7663–81.

the cabinet meeting that morning, and Magruder had tendered his oral resignation, which could be accepted by the commerce secretary whenever he
wanted it. Petersen said he was suggesting that the resignation be put in
writing in case Magruder had any second thoughts. The president said that
there was no change in the status of anyone at the White House, and Petersen agreed they were in a different position than Magruder. Nixon reported that he was heading for Florida, but if Petersen had anything Nixon
should know, he could call him. "But otherwise don't bother me."

Kissinger soon arrived in the Oval Office.[98] Nixon observed that what he
was going through with Haldeman and Ehrlichman was not as difficult as
some of the life-and-death decisions they had made regarding "Cienfuegos,
Jordan or Cambodia."[99] Still, he faced a conundrum: If he did nothing, he
would be criticized; he did not want to do anything to harm his aides, but
then if he did have to let them go, people would call him "a God damn fool"
for keeping them so long. "How could I have been misled for nine months?"
Nixon asked plaintively, and Kissinger replied that it had been his understanding that the president had not been misled, and this was all about public posturing. Nixon said it was a question of how best to do what had to be
done and whether taking action would remove any of the poison. With increased bitterness, he said, "Mitchell was the culprit," and he ended the conversation by complaining that the fight ahead was pure politics.

Shortly after noon, while waiting for his helicopter to arrive on the South
Grounds, the president asked Haldeman, Ehrlichman and Kissinger to the
Oval Office, though Kissinger would only remain for a minute. It had originally been planned that Haldeman and Ehrlichman would accompany the
president to Florida over the Easter holiday, but he had decided to go alone,
because he wanted private time to think.[100] Ehrlichman indicated that they
had just come from another session with their lawyers, who were now getting down to serious business and wanted Haldeman and Ehrlichman to
have an informal session with the prosecutors, if requested.[101] The president
told them that George Bush was letting Rietz go. Ehrlichman was aware that
Rietz had paid the expenses of the spy they had working for presidential
candidate senator Edmund Muskie as a chauffeur. "Well, nothing wrong
with that," the president said. Ehrlichman thought Bush, whom Haldeman
called "Mr. Clean," was overreacting.

The president reported that he had raised with Petersen Ehrlichman's
hope about speeding up the grand jury, but Petersen said that was a problem,

because each person talked about others who were involved, and not only were they running out leads, but they had to study the record, so all of it was taking time. "Well, I understand," Ehrlichman said, clearly not happy with this news, "but I think it would be just a matter of letting him know you were in a hurry, and then periodically keeping the heat on him. The thing to fear here is that Silbert will deliberately try to stretch this thing out, hoping for some kind of apple to fall off the tree." That, Haldeman added, was what their attorneys were convinced he was doing.

"Dean's just changed the terms," Ehrlichman announced, referring to the fact that I was no longer talking with the prosecutors—information that Wilson could only have learned from the prosecutors themselves. "Changed the terms?" the president asked. "Why, I wonder?" Ehrlichman answered, "Probably because these guys didn't deliver what they said they would." He added, "[Dean's] got a guy [who was] Humphrey's field director in '68." "He's cousin of the sister of Dean's first wife," Haldeman clarified.[102] Not surprisingly, Nixon reacted, "Well, I just hope the poor son-of-a-bitch is not going to turn him completely rat. But what is Dean going to try to negotiate now, I don't know. But Christ, I think he must have. It seems to me he's told them whatever he can so far. Don't you think he has?" Ehrlichman said, "It sounds like to me, if he is into that Hunt business, that's pretty far." (In fact, I had still not gone into detail with Shaffer about the president's role.) Based on his conversations with Petersen, the president told Haldeman and Ehrlichman, "Dean has not yet cooperated, you know what I mean."

"You got one sticky wicket there. Dean has the administrative responsibility for the Secret Service, who in the Technical Security Division have responsibility for all document protection and White House guards," Haldeman pointed out to the president.* As his helicopter was landing on the South Grounds, Nixon remarked that he did not think my relationship with the Technical Services Division was "that much of a problem."

The recording system, which was seldom good, made much of the remainder of this conversation difficult to hear. Nixon told Haldeman and Ehrlichman that he wanted to have a further conversation with Dick Moore about the La Costa meetings, reminding them that Moore was a "special

---

*The fact that apparently Haldeman halted here and did not mention that the Technical Security Division also operated Nixon's secret taping systems suggests that Ehrlichman still had not been told of the recording operation. Notwithstanding my administrative responsibilities, I, too, was unaware of the system.

counsel to the president," for he was an attorney on the staff. But he added
that Petersen had told him that my status as an attorney did not mean I could
not testify about criminal matters under attorney-client privilege. Both
Haldeman and Ehrlichman chimed in, almost simultaneously, "Except his
client." The president said, "His client, I figure, is not a member of the White
House staff." Ehrlichman countered, "Well, is the client's [employee] not part
of the client when acting on behalf of the client?" Meaning, weren't he and
Haldeman covered by attorney-client privilege? Nixon did not engage further in this line of discussion but urged Ehrlichman to talk to Moore; Ehrlichman, however, thought it was too late, given that everyone had now
retained counsel. He wanted the president to give Moore a message about
his memory of the La Costa meetings: Ehrlichman (falsely) claimed that
Nixon had called the La Costa session to come up with a paper on the whole
Watergate episode, and as Ehrlichman now recalled, it was I who was "the
major impediment" to that effort.

Nixon asked yet again about the money, and Ehrlichman continued: "The
money business was nothing new. Dean continually, through this period of
time, was coming to us on an episodic basis and saying, Jesus, Mitchell needs
money, and what are we going to do? And invariably and inevitably, with the
exception of the one little, of the Herb Kalmbach episode, we said, John, God
only knows what he's going to do. And my remark about Nelson Rockefeller
is typical. You know, tell Mitchell to go borrow it from his friend Nelson
Rockefeller." Ehrlichman continued, raising his protestations of his innocence
to new levels: "See, our sense of this is, throughout, was Dean saying to us,
nobody in the White House is involved. And our sense of it being, well, look,
if Mitchell needs money, for whatever reason, that's Mitchell's problem." He
added, "I have no interest, for instance, in obstructing justice. I had no exposure myself. I was satisfied from Dean that none of my colleagues in the White
House had exposure, and that Jeb Magruder was a horse's ass and got himself
into this." He quickly admitted, "Well, in all candor, I knew that Mitchell was
trying to raise money for these people. And I knew that LaRue was, and I
knew that because Dean told me so. I don't have any personal knowledge either from Dean or anybody else of any correction in that process."

Nixon now added own his spin to Ehrlichman's account: "You didn't have
any reason to think of it being raised for an improper purpose until two
things: one, until McCord said it was for payoff purposes, and two, until
Dean came in and said that Hunt is shaking us down." "Bob and I have

shared a suspicion that Mitchell was at the bottom of all this," Ehrlichman replied. "There's no two ways about that. And we've shared that suspicion for many months. But Dean very effectively kept between me and any intimate knowledge." (More accurately, Mitchell simply did not want to deal with Ehrlichman.) "Good," the president responded.

Haldeman and Ehrlichman soon departed, sharing Easter good wishes, and Dick Moore, who had been waiting, was asked to enter the Oval Office for a quick meeting before the president left.[103] Nixon had one point to make, which he buried in other conversation, although his message was clear: "You had nothing to do with the money!" He told Moore that Ehrlichman had explained to him that I had repeatedly raised the need for money, which was being raised for the Watergate defendants' legal fees and support. That point made, Moore departed, and the president soon headed for his awaiting helicopter.

In his memoir Nixon included a touching, symbolic scene, with Ziegler joining him that evening in Florida at his Key Biscayne residence, where they "watched the sun setting into Biscayne Bay" while they discussed Haldeman and Ehrlichman resigning. The president's schedule reveals this never happened.[104]

Nixon did, however, speak by telephone with Ziegler, who was at the Key Biscayne Hotel, and learned that Ziegler was distressed by the negative television coverage of Mitchell emerging from the grand jury, which Ziegler believed was clearly intended to "humiliate him." The press secretary was concerned that the same not happen to Nixon's chief of staff and top domestic adviser. He also reported that during the previous three days he had been asked over three hundred Watergate-related questions. Nixon later wrote that because Haldeman had asked him to get a broad spectrum of advice before asking for their resignations, he solicited Pat Buchanan's thoughts, and he asked Ziegler to call Haldeman and read him what Buchanan had to say. Buchanan thought that anyone who could not "maintain [his] viability should step forward voluntarily," and the sooner he did so, the better for all. Buchanan cited conservative columnist and television commentator Howard K. Smith as saying that Nixon could either act like Eisenhower, who "cleans house himself," or Harding, "who covered up for his people."* Buchanan also

---

*Howard K. Smith was wrong in his historical example of Harding. See John W. Dean, *Warren G. Harding* (New York: Times Books, 2004).

noted the impact that Watergate was having on the president's staff: "There is a *Titanic* mentality around the White House staff these days. We've got to put out the life rafts and hope to pull the presidency through."[105]

## April 21–24, 1973, Key Biscayne

At the president's request, the log of his personal contacts from April 21 through April 24 were not recorded in his official daily diary, because he had asked Pat Buchanan and Chappie Rose (if not others whose names have never been disclosed), to come to Florida to discuss Haldeman's and Ehrlichman's leaving the White House. He also made a number of telephone calls soliciting advice: On Easter morning, April 22, the president phoned Colson (7:55 A.M. to 8:21 A.M.), me (8:24 A.M. to 8:39 A.M.), Haldeman (9:45 A.M. to 10:16 A.M.) and Ehrlichman (10:26 A.M. to 10:38 A.M.) and also wished everyone well. As I later wrote, all I remembered of the conversation (since I had stayed up late and Nixon had phoned so early) was his ending the call by saying, "You're still my counsel." In Nixon's own account he told me, "You said this is a cancer that must be cut out. I want you to know I am following that advice." He maintained that I told him I appreciated the call, which I am sure was the case, and that I had not decided if I should take the Fifth Amendment, to which he responded that I should feel free to come and see him. Nixon noted, "Dean said rather coolly, 'I know how that line got in the statement, the one about no immunity,'" which I had only learned about because Len Garment, with whom I remained friendly, had told me. Nixon wrote that we spoke about Gray's destruction of documents and the events relating to Hunt's demands, which led to the March 21 meeting.[106] Even at this late date I was still loyal to Richard Nixon, and had not taken my lawyers through any of my personal dealings with him, other than to allude to the fact that there were problems in explaining the cover-up without involving him. In fact, I continued to hope that Haldeman, Ehrlichman, Mitchell and Colson would join me in admitting the mistakes we had made, believing it was the only way the president would survive. No one person could solve this problem by taking the blame, particularly anyone at a lower level of the staff. But my superiors were prepared to risk it, or they were in a remarkably deep denial of reality.

It was apparently during a meeting at his Key Biscayne home on Monday morning, April 23, that the president made a firm decision that Haldeman and Ehrlichman had to go. It was a protracted and emotional session lasting some three hours, and it included Ziegler, Buchanan and Chappie Rose. Nixon recalled Chappie Rose's quoting Gladstone: "The first essential for a prime minister is to be a good butcher." Nixon wrote in his memoir that, as the session ended, "we all agreed that Haldeman and Ehrlichman had to resign." Nixon asked Buchanan to deliver the message, but he protested and suggested Ziegler, who got the assignment to call Haldeman, who would, in turn, talk with Ehrlichman. Ziegler reported that while Haldeman disagreed with the decision, he would accept it. Ehrlichman, however, did not only not accept it but persuaded Haldeman to change his mind. Nixon, in turn, backed down, and rather than tell them they had no choice in the matter, the president began calling other advisers, such as Bill Rogers, John Connally and Bryce Harlow, who had headed the president's congressional relations office during his first term, thinking they would bolster his position, which they did. But when that information was relayed to Haldeman, he said Rogers and Connally had told them just the opposite. The president returned to the White House on Tuesday evening, April 24.

### April 25, 1973, the White House

The president had had several unrecorded conversations with Henry Petersen while in Florida, and called him almost immediately after arriving in the Oval Office on Wednesday morning, April 25.[107] After scheduling a meeting for later that afternoon, Nixon badgered Petersen about his prosecutors, who were tracking a leak of grand jury information. The president suggested this was another reason for Petersen to give lie-detector tests to the prosecutors. When Nixon brought up Magruder, Petersen replied that, while it still was not public, the secretary of commerce had accepted Magruder's resignation effective Friday, April 27.

After Steve Bull, who had taken over Haldeman's scheduling duties, departed the Oval Office, the president spoke with Ziegler.[108] Ziegler reported on his conversation with Bryce Harlow, who supported Haldeman's and Ehrlichman's departures. Nixon acknowledged that he was having trouble with them: "They're never going to do it, they won't resign. So let's just see if we can get them to resign today. What would you do, tell them to resign?" Before Ziegler could answer, Nixon added, "Or would you say, 'Alright, fellows, you've got a week?' That's about all you can do." Ziegler passed over the question and reported "the Connally view and Harlow's view is that the time to act is instant, and not in a panicky way and not in a the-presidency-is-crumbling-type of emotion." Connally also thought the president should announce a reorganization when he moved on Haldeman and Ehrlichman.

The two aides, however, persuaded Nixon to allow their lawyers to make the case for why they should not resign, and Nixon met for almost an hour and a half with John Wilson and Frank Strickler in the Oval Office that morning.[109] Claiming they were "much better informed about things than they were the other night," the lawyers focused on the troubling area for both their clients—namely, the payment of money to the Watergate defendants. (Clearly, however, the president was better informed than Wilson and Strickler.) Wilson then briefed the president on what they believed was the applicable law, the obstruction of justice statutes, 18 USC §§ 1503 and 1510, which they paraphrased for the president, and whose requisite state-of-mind requirement they clearly did not appear to fully understand.[110] Wilson did mention the law regarding conspiracy, which would instead become the core case against all the Watergate actors involved in the cover-up, but instead briskly dismissed it: "But I do not think that these men criminally breached these statutes," and this was true "even if you make this a shotgun [i.e., broad] conspiracy."

After arguing that his clients had not violated the law, Wilson said he wanted to "drop my role as an advocate for a moment and be a recommender— may I be permitted to suggest certain things?" Nixon encouraged him to proceed. Wilson wanted the president to have Petersen state in writing exactly how his clients had violated the law. (Needless to say, such a document would have been uniquely valuable, not to mention unprecedented.) Although Wilson did not dwell on this, he assured the president he was not asking for anything improper. He mentioned that they had run into Glanzer at the federal courthouse: "Glanzer is destroyed. He's always tense. He looks terrible. He looks like he's been through a bad illness. I said to him, 'Seymour, your hair has turned gray.' He said, 'Well, they haven't found us a leaker yet.'" While Wilson solicited information from Glanzer, he got little, only an agreement that they would get an opportunity to bring their clients in informally.

Wilson then turned to the reason for their visit: to argue why Haldeman and Ehrlichman should not be forced out of the White House. He went through his notes, and his seven points boiled down to: (1) If Haldeman and Ehrlichman departed, it "takes all of the White House cover away" and would embolden the prosecutors to go after them; (2) if should they be in-dicted it "would relate to acts which while in the White House [but] have no effect upon the presidency"; (3) in the present climate the press would place the worst connotation on their resignation; (4) if I resigned at the same time, it would "place all three in the same boat," which would put an awful shadow "upon these boys"; (5) if they remained and were indicted, the president had already said that anyone who was indicted would have to leave; (6) to act now "simply helps nobody but the press, [which] will claim credit for driving you to it"; and (7) if they remained in the White House and were indicted, "we're prepared to write you a very brief letter, as counsel to these two men," stating that, based on the facts they had been given, "we do not believe they have committed a crime." In fact, they would write that letter immediately, so the president could produce it and say he had it before they were indicted.

The president, however, was not convinced by the lawyers' arguments, and told them he was being advised the aides should leave by "hard-liners" such as John Connally. Much of the conversation that followed focused on how they might deal with me, if I testified or was given immunity. Their lawyers' conclusion was that they would effectively have to destroy me, which understandably troubled the president, who feared that I might then strike at him. Strickler noted, "This is possible for a Judas to do." Nixon explained that notwithstanding his recent statement on immunity, he had told Petersen that the decision on granting immunity was Petersen's own. But the president agreed with these lawyers: "I would think that we'd really have to destroy [Dean] in the public mind." Wilson added that, if I said anything untrue, I could be indicted for perjury.

Returning to Henry Petersen, Wilson said, "I want to be sure that you understand we are not meaning to suggest anything improper with Petersen, as you're Petersen's boss. All you wanted to know is certain vital information affecting the office of the president, not with regard to the protection of in-dividuals." (Obviously they wanted the prosecutorial information for their clients Haldeman and Ehrlichman, since they did not represent the office of the president.) Again Wilson argued that Haldeman and Ehrlichman had to be treated differently from me, for as Wilson described me, I was "a self-confessed crook." Not too subtly Wilson made it clear he wanted me fired, for it would start a necessary discrediting process and weaken any case against his clients. The president's argument, for which these lawyers had no real answer, was that Republicans in Congress were now calling, and would continue to call, for Haldeman and Ehrlichman to resign. As this conversation wound down, Wilson took a few more shots at Henry Petersen, calling him "a dangerous man, and I think, if he's your friend, he's only your friend because he's got his tail in a crack, and I'm afraid he's your enemy. I don't trust Petersen. I told you so the other night."

"Is his tail in a crack because he basically cooperated with Dean in the cover-up?" the president asked. "Yes, sir," Wilson answered, and went on to explain why he was also less than happy that Mitchell had hired attorney Bill Hundley, a former Justice Department prosecutor and longtime friend of Petersen's. He thought that Hundley and Mitchell would sway Petersen in an alliance against Ehrlichman. Wilson was also unhappy with my comment to Haldeman aide Larry Higby, whom I had told that Haldeman had made a mistake in having the same lawyer as Ehrlichman, for it had the appearance of being collusive. But Wilson told Nixon, "That's the last thing that exists here, is collusion." In fact, it was an accurate observation, but Nixon and Wilson agreed that I was "a very desperate man"—although neither had any actual information about what I was or was not doing.[111] On the other hand, Wilson did like the fact that I told Higby that the president needed to be careful with Petersen to not get into a position of obstructing justice, and that Petersen was the president's best counsel but not his friend. Wilson chose to interpret this as my sending threatening messages to the president. Strickler warned the president that the prosecutors would put pressure on me in an effort to "psych" me into giving false testimony against higher-ups.

The conversation turned to Judge John Sirica, who Wilson reported was an old friend, as they had been in the prosecutor's office together "almost forty years ago." "I think, without boasting," Wilson quickly added, "that we could get rid of Sirica." He explained that he was currently "representing Sirica in the Court of Appeals in the controversy over the district attorney. And if my man gets indicted, he can't sit with me [as judge], because he goes around town telling everybody, 'John Wilson's my lawyer.'" When Wilson added, "I don't know a more emphatic Republican than John," Nixon countered that he felt that Sirica had "gone far beyond what he should have" in sentencing people like Liddy: "That's just unconscionable." Wilson observed, "He's lost his head about the whole thing. [Still], I'm very fond of him personally," and then he repeated, "We can get rid of him. We can get another judge here who will be—" "Worse," Nixon interrupted, and everyone laughed. As Wilson continued to make his point that they could get Sirica off their case, the president got up from his chair and retrieved two small boxes of cufflinks with the presidential seal on them, which he gave to Wilson and Strickler as they departed this second and final meeting with the president. They had made their case, but they had not changed his mind: rather, they succeeded only in delaying the implementation of his decision.

After the lawyers departed, the president went to his EOB office, where he was joined by Ron Ziegler.[112] Ziegler wanted to clarify Connally's recommendation on Haldeman and Ehrlichman, which was more nuanced that he had initially portrayed it. The president then asked Haldeman and Ehrlichman to come to his EOB office. They arrived at 11:06 A.M. for a conversation that lasted almost three hours, and in which Ehrlichman became increasingly confrontational.[113] The conversation opened with Haldeman's taking them all through his notes of his lengthy conversation with Connally, which was so nuanced that no one could disagree with any of his points, for Connally had managed to take all sides on the question of whether or not the president should force the resignations of his aides. Connally was, however, blunt about "moving Kleindienst out of the Justice Department" and getting "a new attorney general." Nixon's former treasury secretary also believed, as Haldeman reported, that "the money payoffs" to the defendants was "as big as the bugging" and "maybe bigger." Connally was likewise concerned "about the stories of the feud between Ehrlichman and Mitchell, and that they've sworn vengeance on each other." Nixon asked, "What about that?" and then quickly added, "I would agree there's some truth in it. Not on your part, but Mitchell's." Ehrlichman assured the president that there was none on his part. The president mentioned a story by syndicated columnist Joe Alsop that alluded to the supposed feud, and Ehrlichman explained that when Mitchell was attorney general, he "got drunk at a party and fell on me in the presence of Kay Graham," publisher of *The Washington Post*. Ehrlichman said Mitchell had been busy attacking Ehrlichman's positions as "too liberal" and charging that he "was misadvising" the president, who should remove him from the White House. When they all agreed that he had lied at least once in the Watergate case (regarding meetings with Liddy), Ehrlichman asked the president, "Is Petersen telling you anything about Mitchell's problems in New York with that grand jury?" in the Vesco case.[114] When Nixon said not yet, Ehrlichman reported, "I understand they're very close to indicting him for perjury." Throughout the conversation Nixon alluded to his meeting with Wilson and Strickler and the fact that he liked the idea of the lawyers' giving him a letter stating that they did not find the aides had any criminal liability.

This long, rambling, highly repetitive rehashing of what they did and did not remember, coupled with their attacks on others with whom they were having problems, revealed that both Ehrlichman and Haldeman were in serious denial about their standing and fixated on rationalizations. Nixon, however, remained a realist. Although he was careful not to cross them, and conversationally agreed with them, he did pick up some new information and insight. For example, he certainly took note when Ehrlichman raised the prospect of his impeachment. Ehrlichman began by "spinning something out" for him: "I think it's entirely conceivable that if Dean is totally out of control, and if matters are not handled adroitly, that you could get a resolution of impeachment." The president, though a bit taken aback, agreed. Ehrlichman continued, "I don't know if you've thought of this or not, but I got thinking about it last night. On the ground that you committed a crime and that there is no other legal process available to the United States people other than impeachment. Otherwise, you have immunity from prosecution. And so I think we have to think about that." Ehrlichman suggested that the president needed to determine how great a threat I might be, although in Ehrlichman's analysis, "what he has falls far short of any commission of a crime by you, so far as I know."

Ehrlichman had Nixon's full attention as he proceeded, explaining that, in fact, he had no idea what we had discussed during the ten or twelve hours we talked in February and March. "But you get down to a point where you've got John Dean prancing in there and saying, 'The president said this' and 'the president said that' and having somebody in your behalf come back and say, 'No, the president didn't say that, and that's ridiculous.' So you get a kind of credibility thing." Although, Ehrlichman said, he thought I had been "very busy dredging up corroborating evidence and looking for documentation or taking statements from people based on leads that may have developed from those conversations." But Ehrlichman had a recommendation: "I think really the only way that I know to make a judgment on this is for you to listen to your tapes [the existence of which Haldeman had recently informed him, but apparently not that the system was still operating] and see what actually was said, or maybe for Bob to do it, or somebody. See what was said there. And then analyze how big a threat he is."

"Right," Nixon agreed. Ehrlichman continued, "If it didn't come out of those meetings, then I think it's imaginary. Because it then does not come out of your mouth, it comes by reason of the actions or something that one of us said or did, and it can be handled. But if you're really confronted with that kind of a dilemma, or that kind of crisis in this thing, I think, before any other steps are taken, any precipitous steps," Ehrlichman told the president, "you better damn sure know what your hole card is." Nixon agreed. "Beyond that," Ehrlichman continued, "hell, I'm not afraid of Dean and what he might say about me, for instance. I think it can be handled. I don't think Bob has anything to fear from Dean, basically, then, particularly based on what the attorneys tell us; he has an almost unlimited capacity to dredge up anecdotes from a dim and murky past, and we're just going to have to handle it one by one. You mentioned the La Costa plan. Our fellows [i.e., their attorneys] probably didn't tell you this, but Dick Moore's attorney called John Wilson and indicated that Dick Moore just doesn't have any memory at all about La Costa. He can barely remember even being out there."

"Dick Moore told me—" Nixon tried to explain what Moore had related, but Ehrlichman kept interrupting, saying, "I understand," until Nixon did understand that Moore's memory had gone from bad to none. Ehrlichman explained, "His memory is, apparently, feeble beyond measure, because his attorney has explained to him what his exposure is, and Dick is scared shitless, apparently. To the point where he has contacted Silbert to ascertain that he will not be indicted prior to his daughter's wedding, so that he can go to his daughter's wedding."

Notwithstanding the fact that Haldeman had agreed to listen to the March 21 conversation, which would confirm what was or was not said, they proceeded to speculate about the content of that discussion. Ehrlichman reminded the president that he had no exposure whatsoever on the Ellsberg break-in—or, as Ehrlichman described it, "the Hunt escapade on the coast"— as it had been totally outside the president's knowledge and did not reach him. Ehrlichman reported, though, that he himself might have some culpability for the "Hunt escapade" after thinking about the fact that "it was a legitimate national security subject and that we are to stonewall it"; he was then no longer concerned.

About halfway through this conversation, while discussing Haldeman's listening to the March 21 recorded conversation, Ehrlichman said that with that information they might "try and disarm" me, adding, "I'm morally certain he does not know that he is on tape." This led Nixon to ask, "I wonder if he has a tape himself." "That might be," Ehrlichman replied." Nixon then asked, "Is it possible that he carries a tape? Does he do that?" Nixon wondered if I carried it in my "hip or something," but Ehrlichman was not concerned, because "those things almost always go haywire," while Haldeman pointed out that I would have been recording "privileged communications."

Ehrlichman questioned if privilege remained in force if a crime was involved, and thought that might be why I was pushing for immunity. Haldeman shared a thought, based on a misunderstanding of how immunity worked, including the idea that it might enable me to use information I still had against them: "My argument would be that that's the worst thing you can do, because that then puts you in as a permanent hostage the rest of your life to John Dean, and if you look beyond that to Henry Petersen, and beyond that probably to Silbert and Glanzer, and to the court reporters, and others." Ehrlichman added my lawyers to the list of those who would hold them hostage. Haldeman agreed and concluded, "Really, your only real route is to destroy Dean."

Everyone agreed, but the president wanted to know precisely how they would do that. Ehrlichman suggested Nixon call in Henry Petersen, and tell him, "'Henry, I had a conversation with Dean,' whenever the last time it was that you had a conversation with Dean, where he was asked to sign those letters, and maybe it was on another occasion. Say, 'Henry, I do not have any overt, concrete, satisfactory documentary evidence that I'm being blackmailed here, but that is the distinct impression that Mr. Dean gives me. I want to tell you that this president is not subject to blackmail, and I want this turned on Dean. I want you to lay a trap for him. I want you to determine whether or not he is attempting to blackmail me. And I want the full weight of the law to fall on him if that's what he's up to.' Now you may not catch him. Petersen may not want to, may not want to do it." Haldeman soon added, "He's probably bought Henry Petersen already," but then had a further thought and suggested that Petersen was "allied with the president as a fellow blackmailee." Ehrlichman said, "All I'm suggesting is that there is another direction to go, and it's stronger, I think, from the standpoint of the president, than the immunity thing, which—"

"Well, I can't, I don't know," Nixon said, gathering his thoughts. "I guess you're right. You go the immunity route—" at which Haldeman interrupted and said, "It's one more cover-up." Nixon liked that analysis, observing,

"Yeah, it's another cover-up. I'm trying to cover up because [I'm] trying to silence Dean." Then he made a startling admission: "And frankly, if I said something was wrong [referring to involving himself in the cover-up], then I deserve to be impeached." Accustomed to Nixon's propensity for self-pity, neither Haldeman nor Ehrlichman reacted, but Ehrlichman effectively dismissed it by not taking it very seriously: "Well, look at it this way. If you did, and you try to live it out that way, you talk about you getting this cloud over, and you got to start moving on to new directions and doing your job. You sure as hell can't do it that way." Nixon said he was serious, and was distressed because, "Jesus Christ, I thought at least we could talk to our people [privately, including] Dean and everybody."

"Well, see that's the other way to destroy Dean, is not only by Petersen trapping him but by the president," suggested Haldeman, who wanted Nixon to go public, to present himself as a leader "in a time of crisis, even when it's your own crisis. And that they've got to understand and share the agony that you've been going through, that you can and must take the resignation of John Dean. You can't operate the presidency by threat. You have to remove the threat in order to do it, and you say that that's what you've done. This is a man who's disserved you." Ehrlichman supported this idea and added, "You got to go on the assumption that the American people want to believe in their president." Haldeman held forth at some length about this attack on the presidency, and that Nixon could not use "a gimmick to cover up, which I think our pulling out early does. Maybe you then have got to take the offensive in saying [how] this does show there has been something wrong in American politics." Haldeman said that when the president retired he would lead the charge in "changing the American political campaign structure."

From this lofty discussion on reform they were soon back to the reality of their situation, with Ehrlichman reporting that more negative stories were likely to emerge about the campaign, such as bringing the Cubans to Washington "for counterdemonstrations and all that sort of stuff." Nixon felt that was "stuff I think we can survive." "The thing you can't survive," Haldeman said pointedly, "is presidential culpability. And that, I don't think, there is."

"Well, basically, let me put it this way," Nixon replied. "You shouldn't survive if the president was culpable out there." But the president did not think that true of himself. To make the point, he and Haldeman went through a series of his decisions, including the clemency-for-Hunt question, in which all he did, he said, was tell Colson he was very sympathetic to

Hunt's plight after the death of his wife. He also assured Haldeman and Ehrlichman that he had never discussed this subject with Mitchell. The president's only concern remained me, and he wanted both Haldeman and Ehrlichman to find out more about how I might be a problem. Ehrlichman suggested he address the situation before it became a problem, urging, "I'd slam him before he could slam you."

As the conversation headed toward its end, Haldeman produced the notes he had taken during a conversation with me on March 26, when I was at Camp David. He had called to ask if I had any problem going to the grand jury, and he reported that I said I had none. Then I brought him up to date on notes I had been gathering, sorting out what had happened, particularly regarding what I then described as "the blackmail situation" regarding payments to the Watergate defendants. Haldeman read these notes aloud, which were in effect a capsule account of what I would later flesh out more fully before the U.S. Senate and during the Watergate cover-up trial. The others listened and appeared not to disagree with a word. Haldeman had just given them evidence not only that their claims of my inability to write a Dean report at Camp David were not true, but that my draft of that report would have sent us all to prison for conspiracy to obstruct justice.

Ehrlichman explained a project he and Haldeman had been developing: "We made a list this morning to try and see who were in the same boat as I am personally, in this. That is, not charged with anything, with no evidence before the grand jury yet, with an incipient [Watergate] problem, and there are seventeen of us in the same identical situation." "Really?" Nixon asked in a mildly bemused tone. "That's principals," Haldeman noted, referring to seventeen presidential appointees on the staff, and explained, "I mean, you're not looking at secretaries or low-level assistants." They proceeded to read off the names, saying that some were only marginally involved, while others were in more deeply; their list was not restricted to those with ties to Watergate, or even to Segretti, but included those who had taken part in activities that investigations and the media might cause to reflect unfavorably on Nixon's presidency. What follows are the names mentioned by Haldeman and Ehrlichman: Haldeman's assistant Larry Higby; Dick Moore; Dick Howard, a Colson assistant; Powell Moore, who had accompanied Liddy to Burning Tree Country Club to get McCord out of jail; Bruce Kherli, Haldeman's aide who handled personnel and made it appear that Hunt had long been off the White House payroll; Fred Fielding, my deputy, and everyone in my office;

Noel Koch,* who was on the speechwriting staff but reportedly did work with Colson's office; Bill Timmons, who was involved with the convention; Wally Johnson, who handled congressional relations, including matters regarding Watergate; Ron Ziegler and his deputy Jerry Warren, who were given background information so they knew what not to say to the press; Ken Clawson, a Colson assistant; and Bill Rhatican, whom Ehrlichman mentioned twice without an explanation of why he had been included. None of these people would ultimately ever be charged. But because Ehrlichman believed they were in situations similar to his own, he argued that, unless the president was going to clean out the entire White House, Ehrlichman himself should not be forced to leave. But, he added, he was "prepared to take leave the minute the charges surface." To Ehrlichman's surprise, those charges would be made that afternoon, but not in the form either he or the president had expected.

Ehrlichman said that, if he did leave, "I have to go to work, [return to] practicing law." He said he knew where he could go immediately, to a relatively good-paying job. "You wouldn't be terribly happy with it, and I wouldn't be terribly happy with it, but it would be kind of a any-port-in-the-storm situation at that point." (Years after the fact Colson told me that he had offered Ehrlichman a job at his law firm.) "Let me ask you this, to be quite candid," Nixon responded. "Is there any way you can use cash?" He posed the question to both men. Each answered again, "I don't think so." Nixon explained that he thought there might already be as much as two hundred thousand dollars available in the 1974 campaign fund. Haldeman recognized that violating campaign laws was not going to help and told Nixon, "That compounds the problem, that really does." Nixon did not disagree but said he wanted them to know it was available. The conversation ended by returning to the notion of a letter from Wilson and Strickler exonerating them of any criminal conduct. Ehrlichman said he would get Wilson "to gin up a letter in satisfactory form, if you'd like to have that for your file." Nixon said he would, and Haldeman suggested there be two different letters, one for each of them.

Shortly after Haldeman and Ehrlichman left, the president received an urgent call from Dick Kleindienst, who said he needed to meet immediately.[115] Kleindienst said information that I had given to Silbert (in fact, it

---

*Some of these names are difficult to hear. This name sounds like Noel Cook, but there was no Noel Cook, rather a Noel Koch.

was actually Shaffer who relayed it and believed it was an an ongoing ob-
struction of justice to withhold it from Ellsberg) on April 15 regarding the
Ellsberg trial needed to be reported to the judge handling the case. Nixon
instructed Kleindienst to come to the EOB office, but without Henry Petersen, and Kleindienst arrived twenty minutes later.[116] He told Nixon that
Petersen had come to him that morning with a memorandum from Earl
Silbert, and then proceeded to read from it, quoting Silbert's discovery of the
Liddy and Hunt burglary of Ellsberg psychiatrist's office to get his files.
Kleindienst said that the Justice Department did not believe that any such
information had been used to prosecute Ellsberg, but (as Shaffer had advised
them) they still believed they had a duty to inform the judge in the Ellsberg
trial in Los Angeles that afternoon. Nixon, reminding Kleindienst that he
had instructed Petersen to stay out of matters of national security, said that
the Ellsberg break-in was part of "what we call the plumbers operation." As
he explained, "Without any knowledge of anybody, these crazy fools went
out, and they went into the psychiatrist's [office]. They got nothing. It was a
dry hole. Now what happened there is, however, that Dean was aware of that,
because Dean was the one that implemented the whole thing." This was not
confusion on his part, for Nixon clarified precisely what he meant: "When
I say implemented, he carried it out."

Kleindienst advised that they had no option but to turn the information
over. "We can't have another cover-up, Mr. President," he blurted. Kleindienst reported that once they advised the judge, who would have to inform
Ellsberg's lawyers, the information would be on the street very quickly.
"What is Dean, what's he doing, pointing a gun basically at Ehrlichman?"
the president asked. Kleindienst did not know. Nixon continued, "Let me
say I want no cover-up. Good God almighty." After briefly attempting to
justify the action, he soon changed direction: "The fact that these people,
who were designated to do it, burglarized the office of a psychiatrist, shit, it's
the dumbest God damn thing I ever heard of." Kleindienst said he had spoken off-the-record with his friend Judge Roger Robb, who counseled him to
take the very action he was urging on the president. The president wondered
if it would kill the case, but Kleindienst thought not.

Soon Nixon said, "The other point is that Liddy and Hunt, of course, or
Dean, could say he was ordered to [do this] by Ehrlichman." Kleindienst
responded, "Sure. He could say he was [ordered] to by you," but Nixon protested, "No, he won't do that, because I didn't tell him." This led them to a

discussion of whether my trump card might be implicating the president in the Ellsberg break-in. Kleindienst said he told Petersen that, if that was the case, "you have to tell Dean to go fuck himself. You're not going to blackmail the government of the United States and implicate the president in the Ellsberg matter." This prompted the president to ask Kleindienst, for whom I had once worked, what he thought about me. He said he had always trusted me, then added, "Up until two weeks ago I thought he was one of the most able, fine, decent, honest, sensible young kids." Nixon asked Kleindienst what he thought my motives were in giving this information to Silbert.

"His motive is to create an environment whereby he will get immunity," Kleindienst said,[117] and then added, "Dean turns out to be the very weak, selfish, self-directed, you know, the link in this whole operation." If I had anything to say about Kleindienst along the way, Kleindienst had warned Petersen, he would tell "the son of a bitch to get his ass out."

Rather than alert Ehrlichman to the fact that this information was about to surface at the Ellsberg trial in Los Angeles, Nixon decided to sit on it for a while. He surely understood that his attempt to assign responsibility to me for the conspiracy to steal Ellsberg's psychiatric records would not work. The president called Haldeman on the private interoffice line, but Higby answered and said that Haldeman was listening to the March 21 recording of our meetings but would come to the EOB office in ten minutes.[118]

"Well, that is hard work," Haldeman said when he arrived with his notes on the March 21 conversation.[119] "Good God! It's amazing. [The recording equipment] works awfully well in picking up the guest. It doesn't pick up you well. It must be set on the side of the desk or something." Haldeman said both could be heard, but "it's hard as hell to hear you, so you got to keep looking back and reworking." He then presented the highlights of our session: "Dean said, 'The reason for this meeting this morning is that you don't really know what I know, so it's difficult for you to make judgments.' And, he said, 'overall there's, no doubt about the seriousness of all this. There's a cancer close to the presidency. It's growing daily; it's compounding itself. We're being blackmailed. People are going to start perjuring to protect others, and there's no assurance it isn't all going to bust. And, let's face it. First, let me fill you in on the Watergate.' Then he went back to the beginning, went through the whole thing on how it came about."

In all of the recorded conversations before and after this one on April 25, Richard Nixon never had as few comments, nor allowed anyone to speak so long without interruption, as he did while listening to Haldeman report from his fourteen pages of legal pad notes of highlights of our conversation. Haldeman said he had not finished listening to the tape and would return to it later. The president simply punctuated Haldeman's recitation with an occasional "right," except at the point at which Haldeman described Nixon asking me who else had criminal problems, and I told him Ehrlichman, for the conspiracy to burglarize Ellsberg's doctor. Given that this topic was now a matter of some importance, Nixon protested, "I didn't know about that. Alright, go on."

When he finished his account, Haldeman again explained that Nixon should view his reactions to me as merely trying to draw me out to see how much I knew. Haldeman said, "You're trying to see how far it goes. You said, 'Is that your recommendation?' You do that all the time. You ask people questions on the basis of, to try and see what direction they're going. They're leading questions." Nixon was less certain of that, particularly with regard to his declarative statements. "I said 'a million dollars,'" he noted, although he had equivocated a bit on clemency, telling me, "You couldn't do it till after the '74 elections." As Nixon explained, "That's an incriminating thing. His word against the president's, unless he had a tape recorder in his pocket," which apparently had become his worst fear.[120] Haldeman also reminded him of how they were now going to recast this conversation: "At this point, you're investigating."

While Haldeman doubted that I had recorded the conversation, he incorrectly told the president, "He must have been talking from notes, I mean, it sure looked liked it, I mean, sounded like it." "It made quite an orderly report, he'd put together," Nixon observed, and he asked Haldeman to go over the Hunt demand part again. When Haldeman finished he prompted, "You're smoking him out on what he thinks the alternatives are. You're pumping him." As the conversation progressed, the president returned to his incriminating instruction to me to pay Hunt's demand. "What I'm really setting up there," Nixon explained, "putting the best light on a bad situation, is basically, I'm saying, 'Well, get the money, but we should try to cut it off,' and so forth, 'but how do you do it?'" Haldeman reminded him, "You're being blackmailed, here on this specific question of the national security point. Because what Hunt was holding you up on was not on the Watergate. But on the other, the seamy work for Ehrlichman. All the other defendants were also involved in this."

Nixon briefly changed the subject to report that Kleindienst had been over earlier and given him a copy of a memorandum Justice felt they had to send to the judge handling the Ellsberg criminal trial. The president instructed, "Show Ehrlichman that memorandum from Kleindienst and say we had no choice under the circumstances." As he explained, "Dean, see, informed them on the Ellsberg break-in." Realzing it was going to have Watergate repercussions, he said, "It'll break in the paper," and he thought it might "clear Ellsberg." The press would write that the "Watergate buggers tried to do this or that and the other thing. Know what I mean?" Nixon wanted Haldeman to tell Ehrlichman he had had no choice when Kleindienst asked him about doing it.

This discussion ended on the March 21 conversation, when Nixon said, "Let me say, it's got to be, you, Ehrlichman and I have got to put the wagons up around the president on this particular conversation. I just wonder if the son of a bitch had a recorder on him. I didn't notice any, but I wasn't looking." Haldeman thought, "It's almost inconceivable that the guy would try that, because—" Nixon interrupted, acknowledging, "He was really coming in, in fact, to warn me." Haldeman agreed and observed, "He had no thought that you were going to say anything like this. All he was coming in to tell you was that there was a problem. He wasn't expecting you to solve it that way. I think you probably surprised him enormously by even raising this point." Nixon's mind had drifted, and after asking, "What, what?" Haldeman recast his point: "Of, you know, well, we could get the money. I think that's the last thing he expected you to say." Nixon asked, "What did he expect me to say, we can't do it?" Haldeman dodged the question, and Steve Bull entered the office to tell Nixon that Henry Petersen had arrived at his Oval Office.

The president had Petersen brought over to his EOB office, where the poor audio quality of the tape suggests that both seated themselves facing away from the hidden desk microphones for this conversation.[121] Pressed by Nixon for information, Petersen reported that his friend William Hundley would represent John Mitchell and that Sam Dash had informed the Justice Department that the Senate Watergate committee was going to seek immunity for a number of witnesses during their hearings. Petersen was going to try to talk them out of it, but he was not hopeful. Nixon asked how negotiations were going with Magruder's attorney, and mine, and Petersen said no agreements had been reached. With the deeply incriminating March 21 tape fresh in his mind, the president said he thought that that conversation was "probably" my trump card, so he proceeded to spin it for Petersen into an innocuous passing inquiry by him as to how much money the Watergate defendants might want: "I said, 'How much is this going to take?' I mean, 'How about maybe a million dollars.' I said, 'Well, we could get a million dollars, but how the hell are you going to get it to them?' I said, 'It's wrong. You can't go that way.'" Nixon warned Petersen that if I ever tried to testify about the contents of that conversation, I was not to be believed. "But that is the conversation, period. I remember telling Ehrlichman and Haldeman about that conversation," he added, suggesting that his position could be corroborated.

Petersen next reported, "The United States attorney for the Southern District of New York wants Dean to testify in the Vesco thing." Nixon was surprised (as was I), but Petersen assured him that he had been holding them off, trying to make a deal with me. Petersen incorrectly reported that I had made "a couple of calls to the SEC" for Mitchell on Vesco's behalf to get a subpoena quashed. He quickly moved on to report that he had learned the contents of the documents Gray had destroyed (from me via my attorney, for when Gray denied having the documents, I took a lie-detector test and challenged Gray to do likewise, since I had become tired of Gray's calling me a liar publicly, and now privately, to prosecutors). Petersen explained that the documents included "concocted" State Department cables suggesting that, when Kennedy was president, he was actively involved in the murder of South Vietnam president Diem. Nixon, who said nothing, was aware of this undertaking by Colson and Hunt and merely asked why Gray had destroyed the material. Petersen still relied on Gray's account that I had given him the documents to destroy them.

Petersen reported that, based on information "from a very reliable source, a newspaper man" who had interviewed Donald Segretti, they were developing a criminal case against Segretti under the Corrupt Practices Act, and Petersen added that they would probably immunize two people to get an indictment against him. Not surprisingly Nixon continued to bring the conversation back to his own involvement, with him and Petersen repeating that they were not going to allow me to blackmail them, Haldeman, Ehrlichman or Kleindienst. What Nixon ultimately took from this conversation can be gleaned from his subsequent discussions with Haldeman and Ehrlichman.

Nixon tried unsuccessfully to call Ehrlichman first, and failing to reach him, spoke with Haldeman, who was at home when the president reached him shortly before 7:00 P.M.[122] "I had a good talk with Petersen and told him that, you know, about the need to expedite the grand jury," Nixon reported. "Second, I told him I wanted a paper from him with regard to you and John. He said he'd have it by Friday afternoon." The president gave Haldeman more background on the memorandum from Silbert regarding the Ellsberg case, which Nixon characterized as basically "a little blackmail" by Dean.[123] Nixon expected that this would make the news, but Haldeman was not sure that was all bad, explaining, "Well, it adds confusion to the whole thing." "Yeah," Nixon responded, "the Watergate buggers tried to knock over Ellsberg's psychiatrist."

The president asked if Haldeman had given Ehrlichman the memorandum from Kleindienst yet. He had not but said, "I covered it with him."

"I leveled with Petersen on the conversation that we had," Nixon reported, regarding their review of the March 21 recording. "And I said, now I want you to know this, and I said, we'll not be blackmailed on it, we didn't do anything about it, but that's when I started my investigation. And that's our line there, I think," noting, "incidentally, I think that should just be between you and me." Haldeman agreed; they would not tell Ehrlichman. "Did it bother Petersen?" Haldeman asked. "Oh, well, everything bothers him," Nixon quickly answered, and Haldeman could not resist laughing.

Nixon talked about the problem of handling me "in such a way that he doesn't become a totally implacable enemy." He reminded Haldeman, "At least, I have treated him decently. In fact, more decently than he deserves. On the other hand, he may become totally intractable. If he does, you're going to have one hell of a pissing contest." "If you do, you just got to win it," Haldeman replied, leading Nixon to wonder, "What else can you do? And when you think of this, all this kind of thing, you know, I was just thinking a little bit more about the impeachment thing, that I don't see the Senate or any senators starting an impeachment of the president based on the word of John Dean." Haldeman agreed,* and Nixon continued, "That's all it is. I mean, John Dean says that, this, and that and the other thing happened." "And there's no way he can support it," Haldeman added. "I mean, there's no way to make a case." Nixon cautioned, "Well, except it could be he recorded

---

*Needless to say, members of the U.S. Senate only have the power to convict, not the power to impeach, a president, which is left to a majority of the members of the U. S. House of Representatives.

his conversation, made a memorandum, told his lawyers immediately there-after, and so forth and so on. But even there, I mean, here is—"

"Still his word, unless he's got a tape recording. And even with the tape recording, I think you could make the case the other way," Haldeman argued. The president remained silent a while, then thoughtfully added, "I don't know [about] a tape recording. I can't believe that he could have walked in there with a tape recorder that day, because that day, I mean, I'm not trying to be wishful thinking, that particular day he wasn't really out to get the president, I don't think." "That's right, no sir, he wasn't," Haldeman agreed. "He was going just the other way." Nixon noted, "Trying to help?" Although Haldeman agreed, and said he could not conceive that I would have recorded Nixon, they continued to speculate about where and how I might have hidden a recorder. The conversation ended with the president encouraging Haldeman to make a trip to Mississippi with him on Friday and reminding him to fill Ehrlichman in on the Ellsberg matter.

Three minutes after the president ended the call with Haldeman, the operator had Ehrlichman on the line, and they spoke briefly.[124] The president explained that he had given Haldeman information to share with Ehr-lichman following his talk with Petersen. "And the only thing that is partic-ularly relevant is that piece of paper which they brought in here, which I talked to Petersen about, and he said that he felt very strongly, as did Klein-dienst, and Dean's people were trying to blackmail them with that. And that they, therefore, felt it was very important that they get that conveyed to the prosecution. Dean's lawyer having told them this, they feel that it's impor-tant that the prosecution know it. That the judge knows it. Now that's what they've done."

"They passed it on to Matt Byrne?" a mildly mortified Ehrlichman asked. "Passed it on to the judge," Nixon affirmed, and added, "And what is likely to happen is that, well, I don't know. Might call Dean. And then Dean will have to say what it was. So the Watergate buggers are involved in the psychi-atrist's office." He added, "Let me say, though, on that point, I think it was information all those prosecutors over there already [had]," referring to the Watergate prosecutors, and "it's going to come out anyway, John." Ehr-lichman said he would speak to Haldeman.

Nixon knew that this information being released to Judge Byrne had upset Ehrlichman, so he decided to shield his aide as best he could. At 7:22 P.M. he called Kleindienst and instructed him to warn the prosecutors and the judge "that this was a national security investigation of very great sensitivity."[125] Kleindienst thought this was a "good suggestion" and agreed to pass it along. As soon as Nixon completed this call to Kleindienst, he called Ehrlichman to report what he had done.[126] "Great," he told the president, and Nixon proceeded to give him a few highlights of his meeting with Petersen. Ehrlichman confided to Nixon, "I tell you, I made a mistake in joining with Bob in retaining counsel." The president agreed and suggested, "You better change pretty fast." Ehrlichman noted, "If I could, if I can figure out some way of getting a little separation, I think it's wise to do."[127]

During this conversation Nixon ascertained who was involved in the Ellsberg break-in. When he told Ehrlichman that I might be called as a witness in the Ellsberg case on this matter, he said, "He'll probably say he was doing it under Ehrlichman's direction, right? Is that what he'll say?" Ehrlichman answered, "I don't think Dean can say that. They would have to get some other witness, they would have to get Liddy or Hunt or somebody. Dean was not directly involved." "He wasn't?" a surprised Nixon asked. "Then how the hell does he know about this? This is hearsay." Ehrlichman did not recall how I had learned of it, so he said, "Snooping over the fence." "Oh, I see. Oh, I see. He wasn't an actor in this?" Nixon asked, despite having accused me to both Kleindienst and Petersen. "No, sir," Ehrlichman assured him. I had not been involved.

When the president asked Ehrlichman what he would say about the matter, Ehrlichman provided a bit more information than he had in his previous denials: "Well, I'd say what is the fact, that my connection with it was that I authorized their travel, and I authorized them to go out and investigate Ellsberg, and among the things that were to be investigated out there was an examination of his medical records, if that were possible. Now they chose a method that I—" Nixon interrupted and injected, "You did not approve." Ehrlichman agreed, "I did not approve. When I heard about it afterward I disapproved of it. And my shortcoming, my failing, was in not bringing them to account on it and not just having them arrested on discovery. Since it was a—" Nixon interrupted with the response he wanted again: "Highly sensitive thing." But Ehrlichman continued using his own words, "A military area, why, ah—" The president interrupted again to remind Ehrlichman that the FBI was not being helpful, which Ehrlichman acknowledged might be part of the problem. "But here again, I think I'll talk to Wilson about this in the morning, so that he's forewarned. And he can do some briefing on it." But based on Ehrlichman's claiming that he had not approved anything, the president began arguing that it was not illegal, that he had done nothing wrong. Ehrlichman, however, was giving the president a less than full account.

This conversation ended with Nixon relating to Ehrlichman that Petersen had told him that my attorneys (actually, it was only Shaffer) had made a serious error: "[Petersen] says, 'I think Dean's attorneys made a terrible mistake in putting this out to us,'" regarding Ellsberg. "Because they were trying to test us, they were trying to see if we got this information, they didn't think we'd use it. And they thought they would hold that over our heads." (I have not been able to verify Petersen's making this statement to Nixon in their earlier conversation.[128])

After ending his conversation with Ehrlichman, Nixon was still worried about the possibility that I had recorded him, so he called Haldeman again at 7:46 P.M. and asked, "Is there any way that, even surreptitiously or discreetly or otherwise, that you could determine whether Dean might have walked in there with a recorder on him?"[129] "No, I don't think there is any way," Haldeman replied. "I think [it's] so remote as to be almost beyond possibility." They discussed this for several minutes, and Nixon asked if I made memoranda of conversations; Haldeman replied that, to the best of his knowledge, I did not. They agreed again that they would simply have to destroy me if we got into "a pissing match."

At the end of the day Nixon again called Kleindienst to see if he had spoken with the Los Angeles–based Ellsberg prosecutor.[130] Kleindienst reported that he had done exactly as instructed and described the Ellsberg information as sensitive national security material, and he told the president that they hoped they could persuade the judge to consider delaying examining if any improper evidence had been obtained and used until after the trial. "Okay, sleep well, boy," Nixon said. Kleindienst chuckled, "Same to you." Before calling it a night, however, Nixon called Ziegler at 9:07 P.M. to see how his day had gone.[131] Ziegler reported that he was spending a lot of time with the press people, mending fences. Nixon wanted to be sure that he was stressing that "the president has been on top of this every minute of the day, and he's trying to get to the bottom of this thing, and so forth."

## April 26, 1973, the White House

The president called Haldeman into the Oval Office at 8:55 A.M.[132] Haldeman, who was in the process of assembling times and dates for his lawyers, remarked, "It's amazing, when you go back and look through the papers, how little any of us, you or me or Ehrlichman, was involved in any of that stuff."

In this conversation Nixon was again trying to determine what sort of "bomb" or "trump card" or "big play" I might be contemplating in what he perceived as my quest for immunity. In attempting to identify that bomb the president had Haldeman take him through the schedule of our meetings. Tellingly he told Haldeman that the schedule for March 22 was wrong, as it had me with the president when he was in fact meeting privately with Mitchell, following a group meeting that Haldeman, Ehrlichman and I had attended. (I had been at the meeting with Mitchell for only a few minutes and then departed.)

As they attempted to recall Nixon's meetings with me, Nixon paused to instruct Haldeman on his taping system. "With regard to these tapes. I don't know how you can reconstruct it, but I think that, for your information, the directive I've given you is," he began, and then proceeded to what he wanted: "I don't think it should ever get out that we taped this office, Bob. Have we got people that are trustworthy on that? I guess we have." "I think so," Haldeman responded, and Nixon continued that if it ever did become known he taped, then "we only taped the national security information. All other information is scrapped, never transcribed. Get the point? That's what I want you to remember on these, if you will. See my point? That's just a memorandum for your file, basically, that you make." Nixon added, "I think that's very important. You never want to be in a position to say the president taped it, you know. I mean taped somebody."

Haldeman agreed that they would say the purpose was national security, and Nixon further instructed, "I don't want you to disclose that to Ehrlichman or anybody else. I mean, that's just something—I know what you can tell Ehrlichman. Just say you went over it, and it's about the same as—" Haldeman interrupted. "I've already, what I said to him is that the tape, he knows I went over it, of course. Ah, I said, 'It, it basically says what the president recalled.'" Informed that Ehrlichman was aware of the taping system (though Ehrlichman thought Nixon taped only select conversations[133]), Nixon did not press the point further, and they returned to the March 21 conversation and Nixon's concern that I had made a record of our talk. Haldeman was still not concerned: "That area is totally privileged until you come to an impeachment proceeding. There's no way that that can be brought out, because there's no forum for going into presidential guilt except an impeachment." Nixon agreed, and Haldeman continued, "And they have got to impeach you first before the proceeding starts, and they aren't going to impeach you."

Nixon responded, "No, I slept a little on that, and it's good for John to look at it that way," he said regarding Ehrlichman's raising the possibility. But Nixon was not concerned either, asking, "My God, what the hell have we done to be impeached?" Haldeman reminded Nixon, "But John doesn't believe you have either, and John doesn't believe you can be impeached. What he believes is, that's the game Dean is trying to play. Does not believe it's a game of any potential." And they returned yet again to analyzing the March 21 conversation, with Haldeman constantly reminding Nixon that he was merely "trying to smoke out" information from me throughout the conversation. Nixon explained to Haldeman that, when talking about money for the defendants, the reason he had mentioned the Cuban committee is that he "had read about the Cuban committee in the paper, that's true." (The piece apparently ran in a Miami newspaper, for no relevant story was published in either the *New York Times* or *The Washington Post*.)

In going through a drill about what the president did and did not know about the money before our March 21 conversation, Nixon explained: He did not know about the $350,000; he did not know about "the launching of Kalmbach"; and he added, generally, "I did not know, I had read stories to that effect, but I didn't frankly look into them. But basically, I frankly said, 'Well, it must be a bunch of Cubans, or something like that, and I thought of the Cuban committee.'" "I didn't know about La Costa," he added, and the request that Moore tap Mitchell for money. "My point is, and I'm not trying to be selfish, but the point is, the story is very true that I didn't know a thing. Now there's only one weakness in that, the Pappas thing," which Nixon acknowledged he spoke to me about on March 21. Nixon quizzed Haldeman about what he heard regarding Pappas on the March 21 recording: "Did I say, 'I understand that Pappas is helping,' or [did he say], 'Pappas was helping'?" Haldeman reported, "[Dean] said, 'Mitchell has talked to Pappas.' You just quickly lobbed it in, 'I know.'" Nixon resumed, "'Yes, I know.' Well, the point was, what I was referring to only was not that Mitchell had talked to Pappas but that Pappas never mentioned that here in this office. Never mentioned that, I know. All he said is that, 'I'm helping, helping John's [Mitchell's] special project,' and I said, 'Well, thank you very much. I appreciate it very much.' He didn't tell me what it was about." The president was correct regarding Pappas's not knowing why he was providing cash, for he was happy to keep the ambassadorship for his friend that he wanted in exchange for his assistance. Haldeman had clearly explained to Nixon, however, why they needed cash from Pappas, which is reflected in their conversation.*

When they moved on to other matters, Nixon recalled that I had sent him another very clear warning in our final conversation, four days earlier, on Easter Sunday, April 22: "Basically, Dean, it might be that he said he told the president that he was going to do this." He recalled that I had again tried to caution him that he might be obstructing justice in colluding with Ehrlichman to block my testimony and influence my dealings with the prosecutors. "Dean told me when I called him on Sunday, I recollected this, he said, 'You know, I know how that statement with regard to no immunity got into your statement.' And he lobbed that out; this is a guess, of course." Nixon asked Haldeman, "Remember the April seventeenth statement? But I'm just trying to look at things as he may look at them."[134] Haldeman reported that I had told Larry Higby the same thing regarding my scapegoat statement: "He put that statement out, he said, 'That reached the right place.'" Haldeman clarified this for Nixon, "And he said, 'The people that I was talking to got the signal,' something to that effect." He added that I had told Higby, "I'm not out to get anybody." Haldeman thought the signal had gotten through, and Nixon agreed.

When Haldeman said he was not happy with this headline—NIXON CALLS DEAN, SAYS YOU'RE STILL MY COUNSEL—Nixon denied he had made that statement (although Ziegler later corrected him, telling him he had been present when the president said it.) "You doing it privately to Dean is fine," Haldeman said, but publicly he thought created a problem. Indeed, Haldeman wanted to know when they were going to take action on me. "I mean, they have to either indict him or give him immunity, and you've got to move on Dean either way." Nixon said, "One thing you and John got to work on is the game plan on how you handle John Dean. Let's face it: You remember, the only reason I put the immunity thing in there, Bob, was because John

---

*See page 255.

insisted it go in there, do you recall?" Haldeman confirmed, "Yes, I sure do."
Nixon went on, "I think Colson did, too, as I recall. But John was the one.
'Be sure that you say that nobody gets immunity and tell Petersen nobody's
to get immunity, that is it.' Whether that was a good move or not, I do not
know." Haldeman explained that the only reason to grant immunity to any
witness was to nail a more important defendant, and while they had plenty
of witnesses to nail Mitchell, I was the witness who could nail Haldeman
and Ehrlichman.

As this conversation continued, Haldeman admitted to Nixon, "I don't
think that we can pretend that we didn't know there was an interest on
Mitchell's part in raising money for the defendants." "But," he protested, "I
sure as hell don't know what it was for," as if unaware of Hunt's demands.
Nixon noted, "The staff protected me from it, [and] I just wasn't getting involved." "It wasn't a matter of protection," Haldeman explained. "It was not
something that was necessary to get to you. It didn't involve you."

Reviewing the matters that had arisen during the March 21 conversation
caused Nixon to wonder when he had first learned the defendants were being
paid, when this "blackmail stuff" had first come up. Haldeman did not have
a clear answer. "I never got any of this crap about defendants or attorneys'
fees or anything at all here that I remember, with you or anybody else,"
Nixon said.* But he correctly suspected it had arisen before March 21,
whether it was legal or not, so he wanted Haldeman to listen closely for that
when he resumed with the March 21 conversation. Haldeman said he had
discussed this matter with his lawyers, "Because they made the point that
the support thing doesn't hold up [when] the defendants were out on bail
and able to earn their own support."

Nixon wanted to know what their attorneys thought about any potential
charge on "the conspiracy thing, on the support for defendants, in other
words, the launching of Kalmbach and so forth." "We didn't have any motive, and we did not launch Kalmbach," Haldeman replied. "We didn't take
initiative on any of this stuff." It was an evasive answer, but Nixon clearly
did not want to debate Haldeman's conspicuous problems and said, "Okay,
fine." But Haldeman claimed their "thing" was "passive, nondisapproval"—
which he did not understand still placed him solidly in a conspiratorial

---

*In fact, Haldeman first reported paying the Watergate defendants on August 1, 1972 (see page 123),
and Nixon expressed concern that the payments could be bribes during that conversation.

agreement—"because Mitchell said there was a need." Nixon reminded
Haldeman that Ehrlichman had called Kalmbach, according to what he had
been told by Petersen. When Haldeman said he thought Kalmbach had
called Ehrlichman, Nixon responded, "All right, whatever it is, fine," likely
perceiving that Haldeman lacked knowledge of the law. Nixon still pressed
as to what the attorneys had said about "subject A, the purpose of the so-
called hush money. The obstruction of justice. You must have discussed this
with them in some language, Bob?" Haldeman replied, "They've been re-
searching the statutes on the question." Nixon, of course, had already listened to them try to explain that they were searching for (nonexistent) case
law to establish that their clients had not acted "corruptly" or "willfully"
under the obstruction statute.

When not discussing the March 21 conversation, Nixon continued to
question Haldeman on what might be my "big bomb," so they went over my
schedule and activities, which I had openly reported to Haldeman and he
had recorded in great detail in his notes. I had made no secret of the fact that
I had hired an attorney and that he had visited with the U.S. attorneys. While
they merely began going through my day-by-day calendar during this morning conversation, that afternoon they would spend almost five hours examining this material, with Haldeman reading page after page of his notes of
his conversations with me during March and April 1972.

As this analysis progressed, Nixon explained that Haldeman understood
better than Ehrlichman "the human factor." As the president reported,
"Dean says, according to Petersen, he said, 'He's never going to be able to
express anything but the greatest respect for and even affection for the president.' Now I don't know whether that is the case that is with others or not.
But what was Higby's report?" Haldeman replied, "Same thing." Nixon
asked, "What's Ziegler say he said on that?" Haldeman again reported,
"Same thing, that he was trying to give advice to the president," and more
recently, "Don't let the president get caught in the obstruction of justice–type
stuff and all that." Nixon asked, "What do you think he meant by that?"
Haldeman did not know but suggested, "I think that [he was] protecting his
own ass, but not in the way of trying to hurt the president. I think he will
use everything he's got except that. I don't think, unless he becomes a madman, that that is the danger, that I guess you do have to have to possibly
contend with, but so the argument there is, you don't want to do anything
to drive him to becoming a madman, but you, in the same point, cannot let

a record be made of your protecting him." "No, no," Nixon insisted. "Oh, no, no. But Bob, I am in a totally defensible position,"

This conversation ended with the president reminding Haldeman that if I did not receive immunity, "if convicted, there's only one place where he will ever get any possible clemency." Haldeman agreed, and Nixon added, "But I sure wouldn't say that to him." Haldeman agreed, and said he was sure that that had to be in the back of my mind.

Before lunch Ziegler spent not quite an hour with the president in the Oval Office. Ziegler wanted guidance on how to explain John Wilson and Frank Strickler's visit to the president, about which the press had learned. Ziegler was told to say that Nixon was gathering facts, but Wilson and Strickler were not his legal representation.[135] Shortly after noon the president phoned Kleindienst for an update on what was happening in the Ellsberg trial now that the judge had received the information about the Ellsberg break-in. Kleindienst said the message had been given to the judge as instructed, and they hoped he would keep it confidential and that it would not disrupt the trial.[136] Following his conversation with Kleindienst, Nixon went over to his EOB office, where he had lunch, a brief nap and then went through paperwork until he asked Haldeman and Ehrlichman join him. Haldeman arrived just before four o'clock and remained until after nine o'clock; Ehrlichman arrived at 5:57 P.M. and left at 7:14 P.M. Most of this lengthy session entailed Haldeman reporting the remainder of the March 21 discussion and then reading more pages of his notes of his March and April conversations with me.[137] Periodically this session was interrupted by Nixon making telephone calls, nine in all, principally to Kleindienst and Petersen. The president and Haldeman went deep into the minutiae of the conversations as they recalled them to explore Nixon's potential vulnerabilities, and they continued to look for the suspected bomb in my arsenal. Only a few insights and revelations surfaced from this meeting.

Nixon felt that the part of the March 21 conversation when Haldeman joined in was better than the first segment, but Haldeman acknowledged that that was only when looked at in the context of the spin he was placing on the conversation, of "trying to smoke out from Dean what kinds of things he would say to do." He was most concerned about whether he had given me orders to pay off Hunt, and he had not (nor had I ever thought otherwise, for I was trying to prevent him from taking such action). Haldeman read the president a forthcoming story from Jack Anderson attacking me, asserting that everything that was amiss about Watergate was my fault. Haldeman assumed that Colson had given Anderson information, but he admitted that Ehrlichman had assisted Colson, and they "made up a story partly."

After going over the March 21 recorded conversation, Nixon wanted Haldeman's thoughts on how he would deal with the matter when he testified. "It's a privileged conversation, and the president's authorized me to characterize it as I remember it," Haldeman replied, and then proceeded to characterize it as he hoped Nixon would also remember it; namely, Nixon was merely smoking me out. Then they returned to "the Pappas thing," and how to handle that. "Well, Pappas was one of a number of major contributors that we met with," Haldeman said, trying to recall what he had told the president, and added, "I don't think I said the Watergate thing. I said Mitchell wants you to be sure and talk to Pappas. He's very helpful. Well, I may have said 'helpful in raising money for the defense.'"

"Give me a little rundown on your lawyers, if you wouldn't mind," Nixon then asked. "[To see] if there's anything that they've added." Haldeman said they were still going through details and were going to visit the prosecutors that afternoon to arrange an appointment. "Now they very much do not want the appointment until you get the thing from Petersen on what he sees as the potential charges on us," Haldeman said, in effect telling Nixon their attorneys did not want to meet with him until they had a chance to evaluate the charges against them, which Petersen had promised to provide the next day, because the prosecutors would not likely be as forthcoming in revealing the situation to their attorneys when they met as Petersen would be with Nixon. Haldeman and Ehrlichman wanted inside information.

Returning to the Anderson story falsely attacking me, the president had a warning for Colson: "He'd better watch out; Dean will try to nail him." "Yeah, or Dean will lash back," Haldeman agreed. "Now Dean will read this and figure it out. That it ether came from Colson or Ehrlichman or both," although Haldeman noted that the piece implicated both Colson and Ehrlichman as well. Nixon asked if it was true that Ehrlichman had confronted Dean with charges, as Anderson reported. Haldeman said, "Well, he didn't really confront Dean with charges. What Ehrlichman did is say, 'Here's the way the thing stacks up.' I don't think he confronted him with him having advance knowledge, because Ehrlichman still doesn't think he did have advance [knowledge.]"

Nixon and Haldeman had another lengthy discussion of the $350,000 that went back to LaRue at the reelection committee for payment to the Watergate defendants, which prompted the president to ask if Haldeman had talked to their lawyers about this money, "What is their latest feeling as to what the hell your defense is on that point?" Haldeman responded, "Well, they don't feel I have a defense, because they don't feel there's a charge." When Nixon suggested, "Conspiracy to obstruct justice?" Haldeman replied, "They can't make that. Because there's no way that I intended to obstruct justice." Nixon asked about Hunt, and Haldeman said, "They feel I have (A) no motivation to keep him quiet and, (B) no intent to."[138]

When discussing the March 21 conversation, Haldeman repeated that Ehrlichman was not threatened by Hunt's blackmail; Ehrlichman had spoken to Krogh and didn't think he was going to be in any trouble. Haldeman thought I was wrong in the March 21 conversation when I reported that Krogh was troubled by his perjury. Ehrlichman was still claiming all this was "national security," adding, "For that reason, maybe I just don't understand it, but I'm not at all sure that this whole Ellsberg thing coming out is bad."* Clearly Haldeman did not understand it.

Haldeman admitted to Nixon that the part of the March 21 conversation that really shocked him was when I warned, "'Some people may go to jail.' You said, 'Who?'" And he said, 'Well, me, to begin with.' And that really jarred you. You said, 'Oh, hell, no.'" Haldeman said he could tell "by listening to the tape, it startled, came as a blow to you." He added, "As soon as he told you that, a thought process starts in your mind. 'What the hell, you know, who am I dealing with here? What's going on?' Because he was always the dispassionate operator, and you knew he was carrying some water on [unclear] keep Mitchell on, for example. But you didn't know he was [involved himself.]" "I didn't," Nixon agreed. "When they talked about the load, I was not thinking, basically, Bob, of the load taking care of defendants. He never told me that until this damn conversation was made, in February, I don't know." (Although Nixon misspoke here, I had actually previously hinted at my problems—as early as February.) Haldeman continued, "Well, that isn't the load that he was really carrying. He was trying to keep the whole thing on track, as he had all these people lying, bouncing out with all sorts of different tales."

---

*Bud Krogh negotiated a plea agreement with the Watergate special prosecutor regarding his false statements to a grand jury and pled guilty on November 30, 1973. He became a key witness against Ehrlichman regarding the Ellsberg break-in.

Nixon fell silent for almost a half minute, then said, "My God, he should have come to us earlier and said something. But Dean, too, has told you and John, 'What the hell, all we're doing here is protecting John Mitchell.' Correct?" Haldeman agreed and admitted, "We know that, too." Nixon continued, "Bob, I think, we had several conversations on that point. Remember? In February, right? You said, 'This whole God damned thing is about Mitchell. Why doesn't Mitchell get out?'"

The direction of this conversation changed when Ehrlichman joined and the president learned that the *New York Times* had the story of Pat Gray destroying documents from Hunt's safe. Nixon first called Petersen: "I just wanted to get your reaction as to how we how we handle the Gray situation on this *New York Times* thing: You want to think about it a little bit overnight or should we react right away or what?"[139] "Well," Petersen replied, "I told Kleindienst that I'd think about it overnight and then discuss it with him in the morning." He described it as an "unfortunate, almost needless casualty." The president agreed it was "a dumb thing" and asked, "Why the hell did he destroy the damn file?" "I don't know," Petersen responded, and then replied to Nixon's question about how Gray was going respond to the charges: "He said, 'I had implicit confidence in Ehrlichman and Dean; when they gave him documents and said these should be destroyed, he didn't see any reason why they shouldn't.'" "But, well, he can't say that Ehrlichman and Dean told him to destroy them." Nixon, sounding flabbergasted, objected, "It wouldn't stand up for him, I mean, apart from anything else. Why would, for example, Ehrlichman and Dean call the director of the FBI over and say, look, here's some documents, destroy them. Why the hell wouldn't they destroy them themselves?" Petersen said he understood that it made no sense. Nixon reminded Petersen that Gray had previously told him he had not been given the documents, and therefore had lied on at least one occasion. Nixon wanted Petersen to talk sense into Gray, and then wanted to know who should run the FBI. Petersen, somewhat presumptively, said he did not care if he got the job, but added, "I don't want to see anybody from the inside take that job." Nor did Nixon: "It's got to be cleaned out." "I don't think that Gray should pop off with a statement tonight on the thing," Nixon concluded.

At 6:20 P.M. a frustrated Nixon called Kleindienst, complaining that Gray's account of the documents was contrary to what both Ehrlichman and I had told him. Nixon suggested that if Gray took that position, he would publicly call Gray a liar. "Well, I have left the office, Mr. President,"

Kleindienst reported, "I'm at a dinner party of ten people. I have talked to Henry about it. I am going to call Gray on the telephone in the next two minutes." At 7:12 P.M., after talking with Ehrlichman, who was putting out his own statement with the matter still unresolved, Nixon called Petersen again, wanting to know how this was going to be handled. Petersen said he was just commencing a conversation with Gray. At 7:44 P.M. Kleindienst called and said he and Petersen were now in Kleindienst's office at the Justice Department with Pat Gray, who had a new position: He would not say he had been ordered to destroy the documents by Ehrlichman and me, but with a hitch: If cross-examined he would claim, as Kleindienst explained, "He said, 'I had to gather from Dean, as being, you know, a representative of the president of the United States, and I had to just infer from his remarks that these documents should not see the light of day, they were of such a highly sensitive nature they should not be put in the FBI files,' he just concluded himself he ought to destroy them. Now that's quite a bit different, you know, than being given a specific direction."

Nixon still thought it weak, as did Kleindienst, who told the president he had said to Gray: "So suppose that this very statement that you gave us, that you made public tomorrow. You just got the press in and said, this is what happened. What would that do with respect to your ability to manage the Federal Bureau of Investigation?" Gray admitted, "It would be a disaster," but Kleindienst said Gray was resisting resigning: "He feels that for him to resign, it's an admission of guilt of some kind." Kleindienst and Petersen were working on Gray to step down, but they recommended that nothing be done until the following day, because Gray "knows he's got to resign." They now turned to Watergate and me. Like Nixon and Petersen, Kleindienst worried about what I might say about his handling of Watergate: "[Dean] has put himself in the position in opposition to me, you, the government of the United States, everybody he's associated with. John Dean will find himself in a very, very—" before Kleindienst could finish his sentence, Nixon added, "And that's the point. He's going to, you know, as I told you, he will strike a king."

As this conversation proceeded, the president mentioned that Henry Petersen "hated" Ehrlichman and had told Nixon that it was Ehrlichman who had ordered Gray to destroy the Hunt documents. "I don't want Petersen to mislead me like that," Nixon complained. "Petersen doesn't hate Ehrlichman," Kleindienst protested, and told the president how, the previous summer, while Kleindienst was on vacation, Ehrlichman had called Petersen "in a very intemperate way, gave him instructions with respect to what he ought to do in this God damn matter. That really rubbed Henry the wrong way." Nixon now backed down, saying, "I like Petersen, I mean, myself, you know what I mean?" Kleindienst said that if the president trusted him, he should trust Petersen. Nixon said, "Of course," he trusted Kleindienst. (Within seventy-two hours Nixon would force Kleindienst to resign.)

## April 27, 1973, the White House

The president called Haldeman to the Oval Office at 7:50 A.M., before the morning staff meeting, to ask for an update, but Haldeman had nothing new.[140] When the president noted that the Gray story had made the front page of the *New York Times*, Haldeman pointed out that the FBI or Justice Department had gotten their story to the *Times* while the president was talking with Petersen and Kleindienst about what Gray was going to say. Haldeman did not believe that I had instructed Gray to destroy the documents by saying they "should not see the light of day." After briefly discussing the *Times* story, Haldeman said, "Then there is that other story, also a Dean story," referring to an account on the front page of *The Washington Post*, which the president had ignored.[141] Haldeman said, "That, you know, we met on the twentieth and we all agreed to go down with the ship or something." Nixon asked, "What was that?" Haldeman said, "I don't know," and then noted, "Well, I think that maybe there was a meeting on the twentieth when we said he should give you a complete bill on the thing that is quite possible." The *Post* in fact had the date and substance wrong: I thought I had had a tacit understanding with Haldeman and Ehrlichman to tell the truth, regardless of the consequences, when we had spoken without the president on the afternoon of March 21,[142] and Nixon spent the rest of this conversation fixated on this conversation. Haldeman reminded the president that he had to go run the staff meeting, though Nixon wanted to discuss Ruckelshaus's becoming temporary acting FBI director, stating, "I don't want Felt." As the meeting ended, Nixon asked Haldeman what he thought of John Connally or Bill Rogers becoming attorney general. Haldeman did not know about Connally, but thought "Rogers would be superb."

At 8:49 A.M., accompanied by Haldeman and Ehrlichman, the president flew to Mississippi. While they were en route, Pat Gray called to resign. Larry

Higby took the call. It was "John Stennis Day" in Mississippi, with thousands turning out to greet the president, First Lady and Senator Stennis. At the podium, Stennis praised the president: "You don't panic when the going gets rough."[143] Privately Stennis told Nixon that time was running out on Watergate, and he made "the point that down their way they have a saying that the rain falls on both the just and unjust, and when the rain falls on people, they've got to go, whether they're just or not."[144] Flying back to Washington, the president discussed with his aides the appointment of Ruckelshaus as acting director. Haldeman called Ruckelshaus to request he come to the White House at four o'clock, after they returned. During this trip back they also discussed how to deal with the Ellsberg break-in matter, for just as Nixon had feared and predicted, Watergate and the Ellsberg break-in had merged through Liddy and Hunt and exploded in the news.

Nixon was back at the White House by 3:30 and went first to the East Room to say nice words about his secretary, Rose Mary Woods, who was hosting a National Secretaries Week gathering, and then to the Oval Office to meet with Bill Ruckelshaus, whom he simply told that he had a crisis at the FBI and he needed help.[145] Nixon pressed Ruckelshaus to take the job on an interim basis, saying flatly, "Mitchell will undoubtedly be indicted," and assuring Ruckelshaus that he would not have any interference from the White House. Not long into their meeting Kleindienst called and said, "In view of Pat's resignation, Mr. President, it would be my recommendation that you permit Mark Felt—"[146] Nixon cut him off, "No, I tell you, I don't want him. I can't have him. I just talked to Bill Ruckelshaus, and Bill is a Mr. Clean," he said, as Ruckelshaus sat across from his desk, listening. "I want a fellow in there that is not part of the old guard, and that is not part of the infighting in there." Nixon explained. "[Ruckelshaus]'ll do it as acting director until we get a full director." Kleindienst thought it "ideal" and reminded Nixon that the attorney general had the legal responsibility to make the appointment, so Nixon should direct him to do so. By 4:30 P.M. the president had a new acting FBI director.

At 4:31 P.M. Henry Petersen called with an urgent matter: "I just wanted to give you a report on that Dan Ellsberg case. Judge Byrne had opened [the information] last night, and he was inclined to the view that disclosure to him as sufficient, and then apparently, overnight, he changed his opinion and read the memorandum from Silbert to me in open court, indicated that the defendants were entitled to a hearing on it, and requested the disclosure of the source, which I have authorized, and asked for all the information the government has. We don't have anything, you know?" Petersen added that he had asked that the FBI interview me and Ehrlichman to see "if they know anything about it."* Also, Petersen added, they would try to locate Ellsberg's psychiatrist to see whether or not there was a report of a burglary. After briefly reporting how upset FBI officials had been regarding Gray's behavior, Petersen said he felt that Gray "in my judgment's another unwitting victim." "Unwitting victim," Nixon echoed. "There are quite a few in this, Henry. Quite a few." "Now, Mr. President," Petersen continued, "when you asked me for something"—at which point Nixon interrupted, "Yeah, a piece of paper, if I could get it"—"And I don't think I can produce." He explained that the material Nixon wanted was grand jury information. Nixon was annoyed; Petersen was cutting him off, or more likely, Silbert was cutting Petersen off before the entire case against Haldeman and Ehrlichman was corrupted, as Shaffer had warned them. "Now where does the Dean thing stand?" Nixon asked, and Petersen said, "Well, no place." Petersen said I had been served to appear in New York in "the Vesco thing," and Petersen had no idea whether I would take the Fifth Amendment there or not. As for the Watergate investigation, "Our negotiations with him are just no place." For this reason, Petersen said, he was no longer requesting the president take no action regarding my resignation. As Petersen put it, "I think the longer you wait, the worse it gets." Nixon thanked Petersen, and the call ended.[147]

When Haldeman arrived with Ziegler in the Oval Office late in the afternoon for a brief conversation, the president immediately announced that Petersen was now claiming he could not provide information about their case; Haldeman was initially not nearly as annoyed with Petersen as Nixon.[148] "When you're free," Ziegler said, "there are some developments I should discuss with you." Nixon urged him to speak, but Ziegler resisted and said he thought it better they be addressed later. "Well, listen," Nixon said, moving on, "Have you got any more from Dean? Have you talked to him?" Ziegler said he was waiting for a call back, and when he departed, the president turned to the matter of "firing Dean," and his concern that, if he did so, he would set me off against everyone. Nixon made clear to Haldeman that he and Ehrlichman would have to depart soon, which Haldeman thought best,

---

*Ehrlichman was interviewed by the FBI in this matter on May 1, 1973, and later indicted for the false statements he gave the FBI during that interview. See *U.S. v. Ehrlichman et al.*, 379 F. Supp. 291 (1974).

but he acknowledged that Ehrlichman did not agree. They discussed the running of the White House without Haldeman, who suggested his aide Fred Malek could serve as a staff administrator but not chief of staff.

Haldeman returned to the fact that Petersen was cutting the president off from further information: "Well, on further consideration, that Justice Department thing bothers me, though. And I have to agree with John [Ehrlichman]. I think you're being had by Petersen." Haldeman pointed out that the president was not asking for grand jury testimony but rather "for his evaluation of the charges." Nixon, sounding frustrated, said to Haldeman in a tone of despair, "Just pray to God that we live through this thing." "We will," Haldeman assured him,

Nixon indicated that he was going to start drafting a Watergate speech, and Haldeman read language he recommended regarding himself and Ehrlichman, and explained what might happen if someone in the White House was charged. "Bob, we need to make a move," Nixon said, but he became tongue-tied as he continued. "We really have to have to, as I've said, we've got to move so that we aren't, I mean, the way it goes, and they'll say, you know what I mean? I think, I just think you and John are, gosh, you know, it kills me. It's like cutting off both of my arms." Haldeman said that when they departed he was going to still need them for a transitional period with whoever took over their responsibilities.

Haldeman also thought that, once they were out of the White House, he and Ehrlichman could make statements attacking me. "Weigh carefully what you say," Nixon cautioned, and Haldeman proceeded to report a story that Ehrlichman had told him, falsely claiming that while I was at Camp David working on a Dean report, I had told Larry Higby, "I can't do a damn thing on the report, but I've got sixty pages of working out my own defense, and it's beautiful." But while Haldeman had doubts about the truth of the account (as his own notes revealed), he said that, if it was true, it demonstrated that I had hit "rock bottom." And if true, "then you have no more compunction about destroying him, so you go all out on a total basis to destroy Dean, which should be done anyway."

After yet another review of the March 21 conversation, they discussed the fact that Ray Price had sent Haldeman a "long memo" urging him to resign, which, as Haldeman explained to the surprised Nixon, "Yeah, it's a totally asinine memo about purgation and abolition." But Haldeman, trying to remain an honest broker for the staff, advised Nixon that it was something he ought to have a look at. "He may have some good ideas on some of it," Haldeman acknowledged, and he recast it as a "soul-search letter." The conversation ended with Haldeman's offering to talk to Ehrlichman about their departure. He understood that they had to leave and would try to lighten Nixon's load with Ehrlichman.

Nixon asked Ziegler to return to the Oval Office, and after providing guidance for the Ruckelshaus announcement, asked, "What else do you have to report?"[149] Ziegler had new and more serious rumors and inquiries. He had learned that Sy Hersh was a "good friend" of Bill Bittman's, and Hersh had told Bittman that "they have information which would take this matter to a new level." The underlying fact was that "Dean in his testimony or statement is reported to have implicated the president," though Ziegler noted that I, in fact, had not testified anywhere. The second element of Ziegler's report was that Bob Woodward, a college friend of David Gergen, who ran Nixon's speechwriting office, had called several people at the White House "to milk them," hinting that the *Post* had "very serious reports coming in today, stories revealing again a new dimension, a new plateau," one suggesting that someone was "implicating the president, and the other one suggesting that the vice president's going to resign."

"Jesus Christ," Nixon said. "Okay," and he went over the rumors with a clearly concerned Ziegler. Ziegler departed as Henry Petersen was ushered in.[150] Ziegler's report had put Nixon on high alert, and in Petersen he had the very person who would know what had and had not been told to the prosecutor about the president's activities. As Petersen seated himself, Nixon told him that it had come to his attention that reports were circulating in the press that they had to "head off at the pass," because they were untrue and bad for the presidency. After he shared the gist of the rumors, Petersen insisted that no information had come from me implicating the president, for Petersen had spoken with the prosecutors involved, Silbert, Glanzer and Campbell. "Do you mind calling them right now?" Nixon asked. "No, sir," Petersen said. He added that there had been "a kind of crisis of confidence, the night before last [April 25]," so he had met with the prosecutors in his office. The issue had been whether or not his prosecutors were at ease with his reporting to the president, and Petersen thought he had cleared the air on that issue by laying into U.S. attorney Harold Titus. (Clearly this distrust in the U.S. attorney's office had resulted in the cutting off of information about Haldeman and Ehrlichman.)

"You never heard anything like that?" the president asked regarding the rumors Ziegler had heard. "No, sir," Petersen said. "You're certain?" "Absolutely," Petersen assured him. When Nixon asked, "You swear to God?" Petersen responded by repeating what he had told Harold Titus: "We are responsible for enforcing federal law. We have no mandate to investigate the presidency. We investigate Watergate, and I don't know where that line's drawn clearly all the time." Nixon, however, was not satisfied with his answer: "Well, if Dean has implicated this presidency, we're going to God damn well find out. Because let me tell you, the only conversation we ever had with him was that famous March 21 conversation I told you about" and he proceeded to give Petersen another abbreviated and skewed version.

Because Nixon wanted assurance that I had not implicated him, he suggested Petersen use the telephone in the Cabinet Room to call his prosecutors, and he was taken there at 5:43 P.M. At 6:04 P.M. Petersen returned to the Oval Office and reported, "Well, like all things, some substance, some falsity. Last Monday [April 23] Charlie Shaffer was in the office, and the continuation of the negotiations. Charlie Shaffer is the lawyer. Charlie is a very bright, able, bombastic fellow. And he was carrying on as if he was making a summation in a case. And he was threatening, 'We will bring the president in, not this case, but in other things.' What other things are, we don't know what in the hell they are talking about."[151] Other things did not trouble Nixon, though, who said, "Don't worry," and Petersen continued, characterizing Shaffer's remark as similar to his earlier threat that he would "try this administration, Nixon, what have you." Nixon clearly was not interested when Petersen began discussing information unrelated to the president, so Petersen concluded, "There's no more on that, other than I've just told you."

"Why hell can't we stop the paper, Hersh?" Nixon asked. "To think that, to bring the president in with a thing like, good God Almighty. Let me say this, if it were in with the grand jury, I want to know that, too. That I have to know, as president, understand. Good God almighty." He was giving Petersen a new directive, and added, "You've got to believe me, I am after the truth, even if it hurts me. But believe me, it won't. Just like it won't hurt you. We are doing our job. And somebody was in here the other day, and they were saying, 'Well, Dean is going to blackmail you because of something you're supposed to have told me.' And I said, 'Screw him.' I said, 'You have a right to tell me what is going on.'" In response, Petersen further elaborated on material purportedly being leaked by me: "Now Shaffer says it's McCandless that is leaking this stuff to the press," who Petersen explained "was another lawyer that Dean has retained."

With this information in hand the president called Ziegler to the Oval Office and explained that I had not in fact testified, but at best these rumors were a negotiating tactic by my attorney. Petersen described Shaffer's statement to Ziegler as "an emotional statement," though the president insisted it was "crap" and was annoyed that it was being held over their heads, whatever it referred to. Petersen agreed and explained, "That was one of the reasons that was so important, to disclose [the Ellsberg information], because they could've hung that over our heads." Ziegler agreed that it sounded like bargaining by my lawyer, and then added, "I had occasion to talk to Dean a few minutes ago. He's in a very good frame of mind. It was a very quick conversation. He said, 'Ron, I am issuing no statements.' Incidentally, he said, 'I got a telephone call—'"

"A telephone call from the president," Nixon said, cutting Ziegler off midsentence. "You know, Henry, that shows you what a prick he is. I called, you know, to say some nice things. I called six people [on Easter], members of my staff. I called Ron, Henry Kissinger, I called Bob Haldeman and Ehrlichman and Rose, my secretary, and John Dean. You know what I mean. I just go down the list of people, and I just say 'I want to wish you happy Easter.' That's all I did, and it was all over the press!" "Well, you know, we got a report," Petersen said. "Again I got it through Charlie Shaffer that he was pleased and elated and reassured. And you know, as he's a human being—" at which point Nixon began talking over Petersen, "I don't want to hurt John Dean, believe me, I'd like to help him." Ziegler then finished what he had started to say: that I had gone out of my way to say that I had not leaked to the press that the president had called me on Easter, but I thought I knew who had done so from among the few I had told.

Nixon wanted Ziegler to kill the rumored stories, and Ziegler said he had spoken to Clifton Daniel, who had not mentioned them. The president wanted David Gergen to talk to his old friend Bob Woodward and tell him, "They better watch their damned cotton-picking faces. As Henry will tell you, since March 21, when I had that conversation with Dean, I have broken my ass to try to get the facts on this case. Right?" But before Petersen could respond, Nixon reminded them that he had tried to get Liddy to talk, he had tried to get Gray to refresh his recollection, which he had finally done, and he had put Ruckelshaus in the FBI rather than Mark Felt because of what

Petersen had told him. Then he paused to asked Petersen if Ruckelshaus was acceptable to him. Petersen said, "I know him and think well of him."

"So there you are, you've got to knock that crap down," Nixon instructed Ziegler, and then added to Petersen, "If there's one thing you've got to do, you've got to maintain the presidency out of this, because damn it, I've got things to do for this country yet, and I'm not going to have, now this is personal, I sometimes feel like I'd like to resign. Let Agnew be the president for a while. He'd love it." Nixon did not get the protest he expected from Petersen, who merely said, "I don't even know why you want the job." Nixon then turned to the story about Agnew's preparing to resign, and Ziegler explained, "Well, that's the *Post* and the *Times.*" Nixon asked what Agnew had to say, and Ziegler indicated that the story was so "ridiculous" that he had not even spoken with Agnew about it: Agnew's press secretary, J. Marsh Thompson, was going to turn it off.* After again being reassured by Petersen that I had not given information to the prosecutors implicating the president, Ziegler was sent to kill the rumored stories, and Nixon turned his conversation with Petersen back to me.

Nixon again made clear to Petersen that he should understand that, with the April 17 statement regarding immunity, he was not trying "to block Dean giving evidence against Haldeman and Ehrlichman." This was apparently in response to my warning that he and Ehrlichman were obstructing justice by adding the no-immunity directive to that statement. When Petersen explained that, as acting attorney general in this case, the statute expressly gave him the authority to make the immunity decision, Nixon asked if the prosecutors were inclined to give me immunity. "They've vacillated," Petersen acknowledged. "In the first instance they, I think, felt quite strongly that Dean should be immunized, and I was resisting." But Petersen explained that they now felt I would "have the most credibility" if I pleaded and testified "as a codefendant against Ehrlichman and Haldeman as opposed to someone who is given immunity and then testified against them."

Nixon asked what would happen if I began "trying to impeach the presi-

---

*It was not so ridiculous, for within three months Agnew would discover that he was the subject of a federal investigation for extortion, bribery and tax evasion by the U.S. attorney in Maryland, a case that Henry Petersen was overseeing. On October 10, 1973, Agnew resigned as vice president and appeared in U.S. District Court in Baltimore to plead *nolo contendere* to a federal felony for failing to report $29,500 in taxable income he had received in 1967 while governor of Maryland, a plea bargain approved by Petersen. If Petersen had any knowledge of this during this April 27 conversation, he did not give any indication at that time.

dent, the word of the president of the United States, and says, 'Well, I have information to the effect that I once discussed with the president,' the question of this damn Bittman stuff I spoke with you about last time?" The president supplied his own answer: "Henry, it wouldn't stand up for five minutes, because nothing was done, and fortunately I had Haldeman at that conversation," and Nixon said that, in the end, he had told me, "It won't work." The president similarly recast the matter of clemency for Hunt, and he also claimed that any discussion by him of using the Cuban committee sounded ridiculous. "I said, there is no damn thing we can do," Nixon insisted and added, "Mitchell came down the next day, and we talked executive privilege, nothing else. Now that's the total story, and so I just want you to be sure that if Dean ever raises the thing, you've got the whole thing. Now kick him straight." Petersen agreed and acknowledged, "I mean, that's what we have to do."

Petersen then explained in some detail how Bill Bittman's legal fees were being investigated, because McCord had claimed that he had learned from Dorothy Hunt that money was coming to them through those fees. As this discussion proceeded, Petersen noted, "In other words, what we think happened is that a considerable amount within the law firm was paid out in fees, and the balance went on to Dorothy Hunt for distribution to the Cubans and what have you. The strange thing about this one, Mr. President, is that they could have done it openly. If they had just come out in *The Washington Post*, they could have said, 'Well these people were—'" Nixon interrupted to agree and note, "Of course, they helped the Scottsboro people, they helped the Berrigans, and remember the Alger Hiss defense fund?" Petersen said that, because this was done in a clandestine fashion, it had taken on the elements of cover-up and obstruction of justice.[152]

Throughout this conversation Nixon sought to remind Petersen, "But Dean is not credible. He is not credible. He really can't go out and say, 'Look I've talked to the president, and he told me this and that in the other thing.' First, it's not true." Petersen explained that I would become credible by pleading, and then the case would be built with other witnesses, like LaRue and Magruder. After discussing Shaffer's bombast, Nixon said, "Let's come to the Dean thing again. I can give you some more time if you want to negotiate with him. I mean, when I say, more time—"

"He needs more pressure," Petersen said, and explained, "It's become counterproductive. I think he was pressed up against the wall, he's seen the early morning crisis pass and now he's had resurgence. You know, he sees

Ehrlichman here. He sees Haldeman here. He sees John Dean still here. Nothing's happened. His confidence is coming back rather than ebbing." "What is the proper course of action with Dean?" Nixon asked, but then he also turned to the problem of Haldeman and Ehrlichman. He told Petersen that he had two courses of action: They could take leaves of absence until they were cleared, and if they were not cleared, then they would resign; or he could simply ask us all to resign, treating everyone the same. But Nixon worried that resignations could influence the grand jury. Petersen suggested that a leave of absence was the best of both worlds, explaining, "You have given them the benefit of the doubt and you haven't cut the Gordian knot." Nixon also mentioned the possibility of letting Haldeman and Ehrlichman go while keeping me, to see what I did, or some other way of not putting us all "in the same bag." Petersen thought it was a loyalty distinction, but Nixon insisted otherwise. Soon Petersen cut through the chatter with some solid advice: "Mr. President, my wife is not a politically sophisticated woman. She knows I'm upset about this, and you know I'm working hard, and she sees it. But she asked me at breakfast, now I don't want you to hold this against her [if you ever meet her], because she's a charming lady. She said, 'Doesn't all this upset you?' And I said, 'Of course it does.' She said, 'You think the president knows?' And I looked at her and said, 'If I thought the president knew, I would have to resign.' But you know, now, there is my own family, Mr. President. Now whatever confidence she has in you, her confidence in me ought to be unquestioned. Well, when that type of question comes through in my house, we've got a problem." Petersen repeated that Nixon should not try to distinguish between Haldeman, Ehrlichman and me, and Nixon responded, "I will do it my way, and it will be done. I'm working on it. I won't even tell you how."

Mrs. Petersen's concerns appear to have registered with the president, who spent the rest of that evening discussing the departure of Haldeman and Ehrlichman from his White House. Nixon was not only avoiding me but increasingly evading one-on-one conversations with Ehrlichman, who was still not happy about the prospect of being forced from the White House, nor was Haldeman making his own departure easy. Haldeman was sum-moned to the Oval Office as soon as Petersen departed.[153] Nixon had a re-markably difficult time telling Haldeman he wanted him, as well as Ehrlichman, to leave the staff. For over an hour they went around and around, with Haldeman making points such as Pat Buchanan's not understanding why the president hadn't fired me, and Nixon responding with the claim that he had to think "in terms of the presidency." What emerged from this conversation was the understanding that the president was going to go up to Camp David over the weekend and work on "trying to get a statement ready" for Monday night. He would also have Len Garment inform me of his decision regarding my status on Monday, and although Ehrlichman did not want to see Garment become White House counsel, Nixon was inclined to have him take my job.

Nixon suggested he would call on me to submit my leave, but Haldeman erupted. "The president of the United States cannot call upon some little shit that works for him to do something publicly. You can call on a U. S. senator to do something, or Khrushchev to do something, but not an employee." Nixon explained that he had not intended to do that on television but rather would announce that he had requested and accepted my resignation. "Well, now," Haldeman said, "maybe that's the way to separate." As the conversation continued they discussed timing and Nixon's wish "to avoid at all costs getting into any position where John Dean tries to barf on me." He was going to catch me "by surprise" with his speech, and at several points during the conversation told Haldeman, "I'll handle Dean," adding along the way, "Look, that little son of a bitch doesn't have anything. You know what I mean? Really."

Haldeman told Nixon that if he were me and had something on Nixon, he would use it to get out of prison. "I don't think he has any interest in bringing down the presidency," Haldeman said. "I don't think he would want to do that. Unless he goes berserk. And there's that. He just totally flips, and I think he's in, you know, a strange mood." Nixon acknowledged that "every dog could snap," which caused Haldeman to wonder if I would become a "John Wilkes Booth or something." Haldeman quickly added that he did not think I had become that "warped." Still, Haldeman observed, "he's a vicious and evil enough guy to be willing to use everything in his command any way he feels is the most effective way of using it." As this exchange proceeded, Haldeman noted, "He's playing a very large bluff that, to his credit, it's working."

"Well, you know, what he's, he's, he's," a sputtering Nixon began, "Well, the son of a bitch has acquired confidential information," which Nixon felt "unconscionable," and told Haldeman, "The son of a bitch is finished, in my view. I think he's finished with everybody." Haldeman responded, "There

seems to be a place in the world for people like that. They seem to thrive."
After discussing the enthusiastic crowds in Mississippi that morning, which
Haldeman reported had overwhelmingly voted for Nixon, the president said
he was ready to start working on his speech. As Haldeman got up to leave,
Nixon said, "Today we start fighting." It was agreed that Haldeman and
Ehrlichman would come to Camp David over the weekend, and they would
decide how to proceed.

When Haldeman left the Oval Office, Nixon requested Ziegler return to
discuss the logistics of a live television speech the following Monday night.[154]
They talked about Price versus Buchanan, or both, or neither, working on
the speech. When Ziegler observed that Price was likely to "wallow in the
ashes of self-piety, pity and atonement," Nixon agreed that people do not
want their president to say, "Please forgive me, my people, for what I have
done," adding, "I cannot do it, and I won't do it." At 8:22 P.M. this conversation moved to the EOB.[155] Ziegler had by now taken over Haldeman's role as
the staff person to whom Nixon could complain about others on the staff,
and on that night the president was clearly unhappy with Haldeman and
Ehrlichman. "Let me say that this has been a terribly bitter thing for Bob,
and even more for John," Nixon began. "John is a fighter, and thinks he is
guiltless, and, frankly, not aware, you know, of how serious this problem is,
in my opinion." Nixon was still accepting Ehrlichman's dubious claim that
he had not authorized the Ellsberg entry. "Why after that was done did Hunt
stay around?" he wondered.

"Here are two men [Hunt and Liddy] that you reprimand," Ziegler replied, who were then sent over to the campaign. Nixon said, "John probably
thought, these crazy bastards, get them out of here."

The president then turned to the matter of removing Haldeman, Ehrlichman and me or, if Haldeman and Ehrlichman had their way, simply
removing me. He told Ziegler that Haldeman wanted to hold off and wait it
out, but in a frustrated tone asserted, "Well, I can't wait it out." He had made
this point to Haldeman and asked Ziegler, who understood the problem of
forcing me out without Haldeman and Ehrlichman, "Do you want to make
Dean madder than he is? He's a mad dog now, do you agree?" Ziegler did,
and Nixon proceeded to vent his frustration at his intractable aides.

As the conversation progressed, with the usual compulsive rehashing of
information, the president told Ziegler: "Ehrlichman says, 'This is going to
hurt you if I get out.' And I gave them the argument that 'Look, you fellows

can't do your jobs.' Bob made the point to me today, he said, 'Well, half of me is worth more than anybody else,' which is exactly right." "But that isn't the point," Ziegler protested, and Nixon agreed: "Half of him is damaged goods. That's what he doesn't realize. He's damaged goods. Right? We can't have damaged goods in the White House. There's no way." Nixon thought Ehrlichman may have come around with the release of this information about the Ellsberg break-in, remarking, "That shook the shit out of him." Ziegler reported that Haldeman and Ehrlichman had also been shaken by the press attention they received in Mississippi earlier in the day, when swarms of television camera crews began following them at the Stennis Day events. The unwritten rule was that White House staff was not to attract such media attention.

Nixon assured Ziegler, however, that everything was under control, and he was not panicking. "But we're doing something cold," he acknowledged, and if Ehrlichman gave him any problems when he and Haldeman came up to Camp David for a final meeting, he was simply going to tell him it was over. "What the hell else can you do?" Nixon asked. Ziegler agreed he had no other choice, and Nixon confided, "Even though, Ron, I told them a week ago, they knew what the hell I was going to do." Which brought him back to me, leading him to add, with anger, "You know, you've got to fight, though, on Dean. You've got a vicious son of a bitch like this, lying and so forth, there comes a time when you may have to smite him right to death."* Ziegler did not think it would be much of fight, but Nixon was not sure. "Well, I don't know. He's got a lot of shit that he's going to pour out there, but I think your point, as I've said, he's a discredited asshole."

### April 28, 1973, Camp David

After breakfast on the porch of Aspen Lodge, where he read the morning newspapers, the president called Ziegler from his study.[156] "That's quite a collection of headlines this morning, isn't it?" he observed.[157] Ziegler responded, "Oh, boy." Nixon asked after Ziegler's morale, and Ziegler assured him it was fine. Nixon said he was delighted with the timing of all this, for

---

*On two separate occasions I was later asked—first by Jim Neal and later by Richard Ben-Veniste of the Watergate special prosecutor's office—when I was in the U.S. Marshals' witness protection program (at the urging of Watergate special prosecutor Archibald Cox and Senate Watergate committee chief counsel Sam Dash) if I thought Nixon would or could put a hit out on my life. I thought it doubtful, but if he was in one of his dark moods, I said, he might ask Bebe Rebozo to arrange it.

if they had gone sooner, "all this shit" would not have been incorporated in his statement. Mistakenly, the president thought he was through the worst of it. Nixon, a skilled poker player, advised, "You've got to let others play their hand a little bit, and then you crack. This is a time for strong me, Ron. You don't get panicky, and so forth. And our day is going to come. Because we're going to clean a lot of things up." Ziegler asked when Haldeman and Ehrlichman would arrive at Camp David, but Nixon did not know. "As you know," he said, "this is going to be a painful session. And God, I don't—" he started but then went in a different direction, "—Jesus, I mean, with all this, the Congress or, I mean, everybody else saying, Jesus Christ, do something, should they really hang on? What's your feeling on that?" When Ziegler said he favored their leaving, Nixon said, "We've got a lot of big things left to be done," and they could not be addressed until he dealt with this problem, noting, "We can't start that, really, Ron, until after the grand jury indicts." Nixon figured, "Two or three weeks away, I guess, depending on Dean. Dean is the key to the whole thing." But the mere mention of my name caused him to worry aloud, until he finally signed off, telling Ziegler, "I just wanted to cheer you up a little, you know." Ziegler thanked him, and Nixon continued on to spend the day making telephone calls.

*8:43 A.M. to 9:01 A.M. telephone call with Haldeman:* After asking Haldeman about his and Ehrlichman's arrival time, Nixon observed that the timing for his speech would be good, for more had unfolded for him to deal with in the talk. "Now on Dean," Nixon said, "I've been doing some thinking about it. I've got a very tough plan for him. It will be handled properly. It's going to be very preemptory, you know. I'm not going to see him, that's my point. He can't come dicker with me." Nixon said he was merely going to tell me I was out. Haldeman cautioned Nixon not to "antagonize him any more than you have to." As the call ended Nixon said, "Remember, the decision is made," regarding Haldeman's and Ehrlichman's taking leaves of absence, "and I am going to write [my speech] on that assumption." Haldeman said, "Okay."158

*9:02 A.M. telephone call with Rogers:* The president asked Rogers if he "might have time to drop up and we could have a little talk." Nixon said he would arrange a helicopter, but Rogers was fine with driving up. The president said his aides were going to make their move, as "I worked it out with them, finally." Nixon said he was preparing to deal with me "in a preemptory way, but the same way," and he was going to do a broadcast Monday night.

He told Rogers his speech would cover "everything that happened," because he wanted the country to know "that I am in charge, and we're getting to the bottom of it." He closed by telling Rogers, "Frankly, Bill, I'm glad to get it all out. I want to get it done."[159]

*9:13 A.M. telephone call with Petersen:* Nixon told Petersen that he was at Camp David ("I don't come here to look at the Easter lilies") and that things were going to work out, but he did not want any information leaking about people he was seeing. But, he added, "I am not going to see Dean, because I cannot be in a position where he will want to come in and talk to me about how he's going to plea." Petersen approved. When they got onto a tangent regarding the immunity law, Petersen explained, "As a practical matter, when we, as the sovereign, extend immunity it would be almost an impossible situation to prosecute [Dean], even if we came in with evidence from an independent source. Technically, I think that's possible, but a Supreme Court decision has indicated—" Nixon interrupted to say, "In other words, if you give him even use immunity, he gets [full immunity]?" Petersen affirmed, "That's right. Yes, sir." No one understood this body of law better than Shaffer, and this reality was integral to his thinking.[160] Nixon asked about Judge Byrne, and Petersen said he was going to have an evidentiary hearing in open court. Petersen reported that Ehrlichman had spoken to the FBI and told them that "he heard of the incident but had no independent knowledge of it." The conversation ended with Nixon expressing exaggerated disgust that Shaffer had told them, "'Look, we're going to try the president on other things than the Watergate,' Jesus Christ, and then without being specific." They agreed it was evidence of my desperation.[161]

*11:10 A.M. telephone call with Ziegler:* Ziegler said he had spoken with Haldeman, and he wanted to reassure the president that John and Bob were comfortable about taking a leave of absence, but he suggested that the real "master stroke of all this" and a truly "dramatic action" would be if "Rogers is named as the attorney general," and "if Rogers is then in a position to name a special prosecutor." Ziegler said, "That action in itself will then allow the presidency to totally remove itself from the whole process." Ziegler reported that Bob Woodward had information about Henry Petersen's running of the investigation of a fairly recent previous case in which "he can come under some criticism." "The difficulty with a special prosecutor," Nixon noted, was that "it'll be months before they could ever learn the case." Nixon explained that he was going to handle my being placed on leave of absence by having Garment notify me. Returning to Ziegler's master stroke, Nixon said, "I don't think Rogers would ever do it," but that he did have another plan, which he shared with Ziegler: "Maybe I may get Richardson to do it." Elliot Richardson was then serving as secretary of defense and had earlier served as Nixon's undersecretary of state, as well as having been the attorney general of Massachusetts and the United States attorney of Massachusetts. Nixon said he would get back to Ziegler when he knew more. The call ended with Nixon reporting that his daughter Tricia had come to Camp David to tell him that the family had discussed the matter, and "they felt strongly that Haldeman and Ehrlichman should resign."[162]

Bill Rogers arrived at Camp David while the president was speaking with Ziegler. He spent the day with Nixon, talking, having lunch on the patio of Aspen Lodge, and walking the grounds. Nixon later recorded that Rogers, too, felt strongly that Haldeman and Ehrlichman should resign. Nixon asked Rogers to share that assessment with them, but Rogers declined, saying he did not have a good relationship with either.[163] While Rogers had no interest in becoming attorney general, he did agree to try to persuade Elliot Richardson to take the post.

*5:35 P.M. telephone call with Ziegler:* Ziegler reported press interest was running toward the plumbers operations, the Ellsberg break-in, and the bogus cable regarding the overthrow of Diem. Nixon wanted to know how this information had gotten out, suggesting maybe I had leaked it, and Ziegler (incorrectly) assumed that had been the case. Nixon shared what Bill Rogers had said regarding the Ellsberg break-in: "If they did this, and if Ehrlichman knew they did it, and then they were weren't fired, and then went over to the committee, this is going to be very, very tough. Not in a legal way, for Ehrlichman, but in terms of coming back." Nixon said, "Now we've got to make it go, Ron. You're not losing it, are you?" "Absolutely not," Ziegler assured him.[164]

*6:33 P.M. telephone call with Ehrlichman:* Nixon began this call to Ehrlichman by citing Rogers on how the Eisenhower administration handled anyone who took the Fifth or sought immunity: They had to resign. Ehrlichman reported that it was all over that day's newspapers that I would testify, with or without immunity, and he speculated, "Now that means the jig is up. He wasn't able to make his deal, and he's trying to put the best face on it that he can." This caught Nixon by surprise, and they discussed its meaning. In a friendly but pointed tone Ehrlichman said, "Sometime during the time we're there, I would very much appreciate having a few minutes alone with you." Nixon agreed to that, and Ehrlichman continued, "I know that we're sort of coupled like Siamese twins in this, Bob and I, but I do have a couple of things I would like to—"

"I understand, Bob, ah, John. Fine. Of course, you can have some moments alone. Now let me ask one thing. Ron said that today is sort of moving toward the California plumbers operation. Is that right?" When Ehrlichman said he had not been following the news, Nixon asked, "Do you have any thought about it at the moment?" "I really don't," Ehrlichman replied. Nixon then asked, "I suppose that the question was, who was in charge, huh? Now, was Dean in charge?" "No, I was," Ehrlichman acknowledged. "And Krogh and Young, of course, ran the operation." Nixon inquired about its purpose and what happened to Hunt and Liddy after the Ellsberg break-in. "I never saw them again," Ehrlichman said. When the president questioned how the operation had been turned off, Ehrlichman explained, "I talked to either Krogh or Young." However much the president pressed, Ehrlichman would volunteer little other than that the undertaking "got nothing" and that he had given a "negative" when they wanted to go back again. "Well, that's a solid position, isn't it?" Nixon asked, to which Ehrlichman replied, "Well, it's what actually happened." "I'm just trying to put it in terms of saying as far as your part of it was concerned, this was something you never authorized," Nixon clarified, and Ehrlichman (falsely) assured him that was the situation.[165]

The president next shared Ziegler's information about press interest in the fake material prepared by Hunt regarding "Kennedy on the Diem thing." Had Ehrlichman ever heard about this? "Yes, sir, and it leads directly to your friend Colson," Ehrlichman told a startled Nixon, explaining that it was a fake cable allegedly involving President John F. Kennedy. "Oh, my God. I just can't believe that," Nixon exclaimed, as he tried to recall what had occurred, remembering that Ehrlichman and David Young were conducting a study of "the whole Diem thing, and the Bay of Pigs thing." Ehrlichman confirmed that they had done so, and Nixon remarked that he had only asked for the facts. "Well, I don't know where Colson got this inspiration," Ehrlichman replied, "but he was very busy at it." After listening to further explanations from Ehrlichman, Nixon can be heard sighing, and then saying, "I should have been told about that, shouldn't I?" "Well," Ehrlichman said, "I'm not so sure that you weren't."

"But by whom?" Nixon demanded, and Ehrlichman could only concede,

"I don't know. I don't know." The only thing the president could recall was an article being prepared for *Life* magazine, but he had not been informed that it was based on a fake cable. "My recollection is that this was discussed with you," Ehrlichman said, although he admitted he might be wrong. He said he would check his notes when Nixon ordered, "I've got to know about that." Ehrlichman then recalled that it had been Colson, which may have refreshed Nixon's memory, for he decided he did not want to hear any more about the matter, explaining, "Well, it's maybe better I wouldn't know if you told me. Because Chuck didn't."

Nixon then turned to the subject of his Monday speech, which he wanted to keep short. When Ehrlichman observed, "There's no virtue in brevity, I don't think," the president said he was thinking twenty to twenty-five minutes rather than thirty-five or forty. "I gather from Bob that this leave [of absence] business is a closed subject, as far as you're concerned?" Ehrlichman asked. "Yes, it has to be," Nixon replied. "I can't see any way to handle it otherwise." Ehrlichman then questioned, "Do you have anything from Petersen at all that we don't know about?" He did not and would not, which prompted Ehrlichman to tell him that John Wilson had all but fallen out of his chair when he learned that Petersen was refusing to keep the president informed. Nixon did not want to get into a debate with Ehrlichman and returned to the leave of absence: "Well, this is the way I feel I have to move, John. I mean, you know, one of the prerogatives of the president is to make mistakes, and sometimes you have to make some. I've made my share, but on this one, I just feel it's the right thing to do."[166]

*7:06 P.M. telephone call with Petersen:* Nixon called Petersen in response to Ehrlichman's report about my willingness to testify without immunity, wondering if I had been granted some sort of informal or equitable immunity. Petersen said I had not (forgetting that I had been granted informal immunity for my initial meetings with the prosecutors).[167]

### April 29, 1973, Camp David

The president slept in on Sunday morning. When Kissinger called midmorning, Nixon told him, "Now I've got something to tell you in the greatest of confidence, that I've decided I've got to get a new attorney general."[168] He was going to move Elliot Richardson from Defense to Justice, he said, and filled Kissinger in on Richardson's background. Nixon then added, "I am going to get the most mean son of a bitch I can find and put him in the FBI, and let all hell break loose." He also reminded Kissinger, "As you know, Henry, we did do some surveillance with the FBI on these leaks, you remember?" Kissinger answered, "Oh yes." Nixon said they were approved by the attorney general in 1969 and 1970. But when the FBI had failed to investigate Ellsberg, the White House got involved, and "that's why some of that crap was done in the White House. But that's too bad. That's just one of those things. But I just wanted you to know when that comes out, don't back off. Anything that's national security, we're going to fight like hell for." Kissinger agreed, "Absolutely. No, I will certainly not back off."

*10:26 A.M. telephone call with Rogers:* After agreeing that Nixon should announce Elliot Richardson's appointment as attorney general in the speech, and telling Rogers he hoped to appoint Judge Matt Byrne to head the FBI "if he survives Ellsberg," Nixon added, "Can I ask you one other thing, if you would?" To reveal the president's state of mind, the initial section of this passage has been transcribed verbatim: "The, ah, Ehrlichman is hanging terribly tough, and, ah, I wanted, just to get your, just your, your judgment on, ah, on this question again as to, ah, the ah, ah, ah, you, you have, you have no, you believe that we, that they both must, at the very least, take, take a leave of absence?" "Yes, I do," Rogers replied. "As a matter of fact, my own preference is for resignations." Nixon said that that was his preference as well. In something of a pleading tone, he said, "Would it be asking too much if I was asking for you to come up and help me talk to them about this thing a little?" When Rogers said he would, Nixon wondered, "How would you, how would you, just go about talking to them? I mean, I'll talk to them, but what will you say. You'll just, just lay it out?" A surprised Rogers said he thought that this had all already been agreed upon.

"Well, with Haldeman, yes," Nixon reported. "But Ehrlichman, I talked to him last night on the phone, and he said he wanted to raise the question with me again. He feels that not only is his case separate, but I think he probably wants to give the president hell for not getting at this himself earlier, and this and that. You know, he's not behaving well, frankly. Not behaving well, to my surprise." Nixon told Rogers how Ehrlichman's attorney John Wilson had reacted when Nixon did not extract further information out of Petersen: "Ehrlichman says that Petersen's horsing me. He can give me that if he wished." The president, with a nervous laugh, noted, "But the problem is, Petersen may be canned due to the fact that he knows damn well I'll give it to Ehrlichman."

Rogers was appalled that Ehrlichman was putting Nixon in the position of attempting to obtain information from the prosecutor's office and annoyed at Haldeman's and Ehrlichman's obstinacy. "I didn't realize that they were being reluctant," Rogers said, and noted, "They can't perform their duties now. For Christ sakes, the whole government has been in a standstill because these guys are reluctant." When Nixon mentioned Haldeman's claim that "half of them is worth two of anybody else, and nobody else can do it," Rogers replied, "They're nuts." He advised Nixon that their sense of their own indispensability had been trouble all along, and that this matter should have been resolved two weeks earlier. Rogers wanted them to abide by their earlier agreement. As the call ended, Nixon said, "Ehrlichman's coming apart."[169]

*11:46 A.M. telephone call from Rogers:* Rogers, having mulled over his conversation with Nixon, had second thoughts about his own role in dealing with Haldeman and Ehrlichman; he called to urge the president to find somebody else to do it. "I have no idea what they'll say if they get desperate," Rogers conceded, concerned about charges they might make to him against Nixon, information he did not want to have. He was also apprehensive that anything discussed might be leaked, because, as he told Nixon, although he had not spoken with another soul, details of his conversations with Haldeman and Ehrlichman were appearing in news stories. "It seems to me that you shouldn't have to convince them to leave," Rogers pointed out. Nixon said he did not know how they would react, lamenting, "I guess anything can happen, can't it?" Rogers answered, "Well, absolutely. That's the lesson that has to be learned from these things. Men get shaken and desperate, and particularly ones that have been dictatorial in their conduct with others." Rogers had, in fact, been experiencing the dictatorial demands of Haldeman and Ehrlichman for years. As they talked it through, Nixon again asked if Rogers would come up, "and then if it gets into a donnybrook, then could I ask you to come over and help? Would you mind doing that?" Rogers did not think it would become a donnybrook. He said he was happy to help, "as long as I don't get into a pissing match with them."[170]

*12:28 P.M. telephone call with Rogers:* Nixon requested that Rogers come up around four o'clock to help Ray Price refine the draft of the speech, which he thought overall was "pretty good." He had a special reason, he explained, for asking Rogers to join him: "I remember how helpful you were at the time of the fund," the president said, referring to Nixon's 1952 Checkers speech.

He added, "And, frankly, I might not even see you," regarding the meeting with Haldeman and Ehrlichman. The president seemed to take solace just in knowing Rogers would be present, should he be needed.[171]

*12:32 P.M. telephone call with Ziegler:* This brief call reveals that the president had by now firmly changed his thinking from asking leaves of absence from Haldeman and Ehrlichman to demanding their resignations. Rather than deliver this news himself, Nixon decided to deputize Ziegler to do so. He explained the reason for his decision was that leaves of absence would have an uncertain duration, while resignations would provide the certainty he needed. Ziegler agreed, and went about the task.[172]

*12:49 P.M. telephone call from Ziegler:* Ziegler reported on his conversation with Haldeman: "Your [i.e., Nixon's] decision was to ask for their resignations, you talked to Rogers, and thought this through for now three weeks. You feel that a leave of absence would be detrimental to them and to the presidency, and that you intend to ask them for resignations." Ziegler added, "That you recognized that their lawyers don't agree with this approach and that they don't agree with this approach, but the president feels clear in his mind now that this must be done, and that's what he wants. And Bob said, 'Fine.' He understands. He feels it's the wrong decision, but he will abide by it. And in terms of John, he said, 'I think John is going to be more difficult in accepting this.'" Ziegler said he told him, "'I believe the president recognizes that but is prepared to stand by his decision.' And Bob said, 'I'll do what I can with John.'" The president, who was very subdued, said of Haldeman, "Good. A big man." Ziegler added, "He sure is." They discussed the matter briefly, with the president giving Ziegler suggestions to pass on for Haldeman's and Ehrlichman's resignation letters, and wondered aloud what they, particularly Ehrlichman, would do for money. Ziegler offered that they could get advances from friends. "Okay, thank you," Nixon said grimly.[173]

A few weeks earlier Nixon had had the room recording device removed from his Aspen study, so no records exist of his meetings with Haldeman and Ehrlichman after they arrived at Camp David that afternoon, although they all later recounted their memories of the event. Nixon met first with Haldeman at 2:20 P.M. for just over twenty minutes at Aspen Lodge. Haldeman says he found Nixon "in terrible shape." When Haldeman arrived, Nixon shook his hand, which was the first time he had ever done so. They walked out on the patio and looked at the tulips and discussed their beauty, and as they headed back to the study Nixon said, "Well, I have to enjoy it, because I may not be alive much longer." The president said he felt resignation was the right course, and it had been a difficult decision for him. Although Nixon seldom spoke of his religion, he told Haldeman that since becoming president, he got down on his knees every night and silently prayed he would do right in meeting his responsibilities. In Nixon's own account, he told Haldeman, "When I went to bed last night I had hoped, and almost prayed, that I wouldn't wake up this morning." Both Haldeman and Ehrlichman reported that Nixon accepted general responsibility for what had happened at the Watergate. In Haldeman's account; "He said he's thought it all through, and that he was the one that started Colson on his projects, he was the one who told Dean to cover up, he was the one who made Mitchell Attorney General, and later his campaign manager, and so on. And that he now has to face that and live with it, and that for that reason, after he gets his other things completed, that he, too, will probably have to resign." Haldeman added, "He never said that directly, but implied it."

According to Ehrlichman's account, he had been "overwhelmed with self-pity [and] barely civil to Haldeman" on the trip up to Camp David. When he entered the Aspen study after Haldeman's departure he found Nixon in a checked sport coat, his "eyes red-rimmed, and he looked small and drawn." Nixon told Ehrlichman, too, that he had prayed he might die during the night. "It is like cutting off my arm," Ehrlichman recounts the president beginning, but then he could not continue, and began crying uncontrollably. He reports Nixon making an admission of guilt similar to the one Haldeman recounted. Ehrlichman and Nixon both recall that Ehrlichman said, "You can do one thing for me, though, sometime. Just explain all this to my kids, will you? Tell them why you had to do this?" Nixon wrote that Ehrlichman said, "with controlled bitterness," that the president had made a wrong decision that he would live to regret. Ehrlichman added, "I have no choice but to accept it, and I will. But I still feel I have done nothing that was without your implied or direct approval." With that statement, reported by Nixon, Ehrlichman departed. Haldeman says that Nixon called him back to Aspen Lodge after Ehrlichman left and reviewed his meeting with Ehrlichman. Nixon told Haldeman he was concerned, because Ehrlichman wanted him to admit that he ordered illegal acts, which he refused to do.

Haldeman and Ehrlichman remained at Camp David during the afternoon to complete their formal letters of resignation, discussing them with

Ziegler and Rogers. Both had only one last request: That I be fired. Nixon also met with Elliot Richardson and Dick Kleindienst, as well as with Len Garment, who was taking my post. (I had no formal notification of the events taking place at Camp David, but friends connected to the White House grapevine kept me remarkably well informed.)[174]

## April 30, 1973, Camp David and the White House

The president spent the day at Camp David working on the speech he would deliver at 9:00 P.M., gathering information and opinions in a series of telephone calls to complete it.

*10:22 A.M. telephone call with Ziegler:* The only matter of substance Ziegler had to report was that Richardson could not be named "acting attorney general": The president would have to submit his nomination to the Senate, so they should rephrase the announcement and Richardson could not take charge of the Justice Department until confirmed by the Senate. Ziegler also said he had received resignation letters from Kleindienst, Haldeman and Ehrlichman. When Nixon asked, "Now how are you handling Dean?" Ziegler told him that Jerry Jones, a Haldeman aide who handled personnel, would call and tell me that the president had asked for and accepted my resignation. Nixon said that if I wanted to submit a letter or speak with the president, Jones was to say, "No, John, it's all done." They talked about how hard this had to be for Haldeman and Ehrlichman, but Nixon had concluded, "I have a feeling that Dean did a favor in that respect, getting the son of a bitch going."[175]

*10:42 A.M. telephone call with Ray Price:* Nixon sounded out Price on his decision to appoint Richardson, which Price thought an excellent choice. Price had worked late into the preceding night on the draft speech, and when Nixon asked, "Was Rogers helpful?" Price said he had been and had "said he thought that the general tone was good, and it was just about the right amount of sackcloth, and not too much." Nixon replied, "Oh, hell, as far as sackcloth, I'd be willing to go a lot further. I'm one of the few men in Washington that never blames the secretary when the poor damn secretary misspelled a word. I mean, sometimes the boss is always to blame. So the boss did it. Hell, I appointed Mitchell, I appointed Haldeman, I appointed Ehrlichman, I appointed Dean and Colson. These are all my people. If they did things, they did them because they felt that's what we wanted. And so

I'm responsible. The boss can never pass it on." Nixon warned that if you "sackclothed too much, then you no longer can be president," adding, "Well, I take all the blame, and I don't blame these poor fellows, and all the rest. When all is said and done, you think, well, Christ, this poor damn dumb president, why doesn't he resign?" Price laughed, and Nixon continued, "Which is not a bad idea. The only problem is, I mean, you get Agnew. You want Agnew?" Needless to say, Price did not, but he understood Nixon well enough to give him the sympathy he was seeking.[176]

Nixon arrived back at the White House at 7:58 P.M. and first visited the barbershop in the basement of the West Wing. He then went to his EOB office, where he met with his "makeup consultant" before heading to the Oval Office, where he arrived at 8:58 P.M. for the broadcast. For the previous several hours the thermostat had been turned down to chill the office, which heated up quickly with the television lights, making it too easy for Nixon to perspire. At nine o'clock, the red light on the single pool camera went on, the director dropped his arm, and Nixon began his speech to the nation.

Although Nixon had never been seriously accused of having advance knowledge of the Watergate break-in, he began his talk by stating that he had learned of the June 17 Watergate break-in while in Florida and "was appalled at this senseless illegal act, and I was shocked to learn that employees of the reelection committee were apparently among those guilty." He said that as the Watergate investigation progressed, he had asked repeatedly if members of his administration "were in any way involved," and he "received repeated assurance that they were not." He remained assured of that until, based on information he received on March 21, 1973, he became convinced that the charges regarding his staff might be true. So, he said, "I personally assumed the responsibility for coordinating intense new inquires into the matter," which he outlined. He said he was cooperating with the Senate's investigation, and then explained actions he would undertake at the White House: "Today, one of the most difficult decisions of my presidency, I accepted the resignations of two of my closest associates in the White House, Bob Haldeman and John Ehrlichman, two of the finest public servants. It has been my privilege to know them. I want to stress that in accepting these resignations I mean to leave no implication whatever of personal wrongdoing on their part, and I leave no implication tonight of implication on the part of others who have been charged in this matter." Nixon reported that Attorney General Kleindienst was leaving, although he had "no personal involvement whatever in this matter." Nixon disposed of me in ten words: "The counsel to the president, John Dean, has also resigned." Next he announced the nomination of Elliot Richardson to be attorney general, adding that Richardson had the authority to name a Watergate special prosecutor. The rest of the speech, as I later read it, was window dressing.

*May 1 to 10, 1973*

# New Team, Tough Tactics
# and Rough New Issues

T he departure of Haldeman and Ehrlichman in many ways marked the end of the Nixon presidency. All that was good and great during his term in office, and there was much that he had accomplished, was being overshadowed as all that was bad and petty was becoming more and more apparent, despite the president's efforts to keep such information hidden. Richard Nixon seemed to sense this, and following his first Watergate speech he got very drunk. He made a series of telephone calls long into the night of April 30 that reveal him becoming progressively more intoxicated. To Haldeman, at 10:16 P.M.: "I'm never going to discuss the son-of-a-bitching Watergate thing again. Never, never, never, never."[1] To Elliot Richardson, a man he viewed as presidential timber, at 10:34 P.M.: "Do, d-, do your job, boy, and, ah, it may ta-, it may take you all the way."[2] And to Chuck Colson, at 11:24 P.M., he seriously slurred when declaring the plumbers' illegal actions were totally justified.[3]

Having undertaken a radical change in staff to isolate himself from Watergate, Nixon sought to prevent the problems from reaching his presidency. His strategy was very simple: March 21 became his Maginot Line, the firewall that would keep Watergate outside of the Oval Office, for it was the date he claimed he had first learned of a cover-up and before which he had no knowledge of such activity; after learning of it, he had personally taken decisive action. He had spent weeks building this defense, which was based on a fundamental falsehood he had simply concocted.

Nixon had distorted our March 21 conversation to serve his own purposes, and only years later did he begrudgingly admit that he had been totally involved in the cover-up well before March 21:

[W]ithout fully realizing the implication of my actions I had become deeply entangled in the complicated mesh of decisions, inactions, misunderstandings, and conflicting motivations that comprised the Watergate cover-up.[4]

To deal with this problem he had relied on a deception, to which he also confessed:

I gave the impression that I had known nothing at all about the cover-up until my March 21 meeting with Dean. I indicated that once I had learned about it I had acted with dispatch and dispassion to end it. In fact, I had known some of the details of the cover-up before March 21, and when I did become aware of their implications, instead of exerting presidential leadership aimed at uncovering the cover-up, I embarked upon an increasingly desperate search for ways to limit the damage to my friends, to my administration, and to myself.[5]

Remarkably, Nixon devised his March 21 defense strategy without ever personally listening to the actual conversation, yet the recording itself puts the lie to his contentions.* Instead he relied largely on Haldeman's cryptic descriptions (based on twenty pages of handwritten notes, which Nixon also chose to ignore). Haldeman had listened to this conversation twice: first to the part when he was not present, which ran about an hour, and then to the part when he had been present, which ran about forty minutes. It is possible to get the gist of this conversation in real time, which is largely what Haldeman tried to do and indicate in his abbreviated notes. It is not possible for someone who has not listened to the recording, however, to understand it based on a few summary notes made by someone who has listened to it.[6] For example the tone of voice of the person speaking can be very telling. My voice was filled with warning, as I was trying to convey the seriousness of the problem.

*Watergate Special Prosecutor Leon Jaworski would later tell me that the March 21 conversation was the first Nixon tape he would listen to when it became available, and it removed all doubts for him that the president was deeply involved in the Watergate cover-up. Assistant Watergate Special Prosecutor Richard Ben-Veniste, who was with Jaworski when he listened to the March 21 recording, told me it had clearly shaken Jaworski, and as Ben-Veniste would later write, Jaworski understood after hearing it: "[H]e would be confronted with far more difficult decisions than he ever anticipated when he accepted the job as Nixon's second Watergate Special Prosecutor." Richard Ben-Veniste and George Frampton, Jr., *Stonewall: The Real Story of the Watergate Prosecution* (New York: Simon & Schuster, 1977), 209.

Nixon's voice, not merely his words, kept showing that he heard the warning but that we still needed to pay Hunt, because he seemed to be a bigger problem than breaking the law. Yet Nixon was satisfied with this secondhand information and Haldeman's conspicuous spinning of the facts when he reported them, because he and Haldeman had agreed that, if necessary, Haldeman would corroborate Nixon's version of the conversation. Haldeman was good to his word and did indeed falsely testify about this conversation. If events had gone as planned, it would have been my word against theirs.*

Nixon's hope to gain some relief from Watergate with his decisive actions, however, was never fulfilled. To the contrary, as he assembled a new team to assist him in defending his presidency, the April 30 speech simply added more flammable material to this already combustible news story. Throughout April Watergate had escalated from being primarily a Washington story into a full-fledged national scandal. Matters that had only been smoldering suddenly flared into new headline news: The Ellsberg trial in Los Angeles, the earlier efforts to get the CIA to deflect the FBI's Watergate investigation and "national security" documents I had placed in a safety-deposit box† became major stories, forcing Nixon to devote more and more time to refining and reinforcing his defense. And while there was a corresponding increase in the number of recorded Watergate conversations, most of them reveal the president simply treading water, plotting courses of action that were never pursued, talking tough but acting indecisively, often trying to recall precisely what had occurred during the first eight to nine months following the arrests at the DNC but getting it wrong, and educating his new

---

*Haldeman was indicted and convicted for lying to the Senate Watergate committee about Nixon's March 21, 1973, conversation when he testified on July 30–31, 1973. His testimony conflicted not only with what could be heard on the recording but also with the notes he made of what he had heard. Haldeman testified exactly as they had agreed: Nixon had told me that "it would be wrong" to raise money for the Watergate defendants, when, in fact, he had said the exact opposite. The overwhelming evidence of Haldeman's perjury was assembled when he was prosecuted. See counts 8 and 9, Indictment, and closing statement of James Neal, *U.S. v. Mitchell et al.* (December 20, 1974) 11,695–11,699; see also, *U.S. v. Haldeman et al.*, 559 F.2d 31 (1976).

†When I arrived at the White House in July 1970, Tom Charles Huston was placed on my staff by Haldeman. I never really knew what Huston did until after he soon departed, and Haldeman explained that he had developed a plan for the president to remove restrictions of domestic intelligence gathering. Haldeman felt Huston might have offended FBI director J. Edgar Hoover when trying to implement his plan, which the president had approved, and wanted me to see what I could do. Soon the plan arrived in my office with its remarkable label: "Top Secret/Handle Via COMINT Channels Only"—a classification so high that the classification itself was classified. To make the story very short, I did not implement the plan. At the time I broke ranks over Watergate, there was no hard documentary evidence of Nixon's belief that the law did not apply to presidents, a view I did not share. So after consultation with Shaffer, I placed this remarkable document in a safe-deposit box and Shaffer gave the keys to Judge John Sirica. See John W. Dean, *Blind Ambition* (New York: Simon & Schuster), 36–38, 254, 276, 278, and 293.

team of defenders while reassuring them of his innocence, using selective and often erroneous information—selling his March 21 defense to whomever he thought might buy it.

Accordingly, most of the conversations from this period add little to understanding Nixon's defense, or the Watergate story, not to mention that his inclination to dwell on small-bore matters in a repetitive fashion became even more pronounced. As a result I have opted to include only material from these conversations that moves this account forward and toward its conclusion. (As I discovered new information, I have also filled in a few blanks in my own story, as appropriate.[7]) I have also noted the tactics that were used to implement the big-lie strategy with the March 21 conversation, which developed in the days and weeks following his April 30 speech.

## May 1, 1973, the White House

Nixon arrived in the Oval Office in a foul mood, which would only grow worse as the day progressed. When he learned about congressional reaction to his speech—Republicans favorable; Democrats demanding a special prosecutor—he demanded that members of his party "get off their asses" and help, and he made it clear that he did not want his staff walking around with long faces.[8] In a meeting with the bipartisan congressional leaders he mentioned neither his speech nor Watergate.[9] He spent most of his morning with German chancellor Willy Brandt, as he would that evening at a state dinner. Nixon learned from Ziegler that FBI agents had been posted at Haldeman's and Ehrlichman's offices, as well as at mine, which Ziegler explained was to protect the president's files, not to cast aspersions on the individuals concerned.[10] (These files were soon packed up and moved to a central storage location in the EOB basement, where Haldeman and Ehrlichman could copy information by taking longhand notes. I was largely barred from my own files for almost a year.)

"Did Dean pop off yet?" Nixon asked Ziegler, who said no, and that he did not think I would do so. Nixon wanted to make certain that Ziegler emphasized to the press that I had been fired, but also noted: "But, of course, everyone knows that Haldeman and Ehrlichman were fired, too." "Dean came out of this alright, from his standpoint," Ziegler pointed out. "He got what he wanted, which was right. He didn't want to go down alone."

Nixon went to his EOB office for lunch, where he was soon threatening to fire the entire White House staff, beginning with Len Garment, for treating

Haldeman and Ehrlichman like criminals by posting FBI agents at their offices: "I'm going to fire his ass out, believe me."[11] Ziegler tried to calm the president down, but when they walked back to the Oval Office and then to the Cabinet Room, which took them by Haldeman's office in the West Wing, Nixon saw an FBI agent standing by Haldeman's door and asked, "Who the hell are you?" The surprised agent mumbled, "FBI," while an even more surprised bureau agent was grabbed by Nixon, shoved against the wall, and angrily ordered, "God damn it, I want you seated inside."[12] In the Cabinet Room, where his cabinet and senior staff had gathered, the president delivered an emotional and abbreviated edition of the speech he had given the night before, saying complimentary things about Haldeman and Ehrlichman and then mentioning, and rementioning, his displeasure at having FBI agents guarding their White House papers.[13]

## May 2, 1973, the White House

In his morning update Ziegler reported that the Ellsberg break-in story was quickly gaining serious traction, and Nixon instructed him to not comment.[14] Ziegler mentioned that he was thinking about apologizing to *The Washington Post* for criticizing their Watergate coverage, which was fine with Nixon. Ziegler also said that the press had picked up the story about Nixon's shoving the FBI agent, and the president said to tell them he had simply become angry, as the agent had no business in the hallway. Nixon asked who had arranged for the agents—"It was the stupidest thing"—and Ziegler replied that he suspected it had been Garment, which he later confirmed.[15]

Henry Kissinger dropped by and made a special effort to warn Nixon about his new attorney general: "Elliot worries me. He's going to be very ambitious." Kissinger did not think Richardson would protect the presidency: "I know it's all very well to say he should have a free hand, but you should give a free hand only to somebody who is wise enough to use it." Kissinger based his view on what he had seen of Richardson as secretary of defense, concluding that "Elliot is out for himself." Nixon disagreed, saying, "Elliot is a team player, I think."[16]

In a later conversation with Rogers, Nixon asked, "How about making a suggestion to Elliot that he name Pat Brown as the special prosecutor?" A stunned Rogers listened as Nixon ran through his qualifications: "former governor, former district attorney, former attorney general of the state, and basically not a mean man," the president said of the man who had defeated him in his bid to be governor of California in 1962. Rogers dismissed the idea with a simple "That's not going to do it," to which Nixon replied, "Well, [I'm] trying to think of a Democrat."[17]

In midafternoon Nixon had an off-the-record visit with Ehrlichman,* who had a pressing problem. After thanking Nixon for his kind words at the cabinet meeting, Ehrlichman reported that he had just spoken about the Ellsberg break-in situation with Bud Krogh, who had requested guidance. Krogh had refused to talk to the FBI because of their leaks, but he had spoken at length with Elliot Richardson the previous day and had "told Richardson a lot about the whole leak operation," according to Ehrlichman. Krogh wanted to prepare an affidavit for Judge Byrne stating that nothing had been obtained in the break-in so that the Ellsberg trial could proceed. Ehrlichman said that both he and Krogh were troubled by Richardson, who "was asking questions, like, 'Well, when the president heard about these remarks [about the Ellsberg break-in], why didn't he do something? Why didn't he stop the trial? Why didn't he tell the judge? Why didn't he do this or that? Why did he wait until this thing all came out from Dean in April?'"

Ehrlichman explained that Krogh wanted permission when filing his affidavit to take full responsibility for the Ellsberg break-in operation. He noted that Krogh was having trouble recalling what, in fact, he had authorized Hunt and Liddy to do, but it certainly was not a break-in: Liddy and Hunt had exceeded their authority. From Ehrlichman's description of the situation, he was clearly not helping Krogh recall the fact that he himself had also authorized this operation, nor was Ehrlichman revealing his role to Nixon. (Ehrlichman had only days earlier extracted his written authorization for the "covert" action from the files, telling David Young the documents were too sensitive in showing "forethought."[18]) Nixon authorized Krogh's affidavit, and they discussed whether this break-in had been the basis of Howard Hunt's blackmail threat that I had raised on March 21. Ehrlichman was certain it had been, because I had suggested that was the

---

*This meeting with Ehrlichman and a later one, as well as the president's meetings with Haldeman, were not on the president's schedule or the president's daily diary on May 2, 1973, although a two-minute call between 10:02 and 10:04 A.M. with Haldeman was recorded by the White House operator, as was a six-minute call between 8:44 and 8:50 P.M., along with a one-minute telephone conversation with Ehrlichaman between 8:51 and 8:52 P.M. The meeting times (and dates), however, were determined by NARA, because the meetings were recorded. Nixon undoubtedly instructed that they be kept off his schedule so the news media would be unaware of meetings that surely would have prompted questions. Because they were not on the president's schedule, however, investigators were never aware of them either, and they certainly could have been of interest to prosecutors, not to mention to an impeachment inquiry.

case at the time. Krogh had also inquired if he should resign from his post as undersecretary of transportation, though Ehrlichman said both Krogh and David Young felt they had done nothing improper; rather, "their agents exceeded their authority." Without hesitation Nixon said Krogh should make his affidavit and then resign. Young had already left government. (Ehrlichman and the president were unaware that Hunt had appeared before the Watergate grand jury earlier in the day, where he testified that Krogh and Young had authorized the Ellsberg break-in, and the CIA had provided him and Liddy with equipment for the undertaking.)[19]

Less than two hours later Ehrlichman was back with the president for an urgent follow-up: The *New York Times* had the Krogh story, and it would break the following day.[20] While they had no evidence that I had leaked this story, they were both convinced this was my work, based on a *Times* story that had run that morning.[21] "Dean's targets at the moment are you and Haldeman," Nixon said, and asked, "What does that do for him?" Ehrlichman thought I was negotiating with the Senate Watergate committee for immunity. (In fact, that deal had been made earlier, but it was not yet publicly known.) Nixon wondered if the Senate could give me immunity that would affect the prosecution of the case. "Yep," Ehrlichman confirmed. Although the president was not happy to learn this, Ehrlichman felt certain that no one would believe me. It was also during this conversation that the first signs of Ehrlichman's defense for authorizing the so-called covert effort to obtain Ellsberg's psychiatric records began to surface, in a passing remark he made to Nixon. When asked if Krogh had authorized a break-in, Ehrlichman said that Krogh would say, "They [referring to Hunt and Liddy] compromised a covert investigation," explaining that "they [referring to Krogh and Young but excluding himself] did not authorize a burglary. There is a big difference."*

Disclosure of the Ellsberg break-in, along with Judge Byrne's demand for full information, provoked new Justice Department and FBI investigations, not to mention growing press coverage. Ehrlichman requested the president do with Elliot Richardson and the Ellsberg matter what he had done with Henry Petersen: obtain inside information about what was happening, "a progress report" that would "smoke out" Richardson as it had Petersen. To Ehrlichman's

---

*During his trial in *U.S. v. Ehrlichman et al.*, Ehrlichman would argue, unsuccessfully, that a "covert" operation did not mean an illegal one, merely a less than conspicuous activity as, say, when one looks for another job, they don't tell their boss they are job hunting; rather, they covertly look for the new job. See, e.g., William Frates, closing argument, *U.S. v. Ehrlichman et al.* (July 11, 1974) 2403–5. However, as the government pointed out, everyone involved but Ehrlichman, it seemed, understood he had authorized an illegal operation.

surprise Nixon answered, "I don't believe I really want to." Ehrlichman soon pressed an even more important entreaty: "Mr. President, I have one request: If anything ever happens to that boy—Krogh—and he ends up in the pokey, I don't care what happens to me or Bob or anybody else, but I wish we should get him out, because he doesn't deserve this." Nixon did not reply.

Late that afternoon Nixon had an off-the-record Oval Office meeting with Haldeman.[22] It was a rambling, friendly chat, with Nixon personally extending an invitation to use Camp David, which Haldeman declined. Haldeman was not troubled by the FBI's coming in to protect his papers but was instead far more concerned about someone such as Len Garment taking it upon himself to go through them as they contained all his notes of his meetings with Nixon and his dictations based on those notes for his diary. Nixon understood and wanted no one in those documents. Haldeman said former Nixon White House aide, cabinet officer, and longtime California friend of the president's Bob Finch had called him with a recommendation he wished he had thought of: Al Haig for chief of staff. Nixon thought Haig, who had recently returned to the army as a general, would not want the job, but Haldeman told Nixon that, as Haig's commander-in-chief, he should simply assign him to take the post. He reminded Nixon that Eisenhower had had a general running his White House, Andrew Goodpaster, who primarily handled the press. Haldeman observed that "all kinds of people are banging to get into you" and reminded him that he that needed a trustworthy confidant. He also pointed out that Haig not only knew the operation, but that "he's tough, tough as hell. But he doesn't look tough. He doesn't act belligerent," and added, "He can cope with Henry." Nixon asked Haldeman if he could talk with Haig, and Haldeman agreed to do so.

Nixon mentioned telling his daughter Julie the evening before about wishing at times that he could resign. "Do you think I should stick it out?" he asked Haldeman, who said he understood why Nixon might like to "chuck it," but he did not have that option. That night Nixon telephoned both Haldeman and Ehrlichman to wish them well before their grand jury appearances.[23]

## May 3, 1973, the White House

Nixon requested Dick Kleindienst come by the Oval Office for a morning meeting to discuss the Ellsberg case, including a set of 1971 photos of Liddy standing in front of the office of Dr. Fielding, Ellsberg's psychiatrist.[24] Kleindienst did not know what he was talking about, causing Nixon to observe,

"I guess I know more about it that you do." Nixon was trying to figure out how to deal with Richardson's questions to Krogh about why the president had not informed Judge Byrne earlier. But neither Kleindienst nor Nixon was aware of what Petersen did or did not know about these pictures of Liddy, and whether he understood them when they were provided by the CIA.

By default Ziegler had begun taking on some of the chief of staff responsibilities, which became evident in his and Nixon's conversations.[25] Ziegler not only had become the sort of sounding board for Nixon that Haldeman and Ehrlichman had once been but was also coordinating staff functions. Ziegler caused Nixon to have second thoughts about Krogh, who had taken a leave of absence, when he asked if Krogh should resign. "I don't want him to resign," Nixon said. "He should take a leave until this matter is cleared up. And do it quietly." Nixon told Ziegler that I was behind the torrent of negative news stories and warned, "These stories are going to continue. Dean will continue to come out and thrash again," and he said that he expected me to be talking about Hunt's money demands. Ziegler was not concerned, for he, like Ehrlichman, insisted, "They're not going to believe him."

### May 4–9, 1973, Key Biscayne and the White House

Following the April 30 speech Watergate stories dominated the news, so Watergate dominated most of the president's conversations. Nixon, however, became something of a spectator as events quickly unfolded. A new Watergate defense team was assembled that started working from his Florida home, with three central players: Al Haig (chief of staff), Fred Buzhardt (special Watergate counsel) and Ron Ziegler (media and sounding board), with others, such as Ray Price, Pat Buchanan and Len Garment joining the group to deal with particular issues. Nixon had asked his former treasury secretary, John Connally, who had switched to the Republican Party on May 2, to serve as a special adviser to the president on domestic and foreign affairs (a part-time job), but Nixon never seriously turned to him for advice on Watergate.

Although Haig did not wish to return to the White House, nor did he feel himself qualified to be chief of staff given his lack of legal and political acumen, his interim-basis appointment was announced on May 4,[26] as Haldeman had suggested.[27] Rose Mary Woods talked with Kissinger to make sure he would not cause any problems, since Haig's appointment made Henry's former deputy his titular boss.[28]

Nixon returned to the White House on May 8, and in his first morning conversation with Ziegler never got beyond Watergate. Not only was there much speculation about my testimony, but Nixon: struggled with his memory of events, such as when he had learned of the Ellsberg break-in; decided Ehrlichman had been wrong in failing not only "to reprimand [Liddy and Hunt] but to fire their asses"; felt Ehrlichman was not telling all about the Ellsberg break-in because "everybody fibs trying to defend themselves"; conceded he needed a criminal lawyer but did not want a trial lawyer; wanted the Justice Department to obtain the papers I had deposited in a safe-deposit box and given Judge Sirica the key; was unhappy and concerned that I had given an interview to *Newsweek*, in which I said the president had approved of the job I had done when we met on September 15, 1972, after the DNC break-in indictments were handed down, and that I had mentioned the discussion of clemency for Hunt. Nixon asked Ziegler if I was angry, and Ziegler said not as far as he knew.[29]

When Haig arrived at the Oval Office on the morning of May 8 for what would prove to be another long Watergate conversation, he found Nixon pleased that a Harris Poll revealed that a 2-to-1 margin of the public felt he should be given the benefit of the doubt on Watergate, and that his resignation was opposed by 77 percent to 13 percent.[30] Nixon said I was the only person causing him problems, so they needed to time their attacks on me carefully. "Well, he's a sniveling coward," Haig said. "I think we destroy him," Nixon declared, although he was not sure how. "I don't think we can, but I think we must destroy him." "We have to," Haig agreed flatly. Nixon added that that would have to happen "even if he [Nixon] were guilty as hell"—which, he hastened to add, he was not.

The conversation soon turned to whether Elliot Richardson, who had publicly announced he would appoint a special Watergate prosecutor, had made a selection yet. Haig reported that he had not. Although Nixon had assured Richardson of his innocence, and that as attorney general he should conduct a vigorous investigation, the president was now having second thoughts. "Well, he knows quietly that he is to appoint no one [special prosecutor] without checking with you," Haig assured Nixon, who clearly understood that Richardson's confirmation would be dependent on his having named his special prosecutor. Nixon told Haig he had made the big move on Watergate by forcing Haldeman and Ehrlichman to resign, explaining, "They had no friends, let's face it." When Haig agreed, Nixon asked, "You think the stampede has stopped?" "Yes, I do," Haig replied.

When Ziegler returned to the Oval Office, Nixon wanted a Dean update.[31] Still upset about my *Newsweek* interview, the president told Ziegler, "He must be destroyed," but warned that it had to be done cautiously. When speaking with Ziegler, Nixon constantly sought reassurance that the press secretary believed him. Early that afternoon the president likewise took Haig through a forty-five-minute explanation of his innocent behavior during our March 21 conversation, casting me as a man with much to hide.[32]

During the afternoon of May 8, Nixon met with Dick Moore in his EOB office and tried to turn Moore's memory against me, telling Moore he thought they could challenge my account on the basis that I had waited nine months to tell the president about the cover-up.[33] Nixon could not resist, however, admitting that "Tom Pappas, bless his dear soul, came in to see me about the ambassador to Greece. He said to me, 'You know, I'm helping John Mitchell with some things.' And I said, 'Well, thank you.'" He added that I had known about Pappas and mentioned him on March 21, which worried Nixon.

In a late-afternoon Oval Office meeting with Haig, Nixon said they had "to have a strategy" to deal with my appearance before the Senate Watergate committee, when I would be given immunity.[34] "He'll spill his guts on everything, because he's protected," Haig agreed. "He can't incriminate himself." "And he does it on national live television," Nixon added, wondering if the office of the president could survive my "popping off before the Senate committee." Haig was confident it could but warned, "I think it's going to be tough." "Having this little son of a bitch going in there and talking about conversations with the president, unbelievable," Nixon replied, but he claimed that if I told the truth, he was not worried. Haig shared with the president what he had learned about the immunity statute: It was automatic, and the Justice Department could delay the Senate's granting me immunity for thirty days but not prevent it altogether. This conversation produced a tactic they would try to employ to block the Senate Watergate committee; they would claim that if it went forward it would jeopardize the rights of potential defendants. (This was precisely how we had blocked the Patman committee hearing in the House in October.*)

During a meeting with Ziegler later that afternoon the president complained that they had no one in the Senate who was going to take me on, and he remarked, "I don't see why people are playing him up as a great hero."[35]

*See page 159.

When Haig later returned, Nixon made the same point: "I think, if you really want to destroy this office, have me out there fighting John Dean. Somebody else has got to fight him."*[36] When Nixon began to complain about his legal team, Haig recommended that his former roommate from the U.S. Military Academy at West Point, Fred Buzhardt, be transferred on a temporary basis to the White House from his post as general counsel of the Department of Defense. "Get him over right away," Nixon said, but he also wanted his attorney friend from his vice presidential days, Chappie Rose, "for every hour we can get him." Missing Ehrlichman, who he was sure would have a strategy in place, Nixon lamented, "We don't have a good, sound, mature lawyer around right now on the staff." J. Fred Buzhardt, Jr.'s appointment as special Watergate counsel was announced on May 10. Fred's father had been a law partner with Senator Strom Thurmond, and Fred had worked in the Senate for Thurmond for eight years, directly out of law school, so he knew his way around Capitol Hill. But he had no experience whatsoever with federal criminal law.

Meeting with Ziegler in his EOB office that evening, Nixon again insisted that more action be directed at attacking me.[37] Ziegler assured the president that he would "shoot Dean down," but it would be off-the-record. "You know," Nixon said, "sometimes it takes a snake to kill a snake, and you might use Jack Anderson on a thing like this, too, some of these things, you know?" Nixon wanted me discredited before I testified before the Senate or the grand jury; otherwise it would be "impossible for these poor bastards [referring to Haldeman and Ehrlichman] to have a fair trial, and also it will attack the presidency in a way that we've got to answer." "We are working out that strategy now, this meeting with Chappie Rose tonight," Ziegler told him, and he assured the president he had his staff ready to strike me hard at "the right time."[38] Later that evening, when Nixon again telephoned Ziegler, he was still thinking about how he could discredit my testimony and suggested "a sort of white paper," a preemptive report from the White House, on matters I might discuss—an idea that would gain ground in the coming days.[39]

In an early telephone conversation on May 9, Nixon spoke with Haldeman, who was on his way to the grand jury.[40] He said that Ehrlichman had been there for five hours the day before and was scheduled to return that

*Within months, however, Nixon would personally begin attacking me on national television in speeches to the nation, and in press conferences. See, e.g., his August 15, 1973, address to the nation and statement about the Watergate investigations, and hs presidential press conferences of September 5, 1973, November 12, 1973, March 6, 1974, and April 29, 1974.

morning. Ehrlichman had taken great offense at being questioned by prosecutors who were once under his thumb.* Haldeman reported that he had
been through his Watergate notes, and while they would be a problem, he
felt they were a problem "we can live with," if they had to do so. Nixon assured Haldeman they would remain as presidential papers, and he would
"stand absolutely firm" on their remaining so sealed.

When Haig arrived in the Oval Office later that morning, Nixon quickly
launched into a rant about why I had not informed Haldeman and Ehrlichman about the problems with paying money to the Watergate defendants
(which, of course, I had done).⁴¹ Haig was ready with their plan: "Now, what
we've got going now is a very comprehensive game plan on taking this thing
on. We've got to start now building a backdrop, but not shoot our big guns
yet on Dean." Nixon still felt that the best plan was to stop the Senate hearings from occurring by having people like Haldeman claim his "rights will
be jeopardized if these hearings go forward." He wanted the prosecutors, but
not the White House, to join this action. "The main thing we've got to do is
keep our iron hand on presidential papers [and] national security"–related
matters like "the plumbers operation," Nixon said. As for how to deal with
me, they would simply "say Dean's a liar." Although I had yet to testify, Haig
said I was "lying through [my] teeth, [with] one conflict after another in [my]
testimony." Later that morning Nixon instructed Ziegler on a similar approach concerning me: "We've got no choice: Whatever he says, to fight him
to the death."⁴²

That evening the president and Haig had an almost two-hour-long conversation in the EOB office, during which Haig, the seasoned bureaucrat,
boldly began turning Nixon against both Haldeman and Ehrlichman, convincing him that an alliance with them was not in his best interest.⁴³ Haig also
handily eased Len Garment out of a position of influence on Watergate as
he brought Fred Buzhardt into play. As Haig was moving against Garment,
the president also noted, "Bob's lawyer doesn't like Len" explaining the problem as "Bob's lawyer is basically anti-Semitic." Haig noted that Haldeman

---

*Ehrlichman would commit perjury before the grand jury when he pretended his memory had totally
failed him; he claimed he could not recall the answers to 125 questions, including whether I had told
him of my conversation with Gordon Liddy on June 19, 1972, or during that week. Remarkably, when
he was indicted for those false statements, and under cross-examination, he lost track of his false
statements and admitted he had been told about Liddy that week, thus confessing his perjury. See
counts 11 and 12, Indictment, and closing argument of James Neal, *U.S. v. Mitchell et al.* (December
20, 1974) 11,699–11,701.

was, as well. Once again, throughout this conversation Nixon protested his innocence regarding the March 21 conversation and, tellingly did not blame Haldeman, Ehrlichman or Mitchell for not informing him about the Watergate issues, but only me. Nixon instructed Haig to put Buzhardt to work with the congressional relations staff to block the Senate's Watergate hearings.

Partway through this conversation the president asked Buzhardt to join them. Nixon opened by asserting his innocence and noninvolvement: "I just want you to know I didn't know anything about the God damn Watergate, as far as the so-called"—and rather than use the terms hush money or payoffs he rephrased it—"the whole business of payments and all that crap is concerned." While he believed Haldeman and Ehrlichman were innocent, he acknowledged that they might have become part of the problem, "in a tangential way, which may get them in this very mushy area of conspiracy to obstruct justice, which, as you know, is very broad and hard to prove." Speaking in his soft Southern drawl, Buzhardt told the president it would be difficult to involve Haldeman and Ehrlichman in a conspiracy, because "most of the evidence is hearsay, somebody down the line." (Buzhardt was wrong, for there has long been an exception to the rule against hearsay for statements of coconspirators made during the course and in furtherance of the conspiracy.) Nixon instructed Buzhardt that Haldeman and Ehrlichman were to have access to their files, and then with a chuckle added, "Dean has no access."

Buzhardt told the president he would get his longtime friend Senator John Stennis, a former judge and the "one man that rivals Senator Ervin, or outdoes him," to speak to Ervin about "withholding these hearings," which Buzhardt thought was the "best bet to pull it off." Nixon encouraged him to get going as quickly as possible; they had to make a run at stopping them, but "if that fails, then we've got to attack the committee." "We'll have to," Buzhardt agreed, who suspected they would have trouble with some of the Republicans on it, but he was not concerned with the chairman, as "Ervin's gone a bit senile, quite frankly." This conversation ended with a discussion of impeachment: "Impeach the president of the United States for, for why?" Nixon asked.

The president called Haig at home several hours later, shortly after eleven o'clock, to instruct him that neither Garment nor Buzhardt was to have access to presidential papers, and he did not want anyone coming to him and saying public opinion calls it covering up. Or as Nixon bluntly stated it, "Alright, we will cover up until hell freezes over" and signed off with a warning to Haig: "If [Buzhardt] turns out to be a John Dean, we will fire your ass, too." "I would deserve it," Haig responded.[44]

## May 10, 1973, the White House

At a nine o'clock meeting with his cabinet, Nixon discussed the staff changes and reassured his secretaries that these current problems would in "fifty years from now be just a paragraph, and a hundred years a footnote," so everyone should get on with business.[45] Nixon felt confident later that morning when he met with Ziegler in the Oval Office, for the New York Times was reporting that I had "no evidence at all" implicating the president, and neither did the Justice Department or Senate Watergate committee.[46] Now all they needed to do was stop the Senate. Nixon asked Ziegler to speak with Bill Rogers, who was close to Warren Burger, to have the chief justice see if he could not straighten out this problem with Judge Sirica. Ziegler informed the president that I had issued a statement (which I did when I became aware of the concerted effort to block my testimony and totally discredit me[47]), but he did not have any details.

That afternoon Nixon received word that two of his former cabinet officers, and the men who had headed his reelection campaign, John Mitchell and Maurice Stans, had been indicted by the U.S. attorney in New York City for perjury and obstruction in the Vesco case. When Ziegler told him that each man had been charged with six counts of perjury, Nixon was shocked.[48] The only positive Ziegler could note in the news was that all the charges of illegal actions had become "so complex that people can't even follow it anymore." Nixon asked Rose Woods to call Mitchell and Stans to say that "the boss" was thinking of them and was "confident" that "in the end they'll be vindicated."[49]

Nixon's thinking on May 10, however, was still dominated by his hope to solidly reinforce his March 21 conversation defense, and to do so he needed the full support of Haldeman, who could claim he was present during the last part of the meeting and so was aware of what was or was not decided. Haldeman arrived in the Oval Office late that morning, eager to discuss his thoughts on how he and Ehrlichman could be hired immediately as consultants by the Nixon Foundation, since they both had income concerns and no longer had access to their papers.[50] "The foundation has an overriding interest in having an accurate [record] on the Watergate matter, which is going to be a major factor in the history of it," Haldeman noted, so they could work on that project as they prepared their defenses. Haldeman had already spoken with Leonard Firestone and Taft Schreiber, who headed the foundation, and they were "very interested." Haldeman added that "Roy Ash [who headed Nixon's Office of Management and Budget] is anxious to take care of the money." "Do it today, immediately," Nixon said, (This plan was soon rejected, however, when more bad news surfaced.)

The conversation then turned to halting the Ervin hearings, with Nixon wanting Haldeman's lawyers to "raise holy hell, mistrial, Jesus Christ." But Haldeman was not so sure the hearings were all that bad a development. Of course, they would "cover all the facts of the Watergate blunders," but that was old news, and Haldeman was not sure anyone would be interested. Haldeman preferred congressional hearings, which he felt allowed for much more freedom than a courtroom. Nixon turned to the September 15, 1972, meeting he had with me and asked if Haldeman had found his notes on it. He had not been able to, nor could he find the meeting in the president's daily diary, so Haldeman figured I had somehow gotten the archivist to write me into a meeting that had never taken place on that date "In other words," Haldeman explained, "he got the sheet from them and found out there wasn't a meeting, decided this was a useful thing and got it written back in." "My God, my God," Nixon exclaimed.

Haldeman had further recast the March 21 conversation with even more new details. He was now telling Nixon that before March 21, Nixon had told me, "Look, I want the whole facts," which was why I had reported to him—rather than my requesting the meeting. Then, during the conversation, Haldeman claimed, "You probed deeply in trying to draw out of him, and he was reluctant to put it out. You weren't getting a full thing right at the outset from him. You kept saying, but what do you do? You know, raising money is no problem." Haldeman was even more specific: "You were asking a lot of leading questions designed to draw Dean out, because it was apparent that Dean was sort of treading a thin line in how he was talking to you in that meeting. You had told him to give you all the facts. He was not giving you all the facts. He was giving you a selected few of the facts, and you were pushing to get more information."

As Haldeman continued with this reinvention of the conversation, and how he might testify about it, Nixon said little, but he did suggest at one point that Haldeman should not mention Tom Pappas. Haldeman continued and characterized Nixon as probing me "hard to find out what happened," the upshot of which was to instruct me to meet with Mitchell, Ehrlichman and Haldeman; it was then that the president called Haldeman into the meeting. "See, at this point you didn't know what Mitchell's involvement in this was," Haldeman added.

They also discussed Ehrlichman's growing problems with the plumbers and the recent public revelations about his dissembling over the instructions he had give the CIA to provide Hunt with "disguises and all that stuff." (Ehrlichman alleged that I had made these arrangements, when I had never spoken with the person Ehrlichman instructed, not to mention the fact that I had no information about what Hunt was doing at the White House. Fortunately, deputy CIA director Robert Cushman had recorded his July 7, 1971, conversation with Ehrlichman.[51]) This Oval Office discussion ended with a consideration of whether Nixon should resign. His concern was that, if he walked "out of this office, you know, on this chicken-shit stuff, why, it would leave a mark on the American political system." His view, accordingly, was to "fight like hell."

Although Haldeman departed at noon, Nixon continued to think about their conversation, and he called Haldeman that afternoon to ask about his meeting with his lawyers, which Haldeman said had gone well.[52] Nixon told him of the Vesco-related indictments of Mitchell and Stans, saying he was disappointed that I had not been indicted as well. He talked with Haldeman again at 4:18 P.M., but the call was not recorded.[53] At 4:50 Nixon again tried to reach Haldeman, but the call was not completed. While Nixon was having dinner in the residence, Haldeman returned the call, and the president asked if I had been involved with the IRS and Vesco, and Haldeman said no, although I was aware of the efforts to use IRS to get Larry O'Brien.[54] Later that evening Nixon met again, but secretly, with Haldeman in the Lincoln Sitting Room.[55] Neither man has written specifically about this meeting.[56] (After his departure from the White House staff, seventeen of Haldeman's conversations with Nixon were recorded, and it is unknown how many went unrecorded.) But it appears that it was at this meeting that Haldeman assured Nixon that he would testify as Nixon hoped regarding the March 21 conversation, with Haldeman claiming the president had said "it would be wrong" to raise money and pay the Watergate defendants. While they had discussed that topic—which was central to Nixon's defense—earlier, it does not appear in any of the recorded conversations.

# A Preemptive Defense Statement

N ixon found no reprieve from negative news. By the spring of 1973 Watergate had come to represent much more than just a bungled burglary and bugging at the DNC; it was now symptomatic of any and all abuses of power by the Nixon presidency. Old stories were resurfacing, and reporters were digging for information about purported wiretapping of newsmen in 1969 and 1970. Then Deputy CIA director Vernon Walters was summoned back to Washington from the Far East to explain his dealings with the Nixon White House in late June and early July 1972, following the arrests at the Watergate. The Senate's Armed Services Committee, which had jurisdiction over the CIA, had learned of a CIA connection with Watergate.* On the morning of May 11 Walters came to see Haig and Buzhardt to give them copies of memoranda of conversations—known as "memcons"—he had written after his meetings with Haldeman and Ehrlichman on June 23, 1972, along with his later meetings with me. Walters said he had been summoned to testify the following day before the Senate Armed Services Committee, and he wanted guidance as to whether any of his memcons contained classified information.[1]

Those documents were immediately recognized by Haig and Buzhardt as the next Watergate-related disaster for the Nixon presidency, even as Nixon's team was still bracing for further negative reverberations from the unfolding reports from the Ellsberg break-in being addressed by Judge Matt Byrne. On

---

*The chairman of this committee was Senator John Stennis, who was not only fond of Richard Nixon but had been close to Fred Buzhardt for years. Stennis, however, had recently been shot and wounded in an attempted robbery on Capitol Hill and was recovering. The next ranking Democrat on the committee, Senator Stuart Symington (MO), was the temporary chairman when this question of the CIA connection to Watergate arose, which could not have been worse for Nixon, for Symington was a longtime anti-Nixon Democrat.

May 11 Byrne personally delivered a stinging rebuke of the Nixon administration's investigation and prosecution of the case, assailing the government for "improper conduct [in] an unprecedented series of actions" carried out by the plumbers unit, which had broken into Ellsberg's psychiatrist's office with CIA assistance "beyond its statutory authority" in providing "disguises, photographic equipment and other paraphernalia for covert operations." The government had also "requested and received from the CIA two psychological profiles" of Ellsberg. The court was offended by the failure of the government to produce records of these White House undertakings, along with the telephone surveillance records of Ellsberg, which it had belatedly admitted existed yet had failed to produce. Judge Byrne dismissed the government's case, freeing Ellsberg and his codefendant Anthony Russo in a manner insuring that neither defendant could be later retried by the government. Needless to say, this rebuke and dismissal, and the accompanying front-page and network news stories, were devastating.[2] But the Walters memcons had the potential of being worse.

## May 11–13, 1973, the White House and Camp David

When Haig visited the Oval Office shortly after noon on May 11, he was clearly upset as he reported that Walters had been sent to the White House by recently appointed and confirmed (February 2, 1973) CIA director James Schlesinger: "Walters came in to me and gave me eight memcons of meetings here with Haldeman and Ehrlichman in July [sic] of last year, and a series of subsequent meetings with Gray and Dean. When I read them I thought they were quite damaging to us."[3] After Haig explained that he had been shown them to determine if they were classified, and that Walters was also being sent by Director Schlesinger to Elliot Richardson with the documents, he continued, "So I immediately called Buzhardt in, and we both read them. And we said, these papers can't go anywhere. We sent him back to the agency, told him not to take any telephone calls, return here with every copy. And these are vital national security matters and cannot go anywhere."

Haig, who did not have a good understanding of the memcons, did his best to describe them. They revealed that on June 23, 1972, Haldeman and Ehrlichman had directed Walters to see acting FBI director Gray to "tell him that this [Watergate investigation] involved national security matters and that he should quiet down about the investigation. And that it had gone far enough and it was getting wider. It was beginning to get into CIA business, Mexican money." But "Walters refused." And he reported that Gray had called the president to say that Watergate "involved people high up in the White House and he should clean house. This is July." Haig reported that the later conversations with me involved the CIA's providing assistance to the burglars. Haig added that that was not all that was going on, for they had had "some very fast actions here this morning," so he moved on to the next.

Haig had not yet learned that Judge Byrne was dismissing the Ellsberg case although he had been assured that there would be "a mistrial." He told Nixon that Ruckelshaus had been trying to get permission to send the Ellsberg wiretaps, which had been found in Ehrlichman's files the day before, to Judge Byrne. (Failure to produce these wiretaps had been the final straw for Judge Byrne, yet the White House was still not releasing them.) Haig was avoiding Ruckelshaus "until we've got a strategy lined up." They needed a strategy, because by now the Nixon White House's 1969 to 1970 wiretaps of newsmen had also broken in the news, which was also being actively investigated by the FBI. During his earlier stint at the White House, Haig had carried the messages from Kissinger to then assistant FBI director Bill Sullivan as to which newsmen and National Security Council staffers they wanted to wiretap. This would be another major negative story, although the wiretapping had been carried out under the authority of and with the approval of Attorney General John Mitchell. Haig reported that the story had been leaked by Mark Felt, who "was spilling his guts all over the West Coast newspapers" and identifying the newsmen who had been wiretapped. In fact, it was not Felt who was leaking. The leaks were, rather, part of a byzantine plot being undertaken by Bill Sullivan to set up his archenemy Felt, knowing Felt would be blamed and fired.[4] And indeed, Nixon told Haig, "Blame it on Felt," and have Ruckelshaus fire him.

Nixon returned to the memcons, and told Haig, "I'm clean on this thing. I didn't do anything about this CIA thing. That was a Dean plot, period. He cooked the thing up and apparently talked to Haldeman and Ehrlichman about it, and I'll bet you that they didn't approve the God damn thing." Based on his reading of the memcons, Haig agreed that "Dean was operating on his own," though Nixon instructed, "But Walter's memcons should not get out." As they spoke, however, Nixon reconsidered and had a further question: "Do his memcons indicate that Bob and John cooked up the scheme and told Dean to carry it out? Was that the deal?" Nixon understood how his White House actually operated and realized that I would have been fired for undertaking such a plan on my own. Haig looked at the documents again and responded, "Yes. If you read these papers you would get that impression, because of the way the sequence, the timing": Haldeman and Ehrlichman first met with Walters, and "he was told to go over and get Gray to tone down the investigation." "Because of the CIA?" Nixon asked. "Yes," Haig replied.

They would also soon discover that when I had called Walters on June 26, three days after his meetings with Haldeman and Ehrlichman, he had noted exactly what I had told him: "He [Dean] said he wished to see me about the matter that John Ehrlichman and Bob Haldeman had discussed with me on the 23d of June. I could check this out with them if I wished." Walters did call Ehrlichman, who confirmed I had been following up at his request. But even more troubling was the statement in Walters's memcon for June 23, 1972, in which he stated: "Haldeman said the whole affair was getting embarrassing and it was the president's wish that Walters call on Acting Director L. Patrick Gray and suggest to him that, since the five suspects have been arrested, this should be sufficient and that it was not advantageous to have the inquiry pushed, especially in Mexico, etc."

Haig indicated that he was concerned how Ehrlichman, who was increasingly considered more likely to protect himself rather than Nixon, might come out as a result of the information in the Walters memcons. He told the president that Buzhardt had advised, "For God's sake, don't talk to him," warning that if Haig did speak with Ehrlichman, he would soon end up a witness. Nixon said, "Well, maybe I better talk to Bob. Not John, I don't want to talk to John." Haig agreed, suggesting, "Well, to get a feel for how they're going to play that. The FBI is going to see Bob and John, Bob at five tonight." "About this thing?" Nixon asked. "No, not about this but about those [NSC staff/newsmen] taps, and we've got to know how to play that one, too. So we've got to coordinate it all. They're all linked together." After Haig explained that Larry Higby was his connection to Haldeman, Nixon said, "I just think I better get Bob and have a frank talk with him. I know that could be off-the-record." Nixon instructed Haig to have Haldeman "slip into" his EOB office at one o'clock. But Haig, who agreed that Nixon should not be seen talking to Haldeman, felt he could more likely arrive unnoticed in the Oval Office. "Well, one crisis every hour," Nixon said, as the conversation came to an end.

At 12:53 P.M. Haldeman appeared, and Nixon's greeting his aide—whose full name was Harry Robbins Haldeman—with, "Robert, how are you, boy?" must have made Haldeman cringe slightly, given their long association.[5] The president said that he was keeping Haig away from some issues, and reported to Haldeman about the Walters memcons. The main thing he wanted to talk about, though, was how Haldeman and Ehrlichman would testify, for he wanted them "on track in terms of what the story really is." Nixon then explained, based on Hunt's CIA ties, "Our story is that he had done some national security work"—referring to the plumbers operation. But Nixon wanted it made clear that at no time had they tried to "put out a cover story that it was CIA business." Nixon spent most of this meeting trying to reconstruct what Walters had written in the memcons while ignoring Haldeman's request to see the documents. The rest of the conversation involved attempting to recall what had happened on June 23, 1972, when they had summoned Walters and Helms and then sent Walters to see Gray. When Haig joined the meeting, Nixon announced that he would never release the Walters memcons but would hold them "until hell freezes over." As the conversation was winding down, Haldeman shared with Nixon what it had been like to appear before the grand jury: "It's a terrible thing. You're in a big, dark room, with these hostile people, and these merciless prosecutors tearing you up, and you have no lawyer. You're all alone and feel like the bull in a bullfight."

In midafternoon the president called Haig to his EOB, anxious about the damage the Walters memcons would do to his credibility with his own people.[6] Earlier he had pressed Haig to make certain that Buzhardt believed the president was not trying to use the CIA to interfere with the Watergate investigation—which, of course, the memcons revealed was exactly what he had tried to do. Nixon said he did not want his staff to see the documents; he did not want Elliot Richardson to view them; and he was deeply concerned that those who had seen them would no longer believe him. He did not want anyone working for him "to have any doubts about the president. I'm not in this God damn thing," he insisted. He wanted everyone to focus on what he told Gray when he called on July 6—namely, to take the investigation "as high as was necessary"—which Gray had shared with Walters, who had then recorded it in a memcon.

But not even Haig could accept so limited a reading of the documents, and he made it clear that he thought they would create a serious legal problem for both Haldeman and Ehrlichman. "Does [Buzhardt] think they are guilty?" Nixon asked. "He thinks they are guilty, [but] they don't think they are," Haig said, and he shared Buzhardt's assessment of the two men. "He senses that Bob is strong and John is not." Nixon, disagreeing with that analysis, said, "I don't want to get in it with Buzhardt, for reasons which you understand. I trust him and all the rest, but God damn it, after the Dean episode, I don't trust anybody. Do you understand?" Nixon, clearly unnerved by this latest information, complained: "Jesus Christ, I can't trust Garment, Buzhardt, Price, anybody. Jesus Christ, I don't know who the hell we're talking to any more. But if there's one person that is totally blameless in this, I thought Watergate was the stupidest God damn thing I ever heard of." As this rant continued, Nixon insisted, "I really thought it was probably a CIA, because I couldn't think we could have done something that stupid. All this payoff crap. I thought, well, they're taking care of their fees and all this. Believe me, I knew nothing about it, not a God damn thing. And I was busy with other things. But the point that I'm making is this: I'm not going to blame other people for my bad judgment in picking them."

Ironically, this conversation ended with the president's growing realization that he may have made another bad pick, as he told Haig: "Elliot Richardson, they say, is very goosey. If he's goosey, screw him. Out, out, out. He's got to be all the way with the president. No questions." (Five months later Nixon would discover that Richardson was unable "to be all the way.")

Later that afternoon, after digesting the steady flow of calamities and increasingly hostile press coverage, the president telephoned Haig and said, "Let me tell you, the whole game here now, I think you've got to realize, which you and I haven't played much before, it's all PR now."[7] With that, and still unaware of Judge Byrne's decision to dismiss the Ellsberg case, Nixon issued an order not to send the judge the wiretap information: "God damn it, instead of sending it out to that judge and let him sit on it for a week, by God, we'll put it out." The president was now intent on preempting some of the bad publicity that he knew was only going to get worse.

At 3:45 P.M. Haig rejoined the president in his EOB office for a brief session before Nixon headed to Camp David for the weekend.[8] (Because it was raining and windy, he was driving, with Rebozo joining him for the trip.) Nixon said he wanted Walters to meet with Henry Petersen but not Elliot Richardson, who had not yet been confirmed. Walters was on his way, and "he's not going to volunteer anything," Haig replied. He would say that he had refreshed his recollection with his diary but would not mention the memcons. Nixon departed for Camp David shortly after four o'clock, but during the entire weekend he phoned Haig for the latest information, checking in almost obsessively within minutes of his arrival at Aspen Lodge.[9]

That evening at Camp David Nixon learned that Mitchell was denying that, as attorney general, he had approved any wiretaps of newsmen. "That's bullshit,"[10] Nixon remarked, and indeed, later that evening Buzhardt located in the boxes containing the wiretap logs Mitchell's signature authorizing wiretaps of six newsmen and ten National Security Council staffers.[11]

When discussing the memcons with Haig later that night, the president learned that Buzhardt remained adamantly against releasing them, even returning them to the CIA, although the president was inclined to get them out of the White House.[12]

On Saturday, May 12, Nixon decided they could survive the release of the memcons, while understanding the consequences: "It will be very embarrassing, because it'll indicate that we tried to cover up with the CIA."[13] Nixon seems to have overlooked what had apparently concerned Buzhardt: The information in the memcons could give the lie to Nixon's March 21 defense that he had not known about a cover-up until I told him nine months later. Buzhardt advised Haig, who reported to Nixon, that Senator John Stennis was "working covertly" to help the president's cause and trying to bring some sanity to the recent chaos plaguing Nixon.[14] Late Saturday afternoon Nixon and Haig discussed potential Watergate special prosecutors they might recommend to Richardson. Haig's pick was former U.S. Supreme Court justice Arthur Goldberg, whom Haig liked because "he's a little bit obnoxious and doesn't wear well with people, which would be good from our point of view."[15]

On Sunday, May 13, Nixon told Ziegler that timing was key, "And it isn't yet time to go on the offensive."[16] Later that day the president encouraged Ziegler to work on the strategy for dealing with the latest Watergate problems,[17] and then called Haldeman to talk strategy, and to wish him well as he headed back to the grand jury on Monday.[18] He told Haldeman that attempting to stop the Senate Watergate committee proceedings was not going to work, and that as far as the Senate was concerned, "I think we've just got to make an asset out of the liability." He advised Haldeman that when answering questions before the Senate, he had to be as careful as if he were in a courtroom, but at the Senate you can "make a speech each time." And Nixon spelled out the speech he wanted made, with nothing nuanced or subtle: "The president has no knowledge whatsoever, it was never discussed in his presence, you see what I mean?" Nixon also instructed Haldeman on how he should answer questions about Walters: It was all a matter of national security. Together they again tried to remember what had happened on June

23, 1972, but could only guess. So they conjectured (incorrectly) that they had not yet known the true story of Watergate and thought the CIA might have been involved, because CIA personnel had taken part in it.

### May 14 –16, 1973, the White House

Back in his West Wing office on Monday, May 14, the president was gripped with a new concern: Had he written me an incriminating memorandum? During his 8:56 A.M. Oval Office meeting with Ziegler, he raised this question: "Maybe I wrote a memorandum to him saying, look, do everything possible to be sure that John and Bob don't get involved, or everything possible to see that Hunt doesn't talk. Do you know what I mean?"[19] Nixon was sufficiently worried about this possibility that he had Larry Higby check with all the West Wing secretaries who handled presidential matters to see if he had ever written a "confidential memorandum" to me.[20] He was also alarmed about another file regarding Ehrlichman and Hunt: "You know, they were supposed to do a second-story job someplace, and they were going to do this, and they never did, and they just screwed up everything."* "We don't seem to have any file on that," he told Higby, suggesting he take a look. When Higby left, Nixon called Rose Woods into the Oval Office and asked if he had written any memorandum to me since February 27, but she could recall none.[21] She did, however, have an update from psychic Jeane Dixon, who "tells us that May and June are going to be pretty bad. June may be worse than May. But everything will turn out fine and to be of stout heart and all that." By noon Higby assured the president that he had not discovered any memos to me, which he reaffirmed when Nixon called him into the Oval Office at 12:25 P.M.[22]

　　While contrary to Nixon's assumption I knew almost nothing about the wiretaps on newsmen and NSC staffers, for they had been undertaken before I arrived at the White House, he had specifically instructed me on April 16 that this was a national security matter I could not discuss, to preclude my testifying about them. As soon as their existence was made known, as a result of Judge Byrne's inquiry about how Ellsberg had been overheard, however, and additional information about them started to leak, Nixon insisted

---

*On June 30, 1971, Nixon issued the following order to Haldeman: "I want Brookings, I want them to just break in and take it out," he said, referring to a purported copy of the Pentagon Papers at the Brookings Institution. "Do you understand?" "Yeah, but you have to have someone to do it." Nixon added, "You talk to Hunt. I want the break-in, well, hell, they do that. You break in the place, rifle the files and bring 'em out." Conversation No. 533-1.

that the FBI issue a statement that they had been conducted in a legal manner and approved by the attorney general. On May 14, with guidance from
the White House, acting FBI director Bill Ruckelshaus released a statement
acknowledging the activity.[23] While under the circumstances the statement
put the best spin possible on the situation, it inevitably resulted in more bad
press.[24] And the bad news kept coming. Ziegler told the president: Judge
Sirica was reading the classified documents I had placed in the safe-deposit
box, to which I had given him the key; and Walters was testifying before the
Senate Armed Service Committee about the CIA relationship to the Watergate investigation and White House aides Hunt and Liddy.[25] Nixon would
keep asking his staff for an update on my papers, but it would take days for
him to learn of their nature.

By the evening of May 14 the situation at the White House had become
almost frantic. In an Oval Office session with Haig and Ziegler, Nixon
learned that Richardson had given the Senate Judiciary Committee a list of
four potential special prosecutors: U.S. District Court Judge Harold R. Tyler,
Jr., of New York; former deputy attorney general Warren Christopher; William H. Erickson, a judge on the Colorado Supreme Court and chair of the
America Bar Association's criminal law section; and David W. Peck, a former appellate judge on the New York Supreme Court and later a Wall Street
lawyer.[26] (Within days all of Richardson's choices for the special prosecutor
post had turned him down.) The president also learned that Richardson had
publicly criticized both Haig and Garment for suggesting names of special
prosecutors, commenting, "I don't like him pissing on the White House. But
everybody else is doing it at the moment. All right, fine, let's get him confirmed." The Senate Democrats, meanwhile, were hammering the White
House for making its own suggestions for the post.[27]

Haig had more bad news that evening regarding Walters's testimony before the Senate Armed Services Committee: "Well, we got a problem with
the testimony that Walters gave. He twisted it in a way that was bad for Bob
and John." When Haig assured the president that it was not bad for him,
Nixon claimed that Walters had "misconstrued" his own documents. "Every
son of a bitch is a self-server," Haig noted. Ziegler was concerned that they
were getting too involved in "the day-to-day bouillabaisse." Nixon agreed
and said they should just accept the fact that they were in for several months
of a beating, but that they would come back. Only if he was guilty would
they not come back, Nixon noted, but because he was not guilty, they would
survive. This is not to say that Nixon was not outraged by the latest charges

that had surfaced that evening: He had stolen campaign money and put it into his San Clemente house; he had dragged the CIA into Watergate; and he had paid off the defendants. But because none of those were true, he would survive. "There's got to be a way to deal with it," a very frustrated Ziegler said. "I don't know the answer to that yet."

Nixon met with Haig again that evening, complaining, not surprisingly, that day after day and week after week it was all Watergate, all the time.[28] "Now you and I've got to get on with the business of this God damned country," he said, and instructed Haig: "Buzhardt's in charge, and at the end of the day he can tell you, we had this and this pack of shit today, and this pack of shit tomorrow." Ziegler, he said, was concerned with "some attrition in the press and polls," but Nixon's response was, "Screw it. We're going to take it for another two months, and then we'll come back. Don't worry about it. Don't react to the God damned attrition. Al, we just do the job." Haig agreed, and Nixon urged, "Don't react in a jumpy, panicky way every time something comes up." With one exception, Nixon added: the leaked story that he had taken a million dollars and put it in his California property. On that, he said, "We've got to attack them, assault them, destroy them." They spent the next three hours desperately but unsuccessfully trying to kill the story and attacking the Senate Watergate committee, which they believed had leaked it.[29]

In the Oval Office the following morning, May 15, when Ziegler reported that neither the *Post* nor the *Times* had carried the account of the million dollars purportedly taken from the campaign, Nixon pointed out, "It played in the AP."[30] To knock the story down, Ziegler reported, they were bringing in Kalmbach's partner, Frank DeMarco, who did Nixon's taxes as well as those of the Nixon Foundation. But Nixon was now annoyed that they had overreacted to the story and lost their balance again: "You know, there is going to be a story every God damn day, and eventually, they will pass." As this conversation proceeded, and Ziegler raised the fact that they were getting terrible press, the president reminded him, "Ron, we are all getting too obsessed." Nixon asked whether he should consider a press conference, but Ziegler thought not, for it would be all Watergate.

Just before ten o'clock Henry Petersen returned to the Oval Office, for Nixon wanted to make sure he understood that the president had not been trying to block his investigation of the Ellsberg break-in on April 17, when he called him from Camp David and heatedly told him to stay out of national security matters.[31] (Of course, that was precisely what Nixon had been trying to do, at Ehrlichman's request.) Nixon did not want Petersen giving Elliot Richardson the wrong impression. The president also apologized to Petersen for approving the appointment of a special prosecutor, which was effectively a snub at Petersen, who said he understood the changed circumstances. Later in the conversation Petersen explained the problem for the Justice Department if the Senate granted me immunity.[32] But Nixon did not pursue the topic, and instead continued his effort to spin the March 21 conversation.

Following the visit with Petersen, Haig arrived to report that Richardson's nomination was being held hostage to his appointment of a Watergate special prosecutor acceptable to the Senate Judiciary Committee.[33] While Nixon still wanted to influence the choice, they understood that they had to be very careful with Richardson.

On May 16, after weeks of being pressed by reporters, Ziegler told the president when they met that morning in the Oval Office, "This whole question about the Dean report, how it got started, and how you made your August twenty-ninth statement, I think I'm going to just lay that out."[34] To do so he needed some information: "Who asked Dean to conduct the investigation?" Nixon said the "instructions" were his, but a dubious Ziegler caused Nixon to add, "I didn't ask him specifically. I didn't call him in the office and ask him, Ron." Rather, he claimed that all of that was handled by Ehrlichman (even though Ehrlichman himself had told Ziegler that he never asked me about an investigation before the August 29 statement). The point Nixon wanted made was, this was not something he "just made up." (In fact, of course, that was exactly what he had done: Gathering his thoughts on August 29, 1972, Nixon's handwritten notes indicate that he simply claimed he had personally instructed me to undertake an investigation I had never undertaken.*) Nixon instructed Ziegler to simply state that such an investigation was a responsibility inherent to the White House counsel, so Nixon simply retroactively invented this responsibility and sent Ziegler to the press room with that explanation, but instead Ziegler tossed in the towel, admitting that the president had never spoken to me, nor had he directed any investigation by me.[35]

Shortly before ten o'clock Nixon telephoned Fred Buzhardt to see what information he had regarding the documents I had placed in a safe-deposit box. Buzhardt said Judge Sirica had not yet revealed the contents, but Fred had

---

*See Nixon's handwritten notes dated "8.29.72" and prepared for the press conference at page 145.

done "a little snoopin' last night, and I think I've identified the documents" based on the description given the court.[36] He had found a matching document at the National Security Agency (NSA) that did not relate to Watergate, which delighted Nixon. Buzhardt described it as "an intelligence summary of our own collection capabilities and limitation, and a plan for overcoming our shortfalls." That was about as bland a description as possible, so Buzhardt quickly added that "the intelligence people" think it is "quite a hot document." Slowly the issue involved was striking a chord with Nixon, who recalled a meeting with the intelligence agencies, and Hoover of the FBI, about gathering better domestic intelligence. "Fred, damn it, that's not improper," Nixon complained, and though Buzhardt agreed, Henry Petersen, who had received a copy from Judge Sirica, was refusing to give the White House a copy.

A half hour later Buzhardt had more information. In addition to the core document he had described earlier there were White House memos from Tom Huston and Bob Haldeman, as well as others, relating to that document.[37] Buzhardt reported that he was moving "to control this document." Ziegler entered the Oval Office as Nixon was completing his call with Buzhardt, and the president told him that the documents in the safe-deposit box "had nothing to do with Watergate whatever"; he described them as a plan to coordinate the CIA, NSA and FBI for internal intelligence,[38] and added, "It's all highly classified, because it's all supersecret shit. So listen, today we start the fight again."

By midafternoon, when Nixon met in the Oval Office with Haig and Buzhardt, there had been a reassessment of the documents I had placed in a safe-deposit box.[39] Buzhardt had a rather dire analysis, explaining that the study document had called for a number of blatantly illegal actions, ranging from the unlawful probing of the mail of Americans to electronic surveillance to surreptitious entries, tactics that J. Edgar Hoover had also objected to as being illegal, but Hoover had been overruled "in language that will be [viewed as] quite inflammatory." Most important, the material included a memorandum from Haldeman stating that the "recommendations" for all these illegal undertakings had been "approved by the president on all counts," although Hoover soon managed to get this new policy canceled. Buzhardt explained, "Now I think, frankly, that this will be used by the [Senate Watergate] committee, really, to supersede the whole Watergate thing." In short, it was worse than Watergate.

Nixon, rather stunned, listened with only an occasional monosyllablic "yeah" as comment while Buzhardt continued with a recommendation: "I would suggest it be handled in a much different fashion" than Watergate. "I think you can't let this dribble out." "No," Nixon said. "It's my own belief that you have to make your case for doing it." Buzhardt did not report it, but he had surely noticed that much of the core study document set forth rationalizations and justifications for such radical and illegal activity by the government by overstating the problems confronting it, suggesting that the country was on the verge of collapse because of the disruptive antiwar demonstrations that had become commonplace in response to the ongoing conflict in Vietnam. Buzhardt continued, "Think of the environment this was done in. You have to lay it on the record, and there are a number of ways you could do it, with something approaching a state paper, perhaps with a summary by you." He was in effect suggesting a white paper, a formal statement issued by the White House that would preempt the information being used against the president.

Buzhardt had not been privy to the earlier discussions of a preemptive white paper on the Ellsberg break-in, but as they talked, the ideas merged, and the president noted that they could include the Walters memcons with those activities. Nixon was not certain, however, whether it was better to put all this illegal surveillance "into a massive thing" or to "keep it a little bit more confused." Added to this thinking was Buzhardt's further conclusion that these new documents from my safe-deposit box "may precipitate action by the House." Because he was referring to impeachment, he felt they must "make your case in the strongest possible terms. Give everybody all the ammunition you can to help you, and then let's go fight it. Just take them on and fight this thing head-on." No decision was made, but because the president had long been looking for a way to preempt my testimony, he gave the idea serious consideration, as they did more fact-finding, including on the events surrounding the June 23, 1972, meeting of Haldeman and Ehrlichman with Helms and Walters.[40]

## May 17–20, 1973, the White House

On Thursday, May 17, the president began the day confronted with a banner headline on the front page of *The Washington Post*: Vast GOP Undercover Operation Originated 1969: WATERGATE WAS PART OF ELABORATE UNDERCOVER CAMPAIGN, with an accompanying lengthy article by Woodward

and Bernstein, which they had been working on for weeks.[41] The *Post*'s accusations were somewhat vague, but one new charge caught Ziegler's attention, which he raised with Nixon when they met that morning with Haig
and Buzhardt: the fact that John Ehrlichman had obtained the medical records of McGovern's vice presidential running mate, Thomas Eagleton, two
weeks before the story broke that he had had electric shock treatments for
nervous exhaustion in 1960, 1964 and 1966, news that had resulted in his
leaving the ticket.[42] Ziegler, Haig and Buzhardt were worried that the medical records had been the result of another break-in, which they had been
told had occurred in "a letter that came in two days ago," from a doctor
whom Haig did not identify. Nixon dismissed it as paranoia but ordered
Haig to get the facts. (Haig later talked to Haldeman, who knew nothing
about the Eagleton information, and Ehrlichman, who was "upset" by the
story, claiming he could not "conceive of where it came from."[43])

Ziegler had watched a bit of the first day's televised Senate Watergate
committee hearing and reported, "I'll tell you, it is going to be a farce."
"Why?" Nixon asked. "Sam Ervin is just a pompous, fat ass," Ziegler replied.
They discussed the continuing bad news on Walters testifying before the
Armed Forces committee about his memcons and the information in the
documents from my safe-deposit box, which Nixon had started calling
"the Dean papers."[44] What troubled him about these documents was that
they revealed him as authorizing illegal activity. "The bad thing is that the
president approved burglaries as a tactic. That's tough," he explained, and
they discussed how it could be justified. With all this activity converging,
Nixon observed, "the country's looking at Watergate in the context, sort of
as a repressive fascist" undertaking. Haig did not disagree.

By that afternoon Nixon had further warmed to the notion of a preemptive white paper, explaining to Ziegler, following an EOB office meeting with
Buzhardt, "We'll step out there and start putting this all out. What do you
think?"[45] Although Ziegler had embraced such thinking earlier, he had
grown more cautious, and suggested that a statement might be better than
a speech, for there had been consideration by the staff of the president addressing the nation; this was also Buzhardt's opinion, with which Nixon
himself ultimately agreed. "Shit, I can't just speak unnecessarily every God
damn week." When the president called him shortly before five o'clock
Buzhardt reported that he was busy gathering the facts for a white paper,
talking with everyone he could find with knowledge about the Dean docu-

ments, and hopefully ascertaining that no one had commenced any action under the short-lived presidential approval.[46] Nixon advised Buzhardt in planning this counterattack, "You never hit back unless you hit to kill."

At the end of the day Haig, Ziegler and Buzhardt were all agreeing that the Senate Watergate hearings were turning out to be a dull affair. Nixon assured Haig at 7:55 P.M. that the public would "get tired of it, believe me."[47] At 8:01 P.M. he told Buzhardt, "Don't you watch it, don't waste your time on it, please."[48] At 8:07 he asked Ziegler, "Did you survive the television orgasm?"[49] "Well, yeah, I sure did," Ziegler reported, noting that their witnesses "did a pretty good job." But the best news was that the national Nielsen ratings were down. "That's my point, Ron," Nixon said. "People don't want to see this shit" and told him to meet with his team again "just to kick this around." He added, "Because here we are up against it now. The Ervin hearings are started. We got Dean making his move." "He's on [*CBS Evening News with Walter*] *Cronkite*, I understand." "Yes sir," Ziegler confirmed. "We have to coldly assess it and then move accordingly." Nixon and Ziegler agreed that they were not worried about me, and Nixon closed the conversations by saying that they had to "fight the bastards, like we did on November third," which was election day, suggesting that the president viewed his efforts to defend himself as just one more political campaign. A few hours later, at 10:41 P.M., Nixon called Ziegler back to see how his ongoing analysis session had gone.[50] The latest meeting was just ending. Ziegler again assured Nixon that they were doing "a very cold, not weak, but very cold, thorough, calculating analysis of what we are up against." They were assessing "how to approach the battle" and felt "nothing matters" but the presidency. Still, the focus was less than clear, and when Nixon stressed he wanted to address "the Dean problem," Ziegler countered, "We shouldn't dwell on the Dean problem."

Only Nixon and Haldeman truly understood the extent of "the Dean problem," so Nixon framed it broadly: "It is now clear that what we are up against is sort of an attempt to destroy the presidency and so forth." Yet Nixon was still focused on me and wanted to know what I had said to Walter Cronkite. Ziegler replied that, based on a tip from "some plants over there at CBS who edited" the interview, there was nothing new. Nixon wanted to know if there was anything for him to do, saying "Hell, I'm ready to get on my horse, you know, any day." Not yet, Ziegler counseled. Nixon wanted Ziegler's view on who was the best person "to take on Dean," and suggested

Ehrlichman. Ziegler, however, was thinking Nixon-friendly journalists and columnists. Ziegler had begun to become firm with Nixon, keeping him focused and looking ahead rather than endlessly rehashing everything, which was a colossal waste of his staff's time.

On Friday morning, May 18, the president met with Haig and Ziegler in the Oval Office.[51] Despite a great deal of discussion about a battle plan, no plan was set forth. There was more hand-wringing about Walters memcons—faced with no choice, Buzhardt had returned Walters's documents to him, since they had been requested by the Senate Armed Services Committee following his earlier testimony—with the president concluding: "Let me say this: Walters's memcons come out, it's just another blow, but it isn't going to be fatal." This possibility had forced Nixon to think about his June 23, 1972, meeting. Without checking his schedule, not to mention the audio recording, Nixon thought he had met with both Haldeman and Ehrlichman that morning, and "I asked them to have a meeting as part of my efforts to [find out] who the hell was involved and, if the CIA was involved, [keep] them the hell out of it." Nixon was not sure what he should finally do about the Walters memcons, but he felt that Haldeman and Ehrlichman should speak up on this matter.

Haig reported Ehrlichman had called him the night before and said he was about to go public, stating that he had told the CIA precisely what the president had instructed, which he recalled well because he had made "a firm record" at the time. "So John basically is going to turn on the president, do you mean to say?" Nixon asked. "I have a feeling he's going to cave on us," Haig reported. Their debate about what Ehrlichman might say led to a discussion of Haig looking at Haldeman's and Ehrlichman's notes of their conversation with Nixon. Haig wanted Buzhardt also to be fully informed, so he could make decisions, but Nixon vetoed the idea: "They want to pull out all of Bob's papers and John's papers. We can't allow that. We just cannot allow it. If Haldeman's conversations with me ever get into the public record, it will bring the house down." Then Nixon added, "If he looks at them, all it's going to do is drive him up the wall, and he'll probably resign. Now that's just the way it would be. And I feel the same way with regard to John's, and Colson's [papers, too], for that matter." Nixon soon noted that if they got into that material, "you just may as well face up to the resignation right now, to be perfectly frank with you." He said that was the way it had to be, and if "you break that line, we cannot survive it." Nixon felt that that was appropriate, because "the president is not on trial here." Haig noted, "It means the battle will be tougher and less certain," but Nixon was prepared to accept that fact and drew a very clear line for Haig: "My point is this. I am just telling you that from a practical standpoint, if Bob Haldeman and John Ehrlichman and Chuck Colson's memoranda of conversations with the president about any relation to Watergate are spread to the public record, it will destroy us."

After their conversation both Haig and Buzhardt were concerned about Ehrlichman's steadfastness, and they seemed to agree that he would seek "to protect his ass." Nixon and Haig were in accord that Haldeman was the stronger of the two. Nixon wanted Haig to speak with Haldeman and say, "Bob, you have to do what you can to shore up John," who can't "pull the president down. If the president goes down, there isn't anybody to save them. Let's face it, you see? If these men should get convicted, I'm the only one that can save them, putting it quite candidly. They know that."

Haig returned to the Oval Office shortly after noon to report that the Walters memcons were now with the Senate Armed Service Committee, who "read them in their worst-most context."[52] Nixon provided their likely interpretation: "The president told them to go out and fix the case." "That's right," Haig confirmed, and urged that they consider going out and explaining it in a way that would be favorable to the president. To impress upon Nixon the seriousness of the situation, Haig said, "There's impeachment talk in the committee," and for that reason, a report of how it all happened "might sweep the whole God damn thing out of the way. In other words, what we have to think about, sir, is that possibility versus a long bleeding erosion." When Nixon reminded Haig that only the House could impeach, Haig insisted, "But we really have to think about this as a tactic," noting, "We're in a God damn gunfight to maintain you in the presidency." Haig thought that such a report would also help Haldeman and Ehrlichman, and soon he suggested adding information about the plumbers operation, as well. Haig was pushing hard for "getting it all out."

"You'd just put out the white paper? Is that what you'd do? What do you have in mind as to how it would be done?" Nixon asked. But Haig had not thought that through, so they assessed the elements against Nixon in Congress, and the president concluded that "the forces of evil are so malignant at the moment" that he needed to act: "Alright, I am personally going to get a game plan for getting with Ron" to get this information out.

At 12:49 P.M. Haldeman slipped into the president's EOB office for a quick meeting.[53] Nixon again greeted him with a friendly "Robert" and said, "Come in. It's good to see your face." They talked about the Walters memcons and what the June 23, 1973, meeting with Walters had been all about. Haldeman got down to the truth, and referring to the FBI's Watergate investigation, told Nixon that the concern at the time had been "where this can lead outside the Watergate. We were not concerned about the investigation on Watergate." Haldeman bluntly and accurately continued, "We were concerned about the investigation expanding beyond, for reasons that now we have no problem saying, because all that stuff is out." "Is out," Nixon echoed, "We'll say that that's exactly the reason." "And it is exactly the reason, because we didn't want the plumbers operation out."

"In other words, you don't think I should be impeached for that?" Nixon asked. "No. You were doing what you had to do to defend your own operations in here," Haldeman answered. As the conversation continued, Haldeman said that Ehrlichman had very strong feelings that the White House should get out in front of the Congress in explaining "the CIA thing," referring to the Walters memcons. Haldeman wanted to make it part of their offense rather than being forced into defending them. Nixon wanted Haldeman's memory of his role in the Walters matter, but Haldeman (who had not checked his June 23 notes) did not recall if Nixon had directed they meet with Walters and Helms. What he did recall, however, was what he had said at the meeting with Walters and Helms: "I said it was the president's wish that Walters call on Gray and suggest to him that since the five burglars had been arrested, this should be sufficient and was [*unclear*], especially in Mexico, et cetera." Haldeman did not remember if it was he or Ehrlichman who had raised the CIA's involvement. He reminded Nixon that Hunt, who they "knew was involved in the plumbers thing," had not been arrested at the time, adding, "I think we've got to admit to that." "Absolutely," Nixon agreed. Haldeman had also remembered that I had spoken with the Justice Department about the scope of the investigation, although in his account he had me telling them what in fact they had told me. Haldeman reminded the president that they knew Hunt and several of the Cubans had been involved in the Bay of Pigs, which he had mentioned at the meeting, and to which Helms had reacted; Haldeman added that he had gotten the impression from Nixon "that the CIA did have some concern about the Bay of Pigs." Finally, he raised the fact that they had raised the question about the Mexican money and the CIA, and whether that got "into covert sources, because they did not know what the Mexican money involved."

This conversation clarified in Nixon's mind the possibility that he could take the national security wiretaps, the plumbers operation, the Walters memcon issues, and the Dean papers as a whole and issue a report on them: "I would put the whole God damn thing out and let the whole schmear sit there." They would exclude, however, Watergate. Haldeman agreed: "My position is that what you've got to do is put all this out, and I think it should not be the president going on television. It's not a television-type story. It should be a very careful document issued by the White House which puts the matters into perspective." "That's what they're working on now," Nixon reported. Haldeman did not like the idea of a test vote in the House on impeachment, for it was "overgrandstanding." The American people wanted this cleaned up, "so we can watch the soap operas on television."

Nixon again raised the issue that some were calling on him to resign on the basis that he could no longer do his job, and that a resignation would clear his name, but he admitted, "Shit, I can't do it, Bob." Haldeman agreed, explaining that that was the argument Ray Price had made to him as to why he should resign: "My resignation didn't clear my name. My resigning proved to everybody in the world, except a few people that believe in me, that I'm guilty. And your resigning will prove it conclusively. It will prove that you're guilty and that I'm guilty and that everybody else in here is guilty."

Haldeman returned to the president's EOB office for another meeting later that afternoon.[54] He had spoken with Ehrlichman, about whom Nixon remained concerned since their Camp David conversation, when Ehrlichman had given Nixon the impression, "I'm to blame totally, and he's to blame not at all," as the president put it. Haldeman did not think Nixon would have a problem with Ehrlichman. Nixon was pleased with a statement being prepared, which he had been urging for days. The president reported that the plan was to have the white paper completed on Tuesday, May 22. Nixon said it was for the "assholes"—by which he meant the news media. With that clarified, Nixon began reviewing a number of topics along with more immediate questions: Was Ehrlichman talking about the president? Haldeman did not think he was volunteering anything, but the Democratic senators were "fishing on how to get you involved."

Soon they were into another discussion attempting to attribute the blame to me, with Nixon declaring, "We must destroy John Dean. He is a bad, bad man." "He will destroy himself," Haldeman replied. "Why?" Nixon asked. "Because," Haldeman replied," I don't think he is telling the truth, and I think it's all coming around." This dicussion continued through the afternoon and ended with more a hopeful analysis by Haldeman: "I don't see how Dean could hang us, anyway. He's got no evidence."

Nixon asked Haldeman, based on his closed session with the Senate Watergate committee, about the capability of its members. Haldeman thought Senator Daniel Inouye (D-HI) "comes out quite well," and is "capable," "sharp." Senator Howard Baker (R-TN) "comes out very well" and "keeps quoting from *The Washington Post*" to give us the "chance to shoot down all those stories." Senator Edward Gurney (R-FL) "is bad, very bad," "just mean." Senator Lowell Weicker (R-CT) "is a disaster" and "not effective"; his "questions don't make sense," "he is antagonistic," and is "sort of a pain in the ass." Haldeman ended the visit by encouraging Nixon to go out and get some sun. "This is a fight that can be won," Haldeman assured him. Nixon was not so confident, but as he stated it, "The point is, you've got to try, because by God, as you suggested, I sit in this chair with the whole world in [my] hands."

Haig checked in with the president in the late afternoon to assure him that everything was proceeding on schedule in the drafting of the white paper.[55] A few hours later Haig phoned Nixon with some news.[56] When Nixon anticipated the news that Richardson would soon have "his [special] prosecutor and all that horseshit," Haig continued, "I see he got a humdinger." "Who'd he get?" Nixon asked. "A fellow named [Archibald] Cox that used to be solicitor general for Kennedy," Haig reported. "Oh, I know him," Nixon said. "He's not very bright, but he's well respected," and the president did not think the Senate Judiciary Committee could reject him. "Cox is not a mean man," Nixon noted. "He's a partisan, but not that mean," and Haig added that he understood that Cox was "not a zealot." "Believe me, if he'd take Cox, that would be great," the president said.

Nixon stayed actively involved through the weekend of May 19 and 20, checking on the progress of the white paper and all Watergate-related matters. When he met with Haig on Saturday morning in the Oval Office he was thinking about how to roll out the new statement.[57] He thought he would call in the congressional leaders and "take them all for an hour and a half to two hours. And I will lay it all out there, and I'll say, here it is." He would ask for their support and explain it involved "the national interest" and, of course, remind them that he "was not involved in the God damn Watergate." Late Saturday morning Nixon met with Ziegler and Haig and explained why he should not do a television speech with the white paper material: "You can't use the big bullet too often and have it be effective."[58] He wanted to know who was working on it, and he was told Pat Buchanan and Ray Price, and Ziegler assured him they were in sync. Ziegler gave Nixon his reading on the first day of the Senate Watergate hearings: "The overall impact on the public, from a guy like McCord and his testimony yesterday, is zilch."

After much rehashing the president left with the First Lady for Norfolk, Virginia, and then to the USS *Independence* off the Norfolk coast for Armed Forces Day ceremonies. They returned to Camp David around four o'clock. Shortly after seven o'clock the president telephoned Ziegler from Camp David, asking, "How we coming on the project?"[59] Ziegler assured the president they could make the Monday morning deadline, and that in addition to himself, Haig, Price, Buchanan, Garment and Buzhardt were at work on the statement.

On Sunday morning, May 20, the president checked in by telephone with Ziegler, who said they had made good progress the night before.[60] In addition to the congressional leaders, they discussed inviting members of the Armed Services Committee, because of their jurisdiction over the CIA, for the background briefing on the statement. Nixon next phoned Haig[61] and told him that Ziegler had mentioned that Buzhardt thought they could delay releasing the Walters memcons to the Senate until Wednesday, which Nixon thought was favorable, as they would have released the white paper by then. At 12:26 P.M. Nixon called Haldeman to bring him up to date.[62] Haldeman said he was being hounded by the press but telling them nothing other than "the president had no knowledge of or involvement in any kind of cover-up or anything else related to Watergate in any way, shape or form." Most of this conversation involved Nixon once again trying to get Haldeman to tell him what he did and did not know, particularly regarding Ehrlichman and clemency, enlisting Kalmbach, keeping Hunt on after the Ellsberg break-in, and when he first learned of that break-in. Several hours later Nixon spoke again with Haldeman,[63] who had been unable to reach Ehrlichman because he was in California for a new grand jury investigating the Ellsberg break-in. An hour later, however, Ehrlichman had called Haldeman, who then reported back to Nixon.[64] Ehrlichman (who would later change his memory) told Haldeman on "the [Ellsberg] psychiatrist thing, that he doesn't believe you knew about that until February or March," and that he thought that Nixon had learned of it from me. Ehrlichman passed the word via Haldeman that anything Nixon could say in his statement about the Ellsberg break-in situation "would be very helpful." He was looking for "any substantiation" they could get, since it had been under wraps. Nixon responded, "Of course, I suppose that even under the plumbers thing, illegal activity is not," he said with a nervous chuckle, "is not, not impressed with national security."

On Sunday evening Nixon discussed the drafting of the white paper on the telephone with Haig.[65] The president wanted to stress the "national security" angle but did not want to release any of the underlying documents (the memcons or the Dean papers). Nixon said he wanted all this talk about impeachment, particularly by Buzhardt, to cease: "We are fighting to the end. We're going to beat the bastards." A few hours later, at 10:17 P.M., after arriving back at the White House, Nixon talked with Ziegler and learned they were still working on the draft.[66] Ziegler said they had discussed a rapid response team to deal with any charges that arose at the Watergate hearings. Nothing had been decided, nor had a recommendation been offered. Nixon repeated his mantra: "I think the whole thing right now is to play everything very tough, that everybody else is lying."

*May 21, 1973, the White House*

Monday was devoted to editing, rewriting and more editing of the white paper, mixed in with discussions of how to best release it on the following day. The conversations are difficult to follow without copies of the drafts from which they were working during the conversation, but what is clear is that Nixon approved every word of the final draft, often providing his staff information that only he knew. No one was allowed to check Haldeman's or Ehrlichman's notes. Even though Nixon had dictated his contemporaneous thoughts about some of the meetings and issues involved for his diary, he chose not to use it to refresh his recollections. The editing and planning process for the white paper, which would be the most detailed statement Nixon would make of his defense, began when Ziegler entered the Oval Office at 8:40 A.M. to report that Watergate had finally moved off the front pages of the newspapers.[67]

Ziegler explained that they could not have a meeting with congressional leaders to present the white paper, because the Republican leaders—Jerry

Ford in the House and Hugh Scott in the Senate—were "fearful" and did not want to attend a meeting in the White House, so they would be privately briefed in their offices. Ziegler said it had been suggested that Nixon invite the Democratic leaders—Carl Albert in the House and Mike Mansfield in the Senate—down for a glass of bourbon in the Lincoln Sitting Room for their briefing. While considering these and other ideas, Nixon said he had noted in a memo from Pat Buchanan that "he seems to think that it was a mistake for me to refer to Haldeman and Ehrlichman as two fine men. You think so?" Ziegler dodged the question, and Nixon explained that Buchanan did not understand "the problem we had. If I didn't put that in the speech, you could have those two men bitter," which he did not want. Nixon pointed out that fifteen people had left the administration because of Watergate, "And it's a wrenching experience."[68]

As this conversation progressed, Nixon shared his analysis of what had gone amiss with his presidency: "I would never say this to him, but it was Bob Haldeman giving Jeb Magruder the enormous responsibility he did over there at the campaign, and Magruder then taking the Liddys and Hunts and that bunch of jackasses over there." (Absent from this analysis was Ehrlichman's authorizing Krogh to send Liddy to the reelection committee.[69])

To edit the white paper, Haig spent almost a half an hour with the president in his EOB office reviewing the document.[70] When Haig departed Nixon had a particular revision, so he called him back. "One small thing that would help in editing throughout: Never use the word 'criminal'; use the word 'illegal.'"[71] It went on like that throughout the day and evening.[72] During the late afternoon, Nixon asked Ziegler what he made of the designated special Watergate prosecutor's statement that he would conduct an "investigation right up to the Oval Office?"[73] "I'm not the slightest bit worried about Archibald Cox," Ziegler responded, and when Nixon asked why, the press secretary said, "I don't think he's that heavy, and it's basically irrelevant now as to what Archibald Cox does." Ziegler saw it merely as a public relations battle. Nixon and Haig took a dinner break on the *Sequoia* for several hours, cruising down the Potomac, and when they got back at 8:14 P.M., Haig told Nixon the writers needed to work overnight and would have it in the morning.[74]

*May 22, 1973, the White House*

It required down-to-the-last-minute editing to finalize the white paper, which Ziegler assured Nixon was ready to go when they met at 8:50 A.M. in the Oval Office.[75] While Nixon was waiting for the final draft to arrive on his desk, he returned a call from Chief Justice Warren Burger that had come in the previous evening.[76] It was a stilted conversation, a response to Nixon's calling to congratulate Burger on four years on the Court. Nixon assured him he should not be overly concerned about "all the hullabaloo," which he would survive, and it would pass. Nixon did cross the line in raising the difficulty that Mitchell, Haldeman and Ehrlichman would confront getting a fair trial, but Burger only said, "There will be a lot of books written about this, and a lot of law review articles. It's just one of the times when the boat's rocking." With a chuckle, the Chief Justice added, "This kind of separates the men from the boys."

When Haig and Buzhardt arrived in the EOB office at 9:55 A.M. with the draft in hand, Nixon asked who had fact-checked the information.[77] Had Haldeman and Ehrlichman? Buzhardt's answer was vague, saying it had been checked "with a number of people." When Nixon pressed, Buzhardt responded, "We got through, ah, Colson and Petersen." The president did not seem totally satisfied with that reply and said they needed to anticipate every possible question. They then proceeded with work on the document, finishing just before 11:30 A.M. A final revised draft was carried to the EOB office for Nixon at 2:31 P.M. by Ray Price, who was joined by Buzhardt and Haig. Price had added the one-page summary suggested in the morning meeting.[78] Nixon took less than fifteen minutes for a final look and to discuss the release.

That afternoon, shortly after four o'clock, the press office passed out copies of the "Statements About the Watergate Investigations" to the White House press corps.[79] The document ran some twenty legal-size pages, printed on both the front and back sides, and it contained just over four thousand words. It opened with a summary statement, followed by the complete version, which addressed four separate topics: "1969 Wiretaps," "The 1970 Intelligence Plan" (the Dean papers), "The Special Investigations Unit" (the plumbers), and "Watergate." The document from start to finish was written in the first person, clearly indicating that the statement was from Nixon himself.

I first saw the president's new statement that day, when I met with *Time* magazine reporter Hays Gorey, who had come directly from the White

House briefing, at which Ziegler was joined by Len Garment and Fred Buzhardt. I had agreed to give Hays an on-the-record interview, but when he
asked me about this new statement, I was reluctant, because it involved testimony, which I had not discussed with any newsperson. The statement's
summary had seven key items, and Hays asked if I would give him my off-
the-record and for-background-use-only reactions. I agreed to that so he
read from the document, and I briefly reacted with either "true" or "false,"
though an occasional "bullshit" slipped out.[80] Remarkably, while some of
the statements were more artfully worded than others, every declaration by
Nixon but the first was patently false (I have appended to each statement an
endnote that offers several examples of conversations, or other material, that
reveal the sweep of Nixon's mendacity):

> With regard to the specific allegations that have been made, I can and do
> state categorically: (1) I had no prior knowledge of the Watergate opera-
> tion. (2) I took no part in, nor was I aware of, any subsequent efforts that
> may have been made to cover up Watergate.[81] (3) At no time did I authorize
> any offer of executive clemency for the Watergate defendants, nor did I
> know of any such offer.[82] (4) I did not know, until the time of my own in-
> vestigation, of any effort to provide the Watergate defendants with funds.[83]
> (5) At no time did I attempt, or did I authorize others to attempt, to impli-
> cate the CIA in the Watergate matter.[84] (6) It was not until the time of my
> own investigation that I learned of the break-in at the office of Mr. Ells-
> berg's psychiatrist, and I specifically authorized the furnishing of this in-
> formation to Judge Byrne.[85] [And] (7) I neither authorized nor encouraged
> subordinates to engage in illegal or improper campaign tactics.[86]

Following the "line"—to use a Nixonian term—of his April 30 speech,
Nixon dissembled throughout his May 22 summary statement, blending fact
and fiction in the remainder of it. But in providing distorted information
regarding what took place on June 23, 1972, Nixon set a trap for himself, for
no false statements would be of greater consequence than his twisted account of that day's events. He claimed early post-Watergate "reports led me
to suspect, incorrectly, that the CIA had been in some way involved." That
was largely fiction. "They also led me to surmise, correctly, that since persons
originally recruited for covert national security activities had participated
in Watergate, an unrestricted investigation of Watergate might lead to and
expose those covert national security operations." That was mostly fact. He

then added "to prevent the exposure of these covert national security activities," while still encouraging a full investigation of Watergate, he so "instructed my staff, the Attorney General, and the Acting Director of the FBI." That was mostly false, not to mention the fact that he combines events from June 1972 with events in April 1973. Next Nixon completely outmaneuvering himself by stating: "I also specifically instructed Mr. Haldeman and Mr. Ehrlichman to ensure that the FBI would not carry its investigation into areas that might compromise these covert national security activities, or those of the CIA." He simply passed over the Mexican checks, which raised a political problem, and which he could have legitimately said the Justice Department had advised the White House were beyond the scope of the Watergate investigation. Instead he provided misinformation by omitting these facts.

When the truth surfaced fourteen months later with the release of Nixon's recording of the Haldeman conversations of June 23, not only did it establish his deception regarding that day, but it destroyed his claim that he had no knowledge of the cover-up until March 21. It was more than the Nixon presidency could withstand, for these falsehoods revealed that he had been compounding lies to keep his defense in place. But it is not clear from the record that Nixon knew he was lying about June 23. To the contrary, it appears that both Nixon and Haldeman were unaware of the potential trap they had set for themselves. The information needed to understand the June 23 meeting could largely have been gleaned from Haldeman's notes of his conversation with me that morning. But Nixon had also literally banned everyone on his staff from reviewing the Haldeman, Ehrlichman and Colson notes of their meetings with the president. It is clear that Nixon preferred to create his own facts, as he wanted to recall them, and with his May 22 statement he had locked in his defense. It would now be his word versus that of anyone who might dare to challenge it.

*May 23 to July 16, 1973*

# Discrediting Dean
# and the Beginning of the End

Following the release of the May 22, 1973, statement, a newly confident Nixon became convinced his biggest remaining problem was me. For over a month the president, along with his aides and supporters, had been at work trying to discredit me, an effort that would continue not only throughout the rest of his presidency, but for the rest of his life, with Nixon leading the way.[1] The pattern that had emerged in the conversations beginning in mid-April simply continued, though the president's wrath was directed not only at me but at anyone else who presumed to tell the truth if it conflicted with Nixon's defense. During the month between the May 22 statement and my testimony before the Senate Watergate committee, which began on June 25, the president's conversations focused on his efforts to recall and reconstruct his activities, mixed with periodic rants, of which follow a few representative samples:

- *Admissions of error in his May 22 defense statement:* "The question, Ron, of when I knew that funds were being raised for the defense, because, you know, we have nailed ourselves pretty tightly to the twenty-first of March. But I'm confident that I must have had something on it earlier in March."[2] "We don't want to be knocked down on the idea that we said we didn't know anything until the twenty-first of March about any fundraising."[3]

- *False protestations of his innocence:* "I didn't know about any funds before March."[4] Instructions to Buzhardt of what to say to special prosecutor Cox: "The president is cooperating and doing everything he can do on this thing, and that the president is totally innocent and everybody knows it, including me."[5]

- *Falsely recasting the June 23, 1972, conversation*: "Presidential purpose is not to get the CIA in the Watergate [mess]."[6] Nixon learned that Haldeman and Ehrlichman had different recollections of the events on this day, namely that Ehrlichman recalled it was all about the Mexican money, while Haldeman had no memory of that being the reason they met with the CIA. Nixon simply could not recall.[7]

- *Falsely recasting the March 21, 1973, conversation*: "But he [referring to me] didn't tell me about his suborning perjury of Magruder. He didn't tell me the fact that Liddy had told him everything on June nineteenth."[8] "Bob was there, thank God, for the last portion of the meeting. Bob said, he's got his own notes, that the president said, first, it's wrong [to raise money for the Watergate defendants], second, it won't work." "And third, because, basically, you can't provide clemency."[9] This conversation "is what triggered my own investigation."[10] "I said, 'How much would it cost over four years?' But then I said, 'No, we can't go that route.'"[11]

- *How to attack Dean*: In addition to a lot of name-calling—"asshole,"[12] "bastard"[13] and "son of a bitch"[14] were particular favorites—and planting false stories,[15] other tactics were explored. "We've got to hit him right between the eyes [on statements Nixon claimed I had not made to him]."[16] "[Dean] was the fellow that was really doing it all, Chuck, as far as the cover-up was concerned."[17] "You don't want to take him on [from the White House] until you are ready to knock him out of the box."[18] "The guy that can really embarrass the president or raise any questions on him is Dean. The guys that answer that, basically, are Haldeman and Ehrlichman. And to a lesser extent, Colson."[19] "And after thinking a little about that [referring to going through Dean's files], I think it's got to be done, it's got to be done probably in the dead of night."[20] "We're pulling together a chronology of the different statements he's made," Ziegler advised Nixon, material that could be used by the White House staff against me, although it was all pure hearsay.[21] "Well, it will be John Dean's word against a lot of other people."[22] Buzhardt told Nixon: "I don't want to let [Dean] know what evidence exists until he goes under oath, because I would like for him to worry about it."[23] Nixon asked Ziegler, "Has it occurred to you and Buzhardt and the rest that it should be about slapping [Dean] as a traitor, a turncoat, at the proper time, Ron?" Ziegler reported that they had been doing that. "It's got to be done in a brutal slam-bang gut-fight way. We've got to draw the sword on him," Nixon instructed.[24]

Notwithstanding Nixon's concern that I might have secretly recorded him, he kept his recordings going while plotting and planning his effort to cover up the Watergate cover-up. No one on his immediate working staff—other than Steve Bull—knew they were being recorded. Not even the fact that the Watergate special prosecutor demanded more and more of his records gave the president second thoughts about his secret recording. While he had given passing consideration to removing the system, he knew Haldeman had not done so, for he would have been told. He seemed both impervious and oblivious to the fact that this secret system might be revealed, although he was well aware it contained material that could destroy his presidency and create an entirely new set of monumental problems. Executive privilege was then an entirely untested legal concept, more a political stance vis-à-vis Congress than a legal doctrine recognized by any court.*

### May 23, 1973, the White House

When talking with Haig about the Huston Plan, the removal of restraints on domestic intelligence gathering, Nixon said, "I ordered that they use any means necessary, including illegal means, to accomplish this goal. The president of the United States can never admit that."[25] Later that day he told Rose Woods, "Good old Tom Pappas [had] helped at Mitchell's request fundraising for some of the [Watergate] defendants."[26] Nixon said that Pappas had come to see him on March 7 "about the ambassador to Greece that he wanted" but that "we did not discuss Watergate at that point." This was untrue, but as he explained, "It's very important that he remembered that." The president told his private secretary he wanted her to speak to Pappas to make sure he understood this, explaining to her that Pappas's fund-raising activities were not illegal unless "his purpose was to keep the defendants shut up." The president said it was important that he not talk to Pappas about this

---

*Surprisingly, Nixon never did invoke the "state's secrets privilege," which was established law. This common-law privilege empowers the president to refuse to turn over evidence he alone deems a state secret, and the president's decision cannot be reviewed by the courts. See *Reynolds v. United States*, 345 U.S. 1 (1953).

matter, but rather she should inform Pappas that the president's recollection "was that there was no discussion of Watergate."

## May 24, 1973, the White House

At a midday meeting Ziegler mentioned that Kissinger was bitter toward Haldeman and Ehrlichman for "the plumbers activity and so forth."[27] "Bullshit," the president erupted. "He knows what was going on in the plumbers activities. Don't let him give you that crap. He was clear up to his ankles himself." Ziegler was surprised, and Nixon added, "I don't want people around here pissing on Bob and John." In an after-midnight call to Haig, a weary Nixon again raised the possibility of his resigning, since the Democrats controlled Congress and Republicans were weak.[28] Haig would not hear of it, but Nixon was apparently serious, and was also concerned that "Richardson is sort of a weak reed." Haig was spending time with him and thought he was coming along. But Nixon returned to the topic as the conversation progressed, bemoaning the fact that he had "so many weak people in our cabinet." As Nixon viewed it, "Richardson's in the spot where, as you know, he's going to have to prove that he's the white knight and all that bull, and so he and Archie Cox will try to try the president, you know, and all that crap. How do you handle that?" Haig said he had been doing some checking and found that Cox was "not an effective guy." He did not think many of the cases would ever come to trial, for Cox would have them "so screwed-up, nobody will be able to be brought to court."

## May 25, 1973, the White House

Shortly after noon Nixon had Elliot Richardson in the Oval Office for a visit.[29] It was a broad-ranging discussion of the activities of the Department of Justice, with the president praising Richardson and telling him that his experience at the State and Defense departments was of value to the president. Not until the end of this twenty-minute chat did the subject of Watergate come up. Richardson, as he had earlier, vouched for Cox: "He's certainly fair, honorable, scrupulous and so on. He's going to get a fellow who has had some experience in prosecution," Richardson explained, a lawyer like U.S. Attorney Whitney North Seymour, Jr. "You've got complete support there, and you can talk in total confidence," the president assured him, and then he made a point about his papers: "When you're sitting here making a note for me, or if you write a memcon, that's made for me and not for anybody else. Even if we discuss whether or not I'm going to burglarize the ten-cent store. But you can testify. Because, you see, if you ever break into the president's papers, Elliot, we'd have a hell of a problem here."

## May 29, 1973, the White House

During an Oval Office conversation with Al Haig, the president said he agreed with Ziegler on Watergate: "Ron has a good point. This is just a gut political fight now, this whole thing. Cox is going to be a gut fighter."[30] Neither man had any illusions about Richardson's being of much help. Nixon's solution was to "just kick the shit out of them." When meeting later that morning with Bill Rogers, and their discussion turned to Watergate, Nixon said, "There was a cover-up. We know that. And now it's very apparent, the whole God damn thing, frankly, was done because it involved Mitchell." Rogers reported that Mitchell "looks awful," and "I think there's a good chance he'll kill himself."

That afternoon Nixon had another long conversation with Haldeman,[31] who said that he was telling reporters, and would tell the Senate investigators as well, that the president "had absolutely, categorically, nothing to do with any cover-up of any kind in any way, shape or form." And he was going to state "categorically" that he "had nothing to do with any cover-up or with any attempt to cover up." Nixon approved of that and thought Ehrlichman should say the same. Haldeman reminded the president that their involvement with the CIA on June 23, 1972, had related to "the Mexican money," and when the CIA had no problem with that matter, it was dropped. After a great deal of speculation about testimony, and a rehashing of the events now haunting the Nixon presidency, Haldeman mentioned that I was conducting "a very credible campaign" by doing "interviews with Walter Cronkite and *Time* magazine." Nixon said that his "theory of the case now is this: That Mitchell was the one who led Dean around." "I guess so," Haldeman concurred. Haldeman was also worried about his former colleague, reminding the president: "Mitchell hates Ehrlichman, Dean hates Ehrlichman, Colson hates Ehrlichman." Haldeman had concluded that I had broken ranks because the prosecutors had lied to me and told me that Liddy had talked, so I figured it was over, and I should go after others. Haldeman thought the prosecutors had turned Magruder by similarly telling him that "Hunt was going to spill everything." This conversation ended with them attempting to figure out how it had all fallen apart over the last few months.

## June 3, 1973, Camp David

When talking with Ron Ziegler from Camp David by telephone, Nixon had another of his lapses into the truth.[32] While speculating about charges I might make, Nixon pointed out, "What the hell, he can say, I suppose, that I was trying to cover up for Haldeman and Ehrlichman, right?" And before Ziegler could respond, the president added: "Which was somewhat true." Ziegler also told Nixon in this conversation that the addition of Charles Alan Wright to the legal staff "is going to be a big help." Wright, a law professor from the University of Texas, was an a expert in federal court practice and procedures. While a highly respected scholar and acclaimed appellate advocate, he brought no expertise in the federal criminal law, however, which was still the glaring weakness in Nixon's defense team.

In midafternoon that day, Nixon phoned Haig, and both wanted to believe the Watergate story was finally dying, although the president acknowledged that "they're going to try to crap on us about once a week."[33] Nixon did not think the overall situation was bad, however, for "I must say, we're getting a little thicker skin." Late that afternoon, before departing Camp David for the White House, Nixon called Haldeman to set up another off-the-record meeting at the Lincoln Sitting Room an hour later.[34] Although no record was kept of these private sessions, it is very clear from his later conversation with Ziegler that they once again speculated on my testimony regarding the March 21 conversation but this time versus Haldeman's likely testimony about it.[35] They also apparently discussed the president's papers, as he mentioned to Ziegler: "Bob raised this to me today. Around 90 percent of the papers would help us, basically. But the other 10 percent would kill us." Nixon reminded Ziegler during this conversation, "It's going to be a God damned mean pissing match."

## June 4, 1973, the White House

During a morning EOB conversation, Haig told the president that, while he felt "we're over the hump on this thing," he urged Nixon to listen to all of his conversations with me.[36] "I think you should get these tapes replayed for you, alone, and take notes of your discussions with Dean," in order to learn from them "what the son of a bitch" had. "You've got to know what he is specifically going to charge, and then you can sit down with Buzhardt with your notes and give Buzhardt whatever he wants, so that we can strategize whipping this son of a bitch, and structure the kind of strategy we have to have to deal with him." Nixon agreed, however reluctantly, as he was still concerned about what he had actually said in them, although he assured Haig, "I know my motives were right."

Shortly after nine o'clock that morning Steve Bull, at Haig's instruction, had prepared the tapes for Nixon to listen to in his EOB office. Having never been through the tapes before, Bull initially found it difficult to locate particular conversations, since they simply went from day to day, reel to reel, recording whatever was said with no markers to indicate when one conversation ended and the next began. Because of this, it took Bull almost an hour to find the first conversation and queue it up for the president.[37]

From late morning to early afternoon, the president listened to the conversations in the order in which Bull was able to locate them: starting with February 28, followed by three on March 1, and then the February 27 discussion.[38] When Nixon finished with these he took a brief break for cottage cheese and pineapple and told one of the EOB secretaries that he would be working late into the evening: "Be sure they know at the house." Bull told the president he would start queuing up reels for March outside the president's office on another machine, which would speed up the process. When the president learned that all of the March telephone conversations with me were on a single six-hour reel, he asked Bull to listen to that tape and make summary notes of it, as well as of the two conversations with me on March 14 and the one on March 15. The president told Bull he did not want to listen to the March 21 conversation, nor to the one on April 15 and the two on April 16, for he could still recall them.

Because the president eventually started wearing a headset, and some of his EOB exchanges with Bull are inaudible, it is not clear exactly which conversations he ultimately listened to and when, but it appears that during the afternoon of June 4 he proceeded through the following conversations with me: March 6, 7, 8, 13, 16 and 17. It appears that he assigned to Bull a number of my telephone conversationsand ignored the rest.* Nixon apparently decided to pass over any conversation where either Haldeman or Ehrlichman was present, even if only during part of the conversation, on the

---

*Because the president told Bull he was not interested in the April 15, 1973, conversation with me between 9:17 P.M. and 10:12 P.M., it was not learned until much later that this conversation was missing, if in fact at that time it was missing.

theory that they would refute anything I might claim that could present a potential problem for him, or he was continuing to stick to his line that as of March 21, he himself was running an investigation into Watergate, so any information he acquired was then information he later acted upon. Needless to say, because Nixon approached these recorded conversations with the assumption that only he—or possibly Haldeman—would ever learn of their content, not to mention their existence, he would use what he could of them to his advantage. In fact, he began doing so as he listened to them, using select material he heard to reassure Haig and Ziegler of his innocence, and to underscore that press reports of my knowledge of what we had discussed were greatly exaggerated or, more likely, a bluff on my part.

When the president called Haig at five o'clock, during one of his breaks from listening, he said, "This is the hardest work I've ever done in my life. I've really been at it for seven hours now, so [I'm going to] work the rest of the evening though. Just for my own satisfaction."[39] Haig asked how it was going, and Nixon reported, "I'll tell you this: Based on what I've seen so far, that it's a damn fraud, the whole thing"—referring to my knowing anything that would cause Nixon himself any problem. He continued, "But it may be something a little later, that, you know what I mean. I'm only up to the fifteenth of March." Nixon said there were several occasions on which I told him that no one in the White House was involved, "but nevertheless, we can't use this." Nixon added, "And he was talking about, ah, he threw in Strachan's name. This was about the thirteenth [of March]. But he didn't expand on it." He noted, "At the time it made no impression on me. I mean, it didn't even ring any bells, you know what I mean. But on the other hand, looking back, I suppose Dean could say I mentioned the fact that Gordon Strachan had some information or was involved." The president was unconcerned, however, for Haldeman could take care of it.

At 9:39 P.M. the president called Haig again, "I just spent nine hours on this crap, and boy, I got to go to bed."[40] But the effort had been worth it: "The whole damned Dean thing is a fraud. I can see where he may have been involved, but I wasn't involved. And I've listened to stuff till I'm sick." Nixon noted that he had obviously not listened to the four telephone calls with me that were not recorded, nor could he assign those to Steve Bull. They turned to other business, but the conversation ended with Haig reporting that Cox was "running a dogfight," seeking information, giving Buzhardt "an ultimatum today." "Isn't that great?" Nixon responded sarcastically. "But what Buzhardt said he's doing is posturing himself to quit. He's going to resign," Haig advised. That was fine by Nixon: "Okay, we got Richardson confirmed, so we'll just have Petersen do it."

Back at the residence, and with a drink in hand, Nixon called Haldeman shortly after ten o'clock.[41] "I thought you should know that starting at nine-thirty this morning, I have been working until just now. I listened to every tape," he said, exaggerating his undertaking. "You know, the thing that you did, and boy, I know the agony that you went through. And I listened to every damn thing, and Bob, the son of a bitch is bluffing." "Well, sure," Haldeman agreed.

Nixon told Haldeman, "Just for your private information," that Buzhardt had gone through my files and found no memoranda of conversations. The president further reported that he learned from listening to our conversations that I had not mentioned the $350,000 returned from the White House to the CRP until March 21. But he did give Haldeman a bit more of what he had discovered than what he had told Haig: "[Dean] did mention the Krogh thing"—referring to the Ellsberg break-in—"on about the seventeenth [of March], but only in passing, as if it weren't a big thing, or so forth." Nixon noted that I had said, however, that I did not believe anyone at the White House had advance knowledge of the Watergate break-in (as I later testified, and find remains accurate to this day). The president returned to his long hours of listening: "I did nothing else. Just damn near broke me down. But you know how tough it is to listen to that stuff." "Oh, it's nerve-racking," Haldeman said, and added, "and then, of course, I was trying to make notes, which you probably were, too." Nixon reported, "I made notes all the way through."

Nixon explained that he had not listened to March 21, "because I figured you ought to be the witness on that." He suggested that he had listened to March 22, but had made no notes on it, "figuring that you, Ehrlichman and I were there, you know, and you would make notes on that. Nixon noted as they spoke that "the stuff in the EOB doesn't come through." "Oh, really," Haldeman said, indicating he had not listened to any of the EOB tapes. They continued to discuss the conversations Nixon had listened to and the reason they could never be released, because of matters like his opinions of the members of the Supreme Court. After eight hours of listening to our conversations, Nixon now had a slightly revised view of me: "Some way or other I think his lawyer is the one that's moving out here. I don't think Dean, strangely enough, is—" "I think you're right," Haldeman interrupted. "I think his lawyer is out really [slandering]," Nixon began. "I mean, making flamboyant charges and so forth, and they won't stand up. But let's let him get out on a little limb, a little bit more." Nixon asked Haldeman to call Ziegler to tell him the good news, and had no sooner hung up than he had a further thought, and called Haldeman back: "Sorry to bother you again, but the one thing, which, of course, is a sticky point is with, regarding to the twenty-first, and if you'd give some thought with regard to how you would preempt that sometime, I think it would be very good." Haldeman agreed to do so, and said he had a couple of ideas, but did not have his notes at the moment.

## June 5, 1973, the White House

When speaking with Fred Buzhardt in his EOB office in the late afternoon, the president said that John Connally had advised him to stop talking about Watergate, and he planned to do so.[42] Buzhardt reported that in order to protect White House–related materials from subpoenas, Colson, Haldeman and Ehrlichman had returned them to him. The Colson material dealt with his dealings with the plumbers (for which he would have been indicted had he not made a deal with the Watergate special prosecutor). The Haldeman and Ehrlichman material consisted of "tapes of conversations with various people," but Buzhardt assured the president that none of them were with him.

## June 6, 1973, the White House

Still concerned about his conversation with Tom Pappas about raising money for the Watergate defendants, the president spoke with Rose Woods about the matter early on the morning of June 6.[43] She told him she had not yet been able to speak with Pappas, as he was in Greece, but she had left word with "his girl." Nixon explained the situation again, in language almost identical to that which he had used when first raising this problem, and then more pointedly told her, "I don't want to have anything indicating that I was thanking him for raising money for the Watergate defendants. I think he's smart enough to know that, but you know, you just never know."

Haig told the president that morning how delighted he was that former Republican congressman, and Nixon's first secretary of defense, Melvin

Laird, was joining the White House staff, an appointment Haig had been instrumental in bringing about.[44] Former senior congressional relations aide Bryce Harlow was also rejoining the Nixon White House. Laird was taking charge of domestic policy, Ehrlichman's operation, and Harlow was merely formalizing an informal relationship. Nixon also met with the new addition to his legal staff, Charles Alan Wright, whose consultancy was announced with the Laird and Harlow appointments that morning.[45]

During a discussion of Watergate with Haig, Buzhardt and Charles Wright about their assessments of where matters stood, Nixon did acknowledge that Haldeman and Ehrlichman had "collected money in the beginning for the defense attorney," although their "motives were proper, right?" When no one responded Nixon conceded: "I think what you might say, in fairness, maybe they were trying to see that nothing blew the election. That makes sense. But I don't think that it was obstruction of justice." Surely Wright understood what Nixon could not grasp: Obstruction is obstruction, regardless of motive. Buzhardt also reminded the group that Archibald Cox's charter, given to him by Attorney General Richardson, stated "that he'll have jurisdiction over all allegations against the president." To Buzhardt that was "about as stupid a thing as could be," for he told Nixon the courts did not have jurisdiction over him. Charles Wright had no comment.

When talking with Buzhardt that afternoon, Nixon learned that Buzhardt and Wright were going to visit with Cox and offered these instructions: "I want you to say, quite candidly, 'Mr. Cox, it's all over town that you're out to get the president. Now if that is the case, we want you to know we're ready to fight.'"[46] He told Buzhardt to "play a tough game." Late that afternoon of June 6, Buzhardt met with the president in his EOB office to report on his meeting with Cox.[47] It had not gone well, although Buzhardt characterized it as "civil." Buzhardt said that Cox had made it clear at the outset that "he would like to have access to all the documents" that might be relevant. Buzhardt said he told Cox, "He would not have access to the [president's] files." This matter was left unresolved, but Cox said he wanted a copy of the one-page memo prepared by Henry Petersen, which he believed "was a summary of the evidence that they had at that time against Haldeman and Ehrlichman." Nixon did not seem to have a problem with this information.

Buzhardt reported that Petersen had told Cox that Nixon had offered to let him listen to "a tape of a conversation with Dean that you had on the evening of Sunday, April the fifteenth" and added, "We did not comment on that." "I haven't got a tape," Nixon protested twice. "So it was a misunderstanding on his part?" Buzhardt asked. "I have—in fact, I haven't any notes on that," Nixon conceded, avoiding the question. He then falsely claimed that there was nothing in that conversation other than my telling Nixon that "Henry had given him grand jury reports. Now Henry vigorously denies, of course. I don't think it makes any difference." Buzhardt continued, saying that Cox wanted Haldeman and Ehrlichman's Dictabelts relating to these matters, but Nixon said there were none.* When Buzhardt reminded him that Ehrlichman had turned over his, Nixon said that since they had nothing to do with him, "I don't care about that." Cox also wanted a listing of all the president's meetings with me, Ehrlichman, Haldeman and Mitchell from June 17, 1972, on, which, Buzhardt said, would take a lot of time to prepare. Cox asked for a list of the president's meetings from the present back to March 15, 1973. Nixon incorrectly stated that he had not met with Ehrlichman since April 30, and had had approximately ten to fifteen meetings with Haldeman, adding, "But all on transition" and none of them relating to Watergate. When Cox asked for an inventory of Nixon's files, Buzhardt told him he did not think Cox had any jurisdiction to investigate the president. Buzhardt warned Nixon that he fully expected a head-on confrontation with Cox, who would serve them with a subpoena, but that Cox was assembling his research before sending it.

## June 7, 1973, the White House

When meeting with Haig in the morning, the president was still thinking about Cox, and he mentioned that they should start considering that "it may be in our interest to get him out of there" and let the Justice Department "go ahead."[48] Nixon had a lengthy late-afternoon conversation with Buzhardt, who said he was meeting with Henry Petersen the following day, news that prompted Nixon to say he thought he remembered telling Petersen he had "taped" his conversation with me on April 15, but he had misspoken: He had used a Dictabelt, which is what he must have meant when he mentioned it at the time.[49] Throughout this conversation Buzhardt asked a number of questions, but Nixon at best gave vague or inaccurate responses, sometimes

*Dictabelt recordings were made using an analog recording system. These belts were a thin vinyl plastic that fit over metal cylinders that rotated the belt with a stylus engraving the sound on the belt as it turned. See, e.g., www.dictabeltrerecord.com/about.htm.

clearly intentionally and at others because he apparently did not have the answer. Buzhardt, meanwhile, made a number of absurd statements, at one point claiming that Charlie Shaffer had told Jack Miller, the attorney who represented Dick Moore (and after he left office, Richard Nixon), and who Shaffer and I both spoke with, that I was "most worried about Richard Moore," despite the fact that I knew that Moore had a truly terrible memory. Even Nixon dismissed this notion, explaining, "The problem with Dick Moore, if I know him, I don't think he ever made any notes, and I don't know how good his memory is." Nonetheless, Buzhardt kept pushing this notion.*

As this conversation proceeded, Nixon brought up the Pappas situation, telling Buzhardt that, based on the March 21 conversation, he knew that I was aware that Pappas had raised money. After revealing that Pappas had raised that money for Mitchell but none of the actual facts explaining the situation, he asked: "Now that wouldn't make him guilty of anything, would it?" "No," Buzhardt said flatly. "Are you sure?" "Not unless he knew the money was to be used for political purposes, and he was part of the conspiracy," Buzhardt replied, which he felt would depend primarily on Mitchell's statement. "I will check on the Pappas thing and see what I can find out on that," Buzhardt said. He added that he thought "Silbert is probably going to wind up under investigation," regarding his handling of the case, along with Henry Petersen. Buzhardt believed that the special prosecutors were "methodically building a case that Silbert did not really investigate the case as thoroughly as other pending cases." Buzhardt had little confidence that they could make the case but said, "They'll probably smear him pretty bad."[†]

---

*Eventually Nixon, Buzhardt and associates would send Dick Moore to the Senate to impeach my testimony. Moore, accompanied by Jack Miller, appeared before the Senate Watergate committee on July 12, 13 and 14, 1973. After delivering his prepared statement, which really did not contest my facts but rather my interpretation of them, much of the cross-examination was handled by Terry Lenzner. Moore was such an awful witness—still suffering from the terrible memory problem Nixon had first noticed when he quizzed him—that Lenzner was accused in the press of taking unfair advantage of Moore, not to mention that Moore did make a poor showing, diluting his testimony. A *Washington Post* piece reported on Lenzner's cross-examination: "Moore was unable to respond in detail and began stammering slightly as he answered. At one point, asked by Lenzner about an apparent contradiction between an answer he had just given and one he had given earlier that afternoon in a closed-door session with the committee staff, Moore replied that "I'll let my answer stand—whichever it was." Peter A. Jay and John Hanrahan, "Moore: President Was Kept in Dark," *The Washington Post*, July 13, 1973, A-1.

[†]Buzhardt was correct on the fact that the special prosecutors would cast a doubting eye on the work of the U.S. Attorney's Office in its initial investigation, but no formal investigation was ever undertaken, and Earl Silbert certainly made clear when he was later nominated to be U.S. attorney for the District of Columbia that they had done the best possible investigation under the situation with which they were confronted. See U.S. Senate *Committee on the Judiciary*, "Nomination of Earl J. Silbert to be

## June 11, 1973, the White House

During a morning meeting with Haig, the president said he had read in his news summary that "Richardson had given Cox a broader reign. What in the world is that?"[50] "Oh, the ITT merger," Haig answered, and added, "Well, why the hell he did that, I don't know." Nixon, sounding beside himself at the prospect of digging up that old scandal, mused aloud, slowly enunciating each word: "What in the name of heaven made him do that?" He complained that Richardson had not cleared it with the White House. It was another potential scandal.[51]

Haig, ordered to find out what Richardson was up to and why, reported back a few hours later: "I had a good talk with Richardson, and he said that the charter that he gave Cox on the Hill included the mandate to clean up unresolved investigations." Haig continued, "Then he said, you know, 'I feel I can serve the president best by keeping a distance between the president and myself.' And I said, 'Elliot,' I said, 'not right now,'" and told him he could not show any lack of confidence in the president. "He's one fast-stepping smoothie," Haig observed, "and I'll be God damned if we have to put up with that crap." Nixon, still angry, agreed, and Haig reported that he and Richardson had had "a helluva shouting match."[52] The president's morning ended with Kissinger's complaining that Colson was continuing to drag him into the plumbers operation.[53] "Fuck it, he doesn't know," Nixon responded and then advised Kissinger, "They don't pay much attention to Colson, though, Henry."

In early afternoon Fred Buzhardt arrived at the EOB office for a Watergate update.[54] After reviewing the status of the Senate hearings and the order of witnesses—Stans, Magruder, Colson, Dean, Haldeman and Ehrlichman—Buzhardt explained how he was preparing for cross-examining me. Nixon surely understood, but said nothing, about the fact that Buzhardt was looking in all the wrong places: news summaries; my former deputy, Fred Fielding; documents to which I had access; and Dick Moore's information. Nixon noted that Soviet premier Leonid Brezhnev was arriving for the summit with Russia at precisely the likely time of my testimony. The Senate Watergate committee was already concerned about having my appearance conflict with

United States Attorney," *Hearings,* April 23–24 and 30, and June 26, 1974. Silbert served as U.S. attorney from 1974 to 1979.

the summit, Buzhardt said, and was waiting for the White House to request a delay. Nixon said he wanted Congress to make that decision. As this conversation was ending, Nixon, being facetious, said, "Don't worry me with anything I'm not suppose to worry about." "Absolutely," Buzhardt assured him. "I think the fellow's shooting blanks with regard to his insinuation that he had any tapes," Nixon said about my testimony. (In his memoir, which he wrote without transcriptions of all his tapes, Nixon wrote that he did not understand why this had concerned him.*) "Well," Buzhardt responded, a bit disconcerted by the situation, "I just don't think he has any tapes, at all." "We can live with them," Nixon noted. "But it's harder, isn't it?" "Yes, it is," Buzhardt conceded. "You get down to the point," the president said, "if it's his word against the president's, we'll kill him, right?" "I hope it never comes to that," Buzhardt answered. "No, it'd be a terrible thing," Nixon admitted.

Between a visit to his doctor's office and attending a meeting on price controls, the president told Haig in the Oval Office, "If [Richardson's] got any doubt about the president or whatever, then he should resign."[55] "That's a great idea," Haig said. "I mean, I can't have an attorney general who doesn't trust his boss," Nixon said, still smarting at Richardson's reopening of the ITT matter. While the president spent the afternoon in meetings, Haig talked to Elliot Richardson's top aide, since he and Richardson were now at the point of shouting at each other. Haig later reported on that conversation to Nixon, saying that they understand "that Elliot just made a hell of a mistake."[56] Haig did not think there would be future problems, for they had clearly gotten the message: "I said, 'For God's sake, this is the last time I'm going to be surprised.'" The president invited Haig to join him for dinner on the *Sequoia,* but Haig regretted that he couldn't, for he had invited Joe Alsop, a conservative columnist, to dinner and he explained that having postponed the meal twice, he dared not do so a third time: "[Alsop's] writing awfully good stuff, and I'd like to keep it that way."

Following his evening on the Potomac, which he spent with Ziegler, the president did some telephoning, speaking wih Buzhardt shortly after nine o'clock.[57] Buzhardt reported that he had spent the afternoon with Fred Thompson, who was "most cooperative" and "perfectly prepared to assist in really doing a cross-examination" of me when I testified before the Senate

---

*It appears he had by then forgotten that I had told Len Garment, after my April 15 meeting with the president, that recordings existed of one or more of my conversations with him. Years later Garment told me he had reported my comment to him to Haldeman and Nixon.

Watergate committee. Buzhardt also informed Nixon that Henry Petersen was "extremely upset about Cox coming in there and having such wide jurisdiction." He added, "His animosity with Cox, that's showing very firmly." Petersen had told Buzhardt that "I had never given him a hard time," but Ehrlichman had, "about subpoenaing Stans [before the grand jury] last summer." "I didn't know about that," Nixon falsely claimed, adding "But that's alright." Buzhardt added with a chuckle, "Oh, there's very perceptible animosity toward John Ehrlichman among the prosecutors and Cox. Comes through loud and clear. And I'd say, if they were focusing on one man, it would be John Ehrlichman. Much more so than Bob Haldeman. Or even Dean." "Good God!" Nixon replied. "Even Dean?" "They all believe that he was doing it at Ehrlichman's instruction," Buzhardt explained—and with time the overwhelming evidence would establish this fact beyond any reasonable doubt. But the president still believed it was a problem Ehrlichman could handle.

## June 12, 1973, the White House

After checking with Rose Woods on Pappas, whom she had still not been able to reach, the president dictated to her seven questions he wanted me asked during cross-examination.[58] Six of them concerned my relationship with Henry Petersen after the arrests at the Watergate and one related to Pat Gray.[59] The president then asked about the cash funds Woods had in her safe, which he had last checked on following our March 21 conversation. "I have to find a way to get that to the campaign committee," Nixon said, but confessed, "I don't know how it could be done." "You'd have to report it," Woods reminded him. Nixon did not care how she did so, but he just wanted her to get the money out of the White House.

It was a mixed morning of Watergate reports. Haig reported that the Senate was concerned about holding the Watergate hearings during the Brezhnev visit, which was encouraging, and based on his dinner the night before with Joe Alsop, Haig seemed encouraged he would continue "slicing [me] up reglarly." Haig assured the president, "And he's really done a hell of a job."[60] It was left to Ziegler to report the bad news: "Sirica has granted Dean immunity from prosecution, and I just talked with Buzhardt about this, and he feels Dean could possibly go on next week"—during the Brezhnev visit.[61] Fortunately, though, conservative columnist Jack Kilpatrick and others were "attacking Dean's credibility and his immunity." Nixon asked where they were getting material for their columns, and Ziegler said that was being done by Buzhardt. After listening to Ziegler's summary of the coverage in the news media, Nixon complained, "I just can't believe that the country is going to go with John Dean over the president of the United States." "No, they won't," Ziegler assured him.

The president called Buzhardt at 11:44 A.M. for a confirmation of Sirica's decision.[62] Buzhardt did not know whether Cox would appeal the judge's ruling and seek a stay, although Buzhardt explained that the judge really had no discretion in the matter, for when the Senate requested immunity, it was automatic. They discussed matters related to the publicity from the Senate hearings, and Buzhardt said they were debating readying Fred Thompson for my closed-door session with the Senate Watergate committee, which would precede my public testimony. Nixon agreed with Buzhardt that they best not prepare Thompson lest I get any indication in the closed session how they planned to impeach my testimony. Nixon told Buzhardt that he would be available on Thursday morning [June 14] to provide him with his recollection of our conversations.

A conversation with Haig later that morning included another assessment of the president's vulnerabilities.[63] Nixon expressed his doubts about Ehrlichman, but though he did not believe Ehrlichman would turn against him, he noted, "I feel for John [Ehrlichman], because I think that Dean may have reported more to him, and he may have implied more to him, than he's told me." This was a correct assessment. As for Mitchell, while he was fond of him personally, he was unconcerned, because he "had no contact with him whatever," which according to his official diary, was not really correct. Mitchell had joined him with others for a weekend get-together, and then on another occasion, a reunion at their former New York law firm. But saying he had no private time with Mitchell was true. As for Haldeman and Colson, they would both be "like a rock." Haig noted that the problems with the economy and the Brezhnev visit would help deflect from my testimony, and Nixon wanted to "play it up like hell" that the Senate was having me testify while Brezhnev was in the country. Both Haig and Nixon noted that Haldeman would follow me and challenge my testimony as it related to the president. Nixon instructed Haig to make certain they had a strong denial of whatever leaked out of the Senate Watergate committee from my closed-door visit with the committee on Saturday, June 16. "A good, tough statement," Nixon affirmed and suggested Pat Buchanan might draft it. Nixon began to propose cross-examination questions for me regarding my dealings with Petersen, and suggested they might start with these on Friday. The president said that he did not want the White House to deny specific charges I made but rather merely to respond with a flat-out denial of everything I said.

In the early afternoon of June 12 the president telephoned Buzhardt to see if he had received the cross-examination questions that the president had prepared for me; Buzhardt had and thought them an excellent line to pursue.[64] Nixon said that I would claim I could not report to the president because "he has a wall around him," so I reported to Haldeman and Ehrlichman instead. That, in essence, was true; it was not a good defense with respect to Pat Gray and Henry Petersen—hence Nixon's proposed questions about what I had told them. What Nixon did not understand, of course, is that I did not inform Gray and Petersen about the White House cover-up because I was then helping support it as best I could. Buzhardt encouraged the president's less than thoughtful questions, telling Nixon they "should be a very difficult line of questions for him."

Although Buzhardt did not have any further information regarding whether Cox might appeal the grant of immunity to me by the Senate, he was very anxious to get me under oath, so they did not have to guess about what I actually knew. Buzhardt said that while he had not reviewed all the material he planned to go through in preparing for my testimony, he was making good progress, including reconstructing the payments to the Watergate defendants. Nixon then began what was clearly a test of Buzhardt's knowledge: He said that when I had spoken with him on March 21, I had mentioned Tom Pappas, and the president now asked Buzhardt what that was all about. Buzhardt did not know, and instead mistakenly reported that all payments to the Watergate defendants had taken place long before I met with Nixon on March 21, in January 1972 or earlier. Nonetheless, Buzhardt insisted, "this is a very important factor."

Nixon asked if Buzhardt would be ready to meet to discuss the president's recollection of our meetings on Thursday [June 14], and Buzhardt said he would. "All I have are fragmentary notes," the president reported. "It turns out I have more than I realized," referring to notes that he in fact had created only eight days earlier, after listening to a number of our conversations. Buzhardt agreed that going over them together would be helpful, for the more precise their knowledge, the more effective their cross-examination of me would be. Nixon suggested that Buzhardt also consult with Ziegler about other questions I should be asked on cross-examination. Nixon then recapped his reconstructed version of the March 21 conversation.

Buzhardt also had discovered facts that would in time make a lie of Ehrlichman's claim that I had not told him about my meeting with Liddy on June 19, 1972, after the arrests at the Watergate, when Liddy confessed all. Buzhardt told the president, almost a year later, that I had learned about the Ellsberg break-in shortly after the arrests at the Watergate. Buzhardt said that that was the reason why I had sent my deputy, Fred Fielding, to Europe to find Kathleen Chenow, who had been the plumbers' secretary, so that she would not tell the FBI about their operations. The president responded that he didn't know about that, but he did not blame me, for that was a matter of national security. (It had, in fact, been Ehrlichman who had approved Fred Fielding's first-class flight to Europe to retrieve Chenow and to fly them both back to Washington; needless to say, he had been given the full story before he authorized the undertaking.) Nixon was disconcerted to learn I had, in fact, reported about Liddy's confession on June 19, 1972.

Later on that afternoon, while meeting with Haig, the president mentioned that Buzhardt's (erroneous) chronology indicated that payments to the defendants had ended in January, so Nixon now had doubts about my report to him in March that Hunt was demanding money.[65] He also discussed the letter he had recently received from John Ehrlichman, who had written to warn him that Len Garment was leaking information to the news media. But more important to Nixon was his observation: "You can tell from the tone of Ehrlichman's letter that he isn't about to hurt me. He would die first."

Just before six o'clock the president asked Rose Woods into the Oval Office.[66] By now she had finally spoken with Pappas, but apparently on the telephone, so she said nothing about his fund-raising for Mitchell. "Pappas told me Martha called him over in Greece," Woods reported. "Oh, boy," Nixon commented. Woods said she was going to call him back tomorrow, apparently to find out when he was coming to Washington. "God, I hope they don't get Pappas," Nixon said, and then added, "Well, they can't, all he did was raise money," and then speaking over Woods as she was talking, "It wasn't done for the purpose of hushing anybody up." "I didn't even mention it to him," Rose reported. "The only reason I raised it," Nixon said, "Dean mentioned his name to me, you know, that he was helping Mitchell with money for Hunt's lawyer, or something." He was unable to resolve this nagging problem.*

Later that night Nixon called Buzhardt, who had little new information.[67] He said I had refused to testify before the grand jury, taking the Fifth Amendment, and he thought that Magruder would lie before the Senate, for he was trying to get a reduced sentence by implicating anyone and everyone he could, but that he would not be a problem for the president. Nixon said he felt for Magruder, "A hotshot kind of guy with a great future." Nixon judged that Magruder and I were similar. Buzhardt (whom I had met only once, fleetingly, and spoken on the telephone with once or twice long before he came to the White Hous) disagreed: "Dean is not as aggressive as Magruder," he said. Rather I was "bland, seemingly very objective. He's not a flappable-type person." "He was cool," Nixon added. "His memory's not that good," Buzhardt reported (apparently based on my dealing with the prosecutors before I had made any effort to sort out dates and events). "He gets confused as to when things took place. And I think we'll be able to do pretty well on him." Buzhardt quickly added, "Maybe his memory will improve under oath. And maybe I'm misjudging him." This conversation continued with speculation about my testimony and who on the committee would be most helpful to the White House. They hoped they might persuade Democratic senator Herman Talmadge (D-GA) to help them with me. "Oh boy, Herman will kill him," Nixon noted, and asked, When would the White House "draw the sword on Dean?" Buzhardt said it would depend on the cross-examination: The plan was to have one or more columnists write about "my contradictions," even though I had yet to give any testimony or make any testimonial-related statement. But the plan seemed to satisfy Nixon.

The president's final Watergate conversation of June 12 was with Ziegler, who observed that the news media had built my Senate testimony to a crescendo, but what I could "say under oath is not much. I know that."[68] Ziegler noted, "He can't go into the Oval Office in any legitimate way. And if he attempts to do it, he could end up with twenty years" in prison. Nixon gave Ziegler his take on my likely testimony: "Here is a man with an incentive to lie. Here is a man who has given five different stories on this. And here

---

*When I testified before the Senate Watergate committee, I had forgotten about Pappas, and indeed, his name was never mentioned during their inquiry. Ironically it was Nixon himself who surfaced Pappas, when he later produced the tape recording of our March 21, 1972, conversation. Pappas would be investigated by the Watergate Special Prosecution Force, and while they found he had violated the law, no prosecution was pursued. However, they did not have access to the information set forth in this book.

is a man who is lying about the president. Here is a man who had the responsibility and never told the president for ten months." Whatever my testimony turned out to be, Nixon instructed Ziegler: "It doesn't make any difference. Deny it. Do you understand? Deny everything, because he is lying."

## June 13, 1973, the White House

During his Oval Office meeting that morning with Ziegler and Haig, Nixon asked where Ehrlichman could be getting his information that Garment was leaking heavily to the press.[69] Ziegler replied that there was no evidence to support that accusation, and then defended Garment as one of the president's staunchest defenders. Haig did not disagree. Rather than wait until Thursday, the president met with Buzhardt in his EOB office from 11:45 A.M. until 1:29 P.M. to go over his notes on his conversations with me.[70]

Buzhardt said he was going "day by day" through all the president's meetings with me, gathering what information he could from Haldeman and Ehrlichman. This prompted the president to request his briefcase. "It's over at the Oval Office," he instructed a secretary on the telephone. "I've got some notes there," he advised Buzhardt. But when the notes arrrived they did little to trigger the president's memory of our meeting. Rather Nixon walked Buzhardt through his meetings with me, giving him a bare minimum of information. "I don't think I should brief you on all my notes," Nixon explained. "If you go down the wrong track, I should tell you." In effect, the president wanted Buzhardt to tell him what had occurred in our meetings. When that proved unworkable, the president skimmed through the meetings, plucking out occasional statements by me that were consistent with his defense and dismissing matters or spinning them when they conflicted.

When Buzhardt mentioned that Watergate special prosecutor Cox had again requested to hear "a tape of the conversation with Dean" on April 15, which Nixon had mentioned to Petersen, Nixon said that was "a misunderstanding," and explained awkwardly, "what I'm referrng to is that I know I didn't tape. What I'm referring to is that I didn't dictate at the end of the day my recollection, but I was not going to turn that over." Buzhardt reported Cox wanted an inventory of the White House files. "No, sir," the president said without thought. Upon learning that Cox was also seeking tape recordings Ehrlichman made of his conversations, Nixon firmly braced his Watergate counsel: "Well, let me say this. I have no tapes of your very confidential information. Apparently, there are some telephone tapes," he noted vaguely, and added, "but all of them remain in the Oval Office." Nixon declared there were no tapes, but whatever tapes had been made, "I didn't ask for them myself, you understand that?" "Yes," Buzhardt said, reassuringly. After finishing with Buzhardt, the president called Haig.[71] "Well, you know, it's an interesting thing," Nixon said. "At least this week, we're talking about what we're doing, rather than worrying about what they're doing." "Exactly," Haig confirmed. "We're worrying a bit, but not too much. Because what the dickens, they are going to crack us, and that's that," the president observed. Nixon reported that he had just told Buzhardt, "Now be sure that Dean's lawyers [understand] that he better watch his step, because we are, ah, every meeting he was in, we have the record. That's the important thing, that they know that." (No such message was ever relayed to me or my attorneys.)

Nixon requested Ziegler come to his EOB office later that afternoon, and he was given an update on the Senate Watergate committee proceedings.[72] Ziegler liked Senator Edward Gurney's (R-FL) aggressive behavior. Nixon, who seemed to like his new counsel, also noted that "Buzhardt's a real hothead."

Following a sixteen-minute speech to the nation from the Oval Office on the sputtering economy, the president returned to the residence shortly before nine o'clock, where he had dinner in the Lincoln Sitting Room while taking a steady stream of congratulatory telephone calls. At 9:41 P.M. Chuck Colson checked in to lavish praise on the speech and to report how delighted Colson's clients—specifically, the Teamsters union—were with his remarks.[73] Not surprisingly the conversation soon turned to Watergate, when the president said he understood that "Stans had been a good witness." Colson said he had been "superb," but Nixon hastened to add, "I don't watch this crap." Colson liked the fact that Gurney was "really tough" and noted that the *Evening Star* newspaper "had a big piece that Dean and I are now pitted against each other." Nixon moved past this and noted that "apparently Cox has decided not to give him transactional immunity." Colson confirmed that: "Remember, I mentioned to you Sunday, the prosecutors hate his guts." Nixon counseled Colson that he probably did not want to be pitted against me, but Colson said it didn't matter. Nixon assured Colson, "I'm not going to let this little pip-squeak knock you down." "But you pass this way once in this world," Colson said, "and my great satisfaction is seeing what you're doing for the country, and that's all I really care about. This thing with Dean, I've met him head-on."

Concerned I would say "terrible things" when I went before the committee on Friday, Nixon reported, "We've got to be prepared. I've got Buzhardt and all prepared to put out a brief one-sentence disclaimer, but that's about all we're going to do. I don't think the president ought to get in a fight with John Dean. What do you think?" "Absolutely, that'd be the worst thing you could do," Colson agreed. He wanted me "out there all by himself" in making accusations about the president. "And when even *Newsweek* labels him as a turncoat, then you know he's in trouble." Colson said I was getting terrible press, with even the *Star* photo editor featuring a photo that made me "look a little deceitful" and *Newsweek* painting me with "the boy-from-prep-school routine." They agreed this was appropriate. "But he deceived a lot of people," Colson claimed, and Nixon echoed, "But he deceived all of us."

Nixon soon added, "Incidentally, I have not been pleased with Richardson. Not at all," and was particularly annoyed that Richardson had publicly said Nixon should get his own lawyer: "He either shapes up, he's either the attorney general for the president of the United States or he's out." Nixon added, "And I'd put him out damn fast, too," explaining, "We don't owe him a damned thing." When Colson, who knew Richardson from Massachusetts politics, said that he found him to be a "tough politician," Nixon explained how Haig was having to raise hell with Richardson, and noted, "We really rolled him on one thing. You know he violently opposed the appointment of our FBI guy [Clarence Kelly]. Violently." Nixon said Richardson wanted "a Harvard or some Ivy League dean or criminologist. And I turned him down, and so we got this nice cop."

This call ended shortly before ten o'clock, but no sooner did they hang up than they were back on the line for more, for Nixon loved talking to Colson. "This business of attacking the president has got to stop," he said. "As far as the press corps, they can go to hell."[74] Colson assured Nixon that "the great silent majority see right through them." "We've been on the defensive for two months," Nixon began, and then realized it was "because, basically, you see, they were right, in a sense. There was a cover-up, let's face it. But on the other hand, they have built up the first crime and the cover-up to unbelievable things." Citing the departures of Krogh, Haldeman, Ehrlichman and Gray, Nixon did not like the media's characterization of Watergate as "the greatest, you know, corruption in history. That's baloney."

*June 14, 1973, the White House*

Nixon rarely met with his vice president, Spiro Agnew, or included him in anything other than cabinet sessions, but Agnew did join the end of a meeting that morning in the Oval Office with Haig and Ziegler.[75] When Agnew arrived, the conversation had turned to the latest Gallup public opinion poll, which indicated that 44 percent of the American people felt the Watergate matter was important. Ziegler recommended that when I was before the committee the following week, the White House should state that the president was "working on the Brezhnev thing" and would have no comments until I had completed all my testimony. The president solicited Agnew's views, but the vice president soon moved on to another matter, a personal problem he was facing, noting, "What I'm going to tell you about now is something entirely different, to show you the lynch mob psychology that exits over there," in Maryland, where he had served as governor before becoming vice president. Agnew continued, "Now this thing they're calling another Watergate, and this, Mr. President, is the most ridiculous thing I've ever seen." Vaguely the vice president mentioned that "accusations" had been leveled against him, but "nothing that'll stick." And soon the conversation moved on.*

When Agnew and Nixon were alone, Agnew expressed his concern: He had hired Chuck Colson's law firm to represent him, so he wondered if Colson was going to be drawn into Watergate. Nixon thought not and counseled Agnew that if he was happy with the attorney in the firm he should stay with him. Agnew tried to convince Nixon that "what they're really after, Mr. President, they're trying to get both of us at the same time, and get [Speaker of the House] Carl Albert in as the president." "Oh, God," Nixon exclaimed, more in disbelief than concern, which provoked a nervous laugh from Agnew, who insisted, "That's what they're really after."

Late that afternoon the president called Haldeman, from whom he felt he was getting a better read on developments than he could obtain from his staff, and given the information Haldeman was providing, that was undoubtedly true.[76] Haldeman first mentioned that he had talked to Hobart Lewis, the CEO and editor in chief at *Reader's Digest*, as well as a longtime Nixon friend. Nixon had suggested that Haldeman speak to Lewis about funding an undertaking that would allow Haldeman and Ehrlichman to

---

*Only four months later, on October 10, 1973, Agnew resigned.

work for the Nixon Foundation, as well as develop material for publication by Lewis. But Lewis indicated that he had some problems and wanted to speak with Nixon, who said that he would be happy to meet with him after Brezhnev departed. Nixon was most interested in Magruder's testimony that day before the Senate Watergate committee. Magruder had been "lobbing some very rough stuff," Haldeman told him. "He's totally wiped Mitchell out, and he's totally wiped Gordon Strachan out, which is going to be tough to deal with. And it's kind of interesting, because he's covered stuff with Strachan, if it's true, that I had absolutely no knowledge of." Nixon was not surprised. Haldeman reported that Magruder testified that he had discussed the cover-up in January with Haldeman, who disputed that account, saying he had discussed a job for Magruder that month. (Needless to say, Haldeman's conversations with the president reveal that Magruder and Haldeman discussed the cover-up, but unless the specific terms "cover-up" or "obstruction of justice" were used, Haldeman did not consider his actions to be part of a concealment effort.) Haldeman noted that Magruder had absolved me of "preknowledge" but did involve me in the cover-up and in his perjury. He had not involved the president or Ehrlichman, and only indirectly Haldeman. Nixon asked about Ervin, who Haldeman described as "a real jackass, just awful." Nixon asked, "Preening himself?" "Preening himself," Haldeman confirmed.

Late that afternoon Buzhardt brought Nixon up to date in his EOB office, with several discouraging developments.[77] Strachan had requested immunity from the Senate Watergate committee, Buzhardt said, and "they've apparently agreed to give it to him." Buzhardt said that Strachan would "testify that Bob knew about the whole cover-up," for Strachan had told him about it a week after the break-in. Buzhardt said that that information was already running on the news wires.

Buzhardt, however, had additional unwelcome news, which was still inside information: The memo in which Ehrlichman had approved the operation to obtain Ellsberg's psychiatric records had surfaced, as had the fact that Ehrlichman had attempted to remove it from the files but David Young had anticipated this and kept a copy. "So John's got a real problem," Buzhardt reported. "In view of Young's testimony, he's going to have a rough time." Buzhardt said Krogh had also been recalled to the grand jury, since he had tried to assume full responsibility, which was now disproved by Ehrlichman's memorandum. "[Krogh] didn't know it was there," Buzhardt explained.

Buzhardt also reported that I had told Dash and Thompson that afternoon that I had mentioned to the president on two occasions that the Democrats' "civil lawsuit would be taken care of, because one of the attorneys could fix it with the judge, Judge Richey." Nixon, acting flabbergasted, denied that I had ever discussed the matter with him, protesting, "Richey is a decent man, for crying out loud. He said he told me about the civil suit?" Nixon asked several times. "He told you that the civil suit was being fixed until after the elections," Buzhardt reported, and reminded Nixon that I had only seen the president once, on September 15, before the election. Nixon asked if Buzhardt had checked with Haldeman; he had, but Haldeman had no notes of the September 15 meeting regarding me. "[Dean] said that the man who said he would fix Richey was Roemer McPhee," Buzhardt added. Nixon, who knew McPhee from the Eisenhower administration, said he would deny it. When Ziegler joined the conversation, Nixon told him that "Strachan is going to take immunity and dump on Bob. That I just can't believe. I just can't believe it. He said that was on the wire." The president also told Ziegler what he had learned from Haldeman about Magruder's testimony. All this was discussed at length, but no conclusions were reached.

"The prosecutors never believed Dean had anything on you," Buzhardt reported, which led to a remarkable exchange. "Really? How do you know that?" Nixon asked. "They [referring to what would have to have been Earl Silbert, Sy Glanzer and Don Campbell] told me so," Buzhardt replied. "He doesn't?" the president said hopefully. "I told you, he isn't going to talk, okay?" Buzhardt said. "He might have to," Nixon countered. "He won't," Buzhardt insisted flatly. "But what did they say?" Nixon asked, wanting specifics. "They said he just has never come up with anything to implicate the president. And they think Dean was really a key figure in the whole operation, and they want to get the key figures and put them behind bars." If the prosecutors did give Buzhardt this information, they failed to mention that we in fact had never discussed the president; at the time I was dealing with them, I had still not discussed the president with my own attorney. Just as Buzhardt had earlier misinformed the president about the payments to the Watergate defendants ending in January, he was now giving the president a remarkably inaccurate reading of the situation.

This one-hour-and-forty-five-minute conversation rambled along with no resolution, although Nixon did finally have a recommendation: "Incidentally, I think you should start to call Dean a confessed criminal," to which Buzhardt replied, "You know, that's what I'm thinking."

## June 15, 1973, the White House

At ten o'clock the president was aboard Air Force One heading, accompanied by the congressional leadership, for a dedication of the Dirksen Congressional Leadership Research Center in Peoria, Illinois, an event honoring the late Republican minority leader Senator Everett Dirksen. On returning to the capital he prepared to leave for Key Biscayne but before departing met with Ziegler in the Oval Office.[78] Ziegler reported that a private White House poll showed that the economy was the number-one concern of Americans, outranking Watergate by 4 to 1. Gallup's latest poll, meanwhile, indicated that 45 percent of the country thought that "Watergate has been overcovered." Ziegler was also pleased that the columnists Evans and Novak had written another negative piece about me, and Murray Kempton had done a negative radio piece on *CBS Spectrum* on me as well. Al Haig was the next visitor to the Oval Office, and the president told him he was expecting the worst from me when I appeared for the closed session with the Senate committee later that day.[79] As opposed to Magruder's testimony, Nixon told Haig, "You understand the Dean stuff will be rough, and our boys must not panic. I don't think they will." Based on Ziegler's report, Nixon felt there was "a little sense of the balance back." Haig reported that the Senate was feeling the pressure of hearing my testimony during the Brezhnev visit, but nothing had been decided.

## June 18–19, 1973, the White House

On Saturday, June 16, I had attended an executive session of the Senate Watergate committee. It was after that session I learned that the Senate leadership, both majority leader Mansfield and minority leader Scott, would request that the Watergate hearings be suspended for a week during the visit of Soviet leader Leonid Brezhnev, postponing my appearance. While I had written my opening statement, and was prepared to give it to the committee on Sunday, June 17, as originally planned, I learned that the Republicans on the Watergate committee had leaked information I had revealed during the executive session. I told Shaffer that I had no intention of giving them a week to attack my testimony without my having any ability to defend it. While I was breaking the rules of the Senate Watergate committee requiring advanced submission of my testimony, they had broken their rules as well in leaking, so Shaffer notified Sam Dash of my position on Monday, June 18. I would bring my prepared statement with me when I returned to the Senate on Monday, June 25, to testify, but no earlier.

Nixon had returned to the White House late on Sunday night, and the White House was having its own expected problems on Monday morning, when *The Washington Post* ran a banner headline story: NIXON EXPECTED TO ALTER STANCE, ABANDON AIDES. The opening paragraph of Woodward and Bernstein's story reported, "President Nixon is expected to defend himself against increasing allegations of his involvement in the Watergate cover-up by saying he was misled by his former principal deputies, H. R. Haldeman and John D. Ehrlichman, according to White House and other government sources."[80] The story claimed the change in strategy was to counter charges I would make about the president and his aides.

Because Brezhnev was arriving on the South Grounds at eleven o'clock, it would be a rushed morning for Nixon. The president and Haig briefly discussed the schedule for the Brezhnev visit and accompanying Soviet summit, the kind of event that Nixon planned down to the smallest detail.[81] But Haig, believing it more important to discuss the problem created by the *Post* story, said, "We had a vicious, unbelievably vicious story in the *Post* this morning that you were shifting your strategy away from support of Bob and John." "Rubbish. Unbelievable," Nixon exclaimed. "It's just blatant political warfare now. I called Fred and told him to get in touch with Wilson immediately and tell them this was absolutely untrue, and there is just nothing to support it, in any way." Nixon had seen the story and wanted to know where it originated, noting that "White House sources had said Strachan tied ropes around Haldeman's neck. Well, I don't know, I mean, they could have made that up, about a high-ranking White House source. Are we sure Garment isn't talking to anybody?" Nixon asked. "I called Len personally," Haig answered, and reported that Garment said he had not seen Woodward or Bernstein in three weeks. As the president pressed, Haig responded, "The only other person it could be, and I'm checking now, is [David] Gergen, who's close to Woodward. And if it's Gergen, I'll just fire his ass." That was fine with Nixon, who noted of Gergen, "He's not much, anyway." Haig reported that Buzhardt was outraged by the leak and doing his best to repair the problem with Haldeman and Ehrlichman. Haig came back to Gergen and said he would find out if he had been talking to Woodward, for he did not think a speechwriter had any business talking about Watergate. "I'll fire his ass. I don't think he's worth a damn anyhow," Haig added.

As they proceeded to revisit many familiar Watergate issues relating to my testimony, Nixon said the only matter that concerned him was the conversation on March 21 about the million dollars to pay the Watergate defendants. "Al, basically what Buzhardt and the other boys have got to realize, when I learned the consequences of the million dollars, I said, that's when I started my own investigation. I said, get Mitchell's ass down here with the others. That was what triggered it." Nixon said. Then the president turned to my appearance on Saturday before the Senate Watergate committee staff (after starting the session, Senator Baker had departed). "Buzhardt says Dean was not particularly effective the first day," Nixon noted, to which Haig added, "That's right, he was rambling, and there were absolutely no surprises of any kind." Haig said, for that reason, Buzhardt felt very confident that he could handle the situation. (In fact, the Watergate committee staff could not know anything about my forthcoming testimony based on my closed-door session with them. As an experienced former congressional aide, this was a game I knew how to play well.)

When Ziegler arrived in the Oval Office, at 10:14 A.M., he reported that former Nixon speechwriter William Safire, who had become an op-ed columnist at the *New York Times*, had done "the most scathing, cutting, ripping, shredding piece on Dean," which he had entitled "Gunga Dean."[82] But soon this conversation was drowned out by the U.S. Marine Band playing on the South Grounds to mark the arrival of Brezhnev. Not until later that afternoon did the conversations resume, with Haig present and Nixon inquiring if Ziegler had identified the source of the leak for that morning's *Post* story.[83] Ziegler had not spoken to Gergen, for his wife had just had a baby and he was not in, but having further analyzed the story, Ziegler did not think it had come from Gergen, because "it was written in lawyer's language." (Haig was unaware Gergen had attended law school.) Nor did Haig think Garment was the source. The president expressed concern about Fred Thompson's cross-examining me, but Haig said Buzhardt was confident: "Fred's usual explanation is to paint a gloomy picture so it comes out a shade better than he painted. I've worked with him, and I know he's essentially a pessimist, but he's not at this time. He's more optimistic than I'd be. I expect this to be a tough period for us." "But it will be," the president insisted. Haig clarified that his point had been that Buzhardt would be ready for whatever happened. When Nixon asked if they had the crisp, clean denial statement he had requested, Haig assured him it was ready.

At 4:20 P.M. the president called Haig about the fact that the Watergate hearings had been postponed.[84] "Can't we get these hearings put on again, or what's the score? What happened there?" Haig had just received this information from Timmons and had not yet spoken with Buzhardt. Nixon wanted the hearings to proceed, notwithstanding the summit meeting, and thought that halting them was stupid, as were minority leader Hugh Scott and "that poor darned fellow from Tennessee, Baker." Nixon did not like the fact that Baker had been "on my back every minute taking pictures" on the trip the previous day. "He was unbelievable, unbelievable," Nixon complained. Less than a half hour later, after thinking further about the canceled proceedings, Nixon called Haig.[85] First, he wanted someone to get a copy of my statement to the committee. "They've got to have it," Nixon insisted. "The *Post* has got it, or somebody now. Put Gergen on it, if he can tear himself away from his baby long enough." As they spoke, Nixon added, "We ought to make something out of this at the committee," referring to the postponement. "You see, the thing that I'm concerned about is that they're going to let this God damned thing hang over us, and build it up for a week, in order to poison the summit. That's what they're trying to do here, don't you agree?" "Uh, yes," Haig answered noncommittally, as Nixon continued: "Well, somebody ought to say that they backed down, and that, God damn it, the White House didn't ask them to. You know, try to get our little boys together and see if they can think of something, will you?"

Late that afternoon the president met with Buzhardt, who in his campaign to discredit me, had picked up information I had given the Senate Watergate committee: I had used cash in my safe for personal expenses, putting in a personal check to cover the withdrawal.[86] Although I had fully reimbursed the fund* and placed it all in a trust account, Buzhardt was going to try to portray me as a thief as well as a liar.[87] (Ironically, Senator Edward Gurney—who was later indicted but not convicted for bribery, perjury and conspiracy—attempted to create such an impression as well when cross-

---

*This was cash that had been given to me by Gordon Strachan and Colson's aide Dick Howard. They did not know its owner, and they were concerned, because it was apparently left over from larger expenditures that had been made contrary to the campaign finance laws. It was all extremely vague. Indeed, it would take litigation to determine to whom the fund should be given, and it ultimately went to the CRP.

examining me during the hearings, actually giving me a chance to explain my action, which was foolish and expedient but certainly not illicit.[88]) That evening, before heading to his state dinner with Brezhnev, Nixon discussed with Haig and Ziegler in general how to handle my testimony.[89] The debate was whether to fully engage me, or as the president felt, "We should just be enigmatic about it." It came down to the president's instinct: "So I just think that just the one sentence [a general rebuttal] is the thing to do," Nixon said to end the discussion.

The unrelenting White House attacks on me were beginning to have an impact. As Ziegler explained during this conversation, "The discrediting of Dean is taking place below the surface at this point, and I oftentimes think that is the best way." The "kill the son of a bitch" attitude that Nixon and his team fostered, and shared with both friendly and unfriendly reporters, was soon picked up by Nixon supporters, who acted on it. Sam Dash began receiving a steady stream of threats against me, and the first one that appeared serious got his attention: a simple note printed in large block letters, sent anonymously, that read: "JOHN DEAN WILL NEVER BE A WITNESS. HE WILL BE DEAD."[90] Years later Dash told me that this was only the tip of the iceberg, for he received literally hundreds of such threats. After discussing the matter with Senator Ervin, who knew the Capitol Police did not have the capability to protect a witness, he called Cox, who was part of the Justice Department, which had such a program. After Cox conferred with his staff they strongly recommended that I enter the U.S. Marshals' witness protection program: Two U.S. marshals would be posted at our home; others would keep it under surveillance; and two marshals would accompany me on all travels outside my home. After discussing it with Dash, Shaffer strongly urged me to take part in the program. I discussed the matter with my wife, we accepted the offer, and I would remain in the program for slightly more than a year and a half, as the death threats continued until Nixon departed the White House.

In an aside during a summit discussion on June 19 in the Oval Office, Kissinger told the president that he had known Cox at Harvard, and he warned Nixon that "Cox will come after you, I don't doubt it."[91] Kissinger described Cox as "a fanatic liberal Democrat, and all his associates are fanatics." He was critical of Richardson for selecting Cox when he could have found someone who had "a natural interest in us." Cox was on the mind of everyone in the White House, because the front page of that morning's

*Washington Post* had reported, "Special prosecutor Archibald Cox said yesterday that he is studying whether President Nixon can be subpoenaed to testify before the Watergate grand jury here."[92] As the president told Haig and Buzhardt in his next Oval Office meeting, "One thing I noted this morning was that fucking, shocking statement by Cox." Nixon said he was trying to get someone on the Hill to challenge Cox's statement, and suggested to Buzhardt, "Maybe you can write a brief little rejoinder there."[93]

Buzhardt replied (incorrectly, as time would tell) that Cox "knows he can't subpoena the president. He knows he can't indict the president. But he is going to play this game quite the opposite." He also noted that Cox had said "he had made no decision on whether to get into the San Clemente property thing or the gifts," and added, "I'm going to talk to Elliot Richardson." "What does 'the gifts' mean?" Nixon asked, indicating he had not read the full story of the Cox press conference, in which Cox had said "he has not decided whether he will investigate the federal funding of improvements to President Nixon's San Clemente, Calif., home, or the more than $200,000 in tax write-offs that Mr. Nixon built up in 1969 with a gift to the government of his pre-presidential papers." When Buzhardt mentioned Nixon's papers, the president knew exactly what he was talking about and reacted accordingly: "God Almighty." While Buzhardt did not think Cox had jurisdiction, Nixon was complaining: "The San Clemente property, what the hell is he getting into that for? What's Elliot done? What the hell has Elliot done here?" (All these matters would later be investigated by either the special prosecutor or the Congress.)

Buzhardt explained how the committee had voted 6 to 1 to postpone the hearings when it received a letter so requesting from Mansfield and Scott, and he assured the president he should not be concerned by the delay; they would use it to good purpose. Buzhardt was convinced I would be a weak witness, saying, "He is going to be in conflict with every witness practically that's testified, that's been involved," and he added, "Mr. President, he can't go through this whole place and tell a legitimate story and have it stand up under all circumstances. He doesn't know enough, and he doesn't remember enough. He can't put it all together."

Later on the morning of June 19, the president spoke with Haig about the growing problem with Elliot Richardson.[94] Haig said that Richardson had himself grown concerned about Cox—Richardson had not liked the matter about a subpoena for the president to testify, which he thought Cox had taken out of context—and was going to review his charter with him. Haig said that he, too, had also asked for an appointment with Cox to discuss all this with him. "Well, good enough," Nixon said. "I guess we shouldn't get our balls in an uproar about him."

### June 20–21, 1973, Camp David

On Wednesday and Thursday, June 20 and 21, Nixon was preoccupied with the Soviet summit, entertaining Brezhnev, traveling from the White House to Blair House to the State Department to the *Sequoia* and on to Camp David, and he had only fleeting conversations about Watergate. During a morning call Haig reported that I was furious at the committee for having leaked information I had given them in the closed testimony session, and I was now refusing to talk to them.[95] Haig said apparently the IRS investigationof Larry O'Brien had come up during my testimony, which Buzhardt had confirmed. "Don't be concerned about it," Nixon told him.

The weeklong postponement proved to be a significant opportunity for me. My written opening statement ran over sixty thousand words. I had never considered having to read the entire statement, and had I known I would be asked to do so, I would have written something closer to six thousand words. But I knew the committee was not aware of either the information I had or my understanding of what had occurred. Because this was not a criminal proceeding, but rather a legislative hearing, I assumed the committee would want to know how these abuses had occurred and why. Rather than simply testify about what had happened I thought I should place it in context. Contrary to Buzhardt's assumption—and as the president and Haldeman were aware from my March 21 conversation—I had very good recall, but I also fully appreciated that it was my word against that of Magruder, Colson, Ehrlichman, Mitchell, Haldeman and Nixon. Magruder was easy to refute, given that he was hopelessly confused, had told so many different versions of his accounts and was so clearly eager to drag others down. But by the time I was writing my testimony, I knew that the others were prepared to lie, if necessary.

In drafting my testimony I had scrupulously avoided speculating about what others knew and restricted myself to what they themselves had told me of their activity. For example, when Magruder told me that he went to Florida at the end of March 1972 to get Mitchell's approval for Liddy's plans, I did not take this as confirmation of Mitchell's actions, but only of Magruder's. In short, I sought to avoid hearsay. I did, however, have a recurring temptation, when writing my testimony, to include one matter that I did not know for a fact but thought a highly reasonable assumption, based on what I had been told, as well as on firsthand experience: I had been recorded by Nixon in one if not more conversations. I had suggested as much to Len Garment in April to make them worry that "I knew," even though it was actually "I suspected." I decided, therefore, to add a small insert near the end of my testimony. My thinking was that, if I intimated that I believed at least one and perhaps more of my conversations had been recorded, it was unlikely I would opt to lie about the content of them. More important, if I had indeed been taped, the Senate would have no problem in determining the truth. So I had the following statement typed up and inserted, and when cross-examined on this matter I elaborated further about why I believed I had been recorded:

> On Monday night, April 16, I had learned that the President had informed the Government that he allegedly had taped a conversation in which I had told him I was seeking immunity from the Government in exchange for testimony on Haldeman and Ehrlichman. I have no recollection of ever telling the President that I was so negotiating with the Government, and the President told me very specifically that he did not want to do anything to interfere with any negotiations I was having with the Government.
>
> When I learned this from my attorney, I suggested that he request that the Government call for the tape and listen to the tape, because I told him it must be a reference to the meeting I had with the President on April 15, and if that conversation were taped, the Government would have a pretty good idea of the dimensions of the case they were dealing with. I was referring to the fact that the President had mentioned the million-dollar conversation and the fact that he had talked to Colson about clemency for Hunt. I do not in fact know if such a tape exists, but if it does exist, and has not been tampered with, and is a complete transcript of the entire conversation that took place in the President's office, I think that this committee should have that tape, because I believe that it would corroborate many of the things that this committee has asked me to testify about.[96]

It was also during this period, Sam Dash later wrote, that Buzhardt sent to the Senate Watergate committee via Fred Thompson a typed copy of what he called "Fred Buzhardt's reconstruction of Dean's meeting with the President Nixon."[97] Buzhardt had walked Thompson through the information Nixon had given him, if not his notes, but since Buzhardt did not know that it had been drawn from recorded conversations, he merely told Thompson that he had obtained the information, without disclosing its source.* Since it had not come from me, it had obviously originated with Nixon. The White House, meanwhile, had also leaked this document to the press, claiming this "authentic" account of the meeting revealed that I had misled Nixon by never warning him of his culpability. Dash, based on his knowledge of my testimony from our secret meetings, knew this was false, and Dash's staff was struck by how much this information corroborated my testimony. Dash noted that while the material was close to the content the tapes would later reveal, it was always falsely twisted to put me at fault, though that fact would not be established until much later. This document also caused several Dash staffers to wonder precisely how the information it contained had been reconstructed.

## June 22–July 9, 1973, the Western White House

After a signing ceremony for the agreement reached with Brezhnev, the president took his guest to California, giving him a tour of the plane before retreating to his office to work, but visiting again with him as they flew over the Grand Canyon en route. With no recording equipment at the San Clemente offices, nor a Haldeman or Ehrlichman taking notes (Haig took few, and Ziegler less), we have only Nixon's later report of these nineteen days on the West Coast, during which I testified publicly.

The daily briefing of the press office provided no information about Nixon's reaction to my testimony. Ziegler told the press while I was testifying on Monday, June 25, before the Senate Watergate committee: "We do not plan to have any comment on the Ervin Committee hearings as the week proceeds from the White House."[98] Ziegler further explained that the president was following the hearings "much as he did in the past. He will receive a report from his staff," principally Ziegler and Haig.

---

*Buzhardt would not learn of the taping system until June 25, the first day of my testimony, when Nixon was in California and asked him to listen to one of our conversations. See Appendix B.

Much to my surprise, the committee insisted I read my entire written statement, which I had planned merely to submit for the record and then answer their specific questions. My account, which began with a description of the atmosphere out of which Watergate had grown, would take an entire day to read, from shortly after 10:00 A.M. until a lunch break at 12:30 P.M., resuming at 2:00 P.M. until shortly after 6:00 P.M., with three brief recesses while members of the committee went to the Senate floor to vote (approximately twenty-five minutes total). I was even more surprised when the committee spent four days cross-examining me while all three television networks—ABC, CBS and NBC—carried my entire appearance live (approximately thirty hours) and PBS rebroadcast the hearings every night.*

In his memoir Nixon noted that it took me a day to read my opening statement which, the president stated, "contained most of [the] charges against me." Nixon said that, while he had not watched the hearings, the reports of my testimony filled him "with frustration and anger. Dean, I felt, was re-creating history in the image of his own defense."[99] Because even when writing his memoir Nixon decided to use only a select few of the recordings of his Watergate conversations, he effectively remembered Watergate as he wished, rather than as it had actually occurred. For my part, at the time I had no idea of the true depth of his involvement in the cover-up as would later be revealed by his recorded conversations. Nixon would later write that his ongoing attacks on me (which continued long after my testimony) were a miscalculation, for he had set "off on a tangent." His efforts to smear me were no longer the point, or as he put it:

> It no longer made any difference that not all of Dean's testimony was accurate.[†] It only mattered if *any* of his testimony was accurate. And Dean's account of the crucial March 21 meeting was more accurate than my own had been. I did not see it then, but in the end it would make less difference that I was not as involved as Dean had alleged than I was not as uninvolved as I had claimed.[100]

Nixon also noted that my testimony "caught us unprepared." He claimed based on "news reports" that I was asked by the "Ervin Committee's Dem-

---

*An average daily audience of some eighty million Americans.

†Indeed, I had undertestified out of caution, and confused dates of a few events. I had taken pains to make it clear to the Senate that my memory was not a date-stamped tape recorder. See 4 Senate Select Committee on Presidential Campaign Activities (SSC) 1373, 1513.

ocratic members and staff" to include in my opening statement "plenty of 'atmospherics' about the White House," and that I had "readily obliged." That was untrue, for no one on the committee made any suggestion whatsoever about my testimony. But Nixon wrote that "even more than what [I] had to say about Watergate, it was from this that we would never recover." He was referring to the world of the White House in which I found myself, fixated on political intelligence and using government resources to attack the president's countless enemies. Nixon noted that I later said I was surprised how the press overplayed the "enemies list," which was true, for many on the list had not been targets of Nixon's wrath but had merely been designated as enemies by Colson's office. Yet because many on the list had been attacked by the Nixon White House, in response to a question from Senator Lowell Weicker, I produced these lists, believing it appropriate that this underbelly of the Nixon White House be seen for what it was—something that should not be part of the executive branch of the government.

While I had testified in my opening statement about how Nixon had used a national security cover for intelligence gathering and political skullduggery like that carried out by the plumbers unit, I had only hearsay information about other matters in which I had not been directly involved. Only after the fact did I become aware of the Segretti operation. In fact, the Watergate break-in and cover-up section of Senator Ervin's committee report runs 95 pages, while the section on campaign practices and finance, and the uses of incumbency, runs 456 pages.[101] Watergate, as the overwhelming evidence revealed, was merely one particularly egregious expression of Nixon's often ruthless abuses of power. Had Richard Nixon not encouraged his aides to collect political intelligence by any means fair or foul, or insisted from the moment of the arrests that there must be no cover-up, neither would have taken place. Nixon was not only responsible for all that went amiss during his presidency, he was in almost every instance the catalyst, when not the instigator.

## July 10–11, 1973, the White House

When Nixon returned from California on July 10, John Mitchell was scheduled to begin his testimony before the Senate Watergate committee. He was the first of the line of witnesses that Nixon and his aides knew would dispute my testimony: Mitchell, Moore, Ehrlichman and Haldeman. Before leaving for the Cabinet Room that morning for a discussion with Republican congressional leaders on his Phase IV economic controls, he asked Ziegler for "anything else of interest" on Watergate.[102] Ziegler reported: "Mitchell looked very stoic on TV last night. I think he probably will do well today." Nixon had a number of questions for Ziegler about my testimony, and when it fit with Nixon's own view, he agreed it was true, and when it did not, he charged me with lying. Ziegler reported that Ehrlichman, who had given an interview to his hometown newspaper in Seattle, had stated that my testimony "was wrong on point after point after point, and he says it was one hundred and eighty degrees from the truth." Ziegler added that several stories had indicated that Mitchell would not support my testimony. "Dean will be destroyed with these witnesses," the president said confidently. Ziegler reviewed several press accounts, noting that even Nixon's archenemy Jack Anderson had a column that made Nixon look "pretty good" regarding his meeting with Kleindienst and Petersen on April 15 (clearly leaked by Kleindienst).

After the congressional economic briefing, Steve Bull went to the Oval Office to clear with the president giving Haldeman the tape of our September 15, 1973, conversation, since that had become an issue with my testimony, and Haldeman had requested it.[103] Nixon agreed that Haldeman should listen to it. Haldeman was staying at the Statler Hilton, but Bull said he would set the tape up for him at his own home. That afternoon Bull had another tape-related question for the president, with regard to clarifying who could listen to which tapes.[104] More specifically, the following exchange occurred, which is especially interesting in that the April 15 conversation later vanished: Nixon explained, "The general rule on these is that I don't want anybody [listening], except myself, unless I directly authorize it." "Well, you directly authorized me on April 15, did you not, sir, when we were in California?" "Oh, yeah, sure," Nixon said, and Bull reminded him, "That's the only one Buzhardt has heard." "No, no, no. I authorized that. I directed that, because I didn't want that sent out there. Oh, shit. [I'd forgotten about that]," Nixon said. "And that is the only one," Bull clarified. "That was on the day, just April 15," Nixon repeated. "Just that one, yeah, that is correct," Bull agreed. "Yeah, okay," Nixon confirmed. "Other than that there is [none]," Bull added. "Okay, fine. We'll check it out and see, okay, fine, fine," Nixon said.*

---

*Given the fact that this April 15, 1973, conversation later disappeared, the reel containing the conversation believed not to exist because the machine ran out of tape that day, makes this a fascinating conversation. It appears Buzhardt was given this conversation when the president was in California

When Bull departed, Nixon continued his conversation with Haig, who had been present during this discussion of the April 15 tape. Haig reported on his conversation with Elliot Richardson about the White House's concern about Cox. Haig had told Richardson that the White House interpreted the Cox charter "in its narrowest sense here in the context of Watergate and campaign abuses." Richardson protested, "Well, that's not the way to do it," to which Haig said he told Richardson, "That's the way he is going to have to do it." Haig reported that Cox, meanwhile, was investigating any number of matters that the White House felt were beyond his constitutional authority. Richardson gave Haig "his breakdown of things, and there is one in there that I said I just don't accept. It's not going to go anywhere, but that's the De Carlo thing." This was a reference to the pardon that had been sent to Nixon, via my office, in late 1972 commuting Angelo De Carlo's sentence, which apparently arose because of an investigation of Spiro Agnew, who had recommended it. (Haig was correct; it went nowhere, and De Carlo himself died.) Haig explained that Cox was also investigating Vesco (although that was primarily being handled in the Southern District of New York), Watergate, Ellsberg and election law violations. Nixon was not happy but did not feel personally threatened, so his protests went no further than Haig.

To give the president some good news (before relaying more bad), Haig said, "Incidentally, Mitchell has just been superb." "People have told me that," Nixon replied. "They said he stood up like a rock." "Best witness that we've had, by far," Haig noted. "And he handled that God damn creep Dash like a puppy dog." Haig now turned to his unpleasant information: "I've got some bad news that I think you should be aware of. I don't know the full details, but the vice president is in trouble." Haig shared with the president what he knew: Someone who had handled Maryland state contracts for Agnew as governor had been given full immunity to testify about payoffs to Agnew. It surprised Nixon to learn that this witness was now working for Agnew, but Haig assured Nixon this problem did not occur during Agnew's time as vice president. This conversation ended with Nixon telling Haig that things were looking very promising, even if they were keeping the "stinking Watergate" thing going. "Dean, that was their big bullet, and the big bullet didn't hit.

---

during my testimony. This is the conversation I told the Senate caused me to believe I was recorded (4 Senate Select Committee on Presidential Campaign Activities [SSC] 1577). If there was any tape on which the president incriminated himself, and put the lie to his own defense, it was this conversation. And given this exchange with Steve Bull, it certainly appears that Fred Buzhardt solved that problem. (See Appendix B.)

Don't you agree?" When Haig said nothing, Nixon added, "Don't you think they've begun to realize it now?" but Haig remained noncommittal.

Late that afternoon the president asked Haig for an update and was told again that Mitchell had done a fine job.[105] "He will never stand a day in prison if I have any power to solve it. Never. Never. Never. That would be a tragedy of mass proportions. If they would like to try impeachment on that, they can try," Nixon said. He added, "Democrats are going to continue to harass us, of course they are, and that's part of the game."

They continued to discuss Mitchell's performance, until at one point Nixon said to Haig, "Oh, one thing I understand, Ron told me that [the Senate committee] asked him about, well, 'What about the meeting you had with the president on March twenty-second? What did you talk about? The—? You know?' And he said he had never discussed [Watergate with the president]. Isn't that interesting? Watergate was never discussed on March twenty-second. We were discussing executive privilege. That was the entire discussion that day." The president repeated, "That was the entire discussion." Because this was contrary to my testimony (and, of course, contrary to the recording of the March 22 conversation, which shows that conversation was not only about Watergate but that the president had privately told Mitchell to "cover up," if necessary), Nixon observed, "I think Dean will be discredited." After the president added that Colson and others would be taking me on, he said, "Damn it, they are going to show him to be a, a, a liar for immunity. That's what he is, a liar for immunity."

At the end of the day, before telephoning to chat with his daughters and Bebe, the president called Ziegler for a rundown on the evening news coverage of Watergate. Ziegler said that while "Mitchell admitted involvement in some aspects of the cover-up," he had testified that he had not told the president about them, and the president didn't know. Ziegler said Mitchell admitted joining Haldeman and Ehrlichman in coving up "the White House horrors"—as he had described it to the Senate. When he had been asked by Talmadge why he had not informed the president, Mitchell had said that he was concerned "the president would have lowered the boom," and it would have been "extremely detrimental to the campaign." Ziegler reported that Mitchell said "in retrospect he was probably wrong" in not informing the president. "That's good," Nixon said. "Good. Well, it came out as well as we could expect."

On the morning of July 11 Mitchell was returning for his second day of testimony.[106] Ziegler assured Nixon that Mitchell was "getting good reviews." So, too, he reported, had the president's daughter Julie and son-in-law, David Eisenhower, who had given an interview to the BBC in which Watergate had come up. Later on the morning of July 11, Rose Woods was in the Oval Office, and Watergate dominated their conversation. She offered that Mitchell "has handled himself beautifully" and stayed "calm and cool." "I'm glad that good old John came through," Nixon agreed. Since she had been watching the hearings, and he was not, he asked for more detail about Mitchell: "Was he able to put it to Dean at all?" "I think so," she answered, twice. "The press simply didn't say much about Dean. Oh, well." The conversation about Mitchell continued, and Nixon noted, "Nobody got drowned in the Watergate"—an oblique reference to Teddy Kennedy's Chappaquiddick problems, which she understood immediately.* "Rose, they ran the Dean stories for eight weeks. They put him on the cover for two weeks in a row," he complained, referring to the national news magazines. "Right," Rose agreed, and reported, "They put him on three networks. And they're putting John Mitchell on one network." "Oh, they are?" Nixon asked, and she explained the networks were rotating coverage. Rose was incensed that her name had come up in my testimony in response to a question about inquiries at the IRS, for she had called me repeatedly on one case. She told Nixon "the only thing I ever did was call him and ask him to talk to Dr. Riland to tell him what to do." She was upset, because she said I knew "the doctor was indicted, and yet he refused to give the name, so it sounds like a boyfriend almost of mine, and I thought, oh, God.".[107] Nixon easily comforted her by trashing me. "He's a very repulsive character. He really is." Woods soon agreed, "Yeah, he's just, he's an evil man." "Well, I think what has happened is, he's become basically a degenerate, I'm afraid."

That afternoon Ziegler came to the Oval Office with an update: "Mitchell continues to hang in there strong."[108] He further reported, "I'll tell you, people are writing good stuff about Mitchell. I think he is coming out of this alright." Ziegler went over the news commentary at length, particularly that favorable to the president. He noted that one commentator had said, "It is possible that Dean believes his testimony, but there is no question that his perspective has been warped during his passage from pro-Nixon to the

---

*Either Nixon shared this thought, or others had the same thought, for soon Nixon's supporters had bumper stickers that read: Nobody Drowned At Watergate.

anti-Nixon phase of his personal odyssey." This same commentator had also written that "in the president's twenty-seven years in public life" he had "never been caught, as he points out, or accused of, lying in any public statements." Ziegler gave him more information on what was happening before the Senate, and said that the next witness would likely be Dick Moore, possibly Kalmbach, followed by Ehrlichman and then Haldeman. Ziegler mentioned that he had seen John Connally after the cabinet meeting that morning. "I said, 'How do you think things are going?' and he said, 'Watergate is over.' Which is pretty well our judgment," he advised Nixon. This prompted the president to look ahead to his trip to Europe that fall, and to winning back popular support. "Middle American," as Nixon put it.

Later Nixon telephoned Ziegler: "Ron, it occurred to me—just thought of this, but probably nothing could be done—but I just learned it, that they carried Dean on three networks for five days straight. And they carried Mitchell on one."[109] The president thought this was evidence that the networks were simply out to harm him, and he wanted that brought to their attention. "I've done that already," Ziegler reported and had almost mentioned it to a columnist. Nixon wanted to put Colson's successor in charge of attacking the networks on it: "This is one time when I would put [Ken] Clawson and the bomb throwers to work on the thing like that, let them [the networks] bitch a little."

At the end of the afternoon the president met with Haig in the Oval Office.[110] Haig said that he had spoken with Morris Liebman, a senior partner at the Chicago law firm of Sidley & Austin, the preceding evening. Haig undoubtedly knew Liebman from his role as a civilian aide-at-large to the secretary of the army, an advisory post in which he served from 1964 to 1979. The fact that the White House was not winning any legal battles had become conspicuous, and Haig said that Liebman recommended creating a strategy group, which he would be willing to chair, "with Chappie Rose and somebody else to just come in pretty regularly and make an assessment on Fred, and how he's handling the issues." "Not bad," Nixon said. Liebman had also recommended Fred be given more lawyers to assist him, and had suggested names of lawyers in the bureaucracy who could be detailed to the White House. Haig had also spoken with Richardson and Cox. "I just don't trust either of them," he said. "We need to watch them like a hawk."

When Haig departed the president asked Ziegler to come to the Oval Office[111] and repeated a conversation he had had earlier that afternoon with John Connally, one that he had also just shared with Haig. Connally had said, "There comes a time when people get tired, they get tired out of too much ice cream, too much champagne, they get tired of anything, too much sex, anything." This was now happening with Watergate, and come September, Connally urged, Nixon should "go out and attack." When Ziegler agreed, Nixon said he planned to "give them a kick in the ass now and then." Ziegler proposed he start with Cox, since they already had a case on him, and suggested Nixon say: "'Mr. Cox, I'm relieving you of your responsibilities.' Period. And let him squeal. Archibald Cox will not be remembered."

## July 12, 1973, the White House and Bethesda Naval Hospital

The president had awakened at 5:30 A.M. with a stabbing pain in his chest, which he later said reminded him of when he had cracked a rib playing football in college.[112] At 5:43 he called the White House physician, Walter Tkach, who arrived with his colleague William Lukash. After they examined him, Tkach thought it pneumonia, while Lukash diagnosed it as a digestive disorder. Both believed the president should undergo a complete battery of tests. Nixon resisted but remained in bed until early afternoon. At 1:30 P.M. Haig went to his bedroom to tell him that Senator Ervin was calling. As Nixon later reported, "We talked for sixteen minutes. My voice was subdued, because every breath I took caused a sharp pain." Ervin was calling about his request for documents, which had been a front-page story in *The Washington Post* even before the request had been formally made.[113] Nixon accused Ervin's committee of having leaked, and then said, "You want your staff to go through presidential files. The answer is no. We disagree on that." But Nixon said he would think about the letter Ervin had sent to be polite. The conversation with Ervin seemed to have energized him, for he dressed and went to the Oval Office.

But as the president and Haig were talking, a fragment from the bullet Nixon was sure he had dodged was heading his way. As a part of the follow-up on my testimony, the staff of the Senate Watergate committee was informally talking with other potential witnesses, one of whom was Alex Butterfield, whom they were now interviewing in the basement of the Dirksen Senate

Office Building.* Scott Armstrong, one of Dash's investigators, was intrigued by the amount of detail in the Buzhardt information given to Fred Thompson about my conversations with the president, and he asked Butterfield, who had been a top administrative assistant to Nixon during his first term, if he knew how that information might have been assembled. Butterfield, who had been instructed by Haldeman to have the president's secret recording system installed, immediately suspected that someone had listened to the recording of my conversations with Nixon. But rather than say anything, and because they had only asked him about Buzhardt's memo, he set the document aside and said he'd like to think about it. Buzhardt had been concerned that the taping system might come up, and he did not know if the committee had or had not yet discovered it. Butterfield knew it was one of the best-kept secrets of the Nixon presidency, and had decided that only if he was asked a direct question would he answer. And Armstrong had not asked him a direct question.

Donald Sanders, one of Fred Thompson's deputy minority counsel, was also present at the Butterfield interview, and after listening to Armstrong's three hours of questions about how presidential schedule logs were maintained and compiled, the procedures for preparing memoranda of staff conversations with the president and other details of the Nixon White House operations, he had his own question. While no stenographic record was made of the interview, all present recall that Sanders, whose task it was to find errors in my testimony, noted that I had testified that I believed I had been recorded. More specifically, Sanders said, I had testified that the president had asked me a question "in a very low voice concerning a presidential exchange with Colson about executive clemency. Do you know of any basis for the implication in Dean's testimony that conversations in the Oval Office are recorded?"[114] Needless to say, Butterfield did know of a basis for my feeling I had been recorded by the president, and he proceeded to explain the president's secret system to Sanders and Armstrong.

Back at the White House the president arrived at the Oval Office at 2:15, looked over his news summary, and then met with Kissinger and Haig.

---

*While working on this book, a perfect opportunity to discuss the discovery of Nixon's taping system arose at Chapman Law Review Symposium: "The 40th Anniversary of Watergate: A Commemoration of the Rule of Law," Panel 1: "President Nixon's Secret Tapes: Evidence that Politically, Legally and Historically Defined Watergate (and More)," Friday, January 27, 2012, Moderator: John W. Dean; Panelists: Scott Armstrong and Alexander Butterfield, reported in full at *Chapman Law Review* 16 (Spring 2012): 9.

Sounding surprisingly invigorated, he told Kissinger how tough he had been on Sam Ervin when he had called. "Not on your life, there ain't gonna be no papers come out," Nixon quoted himself as telling Ervin. Kissinger reported that the president had a new admirer in Norman Mailer: "He thinks you're going to come out of this eventually stronger. That the public is beginning to identify with you, and somebody gets kicked so much and endures and overcomes it. That is what a lot of people experience in their own lives." Kissinger reported that Mailer wanted "to write that it's all a CIA conspiracy against you because you were on détente." This filled the room with laughter. Returning to his conversation with Ervin, Nixon boasted, "I'm not going to allow this slick Southern asshole to pull that old crap on me. He pretends he's gentle and trying to work things out. Bullshit." They discussed how rough it was going to be at the Senate for Haldeman and Colson, but Haig thought not. And soon Nixon was retailing his version of the March 21 conversation for everyone.

Feeling well enough, the president proceeded with his afternoon schedule: a meeting with a German vice chancellor; a photo opportunity in the Rose Garden; a half-hour meeting in the Oval Office with a visiting dignitary; and a conversation with Bill Timmons about congressional affairs. Nixon complained that Howard Baker had been too easy on me during my testimony and for that would never forgive him: "Howard Baker will never be in the White House again, never, never, never. He will never be on a presidential plane again. I don't care what he does, the softballs he threw up to Dean. But what he did to John Mitchell was unforgiveable."[115] Nixon said he found Baker's actions "despicable," noting, "He thinks he's going to be president. He's finished." When Timmons departed, Nixon did another photo op, this one with a fire prevention group, and then called Rose Woods into the office. "Howard Baker will never be in the White House again, as long as I am in this office," he ordered. "Never. Never. Never."[116] He soon repeated this, and said, "I mean it, Rose." "I agree with that, too," she said. "His name will not be on the Christmas list," he added.

Shortly after five o'clock Haig joined the president in the Oval Office. Nixon had received the results of his preliminary medical examination and said that the doctors wanted him to spend four to five days in the hospital. The doctors wanted him to have a chest X-ray at a nearby naval regional medical clinic (less than two miles and a five-minute drive away), but Nixon was more concerned with discussing protecting his papers from Ervin. He thought senators like Carl Curtis (R-NE) and Barry Goldwater (R-AZ) would support him. He reminded Haig that Harry Truman had made the tough decision to not testify before Congress. Haig observed that the senior White House staff was solid, with the possible exception of Mel Laird. Nixon said letting the Senate have his papers was a no-win situation: If they provided any, they would say that they wanted more, claiming that incriminating documents had not been included or destroyed. Nixon felt as strongly regarding the inevitable demands for documents from Cox.

Nixon called for Ziegler to join the conversation, and when he arrived, the president said, "I've not missed a day in four and a half years. Not a day. Not an appointment, nothing." And then he informed Ziegler that the doctors wanted him hospitalized. Never missing a political opportunity, Nixon told his aides that he could take advantage of the situation, and might even give a speech. President Suffers Viral Pneumonia. Reads Radio Address to Nation, Nixon said, framing the headline. The conversation returned to protecting his papers, and then Nixon mentioned he wanted to send George Bush on a trip: "Best thing with George, he doesn't stand up well." Returning again to the papers, he complained, "They struck out on Dean," so now they wanted documents.

Dr. Tkach arrived in the Oval Office and said he had arranged for an X-ray at the naval clinic at 6:30 P.M. Tkach explained that the X-ray would indicate how serious his condition was, but for "even a mild case," he was recommending the president stay at the hospital that night. He further explained that the risks involved with viral pneumonia were heart attack or stroke or both. Tkach said that Lyndon Johnson, when president, would go to the hospital even with a bad cold. Nixon admitted that he did not feel well, and that he had a 101-degree temperature, which he had taken himself. But again, he was considering the PR aspects: "People don't go to the hospital for a virus." Tkach, not concerned with PR, corrected him. Shortly before six o'clock the president departed for the naval clinic, ordering Ziegler to make no announcement until he decided what he was going to do after he got the X-ray results. He said he was unconcerned about the press, and as he headed out the door, remarked: "The only time the press will be happy is when they write my obituary."

The X-rays were not good, and after his dinner at the residence, the president was driven to the Bethesda Naval Hospital, where he was admitted at 9:15 P.M. on July 12. He remained in the hospital until the morning of July

20, when he returned to the White House. While he was hospitalized, the entire dynamics of Watergate shifted with the revelation of his taping system. On Monday, July 16, at just after 2:00 P.M., Alex Butterfield appeared as a surprise witness before the Senate Watergate committee, where he told the world of the system, until then known only to Butterfield, Haldeman, Bull, Higby, the Secret Service technicians who installed and maintained the system and the president. Haig and Buzhardt were aware that select conversations of mine had been recorded, but as Haig later said, he thought the system could be switched on and off: "It never occurred to me that anyone in his right mind would install anything so Orwellian as a system that never shut off, that preserved every word, every joke, every curse, every tantrum, every flight of presidential paranoia, every bit of flattery and bad advice and tattling by his advisers."[117] Butterfield's revelation confronted Nixon with the decision of whether he should or could destroy the tapes, and since they had not yet been subpoenaed, it was a choice he would have to make quickly, if it was not already too late.

There are three first-person accounts of Nixon's decision to keep the tapes: Garment's, Haig's and Nixon's own. Woodward and Bernstein also prepared an account based on off-the-record interviews with sources that cannot be evaluated. While there are minor differences in these accounts, their gist is consistent. With time seemingly of the essence if the president was going to have any options, the White House appears not to have learned about Butterfield's Thursday, July 12, disclosure, until three days later:

- Fred Thompson said he informed Fred Buzhardt of Butterfield's disclosure on Sunday, July 15, when he telephoned him to advise him of it, and Buzhardt did not seem particularly troubled by the information.[118]

- Len Garment reported that he first learned of the taping system from Larry Higby on July 10, when Higby was heading for a staff interview with the Senate Watergate committee. Higby wanted to know what to say if asked about the system. Garment counseled him not to volunteer anything, but if asked, he should answer honestly. Garment was informed of Butterfield's disclosure to the Senate when he returned from out of town on Sunday, July 15, and was asked to come to his White House office on Sunday evening, where he met with Buzhardt.[119]

- Haig claimed that he did not learn of Butterfield's disclosure until Monday, July 16, when Butterfield testified before the Senate. Haig says Nixon was incorrect in his account that Haig telephoned him early Monday morning to warn him of Butterfield's disclosure and forthcoming testimony.[120]

- Nixon wrote in his memoir that he was informed early Monday morning, July 16, when "Haig called me to tell me that Haldeman's former aide Alex Butterfield had revealed the existence of the White House taping system to the Ervin Committee staff and that it would become public knowledge later that day."[121]

Nixon said he was "shocked" by the news; everyone else was shocked either by the fact that Nixon taped himself or that it had been disclosed, or both. Many on the White House staff thought the exposure of the system had been engineered by Nixon himself: "There were expressions of relief. At last there was something definitive. The tapes had been deliberately exposed. They would prove that John Dean was lying."[122] There was an almost universal consensus that Nixon's tapes would provide a near indisputable way to answer the question Howard Baker had asked me during my testimony: "What did the president know and when did he know it?"[123]

The revelation created a very delicate problem for Nixon's staff, for they, too, understood that the recordings could establish his innocence or his guilt. While many secretly believed he was guilty, such thoughts had to be suppressed in order to remain loyal and work for him. Based on Butterfield's testimony that the Secret Service had installed the system, Al Haig had his deputy call them to "immediately" dismantle it and secure all the existing recordings. Haig made this decision without consulting the president, but then went to the hospital to discuss this situation. "Mr. President, it seems to me that you have two options. You can either keep the tapes or you can destroy them." Nixon wanted to know the consequences of each option. "If you keep the tapes and refuse to make them public, you'll spend the remainder of your presidency beating off the prosecutors, the Congress and the news media. In the end, you may very well have to give them up." And if he destroyed them? "You will be violently attacked. Some will describe it as an admission of guilt. Others will admire your common sense. You will take a tremendous amount of heat, but, whatever happens, it will be over fairly quickly." Haig noted if he did not destroy them, the disclosure process would last forever, and reach into history.[124]

Nixon wanted to know what the lawyers thought of the legal implications. Garment reported that upon learning of the situation he had sent his associate Doug Parker to the law library, where he soon found *U.S. v. Solow*, a ruling with a similar fact pattern to Nixon's tapes and an obstruction of justice under federal criminal law.* Because a president cannot be indicted while in office, but a presidential "felony" could be the basis for impeachment, Garment said the question of destroying the tapes was a matter of "virtually nonstop discussion among Haig, Buzhardt, Parker and [himself]" for the next two days.[125] Both sides were presented to the president at the hospital: by Garment, who argued it would be an obstruction of justice under federal law, and the president should not destroy the tapes; and by Buzhardt, who said the tapes were his property and had not been subpoenaed, so he could do with them as he wished. Buzhardt did not believe Congress would impeach him if he did destroy the tapes. Nixon was also told that Charles Alan Wright had given them a "near categorical opinion" that the president had a powerful executive privilege argument, which the Texas law professor believed he could win should the case go to the U.S. Supreme Court.

While Nixon considered this matter on July 16, Haig later wrote—and undoubtedly the others also worried—what if Nixon did order them to destroy the tapes? To do so after a subpoena had been issued they would be knowingly engaging in a criminal conspiracy to obstruct justice. Garment noted, "We also talked about various technical means for destroying the tapes (by electronic erasure, for example) and about who, other than Nixon himself, might undertake the deed." Garment adds he "made everyone slightly edgy by noting that, even if Nixon could not be indicted, conspirators who facilitated a nonindictable felony, including lawyers and ex-generals, could."[126] Haig wrote, "The awful thought occurred to me that he might even order me to return to the White House and burn the tapes myself. I knew I could not do this; I would resign first. The tapes were not my property or my responsibility. Only the president could destroy them or order them destroyed by someone who was completely outside his inner circle, such as a member of the Secret Service."[127]

---

*138 F. Supp. 812 (1956). Note: A highly respected federal trial judge had ruled that it was obstruction of justice under 18 USC 1503 to destroy four letters it was known a grand jury was interested in, even though the letters had not yet been subpoenaed.

The Watergate special prosecutor's office was as stunned as everyone else but thought the revelation of the tapes was almost too good to be true. Assistant prosecutor James Neal, a seasoned veteran who had left his highly successful private practice to assist Cox, said, "It's bound to be a ruse." Neal wondered if the cunning Nixon might be leading them into a cul-de-sac. Nonetheless, they felt they had to move quickly to subpoena the tapes, particularly those of Nixon's conversations with me, which they concluded were "certain to make or break John Dean's testimony. Probably they would determine the outcome of our case against Haldeman and Ehrlichman. In the bargain, the tapes, if legitimate, would undoubtedly tell us a good deal about the extent of the president's own involvement."[128] The prosecutors felt "[o]nce under subpoena" the tapes could be tampered with only at the risk of criminal liality so, given the uncertainty of the law, they moved quickly and delivered a letter to Buzhardt early on the morning of July 17, informing him that a subpoena was forthcoming.

That same morning Nixon, who had had only a few hours of sleep, told Haig he had made his decision: "Al, I've thought about this all night. Maybe Alex Butterfield has done us a favor. These tapes will be exculpatory. I know I never said anything to anybody that could be interpreted as encouragement to cover things up. Just the opposite."[129] A surprised Haig asked Nixon to consider his decision carefully. Later that day Haig tried to persuade him to change his mind, and had Vice President Agnew visit him, for Agnew strongly believed he should destroy the tapes—as did John Connally, Henry Kissinger and Pat Buchanan. Nixon had someone (probably Ziegler or Haig) contact Haldeman for his thoughts. Haldeman's advice was to claim executive privilege and not give them anything. He opposed destruction of the tapes, for he felt they were the president's best defense.

While I was very worried that Nixon would destroy the tapes, which I knew would not only corroborate my testimony but establish the depth of the president's involvement in the cover-up, that clearly would have been a fatal decision for his presidency. Had he destroyed the tapes he would have survived, tarnished but intact. For that reason, his explanation of his ultimate choice is not unimportant. Nixon said he made the decision not to destroy the tapes for three reasons.

First, he believed "they indisputably disproved Dean's basic charge that I had conspired with him in an obstruction of justice over an eight-month period." This is fundamentally a straw-man argument, for I had never made such a charge: I testified that I had the strong "impression" that he had been involved in the cover-up from the outset. As the conversations transcribed for this book show, my impression was well founded, and had Nixon made the slightest effort to verify what he had actually said and done, it is clear his tapes provide overwhelming evidence that he was involved in the cover-up from the earliest stages.

Second, Nixon says he was persuaded by "Haig's reasoning that destruction of the tapes would create an indelible impression of guilt." He did not think anything he had, in fact, "actually done would be as bad as that impression." To support this notion he cites and quotes notes he made when he returned from the hospital, when he wrote: "If I had discussed illegal action, I would not have taped. If I had discussed illegal action and had taped, I would have destroyed the tapes once the investigation began." In February 1971 the president was told the taping system was installed in the Oval Office; in April of that year he was informed it was working in his EOB office. By June of 1971 Nixon was giving repeated orders to break into the Brookings Institution and "rifle the files" for copies of the Pentagon Papers. In the March 21 conversation, during which I repeatedly told him that paying Hunt would be an obstruction of justice, he insisted this obstruction go on a little bit longer. He clearly knew he was discussing illegal activities that were being recorded, so this second reason appears to be a reconstructed rationalization for his memoir.

Third, he claims "the tapes were my best insurance against the unforeseeable future." Accordingly, he found this "would give me at least some protection" in the event that Haldeman, Ehrlichman or Colson turned on him. In fact, as time and the special prosecutor's subpoenas proved, they had as much if not more to lose, but this argument is more credible than his two prior claims. Without their notes, however, Haldeman and Ehrlichman were also having difficulties in reconstructing the past, so Nixon was making it difficult for them as well. While Ehrlichman did eventually turn on Nixon, Haldeman remained mostly loyal, other than being upset with Nixon's comments about him during the Nixon/Frost interviews suggesting that he had bad judgment when, in fact, he had been carrying out Nixon directives, while he was in prison. As a result, he became very candid, noting, for example: "The president was involved in the cover-up from Day One, although neither he nor we considered it a cover-up at that time." Keeping the tapes proved to be the higher risk, while Haldeman's and Ehrlichman's turning on him was a low one. Indeed, they did not turn until he departed office, having ignored their pleas for pardons, which was very telling. Because they could no longer do anything for him, he was not about to do anything for them.

The decision to keep the tapes changed Nixon's defense only slightly. Notes in his files that he prepared the day after he returned from the hospital have a heading: Tapes, under which he wrote as follows: "These tapes were not for public disclosure: (1) None have been transcribed—or will be. (2) Only [a few] hours have been listened to [by] me personally or for me under my specific direction and control." Beside this note he has placed a little box, clearly containing the names of the others he has authorized to listen: Buzhardt, Haldeman, Bull. "(3) Only notes are in my personal possession and available to me only. (4) No one can use as basis for testimony." Nixon drew two lines across his legal pad after these notes on the tapes, and beneath them added further thoughts: "My statement of May 22 stands and is fully corroborated by the tapes. Nothing in any way questions any of the statements of May 22."[130]

In short, he intended to keep his core defense in place, and its entire thrust would now be on preventing anyone's gaining access to that material. The way he would handle the matter of the tapes would only provoke further outrage regarding his behavior. He had locked himself into his April 30 defense as refined by his May 22 statement—the claim of no knowledge of a cover-up before March 21—and in the coming months of his presidency, which would last just over another year, he would remind Americans that only I had accused him of involvement in the cover-up, and he would continue his efforts to discredit me. Haldeman and Ehrlichman, more out of self-protection than on Nixon's behalf, would testify before the Senate Watergate committee, and like Mitchell, would commit perjury, for which all three would later be charged and convicted. Nixon's defense after the revelations of his taping system, and the filing of subpoenas by the Watergate special prosecutor and the Senate Watergate committee, shifted principally to the federal courts, where they would be resolved. Charles Alan Wright was wrong, and a unanimous Supreme Court (Justice Rehnquist recused himself) ruled that Nixon had to turn over the tapes that the special prosecutor had requested on behalf of the Watergate grand jury. I have highlighted the events that followed in an epilogue. When the Nixon defense finally failed, impeachment was a certainty. On August 8, 1974, Nixon announced his resignation, effective the following day. A Gallup poll immediately after

Nixon's speech revealed that 79 percent thought Nixon did the best thing by resigning, with only 13 percent believing he should have remained in office.[131]

While in the hospital with pneumonia, Nixon made a note: "Should have destroyed the tapes after April 30, 1973."[132] Had he done so, his presidency and its history would have ended much differently.

# Epilogue

F ollowing the revelation of the White House secret taping system, the president and his Watergate advisers decided that no tapes could or should be released. Nixon's defense quickly became focused on protecting the tapes, which kept his statements of April 30 and May 22, 1973, viable. Because no secret recordings exist of this final chapter of Watergate, and this period has been well reported by others, I offer here only a chronological summary of the events that brought the Nixon presidency to an end.[1]

## 1973

*July 18*   Special prosecutor Cox sends a letter to Nixon requesting eight taped conversations based on my testimony before the Senate Watergate committee, arguing that since Cox is part of the executive branch, there can be no separation of powers (executive privilege) issue. On this date the White House taping system is fully dismantled.

*July 20*   Cox writes Buzhardt to make certain the tapes are being preserved intact and their integrity protected as possible evidence and requests that Buzhardt put in place procedures to protect the recordings. Buzhardt now has to be prepared to go to jail if he allows the destruction of the tapes.

*July 22*   Harris Poll: 60 (versus 30) percent think that Nixon was more wrong than right in refusing to turn over documents to the Senate Watergate committee; 50 (versus 30) percent now believe my Senate testimony that Nixon knew of the cover-up.

*July 23*   Nixon rejects the request of the Senate Watergate committee for copies of the tapes and informs Judge Sirica that he will not provide the eight tapes requested by Cox, based on executive privilege. Cox subpoenas nine tapes, six from conversations with me and three from the first week after the arrests at the DNC.

*July 25*   Pat Buchanan sends a memo to the president recommending he burn the tapes that might be damaging to him. John Connally resigns as a part-time presidential adviser and is soon indicted, tried and acquitted of taking a ten-thousand-dollar bribe to raise federal milk-price supports for the dairy industry.

Buzhardt writes to Cox to assure him the tapes are intact and under Nixon's sole personal control, with access to them carefully controlled and documented.

*July 26* Senate Watergate committee votes unanimously to go to court to enforce its subpoena against the president for his tapes. Judge Sirica grants Cox's request for a "show cause" order that requires Nixon to explain by August 7 why he should not compel the president to provide the nine requested tapes to Cox. The White House press office announces that the president will "abide by a definitive decision of the highest Court" regarding his tapes. When Cox, the following day, states that all Supreme Court rulings are "definitive," the Nixon press office responds that some Supreme Court rulings were "less than definitive." This discussion did not escape the attention of the Supreme Court justices.[2]

*July 30* In his testimony to the Senate Watergate committee, Haldeman says he listened to the tapes of my conversations with the president on September 15, 1972, and March 21, 1973, and claims that Nixon did say "there is no problem raising a million dollars" for the Watergate defendants, but "it would be wrong." (The fact that Haldeman heard the recordings after he left the White House on April 30, 1973, offends many both in and out of government, since a private citizen being investigated for criminal conduct was given access while government investigators were being denied.) Harris Poll: 22 percent think Nixon should resign; 65 percent believe he has not been honest regarding Watergate.

*August 9* Senate Watergate committee files an action in federal district court in Washington seeking Nixon's tapes.

*August 15* Nixon addresses the nation from the Oval Office. He repeats his no knowledge of the break-in or cover-up defense and embraces his May 22 statement, adding: "As for the cover-up, my statement has been challenged by only one of the thirty-five witnesses who appeared—a witness who offered no evidence beyond his own impressions and whose testimony has been contradicted by every other witness in a position to know the facts." He proceeds to name me as the person who had failed to give him information before March 21, but when I did, it prompted his investigation. As for his tapes, the "principle of confidentiality of presidential conversations is at stake in the question of these tapes. I must and I shall oppose any efforts to destroy this principle, which is so vital to the conduct of this great office." Nixon issues another detailed statement of his defense, again attributing blame to me and reinforcing the May 22 statement.

*August 16* Magruder pleads guilty on a one-count indictment for conspiracy to obstruct justice and the unlawful intercept of wire and oral communications by eavesdropping at the DNC. Sirica postpones sentencing until he can evaluate Magruder's assistance to the government.

*August 20* Harris Poll: 67 percent believe that Nixon had failed to give "convincing proof" that he was not part of the cover-up; 71 percent think he is withholding important information about Watergate.

*August 22* Cox and Nixon's special counsel Charles Wright argue their respective cases before Judge Sirica regarding the tapes. Wright tells Sirica that one of the subpoenaed tapes of Nixon's conversations with me contains such sensitive national security information that the president could not even hint to Wright of its contents. Sirica says he will rule within a week. Nixon also holds a press conference on this day, and the second question concerns the tapes: "You have said that disclosure of the tapes could jeopardize and cripple the functions of the presidency. Two questions. If disclosure carries such a risk, why did you make the tapes in the first place, and what is your reaction to surveys that show three out of four Americans believe you were wrong to make the tapes?" Nixon replies that his advisers recommended taping for national security reasons. As for the second question, he says that Kennedy and Johnson taped their presidential conversations, but Nixon says he actually preferred dictating notes at the end of the day. When asked why he allowed Haldeman to listen to tapes, Nixon claims (falsely) that he only allowed him to listen to September 15 to be certain they would be accurate in responding. When asked about the March 21 conversation, Nixon asserts that Haldeman's testimony (for which he would later be indicted and convicted) is accurate.

*August 29*    Sirica orders Nixon to produce the eight tapes subpoenaed on July 23 by Cox. In turn the White House issues a statement that Nixon will not comply and is considering an appeal, which they would do on September 6. The White House also files papers denying the Senate Watergate committee's tapes request, charging the committee with conducting a criminal trial that exceeds its authority.

*September 4*    A Los Angeles grand jury returns a secret indictment against Ehrlichman, Liddy, Krogh and Young for conspiracy to commit burglary of Ellsberg's psychiatrist's office, and also charges Ehrlichman with perjury. (At the request of the Watergate special prosecutor, these charges will be dropped when he files his actions involving the same individuals.)

*September 5*    While Nixon has earlier been reluctant to publicly attack me, at his second news conference in two weeks he claims that he personally ordered me on March 21 to undertake an investigation, and when I could not write a report, he turned to Ehrlichman. He refuses to explain what he meant by a "definitive" Supreme Court ruling and admits that confidence in the president has been "worn away" by the "leers and sneers of commentators."

*September 6*    Nixon's attorneys appeal Sirica's August 29 ruling to produce the tapes to Cox, claiming the court does not have power to deal with his private records. The following day Cox petitions the Court of Appeals to order Nixon to deliver the requested tapes.

*September 10*    The White House and Cox both file lengthy briefs with the Court of Appeals regarding production of the subpoenaed tapes. Nixon's lawyers argue that under executive privilege the courts have no power to require a president to reveal information about the presidency. Cox argues that enforcing the criminal law outweighs presidential privacy. On the following day, September 11, they have a three-hour argument before the court. Wright claims that even if Nixon did engage in a conspiracy to obstruct justice, he cannot be indicted, only impeached by Congress.

*September 13*    The Court of Appeals (with seven judges sitting on the case) unanimously adopt a six-hundred-word memo urging an out-of-court resolution to the tape issue. The court suggests allowing Cox to examine the tapes with the president's lawyer and jointly decide which portions can properly be given to the grand jury. Cox approves of the proposal; the White House will consider it.

*September 19*   In response to the Court of Appeals proposal White House lawyers file a brief that states that Nixon will not "tear down the office of the American presidency" for Watergate. The following day the White House lawyers, with Cox, file a joint letter that states that after three meetings, they have not been able to agree on an out-of-court settlement regarding the tapes.

*September 23*   Gallup Poll: 61 percent to 32 percent believe Nixon should release the White House tapes to Judge Sirica.

*September 24*   Senate Watergate committee hearings resume, and White House lawyers file papers with Sirica asking that he reject the committee's request for a summary judgment to provide them the tapes. Cox tells Richardson that Haldeman and Ehrlichman are preventing him from subpoenaing documents by placing them with Nixon's presidential papers. (As long as Nixon remains in office, the strategy works.)

*September 28*   Nixon, who has been considering a compromise on the tapes requested by Cox, instructs Rose Woods to begin transcribing the subpoenaed tapes at Camp David in order to provide transcripts to his lawyers. But he tells Haig he did not want to listen to the tapes personally.

*September 29–30*   During this weekend, Nixon is told by Steve Bull that he cannot locate the June 20, 1972, conversation between Nixon and Mitchell or the April 15, 1973, conversation between Nixon and Dean. (See Appendix B.)

*October 1*   Using a new Uher 5000 tape-deck recorder purchased that day, Woods continues transcribing the June 20, 1972, conversation with Ehrlichman. As she progresses she discovers a gap, a shrill buzzing noise, and informs Nixon, believing she was responsible for it. (See Appendix B.)

*October 4*   Harris Poll: 54 percent to 34 percent believe Congress would be justified to begin impeachment proceedings if Nixon refuses to turn over his tapes.

*October 10*   Vice President Agnew resigns and pleads nolo contendere (no contest) to negotiated charges of failure to pay federal income taxes (on kickbacks from state contracts while serving as governor of Maryland).

*October 12*   Court of Appeals upholds Sirica's ruling requiring Nixon to produce the subpoenaed tapes and calls for Sirica to do an in camera review. Nixon nominates Michigan congressman Gerald Ford, the House minority leader, to be vice president. (Ford will be confirmed by the U.S. Senate on November 27 and by the U.S. House of Representatives on December 6.)

*October 17*   Sirica denies the Senate Watergate committee's effort to obtain the tapes on the grounds that the court could not invoke jurisdiction in a congressional civil suit. Richardson sends a White House proposal to Cox that, rather than have Sirica do an in camera review, transcripts of the tapes could be verified by Senator John Stennis—the so-called Stennis compromise.

*October 18*   Cox tells Richardson he cannot accept the Stennis compromise. The transcripts prepared by the White House, and verified by Stennis, would not have been admissible in court, not to mention that it was well known that Senator Stennis was partially deaf and a strong Nixon supporter.

*October 19*  Notwithstanding the fact that Nixon knows it is unacceptable to Cox, he announces he will not appeal the Court of Appeals ruling on the tapes to the Supreme Court, but instead publicly proposes the Stennis compromise. The Senate Watergate committee accepts the proposal; Cox refuses it.

*October 20*  Cox defends his decision not to comply with the president's proposal during an afternoon televised news conference and asserts that he can be fired only by the attorney general, for Cox was well aware of Nixon's earlier threats. At an 8:25 P.M. news conference the White House announces that Attorney General Richardson and Deputy Attorney General Ruckelshaus have both resigned rather than fire Cox. Solicitor General Bork, as acting attorney general, is responsible for dismissing Cox. Television networks interrupt regular programming to announce this action by Nixon, which becomes known as the Saturday Night Massacre.

*October 23*  Following a tumultuous weekend in the aftermath of the Cox firing, eight impeachment resolutions are introduced in the House of Representatives, and within days the House Judiciary Committee commences a serious impeachment inquiry.

*October 26*  In response to nationwide public pressure, the White House announces that Nixon will give the tapes to Sirica, and the Stennis plan is canceled. In a press conference Nixon announces that acting attorney general Bork will appoint a new Watergate special prosecutor.

*October 30*  The White House publicly discloses that two of the subpoenaed tapes are missing: Mitchell's conversation on June 20, 1972, and mine on April 15, 1973.

*November 1*  Leon Jaworski is appointed as the new Watergate special prosecutor. Both Haig and Nixon believe that in Jaworski they have a conservative Democrat and an establishmentarian who will not cause trouble and go after the president as had Cox.

*November 12*  In a statement from his lawyers to Judge Sirica, Nixon claims neither the June 20, 1972, conversation with Mitchell nor the April 15, 1973, conversation with me was recorded.

*November 14*  Buzhardt learns of the 18½-minute gap in the June 20, 1972, conversation with Haldeman. (See Appendix B.)

*November 21*  The White House informs Judge Sirica and the public of the 18½-minute gap, which leads to an investigation by the Watergate special prosecutor's office that runs throughout November and into December. The investigation determines that the only persons to have had possession of the tape were Woods, Bull and Nixon, though others had access to it. Woods believes she erased about five minutes; Bull says he did no erasing; Nixon is not required to respond. (See Appendix B.)

*December 10*  Jaworski receives two of seven existing subpoenaed tapes from Sirica.

*December 19* Sirica rules that two of the additional subpoenaed tapes and part of a third will not be turned over to Jaworski, because they have no relationship to Watergate.

*December 21* Jaworski receives all the subpoenaed tapes that Sirica believes relevant to Watergate. Soon thereafter Jaworski listens to a segment of the March 21 conversation in the special prosecutor's office. He is shaken when he hears Nixon's "scheme" and is particularly disturbed by how Nixon "coach[es] Haldeman on how to testify untruthfully and yet not commit perjury. It amounted to subornation of perjury."[3]

*December 24* Harris Poll: 73 percent to 21 percent think Nixon has "lost so much credibility that it will be hard for him to be accepted as president again."


## 1974

*January 3* Nixon turns down the request of the Senate Watergate committee for some five hundred tapes and documents they believe relevant to their inquiry. The new attorney general, former Ohio senator William Saxbe (R-OH), is sworn in. Nixon did not know Saxbe well but needed a candidate who would be confirmed by the Senate.

*January 6* The White House announces the appointment of James St. Clair, a Boston-based trial lawyer recommended by Colson, to head the president's Watergate legal team. Buzhardt is appointed to fill my former post of counsel to the president.

*January 7* Harris Poll: Nixon's approval rating is at an all-time low of 30 percent; 48 percent to 40 percent believe he should be impeached if his tapes were destroyed. Gallup Poll: 46 percent to 46 percent on Nixon resigning; on impeachment, 53 percent opposed and 37 percent favored.

*January 15* Panel of court-appointed experts determines that the 18½-minute gap was caused by five to nine separate manual erasures.

*January 18* After a hearing in open court, Sirica recommends a grand jury investigate possible "unlawful destruction of evidence" in connection with the 18½-minute gap and the missing April 15 tape.

*February 3* Jaworski corrects the president's State of the Union claim that he had turned over all of the tapes requested.

*February 4* St. Clair claims that my sworn testimony implicating Nixon was not borne out by the White House tapes and announces that the president will not comply with Jaworski's requests for additional tapes.

*February 6* The House of Representatives votes (with only four nays) to authorize impeachment proceedings against Nixon and to give the House Judiciary Committee broad subpoena powers to undertake the inquiry.

*February 14* Jaworski publicly states that Nixon has failed to provide him additional requested tapes. The following day, St. Clair announces that Nixon believes the prosecutor had been given sufficient evidence to determine if crimes have, in fact, been committed.

*February 22*   Jaworski provides the House impeachment inquiry with a list of tapes and documents he has sought from the White House, as the House Judiciary Committee prepares to request information.

*March 1*   The special prosecutor indicts seven former Nixon aides for conspiracy to obstruct justice in connection with the Watergate cover-up, and several others are additionally charged: Mitchell (conspiracy, false statements to the FBI, grand jury perjury and Senate perjury), Haldeman (conspiracy and three counts of Senate perjury), Ehrlichman (conspiracy, false statements to the FBI and two counts of grand jury perjury), Colson (conspiracy), Mardian (conspiracy), Parkinson (conspiracy) and Strachan (conspiracy and grand jury perjury).

*March 6*   At his press conference the president is asked about Haldeman's perjury indictment on the March 21 conversation for claiming Nixon had said "it would be wrong." Nixon offers his by now standard version of this conversation, but since Haldeman has now been indicted based on the recording of that discussion (which only the prosecutors have heard), the president adds, "Now when individuals read the entire transcript of the twenty-first meeting, or hear the entire tape, where we discussed all these options, they may reach different interpretations, but I know what I meant, and I know also what I did. I meant that the whole transaction was wrong, the transaction for the purpose of keeping this whole matter covered up." At a hearing that day in Sirica's courtroom, St. Clair announces that the president has agreed to submit over eighteen recorded conversations to the House impeachment inquiry, which have earlier been provided to Jarworski, although the House had requested forty-two additional conversations.

*March 7*   Ehrlichman, Colson and Liddy are indicted by the Watergate special prosecutor for conspiring to violate the rights of Dr. Fielding in the Ellsberg break-in. Ehrlichman is also indicted for perjury.

*March 12*   Jaworski sends a letter to St. Clair seeking sixty-four additional recorded conversations, which include the June 23, 1972, tape, in connection with the criminal proceedings against Mitchell, Haldeman, Ehrlichman, Colson, Strachan and the others in the case, which has been designated *U.S. v. Mitchell et al.*

*March 28*   The White House press office states that the court records show that ten of the forty conversations sought by the House impeachment inquiry were never recorded.

*April 11*   The House impeachment inquiry votes 33 to 3 to subpoena the forty-two recorded conversations it has requested. Jaworski sends St. Clair a follow-up letter advising him that if the White House refuses to voluntarily produce the sixty-four recorded conversations requested, a subpoena will be issued.

*April 16–18*   Jaworski requests that Sirica issue a subpoena to the president for the sixty-four requested conversations, which Sirica does on April 18.

*April 29–30*   In an address to the nation, Nixon announces he will turn over to the House impeachment inquiry, and make public, edited transcripts of Watergate conversations. He claims this submission "will at last" and "once and for all" confirm that his role in Watergate has been "just as I have described them to you from the very beginning." On April 30 he releases 1,308 pages of edited transcripts. The document opens with a 50-page introduction that attempts to point out discrepancies in my testimony of my memory of our discussions versus the recorded conversations. It next includes a 4-page listing of the forty-seven select transcripts included, beginning with our September 15, 1972, conversation; then February 28, 1973; followed by select meetings and telephone conversations in March and April 1973, most of the latter featuring Haldeman and Ehrlichman considering how to deal with me; and nine conversations when I spoke with Nixon.[4] Largely ignoring the White House's effort to frame the conversations, newspapers throughout the country print verbatim copies of the massive collection. Commentators quickly note the conspicuous absence of conversations that had been requested by the House impeachment inquiry.

*May 1*     The House impeachment inquiry votes 20 to 18 (along partisan lines) to reject Nixon's edited transcripts and formally declares that the president had failed to comply with its subpoena for forty-two requested conversations. Nixon's lawyers seek to quash Jaworski's subpoena for sixty-four conversations related to the cover-up. St. Clair informs the impeachment inquiry that it has been given everything that the White House will consent to provide. The impeachment inquiry announces it has discovered discrepancies between parts of the newly released White House transcripts and the transcripts that it has had prepared.

*May 7*     Republican Senate minority leader Hugh Scott calls the White House–edited transcripts a "deplorable, shabby, disgusting and immoral performance." St. Clair reports that the president would provide no further tapes to Jaworski or the House impeachment inquiry.

*May 11*     Harris Poll: 49 percent to 41 percent favor Nixon's impeachment (April results were 42 percent to 42 percent).

*May 20*     Judge Sirica orders Nixon to produce the sixty-four tapes subpoenaed by Jaworski for his inspection by May 31.

*May 24*     Jaworski takes Nixon's appeal of Judge Sirica's order to produce sixty-four taped conversations directly to the U.S. Supreme Court.

*May 30*     House impeachment inquiry informs Nixon that defiance of its subpoenas may "constitute a ground for impeachment."

*May 31*     The U.S. Supreme Court accepts Jaworski's appeal seeking sixty-four taped conversations.

*June 4*     A court-appointed panel of experts issues its final report on the 18½-minute gap, stating "the only completely plausible explanation" for the gap was "pushing the keys" at least five times on the recorder. (See Appendix B.)

*June 13*     Buzhardt has a heart attack and is reported to be in serious condition.

*June 23*     Len Garment, asked by a reporter, refuses to say if Nixon would comply with a Supreme Court order to provide the subpoenaed conversations to Jaworski.

*July 1*     Jaworski's brief to the Supreme Court argues that Nixon was involved in the cover-up and names him as an unindicted coconspirator, which makes his conversations relating to the conspiracy to obstruct justice relevant and admissible in the trial of members of the conspiracy (principally Haldeman,

Ehrlichman and Mitchell; a "born-again" Colson had negotiated a plea to be dropped from *U.S. v. Mitchell et al.*, in exchange for pleading guilty to obstruction of justice in the Ellsberg and Russo case).

*July 8*    Eight justices of the Supreme Court hear Jaworski's oral arguments regarding the sixty-four taped conversations that he seeks; St. Clair argues the president's case. Justice Rehnquist, because of his relationship with many of the parties involved, recuses himself.

*July 9*    St. Clair reveals that in the "public interest" Nixon might defy a Supreme Court ruling forcing him to produce the tapes.

*July 17*    Harris Poll: 53 percent to 34 percent favor Nixon's impeachment; 47 percent to 34 percent believe the Senate should convict.

*July 22*    St. Clair again refuses to say whether the president will comply with an order of the Supreme Court to turn over his subpoenaed conversations to Jaworski.

*July 24*    At 11:00 A.M. a unanimous Supreme Court rules that the president must turn over the sixty-four requested conversations to Judge Sirica. When Buzhardt calls Haig at the Western White House to inform him of the Court's decision, to his surprise, Nixon joins in on the call and tells him, "There might be a problem with the June 23 tape, Fred," and instructs him to listen to the tape.[5] Nixon's staff has by now already concluded that one or more of the tapes would be problematic, or he would not have fought so hard to keep them buried. Buzhardt quickly discovers the disaster. St. Clair, who realizes he has made material misrepresentations to the House impeachment inquiry, is very unhappy with his representation of Nixon. Buzhardt, Garment and others have concluded that Nixon should destroy his tapes, pardon everyone involved (Garment has reviewed over thirty potential pardons, should that option be undertaken), and resign. That evening, after several hours of convincing Nixon he has no choice, St. Clair announces the president will comply with the high Court's order. (St. Clair and others knew that Nixon wanted to stall, possibly for weeks, which would put them all in an impossible position.)

*July 26*    St. Clair, instructed by Judge Sirica to work out a production schedule with Jaworski, agrees to produce by 4:00 P.M. on July 30 the twenty conversations the White House had edited for earlier release as transcripts on April 29; he would produce the thirteen conversations Nixon had listened to in May by August 1; the remainder would be produced as quickly as they were prepared, even one or two at a time, if necessary. When St. Clair advises Sirica that this agreement is subject to Nixon's final approval, Sirica orders St. Clair himself to listen to the conversations, making him personally responsible and a potential witness. At the White House St. Clair refuses to listen to the three June 23, 1972, conversations of Nixon and Haldeman, or to help prepare the other conversations, but departs for a golf tournament on Cape Cod.

*July 27*    The House Judiciary Committee votes 27 to 11 (six Republicans join all twenty-one Democrats) to recommend Nixon's impeachment for obstruction of justice in the Watergate investigation. (Article I of the bill of impeachment.)

Ziegler telephones the president, who is at the beach with his daughter Tricia and son-in-law Ed Cox, to inform him of the vote.

*July 28*   As Nixon returns to Washington from San Clemente, only Buzhardt is convinced that the three June 20, 1972, conversations with Haldeman are the "smoking gun"; St. Clair is uncertain. Nixon himself insists that he knew what he meant: Having Haldeman and Ehrlichman meet with the CIA to deflect the FBI's Watergate investigation was a national security matter and not an obstruction of justice.

*July 29*   With Bull in his EOB office cueing tapes, Nixon listens to conversations he had not heard, including his first discussion with Haldeman on June 20, 1972. Late that afternoon he instructs Buzhardt and St. Clair to listen to the twenty conversations that St. Clair had committed to producing by the following day. That evening Nixon summons Bull back to the White House so he can listen to the two other conversations he had with Haldeman on June 23. The House Judiciary Committee adopts a second article of impeachment by a vote of 28 to 10, addressing Nixon's abuses of power.

*July 30*   As Nixon continues to listen to tapes in the Lincoln Sitting Room, St. Clair arrives at Sirica's courtroom shortly before four o'clock with the first group of twenty conversations for Jaworski. When Nixon completes his audit of eleven additional conversations, they are turned over to St. Clair to give to Jaworski. The House Judiciary Committee adopts a third article of impeachment by a vote of 21 to 17, addressing Nixon's defiance of the committee's subpoenas. That evening Nixon has Buzhardt listen to the two additional June 23 conversations with Haldeman, about the CIA's blocking the FBI. Nixon believes they confirm that he was expressing a national security concern; Buzhardt disagrees and says they confirm they were using national security as a cover. Nixon insists again that he knew what he meant.

*July 31*   By this time both Buzhardt and St. Clair are convinced that the June 23 conversations reveal that the Nixon defense was a fabrication and that he had been involved in the cover-up from the onset. When they confront Haig with their conclusion, he does not disagree. It is now no longer a question of if Nixon will leave office, but rather how. Nixon's aides overwhelmingly agree he should resign but do not want to force the issue lest they be accused of undertaking a coup d'état. Nixon resists Haig's request to make a transcript of the June 23 conversations, but Haig finally prevails. Haig, Ziegler, Buzhardt and others take turns explaining to Nixon the seriousness of his situation so that he can make the decision that only he can make: resignation.[6]

*August 2*   Nixon turns over thirteen more conversations, and Sirica sets an August 7 deadline for Nixon to produce the remaining thirty-one conversations due under the subpoena and ordered by the Supreme Court. California Republican congressman Charles Wiggins, Nixon's strongest and most able defender on the House Judiciary Committee, is invited to Haig's office and given a copy of the June 23 conversation with Haldeman to read. He immediately realizes its implications and asks both men when they had first learned of this new evidence. Both dissemble and tell him it was while transcribing the tapes for release, when, in fact, both had known about it before the impeachment voting had started. Haig reports that the tapes will be provided to the House Judiciary Committee on Monday, August 5, thus becoming public. Wiggins, to the surprise of Haig and St. Clair, does not leak what he has learned.

*August 5*   Nixon publicly releases the "smoking gun" tapes of June 23, 1972. His loyal supporters, both on the White House staff and throughout government and the news media, discover they have been lied to by the president and can no longer support him. Nixon quickly loses all backing on Capitol Hill, making impeachment and conviction a certainty. The White House staff all but implodes.

*August 8*   The president decides he must resign. At 9:00 P.M. he addresses the nation from the Oval Office, announcing, "I shall resign the presidency effective at noon tomorrow." Notwithstanding desperate pleas by Haldeman and Ehrlichman for pardons, he turns them down.

*August 9*   After an emotional farewell speech to his staff, Nixon departs for California. Gallup Poll: 79 percent to 13 percent believe Nixon did the "the best thing" by resigning.

*September 8*   President Gerald Ford pardons Nixon, precluding criminal prosecution for any of his activities as president.

*October 14*   *U.S. v. Mitchell et al.* trial opens. The special prosecutor prepares between sixteen to twenty-two hours of the recorded conversations to play during the trial. For technical legal reasons, Gordon Strachan is dropped from the case, and later the charges against him were dropped as well. The defendants standing trial are John Mitchell, H. R. "Bob" Haldeman, John Ehrlichman, Robert Mardian and Kenneth Parkinson.

*December 19*   Congress passes and President Ford signs into law the Presidential Recordings and Materials Preservation Act of 1974 (44 U.S.C. § 2111), placing all Nixon's presidential papers and taped conversations in federal custody to prevent their destruction.

## 1975

*January 1*   The jury returns a verdict: All defendants are guilty of conspiracy to obstruct justice except Parkinson, who was acquitted on all charges; Mitchell, Haldeman and Ehrlichman are also convicted of perjury. (Colson had negotiated a plea deal and was dropped from the case, and Strachan was separated from the case, and the charges were later dropped.)

*February 21*   Mitchell, Haldeman and Ehrlichman are sentenced to 2½ to 8 years for their crimes. They serve approximately 18 months in federal prisons.[7] (Mardian, sentenced to 10 months to 3 years, had his conviction reversed on appeal, because his lead attorney became ill during his trial. The Watergate special prosecutors decided not to retry him.)

# ACKNOWLEDGMENTS

Any shortcomings in this book are mine. If it accomplishes what I have set out to do—sift through and report on the entire recorded archive of Nixon's Watergate conversations—it is because I had a lot of help from many people.

First there were those too often nameless people at the National Archives and Records Administration (NARA) responsible for the Nixon tapes. I have dedicated this book to their good work, which has been done with a relatively small and evolving staff. Few understand the difficulty of their undertaking. They deserve mention. Forty-two people have been involved in varying degrees over several decades in processing the Nixon tapes, with titles of director, supervisory archivists, archivists, archives specialists and archives technicians, and collectively they have assembled, catalogued, reviewed, developed subject logs, posted online and preserved this rare collection. They are (alphabetically): Daniel Kaplan, Ellen Knight, Maarja Krusten, David C. Lake, A. J. Lutz, Clarence Lyons, Charles Mayn, Sam McClure, Melissa McFee, Richard E. McNeill, Cary McStay, David Mengel, Daniel Milin, Timothy Naftali, Wanda Overstreet, Walton Owen, Sharman Powell, John Powers, Jonathan Roscoe, Amanda Ross, Rodney A. Ross, Lisa Rottenberg, Samuel W. Rushay, Mary Elizabeth Ruwell, Dave Sabo, Carol Sanford, Paul A. Schmidt, Mark Sgambettera, Margie Sherrif, James Shine, Emily Soapes, Ronald Sodano, Sue Ellen Stanley, Robert Storm, Michael Sullivan, Wayne Thompson, David S. Van Tassel, David Van Wagner, Karl Weissenbach, Paul Wormser and Leonard C. Yorke.

When I started this project, the Nixon recordings where located at the NARA facility in College Park, Maryland, where virtually everyone listed above worked on the processing of the tapes. To understand the information found in the tapes I have also drawn on documents from other NARA collections, particularly those created by the Watergate Special Prosecutor Force, which has been processed and maintained by David Paynter, in College Park, and who has been of assistance with several of my books.

When copies of the tapes and the original Nixon documents were moved to the NARA-operated Nixon library in Yorba Linda, California, the materials became even more accessible when Timothy Naftali became the first NARA director of this facility, and he and his staff could not have been more helpful to me in locating material, more specifically: Gregory Cumming, Ryan Pettigrew, Melissa Lew Heddon, Jason Schultz, Meghan Lee-Parker, Jon Fletcher, Carla Braswell, Dorissa Martinez, Craig Ellefson and Pamla Eisenberg.

Next I must acknowledge the terrific work of the graduate students who assisted by transcribing the bulk of the recorded conversations for me, preparing drafts from which I assembled this book. This evolving team was recruited and recommended by a friend who teaches history/archival science at California State University at San Bernardino, Professor Thomas Maxwell-Long. Here are the names of my able transcribers: Michelle Lorimer, Sarah Novak, Michelle Garcia-Ortiz, Aaron Beitzel, Sarah Promritz and Cherity Bacon. Collectively they prepared approximately 750 transcripts starting on the project in June 2010, and it ended in May 2014. Cherity Bacon, who I mention in the preface, alone transcribed over 500 of the conversations. While working on her master's degree in archives and records administration, now working on a Ph. D. and raising a family, she found time for this project. With the exception of your author, she has listened to more Nixon Watergate conversations than anyone else in the world, a distinction and experience I have been reluctant to ask her about.

Finally, there have been those who have been vital to editing this hefty work, and then assembled this book, all very quickly to make the long-planned publication date shortly before the fortieth anniversary of Nixon's resignation as president. Every page reflects the deft touch and insights of my editor extraordinaire, Rick Kot, a gifted professional with whom I have had the good fortunate of doing three books. Also Rick's assistant, Nick Bromley, who works quietly and highly effectively, so he surely must lighten the load for Rick because he certainly does for authors. Copy editor Rachel Burd had questions sufficient to make a companion volume as she caught everything from unidentified characters wandering into this story to my syntax snags and typos, not to mention keeping the style consistent. The book's elegant design was developed by Amy Hill, and for me it gives the material the feeling of importance it deserves. Production editor Sharon Gonzalez has kept the project on track. Rick calls Sharon "unflappable," which has been essential for this project. Keeping an eye over it all, leading the entire Viking publishing ensemble, has been Clare Ferraro, Viking's president, and her motto for this book has made it possible: "Give John the time he needs." Now it is time for the media-savvy Bennett (Ben) Petrone, who has provided invaluable assistance with my prior Viking books, to launch another.

As with all my recent books, literary agent Lydia Wills has shepherded the business side of this book with wisdom and enthusiasm. I feel fortunate to have Lydia's acumen and counsel in my book publishing projects. Last but not least is the most important acknowledgment of them all—for my partner in life, wife Maureen, who provides not merely the support system that enables me to take on such a project but is the editor in chief for everything I write, for it always crosses her desk before it goes anywhere.

Bottom line: Allow me to acknowledge I am a fortunate author.

John W. Dean
Los Angeles, California
May 2014

# Appendix A

## Break-in at the
## Democratic National Committee

Although this book focuses on the Watergate cover-up, it contains many passing references to the reasons for the break-in at the Democratic National Committee that arose in a number of the president's recorded conversations. For that reason, I made reference to Appendix A in a footnote whenever this topic arose during the narrative.

When listening to Nixon's Watergate conversations I noticed Ron Ziegler's description in two of them of a phenomenon that is often referred to as the Rashomon effect (although he did not specifically use this phrase). It is occasionally utilized by scholars and journalists to describe how individual eyewitnesses have differing recollections of the same event after the fact.[1] From police lineups to accident investigations, it is well known that firsthand accounts are notoriously unreliable.[2] Yet those directly involved with the Watergate break-in—Magruder, Liddy, Hunt and the burglary team—have been fundamentally consistent and similar in their explanations of the reasons for the break-in, apart from a few minor variations. So, too, are the discussions in Nixon's Watergate conversations.

### White House Discussions

Although a powerful argument can be made that Nixon's demands for information about the Democrats and Larry O'Brien were the catalysts for the Watergate operation, in fact, there is no evidence in all the Nixon-Watergate–related conversations that anyone in the White House had advance knowledge that Liddy was going into the Watergate, only speculation about Gordon Strachan.* Nonetheless Nixon did ask Haldeman, Ehrlichman and me for our understandings of why Liddy and his team had broken into and bugged the DNC. No one in Nixon's circle had better information than Haldeman, and he and Ehrlichman shared what they knew; I had no information to offer. Because there have been lingering questions raised about the reason for the Watergate break-in, the conversations throughout this book when this subject was discussed can be reviewed to obtain the understandings of those involved as to what the burglars were looking for.

---

*That argument is outlined in the prologue.

On June 20, 1972, just three days after the arrests at the Watergate and on his first day back in his office, Nixon told Haldeman, "My God, the [Democratic National] Committee, isn't worth bugging, in my opinion. That's my public line." "Except for this financial thing," Haldeman commented. "They thought they had something going on that." "Yeah, I suppose," Nixon agreed.[3] This exchange suggests that they had had a prior conversation on this subject, and it is clear that they discussed Watergate on the flight back to Washington on June 19. A little over a month later, when the president was gently chiding Haldeman for having an intelligence operation in the reelection committee, Haldeman explained that Mitchell had wanted it, and he vaguely mentioned his interest had been "on the finance thing."[4] On December 10, when this subject arose in another conversation, Haldeman again mentioned that "Mitchell was pushing" regarding "[s]ecret papers, and financial data that O'Brien had, that he was going to get. I didn't even know about that."[5]

During a January 3, 1973, conversation with Haldeman, shortly after Haldeman had had a long meeting with Magruder (which was really their first meeting since the arrests at the Watergate some six months earlier), Nixon said, "I can see Mitchell, but I can't see Colson getting into the Democratic [Committee]." "What the Christ was he looking for?" Nixon asked, and Haldeman could now explain more fully: "They were looking for stuff on two things. One on financial, and the other on stuff that they thought they had on what they were going to do at Miami, to screw us up, which apparently was—a Democratic plot. That they thought they had uncovered. Colson was salivating with glee at the thought of what he might be able to do with it. And the investigator types were reluctant to go in there; they were put under tremendous pressure [that] they had to get this stuff. None of this, I don't know any of this firsthand. I can't prove any of it. Really, I don't want to know. As I pointed out, because if I ever get involved in it, I want to be ignorant, which I am."[6] This report to Nixon was clearly based on Haldeman's conversation with Magruder, who would have told Haldeman everything he knew.

The reason for the DNC entry and bugging next arose in a conversation with me on March 13. "A lot of people around here had knowledge that something was going on over there," at the reelection committee. I informed the president, "They didn't have any knowledge of the details, of the specifics of the whole thing." "You know," Nixon began, "that must be an indication, though, of the fact that they had God damn poor pickings. Because naturally anybody, either Chuck or Bob, was always reporting to me about what was going on. If they ever got any information, they would certainly have told me that we got some information, but they never had a God damn [laughs] thing to report. What was the matter? Did they never get anything out of the damn thing?" "No. I don't think they ever got anything," I answered. "It was a dry hole, huh?" Nixon asked, which I confirmed, and then he volunteered, "But Bob one time said something about the fact we got some information about this or that or the other, but I think it was about the convention, what they were planning, I said they're [unclear]."[7]

When discussing Watergate with the president on March 16, Ehrlichman shared a well-informed theory of what had happened in considerable detail. He recalled that, about the time Liddy's intelligence-gathering plans were being drawn up, "there was also that [rumor] that the Democrats had entered into an illegal alliance with [Florida governor Reubin] Askew for financing of their convention in Florida," which prompted Nixon to say in confirmation, "So, they were just trying to find that out." Ehrlichman added, "And there were a lot of things floating around that particular job." Nixon also noted, as this conversation proceeded, that the White House had been interested in learning "about the Democratic convention."[8] The next day, on March 17, when I told the president, "I cannot understand why they decided to go in the DNC. That absolutely mystifies me as to what—" I began, but then interjected midsentence: "Anybody who's walked around a national committee knows that there's nothing there." The president, evidencing more knowledge than I possessed, explained, "Well, the point is, they're trying to see what they could develop in terms of the—" Nixon did not complete his thought but seemed to imply that it had been a fishing expedition.[9] During my conversation with the president on March 21, when we were discussing the fact that nothing was found in the DNC, Nixon made the following comment: "But Bob one time said something about the fact we got some information about this or that or the other, but I think it was about the convention, what they were planning, I said they're [*unclear*]."[10] Here the president was repeating what he had told me on March 13.

Haldeman consistently reported that Liddy's undertaking related to Larry O'Brien and the Democratic convention. During the March 28 conversation, Haldeman reported to the president about Magruder's effort to involve the White House in the break-in based, in part, on Colson. He said that, according to Magruder: "Colson called [him] twice to tell him to get going on this thing, and he specifically referred to the Larry O'Brien information, was hard on that. And Jeb says Hunt and Liddy were in Colson's office, and LaRue was in Jeb's office on that phone call." Nixon asked why Larry O'Brien, and Haldeman responded, he was told, "Well, that is what they're bugging the Watergate for." When Nixon pressed for more facts about why O'Brien had been targeted, Haldeman answered, "Information regarding the Florida convention stuff, down there." Later in this conversation Nixon asked, "This stuff on O'Brien had to do with O'Brien's activities at the convention?" Haldeman affirmed, "Apparently." As they talked over each other, Nixon asked if they had gotten into "O'Brien's business with [Howard] Hughes, did he get into that, or not?" Haldeman said, "No." Nixon responded, "Okay, sounds good."[11] The last recorded Nixon conversation about this subject was on April 14, 1973, when Ehrlichman said that, based on his investigation (and conversation with Magruder), when Colson called to encourage him to get the Liddy plans approved by Mitchell, Colson had been pushing for information on Larry O'Brien.

If this obsession with O'Brien and the Democrats' convention seems irrational, there was little about Watergate that was otherwise.

# Appendix B
## The 18½-Minute Gap

*I am indebted to the remarkably thorough background research undertaken by Cleveland-based attorney Jim Robenalt, with whom I do continuing legal education programs (see: www.WatergateCLE.com). Jim became interested in this subject and discovered, in the course of his research as reported below, that it was mechanically impossible for Rose Mary Woods to (as she claimed) have erased part—or, as Alexander Haig suggested, all—of the June 20, 1972, conversation in question.*

This appendix addresses a frequently asked question regarding Watergate: Who was responsible for the 18½-minute gap—leaving behind a shrill buzz—on the tape of the June 20, 1972, conversation between President Nixon and H. R. "Bob" Haldeman, and what was erased? Two observations should be made about these questions. First, the answers to them have virtually no historic significance whatsoever as they provide no information about or insight into Watergate that cannot already be found in abundance elsewhere. If the question still lingers, it is due to the amount of news media attention the gap received when it was first revealed—and to the fact that everyone loves a mystery, even when it is ultimately meaningless. Only because the 18½-minute gap mystery has persisted am I addressing it here. Which brings me to the second observation: Knowing what I now know, after having gone through and studied all the Watergate conversations, it is easier to answer the "what" part of the question than the "who"—though I have some new "who" information as well.

At the time of the gap's discovery in late November 1973, these questions could not be answered, and the matter was dropped when Nixon resigned. Yet a rather detailed record was developed by the Watergate special prosecutor's office in its unsuccessful efforts to investigate the missing material and whether there had been an intentional destruction of evidence. Those records are located at the National Archives in College Park, Maryland. While I have made a quick pass through that record, others, like Jim Robenalt, who find this a fascinating puzzle, have studied this material in great depth. Here I am only going to make a few key points about it.

## Background: How the Issue Arose

Following the public uproar after the Saturday Night Massacre on October 20, 1973, which sent Watergate special prosecutor Archibald Cox back to Harvard after he demanded actual copies of the president's recorded conversation, Nixon quickly caved to public pressure, and on October 23 sent his lawyers to notify Judge Sirica that he would comply with the judge's August 29 order (upheld by the Court of Appeals on October 12) to produce the requested tapes: six conversations with me and three that took place on June 20, 1972—the first day Nixon was back at the White House following the June 17 arrests at the DNC—with Haldeman, Ehrlichman and Mitchell.[1]

A week later, on October 30, 1973, Fred Buzhardt returned to Judge Sirica's courtroom to report that two of the requested conversations allegedly did not exist: the June 20, 1972, telephone call with John Mitchell, which Nixon had made from the White House residence using a telephone that was not included in the recording system; and the April 15, 1973, conversation with me in the president's EOB office, of which no record existed because it was claimed that the recording system had run out of tape that weekend. Not surprisingly, in the aftermath of the Saturday Night Massacre, Buzhardt's report of missing conversations created new headlines and even greater suspicion about Nixon's behavior. Why, for example, had the White House waited so many months after receiving the subpoena to divulge that two of the conversations were missing? No good answer was forthcoming from the White House; instead, Buzhardt claimed that they had been so certain that they were going to win in court that they had not bothered to look for the requested information. Judge Sirica wanted to get to the bottom of what had happened, so he called for an open hearing, which began on the last day of October and proceeded for several weeks, into November 1973. The explanation given during these hearings for the missing June 20 conversation with Mitchell—that Nixon had made the call to Mitchell from a telephone that did not record them—made sense. However, the account given for my April 15 conversation being missing was less than satisfactory, even at the time, but given the discovery of the July 10, 1973, conversation with Steve Bull, it makes no sense at all. It appears, rather, that the Nixon White House succeeded in making the April 15 conversation disappear.

## A New Mystery Regarding the April 15 Conversation

During my testimony before the Senate Watergate committee on June 25, 1973, I testified that I believed I had been taped on April 15 when meeting with the president shortly after 9:00 P.M., and I encouraged the committee to determine if such a recording existed.[2] A copy of my testimony was running on the newswires even before I completed it, so it is very possible that it set off an alarm at the Western White House. Later that day, after seven o'clock in Washington and four o'clock in California, at the request of the president, Steve Bull called the head of the Secret Service Technical Division, Louis Sims, and instructed him to get "a certain tape and listening equipment to be sent to California—via Buzhardt," according to the

Watergate special prosecutor's office summary digest of the November 1973 tapes hearing testimony of Sims, who had replaced Al Wong. At some point, however, the plan to send the tape and listening equipment to the Western White House (on the next courier flight) was canceled, and Bull arranged for Buzhardt to listen to the conversation in Washington in Buzhardt's White House office.

Because of the July 10 conversation between Bull and the president, we now know the identity of the tape Buzhardt listened to on June 25. On July 10 they had the following exchange: "Well, you directly authorized me on April 15, did you not, sir, when we were in California?" Bull asked the president. "Oh, yeah, sure," Nixon said. "That's the only one Buzhardt has heard," Bull reported. "No, no, no. I authorized that. I directed that, because I didn't want that sent out there [to the Western White House]. Oh, shit. [I'd forgotten about that]," Nixon said. "And that is the only one," Bull clarified. "That was on the day, just April 15," Nixon repeated. "Just that one, yeah, that is correct," Bull agreed and departed.[3] There is no hesitation or uncertainty in this brief exchange: Bull was clearly confirming that they both recalled that it was, in fact, the April 15 conversation that Buzhardt had been instructed to listen to on June 25.

This conversation in July refutes both Bull's and Buzhardt's later testimony that Buzhardt listened to my March 20 telephone call with the president on June 25. In fact, it makes no sense for anyone to have listened to the March 20 telephone conversation on June 25 when the only purpose was to request a meeting the next day. It is clear that Steve Bull had already listened to this March 20 call, which was consistent with the president's June 4 instruction to Bull to go through my telephone calls. The information provided to Fred Thompson in June (before my testimony) by Buzhardt, about my conversations with Nixon, show that the March 20 telephone call had been reviewed, given the level of detail Thompson had . His notes state what he was told: "The president called Dean that night, and Dean said that there was 'not a scintilla of evidence' to indicate White House involvement and Dean suggested he give the president a more in-depth briefing on what had transpired." This statement by me regarding "not a scintilla of evidence" occurred almost at the end of the conversation. In addition, Nixon told Bull on June 4 that he was not interested in the April 15 conversation, because he could recall it. In the material provided to Thompson, the April 15 conversation is described as follows: "Dean along with almost everybody else was called in that day. The president told Dean that he must go before the grand jury without immunity." It appears no one had listened to this conversation.[4]

In short, there was no reason on June 25 to listen to the March 20 telephone call that Buzhardt later claimed he listened to that evening. On the other hand, given my Senate testimony, the White House had reason for concern about the April 15 conversation. It would, most important, have shown that Nixon's firewall defense was untrue, by his own admissions.

Clearly White House witnesses were volunteering nothing at the November missing tapes hearing. Rose Mary Woods, who also testified, remained silent about what she thought had been a terrible mistake she had made that became known as the 18½-minute gap. To explain Ms. Woods's mistake, it is necessary to go back to an earlier date, before Buzhardt reported the two conversations missing, for the 18½-minute gap did not surface until after November 12, 1973, when the initial tape hearing was ending. But the relevant events that resulted in discovery of the tape gap began well before that time.

## Discovery of the 18½-Minute Gap

The tapes were in the custody of the Secret Service. Their record of who made use of the tapes, such as it was, indicates that there was some activity involving the tapes before Butterfield revealed the system. Haldeman listened to the March 21 conversation on two occassions in April. On June 4, the president spent the day listening to a number of our conversations, assigning Bull to listen to our telephone calls.* No further tapes were removed from the Secret Service vault until June 25, which is when Buzhardt listened to either the April 15 conversation (according to Bull's near contemporaneous statement on July 10) or the conversation of March 20 (according to Buzhardt's recollection after the April 15 one was found missing). On July 10 and 11, Bull pulled tapes for Haldeman—apparently the September 15, 1972, conversation with me was on two reels. It was while Nixon was fighting in court to protect the tapes that Bull next gathered some to take to Camp David for Rose Woods to start transcribing, after they had been placed in the custody of the president or, more specifically, that of his chief of staff, Al Haig.

The first conversation requested in the subpoena was: "(a) Meeting of June 20, 1972, in the President's Executive Office Building ('EOB') office involving Richard Nixon, John Ehrlichman and H. R. Haldeman from 10:30 A.M. to noon (time approximate)." In fact, there was no such meeting, but rather, two separate meetings, first with Ehrlichman and then with Haldeman. Because Rose found the Cox subpoena confusing, she asked for guidance as to which conversation was being requested, and she was told by Buzhardt to transcribe the Ehrlichman one. Other than a flippant comment at the end of the discussion, there was no mention of Watergate whatsoever with Ehrlichman at his first meeting with the president following the arrests at the DNC.† Rose did not finish the transcription that day and resumed when she returned to her White House office on Monday, October 1. Because the recording machine she was using did not have a foot pedal control, it made it much more difficult for her to transcribe, so during the morning of October 1, she asked for a machine with a foot pedal and a smaller headset. The Secret Service did not have such a device, so it purchased a new Uher 5000 recorder, which was equipped as she had requested and arrived at about 1:15 P.M. on October 1. Woods finished up the June 20 Ehrlichman conversation on her new machine, and while checking to be sure she had found the end of it, she went directly into the Haldeman conversation that followed. It was then that she heard a "shrill buzz" on the tape. Believing she had caused a four- to five-minute erasure by mistakenly

---

*See Part IV, page 589. Note: The November 1973 tapes hearing indicates that Bull obtained the April 15, 1973, conversation with me at that time.

†See Part I, page 19.

pressing the record button instead of the off button and then the foot pedal of her new machine while she spoke on the telephone, she believed she had caused the erasure. She immediately told the president what had happened. He assured her that it was not a problem, because the Haldeman portion of the tape had not been subpoenaed, at which she returned to transcribing other conversations.

It was during the following two weeks (with almost daily front-page stories covering the missing tapes imbroglio) that Rose Woods's shrill buzzing on the June 20 Haldeman conversation was discovered by others at the White House. On November 14, as Buzhardt was preparing an index for the tapes he would turn over to Judge Sirica on November 20, he reread the subpoena request for the June 20 material, and the submissions that Cox had made with his own subpoena, and realized that the Haldeman portion had also been cited in the Sirica subpoena, although he would not tell the judge for a week. It is at this time, he claims, that he learned of the gap in the recording. It was next discovered that it was not the four to five minutes that Woods had believed it to be but over eighteen minutes. Haldeman's notes quickly confirmed that the missing part of the conversation was related to Watergate. All this would be investigated in great detail, for Judge Sirica would not only convene another public hearing on the newly discovered tape gap, but would appoint six acoustic and sound-engineering experts to examine it; they would unanimously agree that it had been intentionally erased on the Uher 5000 used by Rose Mary Woods.[5] Sirica would recommend that a grand jury investigate this potential destruction of evidence. Today these records of the investigation into the tape gap are available at NARA, with some available online.[6] The matter has been written about in several books by those directly involved.[7]

## Who Did Not Erase the June 20 Conversation?

Jim Robenalt has discovered and recently reported information that shows that, contrary to what was believed at the time and has remained the received history, Rose Mary Woods could not, in fact, have erased part or all of the tape, as others claim, and as she admitted doing when she discovered the buzzing sound on the tape.* The facts are rather compelling.

The court-appointed experts conclusively found that the machine that had erased the June 20 conversation with Haldeman, leaving a shrill buzzing sound, was the Uher 5000. In the words of the experts: "Support for this conclusion includes recorder operating characteristics that we measured and found to correspond to signal characteristics observed on the evidence tape." These sound experts, however, were not experts on the Uher 5000. But the FBI had located a specialist in the Uher 5000, and had Nixon not resigned and the inquiry into the destruction of the June 20 tape not been largely abandoned, this expert likely would have been called to Washington to testify. Jim Robenalt found this Uher 5000 expert, Doug Blackwell, on the Internet some four decades later and interviewed him.

Blackwell, who at the time was one of the few Uher 5000 (a machine that was built in Germany and imported into the United States) service technicians in the

*See www.cbsnews.com/videos/who-erased-18-minutes-of-nixon-watergate-tapes/.

United States, reported that the accident that Rose Woods described in detail in sworn testimony—she had mistakenly hit the record button, instead of the off button, when she answered the telephone and then pressed her foot pedal—could not have happened. Blackwell explained that the Uher 5000 was designed to prevent exactly that type of accident from occurring. It was mechanically impossible to depress the record button, placing the machine in record mode (which would erase over the content of the tape), while the reels were turning. Also, the foot pedal would not engage in this situation. Without getting too deep into the mechanical operations of the Uher 5000—as Jim Robenalt did when he spoke with Blackwell— by the end of the conversation Jim had no doubt whatsoever that Rose could not have erased the tape in any of the variations or combinations of the testimony she gave to explain how she had erased the material, which was basically as she had told the president: She had accidentally hit the record switch rather than the off switch, and then put her foot on the pedal causing the tape to turn on its reels and thus causing the problem.

So if Rose Woods did not erase the tape, that leaves the even larger question of who did, and of what was erased. Based on my conversations with Jim, I believe there is a very small field of potential candidates who might have been responsible: Richard Nixon, Al Haig, Fred Buzhardt, Steve Bull, John Bennett, Haig's aide, and Nixon's one-time military aide, Jack Brennan, are potential candidates. Who did it can only be established by a preponderance of the evidence, rather than beyond a reasonable doubt, unless a confession should surface. In fairness to all the potential candidates, more than a passing paragraph is needed to set forth the rather extensive and at times complex evidence. After having gone through all Nixon's Watergate conversations, I have concluded that, in the end, while there is no absolute proof about who did it, there really is no mystery at all about what was erased. And then who did it is not as important as what was erased.

## What Was Erased?

To understand what was erased it is necessary to consider why Nixon (or someone acting on his behalf or in his interest) would wish to have such material erased. The answer seems fairly clear and relates to the timing of Nixon's defense. The president adopted his final defense—that he had no knowledge of a cover-up until I told him during our March 21 conversation—in his April 30 speech when firing Haldeman, Ehrlichman, Kleindienst and me, and he doubled down on that defense in his May 22 statement. This, undoubtedly, was why he had only listened to my conversations before March 21, to determine if he could claim that I had not informed him of the cover-up in any of those discussions. While I had strongly suggested it in several of our talks prior to March 21, and in fact had spoken to him as if he was well aware of it, I had not previously done so as strongly and unequivocally as I did on March 21. So as he twisted and reconstituted the March 21 conversation to meet his needs, only a conversation revealing that he actually had knowledge of the cover-up before March 21 would be a threat to his defense.

Undoubtedly Nixon had no idea what he had said in any of the requested June 20 conversations, other than that he had spoken with Mitchell from the residence.

If the June 20 conversations revealed his having knowledge of, not to mention being involved in, the cover-up, the Nixon defense would have been destroyed. For example, had Cox asked for Nixon's conversation at the end of the day on June 20, when he called Haldeman to report on his conversation with Mitchell, it would have revealed Nixon saying: "I gave Mitchell a call. Cheered him up a little bit, I told him not to worry, that we might be able to control this Watergate thing." And one of Nixon's ideas to control it was a Miami-based Cuban defense fund: "They could raise money for the purpose of paying these fines, and all, and so forth."* Or if Cox had requested the tape of Nixon's meeting the following morning, June 21, he would have heard Haldeman explain his discussion with Mitchell earlier that same morning: "Mitchell's concern is the FBI, the question of how far they're going in the process. And he's pretty concerned that that be turned off, and John's [Ehrlichman] working on it." "My God," Nixon insisted, "if you are talking to Gray, it's got to be done by Ehrlichman." Cox did not seek these tapes, because he needed to establish probable cause; since he did not then have probable cause until later, his subpoena likely would have been rejected,

As the conversations from those first days reveal, Nixon took part in the cover-up from the outset. What he was surely discussing during this gap in the Haldeman conversation was not some great confession to Haldeman of White House involvement in the Watergate break-in, for contrary to media speculation, there was no such involvement. What he most likely said to Haldeman was what he had to Mitchell, or indicated his approval of an earlier version of Ehrlichman's scenario. While it was not a major issue at the time, after Nixon had announced his defense, it became a potentially drastic problem, for the tape would put the lie to his own claims. Based on the conversations that transpired later that day, as well as over the next several days, it seems clear that the June 20 tape must have contained some general comment that revealed his involvement in the cover-up. For example, during these early days Nixon repeatedly said that he did not want Mitchell to be ruined by Watergate, when he clearly suspected Mitchell had a serious problem. During this first week he did not want the FBI to get out of control, as he made clear on June 21, and ordered action via the CIA to control the FBI on June 23. In fact similar broad, as well as specific, cover-up–type comments and instructions can be found in conversations that took place throughout the months before the March 21 discussion. While there was never any doubt in my mind that the cover-up would never have proceeded without Nixon's approval, until I had transcribed all the conversations found in Parts I and II of this book, I could not be certain. But today I have no doubt of the nature of the material that was erased on June 20 during the 18½-minute gap.

*See Part I, page 30.

# NOTES

## Preface

1 When listening to a conversation, we seldom notice the "ah," "ah," "ahs" and "you know," or "well, ah," and the like—the false starts, changes in direction midsentence and awkward phrases that so often are part of the spoken word. And we certainly do not include such matter in our notes of conversations. While I prepared verbatim transcripts for all of the conversations involved in this project, those are generally very difficult to read, if not distracting. Indeed, the work of even stenographic reporters, which comes close to verbatim, is not really a transcript of what they are recording. For that reason, as I did with my earlier book based on Nixon's tapes (*The Rehnquist Choice: The Untold Story of the Nixon Appointment That Redefined the Supreme Court* [New York: Free Press, 2001]), I have used my verbatim transcripts as the basis for the dialogue and narrative in this story but cleaned it up to make it readable, without making changes in the substance, or gist, of the statements I have chosen to tell the story. In short, the material in this story is based on exactly what was said, when it was said and whenever possible exactly as it was said, but occasionally I have added a word to clarify using [a bracket] to indicate that I have done so, and I have occasionally paraphrased spoken material in brackets. Also I have simply corrected a tangled phrase without changing its meaning. But I have not [bracketed] every such minor change, because it would make reading difficult. Nor have I used ellipses when I have compressed statements, and no empty brackets [] or [*sic*]s. I have added a bracket when adding a word, or when something was not clear but I felt I could take an educated guess at the word that was used. Anyone who wants a verbatim record is welcome to prepare their own transcripts, for the conversations underlying this story are readily available to anyone who wishes to listen to them. Indeed, they are fascinating. See Nixon White House tapes online, at http://nixon.archives.gov/virtuallibrary/tapeexcerpts/index.php.

2 Richard Nixon, *RN: The Memoirs of Richard Nixon* (New York: Grosset & Dunlap, 1978), x.

3 Butterfield impeachment inquiry testimony, Testimony of Witnesses, Hearings Before the Committee on the Judiciary, House of Representatives, 93rd Congress, 2nd Session, Book I (Washington, DC: Government Printing Office, 1974).

## Prologue

1 June 16, 1972, president's daily diary (hereafter PDD), National Archives and Records Administration (NARA). All dates and times of the president's activities in the following pages, unless otherwise indicated, are taken from the PDD. In his diary, Haldeman noted that Nixon was "extremely tired" at the end of the recently completed trip to Russia, so tired that he questioned his judgment on domestic issue questions, and if there were any decisions that needed to be made, Ehrlichman "should go ahead and make them." Two weeks of a heavy schedule that followed did not help. June 1–16, 1972, H. R. Haldeman, *The Haldeman Diaries: Inside the Nixon White House* (New York: G. P. Putnam's, 1993), 469-71.

2 Richard Nixon, *RN: The Memoirs of Richard Nixon* (New York: Grosset & Dunlap, 1978), 617, 622.

3 The highly disciplined Haldeman made 1,521 diary entries during his service at the White House, from January 18, 1969, to April 30, 1973, typically at the end of each day, first in longhand in a journal and later by dictation to a cassette recorder. For safekeeping, and later to prevent the information from reaching investigators and prosecutors, each journal and tape cassette, when completed, was marked Top Secret and placed in a safe in the office of the White House staff secretary and commingled with the president's records, where its existence remained unknown until Haldeman retrieved the material from Nixon long after his resignation and both had left Washington. It was not transcribed by Haldeman for almost twenty years after he left Washington. In the foreword of the diaries, when he was preparing them for publication shortly before his death, he explained that they set forth "actions I would now prefer had not been taken, conversations I would now like to forget or disavow, and opinions with which I now strongly disagree. In the interest of historical accuracy, the content remains unchanged from the day it was written." Haldeman, *Diaries*, 471.

4 Ibid.

5 Ehrlichman Senate testimony, 6 Senate Select Committee on Presidential Campaign Activities (SSC) 2580–82; Caulfield Senate testimony, 1 SSC 279; April 23, 1973, Summary of Investigative Reports, FBI (April 1973 Summary), 1. Ehrlichman recalled Boggs mentioning the check from Howard Hunt many years later, when writing *Witness to Power: The Nixon Years* (New York: Simon & Schuster, 1982), 347. By long-standing protocol, when the FBI name check came up on Howard Hunt—they had done a background investigation of him when he was being considered by the White House as a consultant—the Secret Service was informed, because of their protective responsibilities for the president.

6 Ehrlichman Senate testimony, 6 SSC 2580–82.

7 Caulfield Senate testimony, 1 SSC 267–68; 21 SSC 9687, 9700–7.

8 Ibid., 21 SSC 9729–37; 22 SSC 10341–56

9 Ibid. Caulfield testified that he told Ehrlichman only that it was a "disaster." Knowing Jack, however, since what he told me was that it was "a fucking disaster," he undoubtedly made that point to Ehrlichman as well. Ehrlichman does not recall Caulfield's telephone call but does not deny it may have occurred. 1 SSC 279, 6 SSC 2580.

10 Ibid., 1 SSC 253–60, 264–67.

11 Colson impeachment inquiry testimony, Testimony of Witnesses, Hearings Before the Committee on the Judiciary, House of Representatives 93rd Congress, 2nd Session, Book III (Washington, DC: Government Printing Office, 1974), 199–207. The codirectors of the SIU were Egil "Bud" Krogh, an Ehrlichman aide, and David Young, an aide to the assistant to the president for national security, Henry Kissinger. Shortly after being assigned to the SIU, David Young told me that he happened to return home for a Thanksgiving dinner and his grandmother asked him what he was doing at the White House. David explained that he was dealing with leaks for the president. "Oh, you're a plumber," his grandmother exclaimed. Upon returning to work David told Krogh the story, and they laughed, and then they decided to have a sign made for the door of the office of their supersecure location in the basement of the EOB: The Plumbers. After hanging the sign briefly, they removed it, for their mission was supposed to remain top secret.

12 Egil "Bud" Krogh with Matthew Krogh, *Integrity: Good People, Bad Choices and Life Lessons from the White House* (New York: Public Affairs, 2007), 75; and Krogh conversation with the author, February 1999.

13 Ehrlichman, *Witness to Power*, 347–48.

14 Ibid., 347.

15 According to the handwritten notes of FBI special agent Daniel Bledsoe, the extra-duty supervisor of the FBI's General Investigative Division, who was tracking the Watergate break-in case that weekend, he received a report at 8:35 P.M. from WFO agent Harold Sanders, who was assigned to the White House, and with whom Butterfield worked to maintain current White House staff background checks and clearances. Bledsoe noted that "Butterfield advised Ehrlichman Haldeman at White House. No abnormal pressure put on CIA per Haldeman at White House." I located Bledsoe's notes regarding the unfolding Watergate case, and

I went searching for them because of an astonishing reconstruction by Bledsoe of an event that weekend, information that has been buried in the FBI's files for decades.

When Bledsoe provided an oral history to the Society of Former Special Agents of the FBI in October 2009 he reported information about the White House reaction during this fateful weekend never previously reported (until some thirty-seven years after the fact). Bledsoe's interview was a recorded telephone call that was later transcribed and published. Factually, the 2009 account is deeply flawed and confused. For example, Bledsoe has "Al Hunt" trying to bail out the men arrested at the Watergate that weekend, when it was a Washington, DC, lawyer, Douglas Caddy. He has G. Gordon Liddy, whom Bledsoe knew from their days together at the FBI, being arrested at the DNC. That never happened. However, Bledsoe remembers "keeping a running log (on paper) about who called, the time, date and their reports." This did happen, and these are the notes I located, but apparently Bledsoe was unaware they still existed. More striking, however, his oral history indicated that the information from Ehrlichman was far more significant than the notes suggest. In his oral history Bledsoe claims that on Saturday, June 17, his secretary told him he had a call from the White House, which he recalled as follows:

"This is Agent Supervisor Dan Bledsoe. Who am I speaking with?" Bledsoe says that a belligerent-sounding Ehrlichman was on the line. "You are speaking with John Ehrlichman. Do you know who I am?"

"Yes. You are chief of staff there at the White House," Bledsoe responded, and although Ehrlichman was never chief of staff, he says Ehrlichman replied, "That's right. I have a mandate from the president of the United States. The FBI is to terminate the investigation of the break-in over there on Virginia Avenue [the location of the Watergate complex] that occurred during the night." When Bledsoe remained silent, he says Ehrlichman repeated his demand, and finally asked him, "Are you going to terminate the investigation?" When Bledsoe said no, he reports that Ehrlichman became upset and profane and wanted to know why not. Bledsoe says he told Ehrlichman, incorrectly if it happened, that the FBI had a constitutional obligation "to initiate an investigation" to determine if there had been a violation of the illegal interception of communications statute. Ehrlichman, according to Bledsoe, asked, "Do you know that you are saying no to the president of the United States?" A defiant Bledsoe said, "Yes." An angry Ehrlichman warned, "Bledsoe, your career is doomed," and slammed down the phone. According to Bledsoe, he then telephoned Assistant FBI Director Mark Felt, the number two man at the Bureau at the time, who had taken charge of the investigation and who told him not to worry: "That sounds like John," Felt advised, then continued, "Dan, just keep up the good work and keep me up to date." Daniel F. Bledsoe interview, August 19, 2009, Society of Former Special Agents of the FBI, at http://www.nleomf.org/assets/pdfs/nlem/oral-histories/FBI_Bledsoe_interview.pdf.

It's a remarkable account. Bledsoe is a well-respected former agent, with no signs of dementia, and thus credible. Before I found his notes, others familiar with the Watergate investigations, who find his story incredible, spoke with him. They do not know what to make of it, but Bledsoe recalled the incident clearly and is sticking by his story, although he did acknowledge he confused Hunt and Liddy, and a few other details. While Ehrlichman was seldom profane, I cannot say this exchange is out of character, for I have seen him act in this manner. Nor is it impossible that Alex Butterfield might have been the one who called Bledsoe and, taking a strong position on Ehrlichman's behalf, delivered this message, although Alex does not recall doing so. What is most remarkable about this information—or, more to the point, the information in Bledsoe's notes—is the fact that this information was never given to anyone in the U.S. Attorney's Office, nor later to the Watergate special prosecutor's office.

Bledsoe's notes, and his memory of the exchange, cannot be ignored, so I have included them in this endnote. I spoke with him, and he clearly remembered these events and sounded as though he had an excellent memory. At the same time, this is a good example of why reconstructed memories like his have been avoided in this book, for they are too often erroneous. The weakness of memory becomes glaring when comparing testimony based on memory with actual information secretly recorded by Nixon. This is true of everyone, including yours truly. Nonetheless, what does appear to be the case is that, while memory is not time-and-date stamped, and it can confuse and commingle facts and events, honest memory does typically recall the general gist of events. Clearly something occurred between Bledsoe at the FBI and the White House on June 17, 1972, and that is confirmed by Bledsoe's June 17, 1972, notes. Ehrlichman, either directly or through Butterfield indirectly, passed a message to the FBI to push back on the aggressive investigation they launched from the moment they entered the case, as they pursued Hunt's CIA relationship, which was a problem for Ehrlichman.

When I spoke with Bledsoe he told me that his handwritten notes were different from the memorandum he recalled dictating to his secretary on just his conversation with Ehrlichman. I have shared this information with others, who requested that the FBI historian see if he could find that memo. So far, it has not turned up.

16  "5 Held in Plot to Bug Democrats' Office Here," *The Washington Post*, June 18, 1972, A-1.

17  "Intruders Foiled by Security Guard," *The Washington Post*, June 19, 1972, A-23.

18  Ehrlichman grand jury testimony, WSPF, May 3, 1973, 55–60.

19  Haldeman, *Diaries*, 471; and June 18, 1972, H. R. Haldeman notes, NARA.

20  Magruder Senate testimony, 2 SSC 815–16.

21  Ehrlichman Senate testimony, 6 SSC 2581. See also Haldeman testimony, *U.S. v. Mitchell et al.*, November 29, 1974, Transcript, 8439–41

22  Haldeman, *Diaries*, 472.

23  Ibid.

24  Nixon, *RN*, 625–26.

25  Colson impeachment inquiry testimony, Testimony of Witnesses, Hearings Before the Committee on the Judiciary, Book III, 259. Colson made his own testimony hearsay, claiming he could only testify to what he told his aide, Desmond Barker, who later reminded him.

26  Haldeman, *Diaries*, 472.

27  This account is distilled from Dean Senate testimony, 3 SSC 993; Dean testimony, *U.S. v. Mitchell et al.*, October 16, 1972, 2649–51; Dean, *Blind Ambition*; and G. Gordon Liddy, *Will: The Autobiography of G. Gordon Liddy* (New York: St. Martin's Press, 1997), 257. Until reading Liddy's account I had forgotten that he had told me he and Hunt had used Bernard Barker and Eugenio Martinez for the Ellsberg break-in in California; Jack Caulfield gave me the same information in broader terms.

28  Dean Senate testimony, 3 SSC 929–31.

29  When I took over Butterfield's responsibilities liaising with the Secret Service, and I had to sort out problems such as Bebe Rebozo driving the president when they were together, I once had a discussion with the head of the protective detail about what the president and Rebozo did on their periodic boat rides on Bebe's houseboat. The agent in charge told me that he was once curious himself, because he was posted in the back of the boat on the roof, and on one trip, when he heard no activity for a long time, he took off his shoes, went down the ladder and peeked in the window to see what was going on. He said Rebozo and the president were stretched out on separate chairs simply reading and not saying a word to each other. The agent also told me that frequently, on their long walks, they would never exchange so much as a single word. He had concluded, based on conversations with other agents, that the president simply enjoyed Rebozo's company, so much of the time spent together was in silence.

30  June 19, 1972, PDD, and Nixon, *RN*, 627–28.

31  Nixon, RN, 627–28.

32  Jack Anderson, "Secret Memo Bares Mitchell-ITT Move," *The Washington Post*, February 29, 1972, B-11.

33  The Watergate special prosecutor's investigation of ITT found that an ITT commitment was raised and discussed for the first time on May 11 or 12, 1971. Richard J. Davis, "Report of ITT Task Force," Memorandum to Special Prosecutor Henry S. Ruth, August 15, 1975, 16.

34  For example, in February 1972, Jack Anderson legman Brit Hume interviewed Dita Beard, and she boasted about her memo, saying, "Of course I wrote it." Mark Feldstein, *Poisoning the Press: Richard Nixon, Jack Anderson, and the Rise of Washington's Scandal Culture* (New York: Picador, 2010), 228–29. Yet on March 27, 1972, Beard testified under oath from a hos-

pital room in Denver that she never wrote the memo. Sandford J. Ungar, "Senators Hear Dita Beard Deny Writing Memo," *The Washington Post*, March 27, 1972, A-1.

35  Both the Watergate special prosecutor and the House of Representatives impeachment inquiry investigated the ITT settlement and found no quid pro quo. But in the process it was discovered that President Nixon had called Kleindienst on April 19, 1971, to demand the ITT case be settled, a recorded conversation that put the lie to both Mitchell's and Kleindienst's testimony in March 1972 before the Senate Judiciary Committee. Because Kleindienst later volunteered this information to the Watergate special prosecutor, Archibald Cox, Special Prosecutor Leon Jaworski agreed Kleindienst could plead to a misdemeanor, over the protest of his key staff working on ITT (who resigned). The fact that President Nixon allowed Kleindienst to become attorney general knowing that he had committed perjury during his second-round confirmation proceeding became a charge in the bill of impeachment against Nixon that was approved by the House Judiciary Committee. Statement of Information, Hearings Before the Committee on the Judiciary, Book V-Part I, Department of Justice/ITT Litigation-Richard Kleindienst Nomination Hearings; and Richard J. Davis, Memorandum to Henry S. Ruth, Special Prosecutor, "Report of the ITT Task Force," August 25, 1975. NARA, Files of the Watergate Special Prosecutor. Mitchell was never charged.

36  The author has personal knowledge that Ehrlichman had a direct link to the IRS through Roger Barth, a special assistant to the commissioner, who regularly advised him of information relating to IRS activities with political figures. In early 1972, the IRS was investigating Howard Hughes's organizations and operations and learned that substantial amounts of money had been paid to Larry O'Brien. See also Statement of Information, Internal Revenue Service, Hearings Before the Committee on the Judiciary, Book VIII, 23, 218–19.

37  H. R. Haldeman, with Joseph DiMona, *The Ends of Power* (New York: Times Books, 1978), 155.

38  March 4, 1970, Haldeman, *Diaries*, 134.

39  Haldeman, *Ends of Power*, 154.

40  Statement of Information, Internal Revenue Service, Hearings Before the Committee on the Judiciary, Book VIII, 23, 218–35.

41  Haldeman's aide Gordon Strachan testified before the Senate Watergate committee (and most of his testimony is supported by contemporaneous notes from meetings with Haldeman and Jeb Magruder) that he followed the creation of the political intelligence-gathering operation at the CRP. It began with an April 22, 1971, memo from Haldeman reporting his meeting with John Mitchell and the president on April 21, 1971. The third paragraph of Haldeman's memo read: "It was obvious in some of the points he [Mitchell] was reporting that we need to do a better job of coordinating infiltration activities, polling, intelligence, etc." A year later, on March 30, 1972, Magruder called Strachan to give him a list of decisions that John Mitchell had made when they visited in Key Biscayne. Included in those decisions was approval of G. Gordon Liddy's political intelligence-gathering operation. Strachan wrote a memo to Haldeman that included this information, which was later returned to him with a check mark indicating that Haldeman had read the paragraph. Strachan Senate testimony, 6 SSC, 2489–90. The Nixon library located Strachan's handwritten notes, long believed destroyed, dated April 4, 1972, which state: "17) Liddy—appr w/ 2 opers not 4," a shorthand note reporting that Magruder had advised him that Mitchell had approved Liddy for two operations. (See www.nixonlibrary.gov/virtual library/documents/donated/040472_stra chan.pdf.) On a date in April 1972 that Strachan could not recall (but most likely shortly after McGovern won the Wisconsin primary, based on April 5, 1972, Haldeman, *Diaries*), it appears that Haldeman instructed Strachan to contact Liddy to tell him to transfer his intelligence capabilities from Muskie to McGovern, with particular interest in discovering any connection between McGovern and Senator Kennedy. Strachan, in turn, called Liddy to his office—who reached over and turned on the radio to prevent any bugs from picking up the conversation—and Strachan passed along Haldeman's instruction. Strachan Senate testimony, 6 SSC, 2455. Although Haldeman instructed me to have nothing to do with Liddy's illegal intelligence operation, and I did not, he clearly did, and fully understood the implications of his actions after the arrests at the Watergate.

42  Liddy, *Will*, 237, 241.

43  *Final Report*, SSC, 27–28. See Strachan handwritten note, April 14, 1972, Nixon library, NARA ("Liddy—Switch Musk to McG") at www.nixonlibrary.gov/virtuallibrary/documents/donated/040472_strachan.pdf.

The following exchange transpired between the president and Haldeman on April 5, 1972, in National Archives and Records Administration (NARA) Tape Subject Log Conversation No. 330-13:

> PRESIDENT: One thing you must do is plant somebody in the McGovern crowd, you know. Can we do that? [That is the question.] We had one, as I recall, in the Muskie crowd.
>
> HALDEMAN: That's what I've been doing [*unclear*].
>
> PRESIDENT: Ah, the reason for having one at McGovern is to know how close the Kennedy alliance is. But we really want to see [is] what McGovern's doing.

# Part I

## *June 20, 1972*

1  It appears I was there because Haldeman's top office assistant, Larry Higby, gave him a note as he headed out to the morning staff meeting that read: "Reminder—Dean should be included in your 9:00 A.M. meeting. Somebody should keep track of all the elements of this thing and Dean is probably the best man to do this."

2  John W. Dean, *Blind Ambition: The White House Years* (New York: Simon & Schuster, 1976), 108.

3  June 20, 1972, H. R. Haldeman, *The Haldeman Diaries: Inside the Nixon White House* (New York: G. P. Putnam's, 1993), 473.

4  National Archives and Records Administration (NARA) Conversation No. 342-12. Note: This one was not transcribed; rather, I listened to the audio. It is found on Tape No. 342(b) in the Miller Center collection at the University of Virginia (http://web2.millercenter.org/rmn/audiovisual/whrecordings/) beginning at 35:40 and ending at 1:30, when the office door to his bathroom slams (the toilet can be heard flushing shortly). We know the discussion of Watergate ended at this point, because the president entered his bathroom, slamming the door behind him, and Ehrlichman left the office. The passing reference to Watergate occurs at 1:29:30 on this tape:

> NIXON: The newspapers, the politicians, the rest, for crying out loud, the attempt to steal photographed documents [*tape-whip sound*], the Pentagon Papers and so forth—
>
> EHRLICHMAN: Hum, hmm.
>
> NIXON: Where were those voices when [Jack] Anderson [*unclear*]? They gave the sons of a bitch a Pulitzer Prize. Published the damn things. Now [*unclear, as Ehrlichman and Nixon can be heard getting up*], getting a Pulitzer Prize.

5  Conversation No. 342-13 (Nixon: "Chief, I'd like a little of that consommé, if I could have it please." Waiter: "Yes, sir, sure."); Conversation No. 342-14 (Nixon, on intercom to Haldeman: "You free to come over, I just finished with John."); and Conversation No. 342-15 (Nixon to Secret Service agent: "Ah, Chief, I wanted to tell you . . ." regarding dictation equipment. He wants small machines rather than the large ones presently available). Also see http://nixon.archives.gov/virtuallibrary/tapeexcerpts/index.php; http://millercenter.org/president; http://web2.millercenter.org/rmn/audiovisual/whrecordings/.

6 Conversation No. 342-16. Note: The conversation with Haldeman begins at 1:34.22 on tape number 342(b) of the Miller Center collection. The Watergate portion of this conversation—and 18½ minutes of buzzing—begins at approximately 1:41.22.

7 NARA, June 20, 1972, Haldeman notes, EOB, 11:30 A.M., on page 2, read as follows:

> be sure EOB office is thoroly ckd re bugs
> at all times—etc.
> what is our counter-attack?
> PR offensive to top this
> hit the opposition w/ their activities
> pt. out libertarians have created public callous
> do they justify this less than
> stealing Pentagon papers, Anderson file, etc
> we shld be on the attack—for diversion—
> what is sched on SFR SALT hearings?
> go to Calif on Fri—w/ PN
> Julie come out later
> PN not to the shower

8 Richard Nixon, *RN: The Memoirs of Richard Nixon* (New York: Grosset & Dunlap, 1978), 632.

9 Ibid.

10 Haldeman, *Diaries*, 473.

11 Conversation No. 342-27.

12 Conversation No. 344-6.

13 Nixon, *RN*, 632.

14 NARA, June 20, 1972, Haldeman notes, EOB.

15 Conversation No. 344-7.

16 Nixon, *RN*, 634.

17 H. R. Haldeman, *Ends of Power* (New York: Times Books, 1978), 25–26. Both Haldeman's and Ehrlichman's calendars indicate they were together the next morning, as Haldeman writes.

18 Ibid., 24.

19 Nixon, *RN*, 635.

## June 21, 1972

1 Tad Szulc, "Ex-G.O.P. Aide Rebuffs F.B.I. Queries on Break-In," *New York Times*, June 21, 1972, 1.

2 Bart Barnes, "Cast of Characters Involved in Democratic Office Bugging Case," *The Washington Post*, June 21, 1972, A-7.

3 Hunt Senate testimony, 9 SSC, 3688.

4 Alfred E. Lewis, "Espionage Possibility Probed in 2d Break-In at Watergate," *The Washington Post*, June 21, 1972, A-9. Years later Liddy admitted his men tried unsuccessfully to remove the lock at the DNC headquarters on May 28 but in fact had successfully picked it on May 29, 1972, planting bugs in the DNC offices and taking pictures of documents. The April 28 date appears incorrect, for Liddy says his men were registered at the Watergate Hotel from May 26 to May 29, 1972. G. Gordon Liddy, *Will: The Autobiography of G. Gordon Liddy* (New York: St. Martin's Press, 1997), 229–33. Nor is there any indication of other break-ins at the Watergate complex by these men.

5 Presidential News Summary, "DNC Break-In," National Archives and Records Administration (NARA), June 21, 1972, p. 15. Note: It is clear that Nixon was aware of this information, because he had made notes and underlined material on this page of his news summary.

6 H. R. Haldeman, *The Haldeman Diaries: Inside the Nixon White House* (New York: G. P. Putnam's, 1993), 473–74.

7 No one attending the meeting in Mitchell's office at CRP—LaRue, Mardian or Mitchell—denies it took place, and there is little disagreement on the substance of the meeting. But there was some confusion about when it occurred. For example, see Mardian testimony, *U.S. v. Mitchell et al.* (December 16, 1974), U.S. District Court for the District of Columbia, 10, 748. Mardian testified: "My recollection when I was first questioned about the matter was on the 21st or 22nd. I wasn't sure. I was told that it was on the 20 and I have no independent recollection honestly whether it was the 21st or 22nd and I previously testified if they said it was the 20th, it could've been the 20th." When further pushed by his own attorney, Mardian testified: "I honestly can't testify as to my own recollection." LaRue testified that the meeting occurred on June 20, 1972. LaRue testimony, *U.S. v. Mitchell et al.* (November 13, 1974), 6598–99, 6601–5. Mitchell thought the meeting had occurred on June 21 or 22, 1972. Mitchell testimony, *U.S. v. Mitchell et al.* (November 26, 1974), 8055. But Liddy, who had been debriefed, had a clear memory that he had met with LaRue and Mardian on June 20, 1972. Liddy, *Will*, 262–64. And the dramatic change in Mitchell's position on the morning of June 21, 1972, confirms that he had been briefed by LaRue and Mardian the preceding evening.

8 Mitchell Senate testimony, 4 Senate Select Committee on Presidential Campaign Activities (SSC), 1653 (July 10, 1973).

9 The strain that had always existed between Ehrlichman and Mitchell, meanwhile, grew more pronounced, and I would soon hear Ehrlichman criticizing Mitchell for having allowed Liddy and Hunt's Watergate burglary, while Mitchell disparaged Ehrlichman for having permitted Liddy and Hunt's break-in at Dr. Fielding's office. Each was leveraging against the other.

10 National Archives and Records Administration (NARA) Conversation No. 739-4.

11 Richard Nixon, *RN: The Memoirs of Richard Nixon* (New York: Grosset & Dunlap, 1978), 636.

12 I knew Silbert before Watergate and Glanzer after. Neither were partisans and both were rather good federal prosecutors. Silbert would be appointed U.S. Attorney for the District of Columbia during the Ford administration, and his opponents on the Senate Judiciary Committee were only Democrats, Senators John Tunney (D-CA) and James Abourezk (D-SC). See Helen Dewar, "Senate Committee Backs Silbert for Confirmation, 10–2," *The Washington Post*, October 1, 1975, A-1.

13 Conversation No. 739-11.

14 See Maurice H. Stans, *The Terrors of Justice: The Untold Side of Watergate* (New York: Everest House, 1978), 202–4. Stans's records as finance chairman of Nixon's reelection committee show that playing by the rules was not enough.

15 Haldeman, *Diaries*, 429.

16 Conversation No. 343-27.

17 Nixon, *RN*, 637.

## June 22, 1972

1 Walter Rugaber, "4 Being Hunted in Inquiry in Raid on Democrats," *New York Times*, June 22, 1972, 1.

2 Telephone interview with author, July 16, 2010.

3 For example, the *Post* reported:

- Hunt's employer, Robert F. Bennett, the president of the Mullen & Company public relations firm, who had been a fund-raiser for the Nixon reelection committee, set up dummy committees for anonymous donors.

- The DC Police and FBI were looking for the four men who had signed into the Watergate Hotel (unaware that they were aliases).

- Larry O'Brien was claiming that Jack Anderson's June 20, 1972, column about his travels and expenses had come from a missing file at the DNC's Watergate office. (Remarkably,

Anderson had run into the Miami burglary team at the airport when they arrived at Washington National Airport on June 16, 1972. Frank Sturgis was an old friend, so he said hello, and Sturgis introduced him to Virgilio Gonzalez, who was carrying a bag filled with lock-picking tools. Anderson asked what they were doing in town. Sturgis said they were visiting friends. Forty-eight hours later Anderson tried to bail Sturgis out of jail, smelling a gigantic story. But Assistant U.S. Attorney Earl Silbert objected, and the presiding judge agreed that giving Anderson custody of a Watergate burglar might not be a good idea.)

- Woodward had "reliable sources" in the Nixon reelection committee saying that Mitchell had ordered "an independent private investigation" of the bugging incident.

- In Miami, "federal sources" said the one-hundred-dollar bills found on the suspect had been traced to the Republic National Bank of Miami, which was in a Cuban neighborhood.

- U.S. District Court Judge Charles R. Richey (a Nixon appointee) had been assigned the DNC lawsuit and had scheduled a hearing for Monday, June 26, 1972.

- Superior Court Judge James Belson was holding another bail-reduction hearing that morning for the four Miami men, whose bail was set at $50,000, and McCord, whose was set at $30,000.

From Bob Woodward, "Democrats, GOP Tighten Security After Watergate 'Bugging' Case," *The Washington Post*, June 22, 1972, 1.

4 Jon Katz, "White House Aide Missing from Job," *The Washington Post*, June 22, 1972, A-8; and William L. Claiborne and Alfred E. Lewis, "Four More Sought in Wiretap Case," *The Washington Post*, June 22, 1972, A-8.

5 National Archives and Records Administration (NARA) Conversation No. 344-14.

6 The entire White House staff, as well as the cabinet departments, became involved in preparing the president's briefing book under the direction of Pat Buchanan. A significant number of presidential and policy decisions were made at the Nixon White House in the process of preparing for his press conferences. White House staff would reach out to the departments and agencies to get their input on issues likely to arise at the press conference, add their own thoughts, and submit the material to the president through Haldeman's office. When Ron Ziegler earlier said that he had sent the president a series of questions and answers regarding Watergate, the reason the document had not arrived on the president's desk was that it needed to go first through Haldeman's office. John Ehrlichman once suggested I send a memorandum to the president on a matter, and when he took it to Alex Butterfield to give to the president, Haldeman discovered it and sent it back to me, with instructions that it was to go to the president though his office. As the president worked his way through background material for his press conferences, he would make decisions, and when he announced his position at the press conference, it became the final decision. A similar process was followed for the release of presidential statements, and when they were released, they became final decisions and the president's policy.

7 Conversation Nos. 740-2, 740-3. An edited transcript of this press conference appears in *Public Papers of the Presidents: Richard Nixon 1972* at www.presidency.ucsb.edu/ws/index. php?pid=3472.

## June 23, 1972

1 Tad Szulc, "Cuban Veterans Group Linked to Raid on Democratic Office," *New York Times*, June 23, 1972, 1.

2 Bob Woodward and Jim Mann, "Bond Cut for Bugging Suspects," *The Washington Post*, June 23, 1972, C-1.

3 Peter Jay and Kirk Scharfenberg, "Exiles' View of 'Bugging,'" *The Washington Post*, June 23, 1972, C-5.

4 See Max Holland, *Leak: Why Mark Felt Became Deep Throat* (Lawrence, KS: University Press of Kansas, 2010).

5 Dean Senate testimony, __ Senate Select Committee on Presidential Campaign Activities (SSC), __; Petersen Senate testimony, __ SSC __. [TKs]

6 National Archives and Records Administration (NARA) Conversation No. 741-2.

7 Dean testimony *U.S. v. Mitchell et al.* (October 16, 1974), 2697–728; Haldeman testimony *U.S. v. Mitchell et al.* (December 3, 1974), 8478–88, 8799–824.

8 When Haldeman later met with CIA director Richard Helms and deputy director Vernon Walters, he only addressed the Mexican money, not the entire FBI investigation. See testimony of Vernon Walters, *U.S. v. Mitchell et al.* (November 11, 1974), 6124.

9 See Richard M. Nixon, *Six Crises* (New York: Doubleday & Co., 1962), 1–71.

10 June 23, 1972, Haldeman office log, NARA. Haldeman returned from the staff meeting with Colson and Mitchell. The log does not state when Colson departed, but it appears that Haldeman and Mitchell could well have discussed this between 9:00 A.M. and 9:30 A.M., when he went to the Oval Office.

11 As he later explained, Helms had rarely approached him personally for any kind of assistance or intervention but had done so less than a year earlier, regarding the possible publication of a book by two disaffected CIA agents. Helms wanted White House support for legal actions by the CIA, despite the fact that there would be cries of suppression. Nixon gave him that support. See Richard Nixon, *RN: The Memoirs of Richard Nixon* (New York: Grosset & Dunlap, 1978), 640. In March 1972, a security problem arose at the CIA when a former Russian language specialist, analyst and aide in the director's office became disenchanted with the CIA and decided to write a book. Victor Marchetti was a security problem because he knew how the place worked. According to Helms's biographer, Thomas Powers, on March 12, 1972, a CIA officer in New York learned that Marchetti had submitted his book proposal to nine publishing houses. The agency read it with alarm. Helms decided to go directly to Nixon, because the new attorney general, Dick Kleindienst, had not been confirmed, and he wanted White House backing to be sure the Justice Department aggressively pursued enforcing the confidentiality agreement Marchetti had signed—like all CIA officers. Following an unrelated meeting in the Cabinet Room with the president, on March 20, 1972, Helms asked the president if he could have a word in private with him. Together they went to the Oval Office and met from 4:48 P.M. to 5:15 P.M. Their discussion—Conversation No. 698-6—has been withdrawn for national security reasons. Powers reports that the president listened to Helms's request, promised support and told him to take it up with John Ehrlichman, which he did. Ehrlichman called the Justice Department, which aggressively pursued the lawsuit, forcing Marchetti to remove some 168 passages from his book. See Thomas Powers, *The Man Who Kept the Secrets: Richard Helms and the CIA* (New York: Alfred A. Knopf, 1970), 244–45.

12 See testimony of Vernon Walters, *U.S. v. Mitchell et al.* (November 11, 1974), 6124.

13 Conversation No. 741-10. Note: The audio quality of this recording is very poor, but I found it possible to transcribe more of the digital edition than the WSPF was able to accomplish with the analog version of the conversation. And because of its historical importance, I tried to dig out as much as possible.

14 Nixon, *RN*, 642.

15 A close listen to the conversation reveals Haldeman was not called back, but rather had returned to meet with the president for totally unrelated reasons, namely to enable Ehrlichman to join him in meeting with Helms and Walters. Ehrlichman had planned to go over the president's statement on the higher education bill at the only time that Helms and Walters could meet. The president's statement could not be delayed, because the White House had announced it, and the TV networks were setting up for a live presidential statement at 3:00 P.M., which the president needed to rehearse. Haldeman had tried to call the president at 10:41 A.M. to explain the situation after their earlier meeting, because Ehrlichman had arranged for Helms and Walters to come to his office at 1 P.M., but given his tight schedule, it called for logistical changes. Rather than Ehrlichman, Haldeman would handle the signing statement

for the higher education bill. The president understood that releasing a statement that afternoon, and preparing his remarks for the teleprompter, which was done on a larger font typewriter, required several hours lead time. Because Ehrlichman had attended the meeting the president held with his economic advisers in the Oval Office from 10:30 A.M. until 12:15 P.M., and then was scheduled to appear in the White House press room to do a background briefing on the higher education bill with then secretary of health, education and welfare Elliot Richardson, he would be busy right up to the time of the meeting with Helms and Walters. Thus, Haldeman took care of the statement for the higher education bill rather than Ehrlichman.

When Haldeman entered the Oval Office at 1:04 P.M. Haldeman asked whether the president would read his statement on busing from a draft or did he want to read it off the teleprompter. He decided to use the teleprompter, and Haldeman gave the president copies of the draft statements. With pen in hand, Nixon can be heard editing the statements. The sound of his pen scratching sentences and adding new material was easily picked up by the microphones planted in his desk, and the edited drafts are in the Nixon library. In addition, the recording equipment also picked up the sound of an electric typewriter, which was not unusual. This meant that a door to the Oval Office remained open, so it is very likely, given the time pressures, that Haldeman was taking the president's edited copy to one of the secretaries as he finished his editing. When the president finished editing, he added his comment about meeting with Helms and Walters.

16 Conversation No. 343-36.

## June 24 to July 1, 1972

1 Helen Thomas, "Martha's 'Ultimatum,'" *The Washington Post*, June 24, 1972, B-3.
2 In addition to the conversations that follow, see Winzola McLendon, *Martha: The Life of Martha Mitchell* (New York: Random House, 1979), 63.
3 National Archives and Records Administration (NARA) Conversation No. 194-14.
4 H. R. Haldeman, *The Haldeman Diaries: Inside the Nixon White House* (New York: G. P. Putnam's, 1993), 475.
5 Joseph Kraft, "The Watergate Caper," *The Washington Post*, June 25, 1972, B-7.
6 Ibid.
7 Helen Thomas, "Martha Is 'Leaving' Mitchell," *The Washington Post*, June 26, 1972, A-1.
8 Haldeman, *Diaries*, 475.
9 Conversation No. 742-8.
10 Conversation No. 742-14.
11 Conversation No. 343-37.
12 John W. Dean, *Blind Ambition: The White House Years* (New York: Simon & Schuster, 1976), 126.
13 Haldeman, *Diaries*, 476–77.
14 June 28, 1972, Haldeman office log, NARA.
15 Conversation No. 346-8.
16 Conversation No. 345-10.
17 Haldeman, *Diaries*, 478.
18 Conversation No. 347-4.
19 Richard Nixon, *RN: The Memoirs of Richard Nixon* (New York: Grosset & Dunlap, 1978), 648–49.
20 See, e.g., John W. Dean, *The Rehnquist Choice, The Untold Story of the Nixon Appointment that Redefined the Supreme Court* (New York: Free Press, 2001).
21 Conversation No. 744-21.
22 Conversation No. 744-22 and 745-1.
23 Ziegler news conference, June 30, 1972, 10–13.
24 The only substantive matters discussed were that the Justice Department would prepare a statement for the president on a recent Supreme Court ruling on the death penalty, and that they would stay out of law enforcement activities during the Democratic National Convention in Miami, so they would not be responsible if demonstrators caused problems.

25 Haldeman later added to his diary for June 30, 1972: "There's some new problems on the Watergate caper. Leading us to a probable decision that the way to deal with this now is to put all of them together, tie it all into Liddy's lap and let him take the heat for it, which is actually where it belongs anyway." Haldeman, *Diaries*, 479.

26 G. Gordon Liddy, *Will: The Autobiography of G. Gordon Liddy* (New York: St. Martin's Press, 1997), 173–80.

27 Conversation No. 745-2.

28 Strachan Senate testimony, 6 Senate Select Committee on Presidential Campaign Activities (SSC) 2455.

29 Sloan Senate testimony, 2 SSC 578–88, 617, 620.

30 The *New York Times* apparently felt that the arrests at the DNC were a local Washington police story. Famed *Times* reporter and columnist Scotty Reston had just relinquished the post of head of the Washington bureau to Max Frankel, and Reston's biographer reports that both men had a disdain for muckraking. See John F. Stacks, *Scotty: James B. Reston and the Rise and Fall of American Journalism* (New York: Little, Brown, 2003), 223. As a result, the *Times* missed the biggest story in modern American journalism, not to mention that the *Times* is an institution.

31 Conversation No. 746-3.

32 Nixon, *RN*, 646.

33 Ibid.

34 Ibid.

# Part II

1 Carl Bernstein and Jim Mann, "FBI Seeks Man Linked to 'Bug' Case," *The Washington Post*, July 2, 1972, A-1.

2 "Gallup Finds Nixon Continues to Lead Top 2 Democrats," *New York Times*, July 3, 1972, 18.

### July 6 to July 18, 1972

1 In an effort to hide the CIA's earlier involvement with Hunt (at Ehrlichman's request), and before departing on a three-week foreign trip, Helms drafted a memo for Walters on June 28, 1972, in which he told Walters, "We still adhere to the request that they [the FBI] confine themselves to the personalities already arrested or directly under suspicion and that they desist from expanding this investigation into other areas which may well, eventually, run afoul of our operations." Thomas Powers, *The Man Who Kept Secrets: Richard Helms and the CIA* (New York: Alfred A. Knopf, 1979), 263–64. Walters told the Watergate special prosecutors that he never received the memo, which the CIA later produced. It worried the prosecutors that it provided corroboration for Nixon's instructions on June 23, 1972. They never did get a satisfactory explanation of why it was written. Richard Ben-Veniste and George Frampton, Jr., *Stonewall: The Real Story of the Watergate Prosecution* (New York: Simon & Schuster, 1977), 76–77.

2 Gray later testified, "I spoke to Mr. MacGregor at San Clemente, California, via the White House switchboard, and I told him that Dick Walters and I were uneasy and concerned about the confusion that existed over the past two weeks in determining with certainty whether there was or was not CIA interest in the people that the FBI wished to interview in connection with the Watergate investigation." While Gray could not repeat his precise conversation, he added, "I also conveyed to him the thought that I felt the people on the White House staff were careless and indifferent in their use of the CIA and FBI. I also expressed the thought that this activity was injurious to the CIA and FBI, and that these White House staff people were wounding the president." Following Gray's call to MacGregor, the president called Gray. He congratulated the FBI on their handling of a hijacking the previous day, and then Gray told the president what he had told MacGregor. Gray said that after a slight pause, the pres-

ident said, "Pat, you just continue to conduct your aggressive and thorough investigation." After this, Gray said, he never had any further concern with White House interference with the FBI investigation. Gray Senate testimony, 9 Senate Select Committee on Presidential Campaign Activities (SSC) 3462.

3 Richard Nixon, *RN: The Memoirs of Richard Nixon* (New York: Grosset & Dunlap, 1978), 650.

4 Ibid., 651.

5 July 6, 1972, H. R. Haldeman, *The Haldeman Diaries: Inside the Nixon White House* (New York: G. P. Putnam's, 1993), 481.

6 See Ehrlichman office logs, NARA, John Ehrlichman, *Witness to Power: The Nixon Years* (New York: Simon & Schuster, 1982), 353–55; and July 8–9, 1972, Haldeman, *Diaries,* 481.

7 Nixon, *RN,* 651.

8 Ehrlichman, *Witness,* 354.

9 Ibid., 354–55; Nixon, *RN,* 651–53.

10 Ehrlichman, *Witness,* 356.

11 For his memoir, Nixon did not transcribe all the relevant recorded conversations to discover when, in fact, he learned of Hunt and Liddy's White House activities. Nonetheless, he wrote, "Ehrlichman says he did not know of it in advance [of the Liddy/Hunt break-in at Dr. Fielding's Beverly Hills offices], but that he told me about it after the fact in 1972. I do not recall this, and the tapes of June–July 1972 indicate that I was not conscious of it then, but I cannot rule it out." Nixon, *RN,* 514. However, Nixon expressed genuine surprise when I told him of this activity eight months later. (It will be noted that between July 8, 1972, when Ehrlichman later claimed he told Nixon about the Liddy/Hunt break-in at Fielding's offices, and March 17, 1973, when I told the president about it, there is absolutely no mention of it on any other recorded conversations, other than the vague types of references made earlier by Haldeman.) In fact, what Ehrlichman told Nixon some ten months earlier, on September 8, 1971, right after the Liddy/Hunt break-in at Fielding's offices, shows his disposition to withhold this information from the president: "We had one little operation. It's been aborted out in Los Angeles which, I think, is better that you don't know about." Stanley I. Kutler, *Abuse of Power* (New York: The Free Press, 1997), 28. When testifying before the Senate Watergate committee in 1973, Ehrlichman said he had not told the president about the Fielding break-in. Ehrlichman Senate testimony, 7 SSC 2804. When Ehrlichman was later charged for criminal activity and tried for his role in the Fielding break-in, the president (still in office) submitted a sworn answer to an interrogatory asking: "On what date were you first informed of the Fielding break-in?" Answer: "March 17, 1973." *U.S. v. Ehrlichman* (July 10, 1974), 2304. That, of course, was the date I told him, when we starting having our first discussions about Watergate.

12 July 18, 1972, Haldeman, *Diaries,* 483.

13 A few of Stanley Kutler's transcripts allude to this activity but do not report the depth of Nixon's involvement in the suborning of Magruder's false testimony.

## July 19 to August 16, 1972

1 National Archives and Records Administration (NARA) Conversation No. 747-14.

2 Jim Mann, "Lawyer in 'Bug Case' Loses Bid to Keep Mum," *The Washington Post,* July 19, 1972, C-1.

3 Haldeman later explained to the president that Ehrlichman, at this stage, wanted everyone to fall on their sword—except Ehrlichman. He was pushing to get the Watergate investigation completed quickly so the Hunt and Liddy contagion did not cause him any problems. Magruder, in fact, could have pleaded the Fifth Amendment, and had he done so, the only immediate consequence would have been that he would have had to leave the campaign. Mitchell, however, had rejected this approach, because Magruder was a buffer against the investigation reaching him. If neither Liddy nor Mitchell testified, no one else had anything other than suspicion or hearsay knowledge about Magruder's role in Watergate.

4 Conversation No. 348-10.

5 July 19, 1972, H. R. Haldeman, *The Haldeman Diaries: Inside the Nixon White House* (New York: G. P. Putnam's, 1993), 484.

6 July 20, 1972, Ibid.

7 Conversation No. 748-7.

8 Conversation No. 349-12.

9 Conversation No. 197-17.

10 Conversation No. 756-3.

11 Conversation No. 758-11.

12 Conversation No. 759-2.

13 Conversation No. 760-9.

14 Conversation No. 353-24.

15 Conversation No. 761-7.

16 Conversation No. 763-15.

17 By August 16, 1972, based on a diary entry, Nixon wrote in his memoirs that he found it "particularly nettling" that "McGovern [was] striking out more wildly now, trying to say that I was indirectly responsible for the bugging of the Democratic headquarters." Richard Nixon, *RN: The Memoirs of Richard Nixon* (New York: Grosset & Dunlap, 1978), 675.

18 August 13, 1972, Haldeman, *Diaries,* 492.

19 Conversation No. 768-4. Note: The audio on this conversation is good for Mitchell and Haldeman but poor for MacGregor, and at times awful for Nixon. But after repeatedly listening to the key statements of the president, what he is says is very clear. To hear his statements I played the recording using several software programs at several speeds, which enabled me to assemble the gist of his remarks.

20 When Bob Mardian brought Ken Parkinson to Jeb Magruder's office and instructed Magruder to tell "*the* truth," he did so for several hours. Mardian was horrified. So, later, was Mitchell. As Magruder wrote in his autobiography, he was soon called to Mitchell's office: "'Jeb,' Mitchell said gravely, 'I gather that you told Ken Parkinson the true story.' I was astounded [Magruder wrote]. 'Mardian told me that you wanted me to tell him the true story,' I said. 'No, we should discuss it with our lawyers,' Mitchell said. 'We have to protect the lawyers.'" Jeb Stuart Magruder, *An American Life: One Man's Road to Watergate* (New York: Atheneum, 1974), 241–42. Magruder also testified under oath to these facts during *U.S. v. Mitchell et al.* (October 30, 1974), 4571. Apparently Mitchell and company did leak the claim that they had conducted "an investigation," which was picked up by no less than Bob Woodward; his source, Deep Throat/Mark Felt, told him on October 8, 1972: "Mitchell conducted his own—he called it an investigation—for about ten days after June 17 [the date of the arrests at the DNC]. And he was going crazy. He found all sorts of new things which astounded even him. At some point, Howard Hunt, of all the ironies, was assigned to help Mitchell get some information." Carl Bernstein and Bob Woodward, *All the President's Men* (New York: Simon & Schuster, 1974), 132.

21 Petersen did not remember making that comment, but I repeated it to Haldeman, Mitchell and Magruder, and so testified before the Senate. See Petersen Senate testimony, 9 Senate Select Committee on Presidential Campaign Activities (SSC) 3651.

22 August 16, 1972, Haldeman, *Diaries,* 494.

## August 17 to September 15, 1972

1 Carl Bernstein and Bob Woodward, "GOP Aide Says Funds Used to Study Radicals," *The Washington Post*, August 18, 1972, A-6.

2 August 18, 1972, H. R. Haldeman, *The Haldeman Diaries: Inside the Nixon White House* (New York: G. P. Putnam's, 1993), 495–96.

3 UPI, "Watergate Break-In to Be Probed," *The Washington Post*, August 20, 1972, A-7.

4 Martin Weil, "Watergate Bug 'Ears' Linked to Motel," *The Washington Post*, August 21, 1972, A-1.

5 Bob Woodward and Carl Bernstein, "Violations by Nixon Fund Cited," *The Washington Post*, August 22, 1972, A-1.

6 Jim Mann and Bob Woodward, "Judge Seals Watergate Testimony," *The Washington Post*, August 23, 1972, A-1.

7 Jim Mann, "Indictments in 'Bug' Case May Be Tried After Election," *The Washington Post*, August 24. 1972, A-17.

8 Carl Bernstein and Bob Woodward, "Judge Wants to Start Watergate Trial," *The Washington Post*, August. 25, 1972, A-1.

9 Sanford J. Ungar, "Kleindienst Vows Tough Watergate Case Probe," *The Washington Post*, August 29, 1972, A-1.

10 *Public Papers of the Presidents: Richard Nixon 1972* at www.presidency.ucsb.edu/ ws/index.php?pid=3548.

11 On October 11, 1972, Ziegler was publicly pressed for a copy of my report during a morning briefing:

> Q: Ron, the Dean report on the Watergate, were you able to find out
> whether it was in writing or an oral report to the president?
> Ziegler: No, I didn't ask.
> Q: Why didn't you ask?
> Ziegler: Are there any other questions?
> Q: Do you plan to ask?
> Ziegler: No, I have all the information I need on the subject.
> Q: Do you plan to inform us whether this was a written or an oral report?
> Ziegler: If I run into Dean, I may ask him.

News conference, 11:21 A.M., October 11, 1972, National Archives and Records Administration (NARA), the Nixon library. It is my recollection that Ziegler asked me shortly after I returned from San Clemente in August about my so-called investigation, and I had told him then that I had done no such investigation.

12 As Nixon's recorded conversations reveal, the president had volunteered during his June 22, 1972, press conference that no one in the White House was involved, based only on his conversations with Haldeman, with no investigation whatsoever other than what Haldeman had learned from Ehrlichman, Mitchell and my conversation with Liddy. See National Archives and Records Administration (NARA) Conversation No. 344-14. According to Nixon's memoir, he created my purported investigation because "Ehrlichman assured me that there was still one thing of which we were certain: John Dean, the Justice Department, and the FBI all confirmed that there had been no White House involvement." Richard Nixon, *RN: The Memoirs of Richard Nixon* (New York: Grosset & Dunlap, 1978), 680. Nixon was correct: There was no White House involvement in the Watergate break-in, notwithstanding the fact that I had not conducted an investigation under his direct guidance, as he claimed, nor had anyone else conducted an investigation. In fact, I had not spoken with the president about Watergate and had been in his office only once since the arrests at the DNC's Watergate office—on August 14, 1972, when he and his wife signed an updated estate plan; I was there with Haldeman, Ehrlichman, Butterfield, two of his former law partners, who had prepared the testamentary documents, and a White House clerk and a photographer. And I had advised Ehrlichman that I had told Haldeman of Liddy's plans in Mitchell's office and tried to kill them.

13 Joseph A. Califano, Jr., *Inside: A Public and Private Life* (New York: Public Affairs, 2004), 271–72.

14 Bob Woodward and Carl Bernstein, "Liddy and Hunt Reportedly Fled During Bugging Raid," *The Washington Post*, September 1, 1972, A-1.

15 Califano, Jr., *Inside*, 272.

16 Bob Woodward and Carl Bernstein, "Democrats Called in Watergate Case," *The Washington Post*, September 6, 1972, A-1.

17 Conversation No. 772-6.

18 Conversation No. 773-1.

19 Conversation No. 773-17.

20 Conversation No. 360-9.

21 Bob Woodward and Carl Bernstein, "Bugging 'Participant' Gives Details," *The Washington Post*, September 11, 1972, A-1.

22 Conversation No. 774-3.

23 Conversation No. 360-12.

24 Conversation No. 360-20.

25 Nixon, *RN*, 680.

26 Conversation No. 775-6.

27 Several days earlier both Haldeman and Colson had told me that the president wanted to know what counter lawsuits might be filed against the Democrats. In turn, I spoke with Mitchell and the reelection committee lawyers, who had been developing potential counter-claims, and counter lawsuits, against the Democrats, based on abuse of process, libel and malicious prosecution, saying that they were using their lawsuit to harass the Nixon reelection committee. In addition, the reelection committee lawyers, and particularly Henry Rothblatt, whose showboating made the reelection committee lawyers cringe, were looking forward to taking depositions against the Democrats because, as they explained to me and I noted in my September 12, 1972, memorandum:

> Depositions are presently being taken of members of the DNC by defense counsel in the O'Brien suit. These are wide ranging and will cover everything from Larry O'Brien's sources of income while chairman of the DNC to certain sexual activities of employees of the DNC. They should cause considerable problems for those being deposed.

Dean Senate testimony, 3 Senate Select Committee on Presidential Campaign Activities (SSC) 1178.

28 Conversation No. 210-13.

29 In his self-published book, James W. McCord, Jr., *A Piece of Tape, The Watergate Story: Fact and Fiction* (Washington, DC: Washington Media Services, Ltd., 1974), McCord writes on page 25 of the first Watergate entry into the DNC offices on May 28, 1972:

> I had been asked to install only one device but had brought a second "for insurance" in case needed. I found an office with a direct view from across the street at the Howard Johnson Motel, pulled the curtain and made the installation in the telephone in about five minutes, tested the device and found it working. I did the same on an extension off a telephone call directory carrying Larry O'Brien's lines in an adjoining room. Surprisingly, both devices were to remain in place and both to operate for months after the arrests. The first was to remain in place until early September 1972. Al Baldwin was to tell of its location in July 1972. In September 1972 one of the lights on the telephone lighted up, a repairman was called and it was found. The second was to remain in place for almost a year, until early April 1973, when I told the federal prosecutors of its exact location. It was still in operating condition and transmission from it could possibly have been picked up in the Watergate apartments and office building during the 10 month period.

30 *Facts on File, Yearbook: 1972* at 742–43.

31 Conversation No. 778-5.

32 Conversation No. 779-1.

33 Conversation No. 779-2.

34 Haldeman may have been referring to an infamous memorandum I had written on August 16, 1971, entitled "Dealing with Our Political Enemies." As I later testified, Haldeman's junior staff pestered me for months, even threatening to have me fired, before I produced a plan, which I wanted nothing to do with. I summed up what they wanted in an opening paragraph that addressed what they wanted to hear: "[H]ow we can maximize the fact of our incumbency in dealing with persons known to be effective in their opposition to our Ad-

ministration. Stated a bit more bluntly—how we can use the available federal machinery to screw our political enemies." The memo went on to explain a process and structure to accomplish this goal, but while doing so excluded me and my office. When Haldeman's staff later sent me the names of people for the "enemies project," other than to toss them into a file, I did nothing. By April 4, 1972, Higby was having his assistant prepare "a talking paper for Mr. Haldeman on the problems we are having with Dean" on this and similar projects. On April 17, 1972, Gordon Strachan sent Higby a note pointing out that "Dean has not implemented the political enemies project." So on May 17, 1972, Higby drafted "Talking Points—John Dean," a document for Haldeman in which Higby emphasized that I was not "putting enough emphasis on some areas" where he thought I could be of unique assistance, namely the enemies project. All noted documents can be found in H. R. Haldeman's chronological files at the Nixon library in the NARA. (Copies are also in the author's files.) When Watergate occurred, Haldeman's eager beavers backed off the enemies project. But soon Ehrlichman ordered me into action. In a meeting with Ehrlichman in his office, on September 6, 1972, he asked me if I knew Johnnie Walters, the head of the IRS. I said I did, for we had served together at the Department of Justice, where he had been the head of the tax division. Ehrlichman told me that within the next few days he would be sending me a list of McGovern's staff and contributors that had been prepared by Murray Chotiner, and Ehrlichman wanted me to call Johnnie Walters to the White House to request that the IRS undertake tax audits of them. He did not explain why he wanted me to do this, but the instruction was given in a manner that both made it clear that I was not to ask and that it had come from the president. When the list arrived, however, it was sent from Haldeman's office, so I knew the president's most senior aides were involved. It was a remarkable document: It had 617 names, including former IRS head Mortimer Caplin; prominent Washington Democratic attorney Clark Clifford; Democratic activist and candidate for governor of Texas and vice president Sissy Farenthold; McGovern campaign manager Gary Hart; actress Shirley MacLaine; Senator William Proxmire; former JFK press secretary Pierre Salinger— and two dozen other prominent members of the Democratic Party, plus almost six hundred McGovern contributors from all over the United States. Statement of Information, Hearings Before the Committee on the Judiciary, House of Representatives, 93rd Congress, 2nd Session, Book III, Internal Revenue Service, "List of McGovern Staff Members and Campaign Contributors" (Washington, D.C.: Government Printing Office, 1974), 248–71.

While I could ignore Haldeman's staff, for they were my juniors in the pecking order, I could not do so with Ehrlichman and Haldeman. At the time it occurred to me that they were testing me, for I had become rather adept at ignoring, finessing or even blocking requests of this nature since I arrived on the White House staff. While I suspected the true source of a request of this magnitude, at the time I did not know for certain. But I proceeded as instructed, literally. I called Johnnie Walters and requested he come to my office on September 11, 1972. Fortunately, he made notes during our meeting. I simply told him that I had been instructed—although he wrote "directed" in his notes, which was not inaccurate—by John Ehrlichman to provide him with a list of McGovern staff and contributors because the White House wanted the IRS to investigate them for any tax problems. Walters asked me if this request had come from the president. I said I had not discussed the matter with the president. He asked me if I had discussed this with Secretary of the Treasury Shultz, and I said I had not. When he advised me that he must discuss it with Secretary Shultz, I assured him I had no problem with that: I was trying to make it clear that this was not my idea. I merely hoped it could be done in a manner that would not cause ripples. September 11, 1972, John Walters Affidavit and John Walters Notes, Statement of Information, Internal Revenue Service, Hearings Before the Committee on the Judiciary, Book VIII, 237–44. That was where the matter sat when Haldeman called me to come over to the Oval Office on September 15, 1972; I was totally unaware that Haldeman had painted me as "ruthless," which he undoubtedly did, because he knew this was what the president wanted on his staff.

35 Conversation No. 780-16.

## Late September Through October 1972

1 National Archives and Records Administration (NARA) Conversation No. 143-9.

2 Conversation No. 783-25.

3 Conversation No. 30-21.

4 Conversation No. 213-31.

5 Conversation No. 787-4.

6 Carl Bernstein and Bob Woodward, "Mitchell Controlled Secret GOP Fund," *The Washington Post*, September 29, 1972, A-1.

7 Conversation No. 788-1.

8 Conversation No. 789-6.

9 Conversation No. 789-7.

10 Conversation No. 790-16.

11 Conversation No. 791-2.

12 Conversation No. 791-7.

13 *Public Papers of the Presidents: Richard Nixon 1972* at www.presidency.ucsb.edu.

14 H. R. Haldeman, *The Haldeman Diaries: Inside the Nixon White House* (New York: G. P. Putnam's, 1993), 513.

15 Carl Bernstein and Bob Woodward, "FBI Finds Nixon Aides Sabotaged Democrats," *The Washington Post*, October 10, 1972, A-1

16 Carl Bernstein and Bob Woodward, *All the President's Men* (New York: Simon & Schuster, 1974), 112–21.

17 For a summary and overview of the Segretti matter, see Senate Select Committee on Presidential Campaign Activities (SSC), Final Report, June 1974, 160–87.

18 G. Gordon Liddy, *Will: The Autobiography of G. Gordon Liddy* (New York: St. Martin's Press, 1997), 202, 204.

19 Dean Senate testimony, 3 SSC 962–66. See also SSC, Final Report, June 1974, 160–87.

20 The Senate Watergate committee's final report contains an excellent summary of their Segretti investigation. See SSC, Final Report, June 1974, 160–87.

21 Notwithstanding the fact that Felt had access to everything collected about Segretti and related activities, both *All the President's Men* and the October 10, 1972, *Post* story, which contained some of the same information, reveal that his account is filled with falsehoods. For example, Felt reportedly told Woodward, and the *Post* reported, that the Nixon campaign was "investigating potential donors . . . before their contributions were solicited"; "[a]ccording to FBI reports, at least 50 undercover Nixon operatives traveled throughout the country trying to disrupt and spy on Democratic campaigns"; "[b]oth at the White House and within the reelection committee, the intelligence-sabotage operation was commonly called the 'offensive security program,' according to investigators." Not only did I know this information was hogwash when I read the October 10 story, and later *All the President Men*, but over the years I have plowed through the massive FBI Watergate investigation and discovered that there are absolutely no documents to support Felt's less than accurate statements to Woodward. Except for a few redactions, and possible missing files, that investigation is now online at http://vault.fbi.gov/watergate. Woodward and Bernstein and the *Post* did phenomenal work reporting on Watergate, but they did not get it all correct, for they were only as good as their sources, and off-the-record sources cannot be held accountable. For a full account of the games played by Mark Felt, and why, see Max Holland, *Leak: Why Mark Felt Became Deep Throat* (Lawrence, KS: University Press of Kansas, 2012).

22 Conversation No. 795-1.

23 Anonymous editorial, "Now, More Than Ever," *The Washington Post*, October 12, 1972, A-18.

24 Conversation No. 366-6.

25 Conversation No. 797-3.

26 Carl Bernstein and Bob Woodward, "Key Nixon Aide Named As 'Sabotage' Contact," *The Washington Post*, October 15, 1972, A-1.

27 Conversation No. 220-12.

28 Dean Senate testimony, 3 SSC 965.

29 Conversation No. 799-6.

30 Carl Bernstein and Bob Woodward, "GOP Hits Post for 'Hearsay': News Stories on Sabotage Held Malicious," *The Washington Post*, October 17, 1972, A-1.

31 Conversation No. 801-24.

32 Lawrence Meyer, "Sirica Sets Watergate Trial Nov. 15," *The Washington Post*, October 18, 1972, A-1.

33 Conversation Nos. 803-22, 804-1.

34 At the time I assumed it must be Edward Bennett Williams who represented *The Washington Post*. But Max Holland reports in *Leak* (p. 235, note 26) that "John Mitchell learned, reportedly from Wall Street lawyer Roswell Gilpatric [who never worked for the FBI or Justice Department], that Felt was leaking to *Time* magazine." Nixon will refer to this in later conversations as the basis of his knowledge that Felt was leaking. Holland was unable to determine if one or more sources were involved in revealing Felt was a leaker. After listening to the conversations and examining the relevant schedules, I believe it is entirely possible that I spoke with John Mitchell before giving this information to Haldeman, who was not available when I first learned about Felt. And, in turn, Mitchell may have made some inquiries on his own and determined or speculated that it was Roswell Gilpatric. I doubt my meeting with Haldeman lasted more than a few minutes, and based on the conversation that followed with the president, it appears he had spoken with John Mitchell as well. Haldeman's diaries are silent on this matter. There is, however, no hard evidence that Gilpatric was involved in any manner.

35 Conversation No. 370-9.

36 Conversation No. 371-1.

37 Conversation No. 371-12.

38 While it appears that Felt was generally aware of the plumbers operation, because of the Watergate investigation, there is no evidence that he was knowledgeable about their other illegal activities, nor of anything else that could create problems for Ehrlichman. Nor did any information not widely available in news accounts later surface in either of Felt's ghosted autobiographies, *The FBI Pyramid: From the Inside* (New York: G. P. Putnam, 1979), written by Ralph de Toledano, or *A G-Man's Life: The FBI, Being "Deep Throat," and the Struggle for Honor in Washington* (New York: Public Affairs, 2006), which was written (published posthumously) by John O'Connor and largely rehashed the earlier de Toledano work after Felt had been identified as Deep Throat.

39 Conversation No. 806-6.

40 Anonymous, "CBS Says Bug Probe Reopened," *The Washington Post*, October 24, 1972, A-12.

41 Conversation No. 806-13.

42 Conversation No. 373-1.

43 Carl Bernstein and Bob Woodward, "Testimony Ties Top Nixon Aide to Secret Fund," *The Washington Post*, October 25, 1972, A-1.

44 Peter Osnos, "White House Denies Story on Haldeman," *The Washington Post*, October 26, 1972, A-1.

45 Bernstein and Woodward, *All the President's Men*, 193, 195.

46 Conversation No. 32-29.

47 Conversation No. 372-24.

48 Conversation No. 807-2.

49 Richard Nixon, *RN: The Memoirs of Richard Nixon* (New York: Grosset & Dunlap, 1978), 711.

50 Conversation No. 809-2.

## November 1 to December 30, 1972

1 National Archives and Records Administration (NARA) Conversation No. 391-5.

2 Conversation No. 390-14.

3  Conversation No. 389-19.

4  Richard Nixon, *RN: The Memoirs of Richard Nixon* (New York: Grosset & Dunlap, 1978), 717.

5  H. R. Haldeman, *The Haldeman Diaries: Inside the Nixon White House* (New York: G. P. Putnam's, 1993), 530–31.

6  John W. Dean, *Blind Ambition: The White House Years* (New York: Simon & Schuster, 1976), 151.

7  Conversation No. 224-15.

8  Conversation No. 815-6.

9  Conversation No. 815-19.

10  Haldeman, *Diaries*, 543. I had been working gathering information for a Segretti report, but neither Ehrlichman nor I had a clue of how to write an honest report on Watergate that would not widen the case rather than end it all. The problem was that all three of us were involved. Ehrlichman had approved Liddy's departure from the White House staff because of his botched break-in attempt in California at Ellsberg's psychiatrist's office and other illegal suggestions, thinking he would not cause a problem at the reelection committee. Haldeman had been told by me of meetings with Mitchell at the reelection committee during which Liddy discussed illegal plans for intelligence gathering, at which I had been present and tried to kill them. Yet Haldeman had instructed Strachan in April 1972 to have Liddy move his intelligence gathering from Muskie to McGovern. (The tapes reveal that neither Haldeman nor Ehrlichman explained these problems to Nixon.) These facts made writing a truthful Watergate report virtually impossible, for there was no assurance that this information, known to varying degrees by Mitchell, Magruder, Strachan, Liddy and Hunt, would not surface at some point and unravel the cover-up. Every time I discussed this with Haldeman and Ehrlichman, regarding how such facts should be addressed, they had no answer other than to shelve the idea of my writing any report on Watergate.

11  Conversation No. 387-4.

12  Conversation No. 157-26.

13  Conversation No. 384-4.

14  Conversation No. 819-2.

15  Conversation No. 820-18.

16  Carl Bernstein and Bob Woodward, "Executive Phone Used to Hunt 'Leaks,'" *The Washington Post*, December 13, 1972, A-10.

17  Conversation No. 822-12.

18  Conversation No. 381-18.

19  Joseph Kraft, "Desperate Signals or Sour Grapes at the FBI?" *The Washington Post*, December 28, 1972, A-21.

20  See, e.g., *Final Report of the Select Committee to Study Governmental Operations with Respect to Intelligence Activities,* United States Senate: Together with Additional, Supplemental, and Separate Views at http://archive.org/details/finalreportofsel01unit; Curt Gentry, *J. Edgar Hoover: The Man and the Secrets* (New York: W. W. Norton, 1991); and Tim Weiner, *Enemies: A History of the FBI* (New York: Random House, 2013).

# Part III

1  Richard Nixon, *RN: The Memoirs of Richard Nixon* (New York: Grosset & Dunlap, 1978), 741.

## January 1973

1  National Archives and Records Administration (NARA) Conversation No. 829-6.

2  Senate Select Committee on Presidential Campaign Activities (SSC) 1233–34.

3  Conversation No. 830-6.

4  Magruder Senate testimony, 2 SSC 806, and Jeb Stuart Magruder, *An American Life: One Man's Road To Watergate* (New York: Atheneum, 1974), 278–79. When Magruder later tes-

tified (and wrote) about why he had wanted this meeting, he was a bit more subtle: He claimed it was to make sure that Bart Porter was offered a good job in the second term, since Magruder had promised him one when he agreed to corroborate Magruder's perjury regarding the campaign's payments to Liddy.

5 Conversation No. 831-6.

6 When all this later surfaced, Colson did not deny his February 1972 meeting with Liddy (and Hunt as well, with Liddy doing all the talking), nor making the call to Magruder, but Colson claimed that he had no idea they were contemplating anything illegal. Knowing both Liddy and Colson, I have always found this claim less than credible. Based on the information that Haldeman provided the president on January 3, it appears that this was the first Haldeman had learned of Colson's role in moving Watergate forward. Only later would Haldeman tell the president he too had pushed Liddy's plans, in April 1972, by having Strachan tell Liddy to focus his intelligence gathering on McGovern rather than Muskie.

7 John D. Ehrlichman 1972 Typed Logs, Watergate Special Prosecution Force (WSPF), National Archives and Records Administration (NARA), Box 25.

8 Conversation Nos. 394-3 and 397-7.

9 Ibid. For example, keywords used by the National Archives archivists for the subject log reveal that they could hear subjects such as: Watergate, -E. Howard Hunt Jr., -Possible plea, -Colson's meeting with Ehrlichman, -Colson's role, -Contacts with [William O. Bittman], -US Attorney, -Hunt cooperation, -Jeb Stuart Magruder, -Haldeman" and later "-Possible clemency, -Jail sentence, -Duration," as well as "-Roles,-John N. Mitchell, -Magruder—to mention only a few.

10 Richard Nixon, *RN: The Memoirs of Richard Nixon* (New York: Grosset & Dunlap, 1978), 754.

11 Ibid., 745.

12 H. R. Haldeman, *The Haldeman Diaries: Inside the Nixon White House* (New York: G. P. Putnam's, 1993), 563.

13 Ibid.

14 Conversation No. 835-6.

15 Conversation No. 835-8.

16 Martin Schram, "Watergate Case Called Broad Plot," *The Washington Post*, January 7, 1973, A-19.

17 Conversation No. 394-21/395-1.

18 Lyndon Johnson's bugging of the Nixon campaign airplane in 1968 would continue to come up in conversation after conversation, for months. For example, when the president met with Haldeman later that evening in the Oval Office, between 5:59 P.M. and 6:04 P.M., the president instructed him to get more information from DeLoach. Three days later, Haldeman reported that Mitchell was talking to DeLoach, and it was believed that he might produce some hard evidence of what transpired in 1968 or be able to tell Nixon where it could be found. To make a long story very short, there was no hard evidence or documentary traces of a 1968 incident relating to FBI surveillance of Nixon's campaign plane because it never happened. Years later DeLoach explained the entire bizarre story in his 1995 memoir, after he had been forced to testify under oath about these events. In 1968, through DeLoach, LBJ did call for and the FBI did agree to wiretap the Vietnamese embassy in Washington and Mrs. Anna Chennault (an adviser to the Nixon national security team) in the final weeks of the 1968 campaign. There was a rumor, later proven false, that when Nixon's campaign plane landed in Albuquerque, New Mexico, he had called Mrs. Chennault to request that she make sure the South Vietnamese would not participate in the Paris peace talks, thereby sabotaging LBJ's peace efforts, which might have helped Nixon's Democratic presidential opponent, Hubert Humphrey. But Nixon's plane was never in Albuquerque. However, vice presidential candidate Agnew's plane was there, and at LBJ's request the FBI did check the toll records of phone calls from his plane, but none were to Mrs. Chennault, nor to anyone else related to national security. DeLoach said that when Nixon was elected J. Edgar Hoover misled Mitchell and Nixon about the purported bugging of his plane to curry favor. In fact, DeLoach asserts that wiring that plane— which was protected by the Secret Service around the clock—would have been impossible

with the technology of the time, and it never happened. Cartha "Deke" DeLoach, *Hoover's FBI: The Inside Story by Hoover's Trusted Lieutenant* (Washington, DC: Regnery, 1995)

19 Haldeman, *Diaries*, 567–68. Because of the denials of Colson and Mitchell, Hersh's January 14, 1973, *New York Times* story was not nearly as threatening as when he asked for comments. It appears that Hersh relied on an inaccurate *Time* magazine story "that the Watergate defendants had been promised a cash settlement as high as $1,000 a month if they pleaded guilty and took a jail sentence. Additional funds would be paid to the men upon their release." Hersh reported that Rothblatt was complaining that his clients were being pressured to plead. See Seymour M. Hersh, "Pressures to Plead Guilty Alleged in Watergate Case," *New York Times*, January 14, 1973. In fact, this was a decision made by the Cuban Americans by themselves after Hunt pled. See, e.g., the Senate testimony of Bernard Barker, May 24, 1973, 1, SSC, 359.

20 See, e.g., *The Washington Post*'s headlines covering the trial: "GOP Aides Listed as 'Bug' Witnesses," January 9, 1973; "Watergate Trial Judge Wants 'Exploration,'" January 10, 1973; "Watergate 'Bug' Suspect Pleads Guilty," January 11, 1973; "Hunt Pleads Guilty, Denies 'Higher-Ups' In Plot," January 12, 1973; "Six in Watergate Case Implicated by Witness," January 12, 1973; "Plea Shifts Hinted in Watergate Case," January 13, 1973; "Evidence Is Curbed in Watergate Case," January 13, 1973; "Hunt Said Urging Suspects in Bug Case to Plead Guilty," January 15, 1973; "Judge Pushes for Answers: Don't Believe You, Judge Tells Suspect," January 16, 1973; "Watergate Defendant Claims 'Bugs' Legal," January 17, 1973; "Key U.S. Witness Tells of Bugging Democrats," January 18, 1973; "Key Witness Can't Trace Wiretap Log," January 18, 1973; "Debate on Taped Talks Stalls Watergate Trial," January 19, 1973; "Witness Can't Recall Who Got Tapped Logs," January 23, 1973; "Liddy Indicated He Reported to 'Others,' Witness Says," January 24, 1973; "Judge Scorns 'Bug' Defense," January 25, 1973; "Watergate Mistrial Denied: Sloan Testimony Is Read to Jury in Watergate Trial," January 27, 1973; "Jury Expected to Get Watergate Bugging Case Today," January 30, 1973; "Still Secret: Who Hired Spies and Why: Trial Fails to Uncover Who Hired, Paid Watergate Spies," January 31, 1973; and "Ex-Aides of Nixon to Appeal: Jury Convicts Liddy, McCord in 90 Minutes," January 31, 1973.

## February 3 to 23, 1973

1 E.g., Walter Regaber, "Watergate Judge Wants U.S. to Revive Its Inquiry," *New York Times*, February 3, 1973, 61.

2 National Archives and Records Administration (NARA) Conversation No. 840-9.

3 It was not until the cover-up trial of Mitchell and the others did it become clear why Colson was convinced that Mitchell was involved in Watergate. He was called as a "court witness," meaning the government would not vouch for his truthfulness. He was cross-examined by Mitchell's lawyer, an experienced trial attorney, William Hundley, who received a devastating response to a question in the following exchange:

> Q. Well, what evidence did you have? You are a lawyer. What evidence did you have that you could pin on Mr. Mitchell?
> A. Well, a few days before the Watergate break-in, we had had a meeting in Mr. Mitchell's law office at 1701 Pennsylvania Avenue to discuss meetings that were taking place between Dwayne Andreas, a supporter of Hubert Humphrey, and Hubert Humphrey, in the Waldorf-Astoria Hotel in New York, and Mr. Mitchell jokingly said at that time, with a half smile, and I didn't—I took it as a joke—"Tell me what room they are in and I will tell you everything that is said in that room." And, after the Watergate break-in, I mean, I put these two things together.

Testimony of Charles Colson, *U.S. v. Mitchell et al.*, December 5, 1974, pp. 9378–79.

4 Conversation No. 850-5.

5 Conversation No. 850-11.

6 Conversation No. 852-7.

7 On February 7, 1973, the Senate's debate on the investigation of Watergate—the resolution to create a Senate Select Committee to investigate Watergate and the 1972 presidential campaign—began in earnest on the Senate floor. Senator Howard Baker offered the first amendment to restructure the committee's membership to three Democrats and three Republicans. Drawing on the concept of bipartisan fairness in general and a number of historical presidents, he said, "I feel that as we launch into a broad, sweeping inquiry, far broader than any judicial inquiry can be, certainly more comprehensive and broader than any criminal inquiry can be"—noting that they were prescribed by rules of procedure and evidence—"it is incumbent on us that we guard against any question of partisanship in the inquiry on which we are about to embark." Senator Sam Ervin rose to "strongly oppose this amendment." Ervin's staff had done a much more complete research job and found that virtually every select committee established since 1947 had given the majority party control. Senator Ervin recognized the amendment for what it was, and said he opposed it because the provision would make it "difficult, or even impossible, for the select committee to perform its functions." He thought it the height of folly for the Senate to create a committee that could "easily get bogged down in indecision and chaos." After a rather lengthy debate, with Republicans making their best case, the amendment was defeated by a vote of 45 to 35, with 20 members not voting. Howard Baker offered another amendment that was remarkably similar to the one voted down, and it too was rejected, by a vote of 44 to 36, with 20 not voting. It was, however, agreed to expand the membership from five to seven, three Republicans and four Democrats. U.S. Senate, *Congressional Record*, February 7, 1973, 3831–33.

GOP senator Ed Gurney of Florida offered an amendment authorizing the committee to investigate "the last three Presidential elections, or any campaign, canvass, or other activity related thereto." Senator Ervin rejected this amendment too, telling his colleagues, "This amendment would be about as foolish as the man who went bear hunting and stopped to chase rabbits." It was rejected by a vote of 44 to 32, with 24 not voting. Senator John Tower offered an amendment to make sure the minority (Republican) members had "not less than thirty-three and one third percent" of the money provided the committee for its investigation. Senator Ervin rejected this amendment as unnecessary and unprecedented. No select committee had ever had such an arrangement; rather, if he were selected to chair the committee, he would make sure the minority had staff to assist them. A modified version of this amendment was agreed upon and added to the resolution without a vote, and the amendment resolution passed by a vote of 77 to 0, with 23 not voting. The committee has often been described as unanimously agreed upon by the Senate, but that is subject to the caveat that 23 members were not present to vote. U.S. Senate, Congressional Record, February 7, 1973, 3842, 3849.

8 H. R. Haldeman, *The Haldeman Diaries: Inside the Nixon White House* (New York: G. P. Putnam's, 1993), 575.

9 The summons followed Haldeman's meeting with the president at his office in the San Clemente compound at 9:25 A.M., before the president spent the rest of his day at his pool and private golf course with daughter Julie and her husband, David Eisenhower. Haldeman later noted the gist of the meeting in his diary: "He got into Watergate strategy. He wants to get our people to put out that foreign or Communist money came in in support of the demonstrations in the campaign, tie all the '72 demonstrations to McGovern and thus the Democrats movement and its leader, McGovern and Teddy Kennedy." Nixon had told Haldeman to leak to syndicated columnists Evans and Novak the fact that his campaign had been proper and circumspect while the Democrats had used libel and violence. He also wanted Gray to get going on the investigation of who tapped him in 1968. Haldeman, *Diaries*, 577.

10 Haldeman, *Diaries*, 577–78. Conspicuously absent from Haldeman's notes and diary was the fact that Dick Moore had been dispatched to New York to see if he could get John Mitchell moving on raising money for the Watergate defendants, who were making new demands for more money as their sentencing approached. *Final Report*, Senate Select Committee on Presidential Campaign Activities (SSC), 76–78. "Ehrlichman also confirms that Moore was sent

to New York to see Mitchell about raising money for the Watergate defendants." Final Report, SSC, 77. Mitchell testified he told Moore to "get lost." Ibid. Moore confirmed he went to New York and spoke with Mitchell about money for the defendants "for support and legal fees" for the Watergate defendants. Ibid.

11 Conversation No. 854-17.

12 Conversation No. 410-14.

13 Conversation No. 855-10.

14 Conversation No. 856-4.

15 Ehrlichman failed to mention that I told him I thought Pat Gray's confirmation hearing could be a disaster because I had worked with Gray at the Justice Department when I was the associate deputy attorney general and had to arrange witnesses for Justice Department legislation; Gray had consistently been a poor or bad witness, often ignoring the president's or Justice Department's stated policies to promote his own notions. In addition, I gave Ehrlichman far more detail than he chose to share with the president about how Gray had incurred the wrath of much of the FBI, both the old Hoover cronies as well as much of the rank and file, who could be counted on to back channel information to the Senate Judiciary Committee in an attempt to defeat Gray's confirmation. None of my assessments would prove wrong.

16 Conversation No. 858-3.

17 Conversation No. 859-38.

18 Ibid.

19 Conversation No. 411-18.

20 Conversation. No. 43-177.

21 Conversation No. 411-19.

22 Conversation No. 862-4.

23 Conversation No. 862-6.

24 Kleindienst knew more than he was sharing with the president, as noted in the prologue. Liddy had tracked him down on June 18, 1972, at Burning Tree Country Club, where he was golfing, with a message from Mitchell to have him get the men arrested at the DNC out of jail. As Liddy later wrote, he "spelled it out for Kleindienst." G. Gordon Liddy, *Will: The Autobiography of G. Gordon Liddy* (New York: St. Martin's Press, 1997), 252. Liddy says, "I told him that the break-in was an operation of the intelligence arm of the Committee to Re-elect the President; that I was running it for the committee and the men arrested were our people working under my direction when they were caught. I told him that they were good men who would keep their mouths shut," etc.

## February 27 to March 15, 1973

1 In addition to the September 15, 1972, conversation, based on the president's daily diary it appears I had conversations with him on the following days, either alone or with others in the meetings: February 27, 1973 (Oval Office, 3:55–4:20 P.M.); February 28, 1973 (Oval Office, 9:12–10:23 A.M.); March 1, 1973 (Oval Office, 9:18–9:46 A.M.), (Oval Office, 10:36–10:44 A.M.), (Oval Office, 1:06–1:14 P.M.); March 6, 1973 (Oval Office, 11:49 A.M.– 12:00 P.M.); March 7, 1973 (Oval Office, 8:53–9:16 A.M.); March 8, 1973 (Oval Office, 9:51–9:54 A.M.); March 10, 1973 (Camp David phone, not recorded, 9:20–9:44 A.M.); March 13, 1973 (Oval Office, 12:42–2:00 P.M.); March 14, 1973 (White House telephone, 8:55–8:59 A.M.), (EOB office, 9:50–10:50 A.M.), (White House telephone, 12:27–12:28 P.M.), (EOB office, 12:47–1:30 P.M.), (White House telephone, 4:25–4:26 P.M.), (White House telephone, 4:34–4:36 P.M.); March 15, 1973 (Oval Office, 5:36–6:24 P.M.); March 16, 1973 (Oval Office, 5:36–6:24 P.M.), (White House telephone, 8:14–8:23 P.M.); March 17, 1973 (Oval Office, 1:25–2:10 P.M.); March 19, 1973 (EOB office, 5:20–6:01 P.M.); March 20, 1973 (White House telephone, 10:46–10:47 A.M.), (White House telephone, 12:59–1:00 P.M.), (Oval Office, 1:42–2:31 P.M.), (White House telephone, 7:29–7:43 P.M.); March 21, 1973 (Oval Office, 10:12–11:55 A.M.), (EOB office, 5:20–6:01 P.M.); March 22, 1973 (EOB office, 1:57–3:43 P.M.); March 23, 1973 (Key Biscayne

telephone, not recorded, 12:44–1:02 P.M.), (Key Biscayne telephone, not recorded, 3:28–3:44 P.M.); April 15, 1973 (EOB office, not recorded, 9:17–10:12 P.M.); April 16, 1973 (Oval Office, 10:00–10:40 A.M.), (White House telephone, 4:04–4:05 P.M.), (EOB office, 4:07–4:35 P.M.); April 17, 1973 (White House telephone, 9:19–9:25 A.M.); and April 22, 1973 (Key Biscayne telephone, not recorded, 8:24–8:39 A.M.).

2 They were found in either the *Submission of Presidential Conversations to the Committee on the Judiciary of the House of Representative by Richard Nixon* (April 30, 1974), which became known as the "Bluebook" for its cover, or the *Transcripts of Eight Recorded Presidential Conversations (May–June 1974) Prepared by the House Judiciary Committee*, which were more accurate drafts of many of the same conversations as found in the Bluebook. The ten conversations to which I had access were: September 15, 1972 (Oval Office, 5:27–6:17 P.M.); February 28, 1973 (Oval Office, 9:12–10:23 A.M.); March 13, 1973 (Oval Office, 12:42–2:00 P.M.); March 17, 1973 (Oval Office, 1:25–2:10 P.M.); March 21, 1973 (10:12–11:55 A.M.); March 21, 1973 (Oval Office, 5:20–6:01 P.M.); March 22, 1972 (EOB office, 1:57–3:43 P.M.); April 16, 1973 (Oval Office, 10:00–10:40 A.M.); and April 16, 1973 (EOB office, 4:07–4:35 P.M.). Not all of these transcripts were complete, however, for the White House had withheld information.

3 John W. Dean, *Blind Ambition: The White House Years* (New York: Simon & Schuster, 1976), 186.

4 As one psychologist who studied my memory vis-à-vis the tapes reported, "Analysis of Dean's testimony does indeed reveal some instances of memory for the gist of what was said on a particular occasion. Elsewhere in his testimony, however, there is surprising little correspondence between the course of the conversation and his account of it. Even in those cases, however, there is usually a deeper level at which he is right. He gave an accurate portrayal of the real situation, of the actual character and commitments of the people he knew, and of the events that lay behind the conversation he was trying to remember." Ulric Neisser, "Memory Observed, Remembering in Natural Contexts," *Cognition: The International Journal of Cognitive Psychology* (February 1981):1–22. This study does not mention that everything in my testimony did, in fact, occur but that I conflated events or had them on the wrong date. None of my testimony, however, was really date sensitive.

5 Dean Senate testimony, 4 Senate Select Committee on Presidential Campaign Activities (SSC) 1513. Nor was it a tape recorder. Dean Senate testimony, 4 SSC 1373.

6 National Archives and Records Administration (NARA) Conversation No. 864-4.

7 Richard Nixon, *RN: The Memoirs of Richard Nixon* (New York: Grosset & Dunlap, 1978), 779.

8 Conversation No. 865-14.

9 Nixon, *RN*, 779.

10 Conversation No. 866-3.

11 Gray testified that "any Member of the U.S. Senate, this committee or any Member of the U.S. Senate, who wishes to examine the investigative file of the Federal Bureau of Investigation in this matter [relating to the Watergate break-in and bugging] may do so, and I will provide knowledgeable, experienced, special agents to sit down with that Member and respond to any question that Member has." U.S. Senate, *Louis Patrick Gray, III, Hearings Before the Committee on the Judiciary* (February 28 to March 22, 1973), 28.

12 Conversation No. 866-4.

13 Conversation No. 37-37.

14 Conversation No. 866-17.

15 Conversation No. 867-1.

16 Nixon news conference, March 2, 1973, at www.presidency.ucsb.edu/ws/index.php?pid=4123.

17 Conversation No. 867-8.

18 John P. MacKenzie, "Nixon Says He Won't Let Aide Testify on Gray Appointment," *The Washington Post*, March 3, 1973, A-3.

19 In fact, the FBI raw investigative reports, known as "302s" as that is their form number, were useless information, for Gray provided me dated material. The only use I ever made of them

was to try and determine who might be leaking information from the FBI to the news outlets, but that information never did match.

20 Conversation No. 867-16.

21 Journalist Gloria Steinem described Pappas in a 1968 report on the Nixon presidential campaign: "Then there's the matter of Greek-American millionaire Tom Pappas, who was an important backer of Nixon's campaign against Kennedy [1960], and of Spiro Agnew's campaign to become Governor of Maryland [1966]. (Nixon has said Pappas was one of those who 'influenced' him in the [1968] choice of Agnew.) An avowed supporter of the Greek Junta, whose interests include steel, chemical, and Esso oil refineries in Greece, Pappas and his brother also established the Pappas Foundation, which has been named as one of the CIA-backed groups transferring money to Greece, presumably to strengthen the Junta." Gloria Steinem, "In Your Heart You Know He's Nixon," *New York* magazine, October 28, 1968, http://nymag.com/news/politics/45934/.

22 Conversation No. 868-7.

23 Conversation No. 868-20.

24 Carl Bernstein and Bob Woodward, "FBI Says GOP Unit Hurt Case," *The Washington Post,* March 6, 1973, A-1.

25 Conversation No. 869-13.

26 John P. MacKenzie, "Gray Says He Didn't Want Dean at Quiz," *The Washington Post*, March 7, 1973, A-1.

27 Conversation No. 871-4.

28 The leaks were extraordinary. Now it is known what was occurring. With Mark Felt heading the Watergate investigation and seeing all the reports, Felt and his cronies were passing out information to favorite reporters at will, and as it turns out, Bob Woodward of *The Washington Post* was way down on Felt's list. Ironically, the excessive leaking by the FBI helped drive the Nixon White House to cover up. Even more troublesome, much of the information Felt leaked to Woodward and others was false, although the reporters to whom it was given were unaware of this fact. See Max Holland, *Leak: Why Mark Felt Became Deep Throat* (Lawrence, KS: University Press of Kansas, 2010), 128, 143, 159–60, 183, 244–45 n. 40, 252 n. 24, 257–58 n. 12 ; see also, John W. Dean, "Appendix: Why the Revelation of the Identity of Deep Throat Has Only Created Another Mystery," *Writ* (June 3, 2005), at http://writ.news.findlaw.com/dean/20050603.appendix.html.

29 Conversation No. 871-5.

30 Ibid. The shift in tone and style of the president's speech makes clear they both know what the president is talking about when the following conversation occurred. I am not the only person who recognized that they were talking about Watergate, for the archivists at the National Archives label this segment of the conversation as follows: Watergate// - Pappas' activities/ -President knowledge/ -Maurice H. Stans// -Gratitude/ -Stans/ -Innocence// -John N. Mitchell/ -Innocence// -Committee to Re-elect the President [CRP]/ -Involvement/ -Guilt/ -Low level staff// -Break-in// -White House Involvement// -Pappas support// -Break-in/ -Democratic National Committee[DNC]/ -Value.

31 This conversation, along with the March 2, 1973, one with Haldeman, would appear to establish violations of Section 600 of Title 18 of the United States Code (prohibiting the sale of ambassadorships), Section 201 (public official bribery), and Section 371 (the conspiracy statute). These conversations were apparently unknown to the Watergate Special Prosecutors when they called former president Nixon before the final 1975 Watergate grand jury, when his only exposure, given his pardon, was if he committed perjury—and he flatly denied ever selling ambassadorships, notwithstanding substantial evidence to the contrary that could have but did not include the March 2 and 7, 1973, conversations. See, e.g., Ciara Torres-Spelliscy, "How Much Is an Ambassadorship?" *Chapman Law Review* (Spring 2012):71.

32 Conversation No. 872-1.

33 Bob Woodward and Carl Bernstein, "FBI Chief Says Nixon's Aides Paid Segretti," *The Washington Post*, March 8, 1973, A-1.

34 Conversation No. 37-89.

35 Conversation No. 37-93.

36 Conversation No. 878-7.

37 Conversation No. 878-14.

38 Associated Press, "Oilman's Donation Returned," *The Washington Post*, March 10, 1973, A-1.

39 Strachan Senate testimony, 6 SSC 2455-2456.

40 Liddy, *Will*, 238. Liddy reconstructed his account almost a decade after the fact, and I believe he has confused a conversation—which Magruder has consistently reported, in which Mitchell told Liddy his efforts were unsatisfactory—and transposed it coming from Strachan. I think Liddy conflated his meeting in April, in which Strachan gave him instructions from Haldeman to transfer his intelligence gathering operation from Muskie to McGovern.

41 The Chappaquiddick incident occurred on July 18, 1969, just about a year before I arrived at the White House, but I had been told about the Nixon White House activities. Mary Jo Kopechne, an attractive young former worker in Bobby Kennedy's 1968 presidential campaign, was a passenger in the front seat of U.S. senator Teddy Kennedy's car and was killed when Teddy drove his car off a bridge, apparently drunk, and into a tidal wash channel on Chappaquiddick Island, Massachusetts. Teddy escaped from the sinking car as it went under the water, swam to the shore and left the scene, not reporting the accident until some nine hours later, and leaving Mary Jo to die in the vehicle. Given Nixon's feelings toward the Kennedys in general, and Ted Kennedy in particular, I assumed he was well aware of this Chappaquiddick investigation, if he had not ordered it. But this young aide did not proceed presumptuously with the president of the United States, and he treated my report as a revelation. For an excellent account of this political rivalry, see Christopher Matthews, *Kennedy & Nixon* (New York: Simon & Schuster, 1996).

42 Tony Ulasewicz later surfaced and testified before the Senate Watergate committee on July 18, 1973. It was made clear the testimony that day would not focus on the investigative work he had done for Ehrlichman and Caulfield, for Ulasewicz was told "the committee is not going to inquire into that area in any detail at all today." 6 SSC 2220. In fact, because of what Ulasewicz did know about Kennedy and Chappaquiddick, he was never called to testify publicly about that information; rather, it appears the Democrat-controlled Senate protected their colleague. Decades later Ulasewicz did write about it, and it is devastating information. See Tony Ulasewicz with Stuart A. McKeever, *The President's Private Eye* (Westport, CT: MACSAM Publishing, 1990), 187–224. Tony had, by that time he wrote the book, also shared some of his knowledge with *New York Times* reporter Philip Taubman, who pulled open part of the Chappaquiddick cover-up in a March 12, 1980, account, "Gaps Found in Chappaquiddick Phone Data," a lengthy front-page story reported by Robert Pear and Jo Thomas; Kennedy was at the time challenging President Jimmy Carter for the Democratic presidential nomination. Kennedy stonewalled about Chappaquiddick to his death, making his last comments accepting responsibility (but not guilt, nor providing all the facts) in his final memoir, Edward M. Kennedy, *True Compass* (New York: Twelve, 2009), 288–93. Nonetheless, a number of carefully documented books make clear that Kennedy and his enablers obstructed justice during the inquiries into what occurred at Chappaquiddick. For what it is worth, I have always been convinced that Kennedy stayed behind the scenes during Watergate because he feared what the Nixon White House might know, which could reopen this matter. It must also be noted that, given what Tony Ulasewicz, Jack Caulfield and John Ehrlichman did know about Chappaquiddick, it is surprising that Nixon did not make this bit of Senate and Kennedy hypocrisy a part of his public defense.

43 Carl Bernstein and Bob Woodward, "Gray Hearing Calls Nixon Aide," *The Washington Post*, March 14, 1973, A-1.

44 Conversation No. 37-99.

45 Conversation No. 419-20.

46 Conversation No. 879-5.

47 Conversation No. 419-23.

48 Conversation No. 37-108.

49 Conversation No. 37-109.

50 Conversation No. 37-116.

51 Nixon news conference, March 15, 1973, at www.presidency.ucsb.edu/ws/index.php?pid=4142.

52 Conversation No. 880-3.

53 Conversation No. 880-6.

54 Conversation No. 880-18.

55 Conversation No. 880-24.

## March 16 to 20, 1973

1 National Archives and Records Administration (NARA) Conversation No. 881-3.

2 Conversation No. 881-4.

3 Conversation No. 881-7.

4 Conversation No. 420-11.

5 Conversation No. 881-8.

6 The only conversation with me that Nixon can be referring to took place in the Oval Office that morning between 10:34 A.M. and 11:10 A.M. (Conversation No. 881-3), but I can find no reference to Nixon telling me to tell Baker that he had "a record of this conversation," and had he done so, it would have clearly suggested to me that he recorded conversations, which had not yet dawned on me, nor was Ehrlichman aware of this fact when Nixon made this reference to him. It is also possible he was referring to the record kept of all his office visits, which did not, however, include a record of Baker's visit.

7 William M. Blair, "G.O.P. Officially Switches Convention to Miami Beach," *New York Times,* May 6, 1972, 13.

8 Conversation No. 37-132.

9 Conversation No. 37-134.

10 Conversation No. 882-10.

11 Conversation No. 882-12.

12 Conversation No. 883-5.

13 Conversation No. 420-24.

14 John W. Dean, *Blind Ambition: The White House Years* (New York: Simon & Schuster, 1976), 191–93.

15 Dean Senate testimony, 3 Senate Select Committee on Presidential Campaign Activities (SSC) 997.

16 Dean, *Blind Ambition,* 192.

17 See Senate testimony of John Dean, 3 SSC 974-976.

18 Conversation No. 37-162.

19 Ehrlichman telephone call to Dean, 7 SSC 2950-51.

20 Conversation No. 884-3.

21 Conversation No. 37-164.

22 Conversation No. 884-7.

23 Conversation No. 37-166.

24 Conversation No. 884-17.

25 See Senate testimony of John Dean, 3 SSC 997 and 1252.

26 Conversation No. 884-23.

27 Conversation No. 885-1.

28 On the surface, Ehrlichman brushed off the Hunt blackmail, for he was prepared to simply deny any involvement. Bud Krogh was not prepared to lie about it, however. This was a potential problem for Ehrlichman. Bud Krogh learned of Hunt's demands from me on March 20, 1973, and he called Ehrlichman, who told him Mitchell was responsible for the "care and feeding" of Howard Hunt. On March 21, 1973, Krogh met with Ehrlichman in his office; Ehrlichman told Krogh that if Hunt "blew the lid" off the Ellsberg operation they could say

that Hunt and Liddy were on "a frolic of their own." Krogh told Ehrlichman that that was untrue, for they had been authorized. Ehrlichman told Krogh that Mitchell was coming to the White House the next day, March 22, 1973, and Krogh should do nothing until Ehrlichman had spoken with Mitchell. On March 22, 1973, Ehrlichman telephoned Krogh and told him, "Hunt was stable [and] now was the time to hang tough." Testimony of Egil Krogh, *U.S. v. Mitchell et al.* (November 22, 1974) 7653–81.

29 Conversation No. 885-7.

30 And I only knew what I had picked up in casual conversations from Mitchell and Magruder regarding the Watergate break-in and from Liddy and Ehrlichman regarding the Ellsberg break-in; I did not know what, if anything, Haldeman had done after I reported to him that I had heard Liddy's pitch for an illegal political intelligence gathering operation in Mitchell's office in late January and early February 1972. I discovered when working on this book that, contrary to my testimony, I had reported to him twice about this, based on his office records. It had been when I reported to him the second time that I thought I had turned it off by pouring cold water on Liddy's plans, literally ending the discussion by insulting Liddy and Magruder for raising the matter with Mitchell, then the attorney general.

31 Conversation Nos. 37-175, 37-176.

## March 21 to 23, 1973

1 National Archives and Records Administration (NARA) Conversation No. 886-7.

2 As revealed by the recorded conversations, the president's daily diary (PDD) is incorrect on the times and people with whom the president met on the morning of March 21, 1973.

3 Conversation No. 886-8.

4 I had conflated two meetings I had with Haldeman about Liddy's plans. The two meetings in Mitchell's office occurred on January 27 and February 4, 1972. While working on this book I discovered that Haldeman's office diary schedule shows I met with him on February 1, 1972, where I first reported on Liddy's plans, and Haldeman's negative reaction is what had emboldened me to blow up the second meeting, when I heard more of the same. When speaking to the president, and later testifying, I recalled telling Haldeman that I had turned off the Liddy plans. Based on Haldeman's office diary schedule, that appears to have occurred on February 8, 1972, either before or after a staff meeting in Haldeman's office. Although he quibbled about the dates, Haldeman later testified that he recalled my reporting having turned off Liddy's plans at the February 4 meeting. See Haldeman Senate testimony, 8 Senate Select Committee on Presidential Campaign Activities (SSC) 3034–35. However, during a March 27, 1973, conversation, Haldeman acknowledged that I warned him about Liddy's plan and that it had been dropped.

5 Whether the White House received information from the DNC before June 17, 1972, will forever remain unclear, because Haldeman instructed Strachan to clean their files. But it appears no such information, in fact, was received. Magruder later testified that he showed Strachan the fruits of Liddy's DNC wiretapping operation, but in his testimony Strachan denied he was shown such material. At the time I was reporting to Nixon, Strachan believed he had seen it because the reports he had been sent and destroyed at Haldeman's instruction after the June 17, 1972, arrests read very much like wiretap reports; they used the language: "From a source believed to be reliable." In the weeks ahead, Strachan and Haldeman would figure out what had been destroyed were reports from a source planted by Magruder rather than wiretap information. See Strachan Senate testimony, 6 Senate Select Committee on Presidential Campaign Activities (SSC) 2468–69.

6 When Strachan later testified before the Senate that he did not know in advance about the Watergate break-in, I had no reason to doubt that testimony. I think Liddy's claim in his memoir, *Will* (which was written long after the fact), that he told Strachan shortly before the second break-in at the Watergate that they were going back in to fix a bug is a confused reconstruction of the meeting in mid-April; that was actually the meeting during which Strachan instructed Liddy to move his intelligence-gathering capabilities from Muskie to

McGovern. Strachan Senate testimony, 6 SSC, 2476; G. Gordon Liddy, *Will: The Autobiography of G. Gordon Liddy* (New York: St. Martin's Press, 1997).

7 When writing *Blind Ambition*, I described my limited knowledge as follows: "The Cuban Committee was a technical part of only one of our payment schemes. A committee had been set up to collect defense funds for the Cuban defendants, and we had planned it; the committee would be flooded with anonymous cash. As it turned out, Hunt had preferred to have the money delivered directly to him and his wife." At that writing I was unaware of the June 20, 1972, conversation between the president and Haldeman, during which he explained his idea. Conversation No. 344-7; John W. Dean, *Blind Ambition: The White House Years* (New York: Simon & Schuster, 1976), 203.

8 After learning of the president's idea of creating a Cuban committee while working on this book, which he envisioned as open and publicly defending those involved in the Watergate break-in, I have discussed this matter with several former federal prosecutors, curious if they thought this would have been an obstruction of justice. While the answer would, of course, depend on how the committee was set up and funded, as a general rule an open and above-board defense fund is legal. Recently, former Bush II White House and Vice President Cheney aide I. Lewis "Scooter" Libby had a multimillion-dollar defense fund when he was indicted (and convicted) of perjury, with no less than former Senate Watergate committee minority counsel, later Tennessee senator Fred Thompson, on the advisory board. But most everyone agreed that using a Cuban committee cover to get hush money to the Watergate defendants would still have been obstruction of justice.

9 Actually, it was an even more detailed point to which Krogh plead guilty: Had he been aware of Hunt and Liddy's travel while they were working for him in the plumbers unit? He testified that he had not been, when, in fact, he had known of it. On October 18, 1973, Krogh plead guilty to making two false statements to the grand jury in August 1972. *United States v. Egil Krogh, Jr.*, Criminal Case 857-73, United States District Court for the District of Columbia.

10 Conversation No. 886-18.

11 Conversation No. 421-8. Note: While the audio on the conversation is of very poor quality, the gist of the conversation is discernible.

12 This was the way Ehrlichman consistently handled his personal jeopardy, from the moment I first mentioned it on June 19, 1972, after talking to Liddy through my relay of Hunt's black-mail demand. Looking at how he later dealt with his criminal problems, Ehrlichman may have been remarkable naive about the criminal law, which would explain why he did not want me to bring a criminal lawyer on after Watergate, for he believed it unnecessary, or he was even more arrogant than I thought, for he felt, incorrectly, that he could bluff and dis-semble his way through his problems. No one would ever successfully argue that he was stupid, although it could easily be asserted that he was foolish.

13 Conversation No. 421-18.

14 Conversation Nos. 37-204, 37-205.

15 Based on the transcript prepared by the Watergate Special Prosecution Force (WSPF) of the president's cassette recording of his recollections of his meeting with Dean and Haldeman on March 21, 1973. The entry continued, "As I examined him it seems that he feels even he would be guilty of some criminal liability due to the fact he participated in the actions which resulted in taking care of the defendants while they were under trial. As he pointed out, what is causing him concern is that every one of the various participants is now getting his own counsel and that this is going to cause considerable problems because it will be each man for himself, and one will not be afraid to rap on the other." He noted that Haldeman had backed me up on this point, when he mentioned that Magruder would bring him down if he felt he himself was to go down. This caused the president again to tell his diary that Haldeman's selection of Magruder was "still a very hard one for me to figure out. He's made very few mistakes, but this is one case where Rose was right; he picked a rather weak man who had all the appearances of character, but who really lacks it when the chips are down." WSPF files, NARA.

In his memoir, Nixon said, "[I]t was clear that on March 21 John Dean was trying to alert me to the fact that what I assumed for nine months was the major Watergate problem—the question of who had authorized the break-in—had been overtaken by the new and far more serious problem of the cover-up." Nixon then takes the rather remarkable position that he did not really understand what I was saying, because I failed to sufficiently describe my own role in the cover-up, so he treated much of what I said as conjecture and deduction instead of as firsthand reporting on a situation that was "already out of hand." Nixon wrote that my insistence that the payment of further money to the defendants was an obstruction of justice only seemed to him "more a reflection of his personal depression than a statement of a considered legal conclusion." Nixon wrote that it took "three weeks" more for him to "understand what Dean had really been trying to tell me." In fact, I was not depressed, as anyone who listens to this conversation vis-à-vis any other of my conversations will realize; rather, I was deeply frustrated that I could not persuade the president to end the cover-up, and a young White House aide does not tell the president of the United States everything he is really thinking, such as: "This man is either a fool or crook." Within days I would decide it was the latter, and within three weeks I would break rank, explaining to my colleagues that I was going to the prosecutors, because the cover-up was over. It was that action, it seems, that enabled Nixon to understand what I was saying, for my actions spoke more clearly than my words of warning. Richard Nixon, *RN: The Memoirs of Richard Nixon* (New York: Grosset & Dunlap, 1978), 800–01, 817.

16  Conversation No. 422-20.

17  Five days later, on March 27, 1973, Ehrlichman would remove the memoranda from the White House files that included his handwritten authorization for the covert entry into Ellsberg's psychiatrist's office. Had David Young not kept a copy of those documents, Ehrlichman might have succeeded in denying he had any knowledge of this operation, or it would have been his word against Krogh and Young, who admitted their roles in the undertaking, as did Howard Hunt and Chuck Colson; Colson had arranged for the funding to pay the expenses of Liddy and Hunt, and their Cuban operatives. *U.S. v. Ehrlichman*, 546 F.2d 910 (1975).

18  See Dean, *Blind Ambition*, 211.

19  Conversation No. 422-33.

20  The letter had been delivered three days earlier, and Sirica saw its potential immediately, telling his clerks, "This is going to break the case wide open." Fred Emery, *Watergate : The Corruption of American Politics and the Fall of Richard Nixon* (New York: Touchstone, 1994), 269–70.

21  See, e.g., Philip B. Kurland, "The Power and the Glory: Passing Thoughts on Reading Judge Sirica's Watergate Exposé to Set the Record Straight: The Break-In, the Tapes, the Conspirators, the Pardon by John J. Sirica," 32 *Stanford Law Review* (November 1979):217–28; and Anthony J. Gaughan, "Watergate, Judge Sirica, and the Rule of Law," *McGeorge Law. Review* 42 (2010–2011): 343.

# Part IV

1  Political crises have been described as breakdowns of governing systems and processes that create problems that might have been foreseen yet have developed into much more because an incipient situation was not addressed. See, e.g., Michael Brecher and Jonathan Wilkenfeld, *The Study of Crisis* (Ann Arbor: University of Michigan Press, 1997).

2  Richard Nixon, *Six Crises* (Garden City, NY: Doubleday, 1962), xv.

3  Richard Nixon, *RN: The Memoirs of Richard Nixon* (New York: Grosset & Dunlap, 1978), 817.

## March 23 to April 13, 1973

1 H. R. Haldeman, *The Haldeman Diaries: Inside the Nixon White House* (New York: G. P. Putnam's, 1993), 594.

2 Ibid., 594.

3 Richard Nixon, *RN: The Memoirs of Richard Nixon* (New York: Grosset & Dunlap, 1978), 805.

4 Haldeman recorded in considerable detail the information, particularly from me, about what had transpired. I had minced no words about Haldeman's and Ehrlichman's criminal liability in raising money and paying the Watergate defendants after June 17, 1972. Haldeman's notes could have provided solid corroboration for my later testimony, but this information remained buried until he published his diaries in 1994. While Haldeman recorded in his note that I explained his problems to him, as well as Ehrlichman's, he never mentioned this information to Nixon, protecting himself and Ehrlichman to the end, and at Nixon's expense. Haldeman, *Diaries.*

5 They did publish, but when McCord's false statement about me fell apart for total lack of substance, and that fact was reported, I took no action.

6 Lou Cannon, "Nixon Denies Dean Knew of Bugging," *The Washington Post*, March, 27, 1973, A-1.

7 Nixon White House Recorded Conversation, National Archives and Records Administration (NARA) Conversation No. 888-4.

8 Haldeman had urged me to record Magruder if I could, and I did so by holding the dictating machine microphone to the telephone while at Camp David. Secretly recording telephone calls was common at the Nixon White House, but other than Magruder, whose story seemed to change depending on whom he was speaking to, I did not record my phone calls. My Magruder recording of March 26, 1973, was turned over to the Senate Watergate committee. See Dean Senate testimony, 3 Senate Select Committee on Presidential Campaign Activities (SSC)1258.

9 Conversation No. 423-3.

10 Conversation No. 44-21.

11 Conversation No. 423-11.

12 Conversation No. 423-13.

13 Conversation No. 44-30.

14 Conversation No. 424-10.

15 Conversation No. 421-22.

16 Dean testimony, 3 SSC 1005–6.

17 Conversation No. 425-23.

18 Conversation No. 44-58.

19 Conversation No. 44-61.

20 Dean testimony, 3 SSC 1006–7.

21 Haldeman, *Diaries*, 618.

22 Conversation No. 424-30.

23 Conversation No. 426-4.

24 Conversation Nos. 44-69, 44-71, 44-80, 426-5 and 426-16.

25 Conversation No. 426-4.

26 Conversation No. 890-33.

27 Haldeman, *Diaries*, 620.

28 Ibid., 622–24.

29 When writing *Blind Ambition* I thought that Liddy's purportedly talking had first come up in my first meeting with the prosecutors on April 8, 1973. Based on the information in Haldeman's diary it is clear that Charlie was given this information as early as April 5, 1973, and, in turn, I shared it with Haldeman on that date and again on April 7, 1973. As to the practice of prosecutors using false information during plea discussions, as I was exploring, today the American Bar Association's Criminal Justice Standards, Standard 3-4.1 (c) states:

"A prosecutor should not knowingly make false statements or representations as to fact or law in the course of plea discussions with defense counsel or the accused." See http://www.americanbar.org/publications/criminal_justice_section_archive/crimjust_standards_pfunc_blk.html#4.1. As I wrote in *Blind Ambition*, I understood why they had to breach the agreement with Charlie, although they never seemed to understand why I felt I had to go to the Senate Watergate committee rather than deal with them. John W. Dean, *Blind Ambition: The White House Years* (New York: Simon & Schuster, 1976).

30 Haldeman, *Diaries*, 629. Note: The day headings for Monday, April 8, 1973, Tuesday, April 9, 1973, and Wednesday, April 10, 1973, are incorrect and should have been Sunday, Monday and Tuesday.

31 Magruder would later write that my lawyer had spoken with Bierbower, who reported to Jeb that I said: "Well, of course John doesn't have any legal problems, but Jeb has a very serious problem, and we don't know if we can help him." According to Magruder, who seems to have missed the message in the call to get to the prosecutor's office sooner rather than later, wrote that he was furious. See Jeb Stuart Magruder, *An American Life: One Man's Road to Watergate* (New York: Atheneum, 1974), 92. But the purpose of the call was not lost on Magruder's lawyers, who indeed did get him to the U.S. Attorney's Office quickly once Jeb gave up his fabricated story and told the truth, on April 12, 1973.

32 Sifting through the information in the recorded conversations, along with other information now available, such as the Watergate special prosecutor's interviews with Earl Silbert on August 30 and 31, 1973, has enabled me to pinpoint matters I could only address broadly in testimony and *Blind Ambition* and to recall others I had forgotten. See, e.g., Peter F. Rient and Judy Denny, September 6, 1973, "Interview of Earl Silbert on August 30–31, 1973," Memorandum to the Files, Record Group 140, NARA. And while I have not sought to fill in all such detail, I have noted this information generally in my account.

33 Conversation No. 44-103.

34 Conversation No. 891-1. Note: This conversation was partially transcribed by NARA for the lawsuit filed by Haldeman when he was seeking damages from the government for not turning over his diary dictation recordings and notes in a sufficiently timely manner. The court ruled against Haldeman, since he had turned over ownership of this material to protect it from the Watergate special prosecutors under executive privilege in 1973, and then claimed ownership only later. Had the Watergate special prosecutor had Haldeman's diary it would have resulted in multiple additional criminal charges against the president, Haldeman, Ehrlichman, Mitchell and others, not to mention made prosecution of the crimes with which they were charged much easier. See *Haldeman v. Freeman* (the administrator of the General Services Administration), 558 F. Supp. 514 (1983).

35 Conversation No. 425-44. (Extremely poor audio quality.)

36 Conversation No. 44-115.

37 Conversation No. 44-117.

38 Conversation No. 892-4.

39 Conversation No. 892-14.

40 E.g., Seymour M. Hersh, "Pressures to Plead Guilty Alleged in Watergate Case," *New York Times*, January 15, 1973, 63 and "McCord Reported Linking Payoffs to a G.O.P. Lawyer: Says He Believes Parkinson Paid Defendants—Lawyer Denies It," *New York Times*, April 9, 1973, 77.

41 Conversation No. 893-10.

42 Stans later wrote that he did not approve the settlement; rather, it had occurred in "early 1973" at the behest of "lawyers at the White House that we should close out this embarrassing litigation." Stans reports that in 1976, Spencer Oliver, whose telephone had been wiretapped by Liddy et al., and who had filed a separate lawsuit, settled for $215,000. And in 1977 the four Cubans who had been arrested in the DNC, and who had sued the Nixon reelection committee for misleading them into undertaking what they believed was a "national security" operation, settled for $200,000. See Maurice H. Stans, *The Terrors of Justice* (New York: Everest House, 1978), 251.

43 Conversation No. 893-16.

44 Conversation No. 893-21.

45 Walter Rugaber, "Watergate Grand Jury Hears Two Former White House Aides and Segretti: None Will Comment," *New York Times*, April 12, 1973, 41.

46 Conversation No. 894-2.

47 Conversation No. 894-4.

48 Conversation No. 894-7.

49 Conversation No. 428-12.

50 The point that Ehrlichman mentioned to the president—that Strachan had testified to $350,000 when, in fact, he returned $328,000—was not the most serious problem with his testimony. He was later indicted for perjury regarding that testimony on matters Ehrlichman did not raise with the president—namely, to whom he had delivered the money and why. See count thirteen of the March 1, 1974, indictment in *U.S. v. Mitchell et al.*

51 In Strachan's testimony before the Senate he acknowledged destroying these documents. See 6 *SSC* 2490–91.

52 The question of what Gordon Strachan knew and when he knew it has remained an open question, and even years later Strachan hesitatingly responded to questions about his knowledge with "I don't think so"–type answers, seemingly unsure himself. Strachan deposition, May 19, 1995, *Deans v. St. Martin's et al.* It may be that Strachan never had copies of the wiretap synopses at the White House, because Magruder later testified he never allowed them to leave his office; he claims, rather, that Strachan saw them there. See Magruder, 2 *SSC* 797–98, 827. This claim is denied by Strachan. See Strachan, 6 *SSC* 2451–52. While Strachan denies knowledge of the Watergate bugging, he clearly admitted to Ehrlichman seeing what he believed to be the fruit, which is not easy to reconcile. Strachan also failed a polygraph examination administered by the FBI on his denial of advance knowledge of the break-in. See April 24, 1973, Silbert Memo, Watergate Special Prosecution Files, NARA. But this could also have been because of his uncertainty as to his knowledge.

53 While this conversation is difficult to hear, there is no question for me regarding what was being discussed. Similarly, the archivists at NARA, when preparing the subject log for this conversation, clearly understood this part of the conversation related to what they categorized as the discussion "Delivery of G. Gordon Liddy reports."

54 Conversation No. 44-158.

55 Conversation Nos. 895-8, 895-22, 895-23, 38-12 and 38-15.

56 Conversation No. 427-1.

57 Conversation Nos. 895-14, 38-9 and 38-14.

58 Conversation No. 895-8.

59 Conversation No. 895-14.

60 Conversation No. 895-22.

61 Conversation Nos. 427-1.

62 Conversation No. 38-9.

63 Conversation No. 38-12.

64 Liddy later reported that he had learned Greenspun had information in his safe that could defeat the presidential campaign of Senator Edmund Muskie, so they planned such an operation. But since his plans for the reelection committee had not been approved, he sought to do the undertaking with the Howard Hughes organization. Liddy and Hunt met with Hughes's people but could not get the funding from them either, so the plan was abandoned. See G. Gordon Liddy, *Will: The Autobiography of G. Gordon Liddy* (New York: St. Martin's Press, 1997), 204–5.

65 Conversation No. 38-14.

66 Conversation No. 38-15.

## April 14 to 30, 1973

1 National Archives amd Records Administration (NARA), Conversation No. 46-113.

2 Conversation No. 428-19.

3 The "Chicago Seven" were seven defendants—Abbie Hoffman, Jerry Rubin, David Dellinger, Tom Hayden, Rennie Davis, John Froines and Lee Weiner—who were charged with conspiracy, inciting a riot and related offenses arising out of their anti–Vietnam War protest at the 1968 Democratic National Convention in Chicago, Illinois. In February 1970 five of the seven were found guilty of inciting a riot, but on appeal, all the convictions were overturned, and Nixon's Department of Justice decided not to retry them.

4 The "Scottsboro Boys," as they are typically called, were nine black teenage boys who were falsely accused of rape and tried and convicted by an all-white jury, with eight of them given death sentences, in Scottsboro, Alabama. The Communist Party tried to assist them in appealing the verdicts in a long and sordid travesty of justice. This sad story has been recounted in books, movies, documentaries and a Broadway musical. Only in November 2013 did Alabama grant a posthumous pardon to the last of these men, who had been framed and brutalized by Southern justice. Shadows and echoes of this horrific past still exist.

5 Ehrlichman provided a very surface analysis of the rift that actually started during the 1968 presidential campaign, when both were candidate Nixon's senior advisers. In fact, Ehrlichman did not think Mitchell was very smart, and Mitchell thought Ehrlichman arrogant and full of himself, the kind of staff man who used his proximity to Nixon to undercut Mitchell's recommendations to push his own ideas, particularly after he became attorney general in January 1969. Mitchell was far more politically conservative than Ehrlichman, who fell on the moderate to progressive side of many issues. By the time Watergate occurred in June 1972, they could barely speak to each. I attended countless meetings during which Mitchell refused to speak directly to Ehrlichman; rather, he would do so by asking Haldeman or me a question in Ehrlichman's presence to convey information. Privately each man blamed the other for Watergate. Mitchell blamed Ehrlichman for sending a loose cannon like Liddy to the campaign operation without warning them he was a screwball, if not a psychopath. Ehrlichman blamed Mitchell for allowing Watergate to occur on his watch as head of the campaign. But dating it to Haynsworth and Carswell worked nicely for Ehrlichman, because Nixon too felt Mitchell had done a bad job in recommending these judges as candidates for the high Court, and the White House had taken charge of the Supreme Court selection process. This strained relationship was a key reason for my becoming the intermediary among all these parties as the cover-up unfolded, for I had never taken sides. See John W. Dean, *The Rehnquist Choice: The Untold Story of the Nixon Appointment that Redefined the Supreme Court* (New York: Free Press, 2001).

6 Nixon's memory was wrong, as Adams's memoir clearly establishes. Note: Adams writes that the decision was left to him, and made by him. See Sherman Adams, *First Hand Report: The Story of the Eisenhower Administration* (Charleston, SC: reprint, BiblioBazaar, 2011), 447–48.

7 See Dean Senate testimony, 3 Senate Select Committee on Presidential Campaign Activities (SSC) 1013, 1312.

8 As his numbering system indicates, Ehrlichman recorded hundreds of telephone calls, but less than one hundred survived with his departure from the White House. He had some sort of special setup to record both Magruder and Mitchell when he met with them on April 14, 1973. While there has never been a transcript prepared on these meetings, I am told that the cassette with the recorded conversations has survived and resides either in the Watergate special prosecutor's files at NARA, in College Park, MD, or at the Nixon library.

9 Conversation No. 896-4(a).

10 Conversation No. 896-5.

11 Haldeman wrote in his diary for March 28, 1973, when I told him that Mitchell had finally admitted to me that he had signed off on Liddy's plans, he noted: "Mitchell and Magruder both told him [Dean] that they had both signed off on the project, which Mitchell told me,

also." H. R. Haldeman, *The Haldeman Diaries: Inside the Nixon White House* (New York: G. P. Putnam's, 1993), 618.

12 Mitchell makes very clear, as set forth in the transcript of Ehrlichman's secretly recorded session with him, why yours truly and others became involved in the Watergate cover-up after the arrests at the DNC. When discussing my motive, they had the following exchange, which addressed not only my motives but Mitchell's:

> MITCHELL: Well, certainly there wasn't any corrupt motive.
> EHRLICHMAN: [*Unintelligible*].
> MITCHELL: Poor John [Dean] is the guy that just got caught in the middle of this thing.
> EHRLICHMAN: Sure, and that's what I said.
> MITCHELL: Like, ah, like so many others that were first of all trying to keep the lid on it until after the election.
> EHRLICHMAN: Yeah.
> MITCHELL: And, in addition to that, to keep the lid on all the other things that, uh, were going on over here, uh, that—
> EHRLICHMAN: Well, the, ah—
> MITCHELL: —would have been worse, I think, than the Watergate business.

Ehrlichman transcript of April 14, 1973, meeting, Statement of Information, Hearings Before the Committee on the Judiciary, House of Representatives, 93rd Congress, 2nd Session, Book IV Part 2 (Washington, D.C.: Government Printing Office, 1974), 729.

13 Almost everyone on the list that Charlie Shaffer and I drew up was named either as an indicted or unindicted coconspirator in violation of the statutes cited on the list. By the time both Haldeman and Ehrlichman started testifying before the Senate Watergate committee they were unable to recall having ever seen my list or its contents. Haldeman, for example, was asked by Sam Dash: "By the way, did Mr. Dean ever show you, in April, a list of persons who would be involved in the Watergate which included your name on it?" Haldeman responded, "I certainly do not recall that at all." 8 *SSC* 3058. Ehrlichman similarly denied having seen the list. 7 SSC 2857.

I note this because it is representative of the amnesia that overcame these men soon after departing the White House, and it was typical of the fact that no point of my testimony, however minor, would be too inconsequential for them to either deny or not recall. While I have ignored countless similar examples, this was the kind of petty lying that caused me to lose all respect for these former colleagues, who went way beyond any call of duty in their efforts to destroy me. But I have intentionally resisted gathering their later false statements in my recounting of what occurred, and as it in fact unfolded.

14 Conversation No. 428-28.

15 Jeb appears to have gone to some length to exaggerate my role in response to Charlie's telephone call, but as often happened with Magruder's testimony, when he placed his interpretation or spin on events, it was far from accurate. With time this all got sorted out, however. For example, Jeb was unaware of the fact that, after hearing of Liddy's plans, I had tried to turn them off at the White House rather than, as he thought, promote them. In fact, Liddy was being pushed out of the White House by Bud Krogh and John Ehrlichman, because they thought (incorrectly) he would not cause problems at the reelection committee. When Jeb created his bogus testimony, it was a finished product when he enlisted me to support it, which I had never agreed to do. He did have—but was unaware of—the support of Mitchell, Haldeman, Ehrlichman and the president for it, of which they were well aware, as the July and August 1972 conversations reveal. Jeb's perception of the truth and the hard reality of a situation were often at odds.

16 G. Gordon Liddy, *Will: The Autobiography of G. Gordon Liddy* (New York: St. Martin's Press, 1997), 237. Note: Liddy wrote that Magruder called him to his office on June 12, 1972, and instructed him to go back into the DNC. This conflicts with all of Magruder's contempora-

neous explanations, at a time when he had no motive to lie, and with the testimony he gave when he agreed to assist the government.

17 Conversation No. 38-31.

18 When Ehrlichman later understood this, he omitted the key fact that Kalmbach was involved in order to keep the Watergate defendants on the reservation; rather, he would claim it was to raise attorney fees. Senate testimony of John Ehrlichman, 6 SSC 2569. Also, Ehrlichman later denied that Kalmbach had asked him if he had to be involved in this project, notwithstanding the fact Ehrlichman had told him it was of the upmost importance. See count twelve *U.S. v. Mitchell et al.* indictment,.

19 Richard Nixon, *RN: The Memoirs of Richard Nixon* (New York: Grosset & Dunlap, 1978), 821–24. The April 14, 1973, entry noted the irony of the White House correspondents awarding the "libelous" *Washington Post* coverage of Watergate their top prize at the time he had discovered the significance of Watergate "for the first time." He recorded that he had mentioned to Ehrlichman the idea of "Haldeman and Dean taking a leave of absence." But Ehrlichman thought that would not work "because as it turns out Dean has ways he could implicate both Haldeman and Ehrlichman, [and] it would be in effect [Dean] admitting his guilt." Nixon noted Magruder's going to the U.S. attorney had been "a terrible load lifted off him." And added that Colson was now "a major target of the U.S. Attorney, [but if] Dean cracks, Colson will have had it." The president recorded that he had learned both Colson and Mitchell had been interested in "material on O'Brien." The president recorded that while Haldeman did not want to resign, he had mentioned it as potentially necessary, but he was inclined to circle the wagons around Haldeman to protect him, because he was only tangentially involved. He found Kleindienst was "the strange actor" in his disengagement from it all. The only good news for his diary was the forthcoming Gallup poll that showed he had 60 percent approval and 33 percent disapproval ratings.

20 Archibald Cox interview of Henry Petersen, May 29, 1973, NARA, Records of the Watergate Special Prosecution Force. See www.archives.gov/research/investigations/watergate/index.html.

21 Conversation No. 38-34.

22 Conversation No. 38-37.

23 Haynes Johnson and Jules Witcover, "'New Majority' Growing Disillusioned With Nixon," *The Washington Post*, April 15, 1973, A-1.

24 Ehrlichman was correct that I never made such a statement. It was not necessary. Together we had listened to Hunt's recorded conversation with Colson shortly after the election, in early November 1972, and I had told him of Hunt's demands for money in mid-March 1973. Hunt made it very clear if he and the others were not paid, they were going to talk, not only about Watergate but about the break-in at Ellsberg's psychiatrist's office.

25 Conversation No. 428-36.

26 Nixon, *RN*, 826.

27 Nixon wrote of this period in his memoir that he understood the payment of money to the defendants had become the biggest problem: "When it came to the question of motive the real answer lay in each man's mind and each man's conscience." Thus, if everyone said the payments were for humanitarian purposes, Nixon believed there would be no obstruction of justice. Not only would such a spin of the facts have been a lie, but it still would have been an obstruction of justice. Take Ehrlichman's claim that he was concerned that Hunt would write an article. Why would Ehrlichman care if he wrote an article other than that it would have incriminated Ehrlichman in criminal activity. It was an absurd contention. When Mitchell, Haldeman and Ehrlichman attempted this defense against the criminal charges against them, it failed. See *U.S. v. Haldeman, et al.*, 559 F.2d 31 (1976), in which the matter of Haldeman's, Ehrlichman's and Mitchell's criminal intents was litigated at length. In fact, the jury did not buy the claim that these defendants acted for humanitarian reasons. See also Nixon, *RN*, 825, and Philip A. Lacovara, "Relevance of Defendants' 'Good' Motives for Engaging in Burglary, Warrantless Electronic Surveillance and Cover-up Activities," Memorandum by the Counsel to the Special Prosecutor, September 19, 1973. This memo,

and the underlying material by Robert L. Palmer, noted that good motive is no defense for violations of the prohibitions of a statute. As for good motive negating specific intent, the memo specifically addressed the same situation as Nixon. When, as Ehrlichman outlined to the president, there was a dual motive, the bad motive was sufficient under the law for conviction.

28  I reject the claim by the White House that the Secret Service had not anticipated that the office would be used over the weekend so they did not change the tape reel. A second machine began recording when the first ended, and they switched back and forth. While the Watergate special prosecutors could not prove that Haldeman disposed of the tape, all the evidence certainly points in that direction. The box with the recording that was available for the April 15, 1973, EOB conversations is marked "Part 1." But Part 2 disappeared. The hearings undertaken by the Watergate special prosecutor in October and November 1973 show one person with unique access and motive to simply toss the recording in the trash: Bob Haldeman. Haldeman was given some twenty-two boxes of tapes on two occasions. The first time, in late April 1973, was before there was any real record keeping noting which ones he was given. And on a second occasion, during July 10 and 11, 1973, just before the existence of the system was revealed on July 16, 1973, the Secret Service records indicate he was given another batch that included "the EOB from April 11 through April 16, 1973." Recording keeping was so loose and sloppy (until discovery of the missing tapes in October 1973) that it would have been unnoticed had Haldeman simply disposed of the reel that ended during the president's conversation with Kleindienst on April 15, 1973. See Hearings on Missing Nixon Tapes, U.S. District Court for the District of Columbia, November 8–9, 1973.

29  Conversation No. 38-42.

30  Nixon, *RN*, 827.

31  Ibid.

32  April 15, 1973, Haldeman notes, Nixon library, NARA.

33  Nixon, *RN*, 828.

34  Because it was speculative, I did not include it in the first draft of my testimony for the Senate. But when reading my draft I added it, because I believed it highly likely when I learned the president was claiming he had recorded our conversation and that I had told him I had been granted immunity, which I had not. My testimony, however, caused Senate Watergate committee minority counsel Don Sanders to ask Alex Butterfield on July 13, 1973, after I had testified if it was possible, as I believed, that Nixon had recorded me. Butterfield's honest answer changed the entire dimension of the Watergate investigation, which became a fight by the prosecutors for the tapes to determine if I was telling the truth, and Nixon was involved, or whether Nixon was telling the truth, that he knew nothing of the cover-up until March 21, 1973, when I told him.

35  Dean Senate testimony, 3 *SSC* 1015–17. Regarding my belief that I was being taped by Nixon, see 3 *SSC* 1016, 1019–20, 1031, and 4 *SSC* 1373, 1434, 1558, and 1576–77.

36  April 15, 1973, Haldeman notes, Nixon library, NARA.

37  Nixon, *RN*, 828–29.

38  See generally, John W. Dean, *Blind Ambition: The White House Years* (New York: Simon & Schuster, 1976), 258–63.

39  Conversation No. 897-3.

40  Dean Senate testimony, 3 *SSC* 1314–15.

41  Conversation No. 897-4.

42  Conversation No. 897-9

43  Conversation No. 897-11.

44  Conversation No. 897-16.

45  Petersen testimony before impeachment inquiry, Testimony of Witnesses, Hearings Before the Committee on the Judiciary, House of Representatives, 93rd Congress, 2nd Session, Book III (Washington, D.C.: Government Printing Office, 1974), 81.

46  Congress had only a few of Nixon's edited transcripts, which nevertheless, along with some testimony, established that Nixon provided false and misleading information to Petersen

regarding Haldeman and Ehrlichman and personally urged Petersen to deny me immunity in order to make it more difficult to develop the criminal cases against Haldeman and Ehrlichman. While Nixon was feeding Petersen misinformation, the unwitting Petersen was providing information that Nixon passed on to Haldeman and Ehrlichman, which enabled them to distort or alter what had occurred by twisting and manipulating others to provide incorrect corroborating information. Petersen's meetings with Nixon would become a cornerstone for article I of the bill of impeachment against Nixon.

47 April 16, 1973, Henry Petersen notes, Exhibit No. 147, 9 *SSC* 3875–76.
48 Conversation No. 427-2.
49 Conversation Nos. 427-5 and 427-6.
50 Conversation No. 427-10.
51 Conversation No. 427-12.
52 Conversation No. 38-82.
53 Conversation No. 38-84.
54 Conversation No. 898-4.
55 Conversation No. 898-6.
56 Conversation No. 898-12.
57 Haldeman appears to be referring to information he was given by a former attorney general, Bill Rogers, suggesting that Petersen had become a coconspirator. When Watergate special prosecutor Archibald Cox was fired by Nixon, and I was working with the prosecutors, Henry Petersen was temporarily placed back in charge of the case. Assistant Watergate special prosecutor Richard Ben-Veniste asked me at that time if Petersen had been compromised. I said I did not believe he had been unless he had become a coconspirator. Given my dealings with Petersen, it was a close question. But given Petersen's dealings with Nixon after I departed, as revealed in the recorded conversations, a strong argument can be made that Petersen became as foolish as everyone else and unwittingly entered the Watergate cover-up conspiracy. Although he, along with many others, became coconspirators, he was never so named. Dick Moore and Ron Ziegler, along with others who would later join the Nixon defense, were all active coconspirators who were never named. '
58 For purposes of illustration, there were three general levels at the Nixon White House: the top level of presidential assistants, which included, for example, Haldeman, Ehrlichman and Kissinger, along with a few others; a middle level, which included deputy assistants, special counsel and counsel to the president, where you found Len Garment, Dick Moore, former aides Chuck Colson, Dwight Chapin, Jeb Magruder and the like; and then the lower level of staff assistants, where you found Strachan, Higby and others. Thus, the president was going to call anyone from the middle level up "a top White House official," although they reported up through others and had no direct access to the president.
59 Conversation No. 38-86.
60 Conversation No. 898-20.
61 During their earlier conversation on April 16, Petersen had told the president about Liddy: "This man is crazy, Mr. President. He's burning his arms. He showed the prosecutor and said, 'I will stand up to anything. I've made myself endure this to prove to myself that I can take anything. Jail will not break me,' and what have you. You've got to be a crazy man to sit there and burn yourself to see if you can withstand the pain." See Conversation No. 427-2.
62 Conversation No. 898-23.
63 As it turned out, Gordon Strachan would corroborate my testimony when he appeared before the Senate Watergate committee on matters such as: Haldeman instructing him to destroy possible Watergate-related evidence in their files; his role in taking White House funds to the reelection committee; and his involvement in the Segretti matter. Haldeman had a number of small-bore people on his staff who would do as asked without asking questions. Strachan was not one of them. To my knowledge there was no significant conflict in our testimony.
64 Conversation No. 899-4.

65 Conversation No. 429-3. Note: The president's daily diary is incorrect in stating that Haldeman and Ehrlichman attended this discussion from the outset, at 5:20 P.M., for the recorded conversation reveals that they joined it approximately twenty-seven minutes after it started.

66 The question of who is the client of the White House counsel would not be resolved until after Watergate, and today, according to the American Bar Association's Model Rules of Professional Conduct, the client is the Office of the President, not the current occupant or his staff. The attorney-client privilege has never protected criminal behavior, and federal courts now have rules that government attorneys have a limited attorney-client privilege. See, e.g. Nancy Leong, "Attorney-Client Privilege in the Public Sector: A Survey of Government Attorneys," *Georgetown Journal of Legal Ethics* 20:163 (2007).

67 Ehrlichman was not telling the president that he had personally met with Kalmbach on July 26, 1972, to give him instructions—"a directive," according to Kalmbach—to carry out his secret mission of raising and delivering money for those involved in Watergate. When Kalmbach said that he was troubled by the secrecy, Ehrlichman told him it was necessary; otherwise, Ehrlichman said, "Herb, they would have our heads in their laps." In early August 1972, Kalmbach reported to Ehrlichman that he had raised an additional seventy-five thousand dollars from a Nixon contributor for this effort. On April 6, 1973, they met again on this subject in the parking lot of the Bank of America, in San Clemente, California. Ehrlichman requested that if Kalmbach was called upon to testify about his activities that he say he had been directed by me. Kalmbach, knowing that was not true, reminded Ehrlichman that it had been at his direction as well. See testimony of Herbert Kalmbach, *U.S. v Mitchell et al.* (November 12, 1974) 6332–95.

68 Conversation No. 38-90.

69 Conversation No. 38-92.

70 Conversation No. 38-95.

71 Conversation No. 900-1.

72 Conversation No. 900-4. Note: The audio of this conversation is very poor.

73 Conversation No. 38-100.

74 Conversation No. 900-26.

75 Ehrlichman was oblivious to the fact that he had created, with the blessings of the president, a criminal conspiracy when he wiretapped syndicated columnist Joseph Kraft's home and office in Georgetown, and although the wiretap failed, the conspiracy was complete when Jack Caulfield's assistant climbed a ladder and tried to intercept the phone lines into Kraft's home. It was the problem of the criminal conspiracy that I had raised with the president.

76 Haldeman, *Diaries*, 648.

77 Petersen, Watergate grand jury testimony, Testimony of Witnesses, Hearings Before the Committee on the Judiciary, Book IV, 1474–75.

78 Haldeman recorded in his diary, regarding Nixon's conversation with Petersen, that Nixon ordered Petersen "not to get into testimony on what Hunt was involved in with national security. Petersen told the P Dean had already told him about the Hunt break-in in California." Haldeman, *Diaries*, 648. It appears Petersen had just learned about it. My attorney, Charlie Shaffer, reported it to the prosecutors on April 15, 1973, to avoid my becoming part of another obstruction of justice relating to the then ongoing trial of Daniel Ellsberg.

79 Haldeman, *Diaries*, 648–49.

80 Conversation No. 902-1.

81 This was a reference to Patricia Marx, whose father was Louis Marx, who allegedly was a friend of J. Edgar Hoover. But this explanation has never made much sense. Journalist Ronald Kessler writes in his look inside Hoover's FBI, *The Bureau: The Secret History of the FBI* (New York: St. Martin's Press, 2002), on page 162, that during the FBI investigation of the leak of the Pentagon Papers they became aware that Ellsberg was married to Patricia Marx, so they wanted to interview her father, Louis Marx, about his son-in-law, Dan Ellsberg. Kessler reports that, following standard FBI procedure, because Louis Marx was an acquaintance of Hoover's, clearance was sought for the interview. Hoover wrote no on the bottom

of the request memo. But it was mistakenly read as ok. So Marx was interviewed. Bill Sullivan noticed that Hoover had said no and told Bob Mardian at the Justice Department. This tip became the principal rationalization for the FBI's setting up its own investigation, along with G. Gordon Liddy's, speaking as a former FBI agent, claiming that the FBI was not treating the investigation with sufficient seriousness.

82 Conversation Nos. 902-2 and 902-3.

83 Conversation No. 902-5.

84 The statement read:

> To date I have refrained from making any public comment whatsoever about the Watergate case. I shall continue that policy in the future because I believe that the case will be fully and justly handled by the grand jury and by the Ervin select committee.
>
> It is my hope, however, that those truly interested in seeing that the Watergate case is completely aired and that justice will be done will be careful in drawing any conclusions as to the guilt or involvement of any persons until all the facts are known and until each person has had an opportunity to testify under oath in his own behalf.
>
> Finally, some may hope or think that I will become a scapegoat in the Watergate case. Anyone who believes this does not know me, know the true facts, nor understand our system of justice.

85 Conversation No. 38-107.

86 Conversation No. 902-9.

87 Conversation No. 429-15.

88 Conversation No. 429-18.

89 Ehrlichman apparently thought he was absolving himself by telling the president he had not raised the money for the defendants; he seemingly could not imagine that a conversation like this—when the taping system was revealed—showed his solid participation in the conspiracy to obstruct justice. He was recounting his agreement with these actions, even if he was not what he described as an "efficient actor." Conversations like this would later provide proof beyond a reasonable doubt of his deep involvement in the cover-up conspiracy.

90 Dr. Samuel Mudd was convicted and imprisoned for his role in assisting John Wilkes Booth assassinate President Lincoln. On June 29, 1865, Mudd along with others, was convicted of conspiring with Booth to help him escape; he splinted Booth's broken leg and built him crutches. On February 8, 1869, Mudd was pardoned by President Andrew Johnson and released from prison on March 8, 1869. Dr. Mudd tried to get his conviction expunged but failed. His descendants took up the cause, but like Nixon, all subsequent presidents had problems with the matter, as did the army, which had tried and convicted him. Both Presidents Carter and Reagan were sympathetic to the claim that Dr. Mudd had been improperly tried on dubious evidence. There is no comparison, however, between the overwhelming evidence that would convict Bob Haldeman and that upon which Dr. Mudd was convicted. See, e.g., Gregg S. Clemmer, "The Case for Dr. Samuel A. Mudd," *The Washington Times* (February 2, 1982), C-3.

91 Of course, both men would later be convicted of multiple counts of perjury. See *U.S. v. Haldeman, et al.*, 559 F.2d 31.

92 Imagine how the dynamics of Watergate might have changed if Liddy had talked at Nixon's request, for he could then have truly taken credit for breaking the case. Liddy, who pretended to remain silent out of loyalty to the president and his men, was actually only protecting himself. Liddy did not wish to talk because, not only had he bungled everything he had been involved with, but he had consistently exceeded his authority, falsely claiming to have acted in the name of others. In addition, he had spent a substantial amount of money (over $45,000—today's value over $250,000) that he could not provide an accounting for. See *Liddy v. Commissioner of Internal Revenue*, 808 F. 2d 312 (1986). Had Liddy come forward, he would have been uncovered for his duplicity and the self-serving sociopathic behavior that provided the catalyst for the destruction of the Nixon presidency. This is not to say that the Nixon White House had not welcomed his lawless behavior before discovering he was also totally incompetent.

93 Conversation No. 123-2.

94 Conversation No. 903-4.

95 Conversation No. 903-6.

96 Conversation No. 38-129.

97 In fact, I was busy exploring being a witness at the Senate Watergate hearings with or without immunity, and I had just started having secret discussions with Sam Dash to prevent this information from leaking. See Dean, *Blind Ambition*, 270–71.

98 Conversation No. 903-14.

99 See Nixon, *RN*, Soviets in Cienfuegos Bay, 485–89; Syrian invasion of Jordan, 484–85; and Cambodian bombing, 446–55.

100 Nixon, *RN*, 836.

101 Conversation No. 903-19.

102 Charlie and I had privately concluded that the U.S. Attorney's Office would never be able to successfully unravel the Watergate cover-up, because the top coconspirator, Richard Nixon, probably could never be indicted. As for the person Ehrlichman referred to, Bob McCandless, I had no idea at the time what post he had had with the Humphrey campaign. Bob had been married to the sister of my first wife, and he volunteered his legal service to help with the Senate, where he had once worked for Senator Robert Kerr (D-OK) and had many friends and associates, and he had later worked as a lobbyist. I signed him on as a part-time cocounsel with Charlie, but he was to have nothing to do with my representation in any criminal matters, only regarding Capitol Hill. I had no relationship whatsoever with Democrats and thought Bob could quietly help out through his friends on the Hill. Not until 2010, when I was visiting Washington and had not seen Bob in decades, did he join me for dinner to tell me what he had primarily done during Watergate. He told me some four decades after the fact that he mostly worked the press, leaking stories and trying to prevent news organizations from buying the false stories that the White House and Nixon supporters were putting out to try to discredit and destroy me. Neither Charlie nor I knew what he was doing, and only infrequently saw Bob; rather, we figured that information he was giving Democratic friends was, in turn, getting leaked to the news media. I certainly had no idea he was privately meeting with editorial boards, Woodward and Bernstein, and others covering Watergate—and now wish he had kept a diary. It would be interesting, if not informative.

103 Conversation No. 903-20.

104 The log of the president's activities make this scene impossible, for he spoke on the telephone three times with Ziegler from the Key Biscayne compound swimming pool (at 5:29 P.M. to 5:41 P.M., 6:00 P.M. to 6:01 P.M. and 6:03 P.M. to 6:03 P.M.) before returning to his residence for dinner with his family (wife, daughters and son-in-law) and Bebe Rebozo, and called Ziegler again after dinner (7:30 P.M. to 7:39 P.M.). Next the president and his family watched the movie *Some Came Running*, from 7:43 P.M. until 10:00 P.M. These details are only of interest because I have always been curious about when, where and how Nixon made his decision to fire Haldeman and Ehrlichman, along with me. Sunset was not until approximately 7:50 P.M., and Ziegler had not been to the presidential compound. The PDD contains the president's schedule, and those times were noted by his Secret Service detail; the calls were logged by the White House operators. The Web site www.timeanddate.com has the sunrises and sunsets for Key West, Florida, back to 1974, which would be very close to what happened on April 20, 1973, in Key Biscayne.

105 Nixon, *RN*, 836.

106 Ibid., 837.

107 Conversation No. 38-137.

108 Conversation No. 904-6.

109 Conversation No. 904-8.

110 When Haldeman and Ehrlichman were later on trial for violating 18 USC § 1503, Judge Sirica explained the meaning of the word "corrupt" when charging the jury: "The word

'corruptly' as used in this statute simply means having an evil or improper purpose or intent." Being more specific, the judge explained, "If you find, for example, that a Defendant participated in the payment of money to the original Watergate defendants for the purpose of keeping them quiet, you would be justified in finding that a corrupt endeavor to obstruct the due administration of justice occurred."

111 In fact, I was anything but desperate; rather, I was very much at peace for the first time in a long time. I had not been comfortable as their desk officer for the cover-up. At this time I was fully prepared to admit and pay for my mistakes, and to testify honesty, and fully. Anything less would only continue the cover-up. Higby was my last channel of communication to Haldeman, and that information I knew would go to Ehrlichman and the president. I was still hopeful that if they realized I was not going to crumble under their effort to rewrite the facts, they would appreciate that only the truth would end this nightmare, and they would proceed honorably accordingly. What the president, Haldeman, Ehrlichman and the Justice Department did not know was that, while I had offered to testify before the Senate Watergate committee without immunity, Sam Dash had offered me immunity from the outset of our secret meetings, and Charlie thought Senate immunity would make it nearly impossible for the Justice Department to ever prosecute me. In short, I was not engaging in the desperate struggle for immunity the White House envisioned; rather. I was merely trying to get them to do the right thing to save the Nixon presidency.

112 Conversation No. 430-1.

113 Conversation No. 430-4.

114 Mitchell, along with Maurice Stans and longtime fugitive Robert Vesco, would be indicted for obstruction of justice by the U.S. attorney for the Southern District of New York on May 10, 1973. They struck me at the time, and still do, as trumped-up charges by a U.S. Attorney's Office that loved to grab headlines, and they did so by indicting two former Nixon cabinet officers as Watergate was exploding. A year later, on April 27, 1974, Mitchell and Stans were acquitted. I was dragged into this case, about which I really knew almost nothing, as a witness. Assistant Watergate special prosecutor Jim Neal later told me that calling me as a witness in the Vesco case had been "a mistake," and the case against Mitchell and Stans was not one he would have allowed when he served as the U.S. attorney for Tennessee.

115 Conversation No. 38-145.

116 Conversation No. 430-16. Note: I discovered when I was writing this portion that I had somehow not assigned this conversation to my transcribers. Thus, in this instance I relied on the almost full transcription of this conversation, and the summary of it, in Stanley Kutler's *Abuse of Power* (New York: Free Press, 1997), 329–34.

117 Kleindienst was clearly not informed, for this information had been imparted ten days earlier, when Shaffer had ended our working relationship with the U.S. Attorney's Office. Since the Ellsberg break-in was a driving force for the White House cover-up and the last payment to Hunt was made in response to his demand lest he reveal it, Charlie had given this information to make certain neither his client nor he was part of an obstruction of justice that was associated with this information. None of the details associated with the matter, and its relationship to the Watergate cover-up, were provided—only the fact of it. The Justice Department has in its files pictures from the CIA, which were developed in 1971, when Hunt and Liddy cased Ellsberg's doctor's office in preparation for the effort to obtain his psychiatric files.

118 Conversation No. 38-146. (Not transcribed; merely listened to it.)

119 Conversation No. 430-22.

120 Nixon writes in his memoir that around this time that he had a recurring thought: "Before long a disturbing thought occurred to me; I couldn't get it out of my mind: what if Dean had carried a tape recorder at our March 21 meeting, a small tape recorder, concealed in his jacket but capable of catching every word. He would be able to use parts of the conversation in a very damaging way." This thought simply did not occur to him, but it appears that he had forgotten why he had this thought. On April 17, 1973, in a meeting with Len Garment,

I told him I had reason to believe that there were audio recordings of one or more of my conversations with the president. I had come to believe this (as I later testified at the Senate) because of Nixon's behavior during our meeting on April 15, 1973, not to mention the fact that he had told Henry Petersen he had a record of my saying that I had immunity, when, in fact, I had made no such statement. I told Len because he was a gossip, so I knew he would spread the story. Years later he said he had done just that, and when he read the transcripts of Nixon worrying about it, felt he had done a disservice to Nixon. See Nixon, *RN*, 842, and Dean Senate testimony 3 SSC 1016, 1019–20, 1031; 4 SSC 1476–77, 1558.

121 Conversation No. 430-23.

122 Conversation No. 38-150.

123 What, in fact, happened was that Shaffer told them that if they wanted to engage in prosecutorial misconduct and keep this activity secret that was their business. What was our business was disclosing it, because it was an obstruction of justice, and Charlie said neither he nor I were interested in obstructing justice. Nixon, Kleindienst and Petersen decided to read this as blackmail.

124 Conversation No. 38-151.

125 Conversation No. 38-153.

126 Conversation Nos. 38-154 and 38-155.

127 Not until many months later, in late 1973 when Ehrlichman was under investigation in several criminal cases, did he retain new and separate counsel, William Snow Frates, who was something of a buffoon, who was nicknamed and called behind his back "W. C. Frito" by attorneys in the Watergate Special Prosecutor's Office. Frates represented Bebe Rebozo in a number of civil lawsuits.

128 While I was unable to find this statement in the Petersen and Nixon conversation—Conversation No. 430-23—earlier that day, it could not have been a more distorted interpretation; that appears to be the way Nixon was thinking. Charlie provided this information to the prosecutors, because he told them we were moving on, since it was obvious to him we could not do business. But he needed to clear up this ongoing obstruction of justice and potential prosecutorial misconduct. He made no threat. He asked for nothing in return for the information. He merely told them that they had the information in their files, and under the leading U.S. Supreme Court case on the subject, they were duty-bound to act appropriately. It was their choice, and his farewell gift to them. It was our last dealings with the U.S. Attorney's Office, and the information was even given to them in such a manner that neither Charlie nor I could be charged with leaking classified information.

129 Conversation No. 38-156 and 38-157.

130 Conversation No. 38-159.

131 Conversation No. 38-161.

132 Conversation No. 905-8.

133 John Ehrlichman, *Witness to Power: The Nixon Years* (New York: Simon & Schuster, 1982), 311.

134 At the time I was not aware that the warning I had sent him through Len Garment about the immunity statement (during the same conversation in which I had told Len I believed I had been recorded) had gotten through. But the conversations with Petersen reveals that Nixon quickly pulled back on immunity and told Petersen it was his decision alone.

135 Conversation No. 905-12.

136 Conversation No. 45-3.

137 Conversation No. 431-9.

138 Apparently Haldeman's attorneys had not yet explained the way criminal conspiracies work, that once you agree with another to undertake an illegal action, all coconspirators become liable for the actions of the others. Throughout these recorded conversations, particularly in April 1973, Haldeman (and Ehrlichman) openly acknowledge their participation in the conspiracy but appear to believe that, because they were not passing the money themselves to the Watergate defendants, particularly Hunt for his silence, they have no criminal exposure. This was why my attorney, Charlie Shaffer, told me not to deal with any of the poten-

tial defendants other than to confront them as I did, with their criminal problems, hoping to get them to step forward and take responsibility.

139 Conversation No. 45-15.

140 Conversation No. 906-1.

141 Carl Bernstein and Bob Woodward, "Dean Seen Asking Full Bug Disclosure," *The Washington Post*, April 27, 1973, A-1. The story reported that I had told Nixon that "to save the presidency" Haldeman, Ehrlichman and I would have to disclose all [we] knew about the Watergate bugging case and face the possible consequences of going to jail. Hopeful that Haldeman and Ehrlichman would follow suit at the president's urging, Dean on April 6 told federal prosecutors all he knew about the bugging and a subsequent White House cover-up, according to three reliable sources. But Haldeman and Ehrlichman apparently balked at the idea of incriminating themselves, leading to the current state of confusion and warfare between individuals inside the White House, the sources reported.

While the date of the meeting with the president and Haldeman and Ehrlichman is wrong—it was March 21, 1973—the gist of the *Post* story is correct, and this is information I had discussed with both Len Garment and Dick Moore. As of April 27, 1973, I had not discussed anything with my lawyers regarding my dealings with the president.

142 According to Ehrlichman's office schedule he met with Haldeman and me from 3:45 P.M. to 6:00 P.M. on March 21, 1973.

143 John Herbers, "Mississippi Crowds Cheer Nixon at 'Stennis Day' Fete," *New York Times*, April 28. 1973, 17.

144 Haldeman, *Diaries*, 667.

145 Conversation No. 906-8.

146 Conversation No. 45-34.

147 Conversation No. 45-36.

148 Conversation No. 906-12.

149 Conversation No. 906-16.

150 Conversation No. 906-17.

151 Conversation No. 906-23.

152 Ehrlichman and Haldeman will claim it was done in a clandestine fashion because of the political situation, but they were unsuccessful in selling this bogus argument to a jury in *U.S. v. Mitchell et al.* Petersen at this time is unaware that Hunt had made clear following the November election that the continued silence of the Watergate defendants could only be assured if payments were forthcoming, and while this was implicit in his conversation with Colson, it became explicit in his demand for money in March 1973, when he said that if payments were not forthcoming, he would have seamy things to say about his work for Ehrlichman. Nixon did not discuss with Petersen this quid pro quo element in Hunt's blackmail demand.

153 Conversation No. 906-24.

154 Conversation No. 906-25.

155 Conversation No. 432-1.

156 Conversation No. 164-2.

157 For example: *The Washington Post*: "Gray Resigns; Ruckelshaus Heads FBI; Hunt, Liddy Linked to Ellsberg Case"; "After Big Day, Nixon Retreats to Camp David"; "Case Role Ill Defined for Lawyer: John J. Wilson"; *New York Times*: "Gray Says He Destroyed Files from Hunt Given Him When He Met Ehrlichman, Dean"; "Haldeman and Ehrlichman Reported Fighting Ouster"; "Dean Is Reported Asking Immunity: White House Counsel Says He Will Not Testify If He Runs Risk Of Prosecution"; "Grand Jury Nears End of Investigation on Tangled Vesco Case."

158 Conversation No. 164-4.

159 Conversation No. 164-6.

160 Charlie Shaffer understood this law perfectly. Congress had adopted a so-called use immunity statute that allowed the government to collect independent evidence of criminal conduct,

then grant limited immunity that forced the person to testify or be in contempt of court, yet still prosecute that person on independent evidence. The Supreme Court decision that Petersen was referring to was *Kastigar v. United States* 406 U.S. 441 (1972), which cast a long shadow over the use immunity statute. Although I assured Sam Dash I would testify with or without immunity before the Senate Watergate committee, Charlie said that if he was going to represent me he would insist on my having immunity. Sam Dash, a professor of criminal law, understood exactly what Shaffer was doing. For this reason, Dash and I were meeting secretly, going over my potential testimony so he could tell Chairman Sam Ervin that I must have immunity and Ervin would make it happen. With the appointment of a special prosecutor, and notwithstanding the fact that I understood it was likely Archibald Cox would be fired, I knew that when I pled guilty to conspiracy to obstruct justice that Nixon would never get a new attorney general without a special prosecutor. As Shaffer later told me, I had Oliver North's case before Oliver North every dreamed he would have to take *Kastigar* to the next level: that Congress could not compel your testimony and then allow the executive branch to prosecute you with witnesses who had heard that testimony. See *North v. United States* 920 F.2d 940 (DC Cir., 1990).

161  Conversation No. 164-10.
162  Conversation No. 164-13.
163  Nixon, *RN*, 846.
164  Conversation No. 164-18.
165  On Monday, March 26, 1973, Ehrlichman's secretary had requested that David Young pull together his files on the Pentagon Papers investigation and send them over to Ehrlichman's office. Young placed them in an attaché case and sent Ehrlichman the files. On Tuesday, March 27, Ehrlichman requested that Young come to his office, and they discussed the Ellsberg break-in. During this meeting, Ehrlichman told Young, "My present recollection is, I didn't know about this until afterward. What about you?" Young replied, "Yes, I do. I not only recall it, I knew about it beforehand; and my clear recollection is you also were aware of it beforehand. And the memoranda in the file, in the briefcase," which Young pointed at and which was in front of Ehrlichman's desk, "the memoranda reflect that fact that you did." Ehrlichman responded, "Well, there is no question about what actually happened. But I have taken those out, because they are too sensitive, and they show too much forethought." Young commented, "Well, somebody also might have copies, Hunt and Liddy." Ehrlichman replied, "Well, that's a chance we will have to take." In fact, David Young had copies of the memoranda showing Ehrlichman had approved the Hunt-Liddy Ellsberg operation in writing. Ehrlichman also met with Young on this subject on April 30, 1973, so it was clearly fresh in Ehrlichman's mind when giving Nixon a false account. Testimony of David Young, *U.S. v. Ehrlichman* (July 1, 1974), 1048–52.
166  Conversation No. 164-21.
167  Conversation No. 164-24.
168  Conversation No. 164-28.
169  Conversation No. 164-30.
170  Conversation No. 164-32.
171  Ibid.
172  Conversation No. 164-38.
173  Conversation No. 164-39.
174  Nixon, *RN*, 847–48; Haldeman, *Diaries*, 671–73; H. R. Haldeman with Joseph DiMona, *The Ends of Power* (New York: Times Books, 1978), 287–96; Ehrlichman, *Witness to Power*, 389–90.
175  Conversation No. 164-44.
176  Conversation No. 164-48.

## May 1 to 10, 1973

1 National Archives and Records Administration (NARA) Conversation No. 45-41.

2 Conversation No. 45-48.

3 Conversation No. 45-65.

4 Richard Nixon, *RN: The Memoirs of Richard Nixon* (New York: Grosset & Dunlap, 1978), 849.

5 Ibid., 850.

6 Having personally transcribed hundreds of these conversations, I know that there was no way Bob Haldeman, as able as he was, could begin to obtain an accurate account of a conversation with as much nuance as the one Nixon and I had during the first hour, as well as the different tone when Haldeman arrived for another forty minutes. Haldeman's twenty pages of legal pad notes merely track the gist of the conversation.

7 Nixon's speech, along with the information I was sure had been leaked by Ehrlichman and Colson for Jack Anderson's April 26 column, left no doubt where I stood. It would be my word against Mitchell, Colson, Ehrlichman, Haldeman and the president of the United States. On May 1, I had my first conversation with Charlie Shaffer about my knowledge of Richard Nixon's role in the Watergate cover-up. As I talked with Charlie—and about the Nixon White House for the first time with anyone other than Nixon's aides and enablers—I began to understand that I had been working in something of a criminal cabal, with well-meaning and intelligent people who had placed expediency and accomplishing the president's goals above the legal rules we all might otherwise agree are essential for our way of life. That realization, not to mention the fact that I would be the target of an even tighter criminal conspiracy to protect Nixon's presidency, certainly altered my thinking and actions.

8 Conversation Nos. 908-1, 908-2 and 908-3.

9 Conversation No. 123-3.

10 Conversation No. 908-15.

11 Conversation No. 45-93.

12 See H. R. Haldeman with Joe DiMona, *The Ends of Power* (New York: Times Books, 1978), 296. See also Conversation No. 908-24. Nixon told Ziegler to apologize to the FBI agent, explaining, "The guy was standing out there in the hall blocking my path. As I came walking up, I said 'Who are you?' He said, 'FBI.' I said, 'You sit inside that door. Get out of here.' Can you imagine that? Stand out in front of Haldeman's office."

13 Conversation No. 120-1.

14 Conversation No. 909-2.

15 Conversation No. 909-11.

16 Conversation No. 909-6.

17 Conversation No. 909-26.

18 Trial transcript, *U.S. v. Ehrlichman* (July 11, 1974), 2341.

19 Conversation No. 909-27.

20 Conversation No. 909-29.

21 Seymour M. Hersh, "6 MAY BE INDICTED: Promises of Clemency in Break-in Called Part of Scheme," *New York Times*, May 2, 1973, 1. In fact, the gist of this story, and the parts that Ehrlichman reported to Nixon, were highly accurate. Hersh was getting solid information, but not from me.

22 Conversation No. 910-3.

23 Conversation No. 45-149 (Haldeman) and Conversation No. 45-151 (Ehrlichman).

24 Conversation No. 911-2. Ehrlichman, and Krogh for a brief while, were totally confusing information I had given them. Months earlier, when in Henry Petersen's office, he had shown me photographs the CIA had developed for Hunt and Liddy when they worked at the White House. They were pictures made of the office building of Ellsberg's psychiatrist in Beverly Hills, California. Because Liddy had told me of his break-in operation on June 19, 1972, following the arrest of his men at the DNC, I immediately figured out that these were pictures they had taken when scouting the job and casing the offices. Remarkably, one picture

included Liddy standing in the parking space under the sign: Dr. Lewis Fielding. Beside Liddy were cars with California license plates. I said nothing to Petersen but returned to the White House and told Ehrlichman about them. In doing so, I made very clear that I had no indication whatsoever that Henry Petersen knew what to make of them. All Petersen told me was that he had shown them to Earl Silbert and asked Pat Gray about them. I also told Ehrlichman it would probably not take an investigator a half-day to put together what had happened by contacting Dr. Fielding, who was Ellsberg's psychiatrist.

When at Shaffer's instruction (and to make certain we were not obstructing justice) I told Earl Silbert, on April 15, 1973, about the Ellsberg break-in, I did so by telling him about the pictures in Petersen's files. After the Department of Justice revealed this to Judge Byrne, and it became public, Ehrlichman began telling Nixon that I had told both him and Krogh that Henry Petersen had been aware of the Ellsberg break-in because of these pictures. That was untrue. Until April 15, 1973, neither Silbert nor Petersen had any idea what the pictures from the CIA involved. Ehrlichman, in this May 2, 1973, conversation, again told the president that in "late November, early December" I had told Krogh "that Petersen, Pat Gray and Earl Silbert all had seen those pictures." That was true, except none of them knew what the pictures involved, as Ehrlichman was now claiming.

25 Conversation No. 911-16.

26 Alexander M. Haig, Jr., with Charles McCarry, *Inner Circles: How America Changed the World: A Memoir* (New York: Warner Books, 1992), 332–35.

27 Haldeman, *The Ends of Power*, 299.

28 Henry Kissinger, *Years of Upheaval* (Boston: Little, Brown and Co., 1982), 108–9. Kissinger wrote that on the evening of May 2, 1973, he received a call from Rose Woods saying Nixon wanted to bring Haig back as chief of staff for a few weeks, but the president was worried about Kissinger's reaction to having his former subordinate technically becoming his superior. Rose said Henry should not cause any problem, because Nixon needed a chief of staff. Kissinger says he was not happy with the arrangement but knew Nixon needed someone in the post, and he recognized that Haig could handle it. Haig also called Kissinger and told him he would not take the post if Henry had a problem. And finally, after Nixon had used others to deal with Kissinger and gotten it all in order, Nixon called Henry himself to explain that making Haig chief of staff was really his plan to increase Kissinger's influence at the White House.

29 Conversation No. 912-2.

30 Conversation No. 912-3.

31 Conversation No. 912-7.

32 Conversation No. 912-18.

33 Conversation No. 433-67.

34 Conversation No. 913-1.

35 Conversation No. 913-3.

36 Conversation Nos. 913-8 and 433-73.

37 Conversation No. 45-162.

38 Meanwhile, friendly reporters told me—when I did on-the-record interviews—about the incredibly vicious whisper campaign the White House had launched to discredit me. A few that were floated but never printed, because they were too outrageously false: I had been kicked out of college for cheating or bad grades; I had deserted my first wife and son; I had been fired from a law firm for unethical conduct; I had participated in orgies; and I was so terrified of prison I might commit suicide—to mention only a few.

39 Conversation No. 45-164.

40 Conversation No. 45-166.

41 Conversation No. 914-8.

42 Conversation. No. 432-24.

43 Conversation No. 434-9.

44 Conversation No. 45-185.

45 Conversation No. 120-3.

46 Conversation No. 915-9.

47 I knew the way the White House worked, so I had no doubt the effort to discredit me was coming from the top. I quickly learned that it was Al Haig and John Ehrlichman doing much of the nasty work and getting their loyal followers to do their bidding. They were claiming I was a notorious liar who had deceived the president and my colleagues regarding Watergate. The efforts were twofold: hopefully, to block my testimony, in which I would merely spread false stories about my former colleagues, or to discredit it. We also learned that the Department of Justice might litigate the validity of the congressional immunity statute during the thirty-day automatic waiting period they had invoked, another way to prevent me from testifying before Congress. For these reasons I issued a statement on May 10, 1973, charging that there were "ongoing effort(s) to limit or prevent my testimony" concerning Watergate. More specifically, I stated: "Efforts have been made to prevent me from obtaining relevant information and records; attempts have been made to influence the handling of my testimony by the prosecutors; restrictions have been placed on the scope of my testimony as it relates to the White House; and blatant efforts have been made to publicly intimidate me. Finally, I am, of course, aware of the efforts to discredit me personally in the hope of discrediting my testimony." I closed the statement by noting, "The news stories quoting unidentified sources and speculating on the nature of my testimony" did not come from me, nor were they authorized by me, not to mention that they were "neither complete nor accurate." Indeed, I had not leaked anything, as I later testified under oath, and everything I provided the news media I did on the record, and that was very little. Bob McCandless would tell me thirty years later, in 2002, that he simply lied to Charlie and me about what he was doing to keep us unaware and unsullied.

48 Conversation No. 45-199.

49 Conversation No. 45-201.

50 Conversation No. 915-12.

51 Partial transcript of a telephone conversation between Robert Cushman and John Ehrlichman, July 7, 1971. Statement of Information, Hearings Before the Committee on the Judiciary, House of Representatives 93rd Congress, 2nd Session, Book VII-Part 2 (Washington, D.C.: Government Printing Office, 1974), 727.

52 Conversation No. 45-193.

53 According to the Presidential Daily Diary, from 4:18 to 4:20 P.M. the president talked with Haldeman, on May 10, 1973, See www.nixonlibrary.gov/virtuallibrary/documents/PDD/1973/099%20May%201-15%201973.pdf.

54 Conversation No. 45-212.

55 This meeting was revealed the next afternoon when Nixon said, "Bob, as I told you yesterday, and I want you to know how much that meeting meant to me in the Lincoln Room last night, I've kind of reached a [point], where you kind of reach low spots sometimes in life." See Conversation No. 916-19. This meeting in not on the president's PDD log and appears to have occurred after Nixon returned from watching a movie alone in the White House theater, the Hitchcock thriller *Notorious*.

56 But Haldeman later wrote, after his resignation, "Nixon and Haig both called me to discuss their strategy, in which I, as it turned out, would later play a major role. They expected Dean to testify to Nixon's March 21 statements about raising money to pay off Howard Hunt. I said, that because I had been at that same Oval Office meeting, I would testify (unstated: falsely, which was known to Nixon but not Haig) that the overall thrust of the meeting was Nixon's intention to 'probe' Dean to find out what really happened. As to the raising money for Hunt, I *felt* Nixon had at one point said that would be wrong." Haldeman, *The Ends of Power*, 299–300. (Emphasis added.) Haldeman wrote that statement while in federal prison, after having been convicted of conspiracy to obstruct justice and perjury for his testimony before the Senate when he said the president stated "There is no problem raising a million dollars, we can do that, but it would be wrong." His statement that he "felt" is very soft compared with his hard testimony before the Senate, in which he claimed that he was "absolutely positive." As the government pointed out, Nixon had made no such statement during our March 21 conversation; rather, he kept saying

that he thought Hunt should be taken care of. Haldeman's notes, which he said he reviewed before testifying, do not have Nixon saying it would be wrong regarding raising and paying the money; he made that statement after I told him it would be impossible for him to grant clemency. See counts 8 and 9, Indictment, and closing argument of James Neal, *U.S. v. Mitchell et al.* (December 20, 1974) 11,695–11,699; see also, *U.S. v. Haldeman, et al.* 559 F.2d 31 (1976).

## May 11 to 22, 1973

1 Vernon A. Walters, *Silent Missions* (New York: Doubleday & Co., 1978), 605.
2 See, e.g., http://law2.umkc.edu/faculty/projects/ftrials/ellsberg/judgerules.html.
3 National Archives and Records Administration (NARA) Conversation No. 916-16.
4 Max Holland, *Leak: Why Mark Felt Became Deep Throat* (Kansas City, KS: University Press of Kansas, 2012), 145–48.
5 Conversation No. 916-19.
6 Conversation No. 46-3.
7 Conversation No. 46-17.
8 Conversation No. 434-37.
9 Nixon made the following calls on Friday May 11, 1973, to Haig: Conversation No. 165-2 (5:35 to 5:57 P.M.), Conversation No. 165-4 (6:35 to 6:47 P.M.) and Conversation No. 165-8 (7:08 to 7:27 P.M.); on Saturday May 12, 1973: Conversation No. 165-10 (10:11–10:49 A.M.), Conversation No. 165-19 (12:37–12:54 P.M.), Conversation No. 165-21 (12:59–1:03 P.M.), Conversation No. 165-23 (2:04–2:10 P.M.), Conversation No. 165-29 (2:27–2:35 A.M.), Conversation No. 165-31 (5:17–5:44 P.M.), Conversation No. 165-33 (6:48–6:56 P.M.); and Sunday May 13, 1973: Conversation No. 165-40 (10:09–10:43 A.M.).
10 Conversation No. 165-4.
11 Conversation No. 165-8.
12 Conversation No. 165-10.
13 Conversation No. 165-19.
14 Conversation No. 165-23.
15 Conversation No. 165-31.
16 Conversation No. 46-21. Note: It is not clear why the call to Ziegler is on a White House telephone recording, when Nixon was at Camp David.
17 Conversation No. 165-36.
18 Conversation No. 165-38.
19 Conversation No. 917-2.
20 Conversation No. 917-5.
21 Conversation No. 917-6.
22 Conversation Nos. 46-27 and 917-28.
23 Conversation Nos. 436-2 and 46-31. See also "Ruckelshaus' Statement on Wiretaps," *The Washington Post*, May 15, 1973, A-10.
24 E.g., Joseph Kraft, "The Long Shadow of Scandal" *The Washington Post*, May 15, 1973, A-21; William Claiborne, "Kissinger Sought Security Leak Plug: Missing FBI Records Found," *The Washington Post*, May 15, 1973, A-1; R. W. Apple, Jr., "Kissinger Viewed Summary of Taps," *New York Times*, May 15, 1973, 22; and John M. Crewdson, "Week-Long Hunt: Pentagon Papers Trial Ended in Part Over Lost Material," *New York Times*, May 15, 1973, 1.
25 Conversation No. 46-31.
26 Conversation No. 917-44.
27 George Lardner, Jr., "Four Names On List for Prosecutor," *The Washington Post*, May 15, 1973, A-1; George Lardner, Jr., "Probe Job Declined by Top Choice," *The Washington Post*, May 16, 1973, A-1.
28 Conversation No. 436-18.
29 See Conversation No. 46-32 (Haig, 7:12–7:13 P.M.), Conversation No. 46-33 (Garment, 7:19–7:26 P.M.), Conversation No. 46-34 (Garment, 7:27–8:15 P.M.), Conversation No. 46-41

(Ziegler, 9:01–9:03 P.M.), Conversation No. 46-43 (Ziegler, 9:15–9:22 P.M.), Conversation No. 46-49 (Garment, 9:40–9:46 P.M.), Conversation No. 46-50 (Higby, 9:47–9:53 P.M.) and Conversation No. 46-51 (Herb Klein, 9:55–10:02 P.M.).

30 Conversation No. 918-6.

31 Conversation No. 918-14.

32 Petersen, paraphrasing the ruling of Supreme Court justice Byron White, in *Murphy v. Waterfront Commission*, 378 US 52 (1964), addresses the problem of state versus federal immunity. He said: "It becomes a much more difficult problem when you're in the same jurisdiction, the federal jurisdiction." He noted, "If you anticipate that Congress granted X immunity and it was in a televised hearing and all over the front page, and then the prosecutor tries to establish beyond a reasonable doubt that his evidence overlapping was independently arrived at. It's a tremendous—" At this point Nixon cut Petersen off, asking if I had immunity from the Senate, but Petersen did not know, explaining that, if I did, all they could do was hold it up for thirty days. What Charlie Shaffer was doing in insisting I get immunity from the Senate (regardless of my willingness to testify without it) was to protect my options by giving me full constitutional protection. Shaffer was building for me the case that Oliver North would have a decade and a half later. See *U.S. v. North*, 910 F2d 843 (1990). Oliver North sought to, and did, beat the rap. That was not my goal. Charlie laid out my options before I decided to plead guilty to my involvement in the cover-up conspiracy. I did not fully appreciate Charlie's genius at the time, but he had a far stronger case than North, and I'm sure would have enjoyed writing new law. I rejected the option for several reasons, all of almost equal importance: (1) It would have been an expensive and time-consuming undertaking, and given the climate of the time, I did not think anyone involved in Watergate could get a dispassionate judicial ruling. (2) Had I gone this route I would have delayed the prosecution of Haldeman, Ehrlichman and Mitchell, if not have allowed them to walk free, since I was the key witness against them. To protect themselves these men had all lied about virtually everything, and dishonestly blamed me, while shoveling false and misleading information to discredit me. No way I was going to give them and their dishonesty a pass. (3) I truly wanted to end Watergate and get on with my life, and I felt the only way to do it was a full and honest accounting of the facts. Had I decided to fight the government, rather than assist, that would not have happened. When all was said and done, I had no regrets for the decision I made to plead guilty, for I was guilty. I had not gone to the White House to get involved in a criminal conspiracy, but that was what had happened.

33 Conversation No. 918-15.

34 Conversation No. 919-7.

35 White House press briefing No. 1740, 12:22 P.M., EDT, at the White House with Ron Ziegler, May 16, 1973.

36 Conversation No. 46-75.

37 Conversation No. 46-77.

38 Conversation No. 919-15.

39 Conversation No. 919-32.

40 See, e.g., Conversation No. 920-3 (Haig and Buzhardt, 4:55–5:22 P.M.), Conversation No. 920-4 (Haig, 5:22–5:25 P.M.), Conversation No. 920-6 (Ziegler, 5:25–5:31 P.M.), Conversation No. 920-9 (Buzhardt, 5:39–5:53 P.M.), Conversation No. 920-11 (Haig, Ziegler and Buzhardt, 5:53–6:11 P.M.), Conversation No. 920-13 (Haig and Buzhardt, 8:45–9:33 P.M.) and Conversation. No. 46-88 (Ziegler, 9:53–9:59 P.M.).

41 Carl Bernstein and Bob Woodward, "Vast GOP Undercover Operation Originated 1969: Watergate Was Part of Elaborate Undercover Campaign," *The Washington Post*, May 17, 1973, A-1. See also Carl Bernstein and Bob Woodward, *All the President's Men* (New York: Simon & Schuster, 1974), 316–19.

42 Conversation No. 921-8.

43 Conversation No. 921-13.

44 The reason I placed a copy of the 1970 proposed intelligence plans, which Nixon had approved but Hoover had rejected, in a safe-deposit box was because when I broke rank I was not sure

anyone would believe that the Nixon White House operated outside the law, and this was document proof. This plan called for electronic surveillance (illegal), spies, overt mail covers (legal but controversial pictures of envelopes), covert mail covers (illegal opening and copying of both an envelope and its contents) and surreptitious entries (illegal burglaries).

45 Conversation No. 438-15.

46 Conversation No. 46-105.

47 Conversation No. 46-107.

48 Conversation No. 46-109.

49 Conversation No. 46-111.

50 Conversation No. 46-113.

51 Conversation No. 922-7.

52 Conversation No. 922-14.

53 Conversation No. 437-11.

54 Conversation No. 437-19.

55 Conversation No. 437-26.

56 Conversation No. 46-116.

57 Conversation No. 923-2.

58 Conversation No. 923-5.

59 Conversation No. 167-4.

60 Conversation No. 167-6.

61 Conversation No. 167-7.

62 Conversation No. 167-10.

63 Conversation No. 167-25.

64 Conversation No. 167-27.

65 Conversation No. 167-29.

66 Conversation No. 46-120.

67 Conversation No. 924-2.

68 This number would appear to include people at the reelection committee who otherwise might have reentered the Nixon administration in the second term.

69 Bud Krogh would later tell me, and testify under oath, that after the Ellsberg break-in they realized they had a serious problem with Liddy and had to get him out of the White House as soon as possible. When the opportunity at the reelection committee arose, Krogh and Ehrlichman thought it perfect, and a place where Liddy could not get in trouble. As Krogh later wrote, after he cleared Liddy going to the CRP with Ehrlichman, who spoke with Mitchell, Liddy went to the CRP. Krogh says, "I called Magruder and told him that Liddy would require close supervision. I did not go into any details, which I regret, but I did indicate that close monitoring of Liddy's activities would be important." Egil "Bud" Krogh with Matthew Krogh, *Integrity: Good People, Bad Choices and Life Lessons from the White House* (New York: Public Affairs, 2007), 120.

70 Conversation No. 439-2.

71 Conversation No. 46-123.

72 See, e.g. Conversation No. 439-11 (Haig, 12:40–1:10 P.M.), Conversation No. 439-19 (Haig and Ziegler, 3:40–4:25 P.M.), Conversation No. 439-21 (Ziegler and Buzhardt, 4:26–4:40 P.M.), Conversation No. 439-22 (Haig and Ziegler, 4:55–5:25 P.M.), Conversation No. 46-132 (Ziegler, 5:28–5:29 P.M.), Conversation No. 439-29 (Buzhardt, 5:40–5:55 P.M.).

73 Conversation No. 439-21.

74 Conversation No. 46-135.

75 Conversation No. 925-3.

76 Conversation No. 46-138.

77 Conversation No. 438-27.

78 Conversation No. 440-3.

79 For the May 22, 1973, statement (along with related presidential documents): www.presidency.ucsb.edu/ws/?pid=3855.

80 John W. Dean, *Blind Ambition: The White House Years* (New York: Simon & Schuster, 1976), 294–95.

81 Nixon's claim that he "took no part in" the cover-up is clearly more limited than his being "aware of," but once he entered the cover-up conspiracy, he never truly left it, so he was actually taking part from that time. The earliest clear example of his taking part is found in his conversations with Haldeman on June 23, 1973, in which he authorized the use of the CIA to cut off the FBI's investigation in Conversation No. 741-2 and Conversation No. 343-36. But Nixon was also very aware of, and taking part in, a cover-up when approving (thus suborning) Magruder's perjury in the mid-July Conversation No. 747-14, Conversation No. 348-10, Conversation No. 748-7, Conversation No. 349-12 and Conversation No. 197-17. The House Judiciary Committee's impeachment inquiry spelled out in Article I of their bill of impeachment nine distinctive ploys Nixon had personally relied upon to cover up. But this matter is not even debatable, for Nixon admitted in his memoir that he had been involved in the cover up. See Richard Nixon, *RN: The Memoirs of Richard Nixon* (New York: Grosset & Dunlap, 1978), 850–51.

82 Nixon tendered inchoate offers of clemency to Magruder in Conversation No. 428-19 and me in Conversation No. 38-37, and then to Haig for Haldeman and Ehrlichman in Conversation No. 922–7, but as used here he is referring to the original seven Watergate defendants, and he clearly gave Colson an offer to pass along to Howard Hunt on January 5 and 8, 1973, in Conversation Nos. 394-3 and 394-7, and Conversation No. 394-21, and he certainly understood what he had done in Conversation No. 424-10 when talking with Haldeman; see also Haldeman, *Diaries*, 594.

83 On August 1, 1972, Haldeman told Nixon that taking care of the Watergate defendants was "a costly exercise" and Nixon told him that that was what money was for, and he raised the issue of bribery in passing, in Conversation No. 758-11. On December 10, 1972, Nixon discussed with Haldeman whether Dorothy Hunt was carrying "payoff" money, in Conversation No. 384-4. On March 2, 1973, Haldeman discussed the role of Tom Pappas in providing cash for Mitchell to use with the Watergate defendants, and on March 7, 1973, when Nixon met with Pappas (Conversation No. 871-5). And following my March 21, 1973, conversation with Nixon, he asked Rose Mary Woods how much cash she had in a secret fund, in Conversation No. 886-18, because he was looking for the $1 million to pay the Watergate defendants.

84 The claim that he did not authorize the use of the CIA to block the FBI's investigation was established as untrue in his June 23, 1972, conversations with Haldeman: Conversation Nos. 741-2, 741-10 and 343-46.

85 Nixon falsely claimed in his April 30, 1973, statement that he started his investigation on March 21, 1973. However, I told him about the Ellsberg break-in on March 17 in Conversation No. 882-12.

86 Suffice it to say that the Senate Select Committee on Campaign Practices (Senate Watergate committee) included several hundred pages in their final report (June 1974) spelling out in great detail Nixon's illegal and improper campaign practices and finance. Samples of Nixon's campaigning techniques are found in his embrace of the dirty campaigning of Donald Segretti, which he did not find seriously troubling at all: For example, Conversation No. 795-1, Conversation No. 366-6, Conversation No. 830-6 and Conversation No. 878-14. Nixon's requesting the Haldeman use of the Secret Service, while protecting McGovern, to obtain information about him in Conversation No. 750-13. Nixon's demanding of an Internal Revenue tax audit of Larry O'Brien in Conversation No. 758-11 and Conversation No. 760-9 was illegal, not to mention his endorsing the use of the IRS in going after McGovern campaign contributors in the latter conversation. See the Final Report, Senate Select Committee on Presidential Campaign Activities, U.S, Senate (Washington, D.C.: Government Printing Office, 1974), Chapter 2: Campain Practices, 107–214, Chapter 3: Uses of Incumbency, Reponsiveness Program, 361–442, and Chapter 4: Campgain Finance, 445–563.

## May 23 to July 16, 1973

1 That I had become Nixon's arch enemy became increasingly apparent in the conversation that follow, then in the public speeches up to his resignation. After leaving office he purportedly gave his postpresidency assistant Monica Crowley his take on me: "He was a traitor and a liar and out for himself from the beginning. He was the one who was feeding me lies about what was going on. And there I was acting based on what he told me. He had a personal stake in covering up the facts, and I didn't know that at the time." Monica Crowley, *Nixon in Winter: His Final Revelations About Diplomacy, Watergate, and Life Out of the Arena* (New York: Random House, 1998), 297. Note: The Crowley book, if correct, and there are questions about its accuracy, indicates that Nixon never did understand the facts, nor did he make any effort to do so. But the effort to discredit me, and the truth as set forth in the extensive record of Watergate, has continued long after Nixon passed. A small group of Watergate revisionists have sought to rewrite history by ignoring the record, while reinventing it to suit their needs, ranging from scholars with a serious "confirmation bias" to conspiracy theory entrepreneurs twisting history for money. Sadly, but not surprisingly, no group has done more to try to distort this history than the Nixon Foundation, which is still in the control of former Nixon aides who are avowed Nixon apologists.

2 National Archives and Records Administration (NARA) Conversation No. 962-2 (Ziegler, May 23, 1973); Conversation No. 440-65 (Haldeman, May 29, 1973).

3 Conversation No. 168-30 (Ziegler, June 3, 1973).

4 Conversation No. 962-4 (Haig, May 23, 1973).

5 Conversation No. 39-104 (Buzhardt, June 6, 1973).

6 Conversation No. 962-2 (Ziegler, May 23, 1973).

7 Conversation No. 441-23 (Buzhardt, June 5, 1973).

8 Conversation No. 962-4 (Haig, May 23, 1973); Conversation No. 929-7 (Rogers, May 29, 1973); Conversation No. 440-65 (Haldeman, May 29, 1973).

9 Conversation No. 39-37 (Ziegler, June 3, 1973).

10 Conversation No. 441-23 (Buzhardt, June 5, 1973).

11 Conversation No. 441-35 (Buzhardt, June 7, 1973).

12 Conversation No. 962-2 (Ziegler, May 23, 1973).

13 Ibid.

14 Conversation No. 962-4 (Haig, May 23, 1973).

15 E.g. Conversation No. 39-106 (Colson, June 6, 1973); Conversation No. 937-5 (Haig, June 12, 1973).

16 Conversation No. 962-4 (Haig, May 23, 1973).

17 Conversation No. 168-28 (Colson, June 3, 1973).

18 Conversation No. 168-30 (Ziegler, June 3, 1973).

19 Ibid.

20 Conversation No. 39-37 (Ziegler, June 3, 1973).

21 Ibid.

22 Conversation. No. 39-129 (Colson, June 7, 1973).

23 Conversation No. 441-35 (Buzhardt, June 7, 1973).

24 Conversation No. 935-6.

25 Conversation No. 962-4.

26 Conversation No. 926-5.

27 Conversation No. 927-3.

28 Conversation No. 39-16.

29 Conversation No. 928-12. It appears the tape was changed during this conversation, and the first few minutes may have been unrecorded.

30 Conversation No. 929-5.

31 Conversation No. 440-65.

32 Conversation No. 168-32.

33 Conversation No. 168-36.

34 Conversation No. 168-38.

35  Conversation. No. 39-37.

36  Conversation No. 441-2.

37  See Conversation Nos. 442-1 through 442-69. NARA has taken the "Draft Transcript Prepared by the Impeachment Inquiry Staff for the House Judiciary Committee of a Recording of the President's Work-Day, June 4, 1973" and broken this 170-page document into sixty-nine segments, interlaced with the telephone calls that occurred throughout the day. The recording is basically the recording of Nixon listening to select conversations with me, and his reactions along the way, which he shared with Haig and Ziegler. Because the president wore a headset during the afternoon, it is not possible to know precisely which conversations Nixon did actually listen to on June 4, 1973—the only occasion during his presidency that he appears to have listened to the recordings.

38  Conversation No. 864-4 (February 27, 1973); Conversation Nos. 866-3, 866-4 and 866-17 (March 1, 1973) and Conversation No. 865-14 (February 28, 1973).

39  Conversation No. 39-78.

40  Conversation No. 39-79.

41  Conversation Nos. 39-80, 39-81 and 39-83.

42  Conversation No. 441-23.

43  Conversation No. 933-1.

44  Conversation No. 933-3.

45  Conversation No. 933-11.

46  Conversation No. 39-104.

47  Conversation No. 443-35.

48  Conversation No. 934-5.

49  Conversation No. 441-35.

50  Conversation No. 935-4.

51  While there had been no substance to the earlier scandal charge, what Nixon knew but only a few others did was that Kleindienst had lied during his confirmation hearing concerning talking with the president about the ITT merger. Richardson's amendment to the Cox charter would surface Kleindienst's false testimony. But Kleindienst would negotiate a plea deal for a misdemeanor and only receive a slap on the wrist. The investigation of ITT by the special prosecutor's office produced nothing else of note. Re Kleindiesnt: Richard Ben-Veniste and George Frampton, Jr., *Stonewall: The Real Story of the Watergate Prosecution* (New York: Simon & Schuster, 1977), 377–78.

52  Conversation No. 935-7.

53  Conversation No. 935-11.

54  Conversation No. 444-5.

55  Conversation No. 936-1.

56  Conversation No. 936-3.

57  Conversation No. 40-20.

58  Conversation No. 937-3.

59  These were less than challenging question, most of which I answered when testifying before the Senate in my opening statement. It appears Nixon incorrectly thought I was not going to discuss my own role in the cover-up. Several of Nixon's questions are based on incorrect assumptions. His seven questions were: "(1) How often did you see Henry Petersen after the break-in? (2) Did he tell Petersen about the meetings he had had prior to the break-in with regard to it? (3) Did he tell Petersen about his talks with Walters asking him to put 'buggers' on the CIA payroll? (4) Did he tell Petersen about his meeting with Magruder and Mitchell when he suggested that Magruder lie about his role? (5) Did he tell Petersen about the fund-raising activities of Kalmbach that he was aware of, and the awareness of the $350,000 fund? (6) Did he tell Petersen of his offers of clemency to others? (7 ) How often did he see Gray? Did he tell Gray about these offers—or some of these other matters? In other words these are questions concerning all these things that happened before March." Fred Thompson's first questions of me during his cross-examination related to Petersen, but they appear based on my testimony rather than on the questions fed to him by the White House—although it is not clear.

60 Conversation No. 937-5.

61 Conversation No. 937-8.

62 Conversation No. 40-28.

63 Conversation No. 937-19.

64 Conversation No. 40-33.

65 Conversation No. 938-6.

66 Conversation No. 938-12.

67 Conversation No. 40-43.

68 Conversation No. 40-49.

69 Conversation No. 939-2.

70 Conversation No. 445-6.

71 Conversation No. 40-70.

72 Conversation No. 445-22.

73 Conversation No. 40-86.

74 Conversation No. 40-95.

75 Conversation No. 940-2.

76 Conversation No. 40-111.

77 Conversation No. 446-6.

78 Conversation No. 942-1.

79 Conversation No. 942-6.

80 Bob Woodward and Carl Bernstein, "Nixon Expected to Alter Stance, Abandon Aide," *The Washington Post*, June 18, 1973, A-1.

81 Conversation No. 943-1.

82 Conversation No. 943-2.

83 Conversation No. 944-2.

84 Conversation No. 41-1.

85 Conversation No. 41-3.

86 Conversation No. 447-11.

87 Buzhardt would also push this approach in Conversation Nos. 945-3, 945-7 and 447-40.

88 Dean Senate testimony, 3 Senate Select Committee on Presidential Campaign Activities (SSC) 935–36, 1025, 1374–78 and 1390–93; see also, John W. Dean, *Blind Ambition: The White House Years* (New York: Simon & Schuster, 1976), 302, 326–27.

89 Conversation No. 944-7.

90 Samuel Dash, *Chief Counsel: Inside the Ervin Committee—The Untold Story of Watergate* (New York: Random House, 1976) 161.

91 Conversation No. 945-1.

92 George Lardner, Jr., and Timothy S. Robinson, "Nixon Subpoena Studied," *The Washington Post*, June 19, 1973, A-1.

93 Conversation No. 945-3.

94 Conversation No. 945-5.

95 Conversation No. 169-16.

96 Dean Senate testimony, 3 SSC 1019, 1030–31, 1576–77, 1588.

97 Dash, *Chief Counsel*, 159.

98 White House press briefing No. 1762, 10:21 A.M., PDT, at the Western White House with Ron Ziegler, June 25, 1973.

99 Richard Nixon, *RN: The Memoirs of Richard Nixon* (New York: Grosset & Dunlap, 1978), 890.

100 Nixon, *RN*, 893.

101 See, Final Report, SSC (Washington, D.C.: Government Printing Office, 1974).

102 Conversation No. 947-3.

103 Conversation No. 947-5.

104 Conversation No. 947-15.

105 Conversation No. 947-16.

106 Conversation No. 948-3.

107 I was asked about the president's interest in tax cases. I responded: "It gets more and more painful to bring these names out, as it was painful to bring the president's name out. It is painful to bring out other people. It was Rose Mary Woods who kept asking me the status of the case, because this individual was seeing the president a good deal." When pressed further, I said: "I told Miss Woods at one point that she should just stay as far away from the case as possible. She was seeing the individual, having encounters with the individual who was the subject of the tax case, and he would protest his innocence to her. He is a fine man, and she was quite convinced of his innocence and could not believe he was being harassed by agents that were trying to get somebody who was close to the president. The individual was using the president's name a great deal; he was traveling with the president to China and Russia and other places." Without naming the individual, I continued testifying that no one at the White House had tried to influence the case. See 4 SSC 1558–60. And when I testified I did not know that Dr. Kenneth Riland, an osteopathic physician, had been indicted in New York on April 10, 1973. According to news accounts, he later went to trial and was found not guilty, and another of his high-profile patients, Nelson Rockefeller, assisted him with the back taxes.

108 Conversation No. 948-10.

109 Conversation No. 41-61.

110 Conversation No. 948-14.

111 Conversation No. 948-18.

112 Nixon, *RN*, 898.

113 Carl Bernstein and Bob Woodward, "Senate Unit to Act on Nixon Files: Senate Probers to Decide on Subpoena of Nixon Files," *The Washington Post*, July 11, 1973, A-1.

114 Fred D. Thompson, *At That Point in Time: The Inside Story of the Senate Watergate Committee* (New York: Quadrangle, 1975), 83.

115 Conversation No. 949-7.

116 Conversation No. 949-10.

117 Alexander M. Haig, Jr., with Charles McCarry, *Inner Circles: How America Changes the World* (New York: Warner Books, 1992), 374.

118 Thompson, *At That Point in Time*, 87.

119 Leonard Garment, *Crazy Rhythm: My Journey from Brooklyn, Jazz, and Wall Street to Nixon's White House, Watergate, and Beyond* . . . (New York: Random House, 1997), 277.

120 Haig, *Inner Circles*, 373.

121 Nixon, *RN*, 899–900.

122 Bob Woodward and Carl Bernstein, *The Final Days* (New York: Simon & Schuster, 1976), 58.

123 4 SSC 1466.

124 Haig, *Inner Circles*, 375.

125 Garment, *Crazy Rhythm*, 278.

126 Ibid.

127 Haig, *Inner Circles*, 375.

128 Richard Ben-Veniste and George Frampton, Jr., *Stonewall: The Real Story of the Watergate Prosecution* (New York: Simon & Schuster, 1977), 112.

129 Haig, *Inner Circles*, 379.

130 Richard Nixon, Handwritten Notes re Tapes, dated 7/21, Nixon library, National Archives and Records Administration (NARA).

131 Gladys Engel Lang and Kurt Lang, "Polling on Watergate: The Battle for Public Opinion," *Public Opinion Quarterly* 4 (1980): 530–47.

132 Nixon, *RN*, 901.

## Epilogue

1 Unless more specifically noted, the following sources have been very helpful in assembling this chronology: R. W. Apple, Jr. (narrative); Linda Amster (chronology); and Gerald Gold (general editor), *The Watergate Hearings: Break-in and Cover-up; Proceedings* (New York:

Viking, 1973), 219–77; and *Watergate: Chronology of a Crisis* (Washington, DC: *Congressional Quarterly*, 1975).

2 Bob Woodward and Scott Armstrong, *The Brethren: Inside the Supreme Court* (New York: Simon & Schuster, 1979), 287, 295. Note: From law clerks debating what Nixon meant by "definitive" to Justice Brennan leading the effort to get an 8 to 0 vote against Nixon to leave no doubt that it was a "definitive" ruling. Clearly, baiting the high Court had been a foolish ploy by Nixon, for this statement would not have been made by Gerry Warren without direction from the president.

3 Leon Jaworski, *The Right and the Power: The Prosecution of Watergate* (New York: Readers Digest Press, 1976), 47.

4 The following conversations were included (listed here with the later created NARA identifications)—Abbreviations: HRH (Haldeman); JDE (Ehrlichman); JWD (Dean); RLZ (Ziegler); RGK (Kleindienst); JNM (Mitchell); HEP (Petersen); and WPR (Rogers)—National Archives and Records Administration (NARA) Conversation No. 779-2 (September 15, 1972: HRH and JWD), Conversation No. 865-14 (February 28, 1973: JWD), Conversation No. 878-14 (March 13, 1973: JWD), Conversation No. 882-12 (March 17, 1973: JWD), Conversations No. 37-175 and 37-176 (March 20, 1973: JWD), Conversation No. 886-8 (March 21, 1973: JWD and HRH), ConversationNo. 421-18 (March 21, 1973: JWD, HRH and JDE), Conversation No. 422-33 (March 22, 1973: HRH, JDE, JWD and JNM), Conversation No. 44-50 (March 28, 1973: JDE call to RGK), Conversation No. 890-19 (March 30, 1973: JDE and RLZ), Conversation No. 44-103 (April 8, 1973: JDE), Conversation No. 428-19 (April 14, 1974: HRH and JDE), Conversation No. 896-4 (April 14, 1973: HRH and JDE), Conversation No. 428-28 (April 14, 1973: HRH and JDE), Conversation No. 38-31 (April 14, 1973: JDE call to RGK), Conversation No. 38-34 (April 14, 1973: HRH), Conversation No. 38-37 (April 14, 1973: JDE), Conversation. No. 896-6 (April 15, 1973: JDE), Conversation. No. 38-44 (April 15, 1973: RGK), Conversation No. 38-52 (April 15, 1973: HRH), Conversation No. 38-53 (April 15, 1973: HEP), Conversation No. 38-55 (April 15, 1973: HEP), Conversation No. 38-58 (April 15, 1973: HEP), Conversation No. 38-63 (April 15, 1973: HEP), Conversation No. 897-3 (April 16, 1973: HRH and JDE), Conversation No. 897-9 (April 16, 1973: HRH and JDE), Conversation No. 897-11 (April 16, 1973: HRH), Conversation No. 427-2 (April 16, 1973: HEP), Conversations No. 427-5 and 427-6 (April 16, 1973: RLZ and JDE), Conversation No. 427-10 (April 16, 1973: JWD), Conversation No. 38-80 (April 16, 1973: HEP), Conversation No. 898-6 (April 17, 1973: HRH), Conversation No. 898-12 (April 17, 1973: HRH, JDE, RLZ), Conversation No. 898-19 (April 17, 1973: JDE), Conversations No. 898-20 and 898-21: HEP), Conversation No. 898-23: HRH, JDE, RLZ), Conversation No. 429-3 (April 17, 1973: WPR, HRH, JDE), Conversation No. 38-100 (April 18, 1973: HEP), Conversation No. 429-22 (April 19, 1973: Wilson and Strickler) and Conversation No. 906-17 (April 27, 1973: HEP and RLZ).

5 Bob Woodward and Carl Bernstein, *The Final Days* (New York: Simon & Schuster, 1976), 263. Note: This account of the final days has held up remarkably well, and I have always felt the reporting here was much better than their first Watergate book, *All the President's Men*. So I have drawn from their information as well for the final, final days. They interviewed many of the people involved during a relatively contemporaneous period.

6 In addition to *The Final Days*, first-person accounts of this period can be found in Nixon, *RN*, 1040–90 ("Impeachment Summer"); Raymond Price, *With Nixon* (New York: Viking, 1977), 308–52 ("The Last Historic First"); Alexander M. Haig, Jr. with Charles McCarry, *Inner Circles: How America Changed the World* (New York: Warner Books, 1992), 466–505 ("The Smoking Gun" and "The Final Paradox").

7 For the record, my sentence was 120 days, but since I was in the U.S. Marshals' witness protection program during this period, I spent my nights in a safe house at Ft. Holabird Army Base in Maryland and a short drive to Washington, for I spent most days in the office of the Watergate special prosecutor in Washington, DC, assisting them with the *U.S. v. Mitchell et al.* trial.

## Appendix A

1 This phenomenon is named after the great Japanese film *Rashomon* directed by Akira Kurosawa, which portrays the trial of a notorious outlaw who allegedly rapes a woman and then kills her samurai husband. The account seeks to find the truth based on four eyewitnesses who recount the events; each is credible and possible, yet they all contradict each other.

2 Hal Arkowitz and Scott O. Lilienfeld, "Why Science Tells Us Not to Rely on Eyewitness Accounts," *Scientific American* (January 8, 2009) at www.scientificamerican.com/article/do-the-eyes-have-it/.

3 Conversation No. 344-6.

4 Conversation No. 758-11.

5 Conversation No. 384-4.

6 Conversation No. 831-6.

7 Conversation No. 878-14.

8 Conversation No. 420-11.

9 Conversation No. 882-10.

10 Conversation No. 886-7.

11 Conversation No. 421-22.

## Appendix B

1 *Watergate: Chronology of a Crisis* (Washington, DC: *Congressional Quarterly*, 1975), 360.

2 Dean Senate testimony, 3 Senate Select Committee on Presidential Campaign Activities (SSC), 1019–20.

3 National Archives and Records Administration (NARA) Conversation No. 947-15.

4 See Affidavit of Fred D. Thompson, 4 Senate Select Committee on Presidential Campaign Activities (SSC), 1794.

5 Found in exhibits with notes for Nixon grand jury testimony at http://media.nara.gov/research/nixon-grand-jury/9-9/9-9-q-and-a-gap.pdf.

6 See, e.g., Nixon's grand jury testimony and related documents that were made public while I was working on this book. See: www.archives.gov/research/investigations/watergate/nixon-grand-jury/.

7 See, e.g., Richard Ben-Veniste and George Frampton, Jr., *Stonewall: The Legal Case Against the Watergate Conspirators* (New York: Touchstone, 1978); Alexander Haig, with Charles McCarry, *Inner Circles: How America Changed the World: A Memoir* (New York: Warner, 1992); Richard Nixon, *RN: The Memoirs of Richard Nixon* (New York: Grosset & Dunlap, 1978); Bob Woodward and Carl Bernstein, *The Final Days* (New York: Simon & Schuster, 1975).

# INDEX